Christmas 1954.

ROYAL AIR FORCE 1939-1945

by DENIS RICHARDS, *Principal of Morley College, and* HILARY ST. GEORGE SAUNDERS, *sometime Librarian of the House of Commons*

The authors of this history have been given full access to official documents. They alone are responsible for the statements made and the views expressed.

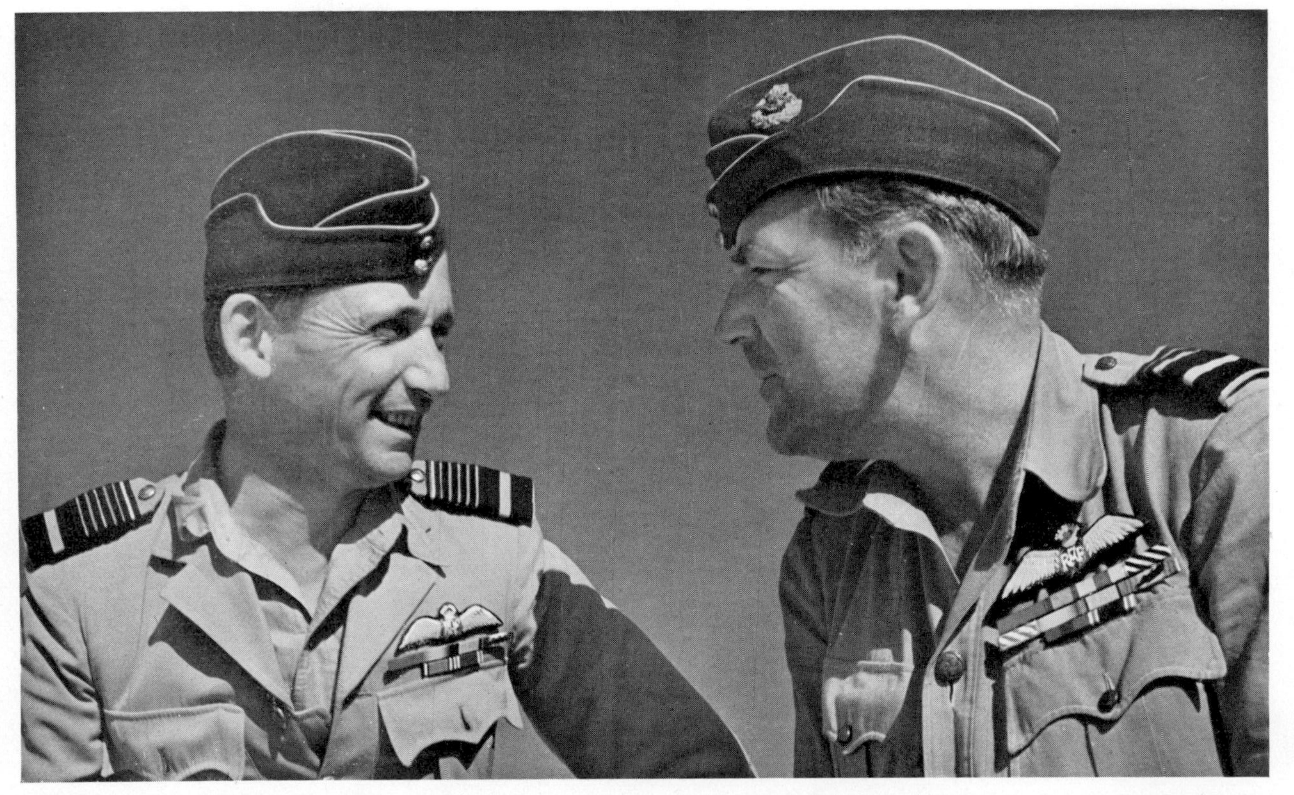

AIR CHIEF MARSHAL SIR ARTHUR TEDDER AND AIR VICE-MARSHAL A. CONINGHAM IN THE DESERT

ROYAL AIR FORCE 1939-1945

VOLUME II
THE FIGHT AVAILS

BY
DENIS RICHARDS
AND
HILARY St. GEORGE SAUNDERS

LONDON
HER MAJESTY'S STATIONERY OFFICE
1954

First published 1954

PUBLISHED BY HER MAJESTY'S STATIONERY OFFICE

To be purchased from

York House, Kingsway, LONDON, W.C.2 423 Oxford Street, LONDON, W.1
P.O. Box 569, LONDON, S.E.1
13a Castle Street, EDINBURGH, 2 1 St. Andrew's Crescent, CARDIFF
39 King Street, MANCHESTER, 2 Tower Lane, BRISTOL, 1
2 Edmund Street, BIRMINGHAM, 3 80 Chichester Street, BELFAST

or from any Bookseller

1954

Price 13s. 6d. net

Printed in Great Britain under the authority of Her Majesty's Stationery Office by McCorquodale, London, S.E.

Contents

Of this Volume Chapters V to XII were written by Denis Richards and Chapters I to IV and XIII to XVI by Hilary St. George Saunders

APPENDICES

MAPS AND DIAGRAMS

PLATES

Preface

THE purpose and scope of this history were described by the late Hilary Saunders and myself in our general preface, printed in the first volume. Here it is perhaps sufficient if I recall that the story is, for reasons of space, confined largely to operations and the policy governing them: that it is not part of the full-length Official History of the War, and is intended for a somewhat wider audience: that it was, nevertheless, officially commissioned, and is based throughout on official documents, to which the fullest access was given: and that the authors, while gratefully acknowledging official help and advice, are alone responsible for the statements made and the views expressed.

For help with this volume, as with the others, our debt was particularly great to the Air Ministry Historical Branch, under Mr. J. C. Nerney. Indeed, without the assistance of that admirable organization, always fully and freely at our service, we could hardly have begun our task, let alone finished it.

The text of this volume, like that of volumes one and three, was substantially completed during 1950. The first four and the last four chapters were written by Hilary Saunders, the middle eight by myself. My friend and collaborator, however, did not live to read the printer's proofs. Throughout the whole period of his work on this history he was in fact struggling against ill health. His premature death was assuredly a direct result of his immense labours, from 1940 onwards, to bring home to his fellow-countrymen the full measure of the achievement of those whose battlefield was 'the blue dome of air'.

D.R.

November 1953.

Preface

CHAPTER I
Japan Strikes

ON a bright morning in the early summer of 1925 three men, each of them at the head of his branch of the profession of arms, were sitting in conference in Whitehall Gardens. The subject of their discussion was the defence of an island, about the size of the Isle of Wight, situated more than eight thousand miles from the United Kingdom near the eastern entrance of the Strait of Malacca. Upon its southern shore lay a large, humid, opulent city, upon its northern the beginnings of a naval base which in course of years was to be variously described as ' the Gibraltar of the Far East ', ' the Greatest Arsenal of Democracy in South Eastern Asia ', and ' an impregnable fortress '. When completed at a cost of some £60,000,000 it was stocked with naval equipment of every kind from a cap-band to a 15-inch shell and off its granite and concrete quays floated a dry-dock, 1,000 feet long and 132 feet wide, able to hold the largest battleship. In February, 1942, the base, the city and the island endured a siege of fifteen days. At the end of it, 70,000 exhausted defenders surrendered to 100,000 Japanese and passed into a captivity, so rigorous and brutal, as to bring about the death of more than half of them. The fall of Singapore was as great a disaster as British arms had ever sustained.

All this was seventeen years in the future when the three men sat at their deliberations that May morning in London. As they proceeded it became evident that they were not in full agreement. The subject of their discussion was how best to provide for the defence of the slowly growing docks and arsenals of the new base. It had been decided in 1921 to remove the main naval base in the Far East from its remote and exposed position at Hong Kong, and the Committee of Imperial Defence had had under scrutiny for two years the strategic problem provoked by the greatly enlarged and continually expanding navy of Japan. Should Great Britain and that country fall to war, a more central and safer spot for the Far Eastern naval base was essential. The Committee thought they had found it on the island of Singapore and their choice was confirmed by the Imperial Conference of 1923. Two years passed and still the experts debated the best methods of defending it. The First Sea Lord and the Chief of the Imperial General Staff favoured that form of defence which a heavy fixed armament of 15-inch guns, accompanied by cannon of smaller calibre, could provide. It was well tried. In one form or another it had stood the test of many wars. Sir Hugh Trenchard, Chief of the Air Staff, preferred a more mobile and far-ranging scheme. To the guns, the submarines, the light surface craft, should be added a squadron of fighter aircraft, two of torpedo bombers and a flight of seaplanes. The installation of immovable 15-inch guns in a fortress where they could have no effect beyond their own range and ' where, in many wars, they would exercise no effect whatsoever ' was, he maintained, a mistake if they were to be the only, or the principal, form of defence. Why not use the air force to strike at the enemy long before he came within their range? Torpedo bombers could do so far out to sea, 150 to 200 miles from Singapore and the great guns.

Such revolutionary notions provoked much discussion. A compromise was eventually adopted, and it was agreed that the first stage of defence should be represented by three 15-inch guns and a complement of ordnance of smaller calibre, and that the second stage should make provision for torpedo aircraft.

For ten years from 1927, the pendulum swung uneasily between guns and aircraft, economy and lavishness. By 1929 the floating dock was in position, and more guns had been added to the defence, and No. 205 Squadron, equipped with Southampton and later with Singapore flying boats, was stationed at Seletar near the still uncompleted naval base. In 1930, when large economies in expenditure on armaments had become necessary, it was reinforced by No. 36 (Torpedo Bomber) Squadron. The completion of the defence scheme as a whole, however, was postponed for five years. Then in 1931 the outbreak of what amounted to war between China and Japan gave rise to apprehensions which two years later led to the despatch of a second Torpedo Bomber Squadron, No. 100, to Singapore, and the leisurely construction of two airfields. At that time the Air Staff was probably alone in believing that Singapore might be assaulted from some other direction than from the sea. The enemy's fleet—and it was obvious to all that the potential enemy was Japan—was expected to attack the base supported by carrier-borne aircraft. To combat this form of assault reconnaissance squadrons were necessary, backed by squadrons capable of a sustained offensive against shipping. They would be provided.

With Singapore primarily in mind, a dual-purpose torpedo bomber aircraft had been developed capable of employment both in frontier warfare and coastal defence. In times of peace squadrons equipped with this new type would form the air garrisons of Iraq and the northwest frontier of India, but should danger threaten in the Pacific, they could be transferred at short notice along the great strategic air route linking Baghdad and Singapore.

These then were the plans, drawn up and carried through by a succession of Chiefs of Staff over a period of twenty years, which, it was hoped, would be enough to guarantee the safety and fighting efficiency of this very important base. By the autumn of 1939 a total of three 15-inch (soon to be increased to five), six 9·2-inch and fourteen 6-inch guns were in position to defend the fortress, their arcs of fire covering a wide area of sea to the south-east, south and south-west of the island. To aid them, four bomber squadrons of the Royal Air Force, of which two were torpedo bomber, were ready with two flying boat squadrons to conduct that long range and flexible defence which Trenchard had so long and so strongly urged.

This situation endured through the opening months of the Second World War. In the last week of June, 1940, however, the surrender of France caused a violent quickening of the tempo and events moved in a direction very detrimental to Great Britain and the Commonwealth, who found themselves carrying on the war unaided and with resources strained to the uttermost. It was in those melancholy circumstances that the Chiefs of Staff met in July and upon the last day of that month gave it as their considered opinion that the defence of Singapore must, in the absence of a fleet urgently needed elsewhere, depend primarily upon air power.

Germany controlled every European port and naval base from Narvik to Bordeaux. With the entry of Italy into the war, the position in the Mediterranean was precarious and the resources of the Royal Navy, great though they were, had been stretched almost to breaking point. This bastion of the Far East lay many miles outside the immediate area of hostilities and was designed to stand against a foe who had not yet declared his intentions and might, if fortune so willed, never do so. Nevertheless, in planning, every possibility must be considered, provision made for every contingency. To enable Singapore to be a firm base from which a fleet could operate, aircraft must, if possible, be provided for its defence. The Chiefs of Staff laid down that by the end of 1941 the strength of the Royal Air Force in the Far East should consist of 336 modern first-line aircraft, supported by adequate reserves and the necessary administrative units. They must be ready to operate from Hong Kong to Calcutta and also from Ceylon. They were to assure the protection of all our interests in the Far East.

This appreciation was considered by the authorities on the spot and judged by them to be insufficient. On 16th October, 1940, a conference at which all Commands in the Far East were represented, urged that the recommended establishment of 336 aircraft should be increased to 566. This in its view was the minimum first-line strength required to meet our Far Eastern commitments. With an increase in air strength in Malaya, a corresponding increase in the army, largely to provide for the defence of the many new airfields it would be necessary to build, was also needed.

To put down requirements on paper, however, was one thing; to translate them into fighters, bombers and reconnaissance aircraft was another. The translation was never made. By 8th December, 1941, the day on which war with Japan broke out, only 362 aircraft belonging to the Royal Air Force had been gathered together. Of these 233 were serviceable.

This weakness in the air, due first and last to the neglect of the Royal Air Force in years of peace, was a reason, perhaps the main reason, why the Japanese were able to achieve complete and overwhelming victory in a campaign which lasted but seventy days. Throughout that brief space of time the squadrons of the Royal Air Force and the Royal Australian Air Force charged with the defence of Malaya were at no moment capable of dealing adequately with those opposed to them or with the naval and military forces of the invader. They had no modern aircraft with which to perform this task. That is the bald truth.

It may seem strange that so vital a bastion of the Empire as Singapore, keystone of our Far Eastern defences, should have been left to defend itself with outmoded weapons in an outmoded manner against the assault of an enemy fully alive to the implications of modern warfare and eager to translate theory into practice. That Singapore was in this lamentable condition was due in the last resort not to any failure in London to appreciate the significance of the air weapon but to the inexorable pressure of events. It had always been understood that, if Singapore were attacked, its defence from the air was to be secured by a prompt use of that most valuable quality of an air force, its flexibility. A chain of airfields, stretching from England to the Far East through the Mediterranean and India had been constructed, so that reinforcements of fighters and bombers could be sent in a matter of days to the fortress. That the chain might be interrupted or that the Royal Air Force might be fully occupied elsewhere had either not been contemplated, or it had been decided, quite rightly, to construct the chain while it was still possible to do so, in the hope that one day enough aircraft to make proper use of it would be forthcoming. When the crisis came, they were not; and the loss of Singapore was part of the price paid for the incurable habit of the English of allowing their armed forces in times of peace to fall far below the lowest level of safety.

This was clear enough, among others, to Duff Cooper, the energetic Chancellor of the Duchy of Lancaster who had been despatched by the Prime Minister to Singapore and the Far East three months before the war with Japan broke out. His orders were to report on the general situation in those territories of the British and Dutch Empires likely to be attacked, were Japan to join Germany. An extensive tour showed him the inadequacy of the defence and the difficulties facing the commanders on the spot. He did what he could by making strong representations, some of them direct to the Prime Minister, to remedy a state of affairs for which there was, in fact, no remedy.

On 18th November, 1940, Air Chief Marshal Sir Robert Brooke-Popham, a veteran of the First World War, took up his duties as Commander-in-Chief, Far East. Placed in operational control of the army and air forces, his instructions were on two points very definite. He was to do all that was possible to prevent war with Japan—'Avoidance of war with Japan is the basis of Far East policy and provocation must be rigidly avoided', telegraphed the Chiefs of Staff in March 1941, and repeated this instruction in September—and to rely for the maintenance of the defence of the Empire in the Far East, 'primarily on air power'.

A brief study of the area covered by his Command, which included Hong Kong, Borneo, Malaya, Burma, Ceylon and the Indian Ocean as far as Durban and Mombasa, convinced Brooke-Popham that the problem was, fundamentally, a naval one. Although the army and air force together might be able to defend many important bases and to repel an enemy, his ultimate defeat could not be brought about unless control of communications by sea was continuous and assured. To achieve this, air superiority over inshore waters was a necessity, and it was here that, knowing the weakness of his air forces, the Commander-in-Chief found himself in so grave a difficulty. Shortage of aircraft, though the principal, was not the only cause of his embarrassment. Problems connected with the attitude of the Services towards each other, with the Intelligence Service, with airfields, with the warning system, with air raid precautions, with co-operation with the Dutch in Sumatra and Java, jostled each other in his office. Compared with these, the fact that the headquarters of the army were five miles distant from those of the air force, that the Governor and other civil authorities were established in Singapore itself and the Naval Headquarters were thirty-five miles by road from the city, was of minor importance.

Brooke-Popham set himself grimly to his grim task. It took him very little time to discover that relations between the army and the air force were by no means happy; there was mutual jealousy and a mutual determination to avoid co-operation. It was not until the command of both Services had been placed in new hands and their headquarters provided with a Combined Operations Room that these troubles began to disappear. Relations on the other hand between the navy and the air force were good. The fact was that all three Services had yet to learn, or rather to remember, that success in the conduct of a war, in which all three are involved, depends on co-operation, mutual and unrestrained.

There was, too, an almost entire lack of what is known broadly as Intelligence. In November, 1940, the Far Eastern Combined Bureau, established with the object of supplying information to all three Services, was in the charge of the Navy and located at Naval Headquarters. The information it produced had, not unnaturally, a degree of naval bias.

The most important weapon in the defence of Malaya and Singapore, the Royal Air Force, was in the hands of Air Vice-Marshal C. W. H. Pulford, destined a few months later to die tragically of exhaustion and malaria, a fugitive from a disaster he had been powerless to prevent. His duties were taken over on 11th February, 1942, four days before the end of the siege, by Air Vice-Marshal P. C. Maltby, who had been his assistant for some weeks, and who, together with so many of his officers and men, was to spend the rest of the war in a Japanese prison camp. Upon these two men fell the responsibility of conducting the war in the air above the tangled jungles of Malaya and the sultry seas that wash her coasts. One had already almost reached breaking point, brought thither by nine months of unremitting labour rendered even more arduous by a severe shortage of trained staff; the other was a newcomer constrained to assume command in the midst of a campaign already lost.

Apart from a grave lack of suitable aircraft, Pulford was continually faced with the difficulty of constructing and maintaining suitable airfields. For this, the topography of Malaya was largely responsible. A rugged, heavily-forested mountain range runs down the centre of the peninsula, dividing the eastern from the western coastal belt and ending at Johore, opposite Singapore Island. The coastal belts themselves are cut up by many broken hills, the plains in between them covered by plantations of rubber or paddy-fields. Rainfall is heavy throughout the year and persistent cloud formations, clinging to the central range of mountains, are a severe handicap to the flight of aircraft from one side of Malaya to the other. Many airfields had thus to be built on the exposed east coast and several were sited in spots where their defence proved difficult, if not impossible. In particular, the landing grounds at Kota Bharu and Kuantan had been placed next to long and excellent sea beaches, a fact of which the Japanese were to take full advantage.

Despite unceasing efforts the construction of airfields progressed but slowly. There were eleven separate provincial government authorities in Malaya, with all of whom negotiations for the acquisition of land had to be conducted. Only when emergency powers had been invoked, were the delays thus caused brought to an end. Other and even more exasperating obstacles were a shortage of mechanical plant and of operators to drive and maintain the few machines available, and a great lack of coolies. All labour was voluntary, and though a permanent labour committee existed to check expensive and wasteful competition between the Services and the Government departments, it could exercise no control over civilian firms which paid higher rates and showed little concern with problems of defence and little desire to co-operate. It had been dinned into ears, perhaps not as deaf as they seemed to be, that the production of rubber and tin was of the first and last importance and the inevitable conclusion had been drawn.

With such an attitude it is scarcely surprising that the Royal Air Force should have found the difficulties of airfield construction so numerous and so great. Nevertheless, by the outbreak of war, nine airfields were more or less fit for use in the north-west, three in the north-east, one in eastern, three in central and six in southern Malaya, though most of them still lacked facilities which in any other theatre of war would have been regarded as indispensable. There were in addition four on the island of Singapore itself, of which the most important was Seletar, close to the naval base. That at Tengah was completed on the day war broke out by the united efforts of officers and men stationed there. They laid 400 yards of metal paving in twenty-four hours.

Of the airfields so built, fifteen possessed no concrete runways but were surfaced with grass, a serious matter in a country where tropical rainfalls are frequent and severe; several, such as that at Alor Star, were out-of-date, with congested buildings close to the runway and few facilities for dispersal; very few were camouflaged, so that they 'stood out stark and bare against the surrounding country'. Ground defences were inadequate or non-existent. The Commander-in-Chief had laid down that each airfield was to be provided with eight heavy and eight light anti-aircraft guns. When war broke out, not one possessed this number. Only seventeen per cent of the quantity authorised had reached Malaya. The best defended airfield was Seletar, which had eight Bofors; the worst those in central and southern Malaya and a number in the northern districts, which had no anti-aircraft defence at all.

Facilities for the repair and maintenance of aircraft were equally deficient and such as did exist were concentrated in the workshops at Seletar, where No. 151 Maintenance Unit was stationed. These workshops, though equipped only to deal with the requirements of at most two squadrons, were called upon to service the whole air force in Malaya. As twenty-seven modifications had to be made in the Brewster Buffalo fighter alone before it could be used in battle, the magnitude of their task is apparent. Of the two additional Maintenance Units authorised—Nos. 152 and 153—the former never progressed beyond the embryo stage whilst the latter though possessed of personnel was lacking in equipment.

Radar units to detect the approach of hostile aircraft and ships were also inadequate. On the east coast of Malaya, where the first landings took place, only two, those at Mersing and Bukit Chunang, were operational. The remaining five were still under construction. On the west coast, one had been completed and two others were approaching completion. Only on Singapore Island itself were all the posts, to the number of three, in working order. With so poor and thin a radar net, adequate warning was out of the question.

As with Radar Units, so with Signals. Teleprinter lines linked Air Headquarters in Singapore with the airfields on the island, but not with those in the Malay Peninsula itself, which were connected with Headquarters by only two telephone lines from north-west Malaya and one from the north-east and east. These had to be shared with the army and the civil administration, they passed through the ordinary exchanges, and there were no provisions for secrecy. On one occasion the Commander-in-Chief, in the middle of an important conversation, was informed by the operator that his three minutes were up and was cut off.

Such were some of the administrative difficulties with which Pulford, and behind him Brooke-Popham, had to contend. Their principal preoccupation, however, remained from first to last the shortage of aircraft and the inadequacy of those which were available. Of these, the most modern, or, more accurately, the least out-of-date, were the Blenheims flown by Nos. 27, 34, 60 and 62 Squadrons of the Royal Air Force and the Hudsons of Nos. 1 and 8 Squadrons of the Royal Australian Air Force. In addition, there were Nos. 36 and

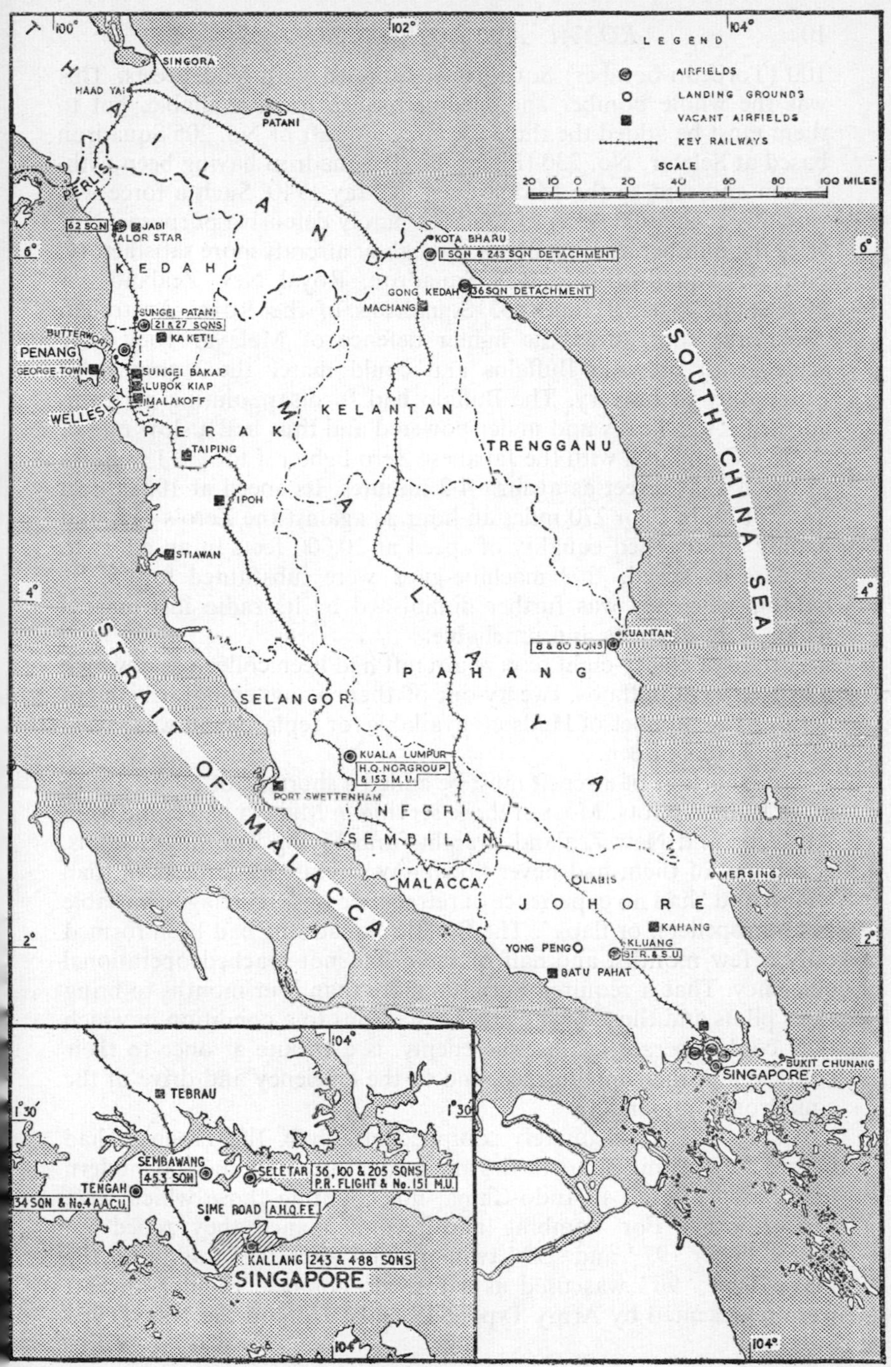

MALAY PENINSULA. LOCATION OF R.A.F. UNITS, 8 DECEMBER 1941

100 (Torpedo-bomber) Squadrons equipped with Vildebeests. This was the whole bomber and reconnaissance force available, but to them must be added the three Catalina aircraft of No. 205 Squadron based at Seletar, No. 230 (Flying Boat) Squadron having been withdrawn and sent to the Middle East in May 1940. Such a force was woefully inadequate even if used for purely defensive purposes. Nor were the number and quality of the fighter aircraft more satisfactory. No. 243 Squadron, No. 488 Squadron, Royal New Zealand Air Force, and Nos. 21 and 453 Squadrons of the Royal Australian Air Force constituted the fighter defence of Malaya. They were armed with Brewster Buffalos and could match the Japanese Air Force only in bravery. The Buffalo had 'a disappointing performance'. It 'was heavy and under-powered and thus had a slow rate of climb'. Compared with the Japanese Zero fighter it took 6·1 minutes to reach 13,000 feet as against 4·3 minutes. Its speed at 10,000 feet was not more than 270 miles an hour as against the Zero's 315, and it only approached equality of speed at 20,000 feet. In an effort to increase its speed, ·303 machine-guns were substituted for ·5. Its fighting efficiency was further diminished by its radio instruments which were obsolete and unreliable.

A total of eighty-eight reserve aircraft had been collected, of which fifty-two were Buffalos, twenty-one of them being temporarily out of action. The number of Hudsons available for replacement was seven, of Blenheims fifteen.

To a shortage of aircraft must be added a shortage of pilots, above all of trained pilots. Most of those serving in Malaya had come from Australia and New Zealand straight from Flying Training Schools, and many of them had never flown any aircraft more modern than a Hart and 'had no experience of retractable undercarriages, variable pitch propellers, or flaps'. The Buffalo Squadrons had been formed only a few months, and half of them had not reached operational efficiency. That it required but little more than four months to bring their pilots and those of the other squadrons to a condition in which they could operate against the enemy, is a tribute at once to their courage and their intelligence, and to the efficiency and drive of the squadron commanders.

Against this inadequately equipped air force, the Japanese had before the opening of hostilities amassed a force of some 300 modern land-based aircraft in Indo-China, not counting those which were carrier-borne. For bombing and reconnaissance they relied on Army Types '97' and '99' twin-engined aircraft. In addition the Navy Type '96' was used as a torpedo-bomber. Fighter aircraft were represented by Army Types '1' and '97' and the Navy Type

'0'—the Zero. This last aircraft proved the greatest surprise of the campaign. It possessed a top speed estimated at some 350 miles an hour, was armed with two 20-mm. cannons and two 7·7-mm. machine-guns, and was extremely manœuvrable. Moreover, its range was appreciably increased by the fitting of an additional petrol tank which could be jettisoned when empty. Such a fighter was more than a match for a Buffalo and also for the Hurricane Mark II, except at 20,000 feet. The Japanese had made use of the Navy Zero against the Chinese in the spring of 1940. Some details of its performance had been divulged by American newspaper correspondents stationed in Chungking, who had seen it in action at that time, and in the same year more details had reached the Air Ministry from other sources in that city. On 2nd September, 1941, this information was duly forwarded to the Far Eastern Combined Bureau for transmission to Air Headquarters. It never arrived there. Moreover, in addition to the information on this fighter provided by the Air Ministry, a detailed description of it, written in Chinese, reached Singapore in July and was duly translated. What happened next is a matter for conjecture since all records have been destroyed; but it seems probable that this very important report formed part of the mass of accumulated files with which the makeshift Intelligence Section, set up at Air Headquarters in October 1941, attempted to deal. When war broke out, they had by no means completed their task and the report remained undiscovered. The result was a disastrous surprise causing many casualties to pilots who had been informed that the Buffalos they were flying were faster and better than any Japanese fighter—not one of which, it was reported, could reach 20,000 feet—and who had in consequence evolved a system of air tactics based on this ill-founded assumption.

The Commander-in-Chief and his Air Officer Commanding strove with might and main to remedy the deficiencies of their air force. On 30th June, 18th August and 20th August, 1941, urgent signals were sent to Whitehall describing the condition of affairs and asking for reinforcements. 'At present', said Brooke-Popham, 'not only is our ability to attack shipping deplorably weak, but we have not the staying power to sustain even what we could now do. As our air effort dwindles . . . so will the enemy's chance of landing increase'. He ended by once more emphasising his main preoccupation. 'I have no doubt what our first requirement here is. We want to increase our hitting power against ships and our capacity to go on hitting'.

His warnings did not by any means fall upon deaf ears, but the Chiefs of Staff were at that time powerless to aid him. As they pointed out, production of aircraft was disappointing—it had been intended to replace the out-of-date Vildebeests with Beauforts manufactured in Australia, but they were not forthcoming; the air forces in the Middle East had to be reinforced in certain expectation of a German attack in the spring of 1942; and finally, and perhaps most important of all, Russia, fighting desperately against a heavy and concentrated onslaught, had to be assisted by every means and to the greatest possible extent. At the end of 1941, there was on every front a shortage of everything, from trained men to up-to-date equipment.

Such then was the general position of the air forces in Malaya on the eve of war. They, together with the small Dutch Air Force of twenty-two Glen Martin bombers and nine Buffalo fighters, were to form the air cover and air support for the navy and army. The Navy received a strong reinforcement on 2nd December in the form of the new battleship *Prince of Wales* and the older battle cruiser *Repulse;* the army was short of the troops and equipment considered to be the minimum for a successful defence. On 8th December, 1941, the total strength of the troops was just under 87,000 officers and men, very few of them trained in jungle warfare. They were without tanks and possessed only a small number of anti-tank weapons.

Behind the armed forces was the civilian population. Their attitude was of importance, for it inevitably affected the spirit of the fighting men. It must be noted with regret, therefore, that at every turn the efforts of the Commander-in-Chief and his subordinate commanders were, if not positively hampered, at least not actively encouraged by the local population, both European and Asiatic. The first had enjoyed many years of prosperity, not seriously impaired even during the slump of the early 1930's. They had behind them a tradition of wealth, or at least of easy circumstances, more than a century old. Yet comparatively few of them regarded Malaya as their home. It was no Kenya nor South Africa nor New Zealand whither a man could go to build his life and raise a family. This was not their own, their native land—this rich, steamy country where a man's shirt stuck to his back all the year round, and where ' the showroom of the house was the cold room . . . the daily retreat from the humid heat '. No doubt the uncomfortable climate was greatly responsible for their lack of energy and determination. Be that as it may, the help and comfort afforded to the fighting forces by men of the same race whose lives and property they were called upon to defend, was far smaller than it should have been.

While relations between the Services and the civilian communities up-country were good and in many places cordial, the planters doing all they could to help the soldiers and airmen, the reverse was so in

Singapore. In that city 'the civilian community', reports the Commander-in-Chief, 'on the whole seemed to resent the presence of the Services as disturbing their ordered way of living'. The Japanese were to disturb it even more. This habit of ease remained with them to the end. Less than a week before the city surrendered, an observer could note that 'there were queues outside the cinemas'.

The attitude of the Asiatic population was, for the most part, one of indifference. The largest part of it was Chinese, but even though their compatriots in China had been fighting for four long years and more against Japan, few recruits from them were forthcoming and it is hard to escape the conclusion that the British administration had not sufficiently explained to them that, were war to break out, Great Britain and China would find themselves allies against a common foe. When this came to pass, the Chinese in Singapore showed themselves, particularly in the Air Raid Precautions organisation, to be calm and steadfast. They never gave way to panic even during the worst raids. The Malays were even more indifferent than the Chinese. The several thousand Indian labourers, mostly Tamils, had been drawn to Malaya by the prospect of high wages. Like their British masters, they had no particular love for the country and intended, like them, to return home as soon as they had made sufficient money.

In passive defence against air raids the inhabitants of Singapore and of Malayan towns in general were especially ill-prepared. Everywhere precautions were primitive and for the most part ineffectual. To achieve a satisfactory black-out was difficult, for to mask lights was to mask ventilation, and in the climate of Malaya the consequences were disagreeable or worse. A 'brown-out' rather than a 'black-out' was therefore adopted and proved on the whole not unsatisfactory. The provision of air raid shelters, however, was a different matter. In Singapore, where the water level is close to the surface, the digging of slit trenches was not only useless but dangerous, because they soon became filled with water and formed breeding places for mosquitoes. The medical authorities were against the construction of surface shelters which they maintained would interfere with the circulation of air and therefore be the cause of epidemics. Such views were doubtless correct in theory, but when the moment came and Singapore found itself subjected to a series of air attacks, which by the standard of 1941 and 1942 must be described as severe, the casualties caused by lack of adequate shelters were unduly high.

Brooke-Popham had not been in command two months before the entry of Japanese forces into Cambodia and Cochin China, often rumoured, became an accomplished fact. At that time, however, and during the months that followed, it was not easy to decide whether this move was intended to prepare the way for an attack on Siam or on Malaya; but by November, 1941, indications that an attack on one or the other was imminent began to multiply. Four Japanese cruisers and some destroyers were reported in the South China Sea; the 5th Japanese Division, highly trained in landing operations, had moved into southern Indo-China and the number of Japanese aircraft there had increased from 74 to some 300 in the space of a month. They did not remain inactive upon their newly seized or constructed airfields, but with increasing frequency carried out long-range reconnaissance flights over Malaya. One of their airborne cameras, which had become detached from its mounting, was picked up in Ipoh about this time. The Royal Air Force did their best to do likewise, but the enemy's main sea base at Kamranh was out of range, and the Commander-in-Chief was unable to persuade General MacArthur, commanding in Manila, to send a Boeing Fortress, which had the necessary range and ceiling, to photograph that harbour. Orders from Washington, said the General, prevented him from carrying out this request. At the time, America, it seemed, was as reluctant as was Great Britain to provoke Japan.

On 28th November, information arrived from Saigon to the effect that it was the intention of the Japanese to land troops in southern Siam on 1st December. The report was not taken very seriously, but as a precaution Air Headquarters were ordered to maintain a daily reconnaissance seaward in an easterly direction; though, in pursuance of the strict injunctions of the Chiefs of Staff, it was made clear that 'a striking force will not be ordered to attack the convoy, if found'. The aircraft flew daily on their appointed courses, but saw nothing upon the wide spaces of the sea until 3rd December, when two large cargo boats were sighted.

It was at this juncture when a Japanese invasion of Siam appeared to be imminent that Brooke-Popham was faced with a most difficult decision. Was this the moment to launch operation 'Matador'? As a plan it had long been matured and did not lack boldness. An advance was to be made into the Kra Isthmus and a line occupied to the north of Haad Yai junction in the area of Singora. From a military point of view such a position was the easiest to occupy and to defend. It would make it possible to attack the enemy when he would be at his most vulnerable, at the moment of landing, and it would add to the number of airfields available and deny them to the Japanese. From the air force point of view this would obviously be a great advantage. The squadrons would be closer to the battlefield and therefore in a better position to support the land forces. They in their turn would be able to protect the air force.

There was, however, a political consideration. The Kra Isthmus is situated not in northern Malaya, but in Siam (Thailand), an ostensibly neutral country. This neutrality would have to be violated, and had not the Commander-in-Chief been directed most firmly to do everything he could to avoid war with Japan? Such a violation would almost certainly lead to immediate war and would do grave harm to our cause in America.

Brooke-Popham proceeded with caution. Detailed plans for operation 'Matador' were drawn up but were kept very secret and for weeks a ban, which could be lifted only by the War Cabinet, was placed on their execution. Two days before the Japanese attack, however, the Commander-in-Chief was informed by Whitehall that he was free to launch the operation if he had reason to believe that the Japanese intended to land on the Kra Isthmus, or if they had already violated any other part of Siamese territory.

To take part in operation 'Matador', Air Headquarters formed Norgroup, consisting of two Blenheim bomber squadrons, Nos. 62 and 34, one fighter squadron, No. 21 of the Royal Australian Air Force armed with Buffalos, and one night-fighter squadron, No. 27, flying Blenheims, to work in conjunction with the III Indian Corps. When the preliminary order was issued on 22nd November, No. 21 Squadron joined No. 27 Squadron at Sungei Patani; No. 62 Squadron was at Alor Star and No. 34 Squadron at Tengah.

With each day that passed it became increasingly obvious that the situation was moving from bad to worse, and moving rapidly. More and more Japanese movements were reported and it presently became plain to the Commander-in-Chief that a decision whether to launch operation 'Matador' or not could not be further delayed. On 29th November the period of warning was reduced from seventy-two to twelve hours. A week went by and then at two o'clock in the afternoon of 6th December the curtain lifted. Hudsons flown by No. 1 Squadron, Royal Australian Air Force, based on Kota Bharu, reported sighting, eighty miles east-south-east of the most southern point of Indo-China, two convoys steaming west. One was composed of twenty-two merchant vessels of an average burden of 10,000 tons, escorted by one battleship, probably the *Kongo*, five cruisers and seven destroyers; the other was made up of twenty-one merchant ships escorted by two cruisers and ten destroyers. Farther to the westward, one Japanese cruiser and three merchant ships were also sighted steering north-west. The achievement of the squadron in finding these ships, more than 300 miles away from the Malayan coast, was a tribute to their training and persistence. The pilots had evidently well digested the first part of the general order issued to the Royal Air Force 'to find the enemy at sea as far away from Malaya as possible'. Was the second part, 'to strike hard and often', now to be put into operation?

The Commander-in-Chief hesitated, as well he might, for until he was aware that the Japanese were apparently moving by sea against the Kra Isthmus or 'had violated any other part of Thailand', he had been forbidden to attack them. He consulted his naval colleagues: Vice-Admiral Geoffrey Layton, Admiral Sir Tom Phillips, who had just arrived flying his flag in the *Prince of Wales*, and Rear Admiral Palliser, his Chief of Staff. These officers were in doubt about the future course of the convoys. Would they continue to sail onwards and thus reach the Kra Isthmus, or would they turn and seek anchorage for the night somewhere on the west coast of Indo-China? The matter was earnestly debated and the conclusion presently reached that this second possibility was the more probable. Brooke-Popham and the naval chiefs were inclined to think that the Japanese expeditions would enter Siamese waters in the hope of being attacked and thus of providing a *casus belli*. In the circumstances, the Air Chief Marshal decided not to launch operation 'Matador' but to wait until further reconnaissance should put the destination of the convoys beyond reasonable doubt. At this point the weather intervened.

The Hudsons had found the convoys at the extreme limit of their range and had not been able to remain in contact with them. A Catalina flying boat of No. 205 Squadron was despatched to shadow the convoys throughout the night. The hours went by, but no signals were received from it, and a second Catalina sent on the same mission was equally silent. The first eventually returned having seen nothing of the enemy. The second was shot down by the air escort of the Japanese convoy based on Phu Kok off the west coast of Cambodia where an airfield had been constructed in less than a month. As soon as day dawned on the 7th Pulford sent out another reconnaissance of Hudsons with orders to regain contact with the convoys and keep them in view. At the same time all the air forces were brought to 'No. 1 degree of readiness', which meant that they were to be prepared for immediate operations against the enemy. But the Hudsons failed to repeat their success of the previous day. Two out of the three despatched returned because of bad weather; the third ranged the Gulf of Siam, but in the low cloud and rain prevailing, saw nothing. The Air Officer Commanding now relied upon the Catalinas of No. 205 Squadron to regain contact with the convoys. They, too, failed, and the approach of the Japanese towards Singora remained, in consequence, undiscovered. Most of their transports had, in fact, made for that Siamese port, sailing a somewhat devious course to reach it. Only eight and a cruiser ultimately

H.M.S. PRINCE OF WALES AT SINGAPORE

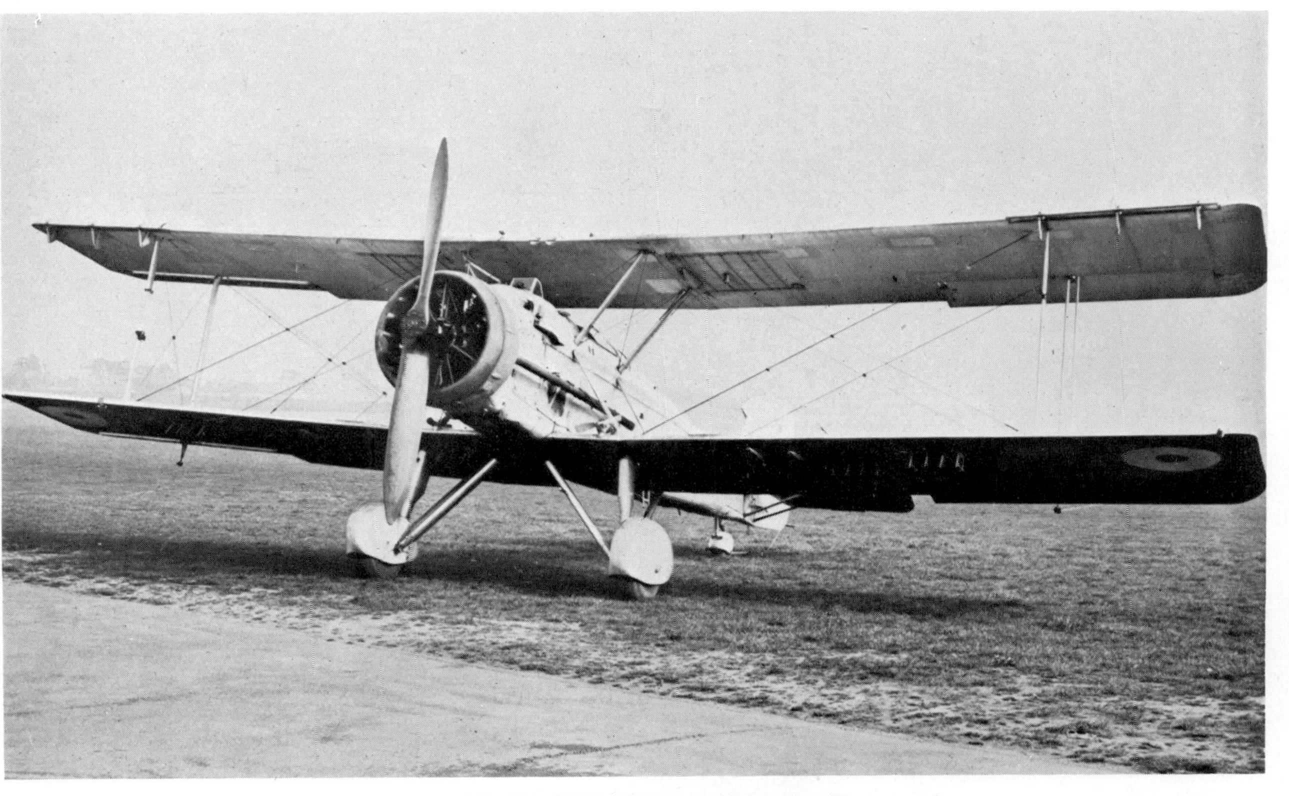

VILDEBEEST IV TORPEDO-BOMBER (Prototype)

made for Kota Bharu. It was, perhaps, part of this force which was seen by a Hudson late that afternoon. Fire was opened upon it by an enemy warship.

All this, however, was unknown to Brooke-Popham, and a final decision concerning operation ' Matador ' had still to be taken. To launch it too late would be useless, for the troops must be in position at least twenty-four hours ahead of the Japanese, and this would be impossible if the convoys were making for Singora and had not turned north-west. The Commander-in-Chief was in a position of the greatest difficulty. Not to move the troops and the air force behind them into the Kra Isthmus would be to lose all hope of gaining the initiative, if war were to break out. On the other hand, to be the first into Siam would almost certainly provoke war. At this juncture a telegram, in which it is difficult not to detect a note of hysteria, arrived from Sir Josiah Crosby, British Representative in Siam. 'For God's sake', wired the Minister, 'do not allow British forces to occupy one inch of Thai territory unless and until Japan has struck the first blow at Thailand'. Sir Josiah went on to state that the attack of the Japanese on Thailand had been planned for 3rd December, had then been postponed, but was due to take place in the immediate future. It was in fact taking place at that moment. But at that moment, too, the Commander-in-Chief decided to cancel operation 'Matador'. His reasons, he explained afterwards, were both political and strategic. If the conclusions drawn from an incomplete reconnaissance, not subsequently confirmed, were incorrect, then Britain would be the first to infringe Siamese neutrality, and this was precisely what the Japanese desired. If they were correct and the Japanese were landing at Singora, it would be too late to take up the chosen line.

As that Sunday dragged on, and no news of Japanese aggression arrived—Pearl Harbour was bombed that day but no report of this reached Singapore until the following morning—Brooke-Popham and the other commanders became more and more convinced that the Japanese, by entering the Gulf of Siam, were doing their utmost to provoke an incident which would give them the excuse for war they needed. The final decision to abandon operation 'Matador' was not taken until nine o'clock that evening, after a report had been received from the pilot of a Hudson that three small Japanese ships had been seen passing Singora, heading south. Four and a half hours later the roar of guns off the coast at Kota Bharu, and an hour and a half after that the loud voices of exploding bombs in the streets of Singapore, scattered the clouds of uncertainty once and for all. Japan had struck. War had come to Malaya and the enemy had gained the initiative.

CHAPTER II
The Fall of Singapore

THE first of the armed forces to go into action on that morning of 7th December, 1941 was the Allied Air Force, whose pilots soon found themselves in close combat with skilful and resolute men of long experience in the Chinese war, flying far superior aircraft. At that time the Japanese Air Forces were allowed a wide measure of freedom in their choice of methods, but were regarded as less than the equal of the Japanese Army and Navy, to which they served as an auxiliary. For this purpose there were two air forces. The Army Air Force was designed to strike fast and hard in close support of the armies in the field. The duty of the Naval Air Force was to attack shipping, to bomb suitable targets on shore, and to cover naval units. In other words, the Japanese air arms were almost entirely tactical and their duty was to secure for the two other arms the highest measure of freedom in action. They were not regarded as wholly independent, and were not therefore used strategically as a general rule, though on occasion they could be and were. In this conception lay a hidden defect. The Army Air Force and the Navy Air Force being kept apart, performed each a different service and were not interchangeable; there was little co-operation between them.

Units of the 3rd and 5th of the five Air Divisions which made up the Army Air Force were used in the attacks on Kota Bharu, Alor Star and the other airfields of northern Malaya. Of the three remaining Divisions, the 1st never left Japan and the 2nd and 4th did so only towards the summer of 1944. Each Air Division was divided into two Air Brigades and two Air Sectors. A Brigade was composed of Flying Regiments of three squadrons made up of sixteen aircraft each. The Sectors were manned by an average of ten Airfield Battalions responsible for construction and maintenance. This was the basis of their organization, the flexibility of which made it possible to meet emergencies. It approximated to that of the *Luftwaffe*.

There was a firm bond between the Navy and the Naval Air Force, whose task it was to control both the skies and the seas. The

Japanese were fully persuaded that, to quote from one of their appreciations, ' The main role in control of the sea has passed from the surface forces to the air forces. Air battles which were formerly considered to be the preliminary skirmishes before the decisive battle of the fleets have themselves become decisive battles . . . Because control of the air precedes control of the sea, it is no longer possible to win and maintain control of the sea only by destroying enemy surface forces in a decisive battle . . . Air power will from now on be the mainstay of the navy . . . It is necessary to discard the relics of the outmoded tactical idea founded on previous theories which stakes everything on a decisive fleet engagement '.

The Japanese Naval Air Force consisted of about ninety Air Groups, with complementary forces beneath them on the ground or on the sea. The groups were not all of equal size and the largest comprised some eighty-four aircraft, manned and maintained by about 2,000 officers and men. Between forty and fifty Groups were organised into Air Flotillas and Fleets, and of these it was the 22nd and 23rd Air Flotillas, part of the 11th Air Fleet, which operated with those units of the Japanese Navy ordered to take part in the invasion of French Indo-China, Malaya and the Dutch East Indies.

The armament used by both air services was more or less identical. Bombs ranged in weight from 15 to 1,000 kilograms. Neither Service used bombers for minelaying, and generally, in bombing attacks, bombs were released simultaneously on a signal from the leading aircraft. In raids on airfields or carriers, aircraft on the ground or on the deck were considered to be the most important targets. When attacked by Allied fighters, bombers would tighten their formation and usually increase speed, but did not lose height. Their pilots had obviously studied the war in Europe very carefully and could cope adequately with all the more usual forms of attack. After a month or two, however, pilots of the Royal Air Force discovered that by varying their tactics and making use of unexpected manœuvres the Japanese bombers were thrown into confusion, of which the first sign was a loud outbreak of conversation on the radio telephone, followed by a breaking up of the formation into individual units which could be dealt with piecemeal.

When bomber formations were given escort, the fighters normally flew in three groups, two at 3,000 feet below, one to port, the other to starboard of the bomber formation and the third at 3,000 feet above it, and slightly to the rear. Three to one was considered to be the ideal ratio of fighters to bombers.

At the outbreak of war the standard formation for bombers was made up of thirty-six aircraft. This number soon fell to twenty-seven, then to eighteen and finally to three. The 'box' formation was thought to be the best protection against fighter attacks and evasive action to counteract anti-aircraft fire was rarely taken. As the war progressed, suicide pilots, all volunteers, were recruited. In the Army Air Force they were known as *Tokkatai* and in the Navy as *Kamikaze* and were sworn to fly their aircraft into the chosen target, there to perish with it. Had it proved necessary for the forces of Mountbatten to carry out the invasion of Japan, plans had been made by the Japanese to use about 1,000 suicide pilots in the Tokio area and about 3,000 in Kyushu. Such were the formidable enemies which the Royal Air Force with the Royal Australian Air Force and their brothers in arms, the American Army and Navy Air Forces and the Dutch Air Forces, were called upon to fight.

The campaign opened with an attempt on the part of the Hudsons of No. 1 Squadron, Royal Australian Air Force, to interfere with the landings of the Japanese Army at Kota Bharu. The weather on the 7th had cleared about midnight over this station, but the surface of the airfield was boggy as the result of recent heavy rain. All was quiet until about one o'clock, when a Japanese cruiser began to shell the coast. At the same time eight to ten transports were observed to be anchored off shore and landing craft to be moving from them towards the beaches. These ships were part of the main convoy, of which the remainder had made for Singora. For the political reasons mentioned in the last Chapter, they had been allowed to approach unmolested, and the Station Commander, mindful of his instructions not to assault the enemy at sea without express orders, had to wait some forty minutes until new orders arrived before attacking the transports. Altogether that night seventeen sorties were made by the Hudsons, which were able to destroy one transport and to damage severely two others. Landing barges were also attacked and the estimated casualties among the Japanese were 3,000. In this affair, two Hudsons were lost. At dawn, Vildebeests of No. 36 Squadron, Royal Air Force, flying from Gong Kedah in heavy rain, unsuccessfully attacked the cruiser with torpedoes. By then the situation at Kota Bharu appeared to be in hand, for the Japanese naval force was withdrawing. It had accomplished its immediate object and was soon to return, reinforced. The attack on Kota Bharu was a secondary operation but its effect was very grave for it lured all the squadrons of Norgroup but one towards that area.

Meanwhile, the main Japanese landings were taking place, unmolested, in Singora, in Siam, the Government of which had surrendered immediately. These were discovered by the only Beaufort in Malaya. On its return, badly damaged, to Kota Bharu, the pilot reported a large concentration of Japanese vessels from which troops were pouring on to the beaches at Singora and Patani. More ominous still, the photographs taken revealed the presence of some sixty aircraft, mainly fighters, on Singora airfield. Tactical surprise had been achieved.

While a fierce and not unsuccessful action was being fought at Kota Bharu, the town of Singapore itself was recovering from its first air raid. This had taken place at four o'clock that same morning, the eighth, and bombs had fallen close to the airfields and the harbour. They caused little military damage but killed sixty-one civilians, mostly Chinese, and injured 133. The defence had received thirty minutes' warning from the radar and observer posts and duly went into action. Although three Buffalos of No. 453 Squadron, Royal Australian Air Force, at Sembawang, were at once warmed up, permission to take off was not granted, to the chagrin of their pilots, one of whom described the oncoming Japanese bomber formation as 'the most perfect night-fighter target which I have ever seen'. Air Headquarters preferred to leave the guns to deal with the raiders. This may, or may not, have been a mistake, but about the behaviour of the Air Raid Precautions organisation there can be no doubt. Its headquarters were not fully manned and no reply was received to repeated summonses by telephone to go into action. Not until a direct approach was made to Sir Shenton Thomas, the Governor, did the air raid sirens sound, and even then the brilliant street lighting of the city was not extinguished. This omission was not so serious as might appear, for there was a full tropic moon that night in the rays of which Singapore in all its detail was clearly visible.

On the following day, the ninth, while its inhabitants were gaping at the bomb-holes—their behaviour was very similar to that of other unhappy citizens in other unhappy cities in other zones of war—the fighting at Kota Bharu was still continuing. By four o'clock in the afternoon, the Japanese had landed in force and reached the boundaries of the airfield. The small military force covering the beaches, fighting with the greatest desperation and heedless of casualties, was driven back and the station could no longer be defended. Its evacuation was ordered and five Hudsons and seven Vildebeests retired successfully to Kuantan. To enable them to do so a stout resistance was put up on the airfield itself, both by the remnants of the Army elements of the 11th Indian Division, and the air force ground staff. 'We fought with rifles and tommy-guns, from billet to billet', says Aircraftman H. G. Edwards, who that day was seeing action for the first time. ' The Japanese would be in one, we in the other, and the range was twenty yards. Very soon all aircraft which had not got away were a burnt mass of twisted metal, and still the Japs came on '. The ground staff held out till the next day and eventually, under cover of the ' merciful rain ', got away, first to Kuala Lipis, then by rail to Singapore.

The quality of the pilots engaged in this, the first action of the war in Malaya, may be judged from the bearing of an unknown Blenheim pilot who, his aircraft on fire, disdained to take to his parachute and dived into a landing craft destroying it and its occupants. A Japanese, subsequently captured, testified to the admiration caused in the ranks of the enemy by this gallant sacrifice.

Before the Royal Air Force bombers could be switched to what should have been the main objectives at Singora and Patani, our airfields in northern Malaya themselves became subject to heavy and continuous attacks from Japanese bombers escorted by fighters. Throughout 8th December Sungei Patani, Penang, Alor Star and Butterworth were assaulted by formations varying in size from twenty-seven to sixty. The bombs used were anti-personnel and fragmentation, and they did serious damage to aircraft and men, but none to the surface of the airfields. These the Japanese were anxious to use as soon as possible, and they wished to capture them in good condition. It was noticed that the raids very often took place when our own squadrons were either landing or taking off, and evidence that information of aircraft movements was reaching the enemy was presently discovered. The most serious of these attacks was that delivered at Alor Star by twenty-seven Japanese aircraft, which succeeded in destroying all but two of the Blenheims of No. 62 Squadron. Two other Squadrons, No. 21 (Fighter) Squadron, Royal Australian Air Force, and No. 27, the night-fighter Blenheims, were reduced, while still grounded, each to four serviceable aircraft. The guns of the Buffalos had proved defective and all were unserviceable.

By the evening of that disastrous day, out of 110 aircraft available in the morning for combat in northern Malaya, only 50 remained in a serviceable condition. It was obvious that the cancellation of operation ' Matador ' was to have a far-reaching influence on the operations of the Royal Air Force in northern Malaya. The airfields at Singora and Patani were in the hands of the enemy; more, they were already being used by him. To attack them without delay was essential if the position was to grow no worse. Accordingly on the next day, the 9th, the two depleted bomber squadrons, Nos. 34 and 62, reinforced by a Blenheim squadron from Kuantan, attempted two counter-attacks. The first, carried out in the afternoon with the loss of five aircraft, was markedly successful and the congested airfield at Singora was repeatedly hit. The second was never launched. As the remnants of the two squadrons were about to take off from Butterworth, the Japanese made a high level bombing attack, followed by low level machine-gun attacks. So successful were these —every aircraft but one was put out of action—that a single Blenheim only, piloted by Flight Lieutenant A. S. K. Scarf, was able to leave the ground. Heedless of the fact that he was alone, he pressed on towards his objective. Over Singora he was attacked by enemy fighters, but dropped his bombs, and turned for home hit in the back and left arm, and mortally wounded. Still conscious, he maintained a running fight until the Malay border was reached. Then, almost dead from loss of blood, he landed successfully in a paddy-field near Alor Star. His navigator was unhurt, but he himself died that night. Five years later he was posthumously awarded the Victoria Cross, the first to be gained in Malaya.

The losses sustained in bombers were so heavy that Pulford reluctantly decided to make no more attacks by day. Already then, before the war was two days old, the situation of the Royal Air Force in northern Malaya, and therefore of the country as a whole, always weak, had become gravely compromised. Further blows were soon to follow, the heaviest of them within twenty-four hours.

It will be remembered that H.M.S. *Prince of Wales*, the latest of our battleships of 35,000 tons displacement and armed with ten 14-inch guns, had arrived in Singapore accompanied by the *Repulse*, an older battlecruiser of 32,000 tons recently reconditioned and armed with six 15-inch guns. These two powerful units had been sent to Singapore to reinforce our Far Eastern defences. By 2nd December, therefore, it could no longer be said that these consisted of a naval base without a fleet. The two great ships, with their escort of four destroyers, reached Singapore six days before the outbreak of hostilities, under the command of Admiral Sir Tom Spencer Vaughan Phillips. Hardly had the first Japanese shells fallen on Kota Bharu, when this short, slight man, in whom the spirit of Drake and Nelson burned with a fierce fire, decided to put to sea with all his force. His purpose was to move north-west up the east coast of Malaya and inflict all the hurt he could upon the Japanese ships, busily engaged in landing troops and equipment in the Singora area of Siam. That such an enterprise was hazardous he well knew, for though there were two powerful ships under his command, either of which was capable of dealing with the Japanese naval escort, there was that unknown quantity, the Japanese Air

Force. Concerning its strength, disposition and efficiency very little was known in Singapore. Admiral Phillips was aware that both the Royal Air Force and the *Regia Aeronautica* possessed torpedo-carrying aircraft with a theoretical range of 500 miles. He was equally aware that no attacks by such aircraft had been made beyond a distance of 200 miles. The best information available led him to believe that the Japanese air forces, both naval and military, were of much the same quality as the Italian and markedly inferior to the *Luftwaffe*. Provided, therefore, that his ships came no nearer than 200 miles to a Japanese air base, they would be immune from dive bombing or torpedo attacks. Bombing from a high level, which he expected, did not unduly trouble him. His ships would be moving at high speed.

The question whether his fleet, which was known as Force 'Z', should be provided with fighter cover and air reconnaissance had been discussed with Pulford, to whom Phillips made three requests. They were, first, that the air force should carry out a reconnaissance a hundred miles to the north of his ships from dawn on Tuesday, 9th December; secondly, that they should reconnoitre Singora at an average distance of ten miles from the coast, the reconnaissance to begin at first light on 10th December; and thirdly, that fighter protection off Singora should be provided from daylight onwards on that same day. At a meeting held soon after noon on 8th December, the Admiral told his Captains that if he could achieve surprise and was granted fighter protection, there was a good chance of 'smashing the Japanese forces' of invasion. He proposed, he added, to attack them soon after dawn on 10th December. Force 'Z' sailed at 1735 hours on 8th December.

It will be noted that at this meeting Phillips made it clear that success depended on the provision of fighter support. For capital ships to enter without it an area dominated by the air power of the enemy would be to run a grave, almost certainly a mortal, risk. Yet it was precisely fighter support which Pulford could not guarantee, and said so. Reconnaissance to the north of Force 'Z' could be provided on the 9th; so, he thought, could reconnaissance up to Singora on the 10th; and in point of fact he was able to provide both on the appointed days and at the appointed hours. Fighter protection, however, could only be given in that area by aircraft flying from airfields situated in northern Malaya. When, on 8th December, Phillips first approached him, Pulford was unaware of the exact situation there, though he knew it was grave. Reports from Kota Bharu showed that it was under heavy attack from sea, land and air; Sungei Patani, Butterworth and Alor Star all reported heavy bombing attacks and great damage. It was, therefore, in the highest degree improbable that fighter squadrons could use them. Since, however, the Brewster Buffalo with which they were armed had a very short range, it was useless, or almost useless, for them to operate over Singora from airfields situated in central and southern Malaya. If they did so, they could give only negligible protection, for they would be unable to remain over the area of operations for more than a few minutes.

Before the day was out, Pulford knew that his fears were realized. The northern airfields had all been put out of action, and the nearest which might possibly be used was that at Kuantan, more than 300 miles to the south of Singora. There could be no fighter cover.

All this Pulford explained to Rear Admiral A. F. E. Palliser, Phillips' Chief of Staff, who had remained behind in Singapore and was in touch with the Commander-in-Chief. By the time he had heard what Pulford had to say, Force 'Z' had sailed. Palliser immediately sent Phillips a signal, of which the relevant passage read: 'Fighter protection on Wednesday 10 will not, repeat not, be possible'. It was received at 0125 hours on 9th December. There is evidence that the Governor of Singapore urged the retention of fighters for the defence of the port and the island and that his views were accepted. Certainly Admiral Palliser sent a signal on the next day, received by Phillips at 2302 hours, reporting bad news of the fighting in northern Malaya and the presence of enemy bombers 'in force and undisturbed' in southern Indo-China. The signal also stated that the Commander-in-Chief was contemplating the concentration of all 'the air effort' on the defence of Singapore. This would seem to confirm the view that the counsels of Sir Shenton Thomas had prevailed. Long before this second signal had reached him, however, Phillips had decided to press on.

Under low clouds the great ships, with their attendant destroyers, ploughed the wastes of ocean. No word came from them until, in the early hours of Wednesday, 10th December, a signal was received in Singapore indicating that they might return sooner than had originally been planned. Then the curtain of silence fell once more, only to be torn apart at 1219 hours, when a report was received from the *Repulse* that she and the *Prince of Wales* were under air attack in a position about sixty miles east of Kuantan. Six minutes after receiving this message, eleven Brewster Buffalos of No. 453 Squadron, which had been specially detailed for the defence of the fleet, took off, led by Flight Lieutenant T. A. Vigors. They reached the scene just in time to see the dark, smoke-enshrouded bulk of the *Prince of Wales* plunge beneath seas already disfigured by patches of oil and crawling with survivors. Of the *Repulse* there was no sign. What had happened was this.

On reaching the open sea, Force ' Z ' sailed first towards the Anambas Islands and then, having passed them, turned to the northward. Throughout the next day, the 9th, weather conditions were excellent for its concealment. Rainstorms were frequent and heavy clouds drifted low above the waves. As the afternoon drew on, however, a breeze sprang up and drove them away. By 1700 hours the weather had cleared, and soon after, what were thought to be three Japanese naval reconnaissance aircraft, were sighted from the *Prince of Wales*. Captain L. H. Bell, who was with the Admiral on the bridge, had no doubt that they were what he has described as ' Japanese float planes '. They kept company for some time with the British vessels but presently flew away. Not unnaturally, Phillips felt certain that they had reported the presence of his fleet at sea and that all chance of surprising the enemy at dawn on the 10th at Singora was lost. Most of the Japanese vessels would now have ample time in which to withdraw. Moreover, if he held on his present course, he would assuredly be exposed to heavy air attack, for he would come well within 200 miles of Japanese bombers and torpedo aircraft. Reluctantly, therefore, he abandoned the enterprise and at 2015 hours on the 9th set course for Singapore.

At the moment when the float planes disappeared in the gathering darkness, Phillips could not possibly have been aware that in fact, they had sent no message. Yet this was so: they had remained silent. Captain Sonokawa, Commander of the *Genzan* Group which sank the *Prince of Wales* and the *Repulse* was quite clear on this point when questioned after the war. No Japanese reconnaissance aircraft were in the air at the time. The float planes were in all probability acting as air escort to two Japanese warships, the *Kongo* and the *Haruma* which, unknown to Force ' Z ', were in the neighbourhood. In the uncertain light the Japanese pilots seem to have mistaken Force ' Z ' for these warships. This explanation may appear extraordinary but, having regard to the fact that they made no report, what other is possible?

Yet though Force ' Z ' had not in fact been seen from the air, Admiral Phillips had nevertheless taken the right decision, for his ships had been sighted by a Japanese submarine, which at 1400 hours that afternoon had reported their position as 7° north 105° east, steering north. The Japanese naval bombers at once prepared to attack them, but it was not until darkness was falling that these aircraft had finished exchanging the bombs, with which they were being loaded when the submarine's signal arrived, for torpedoes. This operation completed, they set off hoping to have the aid of the *Kongo* and *Haruma* in destroying what was obviously a grave threat to the invasion fleet lying off Singora. For six hours they searched in vain the night-shrouded sea and then returned, balked, to their base at Saigon. That they should have failed to find the British ships is not surprising, for the commander of the Japanese submarine had miscalculated and reported Admiral Phillips to be 140 miles north-northwest of his actual position when sighted. In the early hours of 10th December a second Japanese submarine sighted Force 'Z' and sent a signal which showed that it was now heading south, presumably returning to Singapore. This assumption was correct and was to prove fatal to the British fleet.

For nearly four hours it had held on its southerly course when shortly before midnight Phillips received a signal stating that Kuantan was being attacked. This place and its airfield, situated on the east coast some 200 miles from Singapore, was considered a key military position in the defence of Malaya, and to reach it only a small deviation of course was necessary. The Admiral did not hesitate. Though fate had denied him the chance of engaging the main forces of the enemy in the north, he might still strike a blow farther south. He arrived off Kuantan at eight o'clock on the morning of the 10th ready to engage any enemy who might there be found. None was to be seen and one of the destroyers, H.M.S. *Express*, which made a tour of the harbour, reported 'complete peace'.

The 'complete peace' in Kuantan discovered by the navy at 0800 hours was already known to the Air Staff in Singapore, for Hudsons arriving in the area at dawn had reported no evidence of the enemy's presence and no signs of battle. What the Air Staff did not know, however, when this report was received soon after dawn, was that Admiral Phillips and his fleet were approaching Kuantan from the north at twenty-five knots; for he had not informed Singapore of his change of plan, nor did he do so after his fruitless examination of this small port. As soon as the *Express* had rejoined him, he turned east to avoid a suspected minefield and to investigate a number of small vessels observed on the horizon. He was much pre-occupied with the possibility of being attacked by submarines and had no intention of betraying his presence by breaking wireless silence in order to inform Pulford in Singapore of his whereabouts. Of air attacks he had no fear, for being some 400 miles from the nearest enemy air base, he considered himself out of range.

Since Pulford received no signal, he was given no chance to provide the air cover soon so sorely to be needed. Had the Air Vice-Marshal known that Force 'Z' was returning, he could have despatched No. 453, acting as Fleet Defence Squadron, to Kuantan in the early morning of the 10th and it would have been ready to operate at least an hour before the Japanese made their attacks upon the capital ships. True, Kuantan was being subjected to intermittent bombing, but who can doubt that the Air Officer Commanding would have accepted this risk and sent his fighters there had he known that the fleet was to pass so close to that air base?

Meanwhile the Japanese were doing their utmost to put into the air a large striking force. Three groups—the *Genzan*, the *Mihoro* and the *Kanoya*—comprising the 22nd Air Flotilla, and numbering in all eighty-eight aircraft of which twenty-seven were bombers and sixty-one torpedo-bombers, were brought to immediate readiness before dawn. Without awaiting a sighting report from reconnaissance aircraft, they took off from their bases in Cochin China and flew southwards in nine flights along the 105th meridian. They were preceded by nine reconnaissance aircraft which carried out a sector search, for some hours in vain. Not until 1100 hours, when they were on the last leg, did the pilot of one of them catch sight of Force 'Z'. He at once sent a sighting report and twenty minutes later the first flight of the bombers were over their targets. They attacked the *Repulse* and scored one hit, a bomb falling upon the port hangar and bursting on the armour below the marines' mess deck. A fire broke out on the catapult deck but was soon under control. The first round had been inconclusive. There was a pause of twenty minutes and then nine torpedo bombers which had been seen dodging behind clouds came in on the port beam, and 'in no way perturbed by our gunfire' carried out their attack with great coolness. By skilful use of the helm the *Repulse* avoided their torpedoes; but the *Prince of Wales* was less fortunate. She was hit twice, once on the port side aft of the bridge and once in the stern. It was this second torpedo which made her fate certain, for it badly damaged the steering gear and propellers. The balls signifying that the *Prince of Wales* was not under control were hoisted and the *Repulse* immediately began to close, reporting in her turn that she had escaped all the torpedoes fired at her to the number of nineteen. She did not remain unscathed for long. Low on the horizon eight enemy aircraft were coming in again with torpedoes. They split into two formations and dropped them from a distance of about 2,000 yards. Approaching as they did from two opposite directions, it was impossible for the *Repulse* to elude them. She was hit amidships on the port side but still maintained her speed. Almost immediately, a fifth attack, also by torpedo bombers, was made and she was hit four times more. These blows were mortal. She at once took a heavy list to port, and sank in six minutes at 1233 hours, taking with her 444 officers and men. As the remainder struggled in the viscous embrace of the fuel oil pouring out of the gaps in her hull, they beheld the end of the *Prince of Wales*. Ten minutes earlier she had received three torpedoes, two in the afterpart of the ship near the stern and a third on the starboard side under the compass platform. Mortally hit already, these were the *coup de grace*, though even then her modern construction kept her afloat for almost an hour, during which a signal asking for tugs was sent to Singapore. At 1320 hours the *Prince of Wales*, capsizing to port, went down. Admiral Phillips and Captain Leach went with her and with them 215 of her crew. 1,285 officers and ratings were picked up.

The Japanese pilots had shown skill, daring and resolution of a high order. The fiercest anti-aircraft fire, which both great ships developed to the full extent of their armaments, had not deterred them, and they accomplished their task with the probable loss of only four aircraft. On quitting the scene of their triumph, they left behind them a number of reconnaissance aircraft, which made off on the appearance of the Buffalos of No. 453 Squadron. Beneath them the destroyer escort, which had not been attacked, was engaged in the work of rescue. The survivors, officers and men of the Royal Navy, had maintained its traditions with unbroken spirit. 'I passed over thousands', records Flight Lieutenant Vigors in his official report, 'who had been through an ordeal, the greatness of which they alone can understand. . . . It was obvious that the three destroyers were going to take hours to pick up those hundreds of men clinging to bits of wreckage and swimming around in the filthy oily water. . . . Yet every man waved and put his thumb up as I flew over him. . . . Here was something above human nature'.

The loss of His Majesty's Ships *Prince of Wales* and *Repulse*, together with the virtual destruction of the American fleet at Pearl Harbour, gave the Japanese undisputed command of Far Eastern waters within two days of the outbreak of war. It also marked the end of sea power as Mahan preached and Nelson had practised it.

Hardly had the inhabitants of Singapore recovered, if they ever did recover, from the shock caused by the loss of these two ships, when news came that Georgetown on the island of Penang had been severely bombed by Japanese aircraft some eighty strong. The first attack made on 8th December had achieved little result. The second, however, caused heavy casualties among the population, especially among the Asiatics who, with tragic curiosity, swarmed the streets to watch what they thought was to be a repetition of the first which had been carried out against the airfield. In neither case was there any opposition either from the ground or in the air. Such anti-aircraft guns as were available in Malaya had been allotted for the protection of more important targets—the naval base, airfields in general, the harbour of Singapore, and Kuala Lumpur, the Federal capital. No fighters appeared over Penang, for by then the first phase of the Japanese attack, of which the success was hourly more pronounced, was in full development,

Well aware of our weakness in the air, the Japanese commander had decided to strike hard and often against our airfields. The scale of his efforts on the 8th, 9th and 10th December, though small by the standards of the war in Europe, was more than enough to achieve his purpose. A daily average of some 120 sorties sufficed to render all the airfields in north-east and north-west Malaya untenable. Despite the arrival on the 9th of twenty-two Dutch Glen Martins and one Dutch fighter squadron of nine Buffalos from the Netherlands East Indies, in accordance with an agreement for mutual aid concluded before war broke out, the air defences of Malaya were already so gravely depleted as to make withdrawal essential. From Butterworth in north-western Malaya No. 62 (Bomber) Squadron, reduced in numbers to two aircraft, was brought back to Taiping, and No. 21 (Fighter) Squadron, Royal Australian Air Force, with six dubiously effective Buffalos, to Ipoh. No. 27, the night-fighting Blenheim Squadron, did not leave Butterworth. It had no aircraft left in which to do so.

Though the attitude of the pilots towards these heavy losses of aircraft it was their duty to fly was, in general, one of determination to get at grips with a hard-hitting enemy, the demeanour of the ground staff was not always so firm. Some, such as those at Kota Bharu, fought, as has been related, with great courage, abandoning their airfield only when the enemy was upon it. Others showed less stoutness of heart. They became discouraged and more and more inclined to lend an ear to rumours of defeat and disaster, which buzzed about like cockchafers. This attitude can for the most part be traced to the prevailing conditions and to the feeling of helplessness engendered by the frequent bombing of airfields scantily protected. At some stations, such as Butterworth, there was no more effective warning system than that provided by an aircraftman standing on the perimeter and waving a white handkerchief on the approach of hostile aircraft. Nevertheless, the majority of the ground crews continued to carry out their duties in circumstances which grew worse and worse with every day that passed, and to serve a steadily diminishing band of pilots who, flying aircraft markedly inferior to those of the enemy, entered upon the campaign with odds against them of six to one, and still did not falter when at the end of it these had lengthened to fifteen to one.

The misfortunes of the air force were increased by the behaviour of the native labourers, who fled the airfields as soon as the bombing began and did not return. For this they can scarcely be blamed. They did not feel the quarrel to be theirs. Such stores and equipment as had been left intact after the bombing attacks would not have been brought back to the south had it not been for the efforts of a number of the ground staff who maintained the railway in operation when the native drivers had departed. They were in the charge of Flight Lieutenant R. D. I. Scott, who drove a locomotive himself.

Not only had the hard-pressed units to evacuate the northern airfields, they had also to render them unserviceable, if they could. This task was exceedingly difficult, and all their efforts did not retard by more than a few hours the use of the airfields by the Japanese. Bombs were hastily dug into the surface of the runways and exploded (in this the Royal Engineers gave great assistance) and petrol dumps set on fire everywhere except at Sungei Patani, where 200,000 gallons were left behind to the great satisfaction of the enemy. The stocks of road metal accumulated beside each perimeter were used immediately by the Japanese to fill in the craters, native labour being ruthlessly rounded up and employed for this purpose. The attempted destruction of airfields by Norgroup had inevitably a depressing effect on the spirits of the army who, holding positions in front of them, had but to turn their heads to see large fires and columns of smoke in their rear, a truly disconcerting spectacle. Penang had to be abandoned and the army, fighting in northern Malaya, to be robbed of air support. After the bombing of the town on 11th December, the position there grew rapidly worse until it became out of hand. Law and order disappeared; 'The friendless bodies of unburied men' strewed the streets and their stench 'in the tropical heat was indescribable. Rats left godowns where they usually operated for the more lucrative field of the open streets, where food in the shape of dead humans was plentiful'.[1] About 600 persons were killed and 1,100 wounded in the air raids. On 13th December orders were given to evacuate the European and Indian populations, but only Europeans, to the number of about 520, got away.

[1] *In Seventy Days.* E. M. Glover—Frederick Muller.

While these scenes of confusion and horror were being enacted in that lovely city of tall trees, exotic flowers and baroque buildings, where peace and plenty had reigned for more than a century, the army, almost entirely deprived of air support, was struggling back through the jungles. Two or three Buffalos of No. 21 Squadron, Royal Australian Air Force, based at Ipoh, sought to give aid to the hard-pressed 11th Indian Division. These were reinforced by No. 453 Squadron, Royal Australian Air Force, three days after it had witnessed the end of the *Prince of Wales* and the *Repulse*. On arrival at Ipoh they went straight into action, attacked Japanese convoys on the roads and carried out tactical reconnaissance with some effect, for they claim to have shot down five Japanese aircraft over Penang. Six Buffalos of No. 21 Squadron joined them on the 15th, five having made forced landings on the flight from Singapore. The rate of wastage, however, soon proved so high, that Air Headquarters was forced to order the squadrons based on Ipoh to confine themselves to the work of reconnaissance. This task they continued from Kuala Lumpur, to which enemy attacks had driven them on 19th December. While the efforts of the air force to give close support to the army achieved very little success, the attempts to bomb the Japanese Air Force on the northern airfields, which they had seized, had even less. The enemy had enough reserves immediately to replace the small casualties which were all our attentuated squadrons could hope to inflict. As the days went only too swiftly by and the army struggled back, first from Kedah Province to the Krian river, then to the strong Kampar position, then to the line of the Slim river and finally to the northern frontier of Johore, less than a hundred miles from Singapore, the lesson, that airfields which cannot be defended are a liability and not an asset, was driven remorselessly home. Those which had been so laboriously, and with such difficulty, constructed in the months preceding the outbreak of war had now to be held by the army, not in order that the Royal Air Force might operate from them—that had already become impossible—but so that the Japanese Air Force might be denied their use. The effect of this task on the spirit of the troops can easily be imagined.

Throughout this period, and indeed until the fall of Java wiped it out, the air force was served with great gallantry by the Malayan Volunteer Air Force, which, as its name implies, was manned by volunteers, both British and Malay. This small force had been formed in September 1940, and its pilots had carried out their training on Avro Cadets, Tiger and Leopard Moths and other light aircraft, of which none could fly faster than 100 miles an hour; nor were any of them armed. When war broke out they were all that were available for the Volunteer Force, which had taken them over from various flying clubs and unhesitatingly took them into battle. They were used principally to maintain communications, but they also carried out many reconnaissance flights and helped in the work of jungle rescue. The little Moths flew only just above the treetops and, being camouflaged, they were not easy to see. This was as well since camouflage was their only protection. Sometimes, in addition to being bombed on the ground, they found themselves attacked by their own side. On 8th December, for example, a Dragon Rapide arrived with a cargo of explosives at Butterworth during a raid. By flying very low behind the coconut palms, its pilot escaped detection, landed and rid himself of his dangerous cargo. Before he could take off, however, another attack developed and he returned to his Rapide from a nearby machine-gun post to find two burning Blenheims on either hand. The pilot taxied to the runway on one engine, induced the second one to start and was half-way down the runway on the take-off when a Buffalo, cleaving the pall of smoke which hung over the airfield, struck the ground immediately in front of him. The wheels of the Rapide scraped the wreckage, but the machine remained air-borne, to be fired at a moment later by a returning Blenheim which in the murk mistook it for a Japanese. The instrument panel was shattered and one engine put out of action, but the Rapide was successfully flown to Ipoh on the other. These volunteer pilots flew between 1500 and 2000 hours during the eleven weeks of fighting and earned the respect and admiration of their more professional brethren.

With matters in such poor shape in Malaya, it is not surprising that the Japanese attack on Borneo, mounted in the third week of December, should have been immediately successful. During that week a convoy of more than a hundred ships was discovered crossing the South China Sea and by 24th December it was obvious from the frequent reconnaissances made that the Japanese were heading for Kuching in British Borneo. To that island, as to Hong Kong, no air forces had been allotted for defence. With the capture of Kuching on 26th December, Borneo fell into Japanese hands: Hong Kong had been taken by them twenty-four hours before.

It was at this juncture, with the army stumbling back through the thick jungles of Malaya, unable to find any position at which to make a prolonged stand, that the Commander-in-Chief, Air Chief Marshal Sir Robert Brooke-Popham, was replaced by Lieutenant General Sir Henry Roydes Pownall. The new Chief fared no better than his predecessor. He took over at a time when the situation was steadily growing worse. Reinforcements, it was true, were close to hand, and a few aircraft had already arrived, but their numbers were quite inadequate. By Christmas Day, 1941, only six Hudsons and seven Blenheims had reached Malaya but there was a promise of fifty-one Hurricanes in crates and twenty-four pilots. They landed on 3rd January, but on the 18th, excluding the Hurricanes which were still being unloaded, the total stength of the air force was only seventy-five bomber and reconnaissance aircraft and twenty-eight fighters. Moreover the new pilots were quite unaccustomed to local conditions; they had arrived either after a long and arduous flight from as far away as Egypt, or after a long and perilous sea voyage. Circumstances, however, made it necessary to throw them immediately into the fight, where they made up for their deficiencies in experience by the stoutness of their conduct.

Their task was truly formidable. If the aircraft allotted to them were Hudsons or Blenheims, they were required to carry out long reconnaissance flights over the South China Sea and bombing attacks by night, such operations in daylight having been abandoned for lack of fighter cover. If they flew fighter aircraft, they were called upon to protect Singapore, to co-operate with the hard-pressed army on the ground and to give protection to convoys approaching with reinforcements. In view of the ludicrously small number of aircraft available, this programme, which would have taxed the whole strength of the Royal Air Force at that time, was necessarily fulfilled in an imperfect and haphazard manner. The reconnaissance squadrons, aided by the small but efficient Dutch Air Force, made numerous flights over the South China Sea in order to discover any surface vessels which might be moving against Singapore. They also helped the fighters to cover the Banka Strait along the coast of eastern Sumatra, through which ran the route followed by our convoys of reinforcements. Such a task involved daily sorties by at least two Catalinas, six Hudsons and four Glen Martin aircraft, a force far too small but all that could be spared. The remainder had to be kept at short notice to go to the rescue should the convoys be attacked.

The result of this policy of protecting the convoys, indispensable though its adoption was, soon became painfully apparent. After the loss of the *Prince of Wales* and the *Repulse*, no effective aid could be rendered by the Navy, and the task of covering the ships until they reached port fell, therefore, entirely on the Royal Air Force, which could only fulfil it at the expense of the struggling armies in the jungle. They were wholly deprived of air support, and in consequence suffered heavily. All the convoys of reinforcements reached Singapore in safety. Their arrival momentarily raised the drooping spirits of the population, for it was known that fighter aircraft, superior in performance to the Buffalo, were on board. ' It is difficult ', reports Air Vice-Marshal Maltby, who was himself but newly arrived from England, ' adequately to convey the sense of tension which prevailed as these convoys approached Singapore, and the sense of exaltation at their safe arrival. The feeling spread that at last the Japanese were going to be held on the ground, if not driven back, whilst it was confidently expected that the Hurricanes would sweep the Japanese from the sky'.

The Hurricanes, from which so much was hoped, took part in the defence of Singapore for the first time exactly one week after their arrival. On 20th January, 1942, twenty-seven unescorted Japanese bombers appeared over the city. The Hurricanes shot down eight of them. To the inhabitants, who had not quite recovered from the news that the Army had withdrawn from Kuala Lumpur and Port Swettenham, it seemed that at last the tide was beginning to turn. The next day brought disillusion. Once more Japanese bombers attacked Singapore in daylight, but this time they were accompanied by Zero fighters, which forthwith showed their superiority over the Hurricanes by shooting down five of them without loss to themselves. Though not so fast as the Japanese Navy Zero at low heights, the Hurricane possessed the advantage in speed, rate of climb and dive at heights of 20,000 feet and over. Unfortunately, the Japanese often preferred to attack at lower levels. Moreover, as the Hurricanes had been destined originally for the Middle East, their engines had been fitted with special desert air-intake filters which reduced their speed by as much as thirty miles an hour.

Though by then the Air Staff in London was aware of the performance of the Japanese Navy Zero fighter, they were unable to send any type of aircraft better than the Hurricane to meet it. Spitfires were still regarded as essential for the defence of Great Britain and not even the air forces in the Middle East could obtain an adequate number. Outclassed as they were in many respects by the Zero fighters, the Hurricanes none the less contrived to cause losses to the Japanese bombers by adopting tactics which were novel. Such efforts were, however, constantly hampered by the increasing shortness of the warning period. Never at the best more than thirty minutes, it presently fell to twenty, and before the end of the siege almost to nothing. This lack of warning was due to the loss of the radar stations, which were overrun one by one or were dismantled before the enemy reached them. The closing down of the station at Mersing, which took place about the middle of January 1942, some time before the site was lost to the enemy, was of even graver consequence to the depleted Buffalo squadrons than to the Hurricanes. With ammunition reduced to 350 rounds, petrol to 84 gallons and the substitution of the ·303 machine-guns for the ·5, the rate of climb of the Buffalo aircraft still remained far too slow. It took somewhat more than half an hour to reach 25,000 feet, the average height at which, before the arrival of the Hurricanes, the Japanese bombers and their escort carried out many of their raids, and those who had the misfortune to fly the machine were, after the closing down at Mersing, at a great tactical disadvantage, for they were always beneath the enemy. Despite this very grave hardship, 'it says much for the quality of the pilots', reports Squadron Leader Clouston commanding No. 488 Squadron, 'that there was no weakening of morale'.

As the campaign developed, and the army reeled back ever faster in face of an implacable attack sustained by highly trained and fanatical troops, the raids on Singapore increased in numbers and severity, though they never approached the proportions which London had endured without flinching a year earlier. Most of them were carried by formations of twenty-seven bomber aircraft and the maximum number of Japanese bombers which attacked the area of Singapore in any one day was not more than 127. Endeavours, which can only be described as frantic, to provide shelters against the raids, were made by the civil authorities goaded too late to take decisions which should have been reached months before. The original scheme, under which in the event of an air raid the inhabitants were to leave their houses and enter evacuation camps erected in the outlying districts of the city, broke down with the falling of the first bombs. It could, indeed, scarcely have been otherwise. How the inhabitants of a congested city could successfully leave their homes on a dark night and make their way a considerable distance to an unbuilt-on area or a rubber plantation in the brief space of half an hour, was not explained to them. It is hardly surprising that when the moment came they ignored such dubious provisions for their safety.

'The raid took place at eleven o'clock', says an eye witness present throughout the siege of Singapore, 'and resulted in the complete destruction of forty-seven shops and tenement houses. . . . There were no slit trenches, dugouts or bunding in this area, and there were few buildings sufficiently strong to warrant being turned into air raid shelters. Slit trenches were, of course, out of the question. . . . They (the authorities) tried to erect shelters, and even went so far as to buy or requisition concrete-spun pipes, six feet in diameter, and these they placed end to end in the street. . . . They afforded some measure of protection. . . . The Japanese used anti-personnel bombs almost exclusively. . . . I counted eight decapitated bodies in one narrow street. These bombs were made for streets and open places; it almost seemed as if they had been specially designed for Singapore slums, slums which contained no shelters. . . . I looked at the drains on each side of the narrow street. They were full of water—bloody water'. Scenes such as these were soon to become a part of the daily life of Singapore.

With every day, almost with every hour, the war drew closer and closer to Singapore. Whenever the troops in the field attempted to hold a defensive position for any length of time, they were immediately outflanked, either by a swift and silent penetration of a supposedly impenetrable jungle or by landings further down the mangrove-fringed west coast. Moreoever they had to endure attacks from the air of a kind similar to those made by the *Luftwaffe* upon the armies of Poland two years before, deprived, like themselves, of all means of defence against them. On 26th January the Japanese landed at Endau on the east coast of Malaya and moved at once to join with their forces on the west. The Royal Air Force made a desperate effort to prevent them. At one o'clock in the afternoon, nine aircraft of No. 100 Squadron and three of No. 36 Squadron, flying the obsolete Vildebeests with a top speed of 137 miles an hour, accompanied by a small force of Hurricane and Buffalo fighters, attacked the Japanese transports and landing craft off the small port. Zero fighters were there in plenty, but the Vildebeests held on their course, going in to bomb and losing five of their number, including the aircraft flown by Squadron Leader I. T. B. Rowland, leader of the attack. The pilots, who had spent the previous night on operations, did their best to dive-bomb the Japanese shipping but without very much effect. Two hours later the attack was repeated, this time by No. 36 Squadron with a fighter escort, and eight aircraft were shot down, among the pilots lost being Squadron Leader R. F. C. Markham, its commander. The fighter escorts to these assaults did all they could to drive away the Japanese Zero fighters; but they were outmatched by the numbers of the enemy and by the superiority of these aircraft. These two attacks were typical of the attempts made at that time by men who, to quote Major General Percival's Despatch, 'throughout the later stages of the Malayan campaign, went unflinchingly to almost certain death in obsolete aircraft which should have been replaced many years before'.

The landing at Endau meant that any further defence of the Malayan Peninsula was out of the question. From the 28th to 31st January Percival's exhausted troops, their confidence shaken by the supremacy of the enemy on the sea and in the air and by the numbers of armoured fighting vehicles used against them, wound their way across the eleven hundred yard granite causeway into the island of Singapore itself. There they took up defensive positions outside the city and on the edge of the docks. The Japanese immediately increased their air attacks and carried them out by day and night. Their continual pounding, to which shellfire was soon added, made it exceedingly difficult to keep the airfields in serviceable condition. That at Kallang, which was built on reclaimed land, was soon more or less permanently out of action, for the mud oozed up through the bomb craters. Conditions at Tengah were little better. To repair the airfield there was almost impossible, for all native labour had long since vanished. On 7th January, the Singapore War Council, of which Duff Cooper was the Chairman, appointed a Director of Labour, a post which might with advantage have been created months, if not years, earlier. This step was of little avail, for there was no one left to direct.

The harassed, indomitable Pulford was now faced with the grimmest decision of all. There was nothing for it but to order evacuation. The air force had done its utmost to help the army. The fighter squadrons in particular had been employed far beyond wastage point in an unceasing effort to support the troops in the field, to protect the incoming convoys and to try to drive Japanese bombers away from Singapore. The meagre reinforcements of Hurricanes had done their best, but by 28th January, of the fifty-one aircraft torn from their crates and hastily erected barely a week before, seventeen had been destroyed, thirteen were under repair and only twenty-one still remained serviceable. At that date the number of Buffalos was six, made up of the remnants of Nos. 21 and 453 Squadrons of the Royal Australian Air Force. The bombers and reconnaissance aircraft had for weeks been reduced to a 'token' force. They were the first to be withdrawn from Malaya, and by 27th January all had left it for Sumatra where they were presently joined by a small number of Hudsons just arrived as belated reinforcements. The three Catalina flying boats, which had come in on 7th January, were also sent away, and by the last day of that month, apart from the fighters, only three Swordfish under army control, for the purpose of spotting for the coast defence guns, were left on the island. At that date, such fighter squadrons as remained were pinned to the four main airfields. Three of them, Tengah, Sembawang and Seletar, were on the northern edge of the island and could be shelled from the mainland at a range of 1,500 to 2,000 yards. Every effort was still being made by the ground staff to maintain them in operation. On one occasion a bush fire on the edge of the airfield at Tengah was extinguished by the driver of a bulldozer who, at imminent risk to his life, succeeded in creating a fire break between the burning bushes and the petrol and ammunition dump. But with the Japanese artillery in Johore it was impossible to make any further use of these airfields. It was therefore decided by General Sir Archibald Wavell, who had assumed Supreme Command of the Far East Forces on 15th January, to withdraw all fighters except eight Hurricanes and the remaining six Buffalos. Any fighter reinforcements—Hurricanes carried in the aircraft carrier H.M.S. *Indomitable* were expected—would go to Sumatra. In that island, Air Commodore Vincent was ordered to form No. 226 (Fighter) Group with headquarters at Palembang, and No.151 Maintenance Unit was to be established in Java, while Air Commodore Silly was to set up a new air headquarters in Sumatra.

The evacuation of the Air Force proved a task of very great difficulty. By 7th February, the port and shipping arrangements in Singapore were in a state of chaos. Few ships were available and some of their masters were not prepared to take their vessels alongside the crowded, bomb-riven quays to load equipment and stores. Moreover the ships had to be dispersed as widely as possible in an attempt to reduce the size of the targets offered to the Japanese bombers. As their attacks increased in intensity, so did the disorganization. Plans were hastily made, and still more hastily abandoned. Ground units, some of them already shaken by their previous experiences, became inextricably mixed up with each other and the loss of efficiency can hardly be exaggerated. Equipment urgently needed by the bomber force, which had been evacuated to Sumatra, could not be loaded and was left behind. Some 200 motor transport vehicles of inestimable value were lost on passage to that island. More than one ship sailed without her full complement of air force passengers and equipment; others were sunk or badly damaged by the triumphing Japanese Air Force.

The evacuation took fourteen days to complete. During that period the pilots of the Buffalos and Hurricanes continued to fight grimly against overwhelming odds. The first to succumb entirely was the improvised photographic reconnaissance flight of Buffalos which, under the command of Squadron Leader Lewis, had flown over 100 sorties in aircraft unarmoured and without guns. Though repeatedly attacked and many times hit, none of them was destroyed in the air. Hurricane pilots, with an average of only ten aircraft a day at their disposal, maintained the fight for ten days. They took off without any adequate ground control and did what they could, first to give cover to the troops crossing the causeway, then to deal with dive-bombers after the Japanese had landed on the island, an event which took place on 8th February, and finally to protect reinforcements which were still arriving. With the exception of the *Empress of Asia* bombed and set on fire, the Japanese made no very determined attacks upon the ships conveying them. They knew well enough that the troops on board would only serve to swell the army of prisoners who would be theirs as soon as the doomed fortress fell. Instead they concentrated their blows against the shipping moving away, and not all the efforts of the Hurricane pilots could prevent heavy losses. Nevertheless, even as late as 9th February, the day before the last aircraft was withdrawn, six Japanese bombers were shot down and fourteen damaged, our own losses being but one pilot. By then all the remaining air strips but one had been under steady shellfire for four days. At last only boggy Kallang was left. By almost ceaseless labour, a landing strip 750 yards long was kept in operation for three days more. Even so, the pilots had the greatest difficulty in avoiding the numerous bomb craters. On 10th February, the end came, and the last fighter aircraft were withdrawn to Sumatra.

They had fought to the end, and had, since the opening of the campaign, destroyed an estimated number of 183 Japanese aircraft. Now for a few more bitter days they were to carry on the fight from the islands of the Dutch East Indies. They left behind them airfields hastily ploughed up and equipment, for the most part, destroyed or damaged. They also left behind Air Vice-Marshal Pulford who, though he had been given leave to go away on 5th February, preferred to remain with the army commander until the 15th, when he was at last persuaded to depart. This gallant postponement of his departure cost him his life, for the motor boat, in which he left with Rear Admiral Spooner, R.N., was damaged by bombs, and driven ashore on one of the islands of the Juju group. For two months the survivors in this malaria-ridden spot evaded capture; then, after eighteen of them had died, they at length surrendered. Among the dead were the Rear Admiral and the Air Vice-Marshal.

Long before that day Singapore had fallen. On 15th February, hemmed in on all sides with no hope left, the troops of a supposedly impregnable fortress laid down their arms. 'This episode', said Churchill, addressing the House of Commons in secret session on 23rd April, 'and all that led up to it, seems to be out of harmony with anything that we have experienced or performed in the present war'. The verdict of history can only endorse and enhance this most restrained judgment.

CHAPTER III
Sumatra and Java

On 31st January, 1942, a fortnight before the fall of Singapore, statements appeared in the London Press pointing out that now that our forces had retired into the island of that name, they would be provided with 'an air umbrella' and would thus no longer have to endure the dive-bombing and machine-gun attacks of a dominant enemy air force. This umbrella would be furnished by fighter squadrons operating from Sumatra and from the islands south and south-west of Singapore, some of them less than fifty miles away. Those who provided the British public with such glib assurances were ignorant of one major fact. Once the army had been driven out of Malaya, there was no permanent airfield from which fighters could operate nearer than 130 miles, and this distance was far beyond their radius. The airstrips on Singapore Island could be used only as advanced landing grounds. Islands, such as Rangsang and Rempang were useless, for no airfields could be, or had been, built upon them. At no time, therefore, was the umbrella of fighters more than a shadow, a fiction created by commentators 8,000 miles from the scene of events and possessed of no local knowledge. In point of fact, the few airfields available in Sumatra itself were already congested and became more so as reinforcements arrived.

On 30th January, 1942, Air Commodore H. J. F. Hunter took command of the improvised Bomber Group, No. 225, in Sumatra, with Group Captain A. G. Bishop as his Senior Air Staff Officer. Their task was not easy. Sumatra is an island about 1,000 miles long, running parallel to the west coast of Malaya, but extending far to the southward. Its roads are few; so are its railways and the telephone system was primitive. For defence from air attack, seven airfields, including a secret strip in the heart of the jungle, known as P.II, twenty miles south of Palembang with its oilfield and refinery, had been constructed and were more or less in operation. There were no anti-aircraft defences, and the northern airfields were within range of Japanese fighters.

While the much depleted bomber and reconnaissance forces, which had been withdrawn from Malaya, were being reorganized in

Sumatra, the belated air reinforcements originally destined for Singapore began to arrive. They did so in the worst possible conditions. Equipment of all kinds was woefully short. There was a notable lack of tents, and this, since the north-east monsoon was then at its height, was a great handicap to efficiency. At the secret airfield, P.II, for example, accommodation for 1,500 ground staff was required, but provision had been made for only 250. Transport hardly existed—most of it had been lost in Singapore—and even when every bus and lorry which could be found had been requisitioned, remained scarce and inadequate.

In the hurried preparations for defence, the local Dutch authorities played a conspicuous part. They gave every help that they could, and by 7th February, though the Air Force units were still badly intermingled, some kind of order out of chaos had been established. By then, however, most of the reinforcements dribbling in from the Middle East had had to be diverted to Java, for on 23rd January an attack on Palembang by twenty-seven Japanese bombers showed that the main airfield in Sumatra, P.I, could not be adequately protected. This was confirmed when on 14th February a successful Japanese paratroop descent was carried out on the airfield: henceforward bomber operations were conducted from the secret airfield at P.II.

The general policy was to send as many Air Force ground staff as possible to Java and to keep in Sumatra only those required to service such aircraft as remained. The main bombing force was No. 225 (Bomber) Group which was also responsible for reconnaissance northwards from the Sunda Strait, and for the protection of convoys. These tasks were performed with the greatest difficulty. By the end of January only forty-eight aircraft remained and most of these ' required inspection and minor repairs ', or were ' in particularly poor condition '. In keeping them serviceable the efforts of two Flight Sergeants, Slee and Barker, deserve mention.

For twelve days in February the squadrons continued to act as escorts to convoys and to bomb airfields in Malaya, such as Alor Star and Penang, held a few short weeks before by the Royal Air Force. To do so they used the northern airfields of Sumatra as advanced landing grounds. Here aircraft could be refuelled but could not remain for any length of time because of Japanese bombers. The long flights involved in these operations imposed a great strain on the crews, who had to fly through torrential thunderstorms which transformed the tropic night into a darkness so intense that many of the recently arrived pilots, whose standard of night flying was, for lack of training, not high, found very great difficulty in finding their way. At that time the skill and determination of Wing Commander Jeudwine, commanding No. 84 Squadron, was outstanding. It was largely owing to his efforts that the force was able to maintain even a modest scale of attack. Throughout this period, the Malayan Volunteer Air Force, by then evacuated to Sumatra, proved invaluable in maintaining communications between P.I and the secret P.II in their Tiger Moths and other unarmed light civil aircraft.

By 13th February, the headquarters of the Group decided that a reconnaissance must be made to discover whether or not the Japanese intended to land on Sumatra. The position in Singapore was known to be desperate, and it was felt that the enemy would assuredly attempt to extend the range of their conquests. A single Hudson from No. 1 Squadron, Royal Australian Air Force, accordingly took off in the afternoon and presently returned with the report that there was a concentration of Japanese shipping north of Banka Island. This seemed to show that an invasion of Sumatra was imminent. An unsuccessful night attack by Blenheims in darkness and rain was succeeded at first light on 14th February by an offensive reconnaissance carried out by five Hudsons. They discovered between twenty-five and thirty transports, heavily escorted by naval vessels and fighter aircraft. The suspected invasion was on the way. The five Hudsons, subsequently reinforced by all available bomber aircraft, delivered a series of attacks upon the convoy and achieved conspicuous success. Six transports were sunk or badly damaged for the loss of seven aircraft. The squadrons engaged, Nos. 1 and 8 of the Royal Australian Air Force and Nos. 27, 62, 84 and 211 of the Royal Air Force, fulfilled their tasks without fighter protection, for the Japanese had staged an attack by parachute troops on P.I, the fighter airfield at Palembang. The attackers were able to cut the road to the south and west of the airfield and to overpower the meagre ground defences. Wing Commander Maguire, the Station Commander, at the head of twenty men, hastily collected, delivered a counter-attack which held off the enemy long enough to make possible the evacuation of the wounded and the unarmed. He was presently driven back into the area of the control tower, where he held out for some time, short of ammunition and with no food and water, until compelled to withdraw after destroying stocks of petrol and such aircraft as remained.

The fighters which should have accompanied the bomber force attacking the convoy belonged to No. 226 (Fighter) Group, formed on 1st February by Air Commodore Vincent. It was made up partly of the Hurricanes and Buffalos withdrawn from Singapore, and partly of Hurricanes flown direct from H.M.S. *Indomitable*, which had arrived off Sumatra on 26th January. Forty-eight Hurricanes left her flight deck and, of these, fifteen went on to Singapore and the remainder to P.I, where five crashed on landing. The guns of all of them were choked with anti-corrosion grease, put on as a protection during the long voyage, and they were not able therefore to go into action for some time.

Nevertheless, the enemy did not reach Sumatra unscathed. His convoy coming from Banka Island, already once mauled, was again fiercely attacked on 15th February by the Hudsons and Blenheims of No. 225 Group. This time the Hurricanes, though their strength had by then been seriously depleted in attacks made upon them when on the ground at Palembang, were with the bombers. The results achieved were even more successful than those of the day before. The bombers and fighters, operating from the secret airfield P.II to which they had hastily repaired, attacked twenty Japanese transports and their escort of warships either in the Banka Strait or at the mouth of the Palembang River. Between 6.30 in the morning and 3.30 in the afternoon, a series of assaults were delivered, their number being conditioned only by the speed with which the aircraft making them could be refuelled and rearmed. At first, opposition was strong, but the indefatigable Blenheims of Nos. 84 and 211 Squadrons and the Hudsons of No. 62 Squadron returned again and again until it weakened and eventually died away. Before the sun went down, all movement in the river had ceased and such barges and landing craft as survived had pulled beneath the tangled shade of the trees lining its banks. The Hurricanes, too, though flown by pilots most of whom were fresh from operational training units and had just completed a long sea voyage, took their full share in this heartening affair. Their newly cleaned guns did great execution and, as a finale, they destroyed a number of Japanese Navy Zero fighters caught on the ground on Banka Island. These were part of a force thought to have flown off from a Japanese aircraft carrier which had been attacked and sunk by a Dutch submarine. Thus, when the sun set on 15th February, the day on which the fortress of Singapore surrendered unconditionally, the greatest success up till then scored in the Far Eastern War had been achieved, and achieved by the Royal Air Force and the Royal Australian Air Force. The landing of the enemy at the mouth of the Palembang River had been completely arrested, thousands of his men had been killed or wounded, and his plan of invasion brought temporarily to naught. The action fought that day on the coast of Sumatra shows only too plainly what might have been accomplished on the coasts of Siam and Malaya had an adequate Air Force been available.

Sad to say, this highly successful counter-measure had no sequel. There were no troops or naval craft available to exploit the victory and the reaction of the Japanese was immediate and violent. They made another parachute troop landing on Palembang airfield and in the neighbourhood of the town. It was successful and its success jeopardized the situation at P.II, the secret airfield, where stocks of food, ammunition and bombs were running very low. Orders were reluctantly given for a retreat to Java.

All aircraft were to fly; their ground staff were to go by ship and to embark at Oesthaven. Here occurred an administrative blunder which added to the difficulties of the Air Force and considerably reduced its further capacity for fighting. The Dutch authorities at the port had already set on fire the bazaar and destroyed all equipment of a military kind. A dark pall of smoke lay over the town, and beneath it the airmen striving to carry out their orders and to reach Java as quickly as possible found themselves faced with an obstacle created not by the enemy, but by the British Military Embarkation Officer. He was one of those men to whom an order is as sacred and inflexible as are the Commandments of Sinai. All officers and men of the ground staff were to be clear of the port by midnight, but they were to leave, so he ordained, without their motor transport or their equipment. In other words, they were to reach Java in a condition in which they would be quite unable to take any further part in operations. To every remonstrance he returned the same answer: those were the orders. It says something for his personality that they were obeyed. No. 41 Air Stores Park left behind them spare Hurricane engines and other urgent stores; so did the Repair and Salvage Unit of No. 266 (Fighter) Wing, and the anti-aircraft guns and ammunition brought away with such difficulty from P.I and P.II were also abandoned.

This departure, in an atmosphere which can only be described as that of panic, was quite unnecessary, for two days later Group Captain Nicholetts at the head of fifty volunteers from No. 605 (Fighter) Squadron, returned to Oesthaven by sea from Batavia in H.M.S. *Ballarat* of the Royal Australian Navy and spent twelve hours loading the ship to the gunwales with such air force equipment as could by then still be salvaged.

By 18th February, the evacuation from Sumatra to Java of air force pilots and ground staff had been completed and more than 10,000 men belonging to different units, and in a great state of confusion, had arrived in the island. To add to the difficulties of the situation, the civilians in Java, who up till the landing of the Japanese on Singapore Island had shown calmness and confidence, now began to give way to despair and were soon crowding on to any vessel they could find which would take them away from a country they regarded as lost. The confusion brought about by the mass of outgoing refugees and incoming reinforcements is more easily imagined than described, and the scenes enacted a few days before in Singapore were reproduced on an even larger scale in Batavia. Equipment, motor transport, abandoned cars, goods of every size, description and quality, littered its choked quays, and still troops and air force ground staff poured in, hungry, disorganized and, for the moment, useless. Inevitably their spirits and discipline suffered, and the climax was reached when it became necessary to disband one half-trained unit. These few were the only men for whom the burden proved insupportable. The rest rose gallantly to their hopeless task and under the stimulus of Air Vice-Marshal Maltby and Air Commodore W. E. Staton, overcame the chaotic circumstances of their lot and in less than twelve days were ready to renew a hopeless contest.

The fighter strength available had, by the 18th, been reduced to twenty-five Hurricanes, of which eighteen were serviceable. The bomber and reconnaissance squadrons were in equally desperate case. At Semplak airfield, twelve Hudsons, and at Kalidjati, six Blenheims, sought to sustain the war. Behind them, No. 153 Maintenance Unit and No. 81 Repair and Salvage Unit, together with No. 41 Air Stores Park, did what they could to provide and maintain a ground organization. On 19th February all the Blenheims available, to the number of five, attacked Japanese shipping at Palembang in Sumatra, and this attack was repeated on the 20th and 21st, a 10,000 ton ship being set on fire. On the 19th and 22nd, the Japanese delivered two ripostes at Semplak which proved fatal. Of the dwindling force of bomber aircraft, fifteen were destroyed. Yet even after this crushing blow the Air Force still had some sting left. On 23rd February, three Blenheims claimed to have sunk a Japanese submarine off the coast.

By then the hopes originally entertained by Wavell and the Chiefs of Staff in London of building up the strength of the Allies in Java had been abandoned; Supreme Allied Headquarters had left the island and handed over to the Dutch Command, to which henceforward the remains of the Air Force looked for guidance and orders. They came from General ter Poorten, who had as his Chief of Air Staff, Major General van Oyen. Under the swiftly developing menace of invasion, these officers, with Maltby and General H. D. W. Sitwell, made what preparations they could to maintain the defence. Despite the encouraging messages which they received about this time from the Prime Minister, the Secretary of State for Air and the Chief of the

Air Staff, Maltby and Sitwell knew that no help from the outside could be expected for a long time.

General ter Poorten had under him some 25,000 regular troops backed up by a poorly armed militia numbering 40,000. Sitwell could count only upon a small number of British troops, two Australian infantry battalions, four squadrons of light tanks and three anti-aircraft regiments, of which the 21st Light accounted for some thirty Japanese aircraft before the end came. On the sea, Admiral Dorman commanded a small mixed force of which the main units were a British, an Australian, an American and two Dutch cruisers.

No breathing space for the organization of these inadequate and ill-armed forces was afforded by the enemy. On 26th February, a Japanese convoy, numbering more than fifty transports with a strong naval escort, was discovered by air reconnaissance to be moving through the Macassar Strait southwards towards the Java Sea. On the next day, Admiral Dorman put out to meet it. Hopelessly outgunned and outnumbered he fought a most gallant action and lost his entire fleet, a sacrifice which secured a respite of twenty-four hours. Subsequent to the naval battle the Air Force attacked twenty-eight ships of the convoy eventually found north of Rembang on the night of the 28th February. It was in this action, in which a small force of American Fortresses took part, that Squadron Leader Wilkins, the outstanding commander of No. 36 Squadron, was killed. The squadron claimed to have sunk eight ships; the Americans, seven.

By 1st March, the position became clear enough after the confusion of the previous two days. The convoy which No. 36 Squadron had attacked was one of three all making for Java. What remained of the Blenheims and Hudsons after the bombing of Semplak, took off from Kalidjati whither they had been transferred, and did their best to interfere with the Japanese landing at Eretanwetan, some eighty miles from Batavia. They went in again and again, some pilots being able to make three sorties, and accounted for at least three and possibly eight ships, but they could not prevent the landing. By dawn on 1st March the bomber crews, who had operated almost without a break for thity-six hours, were approaching the limit of endurance. Hardly had they dispersed, however, to seek the rest which had at last been given them, when the Dutch squadrons sharing their airfield left without notice. The Dutch aircraft had just disappeared into the clear morning air when a squadron of Japanese light tanks, supported by lorry-borne infantry, made their appearance. The exhausted pilots of No. 84 Squadron, who had by then reached their billets eight miles away, had no time to return to their aircraft, which were in consequence all destroyed or captured; but the last four Hudsons possessed

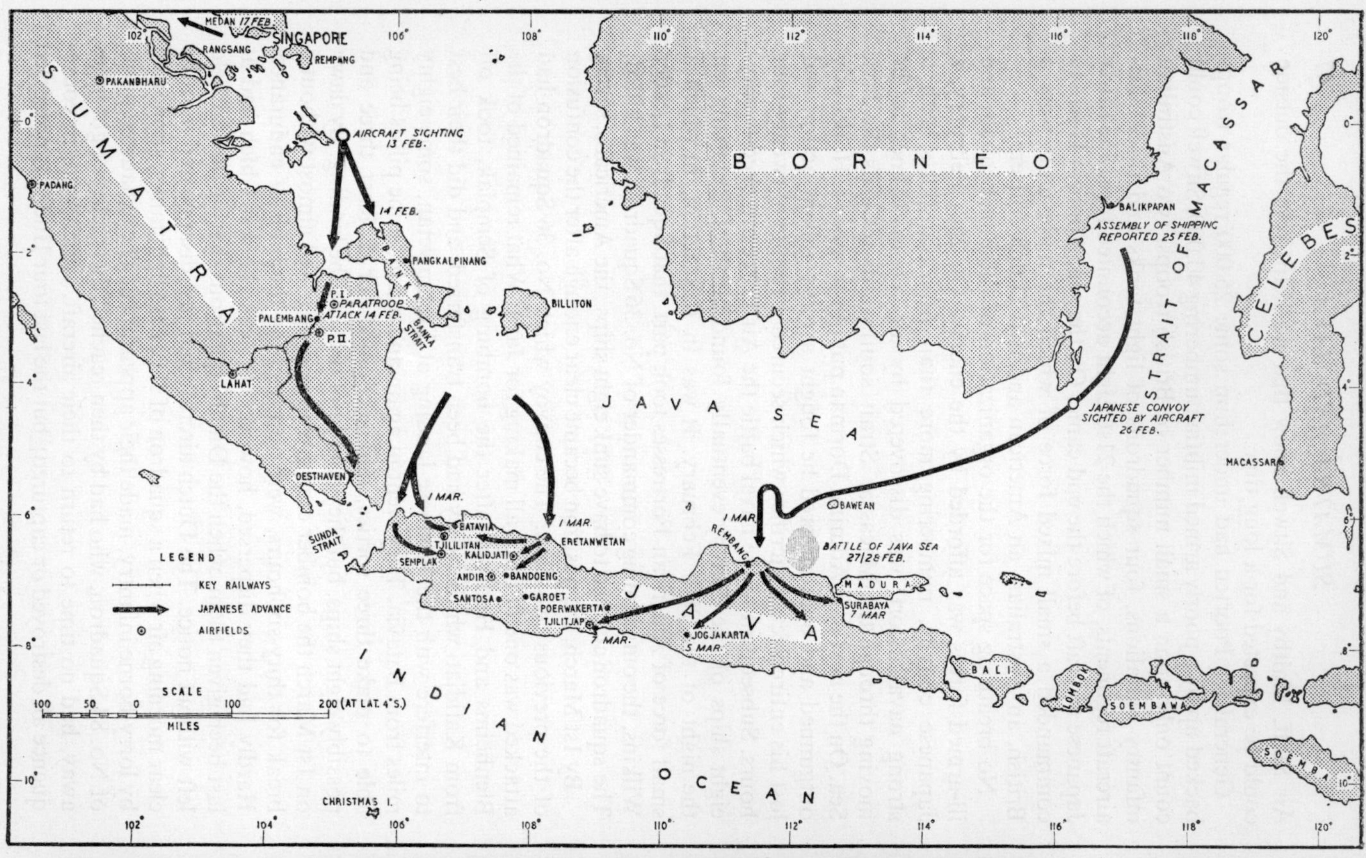

THE CAMPAIGN IN JAVA AND SUMATRA, FEBRUARY - MARCH 1942

by No. 1 Squadron, Royal Australian Air Force, being close to the runway, were taken off under fire and reached a nearby airfield at Andir. Kalidjati had fallen ; a small ground defence party composed of Army and Air Force officers and men, ably supported by the local Dutch defence force, fought with great gallantry to defend it and died to the last man. Their efforts were, however, of no avail, for they had been surprised by the swift move of the Japanese who, after landing at Eretanwetan in the early hours of that morning, had encountered no opposition on the ground either on the beaches or at the various strong points covering the river crossings. The fact was that by then conditions in Java were too confused and desperate to make further defence anything but local and spasmodic.

Nevertheless the Air Force struggled on for a few more days. Nos. 232 and 605 (Fighter) Squadrons had remained in action from the 17th to 27th February doing their utmost to conduct the air defence of Batavia. The normal odds which they were required to meet were about ten to one and they had little warning of the approach of enemy aircraft. Their task would have been eased and might, perhaps, have been successfully accomplished had they received as reinforcements the P.40 fighters carried on the U.S. aircraft carrier *Langley*. After considerable delays this ship had been ordered to sail for the Javanese port of Tjilitjap. She set out on what was a forlorn hope and as soon as she came within range of Japanese bomber and torpedo aircraft based on Kendari in the Celebes, she was attacked and sunk.

By noon on 28th February the total strength of the fighters was less than that of a single squadron, but still the hopeless fight continued. It was decided to retain No. 232 Squadron, under the command of Squadron Leader Brooker, since all its pilots and ground staff had volunteered to remain in Java. Vacancies were filled by volunteers from No. 605 and on 1st March the reconstructed squadron, in the company of ten Dutch Kittyhawks and six Dutch Buffalos, all that remained of a most gallant and skilled Air Force which had been in constant action beside the Royal Air Force, attacked the Japanese, who were engaged on two new landings begun that night at Eretanwetan. Despite intense anti-aircraft fire, twelve Hurricanes went in low and inflicted heavy losses on Japanese troops in barges and set on fire six small sloops and three tanks. They also caused a certain number of casualties and a certain amount of damage to the Japanese troops going ashore at another point on the west coast of Java.

Though the Royal Air Force could hamper the landings and increase their cost in terms of casualties, they could not prevent them, and the next day saw the Hurricanes pinned to their airfield at Tjililitan, whence they were withdrawn with some difficulty to Andir, near Bandoeng. During the withdrawal they maintained a running fight with Japanese fighters.

The last remnants of the Air Force maintained the fight for another three days, attacking the newly captured airfield at Kalidjati on the nights of the 3rd, 4th and 5th March. These assaults were made by the remaining Vildebeests of No. 36 (Torpedo Bomber) Squadron, of which only two were serviceable when the end came. On the morning of the 6th, they were ordered to seek the dubious safety of Burma, but both crashed in Sumatra and were lost. At the same time the gallant remnant of No. 1 Squadron, Royal Australian Air Force, took its three remaining Hudsons to Australia.

In Java, as in Malaya, the attitude of the local white population contributed in no small measure to the swift and overwhelming disaster. The feelings of the Dutch in Java can best be described as those of confused despair. The island on which they lived and from which they drew the source of their great wealth had been at peace for many generations. Now, the prospect of the destruction by fire and high explosive of all that had been built up and handed on to them from the past stared them in the face and their hearts misgave them. If any great show of resistance were to be made, Surabaya and Bandoeng would burn. Why then make it, when the chances of success were infinitesimal? When it is remembered that the chief Far Eastern bastion of an ally far stronger than they were had fallen after a bare fortnight's siege, their attitude is understandable. It was, however, responsible for the grim scenes which were enacted during the last few hours of resistance. 'I was in command that morning', records an officer of the Royal Air Force writing of the events of the last day, 'of a big convoy with all the remaining spare arms, ammunition and such-like equipment of the Royal Air Force in Java. We practically had to fight our way through the mess to prevent the lorries being forcibly stopped, and get them, according to our orders, up on to the hill roads where we understood—poor mutts—that at last we would have another go at the Nips'.

The surrender of Java was thus a foregone conclusion as soon as the Japanese had set firm foot upon the island. Nevertheless it took place in circumstances which, to say the least of it, showed little consideration towards the armed forces, ill-armed and ill-prepared though they were. On 5th March, ter Poorten convened a conference in Bandoeng which was attended, amongst others, by Maltby and the Army Commander, Sitwell. At this meeting, the Dutch Commander-in-Chief painted a picture of the situation which could not have been more gloomy. Bandoeng, he said, might fall at any moment, and if its outer defences were pierced, he did not propose to defend the town. The native Indonesians were very hostile to the Dutch and this hostility made it quite impossible to retire to the hills and there carry on a guerilla war. Nevertheless, though he himself was prepared to surrender, he would, he said, issue orders to the local Dutch commanders to maintain the fight. He had, he averred, instructed his troops not only to do so, but also to disregard any order which he might be compelled to issue calling upon them to lay down their arms. In the event, when discussing the final terms of surrender with General Maruyama, the Japanese Commander-in-Chief, the Dutch Commander subsequently withdrew this order to disobey orders.

The attitude of ter Poorten does not seem to have been shared by General Schilling, commanding at Batavia, who was prepared to emulate the selfless gallantry of Admiral Dorman, but who did not possess enough weight to influence the general situation. After some discussion, the Dutch Commander-in-Chief was induced to name an area north of Santosa as the spot where British forces should concentrate for a final stand, but he made no secret of his opinion that to do so would be folly or worse. That grim evening, therefore, Maltby and Sitwell were brought face to face with the imminence of disaster. One slender hope remained. General Schilling, who had not been present at the conference, was understood to favour a retreat to the hills in south-west Java whither, it was said, he had already been able to transfer a certain quantity of stores and ammunition with the courageous intention of prolonging resistance. Hardly had this faint flame been kindled, when it expired. Ter Poorten made any such move impossible by making Schilling responsible for the defence of Bandoeng while at the same time issuing orders that it was not to be defended, and forbidding any further fighting.

The two British officers took what counsel they could together. The surrender of some of those under their command, those for example at the airfield of Andir, was inevitable. Andir was part of Bandoeng which had been declared an open town, and the officers and other ranks at Poerwokerta had neither rations nor arms. Their position was, in the circumstances, hopeless. For the rest, Santosa seemed to offer the only chance but, when reconnoitred, it was found to be quite unsuitable for defence and to be inhabited by Dutchmen who had obviously no intention of continuing the struggle.

Throughout this confused period, matters were further complicated by the efforts made to evacuate as many men of the Royal

Air Force as could be got away. They left from Poerwokerta, priority of passage being accorded to aircrews and technical staff. By 5th March seven out of twelve thousand had been taken off, but by then no more ships were available for they had all been sunk and about 2,500 of the air force awaiting evacuation were therefore left stranded in the transit camp. In these attempts to send away as many skilled men as possible the Dutch gave but little help. They could not be brought to realize that our airmen were quite unpractised as soldiers and would be of far greater value playing their part as trained members of an aircrew or as technicians on the ground, in some other theatre of war, than they would be trying, without arms or food, to stage a last stand.

Santosa being unsuitable, about 8,000 mixed English and Australian forces, of whom some 1,300 belonged to the Royal Air Force, were concentrated at Garoet; here, too, the Dutch District Civil Administrator, Koffman, proved unsympathetic. He feared what he described as 'a massacre of the whites' if any guerrilla warfare were attempted, and made no effort to collect supplies or to give any aid to the British forces which had so inconveniently arrived in his district. They were by then in a sorry plight and by then, too, the last embers of resistance in the air had expired. By 7th March, only two undamaged Hurricanes were left and on that day these, the last representatives of a fighter force which, during the campaign in Sumatra and Java, had accounted for about forty aircraft, their own losses amounting to half as much again, were destroyed.

On the next day, 8th, came the inevitable climax. About 9 a.m., to their great astonishment, the British commanders received a translation of a broadcast, made an hour previously by ter Poorten, in which he said that all organized resistance in Java had ceased, and that the troops under his command were no longer to continue the fight. The Dutch land forces, in striking contrast to their Navy and Air Force, had capitulated almost without a struggle. They felt themselves to be no match for the Japanese.

This broadcast revoked all previous decisions and was ter Poorten's final word. Maltby and Sitwell were placed in an impossible position. A decision of decisive import had been taken and promulgated without reference to them. If, however, they decided to disregard it, their troops, should they continue the struggle, would, under international law, be subject to summary execution when captured. They had few arms, and what there were, were in the hands of men untrained to them; they were surrounded by a hostile native populace, with little food and, for drinking, they had nothing but contaminated water. In such conditions and with medicine-chests empty, they were in no state to carry on the fight. Moreover their whereabouts and intentions were well known to the enemy. In these circumstances, the two commanders had no alternative but to comply with the Dutch Commander-in-Chief's order to surrender. Four days later they negotiated terms with the Japanese commander in Bandoeng, Lieutenant General Maruyama. He undertook to treat all prisoners in accordance with the terms of the Geneva Convention of 1929.

How they subsequently fared can be gathered from a description of the arrival in Batavia two years later of a contingent which had been sent to one of the numerous islands of the Malayan archipelago, there to work on airfields. It has been set down by a squadron leader, once a Member of Parliament, who survived the horrors of Java, horrors which were repeated in Malaya, in Siam, in Korea, in Japan—anywhere where the Japanese were in control of unarmed and defenceless men—and is one of the few printable pages of a diary kept intermittently during his captivity and hidden from his gaolers :

> Of all the sights that I would like to forget [he writes] I think I would put first some of these returning island drafts being driven into Batavia . . . Imagine a series of barbed wire compounds in the dark with ourselves a gathering furtive stream of all races East and West, in every kind of clothing or none; here an old tunic in rags with a pair of cut down pyjama trousers, there a blanketed shivering malaria case or someone with night-blindness groping along with a stick, blundering over gypsy bundles of still sleeping prisoners. At the side runs a camp road with one high floodlight and all of us waiting to see if any of our friends have made the grade and returned. At last a long procession of stooping figures creeps down the road with jabbering Nips cracking at their shins with a rifle or the flat of a sword. Most of them half naked, and they leading those going blind with pellagra. Others shambling along with their feet bound up in lousy rags over tropical sores (not our little things an inch across but real horrors), legs swollen up or half paralysed with beri-beri, enormous eyes fallen into yellow crumpled faces like aged gnomes. And then a search—God knows what for after months in a desert and weeks at sea. Some Jap would rush up and down hurling anything any of them still possessed all over the place, while as sure as the clock, the dreadful hopeless rain would begin again like a lunatic helplessly fouling his bed. Everything swilling into the filthy racing storm gutters; men trying to reach out and rescue a bit of kit and being picked up and hurled bodily back into the ranks; others clutching hold of a wife's photo or suchlike souvenir of home, small hope for the Nips always liked pinching and being obscene about a woman's picture. And at last after two or three hours when everyone was soaking and shivering with cold, the dreary, hunted column would crawl down the road out of the patch of light where the great atlas moths disputed with the bats, away into an isolation compound, with no light, no food, no knowledge of where to find a tap or latrine, with wet bedding or none at all. The Nips would disappear laughing

> and cackling back to bed, we faded away to our floor space and all was quiet again; and the evening or the morning was the eight or nine hundredth day and God no doubt saw that it was good.

In few respects does a nation show itself in its true colours more clearly than in its treatment of enemies who have the misfortune to fall into its hands. To describe as bestial the behaviour of the Japanese towards their prisoners of war of whatever race or rank is an insult to the animal world.

Of the thousands of Royal Air Force and Royal Australian Air Force officers and airmen who fell into Japanese hands in Malaya, Sumatra, Java and later Burma, 3,462 only were found alive, after due retribution had fallen from the skies above Hiroshima upon the sons of Nippon.

Not by any means all the Air Force was captured in Java. Some, as has been related, were successfully taken by ship to Australia, and a small number to Ceylon. By a combination of good fortune and stern courage a still smaller number escaped. Of these, the most remarkable was Wing Commander J. R. Jeudwine, commanding No. 84 Squadron, which it will be recalled lost the last of its Blenheims at the capture of Kalidjati. Such pilots and ground staff as remained had been sent to the port of Tjilitjap, there to be taken by ship to Australia. No ship, however, was forthcoming; the port was in flames, and the 'Scorpion', the only seaworthy vessel to be found, was a ship's lifeboat capable of holding at most twelve. To try to avoid capture by taking to the woods and jungles near the shore there to await rescue by submarine offered a slender chance. To seek that help in an open boat seemed certain death. Jeudwine and ten others chose this course and boarded the 'Scorpion'. Flying Officer C. P. L. Streatfield alone knew the elements of sailing; Pilot Officer S. G. Turner could handle a sextant and was chosen as navigator; the remainder of the crew was made up of another officer and seven Australian sergeants. On the evening of 7th March, they put to sea, bound for Australia which the navigator calculated would take sixteen days. It took forty-seven. Through all that time they never lost heart, though as day after day passed in blazing sun or torrential rain, the chances of reaching land grew smaller and smaller. They played games, held competitions, but found 'that the mental exercise made us very hungry and that talking and arguing brought on thirst'. Saturday night at sea was kept religiously, a ration of liquor being issued, which was found on closer investigation to be a patent cough cure. Their worst experience was the visit paid to them by a young whale, about twice the size of the 'Scorpion', who came to rest lying in a curve with its tail under the boat. 'Eventually it made off, and when we had regained the power of movement, we passed round a bottle of Australian "3 Star" Brandy . . . after which we did not care if we saw elephants, pink or otherwise, flying over us in tight formation'. At long last, they sighted land near Frazer Islet, were found by a Catalina flying boat of the United States Navy, and taken to Perth. An American submarine sent at once to Java found no sign of their comrades.

Such men as these typify the spirit of the less fortunate who had fought to the end in circumstances which, from the very beginning, made victory impossible, and even prolonged defence out of the question. It was through no fault of theirs that they did not accomplish more. The straits to which they were reduced, flying unsuitable aircraft in the worst conditions, were soon reproduced on the same scale farther north. How the Air Force fared in the first campaign of Burma must now be told.

CHAPTER IV
Burma Falls

TWO days before Christmas, 1941, and a fortnight after Japan had entered the war, some eighty of her bombers, with an escort of thirty fighters, dropped the first bombs on Rangoon, the capital of Burma. They fell on women in the market places, seated, cheroots between painted lips, behind their stalls of dried fish and betel-nuts; upon worshippers on the marble way about the great Shwe Dagôn pagoda; upon coolies sweating beneath their burdens on the quays or in the Strand Road; upon British and Chinese merchants in their clubs or gracious bungalows—in a word upon a people unprepared for war and in whom curiosity had ousted fear. It cost them dear. About 2,000 were killed that day by fragmentation bombs. Forty-eight hours went by and then as the Christian community was celebrating Christmas the bombers came again in like strength and killed some 5,000 more.

As at Pearl Harbour and Singapore, so it was at Rangoon. The Japanese, carefully prepared and ready to the last long-range tank, struck and the blows were swift and deadly. In delivering them there were two objects. An attack on Rangoon, causing panic and disorganization, would make easier the conquest of Burma; but its immediate effect would be to dam up the thin stream of supplies flowing from that port to China. Its course was northwards over range after range of steep, teak-covered hills, along the few but well-built roads, along the railway which ran past the red walls of the King's palace at Mandalay, up the tree-fringed Irrawaddy till all routes merged into one at Lashio and the winding Burma Road stretched its looped, interminable length before the radiators of the creaking lorries. Seize Rangoon and they would come to a standstill or roll on empty to a China deprived at long last of all foreign aid and irrevocably doomed.

Rangoon was not only at the head of the route along which trickled supplies to China, it was also the gateway to Burma itself. No power invading that country could hope to do so with success until it had first captured the city and its port. Burma in shape is somewhat like a man's left hand with the forefinger and thumb extending and pointing southwards from the Himalayan foothills on the wrist. Rangoon is on the ball of the thumb and is situated in a plain formed at that point by the delta of the Irrawaddy. The plains in Burma, not very numerous, all run north and south, being divided one from another by ridge upon ridge of serrated, jungle-clad hills. Her invaders have therefore been compelled by nature always to follow the same route. They can move from south to north or north to south, the direction taken by the rivers, road and railways, but not from east to west. Running down from the Himalayas which seal Burma on the north are two nearly parallel ranges of mountains—the Arakan Yomas to the west and the Shan Hills to the east. Thrusting them apart is the jungle valley of the Irrawaddy, and further east near the Chinese and Tongkanese borders runs the deep and narrow valley of the Salween River. Below these hills and the plain between, a long forefinger, the narrow coastal strip of Tenasserim, points straight at Malaya.

By reason of its geographical position and its natural defences Burma is the bastion between India on the west and China and Indo-China on the east. To seize it meant not only an end of supplies to China, but also the establishment of a firm base lavishly stocked with rice and oil, for an invasion of India. Conversely, should the Allies ever be able to take the offensive, Burma lay on that vital outer perimeter which it was the first aim of the Japanese to establish in order to defend the Pacific with its islands and ultimately their own homeland. This perimeter their early and swift successes soon created and within a few months it was running along a line drawn through the Kuriles, the Marshalls, the Bismarcks, on to Timor, Java, Sumatra and north again through Malaya and Burma.

The main Allied defensive position in that country was that of the River Salween, and to assist the army in the holding of it plans had been drawn up for the construction of eight airfields with their appropriate satellites. By the time war broke out, thanks to the energy and determination of No. 221 Group, commanded by an Australian, Group Captain E. R. Manning, seven of these had been built and they formed the knots of a string joining Lashio in the north to Mingaladon in the south. There were also landing strips still further south at Moulmein, Tavoy, Mergui and Victoria Point, and still further north at Myitkyina, as well as an airfield on the island of Akyab on the west coast. Far out in the Indian Ocean were moorings for flying boats situated for the most part in the islands forming the Andaman and Nicobar groups.

An air force based on this chain of airfields faced almost due east against an enemy advancing, as did the Japanese, from Thailand. It was thus at a disadvantage because owing to the mountainous and difficult nature of the country very few warning posts could be set up and the approach of enemy aircraft could in consequence only rarely be predicted. Had the posts of Toungoo, Heho and Namsang been situated in the Irrawaddy valley, this would not have been so, but they were not, and the most unhappy consequences inevitably followed.

In marked contrast to the difficulties encountered in Malaya, the construction of airfields in Burma was carried out smoothly and with the co-operation of the Government. All were soon provided with one or two all-weather runways able to take modern aircraft of the largest kind. There was also accommodation for staff and for stocks of ammunition, but anti-aircraft guns were lacking and the warning system, as has been said, was defective. The space available in Burma for the use of a defending air force was considerable; unfortunately it was the force itself which was almost wholly lacking. Constituted in April 1941, it was formed as No. 221 Group with headquarters at Rangoon and was subsequently to work side by side with the American Volunteer Group attached to the Chinese Air Force and with the Indian Air Force. In all, however, only thirty-seven front line aircraft, British and American, were available in Burma though the plan of defence stipulated that a figure of 280 was the minimum necessary to meet the invading enemy. Of these thirty-seven, sixteen were Buffalos, these being a flight of No. 67 (Fighter) Squadron, though temporarily under the administrative control of No. 60 (Bomber) Squadron. There was also available a communication flight of Moth types belonging to the Burmese Volunteer Air Force. The American aircraft, a squadron of twenty-one P.40's, were part of the American Volunteer Group stationed at Kunming for the defence of the Burma Road. The Squadron had been specially detached by Generalissimo Chiang Kai-shek for the defence of Rangoon and with the rest of the force was under the command of Colonel, presently General, C. L. Chennault, a modern condottiere, who with his hard-fighting pilots had 'saved the sum of things for pay' in China.

Against this small force the Japanese, whose intention it was to gain control over the Burmese air with the least possible delay, brought some 400 bombers and fighters. Less than three weeks after their attack on Pearl Harbour, they opened the assault with the first of the raids on Rangoon, and they did so comforted by the thought that the success of their campaign in Malaya was already virtually certain. The effect of these raids was immediate and widespread panic. All who could, fled or prepared to do so. The number of men, women and children who began immediately to stream out of the city will never be accurately known, but it was not less than 100,000. As the campaign proceeded, and more and more of their country became absorbed by the enemy, this number increased, until it seemed that half the population were wending their way towards the inhospitable north, disorganised, panic-stricken, without hope. Thousands died by the wayside from cholera, malaria, or the equally deadly assaults of fatigue and hunger. Through the hot jungles, past the steaming paddy-fields, up into the cruel hills, they plodded on, making for the dubious safety of India. Those who eventually reached it made use in the later stages of their flight of a track previously traversed by none but a few head hunters and Lord Curzon in a litter. After covering, many of them, a thousand miles, some 400,000, a broken and disease-ridden remnant, achieved their goal.

This terrible migration of human beings, one of the grimmest recorded by history, was still in the future, however, when the Japanese raiding aircraft drew off from Rangoon on that unhappy Christmas Day of 1941. They had not retired unscathed. The American Tomahawks (P.40's) and the Buffalos of the Royal Air Force claimed to have destroyed thirty-six of them in those two days, some of their victims being long-range fighters. This was no mean achievement, if the difficulties under which the defence operated are borne in mind. Chief among them was, and remained, an almost total lack of warning. There was only one Radar unit in the whole of Burma, and this was already obsolete when it was set up to the east of Rangoon to supplement the chain of observer posts spread thinly along the hills and connected with Air Headquarters by a precarious telephone service. The unit did all that was possible, but its efficiency may be judged by the fact that only on one occasion did the warning which it gave of the approach of enemy aircraft arrive earlier—and then only by a few minutes—than that given by the men of the Observer Corps. In those days, orders to 'scramble' were often delivered to the waiting pilots by messengers riding to them from the operations room on bicycles. The defence was, therefore, at a great disadvantage, and to have even a slight chance of engaging in successful combat, the Buffalos and P.40's, each flying through the wall of dust created by its predecessor, had to climb away from the attacking enemy. Having with difficulty reached the necessary height, they would then turn upon the Japanese bombers, which they usually found flying in one or more formations of twenty-seven with fighters circling round them. Making no attempt to pull out of their dive, and disregarding all opposition, the British and American pilots would head straight for their quarry. If they were not shot down by the Japanese fighters, they pulled out of their dive, laboured once more to gain height and then returned to the fray. Such tactics, though unorthodox, were singularly successful, and for a time kept the enemy at bay. After the Christmas Day attack on Rangoon, he drew off, and a period of precarious calm, lasting almost a month, followed. 'Life in the city has returned to normal' reported a local newspaper, 'Daylight robberies have started again.'

The quality of pilots and aircrews was of the highest, but the ground staff possessed little training in arms, with all that this implies. They had not passed through the usual processes by which discipline is built up and maintained in a force of armed men. They were in consequence subject to all the strains and stresses which bewilder civilians.

During the brief respite which ensued after the Christmas Day attack, reinforcements, desperately needed, and which took the form of a squadron of Blenheims and some thirty Hurricanes, reached No. 221 Group. By then the Air Officer Commanding the R.A.F. in Burma, Air Vice-Marshal D. F. Stevenson, had made his plans. Such bombers as he had would be used to strike the airfields in Thailand from which the Japanese Air Force was operating. The fighters would be sent against the advanced enemy air bases and would give cover to the army on the banks of the Salween. These plans were put into execution as soon as the battle was joined and their soundness immediately proved. By using advanced bases at Moulmein, Mergui, Tavoy and elsewhere, the Hurricanes achieved a fleeting but considerable success. They, and the Blenheims of No. 113 Squadron, which had begun their operations only a few hours after their arrival from the Middle East by dropping 11,000 pounds of bombs on the chief base of the Japanese at Bangkok, had soon accounted for some fifty-eight enemy bombers and fighters on the ground, mainly in the Thailand area, and in so doing had delayed the achievement by the enemy of air supremacy. The small British force was well and resolutely handled by Stevenson, who, to use his own phrase, had decided to 'lean forward' with some of his fighters and, by attacking the Japanese Air Force when it was on the ground, to relieve pressure on the army.

Such tactics, contrasting as they did with those pursued by the air forces in Malaya, depended on an adequate supply of aircraft and on their maintenance, and it was precisely these which were lacking. The Blenheims, for example, after their attack on Bangkok on 8th January, 1942, had to be sent for a refit, urgently necessary as the result of their long flight from the Middle East, to Lashio where they remained out of harm's way, but also out of action until 19th

January. Shortage of tools and spare parts made it impossible for them to take the air again before that date.

In the meantime, the battle in the air above Rangoon, which had for some weeks died away, was renewed and thereafter continued until the city was abandoned. In the eight weeks which elapsed between 23rd December, 1941, and 25th February, 1942, thirty-one attacks by day and night were made upon it by enemy heavy bombers ranging in strength from one to sixteen. The weight of attack may seem small in comparison with the raids by the *Luftwaffe* on London and other English towns in the winter of 1940 and 1941 and with the huge raids carried out by the Allies in the later stages of the war; but for a population ill-supplied with shelters and shaken by a form of warfare to which they were entirely unaccustomed, it was serious enough. Moreover, to defend Rangoon at night as well as by day was too much to ask of the Hurricane pilots and their American comrades. Some repose was necessary, for each day they had to remain at constant readiness between dawn and sunset. Nevertheless they made several successful interceptions at night and succeeded in inflicting casualties upon the enemy, one Japanese bomber falling in flames close to the airfield at Mingaladon.

Between 23rd and 29th January the Japanese made a determined effort to achieve supremacy in the air over Rangoon and to overwhelm Stevenson's small force of fighters. To do so they made use of 200 aircraft or more of which the majority were fighters. They failed and their failure is a measure of the soundness of the defence and the resolution of the Allied fighter pilots. In six days of fighting the Japanese lost a round total of fifty bombers and fighters, a set-back severe enough to drive them once more to the shelter of the dark.

About a month later, on 24th and 25th February, the enemy made his third and last attempt to achieve in the air what his armies were soon to accomplish on the ground. In those two days he used 166 bombers and fighters in a series of resolute onslaughts. On the first day No. 67 (F) Squadron and the Americans claimed to have shot down 37 and seven probably destroyed. On the second day the pilots of the P.40's maintained that they had accounted for twenty-four of the Japanese.[1] Whatever the accuracy of the claims, the fact remains that the Japanese made no further attempt to seek domination in the air above Rangoon until the events on the ground gave them control of our airfields.

The achievement by the Royal Air Force of air superiority, local

[1] When fighting over the soil of China each American pilot received the equivalent of £125 sterling for every Japanese aircraft he shot down.

and transient though it was, influenced the course of the battle on the land, for it enabled reinforcements arriving at the last minute to be put ashore unmolested, and when in the end the army was compelled to retreat from Rangoon, the demolition parties were able to complete the destruction of the oil storage tanks and refinery and the port installations. Even this final withdrawal, both by land and sea, was carried out without interference from the air, so shaken were the Japanese air forces.

Though by the skilful and unlimited use of his fighters, Stevenson was able to postpone the fate of Rangoon, only a predominant force of bombers could have enabled him to postpone it indefinitely. This he did not possess. An average of no more than six Blenheims a day was available for the support of the troops in the field. Handled though they were with skill and courage, they were quite inadequate to stem the onslaught. Inexorably, the Japanese pressed on. On 30th January, the airfield at Moulmein, our main forward airbase, fell, and as a consequence the main warning system, such as it was, was disorganized. Soon it was no more than a solitary 'Jim Crow' Hurricane which patrolled above Rangoon keeping watch. Thereafter no bombing operations could be based on the Tenasserim airfield.

Once the Japanese had obtained control of that narrow strip of territory, through part of which they were soon to construct the infamous Railroad of Death, the fall of Rangoon could no longer be delayed. In assaulting the city, their armies, pursuing their usual tactics, avoided a frontal attack and relied on the penetration of a flank. Before long their movements were observed by the pilot of a lone Hurricane, who reported that the enemy were in strength near Pegu, some seventy miles north-east of the city, and that his light tanks were close to that marvel of piety and sculpture, the recumbent Buddha.

Two escape routes still remained precariously open. Stevenson ordered the remains of his fighter force—three jungle-weary Buffalos, four American P.40's and some twenty Hurricanes—to move northward. Abandoning Mingaladon, which was left strewn with dummies and broken aircraft, they went to a hastily built dirt air strip cut out of the paddy-fields at Zigon. So treacherous was its surface that one landing in five resulted in damage, sometimes severe, to the aircraft. Invariably the tailwheels were rendered unserviceable and bamboo skids were fitted as a temporary expedient in order to fly out the damaged machines for repair. Zigon, however, was the only operational strip—it could hardly be called an airfield—from which the Army retiring from Rangoon could be provided with fighter cover and air support. These operations were controlled by 'X' Wing Headquarters under Group Captain Noel Singer, who, by means of a reasonably efficient system of communications, had striven to preserve our hard-won supremacy over Rangoon until the oil installations at Syriam and Thilawa, together with 'the docks, power stations and stores' had been destroyed, and the army had withdrawn.

On 7th March, the code word 'Caesar', signal for the final stage of the evacuation, was broadcast. Sappers began the work of destruction, and before long a column of tanks and vehicles some forty miles in length began to wend its dusty way northward, covered by the fighters from Zigon. No Japanese bomber attempted an attack. Their work completed, the Sappers too withdrew, and from a wrecked harbour, overhung by the black pall of smoke sent up from burning oil tanks, the last ships moved slowly out to sea.

What remained of No. 221 Group moved by successive stages towards India, covering the long retreat of the Army as best it could, and with complete success as far as Prome. No airfields existed on the Irrawaddy line between Rangoon and Mandalay except the civil airport at Magwe, which possessed no dispersal pens and no accommodation. More 'kutcha' strips were accordingly cut in the jungle and in the hard paddy land bordering the Prome Road.

At Magwe, 'X' Wing became Burwing under Group Captain S. Broughall. It was made up of No. 45 (Bomber) Squadron, No. 17 (Fighter) Squadron, the few surviving American Volunteers and the staff of the R.D.F. Station. Alexander, the Army Commander, controlled its use and it continued to do all it could to support the retreating army. Stevenson with Singer had moved, on 12th March, to the warm, pleasant island of Akyab and set up Akwing. This comprised No. 67 Squadron, flying obsolete Hurricanes, a few communication aircraft, and a General Reconnaissance Flight of No. 139 Squadron with Hudsons. On 20th March reconnaissance aircraft of Burwing reported more than fifty enemy aircraft upon the airfield at Mingaladon. They were attacked the next day by ten Hurricanes and nine Blenheims based on Magwe, and a small but heartening victory —the last of the campaign—was achieved. Sixteen Japanese aircraft were destroyed on the ground and eleven in the air, two of them falling victims to the Blenheims. Such an operation provoked reprisal, swift and all too effective. It was carried out on Magwe by a total of some 230 Japanese bomber and fighter aircraft operating in formations of various sizes over a period of twenty-five hours. This series of attacks accounted for all but six Blenheims and eleven Hurricanes, which, just able to fly but in no condition to fight,

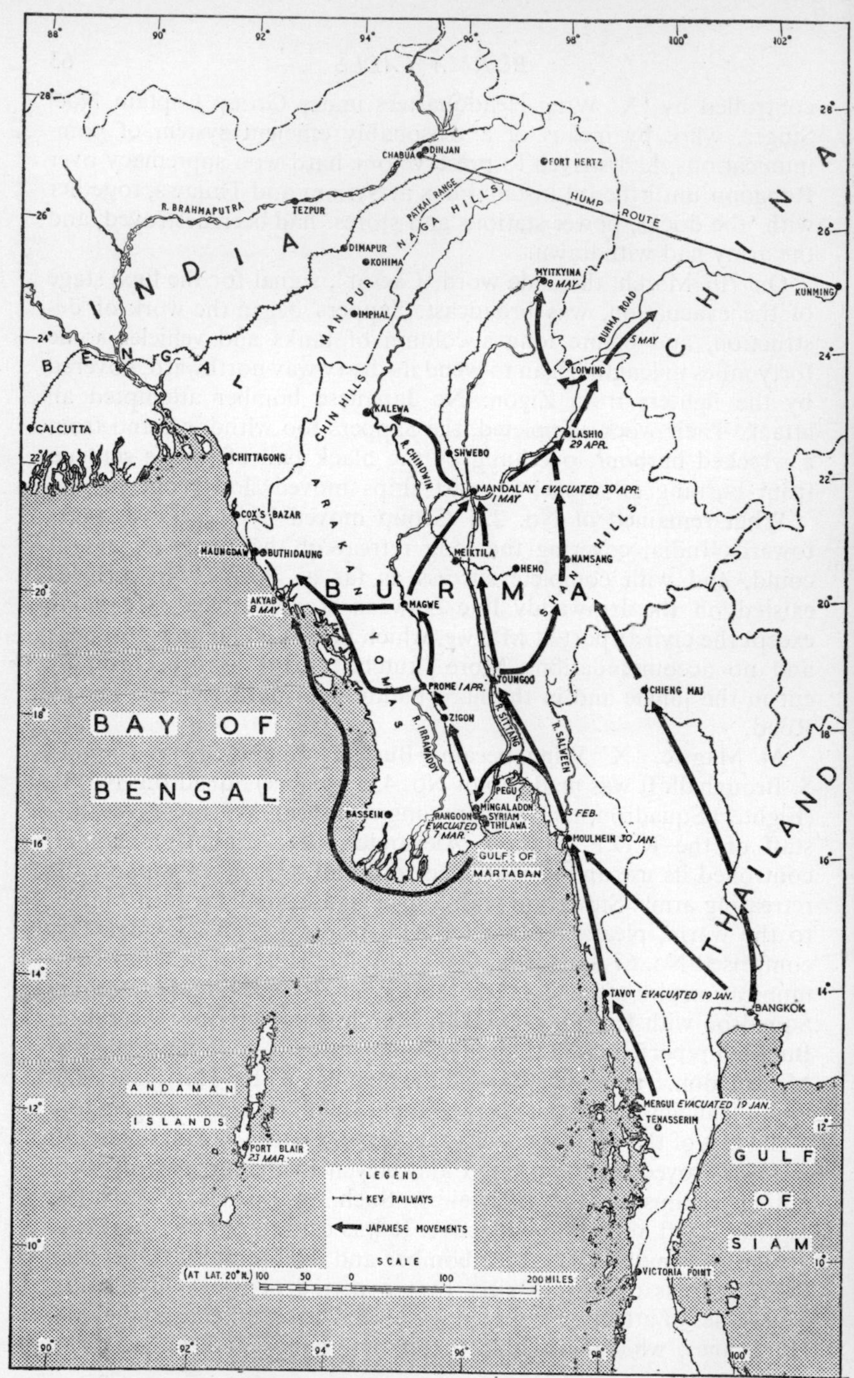

THE JAPANESE ADVANCE THROUGH BURMA, JANUARY–MAY 1942

struggled to Akyab, while the three remaining P.40's moved northwards towards Lashio and Loiwing. The success of the enemy's counterblast at Magwe was due at least very largely to lack of warning. The only radar unit still available was covering the south-east, whereas the Japanese attack came in from the north-east. Flushed with their success at Magwe, the Japanese delivered a final blow on Akyab on 27th March. They attacked in waves for seventy-two hours and destroyed seven Hurricanes and a Valentia.

These two disasters virtually wiped out the air force in Burma. Its pilots had fought with a bitter tenacity equalling that displayed by those of Fighter Command in the Battle of Britain and by the squadrons in Java. Every day for eight weeks at Mingaladon and the other airfields and then at Zigon the pilots of the Hurricanes had remained at two minutes' readiness. Such a strain, continued for so long, was almost past bearing. Yet bear it they did and fought to the end, hopeless but unflinching. One of them caught at last by a Zero fighter above Akyab was shot down in flames into the sea. Struggling from the cockpit, he put the nozzle on his Mae West to his lips and blew. It remained deflated, and continued so until he discovered that the air which he was trying to force into it was escaping through a hole drilled by a bullet in his cheek and jawbone. Unaided by his lifebelt, he kept afloat for three hours till picked up by natives in a canoe. Of such men were the pilots of Burma.

As the result of the Japanese attacks at Magwe and at Akyab, Stevenson was compelled to turn his eyes away from Alexander's armies back to the hot uneasiness of Bengal and the highly vulnerable city of Calcutta, where he had arrived on 17th March. To build up the defences of north-east India and many miles to the southward to Ceylon, was a primary necessity, and the maintenance, therefore, of an air force in Burma, where the battle was already lost, was uneconomical and, indeed, suicidal. Nevertheless, despite the disaster of 21st March, such fighter formations as still possessed aircraft capable of flying, continued, from Lashio and Loiwing, to give what limited support they could to the Chinese Fifth Army in action on the southern Shan front. By the middle of April, however, the Japanese advance against their bases had developed so rapidly and in such strength that they were compelled to withdraw and join the defenders of Calcutta. Not all of them made a successful retreat. Twenty officers and 324 airmen, of Burwing, all of them ground staff, were left behind and, in their determination not to fall into the hands of the Japanese, moved off in some 150 vehicles which they still possessed along the hazardous road from Lashio to Chungtu, in China. There, under the name of 'Rafchin', while awaiting the arrival of Hudson aircraft, which it ultimately proved impossible to send, they spent a year in reorganizing, in providing the Chinese with help at their main air bases, and in training Chinese ground crews. They were also able to make their hosts familiar, albeit to a somewhat limited extent, with the mysteries of Radio Direction Finding, for they had brought with them the Radar Unit from Magwe.

Before their final withdrawal from the battle, the bomber squadrons of No. 221 Group, operating from Tezpur and Dinjan within the frontier of Assam, gave all the support they could to the armed forces still struggling to hold up or at least to delay the enemy. They did so with the knowledge that a resolute thrust by the Japanese anywhere in that remote part of the world might pierce the feeble defences of India and ultimately reach Delhi. For the fact was that India was almost as weak in defence as had been Malaya. These delaying tactics in the air might, and indeed did, help to remove the menace overhanging the red-domed, buff-coloured magnificence of Viceregal Lodge; they could not, however, give any very great measure of support to the army of Alexander, still struggling out of Burma. The Japanese Air Force was at last in the ascendant, and they spread themselves in a series of patrols over a wide area in northern Burma, attacking Lashio, Mandalay, Loiwing and Myitkyina. An assault on Mandalay, delivered on 3rd April, was particularly devastating, for it was carried out against a defenceless city, and one moreover which had lost its fire-fighting apparatus, destroyed by one of the first salvos. In a few hours, three-fifths of the houses had been wiped out by high explosive or fire, and thousands of those who dwelt in them blasted or burnt to death.

By then the ever-thickening stream of refugees, shuffling through dust or mud towards the Naga Hills, had reached its climax. Though conditions were desperate, the Royal Air Force continued to give them such help as it could. A certain degree of protection was afforded by Mohawks based on Dinjan, but their range was very limited and they were no match for the Japanese Zeros. The unarmed and unarmoured Dakotas of No. 31 (Transport) Squadron of the Royal Air Force were able, however, to render great and timely aid. Together with the 2nd Troop Carrier Squadron of the United States Army Air Force, they removed from such centres as Magwe, Shwebo and Myitkyina 8,616 men, women and children, of whom some 2,600 were sick or wounded, and they did so in conditions from which no element of horror was absent. 'When Myitkyina fell on the 8th May, 1942, I was the pilot of the last aircraft to get away', records Flight Lieutenant Coughlan of No. 31 Squadron, 'and the press of refugees surrounding my aircraft was such that we had to hold them off with drawn revolvers. One nursing sister, I remember, offered to give up her place to a favourite dog, and seemed astonished when it was filled instead by a mother and child'. On 6th May, two of the Dakotas, landing in a gathering storm upon the airfield at Myitkyina, were attacked by Japanese dive-bombers. One was hit, the casualties being two women and a child. The remainder of the passengers scrambled out of the aircraft and were immediately machine-gunned. In an effort to defend them, the pilot used his only weapon, a tommy-gun, which he fired at point-blank range as a Japanese bomber swept low over his grounded aircraft. A trail of white vapour was observed to be streaming from one of its engines as it turned away. Among others, the Governor, Sir Reginald Dorman-Smith, was taken away from Myitkyina on 4th May by a Hudson sent from India in anticipation of orders subsequently received from Whitehall.

In this work of rescue it was sometimes necessary to fly as high as 17,000 feet in order to cross the Naga Hills between the Brahmaputra and the Irrawaddy, and at the same time to find cloud cover in which to elude Japanese fighters. The number of daily sorties was exceptionally high, but after the first few days, the crews, having witnessed the scenes on the edge of the runways in the Burma airfields, asked for it to be increased.

The second task of the squadron, in which they were even more successful, was the dropping of supplies to the army and to the refugees on the road to India. At that time the technique of supply dropping had not been learnt or even studied. Mistakes were therefore many. 'In our first efforts', reports Flight Lieutenant Coughlan, who took part in the dropping of supplies as well as the evacuation of refugees, 'we tried putting the rice in a bag and free-dropping it, that is, without attaching a parachute. There were so many burst bags as a result of this method that we eventually evolved another one by which the rice was put into three sacks, one inside the other. After that the losses were not more than 10 per cent. The average load of a Dakota was 5,000 lbs. In daylight we could get rid of this and 1,500 lbs. more in eighteen minutes'. Altogether, with the assistance of the United States Troop Carrier Squadron, 109,652 pounds of supplies were dropped during this period. There is little doubt that the troops of Alexander, and such refugees as survived, owe their lives to this assistance. One of the Dakotas of No. 31 Squadron was able to remove the British Garrison of the small advanced post of Fort Hertz, together with their wives and children. A few months later, aircraft of the same squadron took back to the fort another force which, relying entirely on supplies from the air, successfully maintained itself there and conducted much fierce guerrilla warfare against the Japanese.

Mention must also be made of the Lysanders of No. 28 Squadron, Royal Air Force, and of No. 1 Squadron, Indian Air Force. Their normal function was Army Co-operation, for which the aircraft they flew, out-of-date though they were by then, had been specifically designed. Many uses were found for them and pilots of the Indian Air Force did not hesitate to turn them into improvised bombers. It was during these days of stress and effort that Wing Commander G. Marsland, whose first acquaintance with war had been as a pilot in the Battle of Britain, developed the habit of throwing hand grenades at the Japanese ground forces from the air gunner's seat.

By May 1942 the part played by the Royal Air Force in the first Burma campaign had ended. Overwhelmed by weight of numbers, strong in nothing but courage, they held throughout most resolutely to their duty, and each one of them might have exclaimed with Portius, in Addison's tragedy of Cato

> 'Tis not in mortals to command success,
> But we'll do more, Sempronius, we'll deserve it'.

What they did say was shorter, more idiomatic and unprintable, but it conveyed the same meaning.

By the time the last of the army had reached Imphal, capital of the State of Manipur, where they arrived just before the monsoon broke in full fury, the air force retreating with them had accounted for fifty-four enemy fighters and bombers in the air and twenty on the ground. The American Volunteer Group during the same period claimed 179 and 38 respectively.

In their triumphant sweep to the north and north-west towards the confines of India, the Japanese did not forget the extreme south and, before the war was many days old, began to turn their attention to the island of Ceylon. As far back as July 1940, the British Chiefs of Staff had laid down that at least three General Reconnaissance squadrons for the protection of shipping in the Indian Ocean should be based in that island, and two flying boat squadrons were to be stationed in the Andaman and Nicobar Islands. Fifty-four aircraft would thus be available out of the 336 authorized, for the defence of the Far East; but even this modest figure had not been reached by the time war broke out. Reconnaissance of the Gulf of Martaban and of the Bay of Bengal was controlled by No. 221 Group. From the beginning of December 1941, anti-submarine and coastal patrols were flown over the Gulf, and shipping sailing towards Rangoon was given air cover by No. 4 (Coast Defence) Flight of the Indian Air Force Volunteer Reserve, based on Moulmein, and equipped with Wapiti and Audax aircraft. Our withdrawal under pressure from the Japanese transferred them for a few days to Bassein, on the west coast of Burma, and in a short time to Calcutta. This Flight formed part of a small Coastal Defence Wing, manned by a mixed group of Indian and European business men, which was stationed at the six main ports of India and Burma.

The main work of reconnaissance in the Bay of Bengal fell upon No. 139 (later to be renumbered as No. 62) Squadron which disposed for this purpose of six Hudsons. Of these, one flight was stationed at Port Blair in the Andaman Islands, where a runway 800 yards in length had been built with the greatest difficulty. On 11th February, 1942, this flight was reinforced by Lysanders fitted with long-range tanks, and these aircraft, together with the Hudsons, maintained reconnaissance in the sea approaches to Rangoon and later escorted ships fleeing from that port to the refuge of Calcutta. By the last week of March their base in the Andamans had become untenable, and on the 23rd it was occupied by the Japanese.

By the second week in March, Calcutta, where a quarter of a million tons of Allied shipping was concentrated, was within range of attack from the air. Moreover a Japanese Fleet was in the Bay of Bengal where it was escorting a number of transports carrying reinforcements which arrived at Rangoon on 6th April. Should this fleet, together with the Japanese long-range bomber squadrons based on the newly captured airfields of Mingaladon and Magwe, decide to attack the port of Calcutta, much of, perhaps all, this shipping, of which the value at that stage of the war was particularly great, might, and probably would be lost. The nakedness of the defence, the magnitude of the prize were patent, spread wide for all to see—all including a Japanese reconnaissance aircraft should one choose to fly above the crowded roadstead. Twenty-four hours went by and none appeared. Was it possible that the enemy was unaware that so large a collection of shipping lay in that port? Orders for its immediate dispersal to anchorages on the eastern coast of India were hastily issued; but some days would have to elapse before the fulfilment of them could be completed and in the meanwhile it was essential to prevent the enemy from discovering the state of affairs. An attempt by long-range Fortress bombers of the United States Army Air Corps to damage the Japanese Air Forces in the Andaman Islands was unsuccessful. The five and a half tons of bombs dropped, straddled, but did not hit the targets. There remained the three Hudsons of No. 139 Squadron, which had been driven from Port Blair originally, and which, by refuelling at Akyab, could reach the target. As a forlorn hope, two of them were despatched to attack their former base and both did so. In the first attack on 14th April, two Japanese twin-engined flying boats were set on fire, a four-engined was sunk, and the remainder, eleven in number, damaged by gunfire. Not content with this achievement, the Hudsons returned four days later and, battling their way through a screen of Zero fighters, made a number of runs at a height of only thirty feet to destroy two more and severely damage three others. One Hudson was shot down, and the other returned in a badly damaged state. Their mission had, however, been successful, and for the moment the enemy were blind. Unmolested, some seventy British merchant vessels quitted the Port of Calcutta and dispersed themselves among other Indian ports. So successful, in fact, were these two attacks that no enemy flying boats attempted any reconnaissance flight until the following July.

In Ceylon itself, such preparations as were possible had been made. No. 222 Group, together with a joint Naval and Air Operations Room, was established at Colombo and two new airfields constructed at Ratmalana and China Bay, near Trincomalee. At the outset, this Group consisted only of No. 273 Squadron and part of No. 205 (Flying Boat) Squadron, which had left Singapore before the outbreak of war. It was stationed at Koggala, and moorings with refuelling facilities had been laid out off the Cocos Islands, Christmas Island, the Maldives, the Seychelles and the island of Mauritius. These advanced bases, if they can be so described, were established by the crews of the flying boats themselves, who carried out long flights over vast expanses of sea, in an effort to provide for the defence of the Indian Ocean.

The fall of Rangoon and the imminent loss of Burma changed the situation. The approaches by sea to India and Ceylon were now open, and it became more than ever imperative to provide the Royal Navy in those waters with adequate air protection. Without it, a raid similar to that which had laid low the American Pacific Fleet in Pearl Harbour might well be staged against our naval base in Trincomalee. As Commander-in-Chief India, Wavell, while determining to strengthen Ceylon, wished to concentrate his main force of aircraft in north-east India. Their presence there was necessary to win and maintain air superiority should the Japanese, as was thought most probable, attempt the conquest of that country as soon as they had achieved that of Burma. He was, however, overruled by the Chiefs of Staff in London, who considered that Ceylon was of vital importance in preserving communications between East and West, and that island was accordingly reinforced by Hurricane Mark I's and

Mark II's, belonging to No. 30 and No. 261 Squadrons taken thither from the Middle East in the aircraft carrier H.M.S. *Indomitable*. On 6th and 7th March they arrived and were presently joined by No. 11 Squadron, and No. 413 Squadron, Royal Canadian Air Force.

'Until it is possible to increase our strength in the Middle East', said the Chiefs of Staff in a signal to Wavell dated 12th March, 'you must do everything possible to use to the maximum extent the aircraft and crews available in Ceylon'. Wavell did his best, and by the end of the month fifty serviceable Hurricanes, fourteen Blenheims, six Catalina flying boats and a small number of Fleet Air Arm Fulmars and Albacores were ready and waiting to go into action. Small though these numbers were, the congestion both at Ratmalana and Trincomalee was serious, and one of the Hurricane squadrons was moved to Colombo, where a well-camouflaged runway was hastily constructed on the racecourse. In their subsequent attacks, the enemy never discovered it.

The presence of air reinforcements in Ceylon made it possible to strengthen our Far Eastern fleet which, by the last week in March, when Admiral Sir James Somerville assumed command, was made up to a strength of five battleships, three aircraft carriers, seven cruisers, fifteen destroyers and five submarines. This was no mean force and those in authority began to breathe more freely, when the news was received through a naval intelligence source that a Japanese naval force, made up mostly of carriers, intended to attack Ceylon on or about 1st April. The carriers would be accompanied by a number of 8-inch cruisers with attendant destroyers, and battleships of the *Kongo* class might also be in support. On 31st March, Somerville put to sea from Colombo and later the same day made rendezvous with a portion of his force which had been detached to Addu Atoll. After two days spent off the south coast of Ceylon in a vain attempt to locate the enemy, Admiral Somerville proceeded to Addu Atoll, having detached the cruisers *Dorsetshire* and *Cornwall* to Colombo and the carrier *Hermes* to Trincomalee.

In the meantime, the Catalina flying boats of Nos. 205 and 413 Squadrons had carried out patrols more than 400 miles out from Colombo in an effort to discover the elusive Japanese. Only three of these boats could operate at any one time. A little after four o'clock on the afternoon of 4th April, Squadron Leader Birchall, captain of one of them, belonging to No. 413 Squadron, reported sighting a large enemy force about 350 miles south-east of Ceylon. He sent but one message, and then silence fell. The Catalina has never been seen or heard of since; but its last reconnaissance flight provided just that short period of warning essential to avoid disaster. Another Catalina made contact with the enemy a little before midnight some 250 miles south of Ceylon.

It was now clear that the Japanese were making for Colombo and would certainly stage a heavy air attack at dawn or soon after. They could not be brought to battle by our Eastern Fleet, for it was 600 miles away, refuelling in the Maldives. Admiral Sir Geoffrey Layton, Commander-in-Chief, Ceylon, gave immediate orders for the dispersal of all merchant shipping in the harbour, and some forty-eight seaworthy vessels put out to sea, some sailing west, some north towards anchorages previously chosen, 80 to 130 miles distant from the port. There remained at Colombo twenty-one merchant vessels and thirteen of the Royal Navy, most of them unfit for sea. Among the seaworthy vessels there were the cruisers *Dorsetshire* and *Cornwall*, which were immediately ordered to rejoin the fleet at Addu Atoll.

The expected air attack developed at 7.40 on the morning of Easter Sunday, 5th April, and ended an hour and twenty minutes later. It was carried out by about fifty Japanese Navy Type 99 bombers, escorted by Zero fighters, and they dropped their bombs upon shipping and the dock installations from a height of between 1,000 and 2,000 feet. A high level attack on Ratmalana and Colombo harbour was also made. The workshops there were seriously damaged, but only two naval vessels were sunk, and one merchant ship set on fire. The damage done at the airfield was negligible. Thanks to the timely warning received from the two Catalinas—there were no radar units in Colombo yet ready to operate—the Hurricanes of Nos. 30 and 258 Squadrons, thirty-six in all, together with six Fulmars of the Fleet Air Arm were awaiting the enemy. On sighting them they took off and went into action at once, destroying eighteen, for a loss of fifteen Hurricanes and four Fulmars. The anti-aircraft defences claimed five more Japanese.

The Blenheims of No. 11 (Bomber) Squadron were less fortunate. Sent to bomb the Japanese naval force, they were unable to find it and returned with their bombs still on the racks. Their failure on this occasion must be ascribed primarily to their briefing, which had sent them to an area of sea virgin of the enemy. That these orders were incorrect was due to a mistake made by the wireless operator of one of the Catalinas. He had relayed an S O S sent out by another Catalina in such a manner as to cause it to be mistaken for his own. The flying boat which had appealed for help was further to the westward, under fire from the Japanese warships which the Blenheims had been detailed to assault.

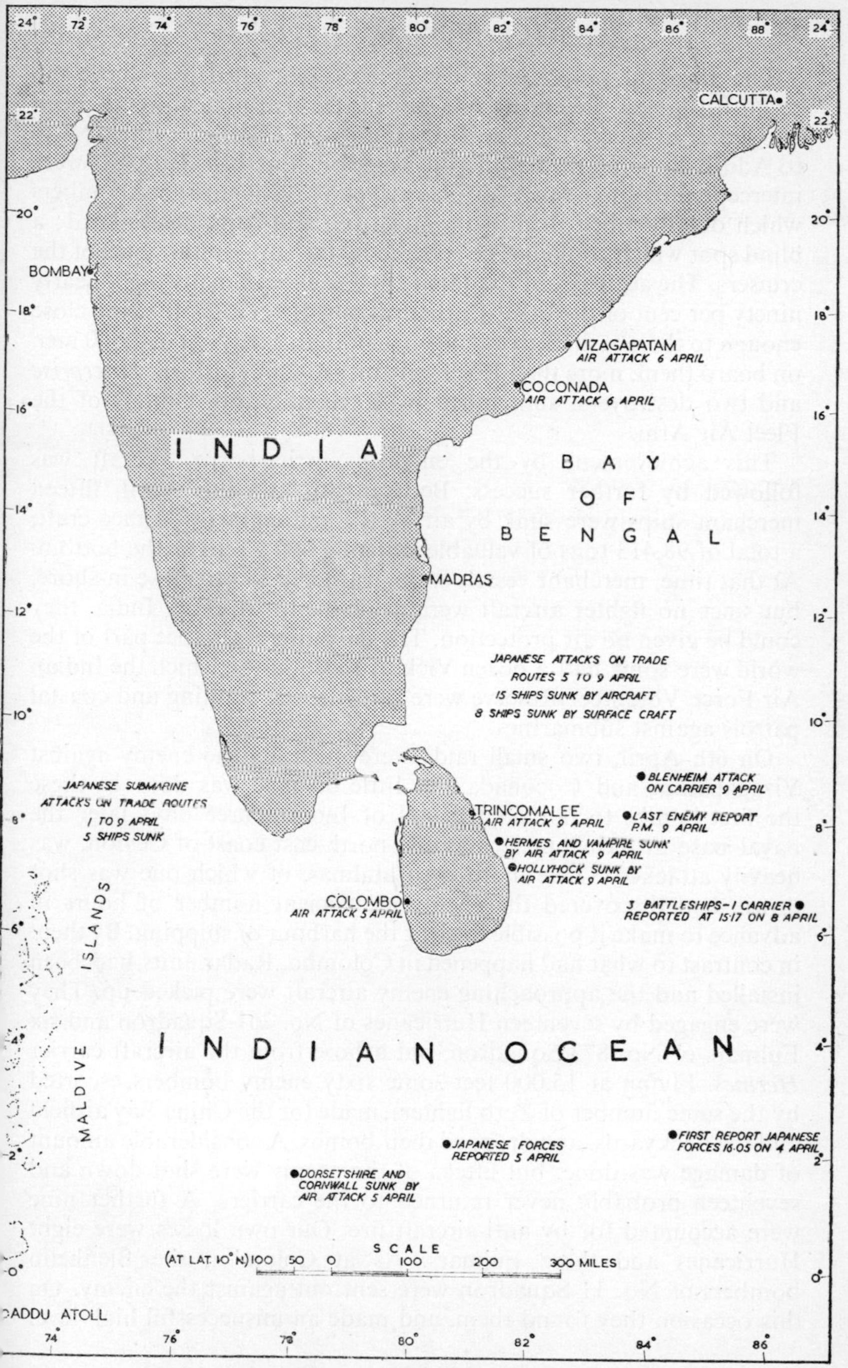

JAPANESE OPERATIONS OFF SOUTHERN INDIA, APRIL 1942

F

The Japanese air attack on Colombo had failed to achieve the result for which the enemy had hoped. He had not, however, been altogether unsuccessful. The *Dorsetshire* and *Cornwall* on their way to Addu Atoll and far beyond the range of shore-based aircraft were intercepted by some thirty-six Navy Type 97 reconnaissance bombers which dive-bombed them from down-sun and from dead ahead; a blind spot which could not be covered by the anti-aircraft guns of the cruisers. The accuracy of the Japanese was exceptionally high, nearly ninety per cent of the bombs either scoring direct hits or falling close enough to the warships to damage them. Both sank, but of 1,550 men on board them, more than 1,100 were picked up by H.M.S. *Enterprise* and two destroyers, summoned by a reconnoitring aircraft of the Fleet Air Arm.

This achievement by the enemy's carrier-borne aircraft was followed by further success. Between 5th and 9th April, fifteen merchant ships were sunk by air attack and eight by surface craft, a total of 98,413 tons of valuable shipping being sent to the bottom. At that time, merchant vessels were instructed to sail close in-shore, but since no fighter aircraft were available in southern India, they could be given no air protection. The only aircraft in that part of the world were some half a dozen Vickers Valentias, in which the Indian Air Force Volunteer Reserve were carrying out training and coastal patrols against submarines.

On 6th April, two small raids were made by the enemy against Vizagapatam and Coconada but little damage was done by these the first bombs to fall on the soil of India. Three days later the naval base at Trincomalee, on the north-east coast of Ceylon, was heavily attacked. Once more the Catalinas, of which one was shot down, had discovered the enemy a sufficient number of hours in advance to make it possible to clear the harbour of shipping. By then, in contrast to what had happened in Colombo, Radar units had been installed and the approaching enemy aircraft were picked up. They were engaged by seventeen Hurricanes of No. 261 Squadron and six Fulmars of No. 873 Squadron, put ashore from the aircraft carrier *Hermes*. Flying at 15,000 feet some sixty enemy bombers, escorted by the same number of Zero fighters, made for the China Bay airfield and the dockyards, and dropped their bombs. A considerable amount of damage was done, but fifteen of the enemy were shot down and seventeen probably never returned to the carriers. A further nine were accounted for by anti-aircraft fire. Our own losses were eight Hurricanes and three Fulmars. As at Colombo, the Blenheim bombers of No. 11 Squadron were sent out against the enemy. On this occasion they found them, and made an unsuccessful high level attack, losing five of their number to Zero fighters, of which they shot down four.

While this assault was being made against Trincomalee, two enemy reconnaissance aircraft, turned away by anti-aircraft fire from Colombo, discovered the aircraft carrier *Hermes,* some sixty miles from that port. She was shortly afterwards attacked, and fought unaided by cover from the sky, for the Hurricanes were engaged in repelling the assault on the airfield at China Bay. The attack was carried out perfectly, relentlessly and quite fearlessly, and was exactly like a highly organized deck display', reported Captain Crockett, R.M., a gunnery officer on the carrier. 'The aircraft peeled off in threes, coming straight down on the ship out of the sun on the starboard side'. Hit repeatedly, the *Hermes* sank in twenty minutes, and the destroyer *Vampire* of the Royal Australian Navy with her was also sunk.

This action was the last to take place in Indian waters in that year. The results were summed up by the Commander-in-Chief, Ceylon. 'As a naval operation', he wrote, 'the Japanese raid must be held to have secured a considerable success. It revealed the weakness of the Eastern Fleet, and induced the latter to withdraw from the Ceylon area, and it did this without the necessity of engaging that fleet in battle. Although the Japanese did not follow up with further attacks on Ceylon, it enabled them to disregard the Eastern Fleet for the time being. The information they gained appears to have convinced them that the Ceylon area itself was not likely to be sufficiently fruitful to warrant attacks on shipping there, and these were discontinued. It would have been a very different story if information of their approach had not allowed us to disperse shipping'.

Admiral Nagumo, the Japanese commander, might indeed have felt proud, as he withdrew eastwards to refuel. Though his carrier-borne aircraft had not inflicted irreparable hurt on Colombo and Trincomalee, his fleet had nevertheless in the course of four months sunk five battleships, one aircraft carrier, two cruisers and seven destroyers and this without loss or even damage to any of his ships. Yet, as fate so willed it, he would have served his Emperor better had he made no move against Ceylon. For in so doing he lost so many of his aircraft to the guns of the Hurricanes and Fulmars that, a month later, only two out of his five carriers were able to take part in the all-important battle of the Coral Sea. The other three had had to return to Japan there to renew their complement of aircraft and pilots. Their presence at that battle might, it is at least permissible to conjecture, have tipped the scale in favour of Japan. Nor was this all. When the Battle of Midway Island came to be fought on 4th June, the new pilots replacing the veterans lost at Colombo and Trimcomalee were, if Japanese witnesses interrogated after the War are to be believed, of inferior quality.

To all appearance, however, the beginning of the summer of 1942 saw the Japanese well launched on a career of victory. They had overrun in succession Malaya, Hong Kong, Borneo, Java, Sumatra and Burma. Their armies were established upon the frontiers of India, amid the broken Naga Hills, prevented from advancing more by the heavy rains of the monsoon than by any opposition which our forces could offer. On the sea their fleet in Indian waters had not been brought to action, and was capable of doing much damage to our merchant shipping. The Japanese attack on Burma and India had, like the dawn in Kipling's poem, come up like thunder out of China. Yet even at that moment, plans were maturing, slowly but inexorably, which in the short space of three years would bring the armies of Nippon to their knees. The success of them depended on a novel and daring use of air power.

CHAPTER V

Coastal Command and the Struggle at Sea:

The North Russian Convoys, Photographic Reconnaissance, and Air-Sea Rescue

HITLER's unconscious admiration of the British Commonwealth was at no time to be seen more clearly than in the opening months of 1942. While the Japanese were stripping us of our possessions in the Far East he continued to believe that we were about to invade Norway. Undeterred by the fate of the *Scharnhorst*, *Gneisenau* and *Prinz Eugen* he therefore proceeded with his plans, and by 20th March, 1942 the *Tirpitz*, the *Scheer* and the *Hipper* were all at Trondheim. This was harmless enough from the point of view of an operation which was never more than a figment of the *Führer's* imagination. It was not so harmless from the point of view of ourNorth Russian convoys, the story of which must now be told.

The first British convoy had sailed to Russia on 21st August, 1941. The second had followed in September, the third in October. From then on the PQ convoys, as they were called, had left Iceland three times a month. Normally they passed west of Iceland through the Denmark Strait, rounded Northern Norway as far to the north as the presence of ice and the land-mass of Spitsbergen allowed, and then turned south for Archangel or Murmansk. Over the first 150 miles of this route they enjoyed the support of Nos. 330 (Norwegian) and 269 Squadrons from Iceland. Thereafter, as all aircraft carriers and long-range coastal aircraft were fully occupied elsewhere, their air support consisted only of occasional patrols flown to detect U-boats off Northern Norway. Like all other convoys, however, the Russian convoys were greatly helped by Coastal Command's constant watch and ward over German warships.

The most dangerous part of the voyage began with the passage north of Norway. From that point, for the rest of the long journey through the Barents Sea, the vessels were mostly within easy range of

German aircraft, U-boats and destroyers based in Northern Norway and Finland. Unfortunately this liability to attack continued even after the arrival of the ships in port, and it was for this reason that the first convoy included Royal Air Force fighters intended to operate from Russian soil. As one of the very few examples of successful co-operation with our Eastern ally, the story of this venture deserves recording in some detail.

No. 151 Wing comprised two newly formed squadrons—Nos. 81 and 134. The instructions of its commander, Wing Commander H. N. G. Ramsbottom-Isherwood, a sturdy, hard-bitten New Zealander, were to help in the defence of Murmansk until the weather stopped intensive flying in October or November. He was then to hand over what remained of his aircraft to the Russians. The force placed under his command numbered thirty-nine Hurricanes, of which twenty-four travelled more or less intact, the rest dismantled.

In due course the twenty-four flew off the *Argus* and touched down at Vaenga airfield, seventeen miles outside Murmansk. German air attacks, however, caused the ships containing the fifteen crated Hurricanes to be diverted to Archangel, some four hundred miles further east. The first task was thus to erect these aircraft at a spot where no arrangements existed for the purpose. Hard work, willing co-operation, and clever improvisation on the part of the ground crews and the Russians overcame all the various local handicaps—including a shortage of airscrew-spanners and a surplus of minor insect life—and the fifteen aircraft were assembled within nine days. The subsequent flight to Vaenga on 12th September was accomplished with only one undue incident. At the refuelling point Russian hospitality proved too much for a couple of the pilots, who found it advisable to postpone their departure until the following morning.

At Vaenga the aircraft from the *Argus* were already installed and operating, ammunition having arrived from Archangel by train the day before. The airfield, which the Wing shared with a Russian medium bomber squadron, was large and reasonably satisfactory, though in wet weather the surface of rolled sand became 'very cut-up and bumpy'. A metalled road about a mile long connected the main points inside the camp, but outside there were only country tracks full of deep ruts and pot-holes. Accommodation in the main brick blocks was good, but the wooden out-buildings were dirty. No complaint could be levelled against the bedding, which was new, and the plentiful food, which was described, according to taste, as 'rich' or 'greasy'. The one really bad feature was the sanitation, which was unhygienic to a degree which revolted the British airmen. It did not, however, destroy their sense of humour. Their main latrine, sited directly over a cesspit and exposed on all sides to the Arctic blast, they at once dubbed 'The Kremlin'.

On the whole our men were pleasantly surprised with their conditions, for they had been warned to expect far worse. The Russians, too, proved extremely helpful, and Isherwood was soon on good terms with the local commander. This officer, at once a general, a skilled pilot and a man of considerable charm, even parted with a set of local military maps—something for which our Military Mission in Moscow would certainly have pleaded in vain. Despite contrary proposals from the Russians, Isherwood was also able to carry out his own plans for making the squadrons operational and escorting the bombers. Indeed, the Wing Commander's most awkward moments were to come not from any obstruction on the part of our allies, but from the difficulty of keeping his own airmen usefully employed after the aircraft had been handed over, and from Slavonic exuberance at, or after, official celebrations. On one occasion, for instance, an extremely drunk Russian Colonel seized the blue-chinned and ultra-masculine Wing Commander in a fierce embrace and endeavoured to smother him in kisses.

Less than twenty-four hours after beginning patrols the Wing scored its first victory. In the afternoon of 12th September five aircraft of No. 81 Squadron intercepted a Henschel and five Me.109's on reconnaissance from Petsamo. Despite the fact that the Hurricanes were as yet carrying only six of their eight guns, they damaged the Henschel and destroyed three of the escort at the cost of one of their own number. No further casualties were suffered in later combats, and at the end of its five weeks' spell of operations the Wing was able to claim, for the loss of this single machine, sixteen enemy aircraft destroyed, four probably destroyed, and seven damaged[1].

The first snows fell on 22nd September, and by mid-October it was time to begin handing over the Hurricanes to the Russians. The keenness of the local military commander, who insisted on being the first to handle the aircraft, was matched by that of his pilots. 'They would turn up', wrote the Commanding Officer of No. 134 Squadron, 'and demand training in the most appalling weather. I remember one pilot doing his first solo in a snow-storm that would have shaken any of us. It took him three shots to get down, and each

[1] The Wing suffered only two fatal casualties after the combat of 12th September These occurred in an unusual and unfortunate manner. The bumpy surface of the airfield made it necessary for a couple of airmen to hang or sit on the tail plane of each Hurricane while the aircraft taxied into position. On 27th September, in a 'scramble' to intercept an enemy machine, a pilot of No. 134 Squadron took off without realizing that his two men were still on the tail. The aircraft crashed from 50 ft., seriously injuring the pilot and killing both airmen.

time he went round again he disappeared completely from sight. I never expected to see him again. However, he made it'. Equal enthusiasm was displayed on the ground, though the Russians' maintenance standards were much less strict than our own, and their technical staffs consisted of a few competent engineers diluted with large numbers of unskilled labourers. No undue difficulties arose in completing the programme of instruction and transferring the aircraft, and at the end of November the Wing was withdrawn to England with its tasks successfully accomplished. Only a few of the signals staffs then remained behind. Equipped by the Russians with sheepskin coats, they afforded great amusement to their departing comrades. 'Their entry into a cinema', records No. 81 Squadron's diary, 'was always the signal for a storm of "Baas"'.

Up to the end of 1941 the PQ convoys and their westbound counterparts (which consisted mostly of empty ships) suffered no damage. Relying on a rapid collapse of Russian resistance the Germans made little attempt to interfere with the traffic, and in any case the long Arctic dark of November and December told in our favour. In the opening months of 1942, however, the enemy set about repairing this omission. In anticipation of the better weather and the longer hours of daylight, reinforcements of German aircraft, U-boats and destroyers were despatched to Northern Norway and Finland. The result was seen at the end of March, when casualties to Allied vessels sharply increased. Worse was to come. In May, when Hitler at last dismissed the bogy of a British invasion, the whole group of twenty U-boats between Norway and Iceland, as well as the three capital ships, became available for action against the convoy route. The seriousness of this new situation came fully home in the closing days of the month, when greatly extended support by Sunderlands and U.S. naval flying boats from Iceland failed to prevent heavy losses in PQ.16. Of the seven ships sunk, six fell victim to attack from the air.

The ordeal of PQ.16 was bound to be re-enacted with other convoys unless we could arrange stronger air protection over the eastern half of the route. But the Navy were still unable to supply an aircraft carrier and our hard-pressed allies could not provide enough support from Russian bases. This led Air Chief Marshal Sir Philip Joubert at Coastal Command to offer three suggestions. The first, that Coastal Command should establish flying-boats at Spitsbergen, proved impracticable: part of the island, from which the Norwegian and Russian mining communities had been withdrawn in August 1941, had just been reoccupied by an intrepid little band of Norwegians, but German forces were also present and the expedition had lost both its ships and all its stores to attack from the air. Other

A SUNDERLAND KEEPS GUARD

A convoy in the Western Approaches, 1942

LOW-LEVEL ATTACK ON U-BOAT
by Coastal Command Liberator from Iceland, 1942

obstacles of remoteness and unsuitable flying weather, as will appear later, were not less formidable. Fewer difficulties attended Joubert's second proposal, to base flying-boats near Murmansk, and it was accordingly arranged that eight Catalinas of Nos. 210 and 240 Squadrons should operate from the Kola Inlet, and from Lake Lakhta, near Archangel, during the passage of the next convoy. The third proposal, to hold the enemy capital ships in check by sending a force of torpedo-bombers to Vaenga, was ruled out by the Admiralty on the grounds that we had at home only two fully trained squadrons of these aircraft.

PQ.17 sailed from the Iceland anchorage of Hvalfiord on 27th June. We were aware that the Germans intended to strike in strength with their capital ships. On 1st July the convoy was picked up by enemy aircraft and U-boats; on 2nd July it began to come under heavy air attack; and on 3rd July *Tirpitz*, *Hipper* and attendant destroyers headed north from Trondheim. The next day the Admiralty, fearing the annihilation not only of the merchantmen but also of the comparatively weak escorting forces, instructed the former to disperse and proceed independently and the latter to withdraw. This gave the Germans what they wanted. Cautiously ordering their big ships back to the shelter of the Norwegian fiords, they directed their aircraft and submarines to hunt down the unprotected merchant vessels. The Catalinas in North Russia, which had thus far been searching for U-boats, accordingly soon found their task transformed into rounding up survivors. In this they did admirable work, and it was in part through their help that fourteen of the thirty-seven merchant ships which had left Iceland eventually reached Archangel.

This disaster, one of the worst suffered by the Allies during the whole course of the war at sea, spurred Joubert to press once more for the despatch of torpedo-bombers to North Russia; for the Coastal chief was quick to point out that had his suggestion been adopted the Admiralty might not have felt impelled to give the order for dispersal. In the two months' interval before the sailing of the next PQ convoy—an interval caused not by our losses but by the demands of the great August convoy to Malta—plans were accordingly made for the temporary transfer to North Russia of a balanced force of search-and-strike aircraft. Under the command of Group Captain F. R. Hopps, this was to consist of four photographic reconnaissance Spitfires, a squadron of Catalinas (No. 210), and two squadrons of Hampden torpedo-bombers (No. 144 and No. 455, R.A.A.F.). The Catalinas were to operate from Grasnaya, on the Kola Inlet; the Spitfires and the Hampdens from Vaenga.

The task of flying these aircraft to distant destinations across enemy territory was in itself formidable. Moreover, the Catalinas were required to operate from their home bases until the last possible moment, which meant that their ground staff and stores had also to be carried by air. The greatest difficulties, however, arose from the limited range and navigational facilities of the Hampdens. The result was a very heavy casualty roll merely in getting the aircraft to their operational bases. One Hampden was shot down by a Russian fighter while coming in over a prohibited area. It 'ditched' off-shore and sank before the wounded air gunner could be released: the rest of the crew were then 'shot up' in the water, but managed to struggle ashore, where they were greeted with rifle fire until their cries of 'Angliski' earned recognition. Two other Hampdens, one of which was damaged beyond repair, ran out of petrol and made forced landings on Russian soil. Worst of all, no fewer than six crashed in Norway or Sweden. Those crews who reached their goal received a well merited tribute from the Prime Minister for having—in the words of one pilot—'got there without wireless, in very bad weather, with very poor maps, and having as our only means of identification the undercarriage, which we put down as a friendly gesture when the quick-fingered Russians started to shoot'.

Equally strenuous efforts to safeguard the forthcoming convoy were made by the Royal Navy. Stronger surface escort, including for the first time an auxiliary aircraft carrier—H.M.S. *Avenger*, with twelve Hurricanes and three Swordfish—accompanied the vessels; arrangements were made for a destroyer group to refuel at Spitsbergen and maintain close escort right through to Archangel; and the main battle fleet stood ready off North Iceland to engage the enemy's heavy ships. Thus protected, PQ.18 sailed from Loch Ewe on 3rd September. At dawn it came under Coastal Command escort and anti U-boat cover, first from North Scotland and then from Iceland, and this continued uninterruptedly for nine days. During this period the convoy suffered no loss, though on 8th September it was sighted by a Focke-Wulf and from the 10th it was trailed by U-boats. Later that day a report came through that the German heavy cruisers and destroyers were putting out from Narvik, and the Catalinas of No. 210 Squadron at once prepared to carry out their task. Between 11th and 13th September the eight flying-boats took off one by one from Invergordon and scoured the waters off Northern Norway for any sign of the enemy warships. Eighteen hours later, each in turn became waterborne at Grasnaya.

On 12th September, a few hours after the last Coastal Command patrol from Iceland had turned for home, the U-boats claimed their first victim. The next day the German torpedo-bombers appeared in force and sank six vessels while the *Avenger's* fighters were repelling high-level attacks. On 14th September the naval pilots, flying with desperate gallantry and resolutely supported by the ships' gunners, beat off four furious assaults with the loss of only one vessel. On 15th September they improved on this performance, entirely frustrating a prolonged attack by seventy bombers. Not even the personal intervention of Göring, who signalled that the destruction of the convoy was of decisive importance and demanded attacks by all available aircraft, could now mend matters for the enemy. Bad weather had settled in, and though the German pilots got through to deliver three further attacks, they sank only one more ship. PQ.18's losses during the whole voyage, at thirteen out of forty ships, were grievous enough; but the effort had cost the enemy three U-boats and thirty-five aircraft, including no fewer than thirty-one torpedo-bombers.

During all this time Group Captain Hopps was making full use of his aircraft in Russia. The Catalinas of No. 210 Squadron continued their watch for U-boats and surface vessels, the Spitfires strove in vile weather to photograph the German anchorages, the Hampdens carried out a long, vain search for major units which in fact had remained in Norwegian waters. Under the cover of these movements and of the German pre-occupation with PQ.18 the westbound convoy QP.14 got through the first stages of its journey unscathed. Later it lost four ships in a fierce battle with U-boats. One of these attackers shot down a Catalina from Iceland, but accounts were more than squared when another of the pack was sunk by a Catalina from Scotland.

With PQ.18 in port and QP.14 well on the homeward leg of the journey, it remained to dispose of the aircraft in Russia. For the Spitfires and Hampdens the return flight against the prevailing wind would have been dangerous, if not impossible. These were accordingly handed over to the Russians. The Catalinas, however, were long-range aircraft, and all the pilots save one were able to fly their machines home. The exception was Flight Lieutenant D. E. Healy, whose previous exploits in visiting Spitsbergen are a story in themselves.

The importance of Spitsbergen in the North Russian convoy route has already been mentioned. When the Allies proposed to reoccupy the island in the spring of 1942 it became essential to discover how far south the ice extended, and whether the enemy was in possession. After Flight Lieutenant D. E. Hawkins of No. 240 Squadron had made the initial reconnaissance on 4th–5th April, 1942, carrying as observers Major Sverdrup, the leader of the projected Norwegian expedition, and the Arctic explorer Lieutenant A. R. Glen, R.N.V.R., the task of visiting Spitsbergen and tracking the ice-edge along the convoy route had fallen largely to Healy. Hawkins' flight from Sullom Voe, a matter of some 2,500 miles and twenty-six hours out and home, had been undertaken exceptionally early in the year for high latitude flying, but Healy's first reconnaissance on 3rd–4th May was little less exacting. Fierce headwinds of up to a hundred knots, huge belts of fog, heavy ice formation endangering the controls, inability to make more than the most occasional use of wireless or astral fixes as an aid to dead reckoning, utter weariness of mind and body from the long hours of flying—these were the perils surmounted on the first two flights, to say nothing of the danger of enemy opposition.

Then followed a period in which the weather made further flights impossible, the expedition sailed and was attacked from the air while landing supplies, and the Admiralty waited in vain for news. It was Healy who broke the suspense. Flying a Catalina specially equipped with long-range tanks, long-range A.S.V., and an extensive selection of compasses, on 26th May he discovered the survivors of the expedition (who had meanwhile existed largely on a 'find' of frozen pork and Russian sweets), and by an interchange of signals on the Aldis lamp learned of the presence of enemy patrols and aircraft. By 29th May he was back again with food, medical stores, arms and ammunition, which he dropped by parachute when his efforts to land on the fiords were defeated by ice. 'The full glory of the scene that followed', recorded Lieutenant Glen, 'could not be properly appreciated from the air. Dirty, bearded ruffians darted out on skis to seize half-buried kit bags, tearing them open and thrusting mixtures of chocolate and boracic powder into their mouths with one hand while with the other they pulled off their tattered bed-sheets to parade back in the full glamour of an Irvin suit. Perhaps the best of all was the sight of a most respectable colonel of the Royal Corps of Signals, sitting on a coal heap oblivious to all else as he devoured large spoonsful of apricot jam and coal dust out of a 4 lb. tin which had burst open on impact'.

Two days later, on the third of these long and immensely exacting trips within a week, Healy was compelled by bad weather to abandon his mission after 17½ hours, but on 7th June his efforts to alight were at last rewarded. Stores were unloaded, and six wounded men were taken on board. Other trips followed in the next two months, that on 27th June being notable for the destruction of a Ju.88 on the ground at Spitsbergen and a sea-fog all the way back to the Shetlands. Finally, after the award of a richly deserved D.S.O. to himself and a D.F.C.

to his navigator, Flight Lieutenant E. Schofield, Healy proceeded with his comrades of No. 210 Squadron to North Russia. He completed his flights for the passage of PQ.18, then took off from Grasnaya for a final visit to Spitsbergen. His instructions were to collect Glen and proceed home. Unfortunately bad weather forced him to abandon the trip, and he decided to return to Murmansk and try again the next day. Some two hundred miles from the Russian coast the clouds cleared and the crew saw a Ju.88 approaching rapidly from astern. The alarm was sounded on the hooter, the crew took up their action stations, and as the enemy drew closer the starboard gunner of the Catalina opened fire. Some of the shots apparently went home, and the enemy, disliking his reception, tore rapidly past and away. This brought him within the arc of fire of the Catalina's front gun; but the weapon jammed, and as the German machine sped off its rear-gunner got in a parting burst. The shells smashed through the windscreen of the Catalina and fatally wounded one member of the crew—the pilot who had done so much to preserve our hold on Spitsbergen, and with it the safety of our convoys.

The death of Healy and the return of the remaining Catalinas from North Russia brought the episode of PQ.18 to a close. All told, the support of the convoy and its westbound counterpart had occupied 111 aircraft from fourteen different squadrons of Coastal Command. Between them these aircraft had put in 279 sorties and 2,290 flying-hours. But by far the greater part of this time had been taken up getting to and from the area of operations. The obvious remedy of stronger escort from aircraft carriers could not yet be applied; and in view of this and the large part to be played by British surface forces in the forthcoming landings in North Africa it was decided for the time being to discontinue the Russian convoys. During October and November several ships sailed to North Russia independently, with a fair measure of success; and convoys were then resumed in December under cover of the winter darkness. They were discontinued during the spring and summer months of 1943, and a similar halt, though for a much shorter period, was made in 1944. By that time the development of the supply line through Persia had made the Northern route less important, while the regular employment of auxiliary carriers had obviated the need for shore-based support by Coastal Command in Arctic waters. The Command continued, however, to help the Northern convoys by reconnaissance, escort and anti U-boat sweeps from Scotland and Iceland. Many gallant actions remained to be fought during these later years, but the Northern route was never again threatened as it had been in 1942. To the crews of the Royal Navy, the mercantile marine and Coastal Command, who in that dire season braved and overcame the worst that the enemy could do, the whole Allied cause thus owed an immeasurable debt of gratitude. The 'iron curtain' has now descended, and on one side of it the deeds of our sailors and airmen are ignored, forgotten, or held in despite and contempt. That is the more reason for honouring them on the other.

* * *

During 1942 Coastal Command continued to execute two essential tasks somewhat aside from its main work. One of these was photographic reconnaissance, the other air-sea rescue. The progress of these two highly important activities must now be briefly recounted.

Long-range photographic reconnaissance over Europe was, as earlier related, the function of the high-level Spitfires of No. 1 Photographic Reconnaissance Unit.[1] To these the fast and versatile Mosquitos had now been added. From the Unit's base at Benson, near Oxford, from the neighbouring satellite of Mount Farm, and from the outlying detachments at Leuchars, Wick, St. Eval and Gibraltar, these unarmed aircraft took off on their hazardous and vital missions. As their numbers grew, and the longer range of the Mosquito enabled still more ambitious tasks to be attempted, so our acquaintance with events in enemy territory improved. 'By May 1942, ten sorties a day, as against four a year earlier, were returning with their precious spools of precise and irrefutable evidence. By that time, too, the Mosquitos were ranging as far afield as Narvik in the north, the Skoda Works at Pilsen in the south.

With the increase in the aircraft resources of No. 1 P.R.U. went many parallel developments. On the technical side, the new F.53 camera, introduced in January 1942, gave a much larger print than the old F.24; its scale of 1 in 10,000 at 30,000 feet at last made possible a completely detailed and accurate interpretation. At the same time larger magazines, capable of taking up to 500 exposures, helped to give better cover. On the organizational side the most striking feature was perhaps the growth of the Central Interpretation Unit. Medmenham, which in earlier days had witnessed the frolics of the Hell Fire Club, now saw earnest figures peering intently through stereos at prints which would have aroused no glimmer of interest among John Wilkes and his cronies. Here was done that 'second phase' and 'third phase' interpretation which would amplify and systematize the information obtained from the immediate interpreta-

[1] No. 2 P.R.U. operated in the Middle East. No. 3 P.R.U. had previously served Bomber Command, but had been absorbed into No. 1 in June 1941; it was later re-formed in India. No. 4 P.R.U. was formed in October 1942 for work in French North Africa.

tion at the operational stations. By the end of 1942 there were at this centre over a thousand men and women of the Royal Air Force; and specialized sections—naval, military, airfields, industries, damage assessment, night photos, and many others—existed to deal with every aspect of the work. Some idea of the size of the organization may be gathered from the year's output, which totalled 204 models, 5,437 reports, and 1,454,742 prints. This last figure was possible only through the introduction of film-processing machines which developed, dried and spooled film at a rate of four feet per second, and of multi-printers which produced a thousand prints to the hour.

The photographic aircraft, it is important to remember, served many masters. Though part of Coastal Command it was as much their duty to obtain information for the Admiralty or the Ministry of Economic Warfare as for the Air Ministry. Among the multitude of their achievements in the period from June 1941 to December 1942 it is perhaps sufficient to mention the discovery of the He.177 and a new class of German destroyer; the constant vigil over the *Scharnhorst*, *Gneisenau* and *Tirpitz*—729 photographic sorties, or on some occasions as many as seven a day, were flown over Brest during the stay of the two battle cruisers; the revelation of what Bomber Command was, or was not, achieving in Germany; the location of some seventy enemy radar stations; and the preliminary reconnaissance for the raids on Bruneval, St. Nazaire and Dieppe, as well as for the invasion of French North Africa. By October 1942, when the continued expansion of No. 1 P.R.U. brought about its division into five separate squadrons (Nos. 540 to 544), strategic photographic reconnaissance was unquestionably among the most vital and rewarding of all our many activities in the air.

* * *

Some account was given in Volume I of the origins of the air-sea rescue organization, and the assignment of Lysander aircraft in Fighter Command to this distinctive task. In the months that followed the Battle of Britain much progress was made, but responsibility continued to be divided among a large number of authorities. In August 1941 it was accordingly decided to concentrate executive control over all air-sea rescue operations in a single person. The choice naturally fell upon the Air Officer Commanding-in-Chief, Coastal Command, and from this date Coastal Command became primarily responsible for the work of rescue. At the same time the Directorate of Air-Sea Rescue at the Air Ministry, which had already done much to develop and co-ordinate methods, was merged in a larger Directorate-General of Aircraft Safety; and over this a distinguished ex-Chief of Air Staff, Marshal of the Royal Air Force Sir John Salmond, was invited to preside. These decisions were a reflection of the increasing interest in work the ever-growing importance of which may be seen from the fact that between February and August 1941 some 1,200 aircrew had crashed into the sea. Thanks to the still-undeveloped rescue services, 444 of these had been saved to fight again.

The increased responsibility of Coastal Command, it should be made clear, in no way lessened the dependence of the rescue services on outside help. The Post Office Radio Stations, the Royal Observer Corps, the Coastguards, the Royal National Lifeboat Institution, the Merchant Navy and even amateur wireless enthusiasts all continued to play an essential part. And behind the rescue services proper—the high speed launches, seaplane tenders and pinnaces of the Royal Air Force, the naval craft, and the 'search' Lysanders and Walruses—still stood the general resources of the Royal Navy and the Royal Air Force.

In September 1941 the Lysanders and Walruses were formed into four squadrons—Nos. 275 to 278. These were the first squadrons to be assigned specifically to air-sea rescue. They remained in Fighter Command, distributed at suitable points around the coast, but their limit of search was extended to 40 miles from the shore. Three other air-sea rescue squadrons—Nos. 279–281—were formed before the end of 1942. The first two, intended for deep search and equipped with Hudsons and Ansons, became units of Coastal Command; the third, another 'close-in' squadron for Fighter Command, was formed on Defiants, then nearing the end of their life as night-fighters.

Together with this growth in the rescue squadrons and a corresponding increase in the number of marine craft went ceaseless progress in devices to sustain life and attract attention to the crashed crews. Such devices, however, were by no means the only points to consider. For the actual rescue was the end of a long chain of circumstance which stretched right back to the design of the aircraft—its reliability, its strength to resist the impact of the water, its facilities for stowage and exit. Equally important, too, was the training of the air crews—the readiness with which they absorbed and practised the drills for ditching and abandoning aircraft laid down by the Air Ministry and tirelessly preached after March 1942 by an air-sea rescue officer at every station. Only if due attention had been given to all these points could the crew survive to take advantage of the safety equipment provided. The great importance of this training may be seen from the fact that of those who crashed into the sea considerably more Allied crews were rescued than British, in proportion to the numbers involved. This was undoubtedly because the Czechs and Poles, knowing the fate that awaited them in the hands of the enemy, were determined if possible to 'ditch' rather than bale out over German territory, and so took the rescue-drills more seriously.

Once the plane had ditched and the crew emerged, then the long list of safety aids came into play. By 1942 all crews were provided, either personally or in their dinghies, with emergency rations, drinking water or fruit juice, chocolate, a first-aid kit, distress signals, Verey cartridges, fluorescine, paddles, a telescopic mast, a flag, balers, leak stoppers, weather-covers, a skull cap, a whistle, a floating torch and a floating knife. With the issue of the one-man, or fighter-pilot's, dinghy to bomber crews, the latter, if forced to bale out, were able to survive when their multi-seater dinghy went down with the aircraft.[1] Other devices issued to crews during 1942 included a miniature wireless transmitter, packed in a waterproof floating case—a piece of equipment, like fluorescine and the one-man dinghy, copied from the Germans; while a further aid, in production but not yet in use, was 'Walter'—an automatic oscillator which registered on the A.S.V. of searching aircraft. As for aids dropped from the air when the distressed crew was discovered, there were the comprehensive packs already well known as the Bircham Barrel, the Thornaby Bag, and the Lindholme Apparatus; and in production there was that masterpiece of ingenuity, the airborne lifeboat.

Thanks to all these devices, to the unstinted co-operation of the outside authorities, and to the unfailing gallantry of the crews of aircraft and launches alike, 1,016 of the 3,000 or so airmen known to have crashed into the sea in 1942 were recovered. Of the many remarkable incidents that occurred there is space to mention only two. The first received some publicity at the time, as it brought into prominence an unusual means of rescue—the carrier pigeon. Such birds were, of course, carried as an emergency aid for communication; but as they do not fly by night, or in bad visibility, or when wet, they were not expected to play any useful part once an aircraft had ditched. The following episode led to their capacities in this respect being taken more seriously.

On the afternoon of 23rd February, 1942, six Beauforts of No. 42 Squadron left Sumburgh for a sweep against enemy shipping. They reached the Norwegian coast, but saw no vessels, and on the return journey the aircraft became separated. Suddenly Beaufort M, piloted

[1] In some aircraft the dinghy was carried in a valise; in others it was stowed in the wings or the outside of the fuselage. In most of the latter types the dinghy was automatically ejected on impact with the water.

by Squadron Leader W. H. Cliff, went into an uncontrollable dive and hit the sea. Cliff and his crew, who only a fortnight before had led No. 42 Squadron's attack on the *Scharnhorst* and *Gneisenau*, thought that their last moment had come; but by some miracle all survived the impact and scrambled out, or were thrown clear, as the aircraft went down. Fortunately one of them was able to secure the dinghy, and this all four men eventually succeeded in boarding. Very soon they were joined by one of the two pigeons carried in the aircraft. They at once captured this welcome arrival, attached to its leg a note of the approximate position of the crash, and launched the bird into the air. But the creature was wet, and darkness was already coming on. After performing a few perfunctory circles the pigeon merely alighted back on the dinghy; and no amount of cajoling, or beating about the head, could persuade it to resume its flight. Its fixed intention was obviously to make a fifth passenger. In disgust the crew therefore abandoned their attempts to drive it off, and huddled together against the rigours of the February night.

By this time the search had begun. The last known position of the aircraft was 150 miles east of Aberdeen, and throughout the night a Catalina sought in vain for the distressed crew. At first light other aircraft went out from Leuchars, Dyce and Arbroath, but several hours' search yielded no sign of the missing men. Meanwhile a pigeon had arrived back at base—not the obstinate creature of the previous evening, but its companion from the same basket. Unknown to the Beaufort crew, 'Winkie'—as the unfortunate bird was called—had made his escape from the aircraft. He of course carried no message; but this did not defeat the acute intelligences at the station. Since he could not have flown in the dark, he must obviously have found somewhere to rest; and an examination of his feathers revealed unmistakable traces of oil. Someone hazarded the guess that he had spent the night on a tanker; enquiry revealed that such a vessel had in fact been passing off the North East Coast; and from a knowledge of its course, and a calculation of the time taken by the pigeon to reach base, the area of search was readjusted to some fifty miles nearer shore. The next aircraft sent out, a Hudson of No. 320 Squadron, flew almost straight to the spot where the dinghy lay tossing on the waves. The crew wirelessed a message to base, then dropped a Thornaby Bag. Three hours later a high-speed launch arrived, and the sufferings of the four bruised and frost-bitten airmen were over.

The second incident was marked by less good fortune, but it exemplifies that determination to succeed without which all the most elaborate preparations would have been in vain. In this case the cost of saving a distressed crew proved heavier than that of leaving them to their fate. Nevertheless the moral value of the episode, in the confidence it inspired in crews that no effort would be spared to save them, far outbalanced any material loss.

On the night of 11th August, 1942 a Leigh Light Wellington of No. 172 Squadron, piloted by Flying Officer A. W. R. Triggs, was on anti-submarine patrol in the Bay of Biscay. In the small hours of the following morning the tail gunner suddenly saw 'excessive sparks passing behind like a cluster of stars', the oil pressure fell to zero, the aircraft lost height, and in a few minutes the pilot was forced to ditch. The crew carried out their drill correctly, including the transmission of an S O S, but when the aircraft struck the water the dinghy failed to blow out of the stowage. This the pilot remedied by prising off the lid of the stowage with his bare hands, while the rest of the crew stood on the wing up to their knees in water. The dinghy then began to inflate and despite the high seas the drenched crew managed to climb aboard.

For the next three hours all six men baled furiously. Then the search aircraft began to appear. No less than eleven of them passed over or near in the course of the morning, but all the efforts of the distressed crew could not attract their attention. There were only two marine signals in the dinghy, and both of these were fired in vain.

The morning turned to afternoon, and at last a Whitley of No. 51 Squadron spotted the six airmen. The Whitley dropped a spare dinghy and a Thornaby Bag, and saw the crew retrieve the latter. It then sent off a signal giving the survivors' correct position and turned for home. Within a short time a Sunderland of No. 461 Squadron, Royal Australian Air Force, escorted by three Beaufighters, was hastening towards the scene. The flying-boat survived an encounter *en route* with a Focke-Wulf Condor ; but another Whitley, which spotted the dinghy and signalled 'Sunderland coming', was shot down on its way home.

The instructions of the Sunderland's pilot were to alight and pick up the survivors if the state of wind and water permitted. The conditions, in fact, were far from good. Nevertheless he decided to make the attempt. As he touched down, the flying-boat hit a wave, bounced, hit the water again, and at once lost the tip of the starboard wing. A second later a starboard engine burst into flames and the aircraft nosed into the sea. The crew just had time to launch one of their dinghies before the Sunderland sank. They had barely clambered aboard when a bulge appeared on the side. Within a few seconds this swelled up and the whole dinghy burst, scattering the crew into the water. The navigator then swam towards the spare dinghy dropped earlier by the Whitley, intending to propel it back towards his comrades. But the dinghy was 400 yards away, and in such seas it was all the utterly exhausted survivor could do to reach it and scramble aboard. The other members of the crew were soon engulfed by the waves.

So 12th August passed. Wet, cold and uncomfortable the six men from the Wellington now faced another night. The next day two more Whitleys arrived over the spot, only to be intercepted and driven off by German aircraft. A French fishing vessel also passed near, but the distressed aircrew pinned their faith to the efforts of their comrades, and made no move to attract its attention. Then the weather closed in. Throughout August 14th and 15th most of the search aircraft were grounded. Meantime on August 14th the six men took their first meal—a biscuit, a Horlicks tablet, a square of chocolate, and a mouthful of water. They also beat off a shark which showed an unwelcome interest in them. Towards the close of the following day they staged a Friday night celebration by drinking a can of tomato juice. On this day, too, they tried to make some progress towards home with an improvised sail—for it was not until later in the year, after a number of fighter pilots had been picked up dead in their dinghies, that proper sails were included in the packs. While the Wellington crew thus kept up their spirits the single survivor from the Sunderland in the other dinghy was without food. He consoled himself by drinking water and chewing at the strap of his wrist-watch.

On 16th August, four days after the first crash, the weather cleared. At midday a Beaufighter of No. 235 Squadron appeared and signalled to the Wellington crew: 'contact other dinghy—injured man aboard'. Guided by the aircraft the six men began to paddle the half mile or so which separated them from the survivor of the Sunderland. While they were doing so a Hudson of No. 279 Squadron arrived over the scene and dropped a Lindholme gear. After five hours' intense effort they reached the other dinghy and pulled the solitary occupant aboard their own. They then rubbed him down and gave him a malted milk tablet and half a can of tomato juice. His first words were: 'I'm all for the open air life, aren't you?' This the crew of the Wellington countered with another question: 'You wouldn't be an Australian, would you?'

By then a British destroyer, accompanied by launches and Beaufighters, was fast approaching. But so were German aircraft. Soon the Beaufighters were shooting down a Ju.88, only to be attacked by F.W.190's. Night fell. The seven men were still in the two dinghies, now lashed together.

Early the next morning a German motor launch, escorted by three

Arado 196's and two F.W.190's, was seen heading towards the dinghies. But the Beaufighters were back on the scene, and they at once dived at the enemy. Under cover of their attacks two of our own launches were then able to approach the dinghies and take aboard the exhausted survivors.

Their adventures were not yet over. On the return voyage German aircraft shadowed and attacked the launches. But the Beaufighters and the gunners on deck held all attempts at bay, and in the evening of 17th August the little convoy reached the safety of Newlyn Harbour. So ended an outstanding rescue which, despite fierce opposition and great mischance, not only snatched seven skilled air-crew from the very jaws of the enemy, but also inspired all others with the knowledge that, in like misfortune, they too would be assured of that 'last full measure of devotion' which is the tradition of the Service.

CHAPTER VI

Coastal Command and the Struggle at Sea:

The Offensive against German Shipping and U-Boats in 1942

THROUGHOUT 1942 Coastal Command continued its routine work of reconnaissance and convoy escort. At the same time it steadily pursued and developed those offensive operations against German shipping and U-boats which in the end contributed so powerfully to the Allied victory.

By the beginning of 1942 the anti-shipping offensive had been waged for over a year. Already Coastal Command was ceaselessly attacking sea-reaches so vital to the enemy as the coastal waters of Norway, the Southern North Sea and the Bay of Biscay. With Bomber Command's Bostons—successors to the heavily-smitten Blenheims—joining in at need, and Fighter Command operating the 'Channel Stop' and supplying escort, there were few occasions on which German vessels could sail completely unchallenged. Unless, of course, they cared to confine themselves to the Baltic.

The year began disappointingly. During the last quarter of 1941 Coastal Command had sunk fifteen ships for the loss of forty-six aircraft, but in the first four months of 1942 it sank only six for the loss of fifty-five aircraft. This was largely a 'seasonal decline'. Better weather, coupled with increased resources in the form of four Hampden squadrons converted to torpedo bombers, soon gave rise to renewed hopes. By May the Command was attacking more fiercely and more frequently than ever before.

Much the larger part of this work against enemy shipping fell to the Hudsons. With the help of the Hampdens, those of No. 18 Group (Nos. 48 and 608 Squadrons) were responsible for strikes off Norway; those of No. 16 Group (Nos. 53, 59, 320 (Dutch) Squadrons, and No. 407 Squadron, Royal Canadian Air Force) concentrated on the traffic between the estuary of the Elbe and the Hook of Holland.

With iron determination the pilots of these squadrons dived through the *flak* and released their bombs from mast-height—or so near it that damage from impact with ship or sea was distressingly frequent. On 28th May, for instance, No. 59 Squadron recorded that one of its aircraft 'struck the sea with port prop—badly bent and homed on one engine at 60 m.p.h.'. The next day No. 407 Squadron reported a still more telling incident. 'For the second time in two nights Pilot Officer O'Connell successfully bombed enemy shipping. After this last episode he is seriously thinking of taking up paper-hanging after the war. He went in so low to attack that he struck a mast and hung one of the bomb-doors thereon'. As material for an impressive 'line' this was probably surpassed only by an incident two years later, when a pilot of No. 455 Squadron, Royal Australian Air Force, returned from a shipping attack near the Dutch coast with several feet of mast attached to his aircraft.

Tactics—and courage—of this kind reaped their reward, and during May alone Coastal Command claimed twelve ships, ten of which have since been confirmed. Many others were damaged. Unfortunately attacks at so low a level also involved severe losses; and at forty-three aircraft for the month these were greater than the Command could possibly continue to accept. The war diarist of No. 407 Squadron, while justifiably stressing the achievements of his comrades, leaves no doubt about their cost. 'Since this squadron became operational again on 1st April we have lost twelve crews, in all fifty persons either missing or killed. During the past month six crews have been designated missing or killed on operations with the loss of twenty-seven lives. This does not take into consideration the fact that after every major operation of this nature at least two or three aircraft are so very badly damaged that they are of no use to this, or any other, squadron'.

In work of this nature even the cloak of semi-darkness was no protection. Whether the strike took place in moonlight or twilight or daylight made little difference—the proportion of aircraft lost steadily increased. By the end of June the grim fact emerged that during the previous three months, out of every four aircraft attempting to attack, one had been shot down. The Germans were applying the obvious remedy. They were arming their merchantmen more and more heavily, surrounding them with more and more escorts—sometimes they now employed as many as four or five warships for a single merchant vessel. This impressive tribute to the work of our crews unfortunately spelled, for the time being, the end of our success; for with his resources stretched to the utmost Joubert could not afford losses of anything like this order. In July he instructed his crews to abandon the low attack, and to bomb from medium level. The resulting fall in casualties was equalled only by the decline in sinkings.

The ineffectiveness of medium-level attack arose partly from the lack of a good bomb-sight for the type of work, partly from the drain of experienced crews—including two of the four Beaufort Squadrons —to the Middle East. The Hampdens, too, were not fast enough for work against the more powerfully escorted convoys—a fact which sometimes led their pilots into desperate expedients. 'There was', records a member of No. 455 Royal Australian Air Force Squadron, 'a very keen type who earned himself the nickname "Hacksaw", because whenever he had the opportunity he sawed off some of the many appendages the old Hampden acquired, to try and squeeze the extra half-knot out of her'.

None of these handicaps was likely to be overcome in the near future. Joubert, however, was far from beaten. Impressed by the remarkable combination of adaptability, speed, strength and endurance to be found in the Beaufighter, he had already suggested that some of these admirable aircraft should be modified to carry torpedoes; and to this suggestion, which was approved by the Air Ministry in June, he now added another—that special Beaufighter 'strike wings' should be formed. These, he urged, should consist partly of the ordinary cannon Beaufighters or Beaufighter-bombers (which would concentrate on the ships' crews and guns) and partly of the new Torbeaus. The whole wing, being composed of the same type of aircraft, could be expected to attack at high speed with cohesion. This proposal also won acceptance, and in September the decision was taken to equip Coastal Command with five Beaufighter squadrons of each type by April 1943.

The first of these new wings, consisting of Nos. 143 (Beaufighter), 236 (Bomber-Beaufighter) and 254 (Beaufighter and Torbeau) Squadrons was assembled in November 1942. It was stationed at North Coates, in No. 16 Group, for work against the heavily escorted traffic along the Frisian coast. On 20th November Spitfires of No. 12 Group, Fighter Command, reported a convoy of twelve to sixteen ships steering south west towards Rotterdam. Two of the Beaufighter squadrons—Nos. 236 and 254—were at once ordered off; but the weather was bad, the formations lost touch, and the convoy was protected by FW.190's. The result was, to say the least, discouraging. The largest merchant ship and two escort-vessels were hit, but only at prohibitive cost to the Beaufighters, three of which were lost and four so seriously damaged that they crashed or made forced landings on return. Concluding that the wing was not yet properly trained as a working unit, Joubert at once withdrew it from the line of battle, leaving the Hudsons and Hampdens to sustain the burden of the offensive.

From the purely statistical angle, anti-shipping operations during 1942 thus showed disappointing results. Over the whole year 42 ships (61,028 tons) were assessed as sunk by the three home Commands. All these sinkings—and three more—have since been confirmed. The total cost was 251 aircraft. These figures are unimpressive, but it would be wrong to conclude from them that the offensive was misconceived or that its effects were insignificant. The Germans were forced to protect their convoys with fighters, guns and minor warships which they could certainly have used to advantage elsewhere. They were driven into adopting rigorous methods which were temporarily effective in repelling attack but greatly reduced the volume of goods they could carry. They were made to haggle about payment with nervous, grasping, or merely sensible Scandinavian crews. In sum, the offensive kept the Germans under pressure on their sea routes, just as other operations kept them under pressure on their land routes. Attacks on shipping by our coastal aircraft were in fact the necessary complement of attacks on ports and marshalling yards by our bombers and 'train-busting' by our fighters. Release the pressure at any point, allow the ships or the trains or the barges to proceed with immunity, and traffic would at once flow from the more to the less threatened routes, with benefit to the whole of the enemy's hard-driven transport system.

These were what Joubert called the 'hidden assets' of the offensive. But even in terms of bare statistics there were some aspects of the campaign which were highly and obviously profitable. There was, for example, a small class of traffic of unique importance in the German war economy—the cargoes of urgently needed primary products carried by blockade-runners from the Far East. The safe arrival of one of these venturesome craft was an occasion for tremendous rejoicing among the enemy. It was the privilege of Coastal Command's No. 19 Group to help the Navy make such occasions few and far between.

The blockade-runners were speedy vessels whose captains were well versed in all the arts of maritime deception. Despite this they rarely managed to avoid the vigilance of the Navy in the outer seas. If luck or good judgment brought them safely past our ships they were almost invariably picked up by Coastal Command as they approached the Bay of Biscay; for though No. 19 Group was on the hunt for U-boats it did not disdain other prey. In January 1943, for instance, there was the case of the *Rhakotis*. Spotted by a Hampden of No. 502 Squadron and shadowed by a Sunderland of No. 10, R.A.A.F., she was finished off by a cruiser which 'homed' on to the flying boat. This single stroke deprived Germany not only of useful quantities of fats, vegetable oils, quinine bark, tea, tin, rice and wolfram, but also of 4,000 tons of rubber—enough to supply four armoured divisions for a year. And the fate of the *Rhakotis* was by no means untypical; in the first four months of 1943 only one blockade-runner out of seven reached the French coast. After that, until the end of the year, the Germans even gave up trying.

By the spring of 1943 the Beaufighter wing at North Coates was ready for action. On 18th April it took off on its first 'strike' since the unfortunate episode of November. The target, located earlier in the day by one of the wing aircraft, was a heavily escorted convoy off the Dutch coast; and the attacking force consisted of nine Torbeaus of No. 254 Squadron, six Beaufighter bombers of No. 236 Squadron and six Beaufighters of No. 143 Squadron, all covered at high level by Spitfires and Mustangs of Fighter Command. 'The role of the escorting Beaufighters', records No. 236 Squadron, 'was to attack the escort vessels with bombs, cannon and machine guns and silence their fire whilst the torpedo carrying "Beaus" attacked the large merchant vessel. Rendezvous with single-engine fighter escort was to be made over Coltishall. The operation went entirely according to plan except that the convoy was encountered some ten miles further north than had been expected (off Texel). Two 'M' class mine-sweepers were hit with bombs, cannon and machine-gun fire, and left on fire, and an armed trawler was also hit. Two certain torpedo hits were made by No. 254 Squadron on the largest merchant vessel (the target vessel of the strike), which was left on fire listing heavily, and thought to be sinking. Many excellent close-up photographs of the attack were secured. The whole operation was outstanding not only in the success of the attack but also in the fact that between 1535 and 1550 hours every one of the 21 Beaufighters engaged landed safely back at North Coates. Only very slight damage due to enemy fire was sustained by two or three aircraft, and no casualties whatsoever to crew'.

Before the end of April a similar operation resulted in the destruction of two merchant vessels and a trawler, besides damage to several escorts, all at a cost of one Beaufighter. The key to success thus seemed within our grasp. A notable indication of this was soon to come. In May 1943 a tally was made of the active shipping in Rotterdam, the most convenient port for the great industrial area of Rhenish Westphalia. It amounted to only 37,000 tons, as against 106,000 tons a year earlier. The work of the strike-wing, coupled with our raids on the port and our ceaseless mining, had forced the Germans to halt most of their traffic at Emden, where handling and transport facilities were greatly inferior.

By the spring of 1943 the anti-shipping offensive thus promised great things. Unfortunately these were not to be achieved as quickly as we had hoped. The demands of the Mediterranean theatre had by then shattered our plan of building up five strike-wings in this country and many difficulties remained to be overcome before our aircraft could seal up Rotterdam and subject the ships' crews off the Dutch and Norwegian coasts to a veritable reign of terror. But if the great days of the offensive were still beyond the horizon, already the clouds were tinged with their approaching light.

Moreover, in the minelaying carried out night after night by Bomber Command, and to a much lesser degree by Coastal Command, there was a weapon at work far more deadly than we realized. Between April 1940 and March 1943 Bomber and Coastal Commands laid nearly 16,000 mines at a cost of 329 aircraft. We now know that these mines sank 369 vessels, totalling 361,821 tons. During the same period Bomber, Coastal, and Fighter Commands delivered some 3,700 attacks on ships at sea at a cost of 648 aircraft. We now know that these attacks sank 107 vessels, totalling 155,076 tons. In other words, it was costing us six aircraft to sink one ship by direct attack, but less than one aircraft to sink one ship by mining. Here was something unappreciated then, and little known now. Taken in conjunction, the two forms of attack were already doing great damage to the enemy, and would soon do much more.

* * *

It is recorded in the first volume of this history that as soon as the United States became involved in the war six of Germany's biggest U-boats were ordered to North American waters. These vessels reached their new hunting-grounds during the second week of January 1942. Within three weeks they had destroyed no less than forty Allied and neutral ships, totalling 230,000 tons.

Well satisfied with this experiment, Dönitz decided to strike while the iron was hot, or rather, while the American defences were still luke-warm. He at once ordered all U-boats lying westward of the British Isles and several lying off the Azores to take up station on the North American seaboard. Shortly afterwards he sent five large boats to operate off Central America. He also began to organize a system of refuelling from other U-boats at sea. One important element in his plan, however, was frustrated. By Hitler's express command twenty-four U-boats—over a quarter of the total operational force in the Atlantic—remained on guard against the expected British invasion of Norway.

For the next four months the German vessels wrought havoc. With a brief exception in April, when sailings were suspended in the most dangerous areas, the sinkings off the American coast grew ever more frequent. For May the figure reached 531,000 tons, or 109 ships, including thirty tankers. All this the Germans achieved at an average cost of less than two U-boats each month.

Such blows, if not mortal, were indeed staggering. Yet there were two facts which offered some consolation. The enemy's easy run of success must surely end as soon as the Americans could develop systematic air and surface escort; and if U-boats were fully occupied in the western Atlantic their capacity for mischief must be smaller elsewhere. During most of the spring the convoys between North America and Great Britain thus sailed relatively unscathed, while in waters covered by Coastal Command only nine merchant ships were sunk within five months. All this enabled the Command, despite the drain of resources overseas and the frequent calls for operations against the German capital ships, to give more attention to the U-boat 'transit areas'.

Two of these transit areas—the northern and the Bay of Biscay—were of particular importance. The former, between the Shetlands and Norway on the one side and the Shetlands and the Faroes on the other, was traversed by new U-boats on their maiden voyage from Germany; the latter was crossed every time a U-boat approached or left the main operational bases in Western France. The most ardent efforts on the part of No. 15 Group in the first area and No. 19 Group in the second at first produced few 'kills' in either zone, but in June 1942 there came a perceptible improvement in the Bay. The reasons for this were very numerous. There was an increase in the anti-U-boat air forces, largely at the expense of Bomber Command[1]; fixed mirror-cameras for recording attacks became more plentiful; new depth charges were introduced, filled with Torpex—thirty per cent more powerful than the old Amatol—and fitted with the Mark XIIIQ pistol. The latter ensured detonation at 34 feet below the surface—

[1] No. 58 Squadron (Whitleys) and eight Liberators were transferred from Bomber to Coastal Command in April, and six Lancasters of No. 44 Squadron followed for temporary work in June. From July onwards a Whitley squadron for coastal duties was also maintained by No. 10 (Bomber) O.T.U. This squadron, to which crews were attached in turn towards the end of their training, did most gallant work, flying some thirty-five anti-U-boat sorties each week until July 1943. In the course of these operations it destroyed one U-boat and damaged four, but only at the very heavy cost of thirty-five aircraft.

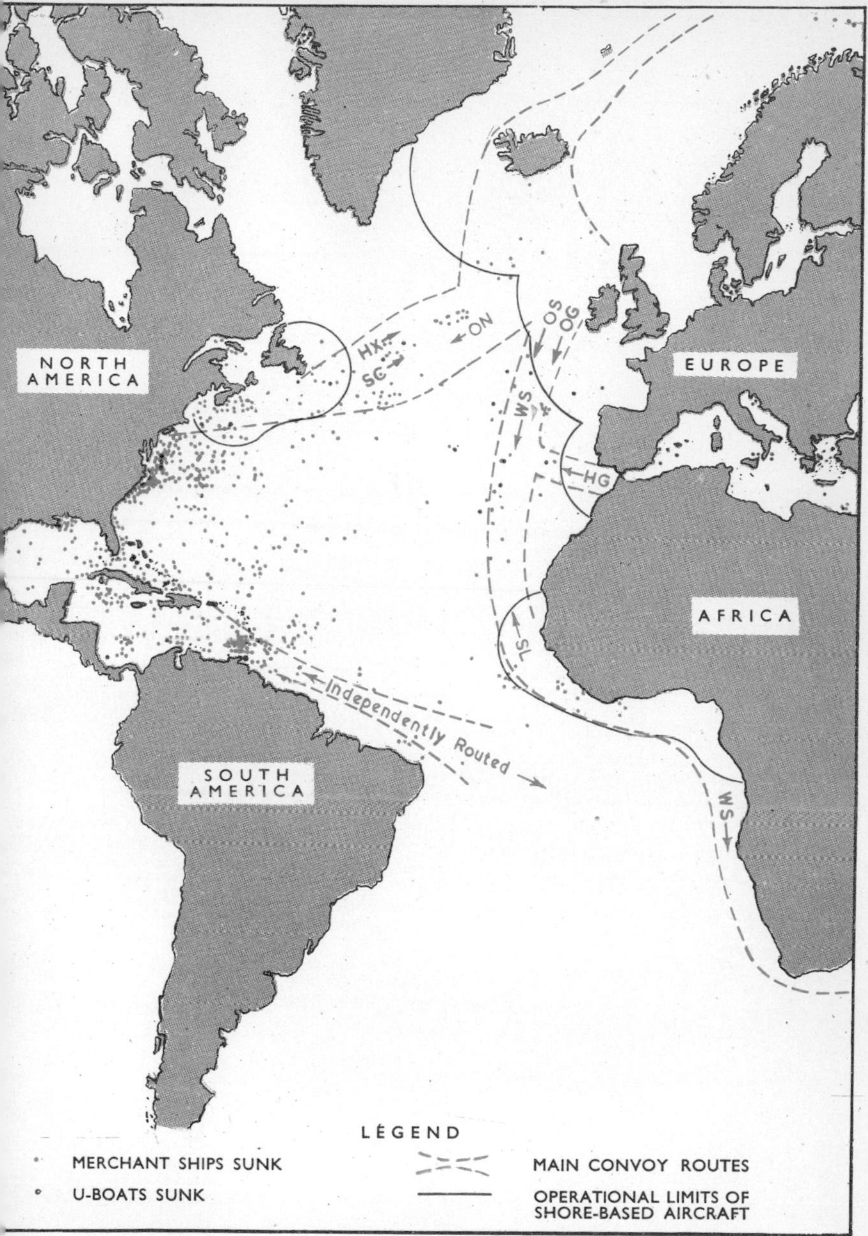

THE BATTLE OF THE ATLANTIC (IV), JANUARY–JULY 1942

Note (i) Extension of patrols over S.W. approaches and off W. Africa.

(ii) Aircraft now operating from Newfoundland and Nova Scotia up to 250 miles from shore.

better than preceding marks, but still deeper than the desired ideal of 25 feet. The effect of all these things, however, was much less than that of another innovation—the Leigh Light.

As is not unusual with inventions of great importance, the origins of the Leigh Light were unorthodox. The need for a good illuminant had been realized very early at Coastal Command; and the idea that anti-submarine aircraft should carry a searchlight, instead of depending on unreliable and swiftly-consumed flares, was born in the mind of Squadron Leader H. de V. Leigh during the summer of 1940. Leigh, who was no specialist in these matters but who had any amount of initiative and common sense, was at that time engaged on personnel duties at Coastal Command Headquarters. He was, however, a pilot of the First World War; and by a fortunate chance the Coastal chief in 1940, Air Chief Marshal Sir Frederick Bowhill, had been his Squadron Commander in the old days. The two men were thus on closer terms than those normally obtaining between the Air Officer Commanding-in-Chief and a squadron leader on 'P' staff.

From the start Bowhill encouraged Leigh to develop his idea. At the end of October 1940 he obtained for him a D.W.I. (mine-detonating) Wellington, complete with generator. The task before Leigh was to fit a 24-inch searchlight into the under-turret of this aircraft, so mounted that the A.S.V. operator could direct it by remote control. The problem, already delicate enough, was complicated by the question whether the weight of the equipment would prevent the aircraft carrying long-range A.S.V., without which it would be useless, besides a full load of fuel and depth charges. But on this score the inventor felt high confidence from the beginning.

By hard work, ingenuity, and help from various sources, among which H.M.S. *Vernon* and the searchlight engineering firm of Messrs. Savage and Parsons take pride of place, Leigh had his prototype installation complete by January 1941. Two months later he carried out his first trials, against an illuminated corvette; and as soon as his A.S.V. equipment was complete, in May, he proceeded to the great test against an unlit submarine. His success was complete. Switching on the light at the last moment just as the A.S.V. reaction was disappearing—for the 'blip', which grows clearer up to about ¾ mile from the detected object, then becomes merged in the general returns from the sea surface—the operator almost instantly trapped and held the submarine in the beam. Long before the vessel could submerge, the pilot had carried out his dummy attack. A new weapon of decisive effect was within our grasp.

The task now appeared to be one of production—of expanding a single prototype into a force of Leigh Light aircraft. By substituting batteries for the generator Leigh had already overcome any difficulty of weight in the Wellington, while for aircraft without under-turrets, such as the Catalina, he was developing a special nacelle-type light to be clamped on the wing. The technical side was well in hand; and for a device of what promised to be revolutionary importance the problems of production should not have been insoluble.

At this stage there occurred an unexpected setback. After the successful trials Bowhill wrote to Joubert, then Assistant Chief of Air Staff (Radio) at the Air Ministry, suggesting that Leigh should be officially entrusted with the task of bringing searchlight A.S.V. aircraft to an operational condition. The reply was discouraging. Joubert had been closely in touch with the development of Group Captain Helmore's 'Turbinlite'; and he considered that Helmore's invention—intended, it will be remembered, for night-fighting—would meet the anti-submarine requirement. So, too, did Helmore. In reality the two lights had little in common; for Helmore's was extremely heavy and not very manœuvrable, gave a strong diffused light instead of a beam, was fitted into the nose of the aircraft, and was used to illuminate the target so that another aircraft could attack. The fundamental differences between the two inventions, however, were not fully appreciated at the Air Ministry; and knowing Helmore to be an expert in his particular field, Joubert met Bowhill's suggestion by assigning responsibility for further trials to the Coastal Command Development Unit (with whom Leigh was already working), and responsibility for further technical progress to Group Captain Helmore.

Events did not stand here. In mid-June Joubert succeeded Bowhill at Northwood. Within a few days he had both recalled Leigh to full 'P' Staff duties and asked for the Helmore light to be fitted in two A.S.V. Wellingtons. At this juncture a lesser man than Leigh might have given up in despair; but the Squadron Leader merely proceeded with his personnel duties at official times, and the development of his invention at others. In particular he persuaded Messrs. Savage and Parsons to carry on with the production of the prototype nacelle and controls, though they had no sort of contract to do so. His quiet persistence was rewarded two months later, when a combined Coastal Command-Admiralty investigation reported that the 'Turbinlite' was quite unsuited for work against submarines.

Joubert, as befitted so acute and agile a commander, now changed his tack right about. He at once became Leigh's firmest supporter. On 7th August he asked for six Wellingtons and six Catalinas to be fitted with the Leigh Light as a matter of urgency; and in November, before delivery had begun, he extended his demand by another thirty

Wellingtons. This was too fast for the Air Staff, who insisted on further trials. When these confirmed the merits of Leigh's device, the Air Ministry then approved an order for twenty more searchlight equipments; but it refused to have these fitted to aircraft until the success of the first six Wellingtons had been demonstrated in operations. Only in response to Joubert's repeated pressure did the Ministry so far relent, in February 1942, as to agree that the immediate aim should be a full squadron (No. 172) of Leigh Light Wellingtons, instead of a flight.

By now, some seven months after Joubert's initial request, the first Wellington had reached Chivenor, a Coastal airfield on the Bristol Channel. There followed a disheartening period during which the aircraft arrived at the rate of about one a month. By May, when there were still only five, Joubert lost patience. Realizing that the laggards and sceptics would be convinced only by a successful operation, he decided to sacrifice the very great advantage of a first appearance in force. On the night of 4th June, 1942, over a year after successful trials, he ordered four of the five Leigh Light Wellingtons to patrol over the Bay of Biscay.

The result was highly gratifying. Three of the Wellingtons found no U-boats, but the ease with which they illuminated A.S.V. contacts which turned out to be fishing vessels left little doubt of the merits of Leigh's invention. The fourth aircraft gave further witness in the best possible way. It contacted, 'homed' on to, and successfully illuminated two enemy submarines. Both fired recognition signals and made no attempt to dive. The first, an Italian vessel, was heavily damaged by the Wellington's depth-charges, and was finished off three days later by No. 10 Squadron, Royal Australian Air Force. The second, profiting from the fact that the Wellington had used all its depth-charges in the first attack, escaped with nothing worse than slight damage from the aircraft's machine-guns.

This was well enough for a start, and the Squadron diary very reasonably recorded: 'the first operational effort was hailed with great enthusiasm throughout the Squadron as it had proved the whole "outfit" to be an outstanding success'. Joubert, equally impressed, within a few hours of receiving a report on the night's activities again demanded an increase in the Leigh Light production programme. Operations during the rest of June fully confirmed the wisdom of his request. One aircraft was lost by flying into the sea—there was still no reliable low-reading altimeter—but between them the five Leigh Light Wellingtons sighted seven U-boats during 230 flying hours over the Bay. In the same period the ordinary night-flying Whitleys, using flares, put in 260 hours without a single sighting.

The new weapon, even though its first use was on so small a scale, had an instant effect on the German crews. Liable to be suddenly transfixed by a dazzling glare which was the sure harbinger of a salvo of depth-charges, they found darkness no longer a protection; and their growing reluctance to break surface at night soon presented our daylight patrols with increased opportunities for attack. Reacting swiftly to the double threat, on 24th June Dönitz ordered all U-boats in the Bay of Biscay to proceed submerged both by day and night. If they surfaced, it must be only to recharge batteries. The result was that life for the German crews became not only more dangerous but more uncomfortable. Their morale, shaken by the British efforts in 1941 and then boosted by their success off the American coast, took a sharp turn for the worse.

During July 1942 the Leigh Light Wellingtons scored their first 'kill', and in August the Air Ministry approved the formation of a second squadron. At the same time nacelle-type lights were ordered for all Catalinas and trial installations for the Liberators and Fortresses. By then some of the secondary effects of the new weapon were becoming clear. One of these was that the U-boats, forced to travel great distances submerged, could now spend much less time on patrol. Another was the reinforcement of the *Luftwaffe* in Western France. On 2nd July Dönitz accused Göring of allowing British aircraft to operate in the Bay with 'absolutely no opposition', and soon twenty-four Ju.88's, which could ill be spared from other fields, were being added to the forces of the *Fliegerführer Atlantik*.

By the summer of 1942 the Bay was thus becoming a scene of danger for the U-boats. By then, too, increased Allied resources and better organization were having their effect along the North American coast. In the air, British as well as American and Canadian units played their part, for in July the Hudsons of No. 53 Squadron began operating from Rhode Island. As the U-boats were driven out of the northern reaches to the Caribbean and the Gulf of Mexico, so No. 53 Squadron followed them south. By August it was based on Trinidad, with detachments in British and Dutch Guiana. The German heyday in American waters was over.

Though Dönitz could still find 'soft spots' to exploit in the Caribbean and off Brazil, the time had now come for a general re-deployment of his forces. Of where the U-boat chief would strike next there was little doubt. Whatever the attractions of the waters off Capetown, West Africa and North Russia, where merchant ships were many and Allied aircraft few, the main offensive must continue in the North Atlantic. And as there was now no safety for U-boats within five hundred miles of Anglo-American air bases, the attack must perforce be concentrated in mid-ocean. The Allied air patrols from Newfoundland, Dönitz was gratefully aware, had not yet been stretched to meet the Allied air patrols from Iceland and Northern Ireland. Those from Gibraltar failed to link up with those from Cornwall. The 'Greenland Gap' in the north, the 'Azores Gap' in the south: here were waters still bright with promise for the German cause.

'Wolf pack' attacks in the Greenland Gap began in the opening days of August 1942. The fierce battles of the next three months displayed at least two consistent features. One was the gallantry and skill with which the surface-escorts harassed the attackers; the other was the fact that the attacks began when systematic air escort ended and ended when systematic air escort began. A good example occurred on 1st September. On that morning the westbound convoy SC.97 was under attack from nine U-boats towards the westward edge of the Greenland Gap. At midday, British and American Catalinas from Iceland began to appear on the scene. Before nightfall they had sunk one U-boat, attacked two more with depth-charges, and forced all the rest to dive. Thereafter the convoy sailed on unmolested. 'I decided to break off the operation', wrote Dönitz in his War Diary, 'as experience had shown that further pursuit in an area under constant air patrol would be useless'.

There was no single answer to the problem of the 'gaps'. On the naval side there was still much that could be done by strengthening surface escorts. Special naval forces, too, could be formed to hunt U-boats rather than protect convoys. The first such group, under that redoubtable destroyer of U-boats Commander Walker, began operations on 22nd September, 1942. In regard to the air forces, our attacks on transit areas or the U-boat operational bases would affect events in the 'gaps' just as much as elsewhere. But the prime need was simply to abolish the gaps. This could be done either by naval aircraft from carriers, or by V.L.R. (very long range) aircraft from shore. But in August 1942 we had no aircraft-carriers to spare for transatlantic convoys; no auxiliary carriers; and only five V.L.R. aircraft in the whole of Coastal Command.[1] Until these things could be supplied our losses at sea were bound to remain grave. From August to October, in fact, an average of nearly half a million tons went down each month in the North Atlantic alone. Worse still, new

[1] These were the five Liberator I's (operational range 2,400 miles) of No. 120 Squadron. Long-range aircraft, as distinct from V.L.R., at this time included the remainder of No. 120 Squadron's Liberators (Mark II 1,800 miles, Mark III 1,680 miles), together with the Catalinas (1,840 miles), the amphibian Catalinas (1,600 miles) and the Sunderlands (1,300 miles). All other aircraft in Coastal Command were medium or short range.

U-boats continued to come into operation very much faster than the old ones could be destroyed.

Despite all this, Dönitz was alarmed at the prospect ahead. 'The number of British aircraft in the East Atlantic', he wrote at the beginning of September, 'has increased, a great variety being seen. They are equipped with excellent location devices against U-boats. U-boat traffic round Scotland and in the Bay of Biscay is gravely endangered by daily, even hourly, hunts by aircraft. In the Atlantic the enemy's daily reconnaissance covers out as far as 20° W., which forces U-boat dispositions far out into the centre of the Atlantic with consequent higher fuel consumption, shorter operational periods, and greater difficulty in finding the enemy convoys in the open Atlantic. There are also some types of aircraft of particularly long range which are used for convoy escort. Such escort has been flown as much as eight hundred miles from English bases. If development continues at the present rate, these problems will lead to irreparable losses, to a decline in ship sinkings, and consequently to reduced chances of success in the U-boat warfare as a whole'. In view of all this Dönitz once more staked a claim on the four-engined He.177's, 'the only aircraft which have a range and fighting power capable of acting as reconnaissance against the Atlantic convoys and of combating the English aircraft in the Biscay area'. In support of this demand he quoted the opinion of his U-boat captains that 'successful operations were perfectly possible against convoys even heavily escorted by surface craft, but only as long as Allied aircraft were not in evidence'.

Admiral Dönitz did not get his He.177's; but it was some time before his worst fears came true. Meanwhile those in charge of Royal Air Force policy and operations made further efforts in two important directions. The first was extremely profitable. The Air Staff—in the person of Air Vice-Marshal J. C. Slessor, who undertook a special mission to Washington—managed to speed up the supply of Liberators. The second was attended with less success: Joubert tried to bring the struggle against the U-boats under a unified Anglo-American direction.

Dissatisfaction with the existing organization on the upper levels was no novelty. It had, for instance, already been voiced by the Rt. Hon. S. M. Bruce. In memoranda to the War Cabinet in June and July 1942 the Australian Representative urged that a small high-level committee, wider than the existing Defence or Chiefs of Staff Committees, should be appointed to assess the relative importance of the war at sea and the air offensive against Germany. Having cleared our minds on that difficult and complex matter, Bruce suggested, we should then approach the United States with proposals for a common policy to be carried out by a common effort. In September Joubert carried this idea a stage further. He proposed a single supreme control for the whole anti-U-boat war, with a central planning staff to co-ordinate the separate and often conflicting policies of the British, Canadian and American naval and air authorities, together with those of the various Service authorities in such areas as the Mediterranean, West Africa and Australia. The scheme was attractive in theory, if liable to give rise to difficulties in practice; and it was pursued for some months before being finally abandoned. In the meantime a concession was made to the critics by the formation in November of the War Cabinet Anti-U-boat Sub-Committee. Under the chairmanship of the Prime Minister, this was normally attended by the political and Service chiefs from the Admiralty and Air Ministry, the Minister of War Transport, some distinguished scientists (such as Lord Cherwell, Sir Robert Watson-Watt and Professor Blackett), and political and naval representatives of the United States. If not what Joubert had hoped for, this body certainly managed to determine priority and secure departmental sanction with great speed, leaving the Admiralty-Coastal Command Anti-U-boat Committee to concentrate largely on technical and tactical matters.[1]

In conformity with the spirit of these proposals for the higher direction of the struggle, Joubert also achieved greater centralization at a lower level. From the end of July details of sorties by V.L.R. aircraft were decided by Coastal Command Headquarters, in accordance with information supplied by the Admiralty, instead of by the Coastal Group Commander in concert with the local naval Commander-in-Chief. At the momentary cost of the Group Commanders' feelings this made the most economical use of exceedingly scarce aircraft.

While these matters of organization were under discussion the struggle had once more taken a sharp turn in favour of the enemy. The offensive in the Bay, which had promised so well with the advent of the Leigh Light in June, was now petering out in failure.

This sombre development was not the result of greater activity by the *Luftwaffe*, though that was real enough. In June German aircraft had managed to intercept only three of our aircraft over the Bay, but with the arrival of the twenty-four Ju.88's which Dönitz had wrung from Göring, opposition warmed up. In July our patrols had to fight some twenty-five combats, in August thirty-three, and in September

[1] The War Cabinet Battle of the Atlantic Committee, after a burst of important decisions in the spring of 1941, had settled down into reviewing progress rather than initiating fresh developments.

forty-four. But though our losses increased from eight aircraft in July to sixteen in October, those of the enemy rose far more abruptly. In July we destroyed over the Bay one German aircraft; in August, four; in September, twelve; and in November (when our own losses were only seven), twelve again. All this was not accomplished without sacrifices in other directions, for the whole effort of two Beaufighter squadrons (Nos. 235 and 248) had to be directed against the enemy. But it was worth diverting squadrons to new tasks when they could record episodes like the following:

> No. 235 Squadron. St. Eval. 18.9.42. Beaufighters N, C, A, H, E, P, J and O. At 1755 hours, aircraft sighted F.W.200 Kurier on easterly course, height 200 ft., over armed trawler of 300 tons. E, P and N attacked F.W.200 from port while O dived from 2,000 feet head on and remainder attacked from starboard. F.W.200 burst into flames, disintegrated, and dived into sea. Three crew were seen in water and one attempting to climb in dinghy. Aircraft H saw C dive into sea from 200 ft., apparently damaged by *flak* from trawler. 1820, three Ju. 88's were sighted flying at 1,000 ft. over fishing vessel flying French flag. Aircraft P climbed and attacked while other Beaufighters converged from various directions. Hits were seen on port engine of one Ju.88 which was further attacked by O and E; flames appeared in cockpit and enemy dived into sea enveloped in flames. When Beaufighters left, tail planes of two Ju.88's were protruding from sea. Aircraft A followed third Ju.88 and delivered two successive attacks, but Ju. disappeared into cloud.

The work of the Beaufighter patrols was well and swiftly done, and by November it was virtually complete. For the time being German interference from the air almost ceased, and our anti-U-boat aircraft were again able to carry out their patrols unmolested.

A greater difficulty than the Ju.88's was the advent of the French tunny-fishing season. In the latter part of July large numbers of fishing craft began to move out after the tunny into the Middle Bay. In earlier years this movement had not mattered, for we had not been operating against U-boats by night. Now it raised an almost insoluble problem. The 'blip' produced on the A.S.V. screen by a fishing vessel was indistinguishable from that caused by a submarine; and the Leigh Light operators found themselves exposing their searchlights only to light up French tunnymen—a waste of effort which ran down batteries and gave unmistakable warning to any U-boats in the vicinity. By mid-August the fishing fleet was so numerous that our night sorties were completely ineffective. Worse still, the U-boats, finding that they could surface with greater freedom during the dark hours, were able to travel submerged through areas covered by our day patrols. Every means of putting pressure on the tunnymen was tried, from leaflet-dropping and appeals over the wireless to sterner measures such as capturing or 'shooting-up' their vessels. Only the end of the season brought relief.

Tunnymen were an accidental and temporary nuisance. The main cause of the break-down of our Bay offensive lay in something much more serious. It had long been realized that if the enemy discovered some means of detecting our A.S.V. radiations, U-boats could dive well before they were sighted by our aircraft. During April 1942 a Hudson carrying A.S.V. had unfortunately crashed in Tunisia; the Germans had obtained the set, including the all-important magnetron valve, more or less intact; and by August they had produced an apparatus which received and recorded A.S.V. transmissions at a distance of thirty miles. By mid-September they had fitted this to large numbers of U-boats. And the vessels not so fitted travelled across the Bay under the escort of those that were.

When we discovered that the Germans had this 'search-receiver'—to use our term—Coastal Command at once strove to apply counter-measures. An attempt was made to 'flood' the Bay with A.S.V. transmissions, so that U-boats would be repeatedly forced to submerge. But all efforts to counteract the new apparatus proved unavailing, and by January 1943 our aircraft had almost ceased to sight U-boats by night. Only one thing could now restore our fortunes: radar of a wave-length beyond the scope of the German search-receiver. The time had come—indeed, was long overdue—for the introduction of A.S.V. Mark III.

A.S.V. of 10 centimetres wave-length, as opposed to the $1\frac{1}{2}$ metres of Mark II, was in fact already in existence. It had originated as an adaptation of the American A.I. set; and an improved version, developed with the help of British scientists, had been tried out with success as early as May 1942. Within a few months U.S. Army Liberators on coastal duties in the western hemisphere were equipped with these or similar sets, but production on this side of the Atlantic was very slow. By August it was clear that the first British models would not be available until the spring of 1943, and that no improvement could be expected while H2S—a new bombing and navigational aid employing many of the same components—was given priority in manufacture. In mid-September a personal approach by Joubert to Harris at Bomber Command failed to persuade the latter to forgo his prior claims, but the discovery of the German 'search-receiver' soon altered matters. The Air Staff quickly ruled that the first forty H2S sets should be converted into A.S.V. Mark III, and the Americans agreed to install the new apparatus in all Liberators intended for Coastal Command. It was January 1943, however, before the first daylight patrols by Liberators equipped with 10 centimetre A.S.V. were flown from British bases, and March 1943 before similarly equipped Leigh Light Wellingtons took up the burden of operations by night. During all this time the offensive against the U-boats in the Bay and the northern transit area was conducted as vigorously as ever but showed little result.

The strain under which Coastal Command was labouring towards the end of 1942 was increased still further by a venture to be described in detail later—the massive Operation 'Torch'. The invasion of French North Africa, the first of the great Anglo-American expeditions under General Eisenhower, set an immense task for our Coastal aircraft. There were photographs to secure of Dakar, Toulon and the Italian naval bases, as well as of the three assault ports—Casablanca, Oran and Algiers. There were weather prospects to be ascertained by 'Met.' flights far out into the Atlantic. There was the ceaseless vigil to be kept over the German capital ships in the Norwegian fiords and over their possible break-out routes on both sides of Iceland. Above all, there were intensified patrols to be flown against U-boats in the Bay and the waters around Gibraltar, and close escort to be provided for the convoys. Nearly all this, and much else besides, would have to be done not merely before and during the sailing of the assault forces but over the whole period of the subsequent 'build-up'.

First and foremost it was necessary to improve the airstrip at Gibraltar, the focal point of the whole operation. By intense efforts, described later, the runway was widened and at the same time extended 450 yards into the sea. This made it possible for three more Coastal Squadrons—Nos. 210, 500 and 608—to be sent out to join Nos. 202 and 233. The airfields in the South-West of England had also to be developed for very heavy operational work. St. Eval, for instance, was organized for a peak load of 72 aircraft, Chivenor for 88. All these measures, and many others, were taken in good time: the reconnaissance was completed, the patrols and escort arranged, the waters off the Biscay ports mined by forces of Bomber Command. At the last minute, after the first vessels had sailed, the Admiralty suddenly asked for air support for five more convoys, but even this unexpected demand was satisfied. Coastal Command aircraft being already fully committed, Joubert was allowed to borrow a Halifax squadron—No. 405, R.C.A.F.—from Bomber Command and eight Liberators from the U.S.A.A.F.

Meanwhile the enemy had fortunately decided to concentrate against our traffic with West Africa. Several U-boats which might otherwise have played havoc with the expedition were thus grouped well to the south-west of our projected routes. Though most of the fourteen invasion convoys crept along at no more than six or seven knots, and some of them crossed the very mouth of the Bay, only two U-boats were seen to approach our line of passage. Both were sunk by Liberators of No. 224 Squadron. In the second case the depth-charges hit the vessel abaft the conning-tower, exploded on impact, and seriously damaged the Liberator—especially in the elevators. 'Aircraft', runs the laconic entry in the squadron diary, 'went into steep incontrollable climb, almost stalling. Climb counteracted by combined efforts of both pilots. Rear-gunner saw elevators disintegrate and wreckage or debris flew up past the tail. Aircraft was extremely tail heavy and A/S bombs could not be jettisoned owing to damaged gear. 1½ hours later flight-engineer managed to open bomb doors and jettison A/S bombs manually. All other loose heavy gear was also jettisoned. Flight back accomplished by both pilots continuously relieved, bracing hands and knees on control column and all crew in nose of aircraft. About one hour before landing control columns had to be tied forward with straps. W/T went u/s. Electrical equipment commenced to function with switches in "off" position. Batteries were switched off in case of fire. Scilly Isles sighted about 1840 to starboard from 14,000 feet. Crew decided to chance crash-landing at Predannack. When over aerodrome, elevator control broke loose becoming u/s. Crash landed, Sgt. Rose suffered compound fracture of leg, rest of crew superficial scratches and cuts. Aircraft destroyed by fire'.

The work of the two Liberators undoubtedly saved the expedition from serious trouble. Still more decisive was the fact that the U-boats to the south-west intercepted a lightly-escorted convoy from Sierra Leone. Other German submarines further out hastened to join in the slaughter, and the unfortunate convoy became a veritable sacrifice for the success of the invasion.

So the majestic array of the 'Torch' armada, which the Admiralty had reckoned might suffer attack by some seventy U-boats, swept on undisturbed. On November 2nd the first convoys came under air cover from Gibraltar, and by 7th November, the eve of the landings, the Coastal aircraft on the Rock were putting up some 48 sorties a day, averaging nearly eight hours each. By then Dönitz's captains were hard on the scent, and twenty-two U-boats were spotted by our air patrols before the assaults were launched. Thirteen of these were successfully attacked and damaged, while on the Allied side not a single ship was lost.

For many days the Gibraltar-based aircraft maintained this effort. Soon it became possible to bring out from home the second squadron —No. 179—to be equipped with the Leigh Light, and the night patrols became as deadly as those flown by day. By mid-December, when Dönitz finally recognized defeat and called off his pack, the Coastal squadrons at Gibraltar had flown 8,656 hours on tasks connected with 'Torch'. In the course of these they had sighted 142 U-boats, attacked 83, damaged 23 and sunk 3, apart from sharing a fourth 'kill' with an Albacore of the Fleet Air Arm. All this they had achieved at a cost of seventeen aircraft, several of which were shot down by our own or the American forces.

During the closing months of 1942 many U-boats began to 'fight back' when attacked from the air. 'Attacked a U-boat which was fully surfaced', records No. 311 (Czech) Squadron on 7th September; 'our aircraft dived to attack from a height of 1,200 feet. U-boat opened fire with cannon and machine gun and our aircraft was hit in the fuselage. Most members of crew injured. The Captain, however, pressed the attack home, and the six depth charges, dropped from seventy feet, straddled the conning tower. Our crew were unable to determine number each side of conning-tower owing to their injuries. Rear-gunner observed the U-boat lift bodily in depth charge explosions. Rear-gunner fired approximately 400 rounds, and observed tracers hit the conning-tower. U-boat dived slowly, and submerged one minute after depth charge attack. Owing to injuries to the crew the Captain left the scene of the attack at once, climbed to 500 feet and set course for base. Crash landed at St. Eval, owing to failure of hydraulics. Navigator seriously injured in both legs, front-gunner small finger of left hand shot away, wireless-operator splinter wounds in right arm, second pilot splinter wounds in leg'.

This practice did not dismay our crews in the least, and a steadily increasing number of attacks ended in 'kills'. A notable occasion was on 8th December, when a Liberator of No. 120 Squadron, joining convoy HX.217 far out in mid-Atlantic, found a 'Wolf-pack' in full cry. '0900 hours began escort', runs the entry in the Squadron diary: '0929 hours sighted and attacked one U-boat with six depth charges, straddling U-boat. Ten feet eruption of water seen, oil streak, numerous pieces yellow wood; many sea gulls collected on and over the oil patch. Aircraft informed Senior Naval Officer of attack and guided Corvette *K.214* to oil patch. *K.214* signalled "You killed him", and that parts of dead bodies were seen'. In the remaining ten hours before this Liberator turned for home its crew spotted six more of the 'pack', but having already dropped their depth charges could attack only with cannon fire. In each case this drove the enemy below the surface and helped to save the convoy.

By the beginning of 1943 successful attacks were no longer the rarity of a year before, and admirable descriptions of the destruction

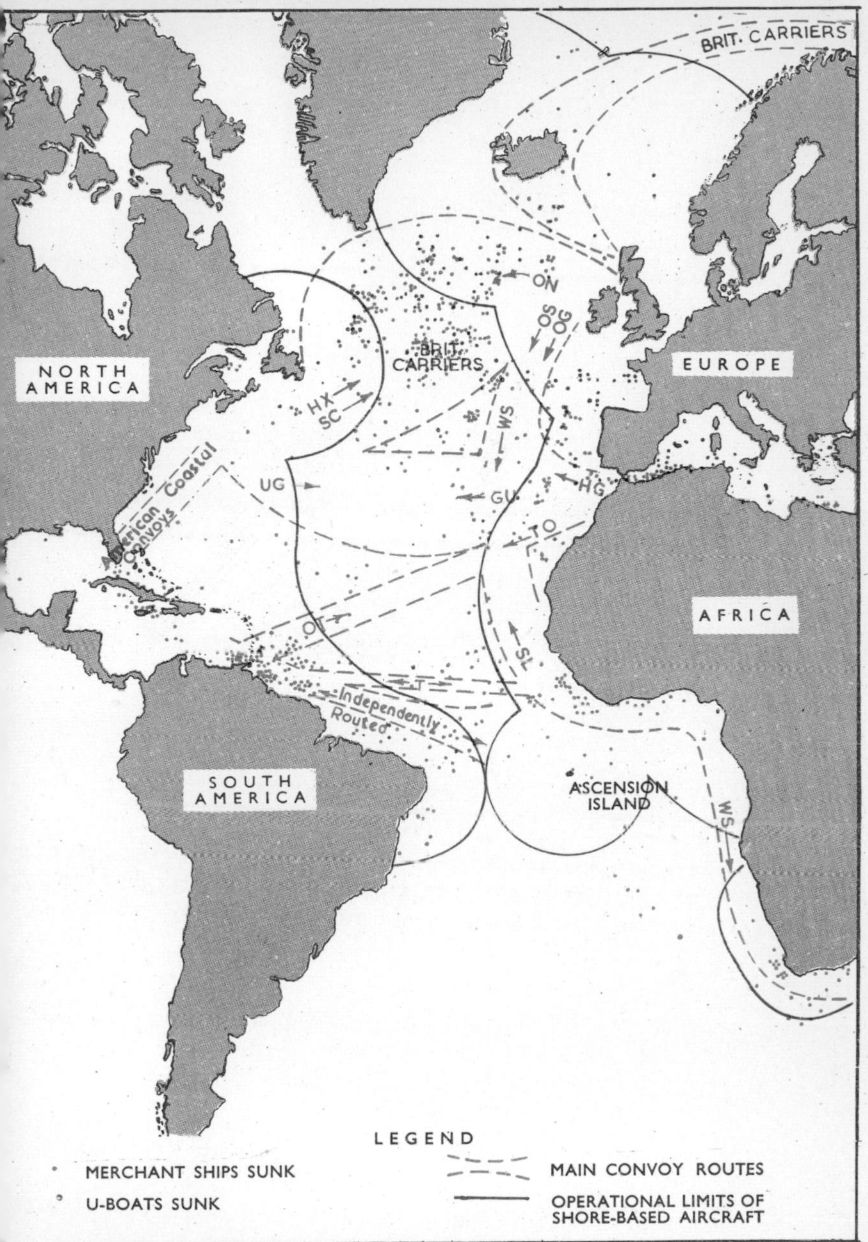

THE BATTLE OF THE ATLANTIC (V), AUGUST 1942—MAY 1943

Note (i) By December 1942 air cover became consistent on N. American seaboard.
(ii) By January 1943 the gap between patrols from Gibraltar and W. Africa was closed.
(iii) Additional patrols off Cape of Good Hope.

of the enemy occur with pleasing regularity in the Squadron Operations Record Books. On 15th January, for instance, No. 206 Squadron (Fortresses) recorded how one of its aircraft 'dived to attack from 20 degrees on the port bow. Air-gunner estimated that the stick was a straddle, depth charges Nos. 1 and 2 falling short and Nos. 3 and 4 engulfing the U-boat in one big explosion. Remaining depth charges failed to release. After the attack the aircraft made a steep climb to port; the bow or stern of the U-boat was observed at a very steep angle bobbing up and down like a half-filled bottle, and boiling foam patches were observed in the depth charge subsidence. Photographs were taken as the U-boat gradually shot under. . . .' Still more graphic was the description by a pilot of the same squadron of a successful attack a few weeks later. 'The aftermath', he reported, 'looked like a dose of Eno's'.

In January 1943, when Morocco and Algeria were firmly in our hands, but a bitter struggle still lay ahead in Tunisia, the British and American leaders met near Casablanca. Of the atmosphere and significance of that great conference more will be said later. Here it is important to note that among the vital decisions then taken was that during 1943 the resources of the two nations would be directed first and foremost to the defeat of the U-boats. No sudden stream of long-sought equipment began to pour into Coastal Command as a result of this ruling, but its effects were nevertheless of the highest moment. For it not only served as a charter of rights for the coastal air forces in disputes over priority and countered the tendency in some American quarters to think primarily in terms of the Pacific; it also made the U-boat bases in the Bay of Biscay Target No. 1 for the Anglo-American bombers.

To understand the precise import of this last fact it is necessary to recall how our bombers were already assisting the struggle against the U-boats. Throughout 1942, as in 1941, much of Bomber Command's effort had been devoted to the war at sea. Apart from lending or transferring to Coastal Command under varying degrees of protest a total of eight squadrons (or nine, if the Whitley O.T.U. squadron is counted) during the year, Bomber Command had helped in many ways. The Bostons of No. 2 Group had joined in the offensive against merchant shipping; the heavier bombers, leaving aside their major effort against the *Scharnhorst*, *Gneisenau* and *Prinz Eugen*, had attacked the *Tirpitz* off Norway and the *Graf Zeppelin* in Gdynia; and the whole night bomber force, under the impulse of Air Chief Marshal Harris, had taken to minelaying whenever the weather prevented operations over land.[1] All these,

[1] The monthly total of mines laid by bomber aircraft, only 62 in January 942, had grown to 1,285 in January 1943.

however, were subsidiary tasks. The main contribution of the Command to the war at sea had taken a different form.

During 1942 over 2,000 sorties had been directed against the Dutch, Belgian and French Channel ports, and more than 2,500 tons of bombs had been cast down upon them. This work, carried out during daylight by No. 2 Group or at night mainly by 'freshman' crews of other groups, had hampered the Germans' transport system, harassed their minor naval craft, and compelled them to retain strong anti-aircraft defences in the West. It had not, however, any more than the subsidiary activities mentioned above, reduced the number of U-boats. No U-boat was sunk by a mine before 1943; and no U-boats used the Channel ports. As for the French Atlantic ports, from which the U-boats did operate, these had been left virtually untouched. No further sorties were made against Brest once the *Scharnhorst* and *Gneisenau* had departed, and although St. Nazaire attracted a steady minor effort in the first half of the year, we had not attempted any major bombardment from the air. This was because, as recorded in Volume I, the U-boat pens by the Spring of 1942 were already covered with several feet of concrete, and we could not expect to inflict direct damage on Dönitz's vessels.

During 1942 Bomber Command's real effort against the U-boats thus took the form of raids on the German North Sea and Baltic ports. These were for the most part 'area' attacks, and part of the wider campaign against German morale and war economy as a whole. But the naval construction yards, or similar objectives, were usually taken as the aiming points; and Bremen, Hamburg and Kiel, which between them were responsible for some 60 per cent of U-boat production, were among the most heavily assaulted towns in all Germany.[1] Severe attacks were also made on Emden, Wilhelmshaven, Lübeck and Rostock. In addition, harassing operations by Mosquito aircraft over all the German ports were a regular feature from July onwards, and small-scale precision attacks were delivered against the submarine yards or slipways at Danzig, Flensburg and Vegesack. A notable and successful attempt to strike at a submarine objective by day was also made in the famous raid by Lancasters on the M.A.N. Diesel-engine factory at Augsburg, to be described later. All told, Bomber Command devoted over 7,000 sorties and more than 11,000 tons of bombs, or 20 per cent of its entire effort during 1942, to objectives in Germany primarily naval in character. When to this is added the 8,500 sorties, or 23·7 per cent of effort, devoted

[1] During 1942, Bremen, with 2,729 sorties and 4,293 tons of bombs directed against it, took second place as an objective only to Essen. Hamburg (1,602 sorties and 2,043 tons of bombs) occupied the fifth place, and Kiel (629 sorties and 927 tons of bombs) sixteenth.

to the other tasks in connection with the war at sea, such as minelaying and the attacks on occupied ports, it will be seen that the Command's effort in the maritime struggle was already by no means small.

During many of these raids, notably those on Lübeck, Rostock, Augsburg and Flensburg, damage of varying degrees was inflicted on the German submarine yards. Of the effect on production there is little detailed evidence one way or the other; but it is probably not without significance that the number of newly commissioned U-boats, which was 22 per month over the last five months of 1941, averaged only 20 per month over the whole of 1942. With this output, however, Dönitz could still increase his fleet at an impressive rate, for his monthly losses at sea averaged something under seven. In other words, however much our bombers were achieving, the fortunes of the battle were still running in favour of the enemy.

It was this which led the Admiralty, in the latter part of 1942, to ask for 'area' attacks on the Biscay bases; for though we had no hope of penetrating the concrete pens, we might conceivably create such havoc among the servicing, power and recreational facilities that U-boat operations would be seriously affected. The demand was long resisted by the Air Staff and Air Marshal Harris, but it was finally approved by the War Cabinet in mid-January 1943, and a few days afterwards reaffirmed as Allied policy at Casablanca. How the attacks were then carried out, and with what results, is described in Chapter XIII.

The decision to give priority to the battle against the U-boats and to obliterate friendly towns in the course of the struggle was the natural consequence of the shipping losses of November 1942. These reached the appalling total of 814,700 tons—the heaviest of the whole war. The following month saw a fall to 374,000 tons, but this improvement was largely 'seasonal'. When Sir Philip Joubert handed over his Command to Air Marshal Slessor in February 1943 a desperate fight thus still lay ahead. On the other hand, the retiring Coastal chief could look back on a period of solid achievement, in which our air patrols had been steadily extended and the aeroplane had developed into a real 'killer'. In June 1941, when he had assumed command, systematic air patrols had extended only 350 miles from the British Isles. Now, in conjunction with those of the American and Canadian forces, they were near to bridging the Atlantic. Up to June 1941 Coastal Command had shared in the destruction of only two U-boats; since then it had destroyed by its own efforts twenty-seven, of which nineteen had been sunk in the last five months. Despite the demands of overseas theatres, the long-range aircraft in the Command had increased from six-and-a-half squadrons in June 1941 to eighteen, of which one was V.L.R., in February 1943. Above all, there had been vital technical progress. The Leigh Light was already a proved success, 10 centimeter A.S.V. was on the way.

In point of fact, the worst was over. Within three months the V.L.R. aircraft in co-operation with the naval escorts, support groups and auxiliary carriers, were to win the battle of the Central Atlantic. A little longer and the Leigh Light, in conjunction with the new A.S.V., would turn the Bay of Biscay into a veritable graveyard for U-boats. These things Joubert was not to know in February 1943. The road ahead seemed hard, the goal very distant. But his work, and that of all those others whose efforts counted equally, had been well done; and triumph, like disaster, is often nearer than we think.

CHAPTER VII

Bomber Command and the Assault on Germany

THROUGHOUT 1942 the Germans retained within the *Reich* and the Western occupied territories only a quarter of their operational Air Force. A fifth was stationed in the Mediterranean Islands, North Africa and the Balkans. Nearly a half remained deeply committed to the struggle in the East.

This disposition, the logical outcome of Hitler's failure to finish off the Russians inside his estimate of eight weeks, had two important results. In the first place England continued to escape serious attack from the air. Seaside 'tip and run', nuisance activity, occasional operations in force against Birmingham or other industrial targets, gestures of exasperation like the 'Baedeker' raids against our lightly defended Cathedral cities—these were as much as the *Luftwaffe* could manage in the circumstances.

The second and perhaps more important consequence of the German deployment was that our own striking forces could wage with increasing violence the campaign against the enemy's homeland. In this they were now to have the help of a new aid. The device known as 'Gee', for which the primary credit must be given to Mr. R. J. Dippy of the Telecommunications Research Establishment, had been under development since 1940. It was a system by which the navigator could calculate the position of his aircraft by observing the time taken to receive pulse signals from three different ground stations.[1] By mid-1941 the three stations had been erected on the East Coast, a few

[1] The centre station, known as the 'Master', transmitted a radio pulse simultaneously with a 'Slave' station situated further North. The time-lag between the reception of these two signals in the aircraft told the navigator how much farther he was from one station than the other, and so enabled him to draw a curve on which the aircraft must be. The same process, repeated with a second signal transmitted by the 'Master' and a 'Slave' to the South, enabled a second curve to be plotted. The aircraft was at the intersection of the two curves.

The task of the navigator was simplified by a special chart which showed curves of distances from the stations in the form of a lattice. The navigator could either work by dead reckoning, using 'Gee' as a periodic check, or he could fly along one line of the lattice and check at the intersections.

hand-made sets had been tried out operationally, and the general results were so promising that the Air Staff, perhaps mindful of the Army's premature employment of tanks in 1916, decided to make no further use of the system until a substantial number of 'Gee-boxes' was available. By February 1942 this moment had at last arrived. Some 200 bombers had been fitted; and in preparation for an assault of unprecedented accuracy the policy of conserving our bombers, applied since November 1941, was now withdrawn.

The decision to begin a new spell of intensive operations against Germany was conveyed to Bomber Command on 14th February, 1942. The Command was instructed to strike with full force for the next six months—the estimated length of time before 'Gee' was discovered and jammed by the enemy. In order to destroy Germany's capacity and will to make war, create the conditions for an Allied second front, and relieve pressure on the Russians, the Air Officer Commanding-in-Chief was to focus his operations on 'the morale of the enemy civil population, and in particular of the industrial workers'. The selection of targets, however, was also to be dictated by the limited range of 'Gee', which was some 350–400 miles, and by the known capabilities of the bomber force. Our bombers, in other words, were to attack the cities of West and North-West Germany. 'Area bombing', already approved when conditions were unsuitable for precise attack, was thus now formally recognised as the standard basis of our policy. It was to remain the official gospel for over two years.

This directive was six days old when Air Marshal A. T. Harris succeeded Sir Richard Peirse at High Wycombe. It is interesting to note that the new Commander-in-Chief, although he was to become the staunchest advocate of the 'area bombing' policy, had no part in its inception. A South African by birth and a pilot of distinction in the 1914–18 war, he had commanded No. 5 Group (Bomber Command) in 1939–40, and had later acted as Deputy Chief of Air Staff at the Air Ministry. From mid-1941, however, he had been in charge of the Royal Air Force Delegation at Washington, far removed from the policy-makers in Whitehall. Misconceiving the province of a Commander in the field, popular opinion has nevertheless regarded Harris as personally responsible for the devastation of Germany. In point of fact, the new Commander of course obeyed orders from the Air Staff, whose policy in turn required, and received, the sanction of the War Cabinet. It must be admitted, however, that Harris's outspoken preference for bombing German towns, and his fearless and trenchant criticism of other policies, made it difficult for the Air Staff—or the War Cabinet—to alter his instructions later.

Nevertheless, by the time of his appointment to command the bomber force, Harris had in fact come to some very firm conclusions. With the means available, attempts to win the war by bombing what he termed 'panacea' targets were doomed to failure. Oil plants, aircraft works, ball-bearing factories, molybdenum mines, submarine yards, and the like—even if our bombers could find and hit them, their destruction would probably have nothing like the effect prophesied by our economic experts. And as, for the most part, such targets could not be found and hit by night, and as our bombers could certainly not survive over Germany by day, it followed that our offensive must be directed against something much larger. The only really large objectives of indisputable value, it was alike clear to Harris and the Air Staff, were Germany's great industrial towns. The destruction of these would unquestionably impede the German war effort, and might at the same time undermine the morale of the whole population. And if, in the course of the attempt, Germany were left with not merely a passing but a permanent reminder of the folly of starting wars, so much the better. In this frame of mind, and with a calculated determination to resist all unnecessary diversions to other ends, Harris embraced his new task. Till then the Germans had escaped lightly. It would not be so in the future.

The force at Harris's disposal in February 1942, excluding five squadrons of light bombers unsuited for work over Germany, amounted to forty-four squadrons, of which thirty-eight were actually operational. Only fourteen of the forty-four were equipped with the new heavy bomber types—the Stirling, Manchester and Halifax—which had been slowly coming forward during 1941. All the rest were the old heavy bombers of 1940, now reclassified as 'medium'—the Wellingtons, Whitleys and Hampdens. Harris himself has recorded in his war memoirs[1]—a first class account of the bombing offensive enlivened by the author's characteristic sniping against his two favourite Aunt Sallies, the Admiralty and the Air Ministry—that on the day he took over, Bomber Command had 378 aircraft serviceable with crews; that about fifty of these were light bombers in No. 2 Group, mainly used as 'bait' in our fighter sweeps over France; and that only sixty-nine were heavy bombers. It was thus with a total force of some 600 aircraft and a normally available force of 300 that the new Commander-in-Chief began his long campaign against the cities of Germany.

Nearly a year later, at the end of January 1943, this force had increased by only seven squadrons, or about 200 aircraft. The drain to the Middle East, the diversions to Coastal Command, the

---

[1]*Bomber Offensive,* Sir Arthur Harris (Collins)

growing shortage of manpower, the entry of the United States into the war (with the Americans' natural resolve to create huge armed forces of their own rather than rest content with supplying ours)—all these things combined to shatter our hopes of building up a great bomber force in 1942. In fact, our plan to achieve a first-line strength of 4,000 heavy and medium bombers by mid-1943 was successively scaled down until all efforts were being concentrated on making fifty heavy and medium squadrons, or some 800 aircraft, operational by the end of 1942. And even this very modest total was not achieved until the spring of 1943.

But if the Command expanded slowly in terms of aircraft, it developed much more rapidly in terms of bomb-lift. At the beginning of 1942 our bombers were predominantly 'mediums'; a year later the 'heavies' made up over two-thirds of the force. During these vital twelve months the Whitleys and the Hampdens were at last honourably retired from Bomber Command, though they continued to operate long afterwards for Coastal. Among the light bombers the Blenheims gave way to newer types—to Bostons, Venturas and, above all, Mosquitos. Of the aircraft with which Bomber Command started the war, only the sturdy and well-loved 'Wimpies'—the Wellingtons—still droned their way over Germany at the end of 1942.[1]

This vital change, which increased our bomb-carrying capacity during the year by nearly seventy per cent, was carried out despite great difficulty with the new 'heavies'. The earliest of these, the four-engined Stirling, took too many men to produce and too many men to maintain. Its 'ceiling' of some 16,000 feet also exposed it to undue risks from anti-aircraft fire. The second type, the four-engined Halifax, at first seemed no better. The tail wheel gave constant trouble, the general performance was unsatisfactory, and many modifications were needed before the aircraft became—as it certainly did—reasonably good. Still worse was the third of the heavy bombers conceived in the great formative period of 1935 and 1936—the twin-engined Manchester. This had many good qualities, but was badly under-powered. Fortunately Avro's were able to re-design the air-frame for four engines; and so, through chance and the happy genius of Roy Chadwick, there soon emerged the Lancaster—the outstanding bomber of the war. Meanwhile the failure of the Manchester

---

[1] Bomber Command Blenheims operated for the last time on 17th/18th August, 1942, Whitleys (apart from aircraft in operational training units) on 29th/30th April, and Hampdens on 14th/15th September. Bomber Command Bostons operated for the first time on 12th February, Mosquitos on 31st May and Venturas on 3rd November.

slowed down the whole scheme of re-equipment.[1]

The expansion of Bomber Command in 1942 was slow enough. Even so, what was achieved would not have been possible without a drastic revision of the training schedule. It has been recorded earlier in this history that the 'export' of trained crews from Bomber Command to the Middle East, coupled with reductions in the length of training courses in the interests of higher output, had seriously impaired the efficiency of the bomber squadrons. In the spring of 1942 these problems were boldly confronted. The Air Member for Training, Air Marshal A. G. R. Garrod, proposed and carried what came to be known as the 'New Deal'. The basic feature of this was the decision, reluctantly accepted by Harris, that henceforth our bombers should carry only one pilot instead of two. This greatly reduced the number of pilots to be trained, and so made possible longer training courses. At the same time a number of compensatory measures were introduced, mainly on the suggestion of Harris. All bombers were to be equipped with automatic pilots; a flight-engineer was to be carried in the heavy bombers; one member of the crew other than the pilot would be given enough training to bring the aircraft back in emergency; and, since the observer (now renamed the navigator) would be too busy with 'Gee', an additional member of the crew would be needed to aim the bombs and act as front gunner. The training commitment for the two new aircrew categories, the flight-engineer and the bomb-aimer, was not so difficult to meet as that for two pilots, and the net gain was substantial. Moreover Harris himself proposed a further economy. It had by now been found that there was little occasion for two wireless-operator/air-gunners in each bomber. One of these posts was therefore filled by a 'straight' air-gunner, so saving many weeks of training in the wireless schools.

* * *

During the first six months of his regime—the vital period in which we expected to enjoy uninterrupted use of 'Gee'—Harris had at his disposal an average of only 250 serviceable medium bombers and fifty serviceable heavy bombers. With these he was expected, if not to shatter, at least to produce some noticeable impression on German morale. The attacking force might be small, but with 'Gee' every blow should strike home. The official view of the Air Staff was that in the opening phase Bomber Command would be able to blot out at least four of the cities of Western Germany.

[1] Manchesters operated for the first time on 24th/25th February, 1941, and for the last time on 25th/26th June, 1942. Lancasters (two aircraft only) operated over land for the first time on 10th/11th March, 1942.

While Harris was waiting for the right weather to begin this main assault, he essayed a subsidiary operation elsewhere. For many months the War Cabinet, reluctant to kill friendly civilians, had refused to permit attacks by night against industrial objectives in the occupied territories. Gradually opinion changed; and on 2nd February, 1942, impressed by the need to destroy German war capacity beyond as well as within the *Reich*, and hoping to deter French civilians from working for the enemy, our political leaders sanctioned night attacks on this type of target. This gave Bomber Command the opportunity to try out under favourable conditions at short range some of the tactical methods of attack, such as a liberal use of incendiaries, which were to be applied over Germany in conjunction with 'Gee'. On the night of 3rd/4th March, Harris accordingly despatched 235 bombers in good weather and perfect visibility against the great Renault factory at Billancourt, near Paris.

The attackers were divided into three waves: a vanguard of all 'heavies' for which fully trained crews were available, a main force of medium bombers, and a rear contingent of such Manchesters, Halifaxes and Wellingtons as were equipped for 4,000 lb. bombs. All aircraft were to carry as many flares as their bomb-loads allowed. The first wave was to light up the target, then bomb, then drop its remaining flares to windward. The second wave was to repeat this procedure, so that the target would be well illuminated the whole time. Two separate groups of buildings were to be attacked, the aircraft of No. 3 Group aiming at the works on an island in the Seine, the remainder at the main plant on the river bank.

The attack went almost exactly according to plan. All but twelve of the 235 bombers reached the target, at which they aimed 461 tons of bombs. The rate of concentration over the objective—a factor of prime importance in 'saturating' the defences, both active and passive, and so increasing damage and reducing our own casualties—worked out at 121 to the hour. This was the highest yet achieved.

Night photographs taken during the operation, reconnaissance the following day, reports from secret intelligence sources and post-war evidence all confirm that the raid was a great success. Disregarding most of the contemporary reports, which were exaggerated, we may accept two documents as sufficiently near the truth. The first of these is M. Louis Renault's report to the Germans. This was obtained for us through a Polish source within three months of the raid. Its estimate of damage was probably on the conservative side, as M. Renault would presumably be reluctant to have the Germans close the works and remove what remained of the machines to the *Reich*. The main damage, according to the French industrialist, was to buildings; but materials, tools and completed products also suffered. Apart from one or two shops that might be at work again in fifteen days, three months or more would be needed before production could be resumed. On the morning after the attack the works seemed completely destroyed: roofs were smashed, walls crumbled, framework overthrown. On the other hand only the machines situated at the points of impact were completely useless; the others could be used again after repair. Of the three thousand workmen on duty only five had been killed.[1]

The second document is the post-war report of the United States Strategic Bombing Survey Unit. According to this, 11·8 per cent of the total area of the plant was seriously affected. Of 14,746 machine tools in the factory, 721 were destroyed and 2,387 damaged; but many others, left roofless or moved into the open to permit clearance, deteriorated rapidly during the bad weather of the next few weeks. Among other achievements, several buildings containing designs, blue-prints and records were consumed by fire; and destruction, partial or complete, overtook 722 vehicles awaiting delivery. The effect on the morale of the workers was also very marked—during the following year the number on the evening shift shrank by nearly a half. Yet despite all this the previous level of production was regained, and indeed exceeded, within four months of the attack.

It was, as Harris points out in his book, somewhat ironical that he, the apostle of area-attack on Germany, should have scored his first great success against a precision target in France. Be that as it may, the raid, with two other successful efforts—against the Matford works at Poissy—within the next few days, acted as a much needed tonic to the bomber force. It was in the warm afterglow of these operations that Harris now struck the opening blow of the main campaign.

* * *

The directive of 14th February gave Bomber Command four primary and three secondary targets within 'Gee' range. Those in the first category—Essen, Duisburg, Düsseldorf and Cologne—were all in the vital Ruhr-Rhineland. Those in the second category—Bremen, Wilhelmshaven and Emden—were on the north-west coast, so giving Harris another chance when bad weather seemed likely over the Ruhr. When experience allowed or conditions were particularly favourable, the Commander-in-Chief might also attack a number of cities in alternative areas beyond 'Gee' range, including Hamburg, Kiel, Lübeck and Rostock in the North, Berlin in the centre, and Frankfurt, Schweinfurt and Stuttgart in the South. Each

[1] Several others, and their families, were killed in neighbouring houses.

of these was an important centre of industry. The general aiming point, however, was not to be a particular factory, but the most heavily built-up district.[1] Among all these areas that of the Ruhr was considered by the Ministry of Economic Warfare by far the most important, for it contained so many heavy industries and was so densely built-up that, according to the Ministry's official estimate, a bomb dropped there at random had 'an even chance of hitting some work of man'. And of all the towns of the Ruhr, the chief was Essen, with the great Krupps works sprawling heavily across it. It was against Essen, then, that Harris aimed the first blow of the new offensive.

The technique of attack had been worked out with great care. An advance force would drop flares for fifteen minutes, relying entirely on 'Gee' and ignoring visual impressions in order not to be misled by decoys. Two minutes after the first flares went down, other aircraft of the advance force would start bombing with incendiaries, taking as their aiming point the big square in the centre of the old town. After fifteen minutes the main force would begin to arrive, and would pile down its bombs on the fires already burning. The tactics, in other words, were to be a form of pathfinder/fire-raiser technique; but whatever the *Luftwaffe* had shown us of these methods in the autumn of 1940 was to be far surpassed. For even if the town was completely obscured by cloud, 'Gee', it was thought, would ensure that at least one bomb in two found its mark.

On the night of 8th/9th March conditions promised well, and 211 bombers, of which eighty-two were equipped with 'Gee', took off for the great attack. The first wave arrived punctually and duly dropped their flares on 'Gee' fixes. The weather held good, apart from the inevitable industrial haze. Unfortunately, many of the incendiaries were dropped after the flares had burnt out. Scattered fires therefore sprang up, and these seriously misled the main force. The result was that though 168 aircraft claimed to have bombed the target area, the brunt of the attack fell on the Southern outskirts. Many bombs also struck the neighbouring towns of Hamborn, Duisburg and Oberhausen. In the Essen area the local authorities noted the fall of 3,000 incendiaries and 127 high explosive bombs, and reported appreciable damage to engineering works, railways and houses. Krupps was virtually untouched.

---

[1] In view of later controversy over Harris's interpretation of this directive, it is worth quoting the following minute from the Chief of Air Staff to the Deputy Chief on 10th February, 1942: 'I suppose it is quite clear [to the C.-in-C.] that aiming points are to be the built-up areas, *not* for instance the dockyards or aircraft factories where these are mentioned'. The D.C.A.S. replied that he had specifically confirmed this point with Bomber Command by telephone.

Despite the favourable reports of crews, Harris at once realized that the raid was no more than a partial success; for none of the forty-three successful photographs taken during the operation showed any recognizable feature of the target area. On the following night he struck again, but once more much of the attack went astray. In this case a Stirling, hit by *flak*, jettisoned its incendiaries over Hamborn. Fires at once sprang up, and these were bombed by the following crews, who were unable to see their objective through the smoke and haze. Hamborn in fact received the main weight of bombs, and the great Thyssen steel works attracted what was meant for Krupps. Two other efforts against Essen before the end of the month were little more successful. On the first occasion the flare-dropping was too scattered, and a good part of the main force was led astray by an unsuspected decoy near Rheinberg. On the second, many of the crews were dazzled by the brilliance of their own flares.

Disappointing as they were, these raids on Essen were not without effect. Dr. Göbbels, for instance, found his plans somewhat disturbed. He had arranged an impressive funeral in Paris for the victims of the Renault raid; but he was now unable to make much of this in Germany, 'since there have also been heavy raids on the Ruhr which we cannot splash in the German press. The German people would consider it an insult and find it hard to understand if German newspapers shed tears for the Parisians but gave only a few lines to our own losses'. More important than the inconvenience of Dr. Göbbels or the actual damage inflicted was the fact that the raids afforded Bomber Command lessons of the highest value. Clearly we had expected too much of 'Gee'. What had seemed a device accurate enough for blind-bombing—or at least for blind-releasing of flares—was turning out to be simply an excellent aid to navigation. It could take our bombers within four or five miles of their objective and it could bring them home—both quite invaluable developments—but it had not obviated the need to identify the target with the human eye. And to do this was proving extremely difficult with the existing flare. Something was required which would not dazzle the bomb aimer, particularly when the brightness of the moon or the reflection from the industrial haze added to the general glare. Such a device was to be produced within a year, in the form of the hooded flare. Some guide to the main force more reliable than fires—which could be lit by the enemy—was also needed. It was to be supplied, within ten months, in the form of the target-indicator bomb.

By remorseless analysis of their failures Harris and his staff at Bomber Command—among whom special mention must be made of the extremely capable and popular Senior Air Staff Officer, Air

Vice-Marshal R. H. M. S. Saundby, and the Operational Research Section under Dr. B. G. Dickins—thus paved the way to eventual triumph. But failure, and the lessons to be derived from it, were by no means all that they could display from the first month's work. For if the opening attacks on Essen were a disappointment, operations outside the difficult Ruhr area showed much more promise. On 12th/13th March, 1942, for instance, fifty-three out of a force of sixty-eight Wellingtons attacked Kiel. The navigators derived great help from 'Gee', which they used up to the limit of its range. Among other successes bombs fell on the great ship-building yards of the Deutsche Werke and about 280 houses were badly damaged.[1] The most significant feature, however, was that though the raid was carried out in the moonless period the results equalled those previously achieved by comparable forces in bright moonlight. Still more encouraging was the attack on Cologne the following night. Photographs taken during the raid showed large fires raging in the Deutz marshalling yards and the built-up areas of the city, while the crews' reports of heavy damage were fully confirmed by agents and by daylight reconnaissance. The local police recorded 237 fires and damage to 1,691 houses.

All this was soon to be overshadowed by the great raid of 28th/29th March. Lübeck, one of the old Hansa ports on the Baltic, was an alternative target well beyond 'Gee' range. It was selected for attack for three main reasons. In the first place, there were so many old wooden houses in the town that it was highly vulnerable to fire; and Harris, who was under pressure from the Air Staff to employ an all-incendiary form of attack was accordingly less unwilling to do so against Lübeck than against the brick cities of the Ruhr. Secondly, we had not thus far raided Lübeck in force, and its anti-aircraft defences were comparatively light. Thirdly, the Baltic ice was beginning to break up, and the Germans would soon be using the port once more for supplying their armies in North Russia and Scandinavia and importing iron ore from Sweden. In addition, the town contained industries of some importance, a depot for military stores, and a training centre for submarine crews.

The general plan of attack was similar to that employed against

---

[1] All statistics of damage to German houses are taken from the local police records. The figures exclude houses which suffered damage only to roofs and windows.

[2] 30 lb. and 250 lb. incendiary bombs were now available besides the old 4 lb. bomb. Neither of the new weapons, however, was a great success. The 250 lb. bomb broke up on impact with only partial ignition and was soon withdrawn from use. The 30 lb. bomb gave off dense black fumes which concealed the target from later aircraft; it proved suitable only for the final stages of the attack. Despite bad ballistics the 4 lb. bomb thus remained the best incendiary weapon in 1942, and indeed throughout the war. After May 1942 a 4 lb. incendiary bomb with an explosive charge also did good work.

Essen, except that nearly half the bomb-load consisted of incendiaries.[2] The moon was bright and visibility excellent, and in the absence of strong defences the raiders were able to press their attacks home from low level. Of the 234 crews despatched, 191 claimed to have bombed the target; night photographs and subsequent daylight reconnaissance fully confirmed their assertion that they had left the town completely ablaze. In all some 300 tons of bombs including 144 tons of incendiaries fell on the built-up area, more than 200 acres of which were utterly devastated. The central power station was destroyed, many valuable warehouses and factories obliterated, the main railway workshops badly damaged. Buildings of historic interest also perished in the general holocaust. German records show that 1,918 buildings were completely destroyed and 5,928 damaged, with the result that 15,707 people lost their homes. No goods could be sent through the town or the port for the next three weeks.

The impression made by the Lübeck raid can be seen from Göbbels' diary. 'This Sunday has been thoroughly spoiled by an exceptionally heavy air raid by the R.A.F. on Lübeck', he recorded on 27th March. 'I was informed of the seriousness of the situation by a long-distance call from Kaufmann. He believes that no German city has ever before been attacked so severely from the air. Conditions in parts of Lübeck are chaotic. . . . Immediately afterwards the *Führer* called me from G.H.Q. and was very much put out about the negligence of the Ministry of the Interior, which did not even succeed in calling departmental heads together on Sunday evening to discuss the necessary relief measures. . . . I telephoned several times to Kaufmann, who gave me a vivid description of the destruction. Eighty per cent of the old part of the city must be considered lost . . .'. A week later Göbbels was still harping on the same theme. 'The damage is really enormous', runs the entry for 4th April, 'I have been shown a newsreel of the destruction. It is horrible. One can well imagine how such an awful bombardment affects the population. Thank God it is a North German population. . . . Nevertheless we can't get away from the fact that the English air raids have increased in scope and importance; if they can be continued for weeks on these lines, they might conceivably have a demoralizing effect on the population. . . '.

The German population, with its natural powers of endurance stimulated by fear of the Gestapo, was tougher than either Göbbels or the Air Staff imagined. The expected demoralization did not occur. Nor was it yet possible to send our bombers to 'Lübeck' a German town every night, or even every week. And the five per cent loss incurred in raiding the Baltic port, though light in relation to the results achieved, was higher than we could consistently sustain if Bomber Command was to develop, as we intended, into a truly formidable engine of war.

The success at Lübeck was not equalled in Western Germany. During the first three weeks of April Harris struck at Dortmund, Essen, Cologne and Hamburg, but to little effect. This was mainly because of bad weather over the targets, combined, in the case of the two Ruhr towns, with the invariable industrial haze—obstacles which 'Gee' was not accurate enough to overcome. In the moon period at the end of the month, however, our raiding forces, normally about 100 aircraft strong, obtained much better results. On the night of 27th/28th April an attack on Cologne destroyed Government buildings, motor factories, important railway offices and much residential and commercial property. The following night a raid on Kiel heavily damaged the Germania ship-yards. But once again the most successful operations of the month were far beyond the range of 'Gee', against another lightly defended port on the Baltic.

The decision to attack Rostock on the night of 23rd/24th April was dictated mainly by the weather. The sky was clear, with a bright moon, and in such conditions our crews stood a good chance of reaching and identifying a distant and unfamiliar target. The general attractions of the place from the bombing point of view included the busy port area, the submarine building yards, and a large plant on the outskirts where Heinkel aircraft were assembled. In accordance with a growing practice of aiming at one precise objective as well as the main built-up area, this plant was given as a special target to selected crews of No. 5 Group. The rest of the 161 bombers were to concentrate on the town as a whole.

The raid was a great success. As the weather remained favourable, repeat performances were accordingly staged the next three nights. All told, 468 of the 521 crews despatched during the four attacks claimed to have reached the target and to have dropped between them 305 tons of incendiaries and 442 tons of high explosive. The effects were certainly impressive. The Heinkel factory was severely hit; if agents' reports may be trusted the destruction included forty-five complete or nearly complete aircraft. 'Reliable sources' also reported that the town was without gas, water or electricity for eighteen days, and that the killed and severely wounded numbered some 6,000. Our own photographs made it clear that over seventy per cent of the old town had been entirely devastated, apart from destruction elsewhere. The cost on our side was twelve bombers.

If Göbbels had been alarmed and angered by Lübeck, he was made positively livid by Rostock. 'It has been, it must be admitted, pretty disastrous', he noted after the second night. 'The anti-aircraft didn't function properly, so that damage to public buildings was more extensive than in all other English air raids since Lübeck. . . . The *Führer* is in extremely bad humour about the poor anti-aircraft defence . . . the *Luftwaffe* wasn't adequately prepared, and this alone made the damage to the Heinkel works possible'. The third raid brought further comments. 'Last night the heaviest air attack yet launched had the seaport of Rostock once again as its objective. Tremendous damage is reported . . . all long-distance communication has been interrupted . . . seventy per cent of all houses in the centre of Rostock are said to have been destroyed. I now consider it absolutely essential that we continue with our rigorous reprisal raids[1] . . . Like the English, we must attack centres of culture, especially those which have only little anti-aircraft. . . . At noon I had lunch with the *Führer*. He is very angry about the latest English attack on Rostock. But he also gave me a few figures about our attack on Bath. . . . The *Führer* declared that he would repeat these raids night after night until the English were sick and tired of terror attacks. He shares my opinion absolutely that cultural centres, health resorts and civilian centres must be attacked now. . . . There is no other way of bringing the English to their senses. They belong to a class of human beings with whom you can talk only after you have first knocked out their teeth'. On 28th April, after the fourth attack, the Propaganda Minister's comments were more severely factual. 'The air raid last night on Rostock was even more devastating than those before. Community life there is practically at an end. . . . The situation in the city is in some sections catastrophic'. Two days later Göbbels received the final report from the local *Gauleiter*. 'Seven tenths of the city have been wiped out. More than 100,000 people had to be evacuated. . . . There was, in fact, panic . . .'.

There was one other outstanding operation in April 1942. With the four-fold object of maintaining pressure against the German fighter force in France, forcing the enemy to disperse his defences, helping in the Battle of the Atlantic and trying out the capacities of the new Lancasters, Harris on 17th April 'laid on' a daylight raid into Southern Germany. The objective was the M.A.N. Diesel Engine Works at Augsburg, the raiding force twelve Lancasters of Nos. 44 and 97 Squadrons led by a South African, Squadron Leader J. D. Nettleton. The plan was for the attacking aircraft to penetrate deep into France and feint for Munich before finally turning for Augsburg. To defeat the enemy radar they would fly at 500 feet until

[1] The German 'Baedeker' raids had begun two nights earlier (24th/25th April).

south of Paris; and other aircraft could help by making diversionary raids against targets in Rouen, Cherbourg, and the Pas de Calais. The attack itself would be delivered at low level with 1,000 lb. bombs fused for eleven seconds' delay.

The Lancasters set off in mid-afternoon, so that most of the return flight could be made in the dark. Unfortunately the diversions were not wholly successful: they served to alert rather than distract the defences in France. Five minutes after Nettleton and his comrades crossed the French coast they were intercepted by twenty-five to thirty German fighters. The first two sections bore the brunt of the attack. Four of these six bombers were shot down in a long running fight which lasted a full hour. But Nettleton and one other survived, and with the second two sections, who had suffered no losses, managed at length to shake clear of the enemy. Apart from *flak* over an airfield, they then met no further opposition until, flying at 'tree-top' height, they neared their objective. Sweeping in so low that the local anti-aircraft gunners knocked down several chimney pots in attempting to shoot them down, they achieved virtually complete surprise. All eight aircraft managed to drop their bombs, seventeen of which hit the target. As the Lancasters roared away, the inhabitants of Augsburg—who according to a German report regarded the attack as 'precision bombing of the highest quality'—saw one of the raiders on fire, heading down towards open ground. The crew were making desperate signs to onlookers to move clear. Two more of the attackers also succumbed to *flak* in the target area. No further losses were sustained on the way home, and the five surviving machines, Nettleton's still among them, eventually regained base in the early hours of the following morning. Every one bore the scars of conflict. The cost was thus severe; but the Lancasters had certainly left their mark on the factory. Though five of the seventeen bombs had failed to explode, the rest wrought havoc in two machine-tool shops, a forging shop and the main assembly shop. Nevertheless, only three per cent of the machine-tools in the whole plant were put out of action.

The repercussions from this gallant venture were not confined to Germany. The extreme daring and skill of the attack were at once recognized on all sides in England, and were signalized by the award of the Victoria Cross to Squadron Leader Nettleton. Several of the other survivors received the D.S.O., D.F.C. or D.F.M., and congratulatory signals—from the Prime Minister, the Commander-in-Chief and the Chief of Naval Staff among many others—poured in on the two Squadrons. On the other hand there was no small volume of criticism against the choice of objective. This came particularly from the

Ministry of Economic Warfare. The Minister, Lord Selborne, addressed a strong protest to Mr. Churchill against the decision to attack a Diesel engine factory when this type of plant was not amongst the six classes of precise objective most strongly recommended by the Ministry. The factory at Augsburg, Lord Selborne maintained, was not specially vulnerable; and even if the whole plant had been wiped out Germany would still have had ample Diesel engine capacity. Harris would have done better, the Minister suggested, to attack certain other targets; and if he had to operate near Augsburg there was always the great ball-bearing factory at Schweinfurt. To this Harris—who had kept his intentions as secret from the Air Ministry as from the Ministry of Economic Warfare—was able to offer a spirited defence. He explained the general motives behind the attack, all of which accorded fully with his directive. He demonstrated that the M.A.N. factory was on his official list, and that it was classed as an objective whose destruction would greatly aid the struggle against the U-boats. He also stressed the importance of tactical considerations, such as the need to choose a compact, easily recognizable target with good land-marks leading to it. Schweinfurt would certainly not have filled the bill in this respect. The Commander-in-Chief's letter apparently convinced the Prime Minister, who in passing it to Lord Selborne referred to it as an 'excellent reply', and characteristically suggested that the affronted Minister should ask Harris to lunch. On the broadest aspect of the operation, however, Harris was as dissatisfied as his critics. Seven out of twelve Lancasters was not a price that he could pay very often for damaging a particular factory. Penetration of the German homeland in daylight was still as difficult as ever: the Lancasters had got away with it little better than the Wellingtons in 1940 or the Blenheims in 1941. The experiment was well worth making, but it had failed; and not until the Mosquitos became available later in the year did Harris attempt further daylight operations against German targets. Even then such attacks were mainly confined to single aircraft working under cover of cloud.

The Augsburg raid caused a storm in a teacup. Of much greater significance was another question under debate at about the same time—the merits of incendiary attack. The Air Staff had for some months regarded fire as the best weapon for attacking cities, and the outstanding success of the operations against Lübeck and Rostock had naturally confirmed them in their view. Harris, on the other hand, had come to Bomber Command with a profound faith in the virtues of high explosive, particularly when it was delivered in big bombs designed for the greatest possible blast effect. At the beginning of the war we had had no such weapons in our armoury; but now the 4,000 lb. and the new 8,000 lb. high capacity bombs offered Harris the chance to put his theories into practice.[1] His expressed conviction—as he put it in a letter to the Air Ministry a few weeks after his appointment—was 'that we had to kill a lot of Boches before we win this war'; and for this purpose fire alone seemed to him inadequate. When the Air Staff invoked the charred ruins of Lübeck, Harris countered that the Baltic city's old wooden houses made it 'more like a firelighter than a human habitation'. His contention that high explosive had a detrimental effect on morale could also hardly be questioned. The Bomber Chief could not, however, ignore photographic comparisons of the two types of damage in Cologne. In the end a compromise was reached: the Air Staff, who had begun to visualize bomb loads consisting entirely of incendiaries, agreed to a normal load of two-thirds incendiaries and one-third high explosive. Such a division could not always be achieved in practice, owing to technical difficulties in loading; but the Air Staff's wisdom in insisting on a high proportion of incendiaries soon became plain. Within less than a year an investigation showed that whereas 8,000 lb. H.C bombs had destroyed or damaged on the average 1¾ acres of built-up property for every ton dropped, and 4,000 lb. H.C. bombs a little less, each ton of incendiaries had laid waste no less than 3¼ acres.

The opening weeks of May were marked by much bad weather over Western Germany, and for some nights Harris was forced to concentrate on other areas. As it happened he had now been instructed to give more attention to the German aircraft industry, and particularly to those plants manufacturing fighters. This was in the interests of the Russians and our own projected return to the Continent. In conformity with these directions Harris now attacked Stuttgart and Warneümnde. Both of these contained important aircraft plants, while in Stuttgart there was also the Bosch magneto factory. The attacks were moderately successful and resulted in damage to all the main objectives. In the middle of May the weather then became so bad that, sea-mining apart, operations by the night bomber force virtually ceased. This, however, only helped the Command to prepare for the great venture now scheduled for the end of the month—the first raid by a thousand bombers.

* * *

The idea of a blow many times more massive than any yet attemp-

[1] The first 4,000 lb. H.C. bomb was dropped on 30th March, 1941; the first 8,000 lb. H.C. bomb on 10th February, 1942. For the development of these and other bombs Air Commodore P. Huskinson's book 'Vision Ahead' (Werner Laurie 1949) is amusing and informative.

ted in the history of air warfare was Harris's own. Even the code name—Operation 'Millennium'—was, in its grim irony, entirely characteristic of the Commander-in-Chief. The whole conception, too, was one of singular daring completely worthy of its author. Up to this time the largest force despatched by Bomber Command against a single target had been 228 aircraft; and the average number of medium and heavy bombers available was no more than 350. To direct 1,000 bombers on a single night against a single town would thus be not only novel, but on the face of it, impossible. It could be done only by husbanding all efforts for some nights beforehand and by bringing into action the bombers from the Operational Training Units. Some of these could be flown by instructors, but others would have to carry a crew of pupils. In any case training would be seriously impeded; and if things went badly wrong both the entire front line and the training organization behind it might suffer a set-back from which recovery would be difficult, if not impossible. On the other hand, lessons of the highest value might be learnt; and in particular the tactics of 'saturating' the defences by heavy concentration over a single target within a short time could be tried out to the full. Moreover, the results of the attack might be so impressive that they would allay all opposition—of which there was plenty—to the creation of a large bomber force.

Harris had no difficulty in convincing the Air Staff and the Prime Minister of the merits of his plan, and it was with a light heart that, after receiving the approval of the latter late one night at Chequers, he drove back home in the early hours of the morning. His headlights, as usual, blazed away unmasked; and he has recorded that, inspired as ever by the Churchillian courage and verve, he found himself humming *Malbrouck s'en-va-t-en-guerre*. There followed a period of intensive preparation. By mobilising all suitable aircraft from Operational Training Units and the Conversion Flights where crews already proficient on twin-engined aircraft learnt to handle the 'heavies', and by manning these aircraft with instructors or pupil crews near the end of their training, Harris hoped to bring his operational strength up to 700 aircraft. The balance he at first thought would have to come from other Commands; and in response to his appeal, Coastal, Flying Training and Army Co-operation Commands all offered substantial contributions. Joubert at Coastal Command alone offered some 250 aircraft. But the response from Harris's own operational and training groups was so overwhelming that he was able to raise the required total of 1,000 aircraft from entirely within his own resources. In the event, only four aircraft from another Command—Flying Training Command—took part in the actual attack, though Fighter Command and Army Co-operation Command helped by raiding German airfields.

In view of the size of the force and the inexperience of many of the crews, the objective had to be one which was reasonably close at hand and easily identifiable, and the raid had to be carried out in bright moonlight. The two obvious possibilities were Hamburg and Cologne, with the final choice between them depending on the weather. The attack was tentatively fixed for the night of 27th/28th May, two nights before full moon, and all aircraft were to be at their allotted airfields by 26th May. The administrative problems raised by this were formidable. If the choice fell on Cologne, as in fact happened, the assault was planned to last for ninety minutes. The first fifteen minutes would be devoted to attack by all aircraft of Nos. 1 and 3 Groups equipped with 'Gee'; and the last fifteen minutes would be given over to the 'heavies' of Nos. 4 and 5 Groups —and to photography and visual observation by eight selected crews. In between, distributed evenly, would come the great bulk of the force. All aircraft were to carry the maximum load of incendiaries, including the new 4 lb. explosive bomb. Nos. 1 and 3 Groups, and aircraft operating with them, were given an aiming point in the centre of the town; Nos. 4 and 92 (O.T.U.) Groups were to aim at a point about one mile to the north of this; and Nos. 5 and 91 (O.T.U.) Groups at a corresponding point about one mile to the south. As the moon would be full, flares and markers were not considered necessary. Aircraft unable to identify Cologne were to set course for Essen, and as a last resort to bomb any built-up area in the Ruhr. A carefully-planned route was laid down, and the crews were left in no doubt of the importance of keeping strictly to the prescribed time table.

On the night of 27th/28th May, the provisional date for the attack, thundery conditions and much cloud over the Continent caused the operation to be postponed. The next night the weather was much the same, and it was possible to carry out only a minor mission over France and a little minelaying. On 30th May, good weather was promised at home bases, but over Germany thundery clouds still persisted. Only the Rhineland offered any hope of a successful attack. The force could not stand by indefinitely. Seizing the chance of landing the vast armada back again in clear weather, and accepting the risk that the target would be covered with cloud and the whole operation prove a fiasco, at midday Harris decided to strike that night against Cologne.

The afternoon turned to evening. On fifty-two airfields the bombers stood waiting. Dusk fell, and their engines awoke to life. One by one the great machines roared down the runways, rose strongly aloft, and set course for the target. Wellingtons, Whitleys and Hampdens—veterans whose days or rather nights of bombing activity were now nearing their end—made up the bulk of the force, numbering in all 708. With them were 338 of the new Stirlings, Halifaxes, Manchesters and Lancasters. Of the total force of 1,046 aircraft, no less than 367 came from the training groups; and of these 259—hitherto regarded as a great force in itself—came from No. 91 Group. While the bomber stream wound its way across the North Sea, fifty aircraft of No. 2 Group and of Fighter and Army Co-operation Commands took off for their part in the attack. 'Intruding' over airfields in France, Belgium, Holland and Western Germany, they maintained their diversion until after the last bomb had fallen on Cologne.

Over the North Sea the bomber stream was now forging through thick clouds and many aircraft were troubled by the weight of ice on their wings. But when Holland was reached the cloud began to break up, and by the time the raiding aircraft sighted Cologne, plainly visible through the *flak* and the glare of the searchlights, the skies were clear except for small wisps of cirrus. At 0047 hours—seven minutes ahead of schedule—the first bombs went down, and at 0225 hours—exactly on time—the last. Apart from some overlapping of the waves everything went according to plan. 'Gee' took the first wave near enough for the crews to identify the target visually in the bright moon. The second and third waves had no difficulty in recognizing the town in the light of the fires started by the first arrivals. The defences were duly 'saturated'. Fighters, *flak* and searchlights were all active, but much less so as the attack progressed; indeed after the first three-quarters of an hour they became, according to the crews, 'weak and confused'. In all, 898 crews claimed to have reached and attacked the target, dropping between them 1,455 tons of bombs, of which nearly two-thirds were incendiaries. High standards of accuracy were achieved—the Air Officer Commanding No. 3 Group (Air Vice-Marshal J. E. A. Baldwin), who personally accompanied his crews in one of the first wave Stirlings, reported fires within half a mile of the aiming point even before his aircraft arrived on the scene. As the last of the bombers turned for home, huge conflagrations were blazing throughout the entire target area. More than 150 miles away they were still plainly visible to our crews.

Early the next morning four Mosquitos of No. 2 Group, in the first bombing operation undertaken by this type of aircraft, penetrated to the stricken city. Their instructions were to deliver a harassing attack and photograph the effects of the previous night's raid. They found fires blazing on all sides and smoke so dense that photography was impossible. Later reconnaissance succeeded in bringing back clear evidence of the chaos beneath. Over 600 acres of the built-up area were completely destroyed—nearly as much as all previous devastation in all the towns of Germany added together. Some 250 factories appeared to be destroyed or seriously damaged, among them metal works, rubber works, blast furnaces, chemical works, an oil storage plant and railway workshops, besides various plants manufacturing submarine engines, accumulators, under-carriages, rolling stock and machine tools. Bombs had also fallen on the Police Headquarters and the Central Telephone Exchange. To this impressive if somewhat statistical picture flesh-and-blood interest was added by reports from intelligence sources. Some of the more sober of these recorded a complete breakdown in the emergency feeding and first aid measures, a drastic reduction in rail, telegraphic and telephonic communication between Cologne and the outside world, and a wave of indignation against the Nazi leaders.

Ample confirmation of all this—except the wave of indignation—is contained in the final report of the raid submitted by *Gauleiter* Grohe to Chief of Police Himmler. This records that 486 persons were killed, 5,027 injured and 59,100 rendered homeless. 18,432 houses, flats, workshops, public buildings and the like were completely destroyed, 9,516 heavily damaged and 31,070 damaged less severely. There was serious interference with the power supply—fifty per cent of the main cables were hit—the gas and water supply, the tramway system and the harbour installations; and the railway repair shops employing 2,500 workers were completely obliterated. Thirty-six Post Offices, including three telephone exchanges, were also destroyed or damaged. The businesses entirely destroyed numbered 484, while 328 industrial plants—about half the total number in the city—suffered in varying degrees. The loss in the larger factories, it was thought, would amount to between three and nine months' production. 'The immense number of incendiary bombs dropped' had caused some 12,000 fires, of which 2,500 had been major outbreaks. As for measures of restoration, 3,500 soldiers, 2,000 prisoners of war and 10,000 labourers had been drafted in to clear the streets and carry out urgent repairs. As a result almost all routes, except in the city centre, were able to function under temporary repair within ten days of the attack. To help in this process of recovery the schoolchildren were at once sent on holiday, for all school buildings still in existence were needed as emergency centres. Finally, the report gave a grim pointer to the excellence of German morale. 'Measures necessary for the keeping of security were taken by the Justice-Administration. The punishable offences committed have been dealt with at once, and have been judged within twenty-

BEFORE AND AFTER—THE 1,000-BOMBER RAID ON COLOGNE

A factory at Deutz, on the east bank of the Rhine

four hours. So far, only one person had to pay the death penalty: the execution was carried out on the very day of passing judgment . . .'.

The cost of Operation 'Millennium' was light considering the untried hazards of the venture. Forty aircraft of the 1,046 and two of the fifty engaged on intruder work failed to return. In addition 116 aircraft suffered damage, twelve so badly that they were 'written off'. Most of the missing aircraft succumbed to *flak*, but at least two were destroyed in collision. Strangely enough the aircraft from the operational groups suffered a somewhat higher rate of loss than the aircraft from the training groups; and among the latter the number of pupils lost (49) was little greater than that of the instructors (40). The rate of loss as a whole was 3·8 per cent—a shade higher than the normal 3·5 per cent against Cologne in the preceding few months, but appreciably lower than the corresponding over-all rate of 4·6 per cent against Western Germany in conditions of cloudless moonlight.

The experiment had thus justified itself to the full. Great damage had been wrought, the loss had been well within bounds, the tactics of 'saturation' had proved a brilliant success. The task ahead was now clear, if formidable—to build up a force which could achieve equal results, not on an odd night or two at the expense of the training organization, but systematically; not against easily identifiable targets in North Germany or the Rhineland alone, but in any quarter of the *Reich;* and not merely in clear moonlight, but in pitch dark and thick cloud.

The entry of 31st May in Göbbels' diary has unfortunately not been preserved. It would doubtless have made interesting reading.

* * *

If 'Millennium' were a success, Harris intended to take advantage of the full moon and the large force already assembled to deliver a second blow the next night. The weather, however, proved unsuitable. The following night the forecast still left much to be desired. But the force could not be kept standing by much longer, and Harris decided to strike where there was least likelihood of low cloud. At nightfall on 1st June, 956 aircraft including 347 from the Operational Training Units accordingly took off against Essen. By the time they got there a layer of thin cloud had shrouded the city. The attack was therefore very scattered compared with that against Cologne. Heavy damage was done in neighbouring towns, notably Oberhausen and Mülheim, but Essen itself escaped lightly and Krupps was once again almost untouched. But though the raiding force failed to achieve an effective concentration it was more than the German defences could cope with. Only thirty-one aircraft (3·2 per cent) failed to return from the most strongly defended district in all Germany.

Raids on this scale, however desirable as an experiment, naturally aroused expectations—on both sides of the North Sea—which could not yet be fulfilled. The British public, eagerly adopting the '1,000 bomber' level as a normal standard, suffered acute disappointment when smaller forces continued to go forth; for the means by which 1,000 bombers had been collected together were naturally not proclaimed from the housetops. In fact only one more raid of this magnitude was attempted in 1942, when 1,006 bombers (including 272 from Operational Training Units and 102 from Coastal Command) took off to attack Bremen on the night of 25th/26th June. Once again, as at Essen, a layer of cloud intervened between the force and its objective. Most aircraft in the first wave bombed blind on 'Gee', and the glow of the fires thus caused, reflected in the cloud, provided the main means of identification for the rest of the force. Serious damage was done at the Focke-Wulf works, and about twenty-seven acres of the business and residential area were completely destroyed. Forty-nine aircraft, however, or five per cent of the force despatched, failed to return—more than in either of the other big attacks. Among these were twenty-two aircraft of No. 91 (O.T.U.) Group, all but one manned by pupil crews.

Despite this warning Harris decided to continue using the Operational Training Units against the nearer or more easily recognized targets. By this means he hoped to mount two or three raids each month of the order of 700 to 1,000 sorties, reserving this effort for the few really fine nights. On the remaining nights activity would be limited to small-scale raids and minelaying. As it happened, however, it was on only one night during the next three months that he managed to put into the air a force exceeding 500 aircraft. His scheme was defeated by the weather, the rising casualties, and the obvious harm which was being done to the training organization.

Apart from the three great raids already mentioned, only four operations over Germany involving the use of Operational Training Units were in fact mounted. These were against Düsseldorf on the nights of 31st July/1st August and 10th/11th September, and against Essen on the nights of 13th/14th and 16th/17th September. Against Düsseldorf, a readily identifiable target at the junction of Ruhr and Rhine, outstandingly successful results were achieved. On the first occasion the raiding force, 630 bombers strong, included 211 aircraft from the Training Units; on the second, 174 aircraft from the Training Units helped to make up a total force of 476. On both nights the Training Units suffered a higher rate of loss than the Squadrons. The two raids on Essen, both carried out by a force of some 400 aircraft—of which about one-third came from the O.T.U.'s—were again frustrated by bad weather and haze.

Raids of this size were exceptional efforts. In general Harris was compelled by the uncertain weather to employ over the *Reich* only the normal operational squadrons. With these he achieved a high rate of effort, despatching forces of the order of 200 aircraft ten times in June. The usual lack of success, coupled with high losses (6·6 per cent) met all attempts to bomb Essen, but good results were obtained at low cost against the more easily located towns of Emden and Bremen. In the last raid against Bremen during the month, 184 aircraft relying only on their 'Gee' fixes released their bombs within twenty-three minutes. This was the highest rate of concentration yet achieved.

In July there were again ten major attacks, carried out by average forces of some 300 aircraft. They resulted in heavy damage at Wilhelmshaven, where the Deutsche Werke again suffered, at Hamburg, where the shipyards of Blohm and Voss and the Deutsche Werft were affected, and at Saarbrücken, where many bombs fell on iron and engineering works. Good results were also obtained against Duisburg and its adjoining towns. Two daylight raids by Lancasters against shipyards at Lübeck and Danzig—the most distant objectives ever attacked in day by our heavy bombers—met with no great success, but avoided heavy casualties.

Though Harris was not using the O.T.U. crews as often as he had hoped, he was thus getting somewhere. Ten raids a month by forces of 200 to 300 aircraft was no small contribution towards victory, particularly as most of the bombs were now falling where they were intended—attacks against Essen always excepted. But the Commander-in-Chief remained keenly dissatisfied with existing methods of illuminating and marking, and uncomfortably aware how much still depended on clear weather over the target. He was also worried by the mounting losses. Many of the attacks had been carried out economically; but others, notably against Essen on 8th/9th June and Hamburg on 27th/28th July, had cost over ten per cent of the force despatched. For the Germans had not ignored the deadly threat implicit in the first 1,000 bomber raid. Everywhere their defences—*flak*, fighters, radar stations, searchlights—were being improved and multiplied. Such developments were unquestionably both a tribute to Bomber Command and an advantage to hard-pressed Russia. But if they proceeded unchecked they could well bring the whole bombing offensive to a standstill, or at least ensure that it grew no more powerful.

So, as the summer of 1942 wore on, Harris continued to address himself to the same essential problems. First, how to get a force of a size equal to the task of destroying at least fifty of Germany's major towns. Secondly, having got it, how to put so many bombers in so short a time over the desired objective that the defenders were helpless. Thirdly, how to do this on moonless nights, when the enemy's night fighters were badly handicapped. By September, despite the failure of exaggerated hopes attached to 'Gee', Harris was nearer to these ideals than at the reopening of the campaign in March. But there was still a long way to go before the bomber force attained either the size that the Air Staff had visualized and the War Cabinet approved, or the accuracy without which size was merely wasteful.

CHAPTER VIII
The Pressure Grows

THE bombardment of Germany by night was not our only means of increasing the pressure on the enemy. When the end of the winter policy of 'conservation' was announced in March 1942 our fighters and light bombers were once more unleashed in full force against objectives on the other side of the Channel. For the Air Staff still hoped to inflict heavy casualties on the German fighters; and the Russians, soon to suffer the shock of another German summer offensive, were certainly in dire need of any help that we could give.

From March to the end of June we waged this cross-Channel offensive with relentless vigour. By day our fighters and light bombers flew the combined sweeps known as 'Circuses', by night they 'intruded' against enemy airfields. Altogether during these four months some 22,000 fighter sorties, or an average of 180 a day, penetrated the German defences in France and Belgium. Over three hundred—three a day—did not return. In the same period the Bostons and Blenheims of No. 2 Group, without whose company our fighters were completely unable to sting the enemy into action, flew some 700 cross-Channel sorties by day for the loss of eleven aircraft. As against a total loss of 314 fighters and bombers, we thought we had destroyed at least 205 of the machines which came up to meet us; but in fact the Germans lost only 90. The balance of casualties thus swung in favour of the enemy even more markedly than in 1941, doubtless because he took care to deploy his latest and fastest fighters—the F.W.190's—on this front. Even so the offensive had the cardinal merits not only of keeping two of Germany's best fighter *Geschwader* at full stretch but also of preserving for us in Western Europe all the moral and other advantages of the initiative.

One of the fighter sorties flown during this period—an individual mission aside from the main operations—has become almost legendary. We had discovered that a company of German troops paraded each day at noon down the Champs-Elysées. Someone at once conceived the idea of sending over one of our aircraft to brighten up this depressing ceremony. Only a fighter stood any chance of getting there, shooting up the parade, and getting back again; among the fighters only the Beaufighters of Coastal Command had the necessary qualities of long range and no secret radar equipment; and among the Beaufighters of Coastal Command a volunteer crew was readily found in the persons of Flight Lieutenant A. K. Gatward and Sergeant G. Fern of No. 236 Squadron. When volunteering, these two men knew only that they were offering to fly 'a hazardous and out of the ordinary single-aircraft mission'. Had they known the nature of the operation and the fact that the original plan of shooting up the parade had now been supplemented by the inspired notion of throwing out a *tricolore* as a parting gesture, their keenness to participate would, if possible, have been even greater than it was.

On 5th May Gatward and Fern learned the details of their mission. They were to carry out the attack only if good cloud-cover extended the whole way from the French coast to Paris. The two men at once began their preparations, making feint attacks each day on an old wreck in the Channel and poring for many hours over maps of Northern France and photographs of Paris. Very soon came the next step. 'One day', records Gatward, 'we went down to the naval dockyard at Portsmouth and drew a very new and grand-looking Tricolour for which we signed several forms. Back at Thorney Island we cut the flag into two and got the parachute section to sew iron bars on to each. In the evenings when few people were around we made tests with the flags, throwing them as high up as the hangar roof to see how they would unfurl when dropped from the air. We soon discovered the best way to fold them. . . .'

On 13th May the weather for the first time promised well. Half an hour before noon the Beaufighter took off. But it had no sooner crossed the French coast than the clouds cleared, and in obedience to their instructions the two men turned back. Two days later they tried again, with the same result. Twice more in the next fortnight they were again baulked; on each occasion the skies cleared when they were well over French territory. Gatward's patience was by then exhausted. As he took the Beaufighter up for the fifth time, on 12th June, he was determined to get through at all costs. How he did so he has himself related:

> The forecast was for cloud but it had broken up when we got there [i.e. to the French coast]. This time we carried on. We flew close to the deck all the way, rarely more than a hundred feet up and often as low as thirty feet. We cruised in at about 220 m.p.h., hedge-hopping over trees and buildings and navigating with a map. Fern did a difficult job magnificently and guided me straight into Paris on course.

The parade was timed for midday. Just before noon we picked up the shape of the Eiffel Tower and at 1202 we were over the Champs-Elysées. I climbed up to 300 feet and banked for the attack. But there was no parade. The boulevards were almost deserted. Somehow the Germans had learned of our mission.

Filled with rage and frustration we dived on to the Champs-Elysées, roared along at below roof-top height and climbed over the Arc de Triomphe. As we flashed past the Arc, Sergeant Fern flung the flags out through the flare chute. They went out rather like harpoons and that was the last we saw of them. By now we were approaching the Place de la Concorde and the Gestapo headquarters in the Ministry of Marine building. This was my secondary target and as we passed I sprayed the place with cannon. We got a glimpse of terrified sentries running for their lives and then we were on our way home. We flew back to the coast as low as we had come but met no ack-ack or enemy fighters. We got away with the whole operation scot-free. The only incident was a minor collision with a big crow which crashed into our starboard radiator. Apart from that our only opposition came from swarms of small flies which, low flying, we had collected in a solid mass on our wind-shield. By the time we got back to Northolt it was getting quite difficult to see through them . . .

* * *

This tonic for French morale, administered by a single aircraft, was at one extreme of our cross-Channel offensive. At the other extreme were the mass operations intended to lead to a clash with the German Air Force. The climax and culmination of these came with the great combined raid against Dieppe on 19th August, 1942.

The Dieppe landing was inspired by several motives, of which two stood foremost. First, in preparation for our return to the Continent—whenever that should be—we needed to try out a large-scale landing at a place where we could supply fighter cover. Secondly, by seizing if only for a few hours an important objective on enemy territory we should be reasonably certain of bringing to battle the whole forces of the *Luftwaffe* in Northern France and the Low Countries. If things went as we hoped, as many as 470 German aircraft—220 bombers and 250 fighters—might appear and dispute supremacy with us over the beach-head; and in that case Fighter Command could be relied upon to seize its opportunity. Control of the air operations was accordingly entrusted to Air Vice-Marshal Leigh-Mallory, of Fighter Command's No. 11 Group, and a force of fifty-six fighter squadrons—Hurricanes, Spitfires and Typhoons—was placed at his disposal. Of other types of aircraft he was given only nine squadrons. The new Mustang tactical reconnaissance squadrons of Army Co-operation Command made up four of these. The other five were Blenheim and Boston squadrons of No. 2

Group with the role of smoke-laying and close support bombing.

The general story of the raid, with its desperately gallant fighting by the Canadians and Commandos, is now familiar. Despite the most heroic efforts our forces were unable to capture some of the commanding points, notably the eastern headland overlooking the harbour, while in the town itself the defences proved too strong for such tanks as we could land. In the matter of air support Leigh-Mallory's squadrons did what was expected of them; but as they consisted of so many more fighters than bombers, they were naturally more successful in protecting the landings from the *Luftwaffe* than in destroying German strong-points on the ground.

Like the raiding forces, the squadrons began their task betimes. 'Everyone was at work by 0300, wondering if this was the much talked-of second front', recorded No. 66 Squadron at Tangmere; 'as dawn breaks, the first aircraft—the Hurricanes—take off . . .'. So it went on, hour after hour. The Mustangs, ranging far afield, kept watch against enemy reinforcements; the Bostons and Blenheims bombed gun-posts and laid smoke; the Hurricanes and Spitfires joined in against the batteries and shot up the defences in the town. Meanwhile, other Spitfires escorted American Fortresses, now beginning to operate from this country, in a raid which put the important fighter airfield of Abbeville-Drucat out of action for two vital hours. And all the time the battle against the German Air Force waxed more and more intense. Caught by surprise, the *Luftwaffe* could at first challenge us only with fighters; but these appeared in growing numbers—twenty-five, fifty, a hundred. Then, at 1000 hours, the enemy's bombers came on the scene. Under strong escort they repeatedly strove to pierce the protective canopy of our fighters. As repeatedly they were driven off or made to aim their bombs awry. Not until the ships were back in harbour and the long August day had closed did their efforts cease.

The raiding forces may have taken a bloody nose, but the results of the air fighting were more to our satisfaction. At any rate there was no doubt that we had succeeded in our object of inducing a great battle. In this we had lost 106 aircraft; but our 'conservative' estimate of enemy losses was ninety-one aircraft destroyed, forty-four probably destroyed and 151 damaged, while a 'reliable' source on the Continent reported the number of German aircraft destroyed as no less than 170. Unfortunately, the enemy's records now reveal that the Germans lost only forty-eight aircraft destroyed and twenty-four damaged. On the more general issues, it was realized at the time that the close support provided by Leigh-Mallory's squadrons was not entirely effective, partly because the cannon of our fighters made little impression on concrete, partly because the situation was at times so confused that the military commanders were unable to indicate the best targets for attack. On the other hand, the all-important task of protecting the raiding troops and the vessels off shore was performed with outstanding success. Our soldiers fought completely unmolested from the air. The *Luftwaffe's* single success against our ships came from a chance hit by a jettisoned bomb.

At the price of over 4,000 casualties the Dieppe raid tested the German defences and brought on the air battle we so ardently desired. The defences proved too strong, the tally of aircraft losses ended two-to-one in favour of the enemy. That is not to say that the whole operation was unjustified. 'Enterprises of great pith and moment' like the invasion of Europe cannot be undertaken without a few realistic and even expensive rehearsals. Whatever Dieppe cost was more than repaid in the lessons it provided for later study. Its epilogue was to be read, not in the communiqués of either side at the time, but in the successful landings in North Africa, Sicily and Normandy.

* * *

Even before the Dieppe raid the conviction was growing that our fighters were not, after all, shooting down two of the enemy for every loss they themselves suffered. The events of 19th August did nothing to dispel this suspicion. And as we had now decided after much anxious probing of possibilities to undertake the invasion of French North Africa later in the year, the cross-Channel fighter offensive was duly relaxed. From the beginning of September to the end of December Fighter Command flew only 10,000 offensive sorties—less than half the number flown in the period from March to June. This brought the Command's total of offensive sorties for the whole of 1942 up to some 43,000, in the course of which we had lost 915 aircraft. Even this great effort, however, was exceeded on other tasks. For during the year our home-based fighters also flew 73,000 sorties on purely defensive work such as the protection of our shores and shipping—a truly astonishing total to be imposed on us by the activity of no more than 500 German bombers, of whom a half at any one time were normally unserviceable.

This naturally gives rise to speculation whether some of our fighter effort might not have been more usefully applied in the Middle East. One point, however, is certain. If it was necessary to keep so many Hurricanes and Spitfires and Typhoons in Britain—and we must remember that the Russian front was far from stable, that German bombers could be switched from East to West much more rapidly than our fighter squadrons could be recalled from overseas, and that we might still be faced with invasion—then there can be no doubt that it was good policy to keep them actively employed. For of all things, what the fighter pilot hated most was inaction. 'Quiet to quick bosoms is a hell', and the Air Ministry was wisely determined that from that particular hell our airmen should not suffer.

* * *

The Fortresses which bombed Abbeville-Drucat during the Dieppe raid were the advance guard of the American Eighth Air Force. They had reached England under their own power the previous month; and to do so they had followed a trail already blazed along much of its length by British aircraft.

The first systematic flights across the North Atlantic had taken place nearly two years earlier. Lockheed Hudsons desperately needed by Coastal Command were at that time taking three months to reach England from California. They were also filling valuable shipping space. But experimental crossings of the North Atlantic by air had already been made in the summer of 1939, and this gave birth to the idea that the Hudsons might be delivered by direct flight. In July 1940 it was decided to make the attempt. On the suggestion of the Ministry of Aircraft Production, the Canadian Pacific Railway set up an Air Ferries Department, under Mr. Woods Humphrey, at Montreal; four distinguished pilots of the British Overseas Airways Corporation and one of the Royal Canadian Air Force were engaged to prepare the venture; and civilian crews were made up from American and Canadian pilots, amateur and professional, and from ground wireless operators willing to exercise their skill in the air. Four months of intense effort were crowned on 10th November, 1940. That evening the first seven Hudsons, led by Captain D. C. T. Bennett, of B.O.A.C., took off from the snow-bound airfield at Gander, Newfoundland. Ten and a half hours later and 2,100 miles farther east all seven put down safely in Northern Ireland. An aerial bridge across the Atlantic was no longer the distant dream of visionaries and cranks, but sober reality.

Within twenty-four hours of their arrival the seven crews were on their way back by ship. Despite very severe weather, three more delivery flights in formation were accomplished before the end of the year. After that it was decided to save time by flying the machines across one by one as they were ready. So began that steady trickle of American warplanes—first Hudsons, then Catalinas, Fortresses and Liberators—which re-vitalized Coastal Command and exercised so profound an effect on the Battle of the Atlantic. To increase that trickle, to turn it into what it eventually became, a broad and steady flow, many things were done in the next few months. Gander airfield, already begun in 1937 thanks to the vision of the Air Ministry and the Newfoundland Government, was developed into a huge airport; on this side of the Atlantic a great reception terminal was built up at Prestwick, on the Ayrshire coast, where weather conditions are abnormally good for these uncertain isles; and return ferry-flights for the delivery crews were operated by B.O.A.C. This last enterprise soon grew into a regular passenger and freight service. At the same time the use of Royal Air Force aircrew and ground staff enabled the work of delivery to be speeded up.

In April 1941 decisions were taken which soon remodelled the delivery organization. Up to this point the aircraft had been flown from California to the Canadian border by American civilians, hauled across, and then flown on to Scotland by the C.P.R. organization. Now the passage of the Lease-Lend Act prompted General Arnold to suggest that the machines should be flown all the way from the Pacific Coast to Montreal by pilots of the United States Army Air Force. The General's idea was two-fold: to train his own crews in long-distance flights and at the same time to speed up deliveries by releasing the American civilian crews for service, if they wished, on the Transatlantic run. The proposal was eagerly accepted. One condition, however, was that the U.S.A.A.F. pilots should deliver the planes at Montreal to a Service and not a civilian authority. So it came about that the existing organization, which had recently come under tighter governmental control as 'Atfero', underwent a further change in July 1941 and became the Royal Air Force Ferry Command.

Under the direction of Air Chief Marshal Bowhill this new Command continued to combine Service and civilian elements, in the air as well as on the ground. As the Canadian Government were already building a great new airfield at Dorval, ten miles outside Montreal, this became the Headquarters of the Command and the hub of its activity—the centre at which aircraft were received from the United States and prepared for the Atlantic crossing. At the same time the problem of the medium-range aircraft was faced. So that these, too, could fly the Atlantic—with a halt in Iceland—the Canadians now agreed to make a departure base in Labrador. There, 850 miles north of Gander, on a sandy plateau set above wild forests and swamps and near a bay with the ideally complementary name of Goose, they built an airfield with incredible speed in the closing months of 1941. Its three 7,000 feet runways were soon capable of taking the heaviest aircraft.

With these important developments in the ground organization went a radical solution to the difficulty of obtaining delivery crews. It was proposed by Bowhill. Thousands of young men were being trained in Canada and the United States to fly for the Royal Air Force; when their training was done, why not entrust the best of them with the task of bringing over an aircraft? The idea was approved; a short course of special preparation was devised; and soon novices from the Flying Training Schools were making flights which three years earlier would have been deemed astonishing for veteran pilots. Moreover they were accomplished with an amazing degree of safety. On the average about one aircraft in a hundred was lost. Many pilots, of course, had terrifying moments, but fortunately the experience of one 'regular' who had three 'S.O.S. incidents' within two months—two crashes in desolate territory and the sudden and irrevocable descent of his flaps and undercarriage in mid-Atlantic—was by no means typical.

By mid-1942 a North Atlantic air route was thus a firmly established fact. And by that time the United States, having decided to build up a great combat Air Force, was anxious to get a large part of it into action in Europe. For the great invasion of the Continent, then projected for 1943, the Americans needed in Britain not only bombers but fighters. With their customary daring they decided to send them across by air. Gander–Prestwick direct would serve for the long range machines; Goose–Reykjavik–Prestwick for the medium range; but the fighters must have some staging post between Labrador and Iceland. The Americans carved what they wanted from the inhospitable soil of Greenland; and with this addition to the airfields already established by the British and Canadians, the bombers and pursuit planes of General Spaatz's Eighth Air Force winged their way across the Atlantic. The first Flying Fortresses of this force touched down at Prestwick on 1st July, 1942. Six weeks later, on 17th August, the Eighth Air Force Bomber Command, with General Eaker, its Chief, among the crews, flew its inaugural mission against the marshalling yards outside Rouen.

* * *

Two days before the Forts went into action over occupied Europe a new unit of great importance formed within Bomber Command. It was aptly named the Pathfinder Force. With equal appropriateness its chief was Group Captain D. C. T. Bennett, who twenty-one months earlier as a civil pilot had led the first delivery flight across the Atlantic.

The Pathfinders came into being only after protracted disagreement between Air Marshal Harris and the Air Staff. That the main force would have to be led by specially selected crews was not at issue, for this was already our practice. But the Air Staff's proposal to take these crews from their squadrons and concentrate them in a single *corps d'élite* seemed to Harris—and to his Group Commanders—destructive of squadron morale. Throughout the spring and summer of 1942 the Bomber Chief had accordingly fought the project with all his accustomed vigour; but his opposition, if spirited, soon developed into a rearguard action. For the Air Staff had one unanswerable argument. 'Gee', it had become clear, was not living up to the more extravagant claims of its champions; and if 'Gee' was falling short of what was desired then the only hope was to pick out a number of the best crews and so organize them that they could not merely lead attacks but give systematic study to the development of pathfinding methods. The final decision came after an interview with the Chief of Air Staff. The Commander-in-Chief emerged having agreed to apply the Air Ministry's scheme, if not to welcome it.

The Pathfinder Force worked no instant miracles. The original four squadrons—Nos. 7 (Stirlings), 35 (Halifaxes), 83 (Lancasters) and 156 (Wellingtons)—were chosen for their high level of skill, but they came to the task as complete units. The less efficient crews had accordingly to be weeded out. Two other handicaps also faced the new force. The only special equipment yet available was 'Gee'; and this the enemy was just beginning to jam. So it was not surprising that the Pathfinders' first operation, flown against Flensburg in bad weather on the night of 18th/19th August, 1942, went entirely astray.

Under Bennett's dynamic direction the new force during the next four months grew steadily more proficient. By ceaseless experiment crews discovered the best methods of attack. Their task, they found, could best be accomplished in three stages—'finding', 'illuminating' and 'marking'. First, 'finder' aircraft, using 'Gee' if they could, and flying on parallel tracks each about two miles apart, dropped extended sticks of flares over the town to be attacked. Next, 'illuminator' aircraft, working in the light thus created, laid a close pattern of flares round the actual target area. Thirdly, 'marker' aircraft, concentrating on this inner ring, put down incendiaries as an aiming point for subsequent arrivals. If there was heavy cloud the target was 'sky-marked' with coloured flares instead of being 'ground-marked' with incendiaries. The Pathfinders having completed their work, the next wave of the attack—the fire-raisers—could then drop a full load of incendiaries. Finally the third wave—the main force—would pile down high explosive and more incendiaries on the fires raging beneath.

Though on the same general lines, all this was rudimentary compared with the refined procedure of 1944 and 1945. The equipment, too, still suffered from serious defects. When the enemy jammed 'Gee' its range was reduced from 350 to only 200 miles, so that in bad weather the force was usually unable to locate the target. In addition the flares still dazzled the bomb aimers, or drifted away with the wind, or silhouetted the aircraft against the sky to the advantage of the defenders. Moreover the incendiary bombs used for 'ground marking' were soon lost to view among the fires—which might or might not be in the right place. If they were the decoys so frequently ignited by the enemy they were definitely in the wrong place. And even the new giant 4,000 lb. incendiaries, or 'Pink Pansies', quickly burnt out and left no distinctive trace.

All these formidable obstacles confronted the Pathfinder Force during the early months of its existence. Despite them all it showed steadily improving results. Between 19th August and 31st December, 1942, Bennett's crews led twenty-six attacks on Germany. Whenever the weather was really bad—as it was on six occasions—they completely failed to find the target; but when the weather was good or even moderate they found and marked the objective three times out of every four. This was certainly a significant improvement on the navigational standards of 1940 and 1941. And though the losses of the main force sometimes amounted to as much as thirteen per cent, the losses of the Pathfinders, at less than three per cent over the whole four months, remained surprisingly and agreeably low.

* * *

By the end of October 1942 the air assault on Germany, resumed with such intensity the previous March, was once more giving pride of place to other tasks. The Allied invasion of French North Africa was timed for early November, and Bomber Command was required to play an important if indirect part in the new venture.

The role of Harris's force was fourfold. There was the minor duty of dropping leaflets over France to explain our motives in descending on French colonies. There was the arduous but not entirely satisfying task of mining Genoa and Spezia to contain Italian warships. There was the more interesting business of bombing cross-Channel targets to occupy German fighters. And finally there was the *pièce de résistance*—the mass bombardment of Genoa, Milan and Turin. The object of this was to compel the Italians to hold back their fighters and anti-aircraft guns from Tunisia, and to strike a blow against the already wavering morale of the Italian people.

On the night of 22nd/23rd October, a few hours after the first 'Torch' convoy sailed for Gibraltar, a hundred Lancasters rained their bombs on Genoa. Apart from an ineffective raid in April this was our first attack on Italy from home bases for over a year. The moon was almost full, the skies were clear, and a new 'Gee' chain in Southern England was operating for the occasion. The Pathfinders therefore found their objective without difficulty. When the last of the Lancasters turned for home many acres of the town lay devastated; the docks, the shipping and the Ansaldo fitting yards were all heavily damaged; and not a single bomber had fallen victim to the defences.

Five times more within the next three weeks was Genoa attacked in like manner. By that time the inhabitants, as Mussolini put it to Ciano, had 'given proof of moral weakness'. Meanwhile on 24th October eighty-eight Lancasters had delivered a daring assault on Milan by daylight. They lost only three of their number in a raid which dotted the town with fires and reduced the railway system to chaos. An attempt to improve upon this damage during the ensuing night was only partially successful. From 18th/19th November the main weight of attack then fell on Turin. Seven raids before the end of the year, mostly by forces of some 200 aircraft, resulted in extensive damage to the arsenal, the railway workshops and the great motor plants of Fiat and Lancia, besides the destruction of many factories, public utilities, military buildings and private houses. Considerable as was the direct effect of all these attacks the indirect results were probably still greater. Intelligence reports spoke with unanimity of disorganization, panic and loss of production throughout the entire northern provinces. It was a far cry, indeed, from the days of 1941 when the *Duce*, to make his people realize they were at war, ordered the alarm to be sounded in Rome every time a raid threatened Naples.

It was during the third attack on Turin, on the night of 28th/29th November, 1942, that there occurred an incident outstanding even in the history of Bomber Command yet entirely typical of the spirit of our crews. On the voyage out, an Australian pilot of No. 149 Squadron, Flight Sergeant R. H. Middleton, had hard work to coax his Stirling over the Alps. The 'ceiling' of this type of aircraft was too low, and in his attempts to gain height the pilot found his engines using too much fuel. Soon it became clear that there might not be enough for the journey home. Ignoring this danger, Middleton pressed on towards his target. He reached Turin, then came down low to identify his aiming point. The night was intensely dark, and he was on his third run across the town, at 2,000 feet, when his aircraft was hit by *flak*. The first shells tore several holes in the mainplanes; then one penetrated the fuselage and burst in the cockpit. The flying metal did its work. One splinter pierced the side of Middleton's face, destroyed his right eye, and ripped the flesh from the bone above it. A second lodged home in his leg, a third in his chest. Other fragments hit the second pilot and the wireless operator, the former, Flight Sergeant L. A. Hyder, being severely wounded in the legs and head.

With Middleton unconscious the Stirling at once plunged down out of control, and only 800 feet separated it from disaster when the second pilot, despite his own injuries, managed to bring it back to an even keel. He then flew the aircraft up to 1,500 feet and dropped the bombs, though the Italian gunners continued to score hits. Then Middleton came round, and immediately insisted on taking over so that Hyder's wounds could be attended to. Once at the controls again, he stayed there. A shattered eye, a wounded crew, a heavily damaged aircraft and a return journey over the Alps with no windscreen and barely enough fuel—none of these dismayed the Australian. He set course for base, determined that neither he nor his crew should fall into the hands of the enemy. He knew that he could scarcely hope to land the damaged aircraft, even if his petrol held out; but if he could struggle back to England his comrades at least might escape by parachute.

His spirit, and that of his crew, conquered. The Stirling staggered back over the Alps; held together across the breadth of France; survived yet further hits over the Channel coast; and at last reached the shores of England. Petrol for only five minutes' flying then remained. The aircraft could not be landed; Middleton himself was too weak to jump. He flew the machine along the shore until five of his crew had safely baled out. The two others insisted on remaining behind to help him. What then happened can only be surmised. It is known that Middleton intended, if he could, to ditch off shore; but apparently the fuel ran out before he could do so. The next day the bodies of his two companions were recovered. He himself probably went down still at the controls.

UVENIR OF A LOW-LEVEL FLIGHT TO THE ARC DE TRIOMPHE

The Grand Palais, in the Champs Elysées, photographed from
Flight Lieutenant Gatward's aircraft

RECONNAISSANCE PHOTOGRAPH OF DIEPPE

Such extreme heroism could be recognized only by the supreme award. The citation with which it was accompanied made a large claim, but recorded the bare truth. 'His devotion to duty in the face of every danger and difficulty is unsurpassed in the annals of the Royal Air Force'.

* * *

Genoa, Turin, El Alamein, Tunisia—from all sides staggering blows had buffeted the unfortunate Italians. Anxious to hasten the knock-out, the Air Staff now proposed that during December and January, when the weather was likely to be bad over Germany, the bomber force should continue to concentrate on Italy. The Prime Minister approved in characteristic terms—'the heat should be turned on Italy, . . . but Germany should not be entirely neglected'.

Various obstacles, notably the decision to obliterate the U-boat bases in Western France, prevented this plan being carried out in full. But the companion project, already begun earlier, of keeping the enemy fighters so occupied in North West Europe that they could not be sent to North Africa—or Russia—was actively pursued. No. 2 Group and Fighter Command continued to fly 'Circuses' over Northern France, with a growing attention to locomotives and rolling stock; and the Mosquitos of Nos. 105 and 139 Squadrons, operating in very small numbers, made daring attacks in daylight against objectives as far afield as the Gestapo Headquarters in Oslo (25th September, 1942), the Burmeister and Wain Diesel engine works at Copenhagen (27th January, 1943), and the main broadcasting station in Berlin (30th January, 1943). On this last occasion the attacks were timed to coincide with speeches by Göring and Göbbels, and kept the former off the air for more than an hour. In addition one or two major operations were also attempted by bombers in daylight with great success. The most notable of these were the dusk raid by ninety-four Lancasters against the Schneider works at Le Creusot (17th October, 1942) and the midday attack by seventy-eight Bostons, Venturas, and Mosquitos on the Philips radio and valve works at Eindhoven (6th December, 1942).

The decision to mount 'Torch' and the rapid advance into Tunisia which followed the initial landings virtually settled the pattern of the rest of the war. Among other things it ensured that the great combined Anglo-American bomber offensive against Germany, planned in 1941 and 1942, would in fact be carried out: for with so much of the Allied resources being devoted to North Africa a major invasion of the Continent in 1943 (the projected

Operation 'Round-up') became only the remotest of possibilities. This was soon apparent to the British Chiefs of Staff. It was accepted more slowly by the British Prime Minister, who might be forgiven his reluctance to inform Stalin that the great venture was to recede yet further into the distance, and who at this stage was anxious to build up American ground forces (more than air forces) in England.

For in truth, although we had formally agreed in September 1942 to a general policy of using Bomber Command against Germany by night and the Eighth Air Force against Germany by day, it was still at that date doubtful whether the Americans could carry out their share of the bargain. Some quarters—outside the Air Staff—in fact spent much time and energy urging the Americans to abandon the doctrine of high-level precision bombing and to concentrate, like ourselves, on 'area' attacks by night. These critics pressed their opinion regardless of the fact that the American aircraft, with their small bomb-load and their unshielded exhaust-glare, were in every way unsuitable for night bombing. By November 1942, however, much of the croaking had died down. Though the American Fortresses and Liberators had penetrated no farther than Lille, and though they had flown under strong British fighter escort—which they could not then hope to enjoy over Germany—their performance had decisively impressed the Air Staff. With bigger numbers, greater familiarity with the European climate and a higher degree of training—for many of Eaker's best crews had been sent to North Africa—the Americans, the Air Staff were now convinced, stood a good chance of succeeding in the experiment which (as Mr. Churchill put it) they so 'ardently and obstinately' wished to make.

It was not, in fact, until 27th January, 1943, when the Eighth Air Force attacked Wilhelmshaven, that the Americans struck their first blow against the German homeland. By that time Mr. Churchill had accepted the viewpoint of the Air Staff and the Chiefs of Staff; and a few days before, in the great Conference at Casablanca, the logical implications of 'Torch' had been formally recognized. The road ahead now became plain. The Anglo-American forces would exploit their success in the Mediterranean by occupying Sicily and increasing the pressure on Italy; and in Western Europe, while regarding the struggle against the U-boats as the first charge on their resources, they would direct a great combined bombing offensive towards 'the progressive destruction and dislocation of the German military, industrial and economic system, and the undermining of the morale of the German people to a point where their capacity for armed resistance is fatally weakened'.

By February 1943, then, the broad strategic problem was resolved. The bombing of Germany would go on with mounting intensity, night and day, until enemy resistance was decisively weakened and the Allied military forces, gathering strength the while, could hurl themselves with confidence at 'Fortress Europe'. By February 1943, too, Bomber Command was at last ready to carry out its share in the great task economically and effectively. The force had reached its immediate goal of fifty squadrons, of which thirty-five were 'heavies'. The target-indicator bomb, with its unmistakeable clusters of red and green candles; the barometric fuse, which could be pre-set to detonate at a given height; the new Mark XIV bombsight, far more accurate than the old 'Course Setting' model; the great high-capacity blast bombs—all these were now at Harris's service. And above all, to guide the Pathfinders, there was 'Oboe'; and to guide Pathfinders and main force alike there was 'H2S'.

* * *

Oboe, an aid so accurate that it could be used for blind-bombing, was born in the mind of Mr. A. H. Reeves of the Telecommunications Research Establishment during 1941. In essence it was another scheme for guiding an aircraft from the ground—in this case from two stations. The first (the 'mouse') directed a radio pulse over the centre of the target. Along this the aircraft travelled, the pilot recognizing his course by a continuous note (of oboe-like quality) which sounded in his earphones. If he deviated to port or starboard he was advised by a system of dots and dashes. At the same time the pulse was radiated back by the set within the aircraft and picked up by the second ground station (the 'cat'). By observing the time taken to receive back this pulse the 'cat' was able to make periodic calculations of the aircraft's progress along the given track. When the aircraft approached the right point for bombing, the 'cat' transmitted the letters abcd, then a series of dashes, then a series of dots. When the dots ceased the bomb-aimer pressed his button. As far as the aircrew were concerned, it was as simple as that.

Such a system, which could guarantee the fall of bombs within a few hundred yards of a selected pin-point even on the darkest night and through the thickest cloud, promised not only heavier damage to the German cities but fewer casualties to our own aircraft; for it would enable us to operate in just those conditions which hampered the enemy's guns and night fighters. Like many good things, however, it had its weaknesses. As with 'Gee', it depended on ground stations, and so was limited in range to about 350 miles. It demanded, too, that the aircraft should radiate signals and should fly straight and level for the last few minutes of its approach. This, of course, played into the hands of the defenders. Further, the system would not work over Germany if the aircraft was lower than 14,000 feet—a height often beyond the reach of the Stirlings. But all these disadvantages were small compared with another—that 'cat' and 'mouse' could between them handle, during the final ten minutes of the approach, only a single aircraft.

This last drawback at one time seemed to condemn the whole system. Then the answer dawned that Oboe should be used, not as a blind-bombing aid for the whole force, but as a target-finding-and-marking aid for the leading crews. An Oboe flight of Mosquitos was accordingly formed in No. 109 Squadron, and in due course became part of the Pathfinder force. Meantime 'cat' and 'mouse' stations were erected on the East Coast to cover the Ruhr, and on the night of 20th/21st December, 1942, six Oboe Mosquitos began their operational career by a calibration raid against a power station in Holland. Other experimental raids followed in January and February 1943; and by the opening of March the Oboe Pathfinders stood ready to lead a major attack.

By this time a further aid of almost equal importance had come into being. Like nearly all the other radio devices which helped to turn the course of the war, 'H2S' ('Home Sweet Home') was produced by the civilian scientists at the Telecommunications Research Establishment. Unlike 'Gee' and 'Oboe' it was a radar apparatus completely self-contained within the aircraft. It could thus operate wherever the aircraft itself could fly. There were already airborne radar sets for detecting other aircraft (A.I.), and ships or submarines (A.S.V.); the function of 'H2S' was to scan the territory over which it passed. Amounting in effect to a kind of rudimentary television transmitter and receiver, it emitted pulses which, when echoed back from the land or sea beneath, presented a rough picture on a cathode ray screen. In this picture land could be easily distinguished from water, built-up areas from open countryside. By giving the crews a clear indication of the shores, rivers, lakes and towns on their route, the device could thus enable them to navigate accurately to distant places, like Berlin, far beyond the reach of 'Gee' and 'Oboe'. We also believed the set to be so accurate that the crews could use it for 'blind' bombing—at least when they were attacking large urban areas. All these possibilities, however, depended on producing short—centimetric—waves of great power; and this introduced a difficulty. For though a set could be built using the simplest generator of centimetric waves—the klystron valve—it would be weak, intermittent and unreliable in performance compared with a set which made use of the magnetron. And the magnetron was at that time—early 1942—our most precious secret in the whole realm of radio.

Up to this point the venture, initiated in late 1941, had gone almost without a hitch. But now an acute difference of opinion entered. The magnetron was to be used in the new ten centimetre A.S.V. of our coastal aircraft; and the Admiralty naturally resented the prospect of its falling straight away into the hands of the enemy—as it would certainly do if it were installed in our bombers. So a battle royal developed between the advocates of the klystron and those of the magnetron. The former were led by Lord Cherwell, who was one of the driving forces behind the whole 'H2S' project, and had even suggested its name. The opposite camp included almost the entire staff of the Telecommunications Research Establishment, who contended that the Germans would take two years to bring the device into effective use from the moment it fell into their hands. This argument carried the day. It would, after all, be poor policy for an air force on the offensive, possessed of greater bombing strength than its opponent, to refrain from employing a weapon for fear of retaliation. In July 1942 the decision was accordingly taken to use the magnetron. Sets were then hurriedly ordered for the Pathfinders as a preliminary to equipping the whole bomber force. By the end of January 1943 the first 'H2S' aircraft were operating over Germany.

For Bomber Command, 'Oboe' and 'H2S' came as the climax to a year of immense progress. But all our newly found accuracy would be useless if our losses became too great. It was therefore well that Harris now had at his disposal a whole battery of weapons against the German radar system. There were jammers, there were radio beams laid across Germany with no other purpose than to distract the enemy from our 'Gee' and 'Oboe' transmissions, there were means of making one aircraft appear as half-a-dozen. And above all, there was that master counter-measure, the innocent-looking little strips of tin foil known as 'Window', which when dropped from the air could reduce a whole radar system to chaos. But this last the War Cabinet, fearing retaliation before we had devised an antidote, would not yet allow Harris to use.

By February 1943, then, the bomber force, after a somewhat painful adolescence, had come of age. Over the past year its capabilities had grown immeasurably. To what it had always had, highly competent commanders and devoted crews, were now added, thanks to British scientific genius, powerful aircraft, huge bombs and vastly more accurate methods of navigation. So, as winter turned to spring, Harris prepared to strike once more, with all the strength he could muster, against the cities of Germany. The order of priority was unchanged. Objective number one was still the Ruhr. Within the Ruhr the main target was still Essen. Within Essen there was still Krupps, virtually intact after nearly three years of attack.

As related more fully later, the new Battle of the Ruhr opened on the night of 5th/6th March, 1943. The target was Essen. Some 450 aircraft operated in all, and the pathfinding force included eight 'Oboe' Mosquitos. More than 500 tons of high explosive and over 550 tons of incendiaries were dropped in an attack which was concentrated within thirty-eight minutes. When the dreadful crash of the bombs had ceased and the fires and the smoke and the dust had died down, the inhabitants of Essen could see what lay in store not only for them but for every other large town in Germany. A great part of their city was in ruins. Krupps, for so long almost untouched, was blasted from end to end.

CHAPTER IX
Middle East: Crusader

BY the spring of 1943 the Royal Air Force was raining blows of unprecedented violence on the German and Italian homelands. The British Army, however, had not yet been able to come to grips again, as it so ardently desired, with the enemy in Europe. How it became free to do so by way of the immortal progress across Africa must now be told.

The first volume of this history has shown how our early success in Cyrenaica was undone by the despatch of British troops to Greece, and how in the spring of 1941 the Middle East Command was beset by a veritable sea of troubles. The storm having been weathered—with the loss of some of the cargo and crew—the vessel could now swing back on course. In the middle of July 1941, a few days after the Vichy surrender in Syria, the Defence Committee of the War Cabinet accordingly met to consider future plans.

It will be remembered that Rommel's forces were then on the Egyptian frontier, with Tobruk still holding out in their rear. In June Operation 'Battleaxe' had attempted to relieve Tobruk and recapture the airfields of eastern Cyrenaica, only to fail ingloriously within three days. The main question for discussion was thus how soon we could stage another and stronger effort in the same direction. The Prime Minister, not surprisingly, favoured an early move. The Russians were expected to succumb to Hitler's onslaught within a few weeks, and it was essential that we should strike at the enemy in Africa while Germany was still committed in Eastern Europe. Mr. Churchill therefore proposed that General Auchinleck, who had just succeeded General Wavell, should be invited to open a major offensive in September. As an inducement he would be guaranteed a minimum strength of 500 cruiser and infantry tanks, to say nothing of 'a large number of ill-conceived light tanks and armoured cars'.

This proposal commanded general acceptance among the political and military leaders present. But in the Middle East it was received with embarrassment. Neither Auchinleck nor Tedder nor the newly appointed Minister of State, Mr. Oliver Lyttelton, believed that we should strike so soon. By the beginning of November Auchinleck expected to have twice as many tanks available as at the beginning of September, while Tedder expected his aircraft strength to increase by nearly fifty per cent. Neither believed that Rommel would grow much stronger during the same period. Their joint views were expressed when Auchinleck wrote: 'I have to choose between a problematical success early in October and a probable complete success early in November. . . . I have no hesitation in advocating patience and the big object'.

Before this weight of responsible opinion the Defence Committee perforce bowed. The offensive was finally set for November, and all movements were then geared towards that date.

The Eighth Army, as it became in September, now settled down to a spell of intense training and reorganization. So, too, though it had to give a larger share of its time to operations, did the Royal Air Force. Four subjects above all demanded Tedder's urgent attention. The organizational framework of his Command needed strengthening; the standard of operational training among the newly arrived crews was too low; there were serious weaknesses in our methods of tactical air support; and under the burden of the successive defeats in Cyrenaica, Greece and Crete the maintenance organization had utterly collapsed.

The weakness in the headquarters organization was the most easily remedied. With the approval of the Air Ministry, Tedder duly strengthened and upgraded the higher formations in Egypt. No. 257 Wing, in charge of the long-range bombers in the Canal Zone, became No. 205 Group—under which style it flew and fought over all the long miles from Egypt to Northern Italy. No. 201 Group at Alexandria remained a group, but in deference to Admiral Cunningham was now labelled, without possibility of mistake or misuse, No. 201 (Naval Co-operation) Group. No. 202 Group was given the status of a subordinate command. It became Air Headquarters Egypt and took over responsibility for local air defence from Command Headquarters. Most important of all, No. 204 Group in the forward area became Air Headquarters, Western Desert. At the same time its squadrons—reconnaissance aircraft, fighters and light bombers—were stripped of unnecessary encumbrances and grouped into wings, each of which, so far as resources allowed, was made mobile. In everything except name this was now the Desert Air Force of legend and history.

The low level of training among the newly arrived crews yielded to treatment more slowly. However, a visit to the Middle East Command by Air Chief Marshal Sir Edgar Ludlow-Hewitt, the

Inspector-General, proved extremely fruitful of results; more Operational Training Units were formed, existing ones enlarged; and leaders of proved skill and recent operational experience, like Group Captain Embry, were brought out from England. By the end of 1941 the general standard of operational efficiency was steadily improving.

Very great progress also took place in the realm of tactical support. An Army-Air Force committee was set up in Cairo and soon produced an agreed statement on the subject. This laid down many of the basic principles—among others, that the Army would find the best protection from air attack not in constant fighter patrols overhead but in a combination of offensive sweeps, raids on enemy airfields, and the determined use of its own anti-aircraft guns. The *sine qua non* of effective support, in other words, was the attainment of a reasonable degree of air superiority. This, the Army now recognized, was the first and most vital task of the Royal Air Force.

The formulation of these basic principles was not a difficult matter for the Air Force, who had all along been aware of them. But it was not so easy to translate principles into action, especially when the equipment for doing so was lacking. Much of our inability to provide air support at once in the right spot had arisen from the immobility of all squadrons except those few actually labelled 'Army Co-operation'. The answer to this was not merely the principle of mobility: it was also more lorries. In the same way, good fighter cover for the front-line troops depended on the supply of mobile radar sets for early warning and mobile anti-aircraft guns for the defence of forward landing-grounds. Meanwhile we could only make the best use of what already existed. And this resolved itself largely into a matter of communications.

Under the impetus of the two Commanders-in-Chief, the Chief Army and Air Force Signals Officers in the Middle East, Major-General W. R. C. Penney and Group Captain W. E. G. Mann, set to work to develop the necessary channels. It was not merely a question of improving Air Force communications; Army communications were so rudimentary that military commanders in the extremely fluid conditions of desert warfare often failed to keep tracks of their own troops. This meant that they were frequently unable to state where they wanted air support. In the same way the results of air reconnaissance, though delivered promptly to Corps Headquarters, often reached the units affected too late to be of use. What Mann and his Army counterpart therefore aimed to provide was a series of channels which linked up all the essential ground and air elements in one comprehensive system.

The nodal points in the system eventually evolved were the Air Support Controls. These were mobile units whose duty was to consider, sift and relay requests for air support. They were manned by the Royal Air Force, with a small Army staff attached, and located at the headquarters of each corps. From them four main channels of communication branched out—to the forward infantry brigades in the field (an Army responsibility), to aircraft in the air, to the landing grounds, and to advanced Air Headquarters, Western Desert. The latter, henceforth invariably alongside Eighth Army Headquarters, would thus have a complete picture of the struggle, and could either reserve decisions to itself or delegate routine matters to the Air Support Controls. The whole system enabled requests from our advanced troops to be considered immediately, and, if approved, met promptly. In similar fashion information from air reconnaissance could be received and relayed in time for both air and ground forces to take proper advantage of it.

Mobility and good communications—these were Tedder's main recipes for effective air support. Many other points, however, needed attention. Rules for laying down a 'bomb-line' beyond which our aircraft could bomb without endangering our own troops, standard means of indicating targets, standard methods of establishing recognition between our air and ground forces (such as by Verey lights, coloured cartridges and ground signs)—all these demanded, and received, consideration. Not everything, even of what has been mentioned above, could be provided in the brief weeks before the new offensive. And what was provided was by no means the end of the story, for tactical air support is a subject infinitely susceptible of improvement. All the same, the months from July to November 1941 saw Tedder and his staff, acting partly in the light of principles already enunciated by Army Co-operation Command but still more in the light of their own experience, hammer out a system of thoroughly effective air support. It was to serve the Army well not only in the deserts of Africa but also, with later refinements and additions, among the swift rivers and frowning mountains of Italy, the green hills and woods of Normandy, and the sombre plains and broken cities of the *Reich* itself.

Even more pressing than the problems of tactical support were those of maintenance. Here the situation was indeed desperate. For a number of reasons unserviceability among our aircraft in the Middle East had by mid-1941 reached fantastic proportions. Campaigns had been and were still being fought in widely separated theatres. All aircraft sufficiently damaged to need major attention had to be carried, usually over vast distances, to the repair bases in Egypt. New aircraft were arriving without guns and wireless. Spare parts were either not arriving at all or were being lost sight of in units hopelessly short of equipment assistants. American aircraft of new types such as the Tomahawks were invariably afflicted with prolonged 'teething troubles'. And all the machines which travelled over the Takoradi route required complete overhaul before they could be put into service. Yet to cope with all this enormous volume of work there existed, apart from the immediate maintenance staff in the squadrons, only the old Aircraft Repair Depot at Aboukir, the more recently formed auxiliary repair depot at Abu Sueir, and one semi-mobile repair and salvage unit in the Western Desert.

On 1st April, 1941, Air Commodore C. B. Cooke, an officer of great talent and energy, arrived in Cairo to take over the position of Chief Maintenance Officer, Middle East. He found the whole repair organization in a deplorable state. Accumulations of damaged aircraft were dotted about the vast Command, and there were practically no reserve machines complete in all respects. Cooke himself has recorded how he arrived at Headquarters in find the Deputy Commander-in-Chief, the Air Officer in charge of Administration, and the Senior Air Staff Officer all in solemn conclave about the fate of one repaired Hurricane.

The size of the job to be tackled was by no means the only difficulty. In accordance with the normal Service organization at the time, maintenance was part of the province of the Air Officer in charge of Administration, Air Vice-Marshal Maund. In the hierarchical pyramid Cooke therefore came below Maund. But Maund was a desperately overworked man: overworked not only because of his immense responsibilities but because he insisted on discharging so many of them personally. When Cooke arrived, Maund was toiling from eight in the morning until ten at night throughout the heat of the Egyptian afternoon and wearing himself out in a conscientious effort to achieve the impossible. Unfortunately Cooke himself had had no recent experience of repair work, and he was quite unable to persuade Maund to relinquish any of his authority over technical matters. The new Chief Maintenance Officer soon developed valuable ideas, such as the need for a big maintenance group on the lines of Maintenance Command in the United Kingdom; but until the advent of Tedder he was debarred from presenting his proposals direct to the Air Officer Commanding-in-Chief.

Despite the arrival of Cooke, nothing much was done at Cairo to remedy the situation during April and May, though by mid-May the flow of supplies from home was fast improving. Meanwhile in London the War Cabinet, alarmed at the Prime Minister's suspicions of 'frightful mismanagement and futility' in the Middle East Command, had agreed to a proposal made by Lord Beaverbrook. This was that Air Vice-Marshal G. G. Dawson, of the Ministry of Aircraft Production, should be sent out to Egypt to ascertain the true state of affairs and to explain the repair organization he had developed at his own Ministry.

Of Beaverbrook's many proposals during the war none bore swifter or better fruit than this. Graham Dawson was a 'live wire' after Beaverbrook's own heart, with a domineering personality and an utter impatience of red tape. He was also an engineer specialist, and therefore, as an Air Vice-Marshal, *rara avis*. Indeed, he would not have attained his exalted rank so swiftly—he had risen from group captain inside seven months—without a determined effort by his political chief. Rapid promotion of this kind, however, did not ease his path in some quarters of the Air Ministry.

In company with two or three skilled engineer assistants, Dawson left England by air on 16th May, 1941. Almost at once a spate of signals, mostly addressed to particular individuals, began to flow in to the Air Ministry, the Ministry of Aircraft Production and the British aircraft firms. From Gibraltar Dawson denounced the faults of the local refuelling system; from Freetown he clamoured for spare engines for the coastal Hudsons; from Takoradi he demanded for local needs not merely many detailed items of aircraft equipment but also more medical supplies, more transport aircraft, more ferry pilots, and a better system of air defence. At the same place he also ordered home all airmen who had contracted malaria more than twice. From Lagos he then proceeded to suggest that one of his assistants should be sent out to replace the chief technical officer. By the end of May he had set an astonishing number of authorities by the ears, and the Chief of Air Staff had ordered him to confine himself to his own province and address his signals to the Air Ministry. But when Portal went on to ask Tedder to restrain the over-enthusiastic investigator, Tedder (who knew the merits of the officer concerned from personal experience at M.A.P.) replied that he was fully aware of what was going on, and that Dawson's activities had his entire support. Such was the state of affairs when the Prime Minister, very appropriately, enquired: 'What has been heard from Air Marshal Dawson since he went to Egypt?'

Though they caused embarrassment and annoyance Dawson's methods worked. All parties, from aircraft firms to Air Ministry, hastened to meet his requirements. Special consignments of stores and spare parts were flown out from home, and 'bottle-necks' became noticeably fewer. Meanwhile at Cairo, Dawson had taken a swift look round and put forward some very novel proposals. These were, in effect, that he himself should undertake the duties of Chief Maintenance and Supply Officer; that this post should be established directly under the Air Officer Commanding-in-Chief, and independent of the Air Officer-in-Charge of Administration; and that Cooke should command a big new maintenance group with executive control of all maintenance units and with greatly enlarged resources.

The proposals were then referred to the Air Ministry. Most of them were quickly approved, but the revolutionary suggestion that Maintenance should become an independent branch at Command Headquarters, on a par with Air Staff and Administration, was turned down. The refusal did not worry Tedder and Dawson, who proceeded with the scheme all the same. Shortly afterwards, Maund's place as Air Officer-in-Charge of Administration was taken by Air Vice-Marshal G. C. Pirie, who was to fill the post with distinction throughout the rest of the Middle East campaigns.

Once firmly in the saddle, Dawson set spurs to his mount. Ably helped by Cooke, he soon had the starveling nag of maintenance running as never before. The new group (No. 206) came into being. The existing repair and salvage unit in the forward area was enlarged and two new ones were created. All were made fully mobile; and more air stores parks, as yet only semi-mobile for lack of vehicles, were formed for them and the squadrons to draw on. As a link between forward and rear areas a Base Salvage Depot was also formed to bring to the Delta such crashed aircraft as the repair and salvage units had collected but could not deal with. Meanwhile at base itself the repair facilities were expanded out of all recognition. By making the utmost possible use of Egyptian labour, two new repair shops were created—one run by the Royal Air Force, the other by B.O.A.C.—on the old established airfields of Helwan and Heliopolis. And when in July the *Luftwaffe* attacked and heavily damaged the repair depot at Abu Sueir, Dawson at once replaced much of the lost capacity by taking over small garages and workshops in Cairo, regardless of the fact that many of them were in unsavoury areas normally out of bounds to British troops. On a more exalted plane, he was also able to find plant, floor space and skilled labour in the engineering faculty of the University.

This was not all. A small equipment store already existed in two of the caves of Tura, in the Mokattam hills outside Cairo. The caves had been excavated, with many others, some thousands of years earlier to supply stone for the Pyramids. Only two had remained open throughout the centuries. The whole hillside, however, was honeycombed with them and Dawson decided to open up the rest. The fallen stone and rubble was cleared, the caves were opened, the floors cemented, the walls white-washed, power and water laid on. When all was done the Royal Air Force had a superb depot for the overhaul of aero engines and the storage of anything from bombs to photo-paper.

By means such as these, Dawson created a system of maintenance in depth. In the forward areas there were the mobile repair and salvage units, at base the extensive repair workshops, in the Sudan and Palestine reserve capacity if Egypt became untenable. Moreover skilful improvisation and use of local labour—over 23,000 civilians were employed in the maintenance organization by the end of 1941—made it possible to carry out repairs of a kind not previously attempted in the Middle East. Worn metal parts, for instance, were built up by chromium plating and then ground down to the correct size. Cracked crankshafts were welded and re-machined; twisted propellers were straightened out and restored to service. All damage of this nature had hitherto entailed replacement from home.

In May 1941, when Dawson arrived in the Middle East, there were only some 200 aircraft serviceable and available for operations in the Western Desert. By the time of Auchinleck's offensive, in November, there were nearly 600. The difference, of course, was by no means exclusively due to Dawson. By November, re-inforcement aircraft and supplies had been coming in for over six months at a much faster rate than in Longmore's time, and we had suffered no serious reverse since Crete. Many other things, too, had helped. The appointment of a Minister of State in Cairo, the formation (in accordance with an Air Ministry plan) of a Master Provision Office to keep check of all equipment, the great work of the Army in extending the Desert railway seventy-five miles west of Matruh and carrying a water pipe-line from Alexandria almost to the same point, the visits of American supply missions under Mr. Harriman and General Brett —all these contributed to the improvement. That Dawson's work was a major factor, however, there can be no doubt. His favourite method of dropping in on some unit unannounced, carrying out an impromptu inspection and departing with a list of deficiencies, either in the equipment or the abilities of the staff, often created consternation. But the process, widely known among the sufferers as being 'Dawsonized', certainly kept things moving.

Dawson, however, would have been entirely powerless without Tedder's support. The most dramatic occasion on which this was given occurred when the Air Ministry sent out a committee to consider the various posts needed under Tedder's plans of reorganization. Before it left home the committee was briefed to give no countenance to the scheme for a Chief Maintenance and Supply Officer of equal instead of subordinate status to the Air Officer-in-charge of Administration. It arrived in the Middle East to find the arrangement a going concern. After meeting the wishes of the Commander-in-Chief on other matters, the committee therefore proved obdurate on this: it refused to regularize Dawson's position as a third air vice-marshal at Command Headquarters. Repeated discussions failed to move either side; whereupon Tedder wrote to the Chief of Air Staff and simply asked him, in the interests of the Middle East war effort, either to withdraw the committee or else to make it recognize his exceptional needs. 'It was only when I separated Maintenance from the A.O.A. that things began to move', he explained. Tedder enjoyed the full confidence of Portal, and the latter met his wishes. The air commander thus got what he wanted; but, as in many other matters, he had to fight for it.

* * *

Throughout the whole period of reorganization Tedder's squadrons kept at grips with the enemy. Among other work they supported the army in Abyssinia, where the last Italian troops capitulated in November, and in Persia, where a three-day operation in August safeguarded our oil and linked forces with the Russians. These, however, were mere 'side shows' compared with Tedder's two main tasks—the battles against the opposing air force and the enemy's supply system.

The reduction of the German and Italian Air Force was achieved in the main by daylight attacks on forward landing grounds like Gambut and night attacks on more remote airfields such as Gazala, Tmimi, Martuba and Benina. The daylight operations were flown by the Western Desert Squadrons, now under the command of the bold and far-sighted Air Vice-Marshal A. Coningham; the night raids were carried out by the long-range bombers from the Canal. The general effect was enhanced by our Malta-based aircraft, which made periodic attacks on airfields in Sicily and Tripolitania.

Unfortunately our fighters could not share in this work to the same extent as our bombers. Against the advice of London and Cairo the Australian Government insisted on the relief of all their troops in Tobruk. All three Services were therefore faced with a difficult and hazardous task at a time when they were straining every nerve to prepare for the forthcoming offensive. In the result, the duty of protecting the relieving convoys made great calls on Coningham's fighters and considerably impaired their activity against the enemy air force. It also bred among our pilots defensive habits which needed special correction later. The convoys, however, were covered with complete success.

Happily the enemy air forces took little advantage of their freedom. They pounded Tobruk very heavily, but failed in their attempt to damage our forward airfields. In their preoccupation with Tobruk they also allowed our strategic bases to escape more or less unharmed. The Italians operated against Malta with faint heart and still fainter success; and *Fliegerkorps X*, established since June in Crete, Greece and the Dodecanese, failed to make any noticeable impression on the keypoints in the Delta. Cairo our enemies left untouched for political reasons, though it was never declared an open city as the Egyptian Government desired. Had they in fact bombed the Egyptian capital we intended to retaliate against Rome.

With the enemy air forces thus held in check by our opposition and their own lack of initiative, Tedder could proceed with the task on which his heart was set. For the fate of the Middle East, as he well knew, was likely to be decided not in the Western Desert but on the seas which divide Africa from Europe. If the U-boats won the mastery of the Atlantic there was an end to our chances of building up decisive strength in Egypt. And if Tedder's own aircraft and Admiral Cunningham's ships and submarines could cut the enemy's life-lines across the Mediterranean, it was farewell to Axis ambitions in Africa. So, while the Desert squadrons wore down their opponents and prepared for the great offensive, Tedder struck with his long-range bombers against the enemy's convoy routes. From Malta, Royal Air Force Blenheims, Marylands and Wellingtons, together with the Swordfish and Fulmars of the Fleet Air Arm, preyed on Naples, Tripoli, and all the wide stretch of water which separates the two. So complete was our intelligence that no important convoy escaped their attention. At the same time the Wellingtons from the Suez Canal raided ports along the enemy's alternative route, which went from Brindisi or Taranto across to Benghazi (or Tripoli) by way of Greece and Crete. Above all, these Wellingtons kept up a ceaseless assault against Benghazi, which was doubly important as a

THREE OF THE VICTORIOUS AIR TEAM IN THE MIDDLE EAST

Air Vice-Marshal G. C. Pirie, Air Vice-Marshal G. G. Dawson, Air Commodore W. E. G. Mann

AXIS SHIPPING AT TRIPOLI WRECKED BY BRITISH BOMBING, JANUARY 1942

terminal of the alternative route and the port to which supplies were moved forward from Tripoli. This task of the Wellingtons was so much a regular routine that it became known as the 'Mail Run'; and it inspired (to the tune of 'Clementine') the best-known squadron song of the war[1].

The general effect of our naval and air operations against the enemy's convoy routes was clear enough at the time, and is clearer still in retrospect. On 29th August, 1941, Mussolini and the Italian Supreme Commander, Cavallero, met Keitel at the Brenner. They informed him that up to 31st July Italy had lost seventy-four per cent of her shipping space employed on the African convoy routes; and that the tonnage left available for this purpose amounted to only 65,000 tons. On 17th September, Raeder reported to Hitler that German shipments to North Africa had 'recently suffered additional heavy losses of ships, material and personnel as the result of enemy air attacks by means of bombs and torpedoes, and through submarine attacks'. In desperation the *Führer*, as recounted earlier, then ordered U-boats into the Mediterranean to offset our naval superiority. This had little effect on our aircraft, and by the end of October the Axis position was so desperate that Hitler decided to re-establish the *Luftwaffe* in Sicily, at the expense of his forces in Russia, for the express purpose of neutralizing Malta. On 13th November Raeder reported: 'The situation regarding transports to North Africa has grown progressively worse, and has now reached the critical stage. . . .'.

So much for the general effect of the joint offensive by our naval and air forces. In terms of figures the result is equally impressive. Between 1st June and 31st October, 1941, we sank at least 220,000

---

[1] Down the Flights each ruddy morning,
Sitting waiting for a clue,
Same old notice on the flight board,
Maximum effort—guess where to.

Seventy Squadron, Seventy Squadron,
Though we say it with a sigh,
We must do the ruddy mail run
Every night until we die.

Have you lost us navigator?
Come up here and have a look;'
'Someone's shot our starboard wing off!'
'We're alright then, that's Tobruk'

Seventy Squadron, etc.

Oh to be in Piccadilly,
Selling matches by the score,
Then we should not have to do the
Blessed mail run any more.

Seventy Squadron, etc.

tons of enemy shipping on the African convoy routes. 94,000 tons of this fell to our naval vessels—mainly submarines—and 115,000 to the Royal Air Force and the Fleet Air Arm. Ninety per cent of the sinkings were of loaded southbound traffic, and at least three-quarters of those attributed to aircraft were the work of the squadrons on Malta. The whole total probably represented something between one-third and one-half of the entire enemy sailings to North Africa over the period.

* * *

In the midst of this preliminary struggle the question of the relative strength of the opposing air forces, which had proved so embarrassing to Longmore, again came dramatically to the fore. Asked by the authorities at home for an estimate of the air forces which would be available on either side at the beginning of the new military offensive, Tedder replied that the enemy would probably enjoy numerical superiority. The air battle, he thought, was likely to be waged between some 650 Axis aircraft on the one hand and 500 British aircraft on the other. If the Russian front became stable the odds against us would be still greater.

This statement caused consternation in Whitehall. According to Air Ministry calculations the enemy had a total establishment in the Mediterranean area of 1,190 aircraft; but the number actually serviceable and likely to be available for the opening phases of a battle in Cyrenaica was only 365, of which 237 would be Italian. Extra help, admittedly, might be forthcoming from the longe-range bombers based in Greece and Crete. On the strength of this Portal described Tedder's comparison as 'most depressing . . . and unjustifiably so'; and, after promises of reinforcement, the Middle East air commander gave a revised estimate of 600 for his own forces. Even then the enemy in his opinion would still be numerically stronger.

Meanwhile Tedder's original statement, had in Portal's words, 'raised acute political controversy'. With bitter memories of Greece and Crete the New Zealand Government asked for an assurance that before New Zealand ground forces were again committed we should be certain of superiority in the air. With Tedder's figures before him the Prime Minister naturally felt unable to give any such guarantee. Tiring of exchanges conducted by telegraph, Mr. Churchill then insisted on sending to Egypt a 'very senior officer' to find out the truth.

Tedder was now on extremely dangerous ground. But fortunately the 'very senior officer', on the inspired suggestion of Lord Beaverbrook, was Air Marshal Sir Wilfrid Freeman, the Vice-Chief of Air Staff and lately Tedder's immediate superior. And if it came to the point, neither Freeman nor Portal was prepared to agree that a commander in whom they still had every confidence, even if he appeared to be undercalling his hand, should be relieved on the eve of a great offensive.

In mentioning his smaller numbers Tedder had certainly not meant to infer that the Axis forces would actually enjoy air superiority; for every British aircraft was worth at least two of the Italians. As a result of this and a little firmness with General Wavell, who as Commander-in-Chief India objected to the movement of squadrons from Iraq, Freeman and Tedder were soon able to adjust matters to their mutual satisfaction. By stripping down Iraq, Palestine, Cyprus, Aden and the Delta almost to the last useful machine, Tedder was able to bring his own strength up to 660, excluding aircraft in Malta; while re-examination of the Axis figure yielded a total of 642 machines, including 435 Italian. Probable serviceability—an important point not dealt with in Tedder's original estimate—was put at 528 for the British, 385 for the Axis; and the British would have reserves of fifty per cent, the enemy few or none at all. This much more favourable comparison, however, ignored the enemy air forces outside Cyrenaica. With Auchinleck also stressing that the New Zealanders would enjoy 'sufficient and adequate' support in both tanks and aircraft, the Prime Minister was now satisfied. The required assurance was given to New Zealand, and preparations for the battle proceeded.

* * *

Operation 'Crusader', to give the forthcoming offensive its code-name, was nothing if not ambitious. The intention was to destroy the enemy's main force of armour, relieve Tobruk and retake Cyrenaica, all as a preliminary to invading Tripolitania. With Libya entirely wrested from the Axis we could then form our main front at the Northern instead of the Western extremity of the Middle East Command, and so stand guard against a German drive through the Caucasus.

The air plan for this very considerable undertaking contemplated four phases, of which two were prior to the Army's attack. Phase One, the intensification of pressure against the Axis air forces and supply routes, began on 14th October, 1941. The effect of all the training and practice of the preceding weeks was at once apparent, and our fighters soon established a high degree of superiority over the forward area. The greatest threat to their supremacy—the new Me.109F, which had an unpleasant habit of 'picking off' stragglers—they kept in check by fresh tactics. Instead of flying straight during offensive sweeps, with one or two 'weavers' in the rear, whole squadrons of Hurricanes and Tomahawks now 'weaved'. 'The squadrons are enthusiastic over their new methods' reported Tedder to Portal; 'they should be a very effective answer to the Hun's "tip and run" tactics. I should hate to tackle one of these formations, which looks like a swarm of angry bees'.

Operations against the Axis supply lines were equally successful. Malta not only continued to take toll of enemy shipping but also struck heavy blows against Brindisi, Tripoli, Naples, the airfield of Castel Benito and the submarine base at Augusta. The raid against the Naples oil storage depot on the night of 21st/22nd October was especially noteworthy; it started a blaze which bomber crews newly arrived from operations over Germany described as the biggest they had ever seen. Meanwhile from Egypt the short-range bombers—the Blenheims and Fleet Air Arm Albacores—attacked the dumps and small ports just behind the enemy's front line, and the longer range bombers maintained their assault on Benghazi. A daylight service operated by the South African Marylands now supplemented the Wellingtons' nightly 'mail run' to this much-bombed port, and the enemy was thus forced to bring up most of his supplies overland from Tripoli. This placed Rommel's motor transport under an intolerable strain—a strain produced quite as much by the moral as the physical effects of the bombing. As Vice-Admiral Weichold (the Chief German Liaison Officer at Italian Naval Headquarters) explained later, 'the dock workers and stevedores were for the most part composed of Arabs who fled at each air attack'; and the 'screaming' bombs (if not the empty beer bottles) of the South Africans doubtless prompted them to an extra turn of speed.

By the end of Phase Two—the six days of intensive attack against the enemy air forces immediately before D Day—enemy supplies were at a very low level, enemy aircraft were thoroughly on the defensive, our reconnaissance had obtained a good picture of the Axis dispositions, and the Eighth Army had moved forward to its striking positions unobserved and unharassed from the air. On 17th November Tedder despatched his eve-of-battle report to the Chief of Air Staff. 'Squadrons are at full strength, aircraft and crews, with reserve aircraft, and the whole force is on its toes'. The following day Auchinleck launched the Eighth Army into action.

The military plan of campaign was for XXX Corps, with most of the armour (including the redoubtable 7th Armoured Division), to move forward on the left round the enemy's open flank. The Corps would then strike boldly towards the coast and Tobruk. The enemy could not ignore a challenge of this kind, and the decisive encounter was likely to be fought near the ridges of El Duda and Sidi Rezegh a few miles south-east of the beleaguered port. In the later stages of this clash, when our victory was reasonably certain, the Tobruk garrison would break out towards El Duda and the relieving troops. Meanwhile on our right XIII Corps, with most of the infantry (including the 2nd New Zealand and the 4th Indian Division) would contain the main enemy positions along the frontier, then advance in the coastal sector to join in the great battle outside Tobruk. As a subsidiary operation a group small in numbers but deceptively large in appearance would create a diversion by attacking the distant oases of Augila and Gialo, far to the south of Benghazi. Another—indeed the main—object of this expedition was to protect the landing grounds of two squadrons detailed to cause confusion in the enemy's rear.

The opposing forces were not unevenly matched. The Eighth Army, under General Sir Alan Cunningham, the brother of the naval Commander-in-Chief and the conqueror of Abyssinia, was seven divisions strong. Against them, under Erwin Rommel, were eight divisions in the forward area and three more in the remainder of Libya. In numbers of tanks the British enjoyed an advantage—655 against the enemy's 505; but Rommel's heavier models with their thicker armour and stronger fire-power were better suited than our own to the open conditions of the desert[1]. In the air Tedder could muster in Egypt and Malta a first-line establishment of some 700 aircraft. Thanks to the great efforts of the maintenance organization actual strength and serviceability considerably exceeded this total. Of his 49 operational squadrons, 9 were in Malta, 11 in the Canal Zone and the Delta, and 29 in the Western Desert under Coningham. The latter's force had a strongly Dominion flavour; commanded by a New Zealander it contained six South African, one Rhodesian and two Australian squadrons, with two squadrons of the Fleet Air Arm and one of the Free French (the Lorraine Squadron) to lend further variety. Against this the Germans and Italians had an official strength of 436 aircraft in Cyrenaica, of which only 283 were serviceable and immediately available. They had also, however, 186 aircraft in Tripolitania, 776 in Sicily, Sardinia, Greece, Crete and the Dodecanese, and over six hundred more in Italy and the Balkans.

[1] The largest gun in the British tanks was the two pounder; the Germans' smallest gun fired a 4½ lb. shell and their largest a 14 lb. shell.

Many of these could play a part in the struggle from their existing bases, while others could be rapidly transferred to Cyrenaica. Moreover the enemy had a powerful air transport fleet, amounting to some 300 aircraft, when we had but two squadrons. The general picture, then, was that we were likely to maintain air superiority over the battle area at least until the enemy could bring his outside forces into play. During this time we hoped to settle the issue.

The opening blow took our opponents entirely by surprise. It anticipated by five days the enemy's long-delayed attack on Tobruk and so caught Rommel 'on the wrong foot'. Good work by the camouflage experts, the failure of enemy reconnaissance in the face of Coningham's fighters and forty-eight hours of atrocious weather all helped to secure this result. This bad weather—torrential rain, low cloud and violent dust-storms—continued throughout 18th November. It imposed a serious handicap on our aircraft. But the enemy were based on softer ground than ourselves and it affected them much more. Our domination of the skies was thus complete. Special features of the day included a successful bombing attack on a group of water-logged enemy vehicles, some long-range strafing of airfields and motor transport by the Beaufighters of No. 272 Squadron, and good work against Italian aircraft and lorries in the rear by the two squadrons (Nos. 33 and 113) with the oases force.

By 19th November the weather was clearer. On our left the reconnaissance squadron (No. 208) attached to XXX Corps pinpointed some 1,800 vehicles and 80 tanks of the Ariete Division, and soon the armoured battle was joined in earnest. The two German Panzer Divisions (the 15th and 21st) nearer the coast were also engaged—though not, as it proved, decisively; and between the two clashes a small British armoured force slipped through and advanced virtually unchallenged as far as Sidi Rezegh. By the 20th the position appeared so favourable that the Tobruk garrison—which was kept informed of developments by four aircraft of No. 451 Squadron, R.A.A.F., based within the perimeter—was ordered to break out the following morning.

During this opening phase Coningham's squadrons continued to maintain complete air superiority. An Army officer back from the forward area described it as 'like France, only the other way round'; and Coningham was able to report to Tedder: 'XXX Corps are very pleased with us, and so is the Army in general'. This was despite mounting opposition as the enemy's landing grounds dried out. On the 20th, for instance, the German bombers made a desperate effort to support their ground forces. They lost eight of their number to our fighters, who repeatedly broke up the enemy formations and

BENGHAZI
BENINA
SOLUK
BARCE
JEBEL EL AKDAR
EL GUBBA
DERNA
MARTUBA
BOMBA
TMIMI
GULF OF BOMBA
EL MECHILI
MSUS
ANTELAT
AGEDABIA
GULF OF SIRTE
EL AGHEILA
EL GAZALA
TOBRUK
EL ADEM
GAMBUT
TRIGH CAPUZZO
BIR HAKIM
BARDIA
GULF OF SOLLUM
FORT CAPUZZO
SOLLUM
HALFAYA PASS
SIDI OMAR
BUQ-BUQ
SIDI BARRANI
FORT MADDALENA
GIARABUB
AUGILA
JALO
CYRENAICA
EGYPT
LIBYAN SAND SEA
QATTARA DEPRESSION
MERSA MATRUH
MAATEN BAGUSH
FUKA
EL DABA
EL ALAMEIN
ALEXANDRIA
ABOUKIR
EL AMIRIYA
SUEZ CANAL
ABU SUEIR
HELIOPOLIS
CAIRO
MOKATTAM HILLS
HELWAN
R. NILE

LEGEND
RAILWAYS
ENEMY POSITIONS
KEY ROADS
TRACKS
ALLIED POSITIONS
ALLIED ATTACKS

SCALE 20 10 0 20 40 60 80 100 120 140 MILES

THE CRUSADER PLAN
NOVEMBER 1941
SCALE 10 5 0 10 20 30 MILES
TOBRUK
70 DIV.
EL DUDA
SIDI REZEGH
15 PANZER
21 PANZER
BARDIA
SOLLUM
SIDI BARRANI
GABR SALEH
ARMD DIV.
4 IND. DIV.
XIII CORPS
2 N.Z. DIV.
XXX CORPS
L.G.123
L.G.122
L.G.124
FT. MADDALENA
L.G.128

CYRENAICA AND THE WESTERN DESERT, 1941

forced them to jettison their bombs. Apart from giving the death blow to the reputation of the Stuka our aircraft also attacked enemy columns, concentrations and landing grounds—the new Hurricane fighter-bombers of No. 80 Squadron joining the ordinary fighters and bombers in this work. In addition six bombers specially equipped for jamming the R/T communications of the enemy's tanks, and popularly known as 'Winston's Wellingtons', flew backwards and forwards at low altitude over the battle area trying to carry out what Coningham described as a 'very thankless and hazardous task'.

With the tide of battle running strongly in our favour, early on 21st November the Tobruk garrison set out for El Duda. At the same time XIII Corps began to move forward in the coastal area. But just then our forward armour preparing to attack Sidi Rezegh became aware that the 15th Panzer Division was approaching from the south-east. The German tanks were held off and Sidi Rezegh was duly captured. Then the 21st Panzer Division, having also shaken off their engaging forces, appeared on the scene. In a fierce two-day battle fought amidst clouds of dust and smoke which at times made it impossible to distinguish friend from foe our tanks were forced away from the ridge and the landing ground. Acting with his usual speed, on 24th November Rommel then sent armoured columns racing towards the Egyptian frontier.

For the next few days the fate of the opposing armies hung in the balance. To add to other complications there was a crisis in the British Command. General Cunningham lost confidence in his forces' power to continue the offensive; Auchinleck lost confidence in General Cunningham; and on 26th November Major General Ritchie, Auchinleck's Deputy Chief of Staff, was placed in command of the Eighth Army. In all this Tedder was strongly on the side of Auchinleck and continuing the offensive. Meanwhile Rommel's raid, undetected by air reconnaissance, had achieved complete surprise. On 24th November the first onrush overran the advanced headquarters of XXX Corps on the airfield at Gabr Saleh. Here the German tank column suddenly appeared while General Cunningham was conferring with the Corps Commander. The ground party of No. 108 Squadron 'left hurriedly, and the Army Commander's Blenheim took off through a stampede of vehicles across the aerodrome'. The whole headquarters was thrown into confusion and for some time afterwards was unable to exercise effective command. According to Wing Commander Gordon Finlayson, the Senior Operations Officer at Air Headquarters Western Desert, there ensued 'a most interesting period, which as a study of panics, chaotics and gyrotics, is probably unsurpassed in military history'.

Sweeping on, the enemy column next menaced our fighter airfields. 'The news of the threatened German tank attack was received at L.G.123 and L.G.124 an hour before sunset' recorded No. 1 Squadron. 'All aircraft were ordered to fly to L.G.128. Other squadrons received similar instructions, and the sky was packed with Hurricanes, Tomahawks and two or three "Lizzies" all making for L.G.128. As most of the pilots did not know the whereabouts of L.G.128, the majority landed at L.G.122. So many aircraft were at L.G.122 they were standing wing tip to wing tip. The pilots, because of the danger of parachute troops, were ordered to sleep under the wings of the aircraft'. In this tense atmosphere, with the ground crews standing guard and the anti-aircraft gunners siting their weapons to engage tanks, the night of 24th/25th November slowly passed. Fortunately the expected attack did not materialize. 'We had 175 aircraft on the 'drome', recorded No. 112 Squadron, 'and as the Hun column passed only ten miles north of us . . . they missed a glorious opportunity of wrecking most of our fighters'. An episode of this kind naturally had repercussions. 'I have left them [the Army], wrote Coningham to Tedder, 'in no doubt as to their obligation to give us security for our bases, and how our work relies on that security. They realize the position but of course could do little about it in the prevailing confusion and lack of information'.

This withdrawal limited the activity of our fighters on 24th November. Nevertheless Coningham's squadrons still maintained their pressure against the enemy's airfields, broke up repeated attacks by Stukas and struck many sharp blows against the marauding columns. In particular, the Tomahawks of No. 2 Squadron S.A.A.F., and the Hurricane fighter-bombers of No. 80 Squadron dealt heavily with 'soft-skinned' vehicles. Several times, however, our aircraft failed to attack or attacked our own forces. This was partly because our troops were not displaying identification flags (they were issued with only forty to a Corps), partly because the Germans were now using captured British lorries. Moreover, in the words of No. 80 Squadron's diary, 'Nearly all columns in the so called "Matruh Stakes" were moving as fast as the ground and their horsepower allowed in an easterly direction, and it was singularly difficult for anyone either on the ground or in the air to pick out whether any particular cloud of dust was friend or foe'. Our squadrons' failures, however, were much less important than their successes. Despite all the confusion, on 24th November our aircraft unquestionably slowed down the enemy.

On the 25th and 26th the work continued. Hurricane fighter-bombers caught the main enemy column near Sidi Omar, Blenheims and Marylands took up the attack, and Fleet Air Arm Albacores continued the assault far into the night. Against groups of lorries the fighter-bombers proved deadly, but their 40 lb. bombs were too small to do much harm to tanks. They were sufficiently powerful, however, to blow off the heads of several tanks crews who 'opened up their lids to see what the noise was about'. By an intense and sustained effort Coningham's squadrons thus helped to stem the tide, so giving the disorganized elements of the Eighth Army time to recover. In the end Rommel's thrust achieved little. 'But', as General Auchinleck wrote later, 'it might have succeeded had the 4th Indian Division shown less determination and [our] mobile columns less offensive spirit, or had the Royal Air Force not bombed the enemy's principal columns so relentlessly'.

Fifty miles or so to the West the New Zealand Division and the Tobruk garrison had meanwhile been relieved of the pressure of the enemy's armour. This enabled them both to make decisive headway. On 26th November the New Zealanders captured Sidi Rezegh and the 70th Division from Tobruk reached El Duda. By nightfall the two forces had made contact. This was far too serious for the raiding columns on the Egyptian frontier to ignore. Strongly opposed on the ground, hammered from the air and now threatened in the rear, on 27th November the Axis tanks abandoned their foray and hastened back towards Tobruk. By 28th November they were ready to dispute our gains. Two days later the ridge at Sidi Rezegh was once more in German hands and Tobruk was again isolated.

This reverse checked but in no way dismayed the Eighth Army. Tedder, visiting the forward area on 3rd December, was deeply impressed with the way the 'new Army management' was facing up to its task. That same day, content with the situation outside Tobruk, Rommel sent off two strong patrols towards the Egyptian frontier. One moved along the coastal road, the other along the great desert track known as the Trigh Capuzzo. Both were spotted and attacked from the air, fiercely resisted on the ground, and routed with heavy loss. The next day the German commander tried again; again the column was detected by our reconnaissance and beaten off by combined air and ground action. Meanwhile an attack on our positions outside Tobruk was held after severe fighting, and on 5th December the main enemy concentrations around Sidi Rezegh withdrew to a fresh line a few miles further west. During this movement great storms of dust grounded our bombers but the fighter-bombers again attacked motor transport with success. The night bombers, too, were soon busy against the enemy's new positions. By 8th December continued pressure had once more brought our troops into contact with the defenders of Tobruk and the eight months' siege was virtually at an end. Completing his withdrawal, Rommel then moved west to well prepared positions at Gazala.

The enemy armour, though not yet destroyed, was now severely mauled. But at this very moment events of decisive importance for the future of the struggle occurred elsewhere. Just as the decision to support Greece had earlier cost us the fruits of Wavell's offensive, so now the Japanese invasion of Malaya prejudiced the success of 'Crusader'.

The full effects of the war in the Far East were to be felt later. For the time being Ritchie's troops still pressed on and Coningham's squadrons gave them all the help within their power. This was now considerably less than Coningham desired. Bad weather, lack of forward landing grounds, difficulty in distinguishing the enemy's vehicles from our own, shortage of information about the movements of our tanks—all these gravely restricted the activity of our bombers. For many hours the Blenheims and Marylands stood by, unable to operate because the Army could suggest no suitable objectives for attack. 'Very hectic today' wrote Coningham to Tedder on 10th December, 'the most intensive fighting on the front is here—my fighting for targets!! Took three and a half hours this morning'. These restrictions did not, however, apply to the fighters, which kept up relentless pressure against the opposing air force and the retiring columns.

On 13th December the Eighth Army attacked Rommel's new line at Gazala. This was well fortified; but the strongest line in the desert, except at one or two very special positions like El Agheila and El Alamein, had an open flank to the south. Three days' heavy fighting and an outflanking movement sent the enemy once more into retreat. By the 16th it seemed that our ultimate ambition, the envelopment of the entire Axis army, might well be achieved. 'Hope you realize the present unique situation', signalled XIII Corps Commander to the Commander of the 7th Armoured Division. 'The enemy is completely surrounded provided you block his retreat. You have more than sufficient force to achieve this and worry him incessantly. You can, and must, inflict shattering blows on his soft stuff. Never in history has there been fuller justification for intrepid boldness. If we miss this opportunity we are disgraced . . .'

The 7th Armoured Division was not, and could not be, disgraced. But the enemy escaped all the same. Soft sand held up our supply vehicles, and Rommel lived to fight another day. 'The battle of

Gazala has been a great disappointment', wrote Coningham to Tedder on 17th December, 'in that there was a promise of a complete encirclement and defeat of the enemy which has not been fulfilled. From my point of view the operational aspect regarding bombing could not have been worse. I pointed out to Neil [General Ritchie] last night that the whole of the enemy land fighting force had been in a comparatively small area south-west of Gazala for nearly three days and had not had one bomb dropped on them, although we had absolute superiority without any hostile interference in the air for two days. During that time squadrons of bombers have been "at call" here, but always their operations have had to be called off because of the lack of identification and the close contact of the enemy forces with our own'.

As the enemy broke away, conditions became right for intensive bombing, and for three days Coningham was able, as Tedder put it, 'to let his hounds loose'. Nowhere in the whole breadth of the Jebel could Rommel possibly make an effective stand, and on Christmas Eve our patrols for the second time swept into Benghazi. There, before their eyes, were the results of the 'mail run', augmented now by the enemy's demolitions. Sunken vessels lay dotted about, huge holes were torn in the quays, the harbour entrance was completely blocked. Desperately though we needed the port to sustain our advance it was a full fortnight before the first British ship could enter.

As our troops moved across Cyrenaica they also found ample evidence of our attacks on airfields. On every landing ground large numbers of damaged and unserviceable aircraft lay abandoned. Not all of these were victims of our air action: many had been shattered by the shells of the ground forces (notably the Long Range Desert Group) or had succumbed to the general wear and tear of desert conditions. But there were enough that bore the marks of our fighters and bombers; and the total numbers were certainly impressive. At Gambut there were 42; at the Martubas 37; at El Adem 78; at Derna 75; at the Gazalas 71; at Berka 71; at Benina 64. All told, between Gambut and Benina 458 enemy aircraft, or their remains, were picked up on airfields alone. Many hundreds more lay in the open desert and in the dumps known as 'graveyards'. Not much of this could be ascribed, as when we counted hundreds of abandoned enemy machines during our first great advance, to bad maintenance by the Italians. Almost exactly half the aircraft concerned were German.

At Agedabia the pursuit once more slowed down. Here the enemy were able to stand while they prepared their final positions on the well-tried line of El Agheila. Prodigious work by the Royal Air Force ground crews—at Gazala they laboured for two days ahead of our forward troops—had thus far enabled Coningham's fighters to keep up with the advance. With the help of the American Kittyhawks now coming into action for the first time, we therefore still maintained our superiority in the air. Our bomber squadrons, however, could not move forward so fast. They accordingly made up for their reduced effort in the forward area by attacking by-passed strong points near the Egyptian frontier. Some 400 sorties contributed to the fall of Bardia, and the bombers then turned their attention to Halfaya. After a Wellington had dropped without effect a forged message from Rommel ordering the garrison to surrender, some 300 sorties of a more orthodox nature helped to produce the desired result, which finally came about on 17th January.

Meanwhile on 6th January the enemy had withdrawn from Agedabia. Within a few days the position of the two main armies stabilised at El Agheila. There, behind a fifty-mile line of salt-pans, sand dunes and small cliffs, with the vast expanse of shifting sand known as the Libyan Sand Sea on the southern flank, Rommel defied our further attempts to advance. He was able to do so not only because of the natural advantages of the place but also because our supply system was now strained to the limit; conversely he himself had come within easier reach of his own bases as he fell back. At El Agheila the Axis forces were some five hundred miles from Tripoli; the Eighth Army was a thousand from Cairo and Suez. Had Ritchie found it possible to press on, Coningham could have given adequate, if reduced, support. But for the moment our troops were at the end of their administrative tether.

Once more, then, it was a race to build up supplies in the forward area. Plans were drawn up for the fresh advance—Operation 'Acrobat'—which would carry us to the Tunisian border; but in no case could Auchinleck hope to strike before the middle of February. And this time, despite the mauling the enemy had suffered, the situation was very different from that of the previous November. Before 'Crusader' our bases had been comparatively near the front line, the enemy's far distant; for several months a generous stream of supplies had been pouring into the Middle East; and Malta, faced only by the Italians, had been free to prey with deadly effect on the Axis convoy routes. Now the reverse obtained in every respect. Our supply lines stretched half way across Africa, while the enemy's were relatively short; men and machines were fast moving out of the Middle East to Malaya, Burma and threatened India; and Malta was once more under fire from the Germans.

* * *

Between the end of May 1941 when German aircraft left Sicily and the middle of December when they returned, Malta faced only the Italians. The island made good use of its freedom. Despite an absence of bulldozers, mechanical 'grabs' and other devices which make modern building so fascinating a spectacle, the defences underwent a remarkable development. With no heavy equipment more up-to-date than a few steamrollers, the Air Ministry Works Directorate pressed on with new airfields, taxi-tracks, dispersals, radar stations and operations rooms. In all this it was helped unsparingly by the local Army authorities. During the same period devoted efforts by the Royal Navy and the Royal Air Force brought in two convoys from the west, so restocking the island with food, bombs, ammunition, aviation fuel and many other vital commodities. The result of this replenishment was not merely a surprisingly high standard of living among the Services (in the words of Air Vice-Marshal H. P. Lloyd, who had taken over from Maynard in May, 'You wouldn't have known there was a war on'). It was also, as already indicated, victory in the battle of supplies that preceded 'Crusader'.

During the opening weeks of Auchinleck's offensive Malta still struck out with vigour. Bad weather and the enemy's determination to route his vessels as far from the island as possible failed to subdue our aircraft and submarines. In November 1941 the confirmed and identified sinkings on the Axis convoy routes totalled 39,000 tons; while the proportion of shipping lost or disabled amounted, according to Admiral Weichold, to no less than seventy-seven per cent of the entire tonnage employed. December showed little decline on this remarkable achievement. The steadily worsening weather cut down the sinkings by aircraft, but another 35,000 tons still went to the bottom. Moreover the passage to Malta of two small west-bound convoys under air cover from our newly captured landing grounds in Cyrenaica promised further successes of the same order.

By then, however, Hitler had resolved to strike at the root of the trouble. On 29th October, 1941 he gave preliminary orders for the transfer of air units from the Russian front to the Central Mediterranean. During November the Headquarters of *Luftflotte* 2, then controlling air operations before Moscow, duly moved to Rome. With it came *Generalfeldmarschall* Kesselring, the soldier-turned-air-commander who had presided over its fortunes from the days of the Battle of Britain. A little later, in December, after a formal directive had placed Kesselring in charge of all German air forces in the Mediterranean, the units of *Fliegerkorps II* followed from the East and began to take up station in Sicily. This meant that the *Luftwaffe* now had three major formations in the Mediterranean —*Fliegerkorps II* in Sicily, *Fliegerkorps X* in Greece and Crete, and the forces of the *Fliegerführer Afrika*. At the same time air reinforcements, German and Italian, were flown to Tripolitania. By mid-December the process was still incomplete. But by that date the German Air Force in the Mediterranean, despite the losses it had suffered in 'Crusader', was over fifty per cent stronger than it had been a month before.

All this was what Tedder had foreseen in October when he had been so reluctant to assess relative strengths merely in terms of aircraft based in Africa. By the third week in December the combined German and Italian air forces in Sicily numbered some 250 long-range bombers and reconnaissance aircraft and nearly 200 fighters. Against these Lloyd could muster only 60 serviceable bombers and 70 serviceable fighters.

According to the orders he had received from Hitler on 2nd December, Kesselring was to concentrate on three main objectives. In the first place he was 'to obtain air and sea supremacy in the area between Southern Italy and North Africa in order to establish safe shipping routes to Libya'. To this end it was 'particularly important to suppress Malta'. Secondly, he was to co-operate with the German and Italian forces in North Africa. Thirdly, he was to 'paralyse enemy shipping traffic passing through the Mediterranean. . . .' He had, then, to attack both Malta and the convoys supplying it. On 22nd December he set about his task.

Up to this point the enemy had not normally flown more than sixty or seventy sorties a week against Malta. Now, in the last week of December, over two hundred aircraft attacked the island. Their objective was the Royal Air Force. Repeatedly, they raided the fighter grounds of Hal Far and Takali, the bomber airfield of Luqa, the seaplane base at Kalafrana; but the Hurricane II's, though outclassed by the latest Me.109's, broke up the enemy formations and kept the damage within tolerable limits. Then the Germans struck still more violently. In the opening days of January 1942 they flew some five hundred sorties against Lloyd's bases. At the same time heavy rains turned the battered fighter airfields into quagmires, and all squadrons had to be concentrated on the equally battered but better drained Luqa.

Under the combined impact of the elements and the German Air Force, the bomber effort from Malta began to wilt. At the beginning of January 1942, Lloyd could still strike some shrewd blows. On 4th January, for instance, ten Blenheims attacked a large force of transport aircraft on the ground at Castelvetrano, destroying eleven and damaging twenty-eight. But the month's total of offensive sorties was only half of that for December. However, more supplies were brought safely into harbour and Malta was not yet without the means of hitting back.

By February the Germans were warming to their work. On 7th February Malta's air-raid sirens sounded sixteen times within twenty-four hours. So frequent and so heavy were the attacks that during the whole month our bombers flew only sixty sorties and sank only one ship. On 22nd February the Blenheims were therefore withdrawn to Egypt, leaving only the Wellingtons and the Fleet Air Arm Swordfish. But for all the violence of the enemy's attacks the morale of the defenders never faltered. The pilots and the anti-aircraft gunners remained as ardent as ever; and willing hands toiled, day and night, to repair the runways and build shelter-pens for the aircraft and the few precious steamrollers and petrol bowsers. These pens they made first from sand bags, then from earth-filled petrol tins, then, as the damage increased, from broken masonry. Maltese civilian labour alone could never have coped with this task, and some 3,000 men of the Army joined their efforts with those of the civilians and the Royal Air Force. 'But for the soldiers', said Lloyd afterwards, 'I should certainly have been out of business'.

So the battle continued. The enemy was striking ever more furiously; Malta still resisted every blow, but was fast losing her ability to strike back. Such was the situation when German aircraft sank the mid-February convoy from Alexandria. In the knowledge that existing stocks of fuel, food and ammunition could last but a few brief months, Malta now faced a future which was indeed grim. For all her sufferings to this time were but the prelude of the storm to come.

* * *

On 5th January, 1942, a Maryland of No. 69 Squadron from Malta spotted nine heavily escorted merchant vessels entering Tripoli. Covered by bad weather and the German assault on Malta these had slipped across the Mediterranean unmolested.

This was the second large group of enemy ships to reach Tripoli within three weeks. In the latter part of December bad weather had also enabled a battleship-escorted convoy to get through. On that occasion Malta's aircraft had sunk two cruisers and two of the merchant vessels, including one loaded with tanks, before the convoy put out from harbour; but the forebodings of Ciano about the actual voyage ('All the ships and all the admirals at sea. May God help us!') had for once proved unjustified.

The arrival of these two convoys with reinforcements and some 2,000 tons of aviation fuel transformed Rommel's position. Having just lost two-thirds of their strength in Cyrenaica, the German and Italian forces might reasonably have been expected to pause for recuperation. But Rommel, being Rommel, now set off eastwards again with something like three days' rations in hand and less than a hundred tanks. According to Kesselring, the decision was taken very suddenly and without the knowledge of, and in opposition to, the Commander-in-Chief Tripolitania, Marshal Bastico. 'On 21st January', recorded Auchinleck, 'the improbable occurred, and without warning the enemy began to advance'.

The move caught us unawares and in poor fettle. The forward landing grounds at Antelat were flooded after exceptionally heavy rains. Reconnaissance had been gravely curtailed and half the fighter force had just moved back to Msus. In addition, the general outrunning of supplies, the withdrawal of squadrons to the Far East, and technical trouble with the newly arrived Bostons had all combined to weaken the Western Desert Air Force. As for the Eighth Army, apart from other difficulties a Support Group inexperienced in desert driving had just relieved that of the 7th Armoured Division. This was ominous; for when a formation new to the desert had previously replaced those hardened veterans, Rommel had burst through and recaptured the whole of Cyrenaica.

The enemy's thrust was at first accompanied by intensive air action. From flooded Antelat our aircraft could not fight back to good effect, and for two days Stukas and Me.109's were able to attack our forward troops with some freedom. By the 22nd the German columns were coming on fast, with the result that the fighters still at Antelat left at remarkably short notice. 'First warning [of the enemy's advance] received by No. 258 Wing, Antelat', Coningham informed Tedder the next day, 'was at 1300 yesterday from Corps, and was merely "Move back at once, enemy coming". Place was being shelled as last aircraft took off. Pure good fortune that most of the fighter force not lost owing to state of ground . . . departure necessitated man-handling each aircraft by twelve men under wings to a strip thirty feet wide and five hundred yards long. All got off except four Kittyhawks and two Hurricanes which required air-crews and small repair'. These six aircraft, however, the squadrons destroyed before their departure, while others officially unserviceable—including a Kittyhawk with a damaged undercarriage—were flown off by pilots determined to risk their lives rather than abandon useful machines to the enemy. The ground parties, too, escaped, aided by spirited action on the part of Nos. 1 and 2 Companies, Royal Air Force Armoured Cars.

By 23rd January our fighters were operating strongly from Msus and had regained superiority over the forward area. But the enemy's drive, once begun, was not easily stopped. At the end of the day the Commander of XIII Corps asked for discretion to withdraw, if necessary, as far back at Mechili; and Coningham, distrustful of future developments, wisely ordered his maintenance and other heavy units, though not his fighting formations, to retire behind the Egyptian frontier.

Meanwhile in Cairo the Commanders-in-Chief could scarcely credit the evidence of the reports before them. Alarmed at what he considered a premature retirement, on the 25th Auchinleck flew up to Eighth Army Headquarters and pressed Ritchie to cancel XIII Corps' orders for a general withdrawal. The instruction was duly countermanded, much to the satisfaction of Tedder, who had accompanied Auchinleck, and who the next day reported to Portal, 'As a result of last night I hope some offensive counter-action on land may now be taken. The only way of stopping this nonsense is to hit back. Our fighters under Cross [Group Captain Cross, Commanding Officer of No. 258 Wing] are in angry mood . . . they appear to be at present the vital stabilising force. Coningham's team working well, angry but keeping their heads. . . .'

By this time the fighters were operating at top pitch. Back now one stage further, at Mechili, they kept up continuous low flying attacks on the enemy's advancing columns. The two squadrons of light bombers still available joined in and by night the Wellingtons of No. 205 Group, operating from advanced landing grounds, bombed concentrations of lorries further in the rear. On 26th January the Tomahawks, Kittyhawks and Hurricanes, repeatedly harrying the enemy as he pressed forward along the desert tracks, claimed 120 lorries destroyed or damaged. For the moment the advance on Msus was held.

All this was done despite frequent and violent sandstorms. 'The rising wind', recorded No. 30 Squadron on 26th January, 'soon developed into gale force. By lunch time our camp, which had a trim appearance ready for an inspection by the C.O., soon assumed the character of a veritable waste. Despite every ingenious device of the occupants of the tents to keep their "homes" intact—including the surreptitious appropriation of earth-filled M.T. petrol tins used to map out the tracks from one part of the camp to another—at least fifty per cent of the whole camp was dispersed flat. Even the arduous endeavours of the Orderly Room Staff to preserve their impeccable filing system failed to subdue the Muses, and eventually the filing system extended from the camp site to the beach—much to the chagrin of the runners who spent the remaining daylight hours collecting elusive bits of paper. The ferocity of the gale continued with unabated fury throughout the whole night. . . .'

Under cover of this storm, the next day Rommel again moved forward. While feinting to continue across the desert towards Mechili he directed his main strength northwards on Benghazi. Though our air effort was instantly applied to the threatened area it could not prevent the port once more changing hands. This happened on 28th January. Again the squadrons at Benina airfield took off only as the enemy approached; and again they left nothing behind.

XIII Corps now withdrew from Mechili to avoid encirclement from the north. But instead of leaving a mobile screen to cover the local landing ground until the last moment the Corps ordered the fighters to retire at once to Gazala. From Gazala, however, they could hardly cover our foremost troops. 'Very concerned to hear XIII Corps have ordered Fighter Wing to withdraw from Mechili', signalled Tedder to Auchinleck. 'Hope you fully appreciate how such a backward movement will hamstring our effort in the forward area. . . .' Auchinleck, still at Eighth Army Headquarters, promptly replied that he was 'infuriated to hear of this avoidable mistake'. 'Blame rests entirely with the XIII Corps Staff', he continued, 'Mary [Air Vice-Marshal Coningham] is getting them back to Mechili as quick as he can, but much valuable time has been lost'. In point of fact Coningham was unable to re-establish the squadrons at the vacated airfield, for the situation deteriorated too fast; he did, however, use it again as an advanced landing ground. Meanwhile our fighter activity over the forward area had inevitably been restricted—a very brief restriction but one in significant contrast with the continuously powerful support given a few months later during the retreat to El Alamein.

This incident, which doubtless arose from XIII Corps' commendable anxiety to avoid another move as unpremeditated as that from Antelat, naturally did nothing to inspire trust in our tactical direction. 'One feels that at present the sole stabilising factors are Auchinleck and our squadrons under Coningham' wrote Tedder to Portal on 29th January. 'I have confidence in both, but wish latter were stronger numerically'. For the enemy continued to advance through the Jebel Akdar, and nothing now but a further and deliberate withdrawal to the line Gazala–Bir Hakim could offer any chance of successful resistance. Such a withdrawal would sacrifice most of Cyrenaica, but would at least retain Tobruk and the eastern airfields.

Closely observed by our reconnaissance, Rommel pressed hard upon our retreat. But to do so he had now to leave behind his aircraft and nearly all his tanks. Having again out-run his supplies, the German Commander could only follow up with motorised infantry. By the same token the *Luftwaffe*, quite unable to keep pace with so rapid a progress—for Rommel kept the great bulk of the lorries and petrol for his own troops—could provide support only with its long-range bombers. These operated for the most part from Greece, either direct or by way of the rear landing grounds in Cyrenaica.

For almost a week the Stukas and the Me.109's made no appearance over the battle area. Of this opportunity Coningham's squadrons took full advantage. The climax came on 5th February when our fighters, now back at Gambut and El Adem, claimed over a hundred vehicles destroyed or damaged. The light bombers also maintained a fine effort and the squadrons from hard-pressed Malta struck what blows they could against the enemy's rear communications. By this time, too, the Wellingtons of No. 205 Group were again busy on the Benghazi 'mail run'. Lacking the weight to press home their advantage the enemy were thus halted. Their advance, begun so brilliantly, petered out from a combination of resistance on the ground, resistance in the air and sheer malnutrition. By the middle of February stability had returned to the war in the desert. The line from Gazala to Bir Hakim held firm.

Just as the disasters of Greece and Crete gave rise to bitter feelings on the part of the soldiers against the Royal Air Force, so the second loss of Cyrenaica led to bitterness among the airmen against the Army. In 1941 the Army had ascribed its defeat to German air superiority, and for this had blamed a hopelessly outnumbered Air Force. Now in 1942 the Royal Air Force had clearly achieved a very fair degree of superiority and the *Luftwaffe* had in no material sense affected the outcome of the battle. Yet the Army had still retreated. What the soldiers had previously imputed to the Air Force's wilful refusal to give proper protection, the airmen now imputed to the Army's faint-heartedness and incompetence.

In fact, of course, each Service was doing the other an injustice. The Middle East Air Force in early 1941 had been battling against impossible odds; the Eighth Army in early 1942, though otherwise well provided for, was struggling along with tanks greatly inferior to those of the Germans. During the three weeks of the retreat to Gazala the 1st Armoured Division lost over a hundred tanks through enemy action or mechanical breakdown—two-thirds of its complement and as many as the entire number of tanks opposed to it. Since this handicap was not commonly understood, and whenever it was mentioned in Parliament invariably received a strong official denial, the Royal Air Force can hardly be blamed for unfairly blaming the Army. Also it was natural for the airmen to seize an opportunity for retaliation. Of so fragile a nature was still the relationship between the Services in 1942, though at the upper levels Tedder was on excellent terms with Auchinleck, and Coningham with Ritchie, while at the lower levels co-operation rarely failed between airmen and soldiers actually working side by side. On the whole the presence of such lamentable sentiments was perhaps not surprising. In victory it is not difficult to overlook a partner's failings; in defeat they tend to occupy most of the picture.

Disappointing as the final outcome of 'Crusader' was, the dividends from the operation were very considerable. Even after the retreat our front line was still well west of the Egyptian frontier, instead of along it, and the airfields of Eastern Cyrenaica were now in our hands. Depth of defence, both in the air and on the ground, had been gained for the whole of Egypt. Moreover Tobruk, a tremendous strain on our resources while besieged, had been relieved; and the temporary possession of the West Cyrenaican airfields had enabled us to run convoys through to Malta. The new methods of tactical support for the Army had also been tried out, and if still capable of improvement had shown themselves a great advance on anything that had gone before. With further developments now foreshadowed, including the Army's long-deferred consent to the painting of some distinctive mark on its vehicles, even more effective support would certainly be given. The scheme of mobile wings, too, had proved a triumphant success; Coningham's squadrons had kept up with every movement in a campaign of extraordinary fluidity. As for the new Maintenance organization, its performance may be judged from a single fact. Between mid-November and mid-March, the maintenance units received 1,035 damaged aircraft—aircraft brought in from points scattered over something like100,000 square miles of desert. During the same period 810 of these machines were delivered back repaired to the battle area.

Certainly, then, the men of the Middle East Air Force could hold their heads high. From 18th November, when the Eighth Army went into action, to 14th February, when the position stabilised at Gazala,

Tedder's forces, including those in Malta, had flown some 16,000 sorties. For a loss of 575 of their own machines in the air and on the ground, they had destroyed, in conjunction with the gunners, 326 German aircraft and probably an equal number of Italian. They had protected our troops, safeguarded our ships, defended Suez and Alexandria, mauled the enemy's ground forces, and virtually eliminated the *Regia Aeronautica* as an effective force in Africa. All this they had done at a time when their aircraft were being drained away—some 300 of them between the end of December and the middle of February—to the Far East.

As the desert war again entered one of its quieter phases, Tedder's forces accordingly settled down once more, with the confidence born of success, to fight the battle of supplies that would so largely decide the next clash between the armies. But this time, though our air bases were farther forward in the desert, there was a new and ominous factor to take into account. So far from striking out with deadly precision against the enemy's convoys, Malta was now struggling desperately for mere survival.

CHAPTER X

Middle East: The Crisis of 1942

WITH the Eighth Army established at Gazala the military position became static. It remained so for over three months. Exhausted by the pace and fury of the exchanges the two combatants glared at each other from their opposing corners of the ring and gathered strength for the next round.

This interval passed less quietly for the air forces. On the British side, Tedder's squadrons continued to scour the Mediterranean for enemy shipping, protect Tobruk and the forward troops, 'deliver mail' at Benghazi five nights out of every seven, and attack the enemy's camps, landing grounds, dumps and lines of communication. Other units meanwhile sent off aircraft to the Far East (nearly 450 of them between mid-January and mid-March), installed mobile radar at Gazala and Gambut, and adapted fighters to carry 250 lb. and even 500 lb. bombs. On the planning side the staffs kept their wits in trim by preparing at one and the same time for a new offensive in the desert, an expedition to Turkey if Hitler threatened Anatolia, and a general redeployment in Persia if the German armies in Russia pierced the Caucasus.

The Axis air forces were almost equally busy. Among other activity they raided Tobruk and the forward area, made sporadic attacks on Alexandria and the Canal, and ran a supply service from Greece and Crete to Derna. They were also fully occupied trying to hold off our aircraft. In all this the *Luftwaffe* came a good first and the *Regia Aeronautica* a very poor second. All the work of the German airmen in Africa, however, paled into insignificance beside that of their comrades in Sicily.

The *Luftwaffe's* renewed assault on Malta had continued with mounting intensity throughout January and February 1942. In the latter month the enemy airmen cast down nearly 1,000 tons of bombs on the island—mainly on and about the airfields. In March the attack grew still hotter. Only one day passed without the wail of the siren, the heavy drone of the approaching 'hostiles', the sharper, angrier buzz of the Hurricanes, the racket of the guns, the swish and crash of the bombs. But on 7th March a new instrument joined this demonic orchestra. On that day fifteen of our best fighters, the first to be spared from home, flew in from carriers; and soon, high above all, sounded the shrill whistle of the Spitfire.

One squadron of Spitfires did not make a Maltese summer, or even a spring. By mid-March the number of serviceable Hurricanes was down to thirty, and all the bombers except a tiny handful of Wellingtons had been driven from the island. Malta's sword was being struck from her hand. From now on she must rely more than ever on her shield.

Kesselring at this stage appeared to be doing well enough. Though Malta's guns and fighters still offered fierce resistance, and though she was not yet out of action as a bomber and naval base, her offensive power and even her capacity for self-defence were fast diminishing. But the German commander remained dissatisfied; and his discontent was shared by the German Naval Staff. Kesselring and Raeder, though different enough in other ways, were both sound strategists; and both were well aware that Germany's interests in the Mediterranean demanded not merely the bombardment but the occupation of Malta. On 12th March Raeder represented this view to Hitler. The situation in the Mediterranean, he urged, was so favourable that Rommel should soon be able to drive forward on Suez. Before this could be done, however, the Axis must first subdue Malta. Direct capture would be preferable, but if that were impossible the island must be completely neutralised by attack from the air.

For once the Admiral's proposals fell on attentive ears. The Italians, explained Hitler, were already planning an expedition against Malta. Clearly something must be done to encourage this intention. The *Luftwaffe* must lend its aid—in what precise form he, the *Führer*, would shortly discuss with the *Duce*. Meanwhile the island must be attacked from the air with redoubled force.

Nothing loth, Kesselring flung his aircraft, by now some 400 in number, still more violently into the fray. The new phase began on 20th March with attacks by estimated forces of 143 Ju.88's and Me.109's. Takali was heavily hit, but Grand Harbour and the submarine base escaped damage. On the 21st the number of raiders rose to 218, and Takali was again badly cratered. On the 22nd 112 aircraft destroyed the barrack blocks at Takali but had less success at Hal Far. Then, on the 23rd, the attack switched to another objective; for a convoy of four supply ships, which Rear Admiral Vian had fought through from Alexandria in the teeth of the Italian Navy and the German Air Force, was now approaching the island. One of the precious freighters was hit and sunk twenty miles from shore, but despite furious attacks two others reached Grand Harbour that day. The third, much damaged, was later brought into harbour on the south of the island. Then followed tragedy. On the night of 23rd March only five of Lloyd's fighters remained serviceable; and some of his airmen wisely decided to take no chances of what might happen on the morrow. They boarded the two ships in Grand Harbour and extracted all the Royal Air Force stores that they could lay hands on, including a consignment of aero-engines. Unfortunately the arrangements for dealing with the rest of the cargo were not marked by equal enterprise. On the 24th there were raids by some 200 aircraft, none of which succeeded, thanks to the guns and fighters, in hitting the ships. On the 25th, ninety-one aircraft again attacked in vain. Such good fortune could not last. On the 26th all three ships were fatally struck. No attacks had taken place during the three nights; but from the total cargo of 26,000 tons only 5,000 tons, including oil, had been unloaded.

So March went out. During the month it was estimated that some 2,850 sorties had been flown against the island and 2,174 tons of bombs hurled down upon her. Yet Malta still survived. Moreover, her guns and fighters had between them shot down in these four weeks sixty of Kesselring's aircraft—a loss he could ill afford. The episode of the vessels sunk in Grand Harbour, however, had not improved relations between Lloyd and Sir William Dobbie. Lloyd, with his air of an attractive buccaneer, was a very different type from the equally valiant but strange, General Gordon-like figure of the Governor. He considered that the Governor had not handled the question of Maltese labour with sufficient vigour; and being an outspoken man, he made his views plain. The Governor for his part had come to regard Lloyd as 'a difficult person to absorb into a team', and also made his views plain. They did not, however, carry conviction with Tedder, who was deeply impressed with Lloyd's bulldog courage and his unfailing determination not merely to keep Malta in being, but to use the island as an offensive base—a use which, since it consumed petrol and invited retaliation, naturally appealed less to the political than to the air and naval authorities.

April, 'the cruellest month', saw no slackening of the enemy's blows. These now rained down even more heavily on the Harbour, and on Valetta and its companion cities in the process, than on the airfields. 200 sorties aimed against the island within twenty-four hours was nothing uncommon; twice—on the 7th and the 20th—there were over 300. Under this weight of attack Malta's destroyers and submarines, like her bombers, perforce departed, and by 12th April Kesselring was able to report—a few days prematurely—that he had knocked out the island as a naval base. But as he had not yet beaten down the resistance of the guns and fighters, he proposed for the time being to continue his attacks. Meanwhile, he urged, the Axis should rush reinforcements across to Africa while Malta was weak, and German forces should join the expedition against the island now being prepared by General Cavallero.

The attacks duly continued. Tedder, visiting the island during the middle of April, found the number of serviceable fighters reduced to six, and that there were times when the defence rested on the guns alone. And the guns, apart from special occasions, were down to a daily ration of fifteen rounds. By then the airfields were a wilderness of craters, the docks and neighbouring Senglea a shambles, Valetta a mass of broken limestone from which the towering frames of her baroque buildings nevertheless still rose majestically aloft. These indeed, in their unconquered grandeur, seemed to typify Malta. Battered and blasted but apparently indestructible, they refused, like those who had inhabited them, to recognize defeat.

For in all this—and no praise could be higher—the civilians of Malta proved worthy of their defenders. Maltese casual labourers did not display, and could not be expected to display, the same fiercely combative qualities as British sailors, soldiers and airmen. But the Maltese gunners in the Army stood firmly to their posts; and ordinary Maltese men, women and children, who had lost their homes and their every possession, and who were reduced to a pitiable and all too public existence in some corner of the shelters, displayed a truly astonishing fortitude. In poverty and rags but with vitality undimmed they still greeted the enemy raider with a curse or a gesture of defiance, the passing British Commander with a cheer. Loyalty and endurance of this kind deserved, and received, an uncommon form of recognition. On 16th April Malta was awarded the George Cross.

Of the spirit which animated the fighter pilots it is not necessary to write. It was the spirit of Dunkirk and of Britain. Their work would have been in vain, however, without a corresponding effort on the part of the ground crews. These men, whose efforts inevitably go so largely unrecorded, numbered only a quarter of the total considered necessary to maintain a similar number of squadrons in England. They were hungry, badly accommodated, badly equipped, and they worked under incessant attack. Yet throughout all their toil they preserved that unfailing humour which is the despair of foreigners and the secret strength of our race. 'One night we were coming back from Safi Strip after attending an incendiary bomb raid', recorded the leader of a fire-fighting party, 'and we met the A.O.C., Air Vice-Marshal Hugh Pughe Lloyd, on his way to the Strip. He stopped us and asked what we had been doing. To emphasize our story I handed him an incendiary bomb which we had extinguished before the case had melted. We, of course, had asbestos gloves on, and the look of surprise on the A.O.C.'s face as he quickly handed me back the still hot bomb was very amusing. . . .' Occasionally this cheerful *sangfroid* on the part of the ground crews surprised even some of our own number. 'Jerry proceeded to properly plaster the 'drome', noted a corporal new to the island, 'and amongst the H.E.'s he dropped literally hundreds of 2 kg. incendiaries. The raiders passed over and we once more came out into the open. All around us were patches of bright light where the incendiaries were burning. There was an immediate rush to fetch out what was left of our meagre daily bread ration, and the boys each picked their own incendiary and sat over it toasting their bread!'

At the very height of the assault, on 20th April, Malta received encouragement of a sort it had long desired. Only our best fighters could possibly cope with Kesselring's Me.109F's, and now at last a substantial force of Spitfires—forty-seven in all—was spared from the many hundreds in Fighter Command. They flew in from the United States carrier *Wasp*; but they flew in observed by the Germans. Within twenty minutes of their arrival the enemy began a series of violent attacks. Unfortunately the guns and wireless of many of the Spitfires were in far from perfect condition—so much so that a whole night's work by the ground crews failed to make them ready for action the following morning. Two of the newly arrived aircraft were destroyed on the ground, six damaged, and nine immobilised, during the first day. On the morning of the 21st only twenty-seven remained serviceable; by the evening, only seventeen. This fresh tragedy—for it was little less—brought the number of fighters awaiting repair to over a hundred. By 27th April Lloyd was signalling, in terms of surpassing urgency, for further reinforcements.

The month at last wore out—a month in which the enemy, according to our estimate, flew 4,900 sorties against Malta and dropped 6,728 tons of bombs. The Valetta sirens had sounded 275 times, or an average of once every 2½ hours throughout the month. And as April drew to its close still greater dangers loomed ahead. On 21st April a Spitfire of No. 69 Squadron had returned from reconnaissance of Sicily with the news that the enemy had started to make a rectangular strip some 1,500 yards long by 400 yards wide at Gerbini, in the Catanian plain. By 24th April further reconnaissance showed the strip to be cut and levelled. By the end of the month there were two more strips. By 10th May work on all three strips was complete and underground cables had been installed. The explanation was clear. The enemy was preparing to invade Malta from the air, using gliders as well as paratroops.

In point of fact the expedition, as the Intelligence departments in London were able to assure the Malta Commanders, was not quite so imminent as appeared. At the end of April Mussolini visited Hitler at the Berghof. There the two dictators finally settled the programme. As the Axis had too few aircraft to permit simultaneous strokes in Malta and Libya, the order of proceedings would be: first, at the end of May or the beginning of June, Operation 'Theseus'—the capture of the rest of Cyrenaica; second, between mid-July and mid-August, Operation 'Hercules'—the seizure of Malta; third, at an unspecified date, the invasion of Egypt and the triumphant march to the Nile and the Suez Canal. On 4th May, Keitel accordingly embodied the first two of these items in a formal directive. This gave Kesselring for the Malta project a force of transport aircraft equipped for paratroops, a battalion of engineers, some thirty tanks (including ten captured from the Russians), and the whole of the German 7th Airborne Division under General Student. All these were in addition to the main Italian forces already assigned to the operation.

But the prospect of invasion, alarming as it was, was not the danger about which Malta was chiefly concerned. For from now on the defenders were haunted by the spectre of starvation. The February and March convoys had both succumbed to German aircraft; no convoy had sailed in April; and no convoy could sail, Lloyd and the Admiralty were alike convinced, until Spitfires were present in sufficient quantity to win a measure of freedom in the skies above the island. On 20th April a substantial number of Spitfires had duly arrived, only to suffer rapid disaster. The chances of a convoy sailing in May were therefore remote; for the time being, Malta must exist on her 'hump', such as it was, and on what could be brought in by submarines, aircraft and fast minelayers like the daring *Welshman*. Expedients like this could prolong but could not avert the end. Without fuller supplies during the next two months Malta was doomed. The guns would fall silent for need of ammunition, the aircraft stand idle for lack of fuel, the defenders weaken and fail for want of food. This, as April gave place to May, was the peril looming on the none too distant horizon—that Malta's epic of defiance might end, not in a last glorious if unavailing fight against the invader, but in the humiliation of impotent surrender.

But the sun, Shakespeare assures us, 'breaks through the darkest clouds'; and so now, even at the blackest moment in Malta's fortunes, hope again dawned. Hitler, with that improvidence characteristic of the master-plotters of war, was short of aircraft. A new campaign presented its demands in Russia; Rommel was due to attack in Cyrenaica; the *Luftwaffe* must exact revenge for Bomber Command's raids on the *Reich*. Each of these projects for the moment seemed more important to Hitler than bombing Malta. So, in the opening days of May, to Russia, to Cyrenaica and to France the greater part of Kesselring's bombers departed.

The German calculation at this stage was that if the Italians played their part, enough aircraft would still remain in Sicily to keep Malta subdued. The Italians, however, were more doubtful. 'The neutralisation of Malta', ran an Italian appreciation of the situation on 10th May, 'is partial and temporary. The forces necessary for the operation remain more or less unchanged since two months ago, and the situation does not call for a slackening of pressure in order to benefit other sectors. Malta [has been] transformed from an offensive-defensive strategical base into an exclusively defensive one . . . [but] the defence . . . was not affected by the operations'.

'The defence was not affected by the operations'. Here indeed was a tribute to Malta's pilots and gunners. From the beginning of 1942 to the end of April the enemy had flown some 10,000 sorties against the island and had cast down some 10,000 tons of bombs—twenty-five times as much as fell on Coventry on the night of 14th/15th November, 1940—against a few restricted and carefully selected targets. Yet the Italians were conscious only that the whole task still remained to be done. Malta's guns seemed as many as ever—if they were less active it escaped the Italians' attention—and her aircraft were unquestionably present in even greater quantities; for on 20th March, at the beginning of the most intensive period of the attack, Italian reconnaissance had detected forty-three, and now on 10th May the photographs showed eighty-seven. Clearly our opponents had a long time to wait before the fruit would fall, ripe from the bough, into their receptive and ever-open mouths.

The Italian cameras had not lied. There were certainly more fighters in Malta on 10th May than two months before. For on 9th May another batch of Spitfires had flown in from the *Wasp* and the *Eagle*. Sixty-four aircraft had taken off from the carriers' decks; sixty-two had reached Malta. There they found that the red carpets were indeed out, and that Lloyd had arranged for their reception with a care that was almost flattering. A combined plan had been worked out by the three Services, ammunition restrictions withdrawn, the gun-barrage concentrated to protect the airfields. Servicing parties, soldiers as well as airmen, stood ready to receive the precious reinforcements; in every aircraft pen there was petrol, oil, ammunition and food, and in most a Malta pilot; runners sprang at the call of the airfield control officer to guide the machines to the right spot; and the first Spitfires were refuelled and ready for action within five minutes of touching down in Malta. Many times that day enemy aircraft, German and Italian, strove to repeat their success of the previous month. They were met, and defeated, by the fighters they had come to bomb.

'The tempo of life here is just indescribable', reported one of the newly arrived pilots. 'The morale of all is magnificent—pilots, ground crews and Army, but it is certainly tough. The bombing is continuous on and off every day. One lives here only to destroy the Hun and hold him at bay; everything else, living conditions, sleep, food and all the ordinary standards of life have gone by the board. It all makes the Battle of Britain and fighter-sweeps seem child's play in comparison. . . .'

The next morning, 10th May, the gallant *Welshman*, having escaped air attack en route by assuming the guise of a French destroyer, arrived in Grand Harbour. Her cargo consisted mainly of ammunition. Within less than half an hour a Ju.88 was over on reconnaissance. Soon strong enemy formations were on their way; but by this time the harbour was cloaked with a smoke screen, the guns were trained ready, the Spitfires were waiting. Every attack was broken up or diverted; while down below, taking shelter only when the red flag denoted 'imminent danger', soldiers, sailors and airmen sweated to unload the shells. Within seven hours the job was done. The guns could shoot for a few weeks longer.

The departure of some of Kesselring's forces and the arrival of the Spitfires and the *Welshman* marked another turning point in the battle of Malta. 'In these last attacks', noted Ciano on 13th May, 'we, as well as the Germans, have lost many feathers'. The attacks still continued, and Malta was still heavily bombed. But the assault was now on a much smaller scale—the Spitfires were there, with a further reinforcement of seventeen on 18th May—and the whole process was becoming very expensive for the enemy. Under the reduced weight of attack Malta began to breathe again, and even—sure sign of her revival—to turn once more towards the offensive. Her other role, that of an air staging post, she had never abandoned even at the very height of attack; in the first four months of 1942 over 400 aircraft had landed, refuelled, and taken off again for the Middle East—invariably at night and usually under fire. Malta's troubles, however, were still far from over. All too close ahead lay the danger of invasion and the day when, failing the arrival of a convoy, the last slender reserves of fuel, food and ammunition would be exhausted.

* * *

At the cost of keeping 600 aircraft tied down to a single objective, the Axis powers secured one great benefit from their assault on Malta: for some months their convoys sailed to Tripoli in comparative freedom. In fact, the first five months of 1942 saw Malta's Blenheims, Wellingtons and Swordfish sink only a fifth of the tonnage they had sunk in the last five months of 1941. It was thus a Rommel much better supplied than ever before who on 26th May, 1942, struck once again in the Desert.

The enemy offensive forestalled one of our own by a few days, but did not catch us unawares. During the preceding fortnight dive-bombers and fighters from Sicily had been joining the forces of the *Fliegerführer Afrika*; and a particularly heavy if more or less ineffective raid on our fighter landing grounds during the night of 25th/26th May, coupled with various other signs and portents, gave warning that the 'lull' was over. The following evening a Hurricane of No. 40 (S.A.A.F.) Squadron reported Italian units moving up to the attack.

The Eighth Army's position, it will be remembered, ran roughly southwards from Gazala, which is some thirty-five miles west of Tobruk. It was well protected by minefields and ended in the isolated strongpoint of Bir Hakim. This was garrisoned by the 1st Free French Brigade under General Koenig. Most of our armour was so grouped in the rear of these positions that it could meet either a frontal assault through the minefields or an outflanking movement round the south of Bir Hakim. It was the latter which Rommel now tried.

The German Africa Corps, consisting of the 15th and 21st Panzer Divisions, moved to the south of Bir Hakim during the night of 26th/27th May. With it went the other 'crack' division of what was now the Panzer Army Africa—the 90th Light Division of mechanized infantry. Rommel's intention was to round Bir Hakim, to strike north in two thrusts towards Acroma and El Adem, destroying our armour in the process, and then to take the Gazala positions in the rear. Four Italian divisions would meanwhile attack from the front. Two days, Rommel thought, would be enough to annihilate the entire British force in the forward area. Two more would see Tobruk at last in German hands.

On 27th May the outflanking manœuvre bade fair to succeed. The 90th Light Division, on the extreme right, swept on and swung up north as far as El Adem. The two Panzer Divisions, nearer the hub of the movement, drove north towards Acroma. But at El Adem the 90th Light were held; and the Panzers got no further than Knightsbridge, a point some fifteen miles short of their objective. Here, where the desert track from Acroma to Bir Hakim crosses the Trigh

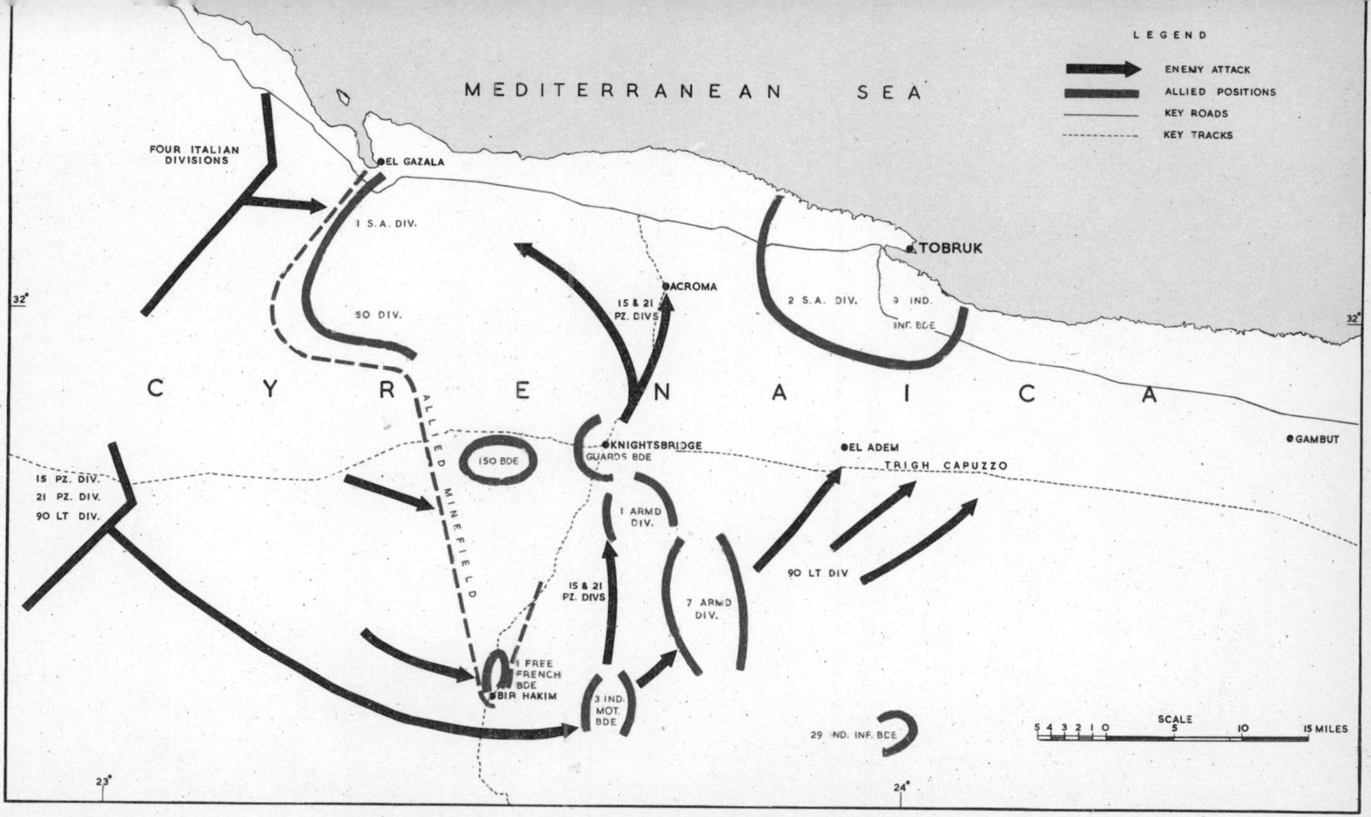

LEGEND
ENEMY ATTACK
ALLIED POSITIONS
KEY ROADS
KEY TRACKS

MEDITERRANEAN SEA
CYRENAICA

FOUR ITALIAN DIVISIONS
EL GAZALA
I S.A. DIV.
50 DIV.
ALLIED MINEFIELD
150 BDE
15 PZ. DIV.
21 PZ. DIV.
90 LT DIV.
15 & 21 PZ. DIVS
ACROMA
KNIGHTSBRIDGE
GUARDS BDE
1 ARMD DIV.
15 & 21 PZ. DIVS
1 FREE FRENCH BDE
BIR HAKIM
3 IND. MOT. BDE
7 ARMD DIV.
90 LT DIV
2 S.A. DIV.
9 IND. INF. BDE
TOBRUK
EL ADEM
TRIGH CAPUZZO
GAMBUT
29 IND. INF. BDE
32°
32°
23°
24°
SCALE
5 4 3 2 1 0 5 10 15 MILES

ROMMEL'S PLAN OF ATTACK, MAY 1942

Capuzzo, a great battle developed which was to rage with intermittent fury for many days to come. Meanwhile the Italians made no perceptible progress in their frontal assaults on our minefields and Bir Hakim.

During this first day the main concern of the Royal Air Force was to achieve air superiority. Coningham's fighters flew over 150 sorties on offensive and defensive patrols, broke up several heavily escorted raids by Stukas, and claimed a good bag of enemy aircraft. The Boston and Baltimore bombers, followed by the Wellingtons at night, played their part by attacking the enemy's landing grounds. In addition the bombers gave close support to our troops, while the fighter-bombers—of which there were now four squadrons—attacked supply columns in the rear of the enemy's armour and put some 200 vehicles out of action.

The next day, 28th May, the opposing troops were still locked in conflict at Knightsbridge and El Adem. At the Eighth Army's request Coningham now virtually ignored the fight for air superiority—it was a tribute to his previous work that he could—and concentrated his entire force against the enemy columns. Three raids by the Bostons and continuous low-flying attacks by the Kittybombers and the fighters helped our armour to hold its own and foiled Rommel's attempts to supply his forward columns round the south of Bir Hakim.

From first light on 29th May Coningham's squadrons were again active in close support. Particularly rewarding were the attacks by 250 fighters and fighter-bombers against Rommel's supply lines south and east of Bir Hakim. Formations of Stukas were also twice forced to jettison their bombs. But after midday sandstorms cut down our operations; and the Italians, spurred by the plight of the German armour, managed to clear a path in the minefield. Through this Rommel now strove, as yet with little success, to pass supplies.

By the morning of the 30th the enemy were in serious trouble. While part of the Panzers withdrew to the south to shorten their supply line, other elements retired westwards. These, however, then smashed their way into our minefield from the rear, so opening a second and larger gap. About these two gaps the fight now swayed. Three raids by the Bostons and repeated attacks by the Kittybombers soon helped to bring the 'Cauldron'—as it became known—to the boil, and our pilots returned to report a stupendous confusion of vehicles shelled, bombed, colliding and running on to mines. Two attacks by the fighter bombers, operating from 6,000 feet but bombing from 1,000, were much remarked upon by our ground forces: both reduced some fifty or so enemy vehicles to blazing wrecks. Attacks against the supply line to the south of Bir Hakim were no less successful.

On 31st May and 1st June the fog of war, in the almost literal form of violent sandstorms, descended over the battlefield. For two days the Royal Air Force was unable to operate with the same freedom; and as the enemy air force, profiting from our previous concentration against military targets, began to show an unwelcome degree of activity, Coningham had to apply much of his effort defensively. During these two days Rommel managed to regroup his forces, strengthen his hold on the minefield gaps, and generally improve his position at the expense of the Eighth Army. Not until 4th June could —or did—Ritchie attempt the counter-stroke that was so obviously needed; and by then the chance of exploiting the enemy's earlier setbacks had disappeared.

Despite these successes Rommel had still not disposed of our armour in the centre. Retaining the bulk of his tanks in the Knightsbridge area as a threat both to the rear of the Gazala positions and to Tobruk, the German Commander therefore mounted a concentrated attack against our southern strong-point of Bir Hakim. For the next few days the armoured units continued to clash around Knightsbridge, but the main interest centred about this attempt to reduce Bir Hakim and so open a clear route for the enemy supply columns.

The fight of the Free French Brigade in this desert outpost has passed down to legend; for at Bir Hakim the military glory of France, so sadly tarnished in 1940, shone out again with undiminished splendour. It was an episode in which the Royal Air Force played no small part. Owing to its isolated position, our ground forces could give Bir Hakim little support either in the matter of supplies or by way of exerting counter pressure elsewhere. Coningham's fighters therefore decided, in their commander's phrase, 'to adopt the Free French and their Fortress'.

The Italians had already begun a renewed attack on Bir Hakim on 2nd June. This was powerfully supported by German Stukas. On the morning of the 3rd, Coningham accordingly switched part of his fighter force over from the Knightsbridge battles to protect the harassed garrison. During the day three raids by Kittybombers on enemy concentrations south of the fort put some sixty vehicles out of action; while our fighters, flying over a hundred sorties, repeatedly broke up the enemy's air attacks. One particularly hard-fought combat occurred at noon, when Tomahawks of No. 5 Squadron, S.A.A.F., intercepted a formation of strongly escorted Stukas and claimed seven for the loss of five of their own aircraft.

These efforts continued on 4th June, when the Kittyhawks and Tomahawks again wrought havoc among enemy transport and frustrated the attempts of the Stukas to dive-bomb the garrison into submission. The highlights of the day were a direct hit on a large ammunition wagon, and the bomb skilfully planted by Squadron Leader B. Drake, of No. 112 Squadron, in the midst of a party of enemy troops 'who were listening to a pep-talk by one of their Colonels'. So much of all this occurred within sight of the French garrison that in the evening their commander sent Coningham a message which gave great pleasure throughout the tents and caravans of the Western Desert Air Force: '*Bravo! Merci pour la R.A.F.*' In best Service style and command of foreign idiom the reply was promptly despatched: '*Bravo à vous! Merci pour le sport*'.

More help was given to the Free French on 5th and 6th June, but by then the Knightsbridge area, where our counter-attack and the enemy's *riposte* were taking place, demanded most of the available air support. On 8th June, however, it became evident that Rommel had decided to reduce Bir Hakim at all costs. The bulk of Coningham's squadrons were accordingly switched back to support the Free French. The plight of the garrison was now more desperate than ever, for the 90th Light Division had joined in the siege and the fortress was being subjected to ceaseless attack by infantry, tanks, artillery, and an ever growing number of enemy aircraft. Despite continuous shooting-up by our fighters and good work by No. 6 Squadron's new Hurricane IID 'tank-busters' (aircraft firing 40-mm. shells), the enemy pressure increased. By 9th June an overwhelming mass of artillery was trained on the fort. That day two Hurricanes under protection from fourteen others dropped supply canisters within 100 yards of the isolated defenders, and in the night a Bombay of No. 216 Squadron brought further relief. None of this, however, could compensate for the lack of adequate support and supply on the ground; the fight, it was becoming clear, could have only one end. On 10th June Hurricanes and the first squadron of Spitfires to appear in the desert saved the garrison from a heavy raid, but two other enemy attacks penetrated to their objective. Raids of this kind might have been endured even when delivered (as they were) by as many as fifty or sixty bombers; but shells from the enemy guns were now pouring in without respite. During the night of 10th/11th June the surviving defenders were accordingly ordered to retire. Some 2,000 made their escape, to complete their withdrawal the next day under cover from our fighters.

The action at Bir Hakim was more than an epic of human endurance. Though at the time the garrison appeared to have fought in vain, in fact they had helped to change the whole course of the struggle. The enemy's intention, it will be recalled, was to defeat our forward forces, capture Tobruk, and advance to the Egyptian frontier. The offensive was then to be broken off while Operation 'Hercules' was mounted against Malta. The timetable for all this was based on capturing Tobruk by 1st June and halting on the Egyptian frontier by 20th June. It was on this supposition that supplies, notably of fuel for the *Luftwaffe*, had been sent across to Africa. The Germans and Italians had allowed no margin of reserves for unexpected setbacks; for apart from their customary difficulty in running their ships across the Mediterranean they had been hard pressed to amass sufficient fuel in Sicily and Italy for the expedition against Malta. Rommel, then, began his attack on 26th May with less than a month's supply of petrol. The resistance of the Free French at Bir Hakim and of our armour at Knightsbridge, sustained so vigorously in both cases by the Royal Air Force, thus put the enemy advance entirely out of joint. Bir Hakim alone absorbed some 1,500 sorties by the enemy air force—and even then, thanks to Coningham's fighters, shelling rather than bombing settled the issue. Like the rest of the Gazala line, Bir Hakim was timed to fall between 28th May and 1st June. No subsequent progress could atone for the fact that it held out till 10th June. 'This meant a nine days' gain for the enemy', wrote a staff officer of the *Luftwaffe* Historical Section, 'and for our Army and Air Force, nine days of losses in material, personnel, armour and petrol. Those nine days were irrecoverable'.

* * *

The struggle for Bir Hakim was barely over and that for Knightsbridge was still raging when Tedder's squadrons faced a further and no less vital task—the protection of a convoy to Malta.

Since the arrival of the Spitfires and the departure of some of Kesselring's aircraft in early May, the Axis attacks on Malta had met with little success. In one sense Lord Gort, who succeeded Sir William Dobbie on 7th May, came at the turn of the tide; but in another the situation was still desperate enough. For as the weeks passed, so the island's diminutive stocks of fuel and food ebbed relentlessly away. 'It was pleasant to realise we had won our battle', wrote Lloyd afterwards in his memoirs[1], 'but starvation looked us in the face. The *Welshman* had been in and out, also the occasional submarine, bringing oil, edible and otherwise, and food; but they could carry little to meet our needs. . . . We wanted convoys. . . . The

[1]*Briefed to Attack*, Hodder and Stoughton

poor quality of the food had not been noticed at first, but suddenly it began to take effect. In March it had been clear enough, but in April most belts had to be taken in by another two holes, and in May by yet another hole. . . . Our diet was a slice and a half of very poor bread with jam for breakfast, bully beef for lunch with one slice of bread, and except for an additional slice of bread it was the same fare for dinner. There was sugar for every meal, but margarine appeared only every two or three days. Even the drinking water, lighting and heating were rationed. All the things which had been taken for granted closed down—the making of beer required coal, so none had been made for months. . . . A crashed aeroplane was a windfall as the oil would provide an extra hot drink for a day or so. . . . [Owing to shortage of petrol] such accommodation as could be found had to be within easy walking distance of the aerodromes. Officers and men slept in shelters, in caverns and dugouts, in quarries . . . 300 slept in an underground cabin as tight as sardines in a tin; 200 slept in a disused tunnel. None had any comfort or warmth. . . . Soon, too, we would want hundreds of tons of bombs and ammunition. . . . Malta was faced with the unpleasant fact of being starved and forced from lack of equipment into surrender. The middle of August was starvation date, and as we should all have been dead before relief arrived, the surrender date was much earlier. . . . Such were the fearful effects of the loss of the February convoy and of the three ships in harbour in March'.

But the Spitfires were now firmly established—and could be increased—and it was at last possible to risk another convoy. Owing to the calls of the Far East and the danger from the *Luftwaffe* the escorting naval forces would inevitably be weak compared with what the Italian Navy, given the necessary fuel and inclination, could bring to bear. The Chiefs of Staff accordingly decided to split the opposition by running a convoy from each end of the Mediterranean. The second would dock in Grand Harbour within twenty-four hours of the first. The story of these two ventures shows at once the stranglehold which land-based air power can exert over sea communications in narrow waters, and at the same time the immensity of the effort required to keep our 'unsinkable aircraft-carrier' in action.

Air operations in support of the convoys began on 24th May, long before they sailed. On that date No. 104 Squadron again began intensive activity from Malta against the airfields and harbours of Sicily and Southern Italy. These the Wellingtons attacked every night until 11th June, when they were withdrawn to make room for six torpedo-Wellingtons of No. 38 Squadron and some reconnaissance Baltimores for No. 69 Squadron. That same day our aircraft from

Gibraltar, Malta and Egypt began the full programme of reconnaissance to detect the Italian fleet. Meanwhile, during the previous fortnight, the *Eagle* had flown off another sixty-three Spitfires, fifty-nine of which had reached Malta. This brought the total of these aircraft on the island to over a hundred, of which ninety-five were serviceable. Of other aircraft on Malta there were sixty serviceable, including two squadrons specially brought in for the passage of the convoys—No. 235 (Beaufighters) and No. 217 (Beauforts). By 12th June all was ready. The east-bound convoy, direct from the Clyde, left Gibraltar behind that morning. The following day the main part of the west-bound convoy assembled off Alexandria.

The convoy from Alexandria (Operation 'Vigorous') consisted of eleven merchant ships escorted by cruisers and destroyers. The duty of meeting a serious challenge by the Italian fleet therefore rested for the most part on our submarines and aircraft. The air striking force available consisted of two squadrons of torpedo aircraft (Beauforts, Albacores and Wellingtons) in Malta, one squadron of torpedo aircraft (Beauforts) in the Western Desert, and some two dozen Liberators based near the Suez Canal. These Liberators were the first long-range bombers to appear in the Middle East. Five were Royal Air Force machines of No. 160 Squadron, bound for India and temporarily detained by Tedder; the remainder belonged to the American 'Halpro' unit commanded by Colonel H. A. Halverson. Originally intended to bomb Tokyo from China, this had been diverted to the Middle East for an operation against the Ploesti oilfields. By special American permission such of the aircraft as survived the raid on Ploesti on 12th June were at Tedder's disposal for work against the Italian fleet at sea. Apart from these forces for direct action against the enemy ships, the Wellingtons of No. 205 Group and the light bombers of the Western Desert Air Force would be available to attack airfields, the aircraft of No. 201 Group would fly reconnaissance and anti-submarine patrols, and fighters from Palestine, Egypt, Cyrenaica and Malta would in turn provide protection for the convoy. The cover from Cyrenaica, however, could not be stretched to meet that from Malta. As a further aid small parties would sabotage enemy airfields in Crete.

A few ships of the west-bound convoy had sailed ahead on 11th June. During the next two days our fighters flew some 240 protective sorties, but on the evening of the 12th about a dozen Ju.88's broke through in 'Bomb Alley'—the passage between Crete and Cyrenaica. One merchantman was damaged and retired; and as another was too slow to keep station the convoy lost two vessels even before the main part sailed. This suffered several individual attacks without harm off

Alexandria, and by the 14th the two parts of the convoy had joined up and were making good progress westwards. Another vessel, however, could not maintain the common speed; it was detached to Tobruk and sunk by German aircraft before it could get there.

Meanwhile the convoy had reached 'Bomb Alley'. Soon some forty Ju.87's and 88's, escorted by Me.109's, attempted to attack; but they were intercepted by twenty-three Kittyhawks and Tomahawks specially 'scrambled' by Coningham (despite the crisis in the desert battle), and were forced to jettison their bombs. Throughout the afternoon and evening of the 14th the enemy's attacks persisted; between 1630 and 2115 there were no less than seven, each by some ten or twelve aircraft. But though the defence of the convoy now rested on the ships' guns and a few Beaufighters and long-range Kittyhawks, these performed to such purpose that during all this time only one more merchant ship was sunk and one damaged. The eleven merchant vessels, however, were now reduced to seven; and as night came on, enemy submarines and E-boats took up the attack. Worse still, a large Italian naval force including two battleships and four cruisers had been spotted by a Malta Baltimore leaving Taranto, and was now steaming south to intercept.

During the night of 14th/15th June this threat caused the convoy to be put about. Meanwhile four torpedo-Wellingtons of No. 221 Squadron from Malta were hastily directed against the Italian vessels. They found them but were foiled by the enemy's smoke screen. By dawn on the 15th nine Beauforts of No. 217 Squadron from Malta were also on the job. They came up with the Italian fleet at about 1600 hours; and though their crews did not (as they thought) hit both battleships, they utterly crippled the cruiser *Trento*. This vessel was afterwards finished off by our submarine *P.35*, whose commanding officer vividly recorded the effect of the Beauforts' attack: '*P.35* was in the unenviable position of being in the centre of a fantastic circus of wildly careering capital ships, cruisers and destroyers . . . of tracer-shell streaks and anti-aircraft bursts. At one period there was not a quadrant of the compass unoccupied by enemy vessels weaving continuously to and fro. . . . One was in fact tempted to stand with periscope up and gaze in utter amazement'.

The reported success of the Beauforts caused the convoy to be turned again in the direction of Malta. Meanwhile, a co-ordinated attack on the Italian ships had also been arranged from Egypt. The two formations, seven American and two British Liberators from the Canal and twelve Beauforts of No. 39 Squadron from the Western Desert, started from bases 500 miles apart. So good was their navigation that the attacks duly synchronized to within a few minutes. One of the American Liberators hit the battleship *Littorio*, but its British 500 lb. S.A.P. bombs (the largest available) did little damage; the Beauforts, now a gallant band of five which had fought their way through a formation of Me.109's, may also have scored one hit. But no further vessel was sunk, and the Italian fleet held to its course. Meanwhile the convoy, having learnt that the enemy was still standing on, had once more turned back towards Alexandria.

It was now midday on the 15th, and our ships were retiring through 'Bomb Alley'. Four times between noon and dusk they were fiercely attacked by escorted Ju.87's and Italian torpedo S.79's. Twice these formations were intercepted by our fighters. Darkness at last brought relief, but though the air attack slackened the activity of enemy submarines increased. Then it was learned from our shadowing aircraft that the Italian fleet, either nervous of carrying the pursuit closer to Alexandria or disliking the treatment it had received from the Beauforts and Liberators, had turned about during the afternoon and was making back towards Taranto. In the words of Admiral Harwood, the new Commander-in-Chief Mediterranean, this was the convoy's 'golden opportunity'; but the harassed escort was by now too short of ammunition to face yet another voyage through 'Bomb Alley', to say nothing of the final approach to Malta. By the 16th Rear Admiral Vian, who would certainly have fought the convoy through if anyone could, was back in Alexandria.

The Italian fleet, however, had still to reach port. In the mid-afternoon of the 15th, No. 217 Squadron's Beauforts had again taken off from Malta—for the second time that day, and after continuous stand-by or operational flying for more than thirty-six hours. Failing to find their target, they returned to face the nerve-racking task of landing at Luqa in the dark after an air raid. Though the crews had little experience of night-flying and three of their undercarriages were out of action, all got down safely. A last strike by Malta's Wellingtons was more successful. Over six and a half hours after the last sighting, five aircraft of No. 38 Squadron found the Italian ships. The time was now shortly before midnight on the 15th; a further ninety minutes of shadowing and one of the bombers, captained by Pilot Officer O. L. Hawes, put a torpedo into the *Littorio*. So it came about that the enemy returned home without the *Trento* and with the *Littorio* badly damaged; but though the foray had earned no laurels for the bare brows of the Italian admirals, it had certainly helped to frustrate Operation 'Vigorous'. All the heroism of our sailors and airmen had failed to bring succour from the eastern end of the Mediterranean. Malta must look to Operation 'Harpoon'—the convoy from the west.

Needless to say, this too ran into trouble. The six merchant ships entered the Mediterranean under a powerful escort which included a battleship and two aircraft carriers. The convoy had one day in peace after passing Gibraltar, and a second during which it was shadowed but not attacked. Then Italian aircraft from Sardinia appeared in force. Four times during the morning of 14th June escorted Savoias and Cants subjected the vessels to determined attack, but the ships' gunners and the Fleet Air Arm fighters kept the losses down to one merchant ship. A damaged cruiser, however—the *Liverpool*—had to be sent back to Gibraltar under tow, and this unfortunate vessel attracted most of the enemy's effort from Sardinia for the rest of the day.

Evening then brought the convoy within range of aircraft from Sicily. Ten German Ju.88's attacked at 1820, a larger number of escorted S.79's, Ju.87's and Ju.88's at 2000. Both assaults broke down before the ships' fighters and guns. An hour later, as the convoy approached the Narrows between Tunisia and Sicily, four long-range Beaufighters arrived from Malta, some 200 miles distant. Shortly afterwards, in accordance with plan, the main escort turned back for Gibraltar. The five freighters and their attendant destroyers sailed on; and at 2200 the Beaufighters beat off yet another attack by Ju.88's.

Meanwhile, an Italian surface force of two cruisers and four destroyers was on its way to intercept the convoy. It was spotted by a submarine leaving Sardinia on the evening of 13th June, attacked by Wellingtons without success in the early hours of the 14th, picked up in Palermo during the evening, and seen again by a Spitfire as it put to sea that night. At 0620 on 15th June the convoy's escorting Beaufighters reported these vessels only fifteen miles away, and an engagement then ensued between the two naval forces. Both sides suffered damage, but the merchant ships meanwhile kept out of range, and it was from Ju.87's, at 0705, that they suffered their second loss. Four freighters then remained, of which one was disabled; and the Italian warships, though held off by our destroyers' action, were still threatening. Owing to the even greater danger of the convoy in the Eastern Mediterranean, only six 'strike' aircraft were available in Malta. Two of these were Beauforts with inexperienced crews, the other four obsolescent naval Albacores. All six were at once despatched under Spitfire cover to attack the Italian ships. What damage they did is problematical; but it is certain that the Italians disliked their presence and withdrew. On their way home the enemy were attacked again by some of the same gallant crews.

This disposed of the threat from the Italian fleet, but not of the danger from German aircraft. At 1040 the *Luftwaffe* delivered a fresh attack, just after the first long-range Spitfires had arrived from Malta over the convoy. This assault the Spitfires beat off, but half an hour later, when they had turned for home with their ammunition exhausted, and before the relief flight could arrive, an attack by ten Ju.87's damaged another of the precious vessels. Two were now intact, two crippled; and the convoy had still 150 miles to cover. Long-range Spitfires were soon overhead, repelling the enemy; but to enable the two good ships to make full speed the officer in charge of the surface escort decided to sacrifice the cripples. They were left behind to be sunk by our destroyers, but were in fact finished off by enemy aircraft. Meanwhile the last two merchant vessels sailed on; and 100 miles from Malta the short-range Spitfires took over. These beat off three more attacks; then, as night fell, Malta at last loomed ahead. Mines took a further toll of the escort; but in the early hours of 16th June, and still under the protective canopy of Spitfires, the two gallant merchantmen berthed safely in Grand Harbour. 'There were a hundred or more civilians near me', wrote Lloyd afterwards, 'and not one of them spoke a word. It was one of those rare occasions on which everyone, without any thought, turns to bare his head in salutation'.

The cost of fighting these two vessels through to Malta was the loss, in the twin operations, of a cruiser, five destroyers, two minesweepers, six merchant ships and over twenty aircraft, besides damage to another thirteen vessels. As against this the enemy had a cruiser sunk, a battleship put out of action for several months, three other warships damaged, and many aircraft shot down—the number cannot be precisely determined but was thought at the time to be sixty-seven. The price paid by our Navy and Air Force was high; but it was not too high for what it bought—the survival of Malta. The only pity is that some at least of all this frightful risk and effort might perhaps have been avoided. 'Had we taken serious notice of our supply situation in 1941', writes Lloyd, 'and had we taken a strong line and brought the Maltese fully into our confidence, we should not have been reduced to our very parlous state in the spring of 1942'.

* * *

On 12th June, when the convoys were about to run the gauntlet, Bir Hakim had just fallen, but the rest of the Gazala line still held. On 16th June, when two of the seventeen merchantmen won through to Malta, the Eighth Army's whole position was in dissolution.

Bir Hakim fell during the night of 10th/11th June. Having won a clear route for supplies round the south of our positions, Rommel

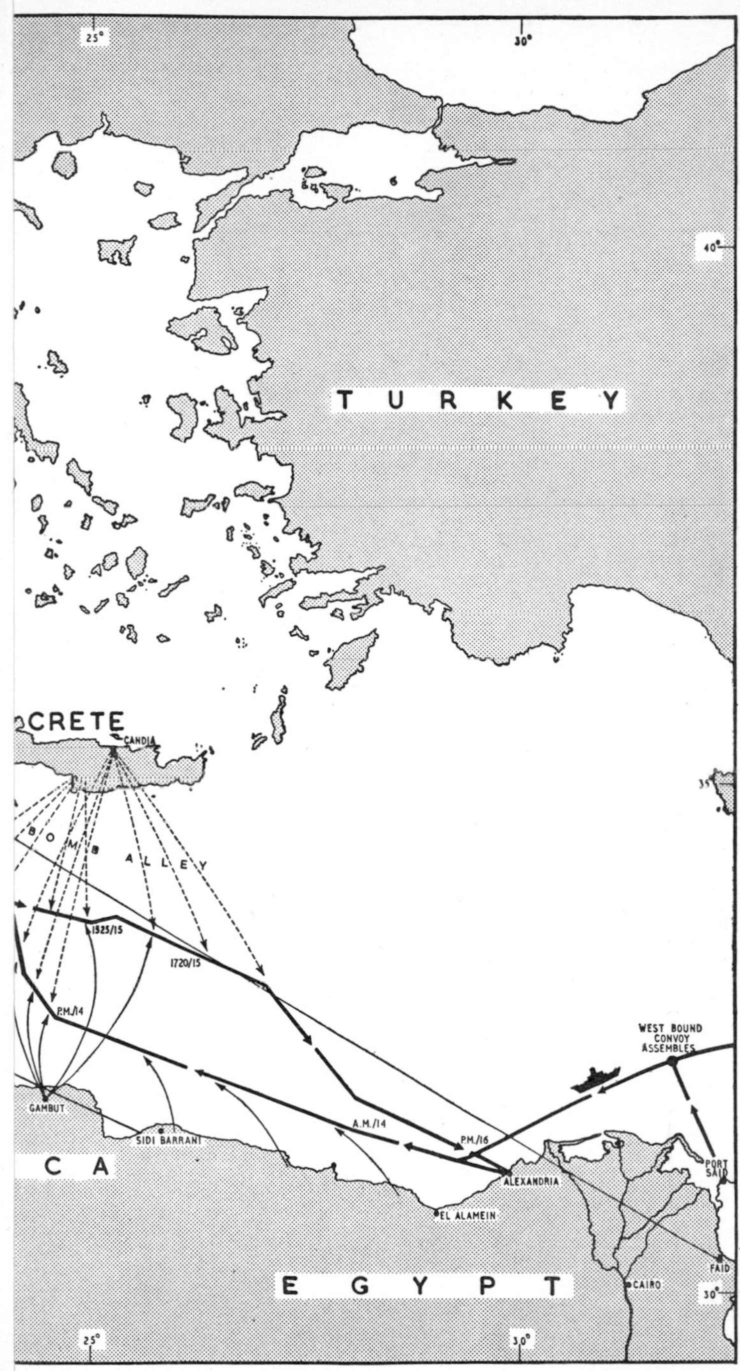

ROUS)

[*facing page 208*

then reverted to his original plan of capturing El Adem and Acroma as a preliminary to taking Gazala in the rear. As usual, he struck with remarkable speed and vigour. By 13th June the 90th Light Division had the landing ground at El Adem, while the two Panzer Divisions, after inflicting heavy losses on our tanks, were driving our armour from Knightsbridge towards the coast. With the Gazala positions thus becoming exposed from the rear, Ritchie had now no option but to pull out his forward forces. By 14th June the road east from Gazala was black with men and lorries as the South Africans, with the 50th Division a little farther inland, set off with all speed towards Tobruk and the Egyptian frontier. For three days and nights this breathless retirement continued, our tanks and aircraft meanwhile holding off the enemy to the south. Unable to cut across to the coast and intercept the retreat Rommel then pushed his advanced columns eastwards. By-passing El Adem and Tobruk, he first made sure of Sidi Rezegh. By the 18th Gambut too was in his hands, and by the 20th he had closed the ring and locked up a large force in Tobruk. On the 21st this erstwhile stronghold, which in 1941 had successfully endured a siege of eight months, succumbed almost in as many hours.

At this stage our enemies changed their plans, with the most far-reaching results. The Axis intention, it will be remembered, was to destroy the British armoured force in Cyrenaica, capture Tobruk, advance to the Egyptian frontier, and then break off the offensive while Operation 'Hercules' was mounted against Malta. But Rommel now found the going so good that he was reluctant to bring his mount to a halt. On 22nd June, as soon as he had Tobruk, he signalled Italian Supreme Headquarters at Rome in these terms: 'The first objective of the Panzer Army in Africa, to defeat the enemy army in the field and take Tobruk, has been attained. . . . The condition and morale of the troops, the present supply situation improved by booty, and the momentary weakness of the enemy will permit pursuit into the heart of Egypt. Request the *Duce* to effect the suspension of the former limitation on freedom of movement . . . so that the campaign may be continued'. This request was at once supported by Hitler, to whom Mussolini replied that he was 'in complete agreement with the *Führer's* opinion, and that the historic moment had now come to conquer Egypt, and must be exploited'. In point of fact the *Duce* had his misgivings, since 'owing to Malta's active revival' the supply of the Panzer Army in Africa had 'once more entered a critical stage'. He therefore stipulated that if Malta was not invaded it must be neutralized by air bombardment. In the absence of sufficient aircraft to attack Malta and support Rommel in Africa at one and the same time, however, the Germans found the point academic. At all events the two dictators agreed to postpone the invasion of Malta until September, and allowed Rommel to go ahead.

So, in defiance of ancient military axioms about neglecting an enemy base on the flank, to say nothing of more modern ones about advancing into territory dominated by hostile aircraft, Rommel pressed on. On 24th June his armour entered Egypt. At this point of crisis Auchinleck took over from Ritchie. Judging his remaining guns and tanks too few to hold the position at Matruh, the Eighth Army's new commander at once decided to fight on a shorter line much farther east. This he had long marked for a supreme emergency; for here, sixty miles west of Alexandria, the traversable desert narrows into a confine only thirty-eight miles wide. On this line, between the coast at El Alamein and the vast impassable Qattara Depression inland, Rommel's attack might at last be held; and on this line, safely gained despite the loss of 60,000 men in the fighting and the retreat, the Eighth Army now took the shock of the advancing enemy.

The drama of this black fortnight, when all that our forces had so painfully won seemed to be slipping inexplicably through nerveless fingers, still lingers vividly in the memory. The collapse of Tobruk was a cruel blow to Mr. Churchill in Washington, softened only by the prompt and generous reaction of the Americans. But the dismay in England and the United States was naturally as nothing to that in Cairo, where there were all the symptoms of a first-class 'flap'. This was not confined to local agitators whose partiality for the Germans and Italians varied in direct ratio to their proximity. On an occasion ever afterwards to be known as 'Ash Wednesday'—a day when Auchinleck and Tedder were forward in the Desert—vast clouds of pungent smoke containing scraps of singed paper billowed upwards from the yards and roofs of the headquarters; and from the evidence of this documentary super-bonfire, coupled with the retirement of the fleet from Alexandria and the exodus of officials' wives to the Sudan, the local population very understandably concluded that the end was near.

It was indeed, but not in the sense they imagined. For there was one feature of our defeat which had not yet been fully appreciated. The Eighth Army had retreated 400 miles in a fortnight; but though its losses had been grievous it had remained a cohesive whole. It had not only escaped destruction on the ground; it had escaped decimation from the air. In some respects this second fact was the more remarkable. For days on end the coastal road had presented the astonishing spectacle of a continuous line of vehicles, nose to tail, stretching out for mile after mile. It was the text-book situation of a defeated army helplessly bunched together and pouring back along a single narrow ribbon of communication—a situation such as might present itself to ardent young commanders of ground attack squadrons in their dreams. A little systematic attention from the Stukas and the Me.109's, and the lorries must have piled up in endless confusion. Yet the *Luftwaffe* allowed the Eighth Army to reach El Alamein virtually unmolested from the air. During the three days when the South Africans and the 50th Division were pulling out of Gazala, and the congestion was at its height, and the Me.109's were based only forty miles away, and the Hurricanes and the Kittyhawks and the Beaufighters were desperately striving to cover El Adem and the Malta convoy as well as the coastal road, the number of British soldiers killed by German and Italian aircraft was precisely six.

The reasons for this almost incredible immunity must be sought in two directions. In the first place, a large part of the German air contingent was unable to keep pace with Rommel's advance. Though demanding and expecting complete air cover for his troops, Rommel had consistently ignored the fact that air forces, like ground forces, depend for mobility on a good supply of vehicles. Only on 26th June, when his tanks were already pouring into Egypt, did he decide to bring his aircraft forward at the expense of the Italian infantry, who had to walk. Beyond this, however, the Germans had simply not developed the highly refined, stripped-for-action mobility of the Western Desert Air Force. By 1942 the much-vaunted *Luftwaffe*, which had been held up by so many of our military commanders as the perfect model for the Royal Air Force, had been completely surpassed, and, indeed, made to look positively amateurish, in its own special field of tactical support.

When all due allowance has been made for these facts, the *Luftwaffe* could still have wrought havoc among our retreating forces had its appearance over the battle area not been so rigorously discouraged by the Royal Air Force. Much of this discouragement took place out of sight of our troops; highly effective attacks on the Gazala airfields, for instance, were made as soon as they were occupied by the enemy, so crippling the German fighter effort from the start. Later, the enemy air force was twice caught on the ground—at Tmimi and Sidi Barrani—at critical moments during the pursuit. And such fighters as the Germans did manage to bring forward—it was to fighters, significantly enough, that they gave priority—were kept so busy trying to protect the German ground forces that they had little leisure to attack ours.

For Coningham's squadrons certainly gave their opponents no rest. After the light bombers and the fighter-bombers and the fighters had finished by day, the Wellingtons of No. 205 Group carried on by night. Released from the Benghazi mail run—the change to other targets was greeted by the crews with cheers—they moved up to the Western Desert and flew a steady sixty or seventy sorties every night against the enemy's troop concentrations. In this they were much helped by the naval Albacores of Nos. 821 and 826 Squadrons, who pinpointed the targets and dropped flares. Moreover, as the retreat continued, and as the Western Desert Air Force retired upon its main bases, so our effort in the air increased. During the first week of the attack, from 26th May to 2nd June, Coningham's squadrons flew 2,339 sorties; during the sixth week, from 1st July to 7th July, when the El Alamein line was withstanding the initial shock, they flew 5,458. The proportion of our aircraft serviceable, so far from declining as the fight continued and the casualties mounted, actually showed an improvement. In the first week of the struggle it was 67 per cent; in the second, 75 per cent; in the fifth, 85 per cent. In the sixth and last week it was still 75 per cent, which was the average over the whole period.

All this was possible because of the strenuous and indeed heroic labours of the servicing, repair and salvage crews, who worked in shifts throughout the entire day and night. It was also possible because of the boldness of Tedder, who withdrew Spitfires from Malta and Hurricanes from the Operational Training Units and hurled them into the fray. The Air Commander also built up his forward forces by stripping down those farther back until the fighter defence of Cairo and Alexandria rested on a single squadron of night Beaufighters. But no *ad hoc* measures, however effective or daring, could have compensated for any fundamental weakness in organization. At root, the work of the Desert squadrons was possible because Tedder, Drummond, Wigglesworth, Pirie, Dawson, Coningham, Beamish, Elmhirst and the rest had prepared in advance for the particular brand of warfare—mobile warfare—that would be fought in the Desert. With the squadrons streamlined and divided into two parts each capable of 'leap-frogging' the other, a landing ground could be kept in operation until the next, farther in the rear and already stocked with bombs, ammunition and petrol, was brought into use. 'I have prepared landing grounds all the way back to the frontier', signalled Coningham to Tedder on 16th June, 'and plan is steady withdrawal of squadrons keeping about twenty miles away from enemy. See our own bombs bursting is rough deadline. As units move, the Repair and Salvage Units clear up. Squadrons fearful of being taken too far from enemy as they like present form of warfare. Squadron Commanders explain situation to voluntary parade of men daily, and point of honour that there are no flaps and nothing left for enemy. Am content that whole machinery working very smoothly. . . .'

In the vital work of 'clearing up', squadrons and salvage units alike performed marvels. During the whole of the retreat they left behind only five unserviceable aircraft—and these they burned or otherwise demolished. And if Rommel kept up the pace of his advance, as he did, on captured petrol, it was on none that he found on the landing grounds of the Western Desert Air Force. The result was that, except at one place, the Eighth Army was given complete and continuous support. The exception was Tobruk, where the Ju.87's had matters all their own way after the loss of Gambut drove our main fighter force beyond range. And the very swiftness and immensity of the disaster at this point, with our aircraft virtually absent, points the contrast to the successful retirement along the rest of the route, where our aircraft were so very much present.

How this air activity of ours appeared to the enemy may be seen from the War Diary of the German Africa Corps. The picture it displays is indeed that of May 1940 in reverse. 'Several fighter-bomber attacks are made on the Panzer Divisions this morning', runs an entry for 12th June; 'the *Luftwaffe* has carried out no operation as yet'. On the 17th the Diary records: 'The enemy air force is very active again today . . . two bombing attacks are made on the 21st Panzer Division while the G.O.C. is there'. On the 23rd it is the same story: 'The enemy air force is very active today, but there is no sign of the *Luftwaffe*'. The next day comes a tribute to the attacks against Rommel's supply system—'15th Panzer Division reports that it is unable to continue its advance owing to lack of fuel'—followed, of course, by the usual complaint: 'The enemy air force was very active today and several attacks were carried out. No *Luftwaffe* operations were observed'. By the 25th the Panzers had picked up fuel from our military dumps, but the situation in the air was no whit better: 'The enemy air force was particularly active again today. Almost continuous bombing attacks were carried out. . . . The enemy also carried out bombing operations at night . . . attacks of long duration were made on G.H.Q. with the help of flares'. The 26th sees the two Panzer Divisions each with about 950 tons of fuel, but 'continuous bombing attacks have been in progress again since dawn'. In the afternoon these become still heavier. 'Enemy air activity continues to increase. Bombing attacks are being made every hour, causing considerable losses. There is nothing to be seen of the *Luftwaffe*'.

This, then, was how our air operations appeared to an enemy staff officer at Corps Headquarters. To the enemy soldier in the field, or rather desert, they doubtless appeared a great deal worse. Equally striking, however, was the appreciation on our own side of the part played by the Royal Air Force. 'During a full and frank discussion at tonight's War Cabinet', signalled Portal to Tedder a few hours after the fall of Tobruk, 'there was no, repeat no, suggestion from any quarter that your forces could have done more. . . . We all realise and appreciate the magnificent effort your squadrons are putting forth in this crisis, and we fully share your conviction that the enemy is in for a rough passage. . . .' And when, with the continued advance of the enemy, mutterings of criticism began to arise against the Middle East Air Force, they found no echo in responsible military circles.

Indeed, so far from expressing any doubts on the handling of the Middle East squadrons at this critical time, Portal's letters to their commander spoke nothing but comfort, physical and spiritual. The physical comfort took the form of arranging for reinforcements and announcing details of future American aid. The spiritual may be judged from the letter of 26th June. 'To end with', wrote the Chief of Air Staff, 'I would like to tell you how much it relieves my worries to have you in command in the Middle East, and from all I hear you give the same confidence to everyone else, both residents and birds of passage. I think you are well set for a great success if only we can get the aircraft to you. . . . I wish you and your men the very best of luck in the coming battle. You certainly deserve it'. This, be it remembered, was from an undemonstrative man not, as might be thought from the tone of his messages, at a time of general optimism, but when Rommel was bearing down on the Delta and panic was rampant. Encouragement of this kind at such a moment was, like the quality of mercy, twice blessed: it spoke as much for the comforter as the comforted. For if Portal reckoned himself fortunate to have the alert, unruffled Tedder in control in the Middle East, it is certain that Tedder, and the Royal Air Force, were fortunate in having the steadfast, far-sighted Portal at the helm in Whitehall.

The merits of commanders are apt to be overlooked when the battle goes against them. All the immense personal contribution of Auchinleck to the stabilization at El Alamein could not—or did not—protect him from the stigma of the earlier defeat of his chosen subordinate. But throughout this critical period the position of Tedder and Coningham remained completely unchallenged. This was mainly because though the Eighth Army was defeated by Rommel's ground forces the Royal Air Force was victorious over the *Luftwaffe* and the *Regia Aeronautica*. But it was also because Tedder took the trouble, and possessed the ability, to keep his superior officer in London informed, not merely adequately, but brilliantly, of the progress of events in his Command. On 29th June, for instance, when Rommel was still coming on fast, he dictated a letter to Portal which covered nearly four pages of closely typed foolscap. To the head of the Service in London, hungering for the flesh-and-blood realities behind the formal operational summaries, and having to justify the performance of his forces before the Cabinet or his fellow Chiefs of Staff, such bulletins came as a godsend. Their main qualities were those of Tedder himself—shrewdness, astuteness, tact, humour, and a sane and measured optimism. 'I went up on Thursday morning (25th)', wrote Tedder in the above-mentioned letter, 'to Bagush, where the Joint Advanced Headquarters were. I had a long review of the situation with Ritchie and Coningham (Ritchie did not then know that Auchinleck was going to take over).... At that time the Hun was massing to the west of the Matruh defences. A concentration of 5,000 M.T. being reported, everything possible was done to produce the maximum scale of effort both by day and night. The Wellingtons, assisted by Albacores, kept at it from dusk to dawn, and at seven in the morning the Bostons started an hourly service which went on throughout the day. This was continued the following night with maximum intensity. I have heard squadrons' accounts of these operations, and there is no doubt that quite impossible things were done. There were instances in fighter squadrons of fighter aircraft doing as many as seven sorties in the day and pilots doing as much as five sorties. The Boston aircraft did three or even more per day.... Credit for this of course lies not only with the pilots and aircrews, but even more with the ground crews, reduced as they are to the minimum in order to effect rapid moves without stopping operations and handicapped as they are by conditions and minor nuisances such as bombs and flares at night. It really does appear that these continuous attacks on the enemy transport columns and concentrations are being effective. I had an entirely unsolicited testimonial from Freyberg when I went to see him in his ambulance fresh from his battle. He had seen the Bostons bomb and was most enthusiastic. . . .

'I think one of the most remarkable things about the recent operations has been the way in which the squadrons have cleaned up behind them and left practically nothing which can be of use to us, and literally nothing which can be of use to the Hun. During the last stage or so this has become progressively more difficult, since there has not been a sufficient interval between moves to allow the articulators and cranes to clear the accumulations. On one fighter aerodrome yesterday I saw about 100 men lifting a Spitfire bodily so as to get the articulator beneath it. There was no crane available there but they were determined not to lose this Spitfire, and that is the spirit one has seen throughout—a full-out determination to give the Hun nothing but knocks. . . .

'The force as a whole is in terrific form and has complete moral ascendancy over the Hun. They are, however, tired, and at the first possible moment I must try and ease the situation—not that there is a hope of being able to do it for the next few days!

'As regards the immediate future, I do feel that our continuous attacks on enemy supplies must ultimately produce an effect which will be disastrous if the Army can take advantage of it. I do not know to what extent it has been possible to complete the El Alamein line, but I have little belief in lines of trenches, nor has Auchinleck, and his plan is, as I understand it, to use the line of defended positions in order to canalize the enemy attack and enable us to deal with him with mixed mobile forces of tanks, guns and infantry. The main failures in the past have, I think, been due to loss of effective control. In this case I know Auchinleck intends to exercise direct control over the battle, and on this restricted front one feels he ought to be able to do so. If he can give them a good smack here I feel that we ought to be able together to clean up the whole party. I have told all my people that the move backwards they are now making today is to be made in such a way as not to prejudice an immediate move forward. The campaigns out here have been starred with a number of lost opportunities; each one lost through the inability of the Army to strike back hard and follow up. I know Auchinleck fully appreciates this and is determined to follow up any successes quickly and ruthlessly. We intend to be ready'.

CHAPTER XI

Middle East: The Alamein Line and Decisive Victory

On 29th June Mussolini arrived at Derna to lead the triumphal procession through Cairo. His mode of transport was a Red Cross plane heavily escorted by fighters. According to a persistent legend for which there appears to be no shred of evidence, he also brought with him a white horse. The cast being thus assembled for the final scene, on the evening of 1st July Rommel swept forward against the Alamein line.

That night the Wellingtons, flying over a hundred sorties, attacked the enemy's concentrations and communications in full force. 'The day was notably lively', recorded the Africa Corps Diary, 'with many successful bombing attacks by the British. . . . In the night continuous [British] bombing raids met with success, and the supply columns were blown up'. All the next day this intense activity in the air continued, and by dusk Tedder's pilots had flown nearly 800 sorties within twenty-four hours. 'Throughout the whole of the day', reported the enemy, 'there were heavy air raids, and our own fighter defence was not nearly sufficient'.

Thanks to the Eighth Army's stout resistance on the ground and to this great effort in the air, the enemy attack made little headway, and as darkness fell the Wellingtons and Albacores again went out with deadly effect. Among their many achievements that night was the destruction of a large ammunition dump which the penetrating eye of Pilot Officer S. J. Thorne, of No. 37 Squadron, had discerned, or rather suspected, beneath a series of eight innocent-looking sand dunes. Thorne's bombs scored direct hits on two of the dunes, whereupon there was a tremendous explosion, a red glare that lit the entire area, and a great cloud of black smoke that rose to 5,000 feet. Unfortunately, the aircraft was so badly damaged by the blast that the crew were soon forced to bale out, and in helping the front gunner Thorne fell through the lower hatch. 'The captain's parachute', records the Squadron Diary, 'was found unopened on the ground, unattached to the body. The harness was also found near the body, broken'.

Throughout 3rd July our squadrons maintained their great effort, flying in all some 780 sorties. 'The continuous raids by day and night are hindering the troops seriously', noted the enemy, '... the supply situation has become even worse'. The next day brought no relief 'The enemy air force is bothering us a lot', an Italian artillery officer confided to his diary; 'from 5 to 11 o'clock it was over more than six times. Night and day it seems to go on without interruption, and there is not a moment's peace. We are becoming like potatoes—always underground'. But by then the work of our troops and airmen had had its effect. In the early morning of 4th July Rommel recognized his defeat and ordered his army over to the defensive. The Alamein line had survived its first and greatest test.

As soon as it was clear that the enemy had been stopped, Auchinleck set about regaining the initiative. During the rest of July he launched a number of fierce attacks, local and general, against the Axis troops in front of the Alamein line. On 10th July, the 9th Australian Division, fresh from Palestine, made useful gains; in the following week there were several sharp engagements; and on the 21st, and again on the 26th, Auchinleck struck in full force. These endeavours inflicted many casualties on the Italians and somewhat improved our general position; but they signally failed in their main purpose of putting the enemy to flight. Moreover our armour, much of which was inexperienced, again suffered heavy losses; our reserves were too few to maintain the initial momentum of the attacks; and many of our troops were so tired as to be near the limits of endurance. On 30th July the Commander-in-Chief accordingly acknowledged that success was not yet within his grasp, and for the time being gave up his attempts to make headway. Expecting, as he did, to receive four fresh divisions (including two armoured) within six weeks, it was only common prudence to break off for a spell of rest and reorganization. Meanwhile Rommel, who also expected reinforcements and whose troops were equally exhausted, had taken a similar decision. The Desert War settled down again into a battle of supplies.

During all these engagements Tedder's forces, besides attacking ports and shipping when occasion demanded, continued to give highly effective support to the Eighth Army. The main lines of their work were by now familiar. The Baltimores and Bostons, based in the Canal Zone since the retirement but operating from forward landing grounds near Cairo, pattern-bombed the enemy's troop positions from dawn to dusk. The 'Eighteen Imperturbables' as these light-bomber formations came to be called, were so well protected by the

Kittyhawks that for days on end they were able to operate without loss. Their efforts were supplemented by those of the fighter-bombers, which ranged ceaselessly over the enemy lines in search of profitable objectives. Like the fighters—which also attacked ground targets in the intervals between shooting down Stukas and Me.109's—these aircraft were based mainly on landing grounds along the Cairo-Alexandria road. At night the task was taken up by the heavier bombers, now withdrawn to Palestine for lack of room in Egypt. The Wellingtons, refuelling in the Canal Zone, attacked troop positions with the help of the Albacores whenever a major battle was in progress; when it was not, they visited Tobruk—for their old love, Benghazi, was now far beyond their reach. The Liberators, however, could still raid the latter port direct from Palestine. In sum, the Middle East aircraft demonstrated the flexibility of well-organized air power. The Western Desert Air Force, Air Headquarters Egypt, No. 201 (Naval Co-operation) Group, and No. 205 Group, to which the American heavy bombers were attached—all existed for distinct purposes. But when need arose all could be, and were, applied to the critical task of slowing down the enemy or helping our own troops forward.

The effect of their work again emerges in the enemy records. On 16th July the War Diary of the German Africa Corps tells how our fighters nearly disposed of Rommel—or rather, how they shot up the car in which he had been sitting until they appeared. On 19th July the same source, after reciting the fact that the Africa Corps disposed only twenty-eight serviceable tanks, details a new order—that all tanks are to be 'surrounded by sand bags and stone walls to protect them from damage in air attacks'. Difficulties of supply, and particularly the shortage of ammunition, receive repeated mention. On the night of 21st July—the eve of Auchinleck's main effort—the Diary records that 'continuous heavy bombing attacks are being carried out. Enemy air activity tonight exceeds anything hitherto experienced. Telephone communications are frequently broken, and there is no contact with the divisions'. That same day Rommel informed Keitel that 'the enemy air force . . . has by continued day and night operations caused considerable losses amongst our troops, lowered the morale of Italian troops, delayed and at times cut off supply . . . the supply situation is tense owing to continual and partially successful attacks by enemy air and naval forces on German supplies at Tobruk and Matruh'.

Unfortunately, our success in the air was not yet equalled on the ground; for as Auchinleck attacked so his tanks again wilted away. How far this was caused by lack of effective communication and control, how far by defective tactics, and how far by the heavier tanks and the 88-mm. guns of the Germans, is a matter for the military historians to determine. But the broad fact was clear enough. On 22nd July the Africa Corps Diary noted: 'Out of an attacking force of 100 enemy tanks, forty have been destroyed for the loss of three German tanks'. The following day the claim increased to 118 British tanks destroyed within forty-eight hours. And at the same time the Germans, by working on their damaged but recoverable machines, were soon able to rebuild a powerful force. On 2nd August the two Panzer Divisions, which a fortnight earlier could muster between them only twenty-eight serviceable tanks, could boast 163. By 15th August Rommel's strength in troops, which three weeks before was down to thirty per cent of establishment, had risen to over seventy per cent; and his strength in tanks, which had been down to fifteen per cent, had risen to fifty per cent. All the efforts of the Eighth Army and the Royal Air Force had for the moment brought about no more than a stalemate.

This, however, if less than Auchinleck and Tedder had hoped, was a great deal more than many on the allied side had thought likely. Certainly to Rommel, and to the Italian dictator impatiently awaiting the cue to appear on his white horse, the consolidation of the Eighth Army at El Alamein was a bitter disappointment. After three weeks of steadily growing disillusionment the *Duce* departed for Italy on 20th July, leaving behind his baggage—more for the sake of appearances than from any anticipation of returning. Shortly afterwards he was visited by Ciano, to whom he soon unburdened himself. Rommel, Mussolini complained, had been discourteous—he had not even troubled to pay him a formal call. The German soldiers were grasping and insolent. The Arabs behaved badly. Even the British prisoners of war left much to be desired. 'He told me', wrote Ciano, 'that he had found groups of fierce-looking New Zealand prisoners who were so far from reassuring that he always kept his gun close at hand'.

The Italian counterparts of these New Zealanders, it may be recalled, were already making admirable servants in British messes. The contrast was instructive. Sooner or later the deadlock between the two armies would be broken. Whoever struck the decisive blow, it was not likely to be the Italians. And Rommel's Germans, after all, amounted to only four divisions. The proposition before the Eighth Army might be difficult. It was clearly not impossible.

* * *

It will be recalled that when our enemies changed their plan and allowed Rommel to drive on into Egypt, Mussolini had made a stipulation. If Malta was not to be invaded until the autumn, it must meanwhile be neutralized. On 1st July Kesselring, who since early May had kept up only a minor scale of attack against the island, accordingly flung his aircraft across from Sicily again in full force.

By then the arrival of the two merchantmen in June, coupled with the continuous reinforcement by Spitfires, had greatly eased the task of the defenders. On 1st July there were nearly 200 aircraft on Malta, of which over half were Spitfires. Among the rest, the Marylands and Baltimores had never ceased to carry out their vital function of reconnaissance; while the Wellingtons, so far as resources of fuel allowed, were already striking out again with great effect. Some, indeed, of the newly arrived fighter pilots had not yet fired a gun in anger—the home Commands had a habit of 'milking' squadrons proceeding overseas of their leading members—but what the newcomers lacked in experience they amply made up for in martial ardour.

When Kesselring once more turned on the pressure, using Italian planes in strength as well as German, his crews were accordingly treated to a warm reception. Able to call on a force of 567 aircraft, in the first fortnight of July the German Commander directed about 1,000 sorties, bomber and fighter, against the island. Many times the attacks struck home against the airfields which were their objective; but our fighters were not to be shaken off, and for the most part caused the bombs to fall wide. Soon it became obvious that the Spitfires, the Beaufighters and the guns were giving quite as good as they got. By 14th July the new 'blitz' had cost Kesselring forty-four aircraft, of which twenty-three were bombers. Malta's fighter losses for the same period were thirty-nine, from which, thanks in large part to the island's admirable air-sea rescue service, twenty-six pilots survived to fight again. At a time when Germany was desperately short of aircraft to meet all her many self-imposed commitments she could not afford even this degree of losses; and from mid-July the attack again weakened.

The defeat of this fresh attempt to subdue Malta marked the end of another phase in the island's story. It was signalized by a change of command. Lloyd was given a well-earned rest—a rest, that is to say, by comparison. He was selected to take over No. 201 (Naval Co-operation) Group from Air Vice-Marshal Slatter. Slatter, whose work at Alexandria had been no less impressive than his early achievements in the Sudan, departed to put his maritime experience to equally good use in Coastal Command; while to Lloyd's place in Malta there succeeded the Air Officer Commanding from A.H.Q., Egypt—Air Vice-Marshal K. R. Park. This vigorous, skilful, and very experienced commander was appointed to Malta because the defence of the island seemed for the time being even more important than its offensive against enemy shipping; and what Park did not know about fighter defence was not worth knowing. Conversely, as the strikes against enemy convoys had come to be directed mainly from the Eastern Mediterranean, it was useful to have Lloyd, whose heart and soul was in this type of work, in charge of No. 201 Group at Alexandria.

Within a few days of taking over his new post Park put his talents as a fighter commander to good use. While Malta's fighter force consisted of a few obsolescent Hurricanes with—for 1942—a slow rate of climb, the tactics of defence had necessarily been restricted; for the Hurricanes had been compelled, when warned of the enemy's approach from the north, to gain height to the south of the island. Their operational height once reached, they could then return to engage the attackers as the latter swept in across the coast. The advent of the latest Spitfires in considerable numbers, however, had opened up other possibilities, and this Park at once saw. He promptly ordered his fighters to gain height while approaching the enemy and to intercept, not over the island, but as far north of it as possible. This increased the strain on the air-sea rescue service and the pilots, who now had to operate many miles out to sea; but both were fully equal to the call. The scheme was an instant success, and Park could soon point not only to the continued slaughter of the enemy but also to a most welcome decrease in the proportion of bombs falling on Malta. In fact by the end of July the enemy had been driven into the same tactics as in the closing stages of the Battle of Britain—the tactics of high-level fighter and fighter-bomber sweeps, which kept the defences at full stretch but accomplished little else.

By this time the island, despite deliveries by aircraft and submarine, was again in desperate need of supplies. The episode of the June convoys had shown that a supply operation from the east was impossible, but that ships might get through from the west if given really powerful air and surface escort. Operation 'Pedestal' was accordingly devised. As a necessary preliminary over 100 machines—including four Liberators—were flown in to Malta, so increasing Park's strength to some 250 aircraft. At the same time convoys to Russia were temporarily suspended, with the result that the fourteen merchant vessels sailed to Malta under the escort of two battleships, three aircraft carriers, six cruisers, an anti-aircraft cruiser and twenty-four destroyers. As part of the deception plan a dummy convoy ran in two parts from the Eastern Mediterranean as far as Alexandria.

The merchantmen and their main escort entered the Straits of Gibraltar on 10th August, 1942. By then Park's aircraft were making ready to bomb the Sicilian airfields. But the striking force available for this type of work was very small, and from the 11th onwards the convoy was shadowed and repeatedly attacked from the air. Despite the heroic efforts of the naval fighters and the ships' gunners casualties soon mounted, while mines, U-boats, and E-boats took a further toll. Even the arrival over the convoy of long-range Beaufighters from Malta at first brought no relief, for they were at once mistaken for Ju.88's and heavily fired on by our ships. However, an Italian naval force was successfully discouraged from intervention by the joint efforts of a single Wellington and Malta's Operations Room Staff. The latter sent a plain language signal directing some largely imaginary Liberators against the enemy warships.

All told, the convoy and its escort suffered attacks by estimated forces of about 150 bombers and eighty torpedo bombers. The ships' guns, the Fleet fighters and Malta's Spitfires and Beaufighters between them shot down forty-one of these assailants. Of the fourteen merchantmen five, including a crippled tanker in tow, eventually reached Grand Harbour, where our fighters and guns held the enemy at bay until the last stores were safely extracted. At the cost of the *Eagle*, two cruisers, a destroyer and eighteen aircraft, the operation had given Malta a new lease of life. Able once again despite all shortages to strike against every enemy vessel that came within her reach, she could now play her full part in the forthcoming, and decisive, phase of the Desert War.

It is impossible to leave Malta and turn back to the African scene without recording an incident which occurred a fortnight before the arrival of the August convoy. Unusual as it was, it typified the spirit of Malta's aircrews and indeed of aircrews throughout the Royal Air Force.

On 28th July a Beaufort of No. 217 Squadron, piloted by a South African lieutenant and carrying as crew a British pilot officer and two New Zealand sergeants, was shot down off the west coast of Greece. As the stricken bomber plunged towards the sea the crew had the satisfaction of seeing their torpedo run true against its target, a 6,000 ton merchant vessel forming part of an enemy convoy. The task of escaping from the aircraft, which sank within ninety seconds, then claimed their full attention. Despite the fact that the pilot was in the submerged nose all four men managed to struggle into the dinghy. After a brief stocktaking they then paddled in the direction of the shore—towards which, when they had remembered to haul in the drogues, they made good progress.

They were still paddling when an Italian Cant float-plane appeared overhead, circled, and put down about a hundred yards away. The Beaufort pilot, Lieutenant E. T. Strever, promptly swam across and was hauled aboard, where he was given brandy and a cigarette. The rest of the crew were then picked up and treated likewise, after which the Cant taxied to a harbour in the island of Corfu.

On landing the prisoners were taken to a camp, where the Italians again showed them every consideration. There followed a mid-afternoon meal built around steak, tomatoes and wine; an excellent supper, with more wine and cigarettes; comfortable beds in rooms vacated by the Italian officers; and eggs for breakfast in the morning. Their captors then informed them that they would be taken to a prisoner-of-war camp in Italy by aircraft. At this their hearts sank, for unlike a journey by train or car the mode of transport seemed to offer no chance of making an escape. The only possibility, they decided, was to capture the plane; but of how to do this they had no idea.

A few hours later they were taken back to the harbour, where their aircraft turned out to be the Cant of the previous day. The Italian crew of four was also the same, with the addition of an armed corporal to stand guard over the prisoners. The seaplane took off and set course westwards, and for a while the flight proceeded uneventfully. Suddenly, one of the New Zealanders, Sergeant J. A. Wilkinson, who in the manner of New Zealanders had been quietly working things out, leant forward and smashed his fist into the face of the Italian wireless operator. Leaping over the latter's falling body he then flung himself on the corporal and wrenched away the revolver, which he at once passed to Lieutenant Strever. Not to be outdone the other two members of the Beaufort crew, Pilot Officer W. M. Dunsmore and Sergeant A. R. Brown, promptly tackled the engineer, while the Italian pilot tried to draw his revolver and the second pilot began fumbling with a tommy gun. This danger Wilkinson countered by advancing up the fuselage holding the corporal in front of him as a shield, while Strever followed brandishing the captured revolver. A few more swift moves and the Italians were disarmed and tied up with their own belts, and Strever had taken over the controls. All this proved too much for the corporal, who was on his first flight, and who now added to the confusion by being violently sick.

The next problem was how to fly a strange aircraft with no maps, no charts and no knowledge of the petrol consumption. Strever soon found it easier to free the Italian second pilot, to place him at the controls, and to give him rough and ready directions which he hoped might bring them to Malta. At length the toe of Italy hove in sight.

VALETTA, MAY 1942

'UNCRATING' AN AIRCRAFT AT TAKORADI, JULY 1942

A SALVAGE CONVOY NEARS ITS DESTINATION
Wrecked aircraft brought in from the Desert for repair at Cairo

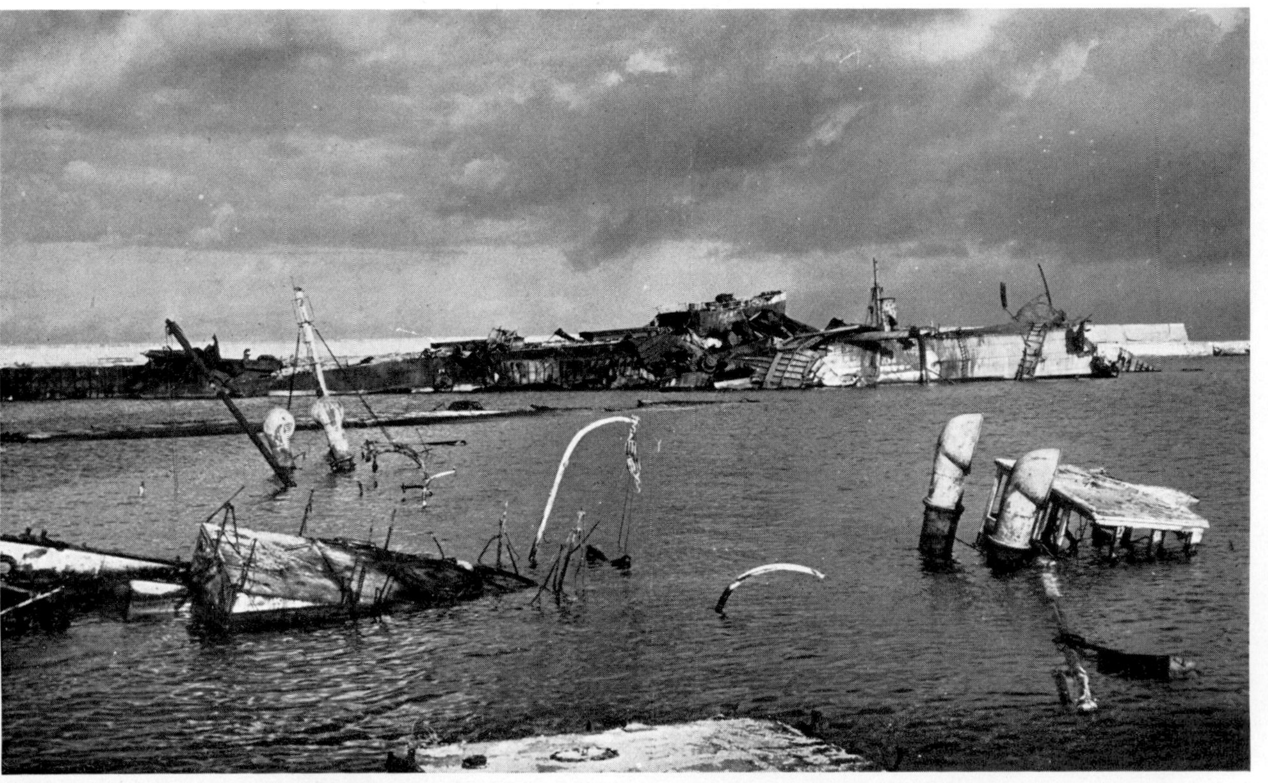

AXIS SHIPPING AT BENGHAZI WRECKED BY ALLIED BOMBING

Taking a chance in the matter of petrol, Strever at once ordered the pilot to turn south. At this the Italians, who were fully aware how Malta's fighters would greet a Cant, registered great alarm. Their fears were soon justified. As the float plane came in low, three Spitfires swept down upon it. All efforts to explain the position—including those of Pilot Officer Dunsmore, who took off his vest (the only white object handy) and trailed it behind the aircraft as a sign of surrender—proved unavailing: the Spitfires continued to attack. When a stream of bullets poured through the wing Strever decided the time had come for a more decisive gesture, and he ordered the Italian pilot to put down on the water. The floats met the surface safely; then the propellers spun idly in the air as the last drop of petrol spluttered in the jets. It remained only for the four airmen to climb out and signal frantically to the Spitfires; for a launch to appear from Malta and tow in the captured machine; and for the Beaufort crew, who were feeling a little conscience-stricken at the way they had repaid the Italians' hospitality, to offer their apologies and do all they could for the comfort of their captives. The latter, cheerfully recognizing that war is war, took everything in good part; and the episode closed with one of them producing from his suitcase a bottle of wine which he insisted on sharing with Lieutenant Strever.

Strever then looked in on the Spitfire squadron, where he had the doubtful pleasure of hearing the pilots slated by their commanding officer for bad shooting.

* * *

During August and September Tedder was mainly concerned to win the battle of supplies and repulse Rommel's next attempt on the Alamein line. But there were also certain organizational matters which demanded his attention.

The retreat from Gazala and the struggle in July had left the Middle East Air Commander keenly aware that there were still serious weaknesses in the organization of tactical support. These no longer sprang from the inability of the Royal Air Force to keep up with a fast-moving battle but from the inability of the Army to maintain an up-to-date picture of its own movements. Moreover, although brigades at once demanded air cover when they were bombed, they very rarely appealed for air support when they were hard-pressed on the ground. During the retreat from Gazala, when many units of the Eighth Army were in desperate straits, Coningham received only twelve requests for air support: all other attacks made by his squadrons were planned on information which they themselves had gathered.

Some improvement was already achieved before Auchinleck departed. That great soldier and gentleman had throughout acted in the closest concert with Tedder, and his final Order of the Day before handing over to General Alexander on 15th August included a generous tribute to the Royal Air Force. 'During these weeks you [the Eighth Army] have stopped the enemy . . . forced him on the defensive, taken 10,000 prisoners from him, and destroyed or captured many of his guns, vehicles and their equipment. You will, I know, join me in acknowledging the great and glorious part our air forces have played in helping us to achieve these results. Without their aid the story would have been very different'.

As part of the reorganization in the Middle East, Lieut.-General B. L. Montgomery was appointed to command the Eighth Army, and this at once brought closer co-operation between the two Services. The last two months of the Auchinleck régime, with the Commander-in-Chief also acting as Commander of the Eighth Army, had naturally led to technical difficulties. It had meant, for instance, that the Eighth Army's headquarters were no longer side by side with those of the Western Desert Air Force. In this respect Montgomery at once restored the previous practice. Beyond this, however, he also brought to his post a remarkably keen, clear and vigorous appreciation of the part that could and should be played by air forces in a land battle. Commanders like Auchinleck and Ritchie had never been anything but highly co-operative; but Montgomery insisted that good-will was translated at all stages into practical action. If air co-operation was the gospel in the G.O.C.'s caravan, it would also be the gospel all the way from base to front line. The result was that within a few weeks of Montgomery's appointment, on the eve of the final battle of El Alamein, Tedder could write to Portal: 'Co-operation with the Army has further improved, thanks undoubtedly in some part to the lead given by Montgomery on the subject. It was very refreshing to see in Eighth Army Advanced Headquarters the embryo of a real operations room copied directly from our own mobile operations rooms. As I told the soldiers, it was the first sign I had seen of their being able to collect and sift information of their battle, and consequently the first sign one had seen of their being able to control it. For the past two years they had been saying such a thing was impossible; now they have started it and realise its potentialities. I think it should develop well and make an enormous difference'.

Another problem at this time—but of a kind with which Tedder was very glad to be confronted—was the arrival of American squadrons in the Middle East. After Operation 'Vigorous' and the attack on Ploesti the Halverson Detachment had remained in the

Command; by 25th June, only four days after the fall of Tobruk and two days after receiving his orders, Major-General L. H. Brereton, Commanding General of the American Tenth Air Force in India, was posting with all speed to Egypt in company with his nine available B.17's; and as the summer passed, other American squadrons began to arrive in the Middle East in obedience to the principle that, wherever possible, American aircraft should now be flown by American crews. At the end of July the 57th Fighter Group, armed with P.40's (Warhawks), crossed the Atlantic in a carrier and thence flew along the Takoradi route; in the first week of August the B.24's (Liberators) of the 98th (Heavy) Bombardment Group followed under their own power; and a week later the B.25's (Mitchells) of the 12th (Medium) Bombardment Group also winged their way across the Atlantic and Central Africa.

These welcome reinforcements raised problems not only of co-ordination and control but also of maintenance—for the aircraft and crews travelled in advance of their full ground echelons. Fortunately, inter-allied relationship was Tedder's *forte*. Royal Air Force maintenance resources were placed without stint at the disposal of the new arrivals; the American groups, though officially only under Tedder's 'strategic direction', were integrated where necessary into the Royal Air Force organization—the fighters and medium bombers, for instance, acted under Coningham's operational control; and the technically very proficient but operationally inexperienced American crews were 'blooded' by flying with a British squadron before going into action on their own. All this, of course, could be done only because Brereton—whose units eventually became the Ninth Air Force—was another devotee of the gospel of co-operation. Naturally the Royal Air Force, with the larger resources in the theatre and over two years' experience of the Desert fighting, was at this stage the senior partner; but the traffic of ideas was by no means one-way. By 21st October Tedder could report to Portal: 'The Americans work in very well with our squadrons. They now have their own fighter wing with two squadrons who have already shown up well in combat. Their third fighter squadron, which has had more experience and which we can make reasonably mobile, is in one of our own fighter wings (No. 239) and will go forward. They are learning from us and we are learning from them—I was glad to hear this from both sides.'

* * *

As the summer wore on, Tedder became very concerned with the problem of enemy air reconnaissance. In June the Germans began to use for purposes of reconnaissance a few unarmed, pressurized Ju.86's capable of flying at over 45,000 feet. No ordinary fighter on the British side could approach this height; yet if these aircraft went unchallenged the enemy would soon have a complete picture of our positions and preparations. One answer was eventually found in the tactical combination of two specially stripped-down (and 'hotted up') Spitfires. One of these was left with armour, R/T and four machine-guns, the other with no armour, no R/T and only two machine-guns. The technique was for No. 1 to guide No. 2 within visual range of the enemy; for No. 2 then to climb to the level of the Ju.86 and direct its fire at the latter's engines; and for No. 1 to wait below and if necessary finish off the winged bird. The first victory—a solo effort—was obtained at 49,000 feet on 24th August by Flying Officer G. W. H. Reynolds, the chief test pilot at No. 103 Maintenance Unit. Fortunately, only five more Ju.86 sorties were reported—of which two were shot down—and the menace was disposed of by mid-September. The last of the raiders was also engaged by Reynolds, who, despite his thirty-eight years, flew at over 40,000 feet some twenty-five times during the month. In pursuit of this final intruder he had to fly above 45,000 feet in an iced-up aircraft for more than an hour, and finally, faint and half paralysed, summon up his last ounce of strength to press the gun button.

* * *

Meantime the battle of supplies continued. The safe arrival of five ships in Operation 'Pedestal', carrying the largest bulk of stores to reach Malta since September 1941, enabled the Navy once more to operate cruisers, destroyers and submarines from the island. The combined attentions of these and Malta's aircraft soon drove the enemy's North African convoys back into the old fantastic detour by way of Greece and Crete. Several vessels started from Italy for Greece only to put back not once, but three or four times, merely because they were spotted by air reconnaissance. Moreover, during the whole period of stabilization on the Alamein line Park was also able to keep up a steady average of fifteen bomber sorties a week—not a remarkable figure at first sight, but impressive enough when it is remembered that supplies were still extremely short, that the island remained under attack, and that every sortie was against a carefully selected and to the enemy altogether precious target.

The anti-shipping effort from Malta, however, was by now less important than that from the Eastern Mediterranean. This continued to be the work of No. 201 Group, which called for striking forces as necessary from No. 205 Group, the American Liberators, and the Western Desert Air Force. Between them, and with the help of the submarines, these formations made the task of the convoys attempting the run across from Greece one of the utmost difficulty. Moreover, their repeated raids on Tobruk prevented the enemy making anything like full use of this port. This in turn forced Rommel to bring up his supplies from Benghazi either in lorries which soon wore out, or in small naval craft which proved attractive targets for the long-range Beaufighters. And even Benghazi, out of range as it was to the medium bombers, could still be attacked by the Liberators. The result of the whole combined effort can be seen in a single figure. According to Admiral Weichold thirty-five per cent of the total Axis supplies despatched to North Africa during August failed to reach their destination.

The importance of this fact was heightened by another. While the enemy's supplies were thus curtailed our own were arriving in an ever-broadening flow—during August in particular, very large numbers of replacement and reinforcing aircraft poured into the Middle East Command. With all this traffic the enemy was entirely impotent to interfere. When a force of U-boats attempted to make trouble off the Levant coast its efforts soon came to grief before the combined vigilance of the Navy and No. 201 Group; and the mines which enemy aircraft repeatedly dropped in the Suez Canal were as repeatedly swept up the following morning.

* * *

Anxious to strike before the Eighth Army was too heavily reinforced, at the end of August Rommel renewed his assault on the Alamein line. In the late evening of 30th August our aircraft reported three concentrations of enemy vehicles in the southern sector, and by midnight it was plain that the Axis forces were beginning a general advance. 'Yesterday evening at eight o'clock', noted Ciano, 'Rommel attacked in Libya. He had chosen the day and the hour well, at a time when whisky had begun to appear on the British tables. . . .' It is not recorded whether the British officers, in the spirit of Drake, paused to complete the task in hand before proceeding to other business; presumably they did. What is certain is that from the start the enemy's punch lacked power, and that Montgomery's tactics of allowing the German armour to batter against our cunningly protected or entrenched guns and tanks paid handsomely. The Axis ground forces, however, were strongly supported by the *Luftwaffe*, which was now well forward. During the night Ju.88's from Crete did great execution among the dummy aircraft thoughtfully provided for their attention on our landing grounds; while other German bombers strove with the help of flares to emulate the work of the Wellington and Albacores against troop positions. The next day escorted Ju.88' and what Stukas the enemy could still muster were again extremely active over the battle area. Indeed, during the whole period of the attack the *Luftwaffe* managed to fly a daily average of ninety-five sorties by bombers and 220 sorties by fighter-bombers and fighters.

This, however, was very small beer compared with what Tedder's forces could now put up. On 31st August and the ensuing night they flew 482 sorties; on 1st September 674; on 2nd September 806; and on 3rd September 902. Throughout the struggle our fighters held the ring over the battlefield and protected our troops from the *Luftwaffe;* and from first to last, bombers, fighter-bombers and fighters alike hammered away at the Axis ground forces. Bunched up by the pressure of our artillery and armour, these offered a superb target which the Western Desert Air Force and No. 205 Group were in no mood to ignore. 'We were very heavily attacked every hour of the day and night', later testified General Bayerlein, who took over the Africa Corps for a few hours after Nehring was wounded by our aircraft, 'and had very heavy losses, more than from any other cause. Your air superiority was most important, perhaps decisive'. 'The continuous and very heavy attacks of the R.A.F.', recorded Rommel, '. . . absolutely pinned my troops to the ground and made impossible any safe deployment or any advance according to schedule'.

Farther removed from the battle but equally effective was the work of Malta, No. 201 Group and the submarines. Between 27th August and 4th September no less than nine Italian vessels were sunk on the African convoy routes—one by a mine, two by our submarines and six by our aircraft. The result of all this was noted by Ciano, who on 2nd September recorded: 'Rommel is halted in Egypt because of lack of fuel . . . three of our tankers have been sunk in two days'. On 3rd September the news was little different: 'Rommel's pause continues, and what is worse the sinking of our ships continues. Tonight there have been two'. And by 4th September, still in the same vein, Ciano could only record that all was over: 'Rommel is drawing back his left flank under the attack of the British Air Force even before the enemy tanks come into action. Tonight two other ships were sunk'. Rommel himself was no less specific: 'The petrol, which was a necessary condition of the carrying out of our plans, did not arrive. The ships which Cavallero had promised us were some of them sunk, some of them delayed and some of them not even despatched'.[1]

[1] Quoted in Brigadier Desmond Young's *Rommel.*

So ended the battle of Alam-el-Halfa—Rommel's second attempt to force the Alamein position, and the last occasion on which his forces were to hold the initiative. The struggle had been won by good generalship, stout resistance on the ground, and overwhelming superiority in the air, all acting in a situation created by relentless interruption of the enemy's supplies.

* * *

The episode of Alam-el-Halfa over, Tedder could again focus his attention on the supply battle. During September his aircraft and Admiral Harwood's submarines sank nearly a third of the enemy cargoes attempting to reach Africa, besides causing many other vessels to turn back with their mission unaccomplished. In all this the renewed striking power of Malta told to such effect that Hitler soon ordered another 'blitz' against the obstinate island. 'Because of the revival of Malta as an air base and the numerous sinkings in the Mediterranean', ran his directive of 14th September, 'supplies for the First Panzer Army have fallen far below normal requirements. Unless Malta is weakened or paralysed once more, this situation cannot be remedied'. At the end of the month Ciano was still more explicit: 'In all, we have little more than a million tons [of merchant shipping] left', he noted on 29th September, 'at this rate the African problem will automatically end in six months, since we shall have no more ships with which to supply Libya'.

The new, and, as it proved, final assault in Malta began on 10th October, 1942. That day the number of enemy raiders rose abruptly from the by then normal twenty or thirty to over 120. Six times the enemy appeared in strength—though each time, significantly enough, with few bombers and many fighters. Five times our aircraft intercepted these formations well north of the island; on the other occasion a formation composed entirely of fighters managed to cross the coast at great height but did no damage. From the day's fighting the enemy lost two aircraft, ourselves none; and, still more gratifying, not a single bomb fell on Malta.

Such was the beginning. The next day the enemy sent over, according to our estimates, 216 aircraft; the day after, 279; and from then on, up to and including 19th October, between 200 and 270 each day. In addition some ten to twenty aircraft carried out 'nuisance' raids at night. But from 20th October onwards the attacks fell away, until in the last week of the month the daily average was no more than 120 raiders, most of which got nowhere near the island. During these final operations the Germans found out once again that fighter sweeps are no substitute for heavy bombardment. The defeat of the enemy, in fact, may be dated from 18th October, when Kesselring withdrew his Ju.88's from the battle. In the period of the most intensive fighting, from 10th to 19th October, we shot down forty-six German aircraft and probably at least an equal number of Italian, as against a loss of only thirty Spitfires; while in terms of aircrew the estimate was that fifteen of the enemy had failed to return to base for every one of ours. More important than any exact calculation of losses was the fact that damage to the island was slight, and that though some bombs fell on the airfields nearly every day they did not impede our operations. On only one night during the month did Malta's bombers fail to take off against enemy shipping. That was a night on which there was no enemy shipping to attack.

This, then, was all Kesselring could show for his final fling against Malta. For this the Axis had kept 600 aircraft in Sicily at a time when they desperately needed every one of these machines in Africa. In the end even the German pilots lost heart; and a final order from Göring at the end of October, that Malta must be destroyed within eight days, was as vain and wind-stuffed as the source from which it came. As Kesselring coldly pointed out in reply, experience had amply shown that only the occupation of the island could put it out of action. And by that time matters were so far gone in Africa that the enemy was quite unable to spare forces for an attempt on Malta. So passed to the grave that still-born conception which the Germans with Teutonic pomposity had termed Operation 'Hercules', and the Italians, with a more prophetic insight into their own limitations, Operation 'C.3'. It was a project which, like the capture of Gibraltar, would have been simple compared with many that the Germans cheerfully and unnecessarily undertook, but which, had it been attempted with success, might well have spelled defeat to the allied cause.

* * *

In October our aircraft and submarines struck with still greater effect against the enemy convoys. Between them the two methods of attack, sharing the honours almost equally, sank some 50,000 tons of shipping on the North African routes. According to Admiral Weichold, forty-five per cent of the entire Italian tonnage despatched, and fifty-nine per cent of the German, failed to reach the other side. Of the German cargo of which Rommel was thus cheated, sixty-five per cent was fuel.

Meanwhile, our aircraft were also busy on operations designed to usher in the last and greatest battle of El Alamein. The plan was for the crews to start intensive attacks against the enemy air force four days before the opening of the land battle; but on 6th October, three weeks before the Eighth Army was due to strike, there occurred an opportunity too good to miss. Very heavy rain began to fall; and by 9th October our photographs showed the Daba landing grounds under water and Fuka usable only with the greatest difficulty. Seizing the chance of catching his opponents grounded, Coningham at once called a halt to training and launched some 500 fighters and bombers against the two sets of airfields. The attack destroyed or put out of action some thirty enemy aircraft and did great damage to airfield transport, dumps, and gun positions. It was thus against antagonists already seriously weakened that the Middle East Air Force opened its full offensive on 19th October.

The force which Tedder disposed on the eve of El Alamein was very different from the attenuated body he had taken over in May 1941. In Malta, under Park, there were eight squadrons; in the Western Desert Air Force, under Coningham, twenty-nine; in No. 201 Group, under Lloyd, seventeen; in No. 205 Group, under Air Commodore A. P. Ritchie, eight; in A.H.Q. Egypt, under Air Vice-Marshal W. A. McClaughry, four. In addition there were a few units directly under the Command Headquarters—and there were the Americans. Of the grand total of ninety-six operational Allied squadrons in the Middle East, including the thirteen squadrons in the outlying theatres, sixty (with the Fleet Air Arm squadrons) were British, thirteen American, thirteen South African, five Australian, one Rhodesian, two Greek, one French and one Yugoslav; and a large proportion of the aircrews in the British squadrons came from the Dominions. All told, the entire force totalled over 1,500 first-line aircraft, of which some 1,200 were based in Egypt and Palestine. Against this the Axis had nearly 3,000 aircraft in the Mediterranean theatre, but only 689 in Africa—and of these little more than half were serviceable. On the ground the enemy numbered about 93,000 men, 470 tanks (excluding light tanks) and 1,450 guns. The corresponding figures for the Eighth Army were 165,000 men, 600 tanks, and 2,275 guns. All the material conditions were present for a decisive victory.

The military plan of campaign struck Tedder as having one important defect. Our incessant bombing had taught the enemy to disperse his troops, and these were unlikely to concentrate, and so provide our squadrons with really profitable targets, unless they were plainly threatened by our ground forces. Montgomery's plan, however, made no provision for this, but staked everything on complete surprise. It thus placed a high premium—justifiably, as it proved—on the efforts of Tedder's aircraft to prevent German reconnaissance, and on the success of the deception plan. Tedder would have preferred the other course. 'I feel we should have made such a threat', he wrote to Portal on 22nd October, 'and given us the opportunity from the air to hammer [the enemy] and weaken him for three or four days before delivering the final blow on land. I am afraid, however, it is too late to do anything about it now, and we shall have a contest on the best Queensberry Rules lines: the two opponents carefully fattened up in their respective corners, fanned and advised by their seconds up to the last minute before the seconds are ordered out and the gong goes. Of course from the air point of view the contest has been going on for some time in the attacks on shipping, lines of communication, and, with the last two or three days, against his air'.

The essence of Montgomery's scheme was to persuade the enemy that the main blow would fall in the south, and then deliver it in the north. To this end XIII Corps, covering the southern sectors, was to display a suitable array of dummy tanks, dumps and the like, while conversely the advanced infantry of the XXX Corps, in the north, were to 'dig-in' during the final stages and lie concealed. After preliminary artillery fire both Corps would then engage the opposing infantry, but the main effort would be in the north, where XXX Corps would open up two gaps in the enemy minefields. Through these corridors X Corps, containing the main body of armour—which would be held at first in the rear—would then advance. Behind the enemy infantry and minefields they would find the enemy armour; and there, in open country, free from the mines, ridges and guns of the El Alamein position, they would engage and destroy the Panzer divisions. After that we could round up the rest of the Axis army at leisure.

Such was the degree of air superiority attained by Tedder's squadrons that all the preliminary moves and dispositions for this plan were made without the slightest interference by the enemy either from the air or on the ground. The assaulting infantry of XXX Corps, for instance, moved forward on the night of 22nd/23rd October and spent the whole day of the 23rd in their fox-holes in advance of our main positions without being in any way observed or molested. As night approached, the hope that our attack would achieve tactical surprise hardened into a certainty. At 2140 hours over a thousand British guns opened up, and the loudest noise ever heard in Africa gave the enemy their first warning that anything

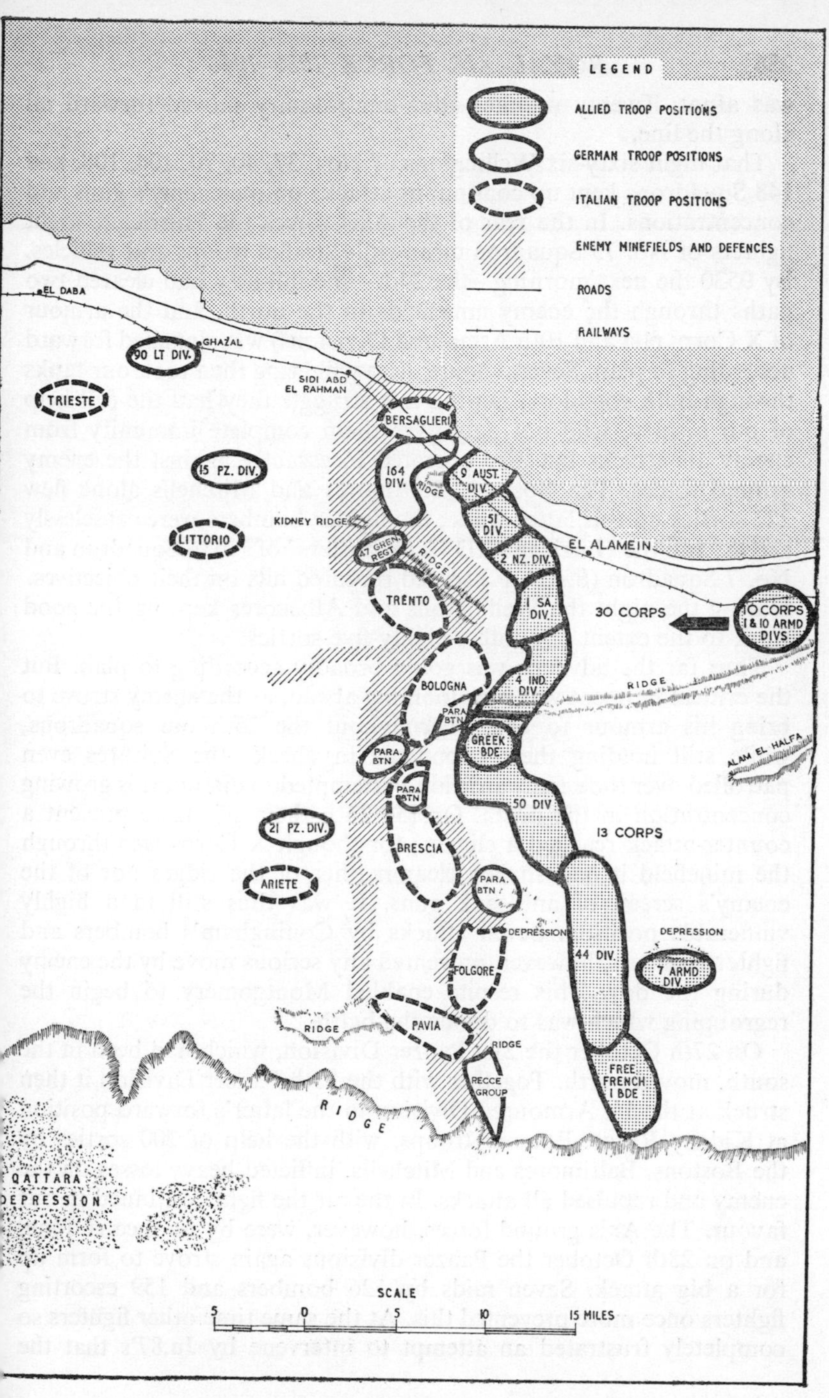
LEGEND
ALLIED TROOP POSITIONS
GERMAN TROOP POSITIONS
ITALIAN TROOP POSITIONS
ENEMY MINEFIELDS AND DEFENCES
ROADS
RAILWAYS
EL DABA
GHAZAL
90 LT DIV.
SIDI ABD EL RAHMAN
TRIESTE
BERSAGLIERI
15 PZ. DIV.
164 DIV.
RIDGE
9 AUST. DIV.
KIDNEY RIDGE
51 DIV.
LITTORIO
47 GREN REGT
RIDGE
EL ALAMEIN
2 NZ. DIV.
TRENTO
1 SA. DIV.
30 CORPS
10 CORPS 1 & 10 ARMD DIVS
BOLOGNA
4 IND. DIV.
RIDGE
PARA BTN
GREEK BDE
ALAM EL HALFA
PARA. BTN
PARA BTN
50 DIV
21 PZ. DIV.
13 CORPS
BRESCIA
ARIETE
PARA. BTN
DEPRESSION
DEPRESSION
44 DIV.
FOLGORE
7 ARMD. DIV.
RIDGE
PAVIA
RIDGE
FREE FRENCH I BDE
RECCE GROUP
RIDGE
QATTARA DEPRESSION
SCALE
5
0
5
10
15 MILES

THE POSITION AT EL ALAMEIN, 23 OCTOBER 1942

was afoot. Twenty minutes later our infantry moved forward all along the line.

That night sixty-six Wellingtons of Nos. 37, 40, 70, 104, 108, and 148 Squadrons kept up continuous attacks on the enemy's guns and concentrations. In the rear of the Axis forces the Hurricane night fighters of No. 73 Squadron meanwhile strafed troops and vehicles. By 0530 the next morning—the 24th—the infantry had cleared two paths through the enemy minefields in the north, and the armour of X Corps (1st and 10th Armoured Divisions) was signalled forward according to plan. Several hours' heavy fighting then took our tanks through both corridors. During this struggle they had the full help of our airmen, who not only gave them complete immunity from enemy air attacks but also operated incessantly against the enemy ground forces. The Bostons, Baltimores and Mitchells alone flew 222 sorties on this latter work; the fighter-bombers were ceaselessly active; and the Hurricane IID 'tank busters' of No. 6 Squadron and No. 7 Squadron (S.A.A.F.) scored repeated hits on their objectives. During the night the Wellingtons and Albacores kept up the good work to the extent of another eighty-five sorties.

Thus far the advance was going broadly according to plan. But the critical moment was now looming ahead, as the enemy strove to bring his armour to bear. Throughout the 25th our squadrons, while still holding their opponents in check—the Spitfires even patrolled over the enemy airfields—attempted to disrupt this growing concentration in the north. On the 26th their efforts to prevent a counter-attack reached a climax; for though X Corps was through the minefield it had shaken clear neither of the ridges nor of the enemy's screen of anti-tank guns. It was thus still in a highly vulnerable position. Seven attacks by Coningham's bombers and fighter-bombers, however, prevented any serious move by the enemy during the day. This respite enabled Montgomery to begin the regrouping which was to decide the battle.

On 27th October the 21st Panzer Division, which had been in the south, moved north. Together with the 15th Panzer Division it then struck at the 1st Armoured Division in the latter's forward position at Kidney Ridge. But our troops, with the help of 200 sorties by the Bostons, Baltimores and Mitchells, inflicted heavy losses on the enemy and repulsed all attacks. In the air the fight continued in our favour. The Axis ground forces, however, were by no means done, and on 28th October the Panzer divisions again strove to form up for a big attack. Seven raids by 126 bombers and 159 escorting fighters once more prevented this. At the same time other fighters so completely frustrated an attempt to intervene by Ju.87's that the once formidable Stukas jettisoned their bombs on their own troops. 'On 28th October', Montgomery recorded in his published account of the battle, 'the enemy made a prolonged reconnaissance of Kidney Ridge, probing it for soft spots while the two German Panzer divisions waited in the rear. In the evening they began to concentrate for attack, but the Desert Air Force intervened to such effect that the enemy was defeated before he had completed his forming up'. So ended our opponents' last attempt to deliver an effective counter-stroke.

Under the protection of our air superiority, Montgomery was now able to carry out the decisive regrouping. To counter the movement of the 21st Panzers, he ordered the 7th Armoured Division to move north from its position in the south; and at the same time, to prepare for the final punch, he withdrew into reserve the 1st Armoured Division and the 24th Armoured Brigade. He then began a very determined and profitable attack with Australian infantry near the coast. His plan at this stage was to direct his new attack, not through the corridors thus far opened, but along the line of the road and railway farther north. But on 29th October he learned that the enemy had divined his intention, for the 90th Light Division had moved athwart his route. The three crack German divisions were now all in the extreme north; and Montgomery—also mindful of the need to capture the East Cyrenaican airfields at once, if Malta were to survive (a consideration forcefully represented to him by Tedder and the Minister of State)—therefore decided to force a new gap in the minefield to the south of the German armoured concentration. The blow would fall near one of the existing corridors, in the northern sector, but south of the main German force and in a position held by the Italians. In sum, the Australians would mislead the enemy by continuing their pressure near the coast; the New Zealanders would open the new gap; and through the gap would pour X Corps, now with all three Armoured Divisions—1st, 7th and 10th.

While Montgomery was preparing this thrust the enemy troops were too dispersed to make good targets for our bombers, but the fighter-bombers flew many hundreds of sorties with great effect. Moreover, the battle against the opposing air force continued to go well: on 1st November, for instance, a formation of British and American Kittyhawks intercepted thirty Ju.87's escorted by fifteen Me.109's. The American fighters held the ring; the British fighters closed in and shot down seven of the enemy without loss to themselves; and the Stukas again jettisoned their bombs on their own troops.

On the night of 1st/2nd November, while 113 Wellingtons and Albacores were about their routine task of making life uncomfortable for the enemy, Montgomery began his new attack—Operation 'Supercharge'. The next day the New Zealanders went right through. Thirteen attacks (211 sorties) by the Bostons, Baltimores and Mitchells and 374 sorties by the Hurricanes and Spitfires gave valuable assistance; and after one raid 200 enemy troops walked over to our lines and declared they could endure no more. But though the New Zealanders had gone brilliantly ahead, a powerful screen of anti-tank guns still held up the 1st Armoured Division. On the morning of 3rd November seven attacks by the light bombers accordingly helped to weaken this opposition. Then our reconnaissance began to return with reports of traffic streaming west along the coastal road: under cover of their guns the Germans and Italians were breaking away. At midday Coningham switched his squadrons on to this retreat, and soon our bombers, fighter-bombers and fighters were all harrying the fleeing enemy. By the time night fell, over 500 sorties had been flown against targets on the ground, the road from Ghazal to Fuka was a mass of blazing wrecks, and the Axis soldiery had drunk deep of the bitter draught that in earlier days the *Luftwaffe* had so often meted out to others.

Well into the night the Wellingtons, Albacores and Hurricanes continued this work. The following day, 4th November, the 51st and the 4th Indian divisions cleared the anti-tank gun screen and enabled the 1st Armoured Division to go ahead. The third and greatest battle on the Alamein line was over. It remained only for XIII Corps in the south to round up four Italian divisions left with no transport and little food or water; and for X Corps to set off in full cry after the retreating Germans. Meanwhile the Western Desert Air Force, in Montgomery's words, 'operated at maximum intensity and took every advantage of the exceptional targets which the fleeing enemy presented'.

The battle of El Alamein was not, as popular impression sometimes has it, the victory of the Eighth Army alone. Nor was it simply the victory of the Eighth Army and the Western Desert Air Force. It was the victory of the Eighth Army and almost the whole allied air force in the Middle East. The first and greatest task of the Middle East Air Force was to win air superiority; that achieved, all other operations could be carried out effectively. During the battle this air force safeguarded our soldiers from the *Luftwaffe*, repeatedly broke up potential attacks on the ground, and in general helped to wear down the enemy troops by its incessant activity. In this last respect the long interval between Montgomery's initial thrust and the final break-through gave Tedder the opportunity which he felt had been denied him in the original plan. Moreover, as Rommel has recorded, our air superiority actually dictated the Axis military dispositions.

> We could no longer put the main burden of the defensive battle on to the motorised formations since these . . . were too vulnerable to attack from the air. Instead, we had to try to resist the enemy in fixed positions . . . We had to accept the fact that in future the enemy would be able to delay our operations at will by strong air attacks by day and similar attacks at night with the aid of parachute flares. Experience had taught us that no man could be expected to stay in his vehicle and drive on when attacked by enemy bombers and that it was useless to try to work to a time-table. Our positions had to be constructed so strongly that they could be held by their local garrisons . . . without support of operational reserves, until, in spite of the delays caused by the R.A.F., reinforcements could arrive. British air superiority threw to the winds all our operational and tactical rules . . . The strength of the Anglo-American Air Force was, in all the battles to come, the deciding factor.[1]

The actual fight at El Alamein, however, was only the crown and summit of all that had gone before—and particularly of the sustained operations by the Middle East Air Force and the Royal Navy against the enemy's supply routes. For these operations had the broad result that the Eighth Army at El Alamein faced an enemy short of almost every vital commodity, including fuel; and fresh attacks of this kind continued to affect the enemy's position even at the very height of the fighting. How they did so, and with what determination they were carried out, may be seen from the episode of Rommel's last tanker.

On the afternoon of 25th October, two days after the Eighth Army had gone into action, a Baltimore from Malta spotted an Italian convoy north-east of Benghazi. It consisted of two merchant ships and a tanker, escorted by four destroyers. Rommel's shortage of fuel was well known, and the report of a tanker immediately put the British aircrews concerned on their mettle. The target was by then beyond range of Malta, but Lloyd at No. 201 Group at once 'laid on' a strike from Egypt. Wellingtons duly found and attacked the convoy during the night, but were unable to claim any definite success. The hunt therefore continued, and the following morning, the 26th, the convoy was again located, this time nine miles north-west of Derna. The ships were then travelling under air escort and obviously making for Tobruk. They were carefully shadowed until they came within range of our day bombers in Egypt. Then, when the convoy was about twenty miles short of its destination, Lloyd

[1] Quoted in Brigadier Desmond Young's *Rommel.*

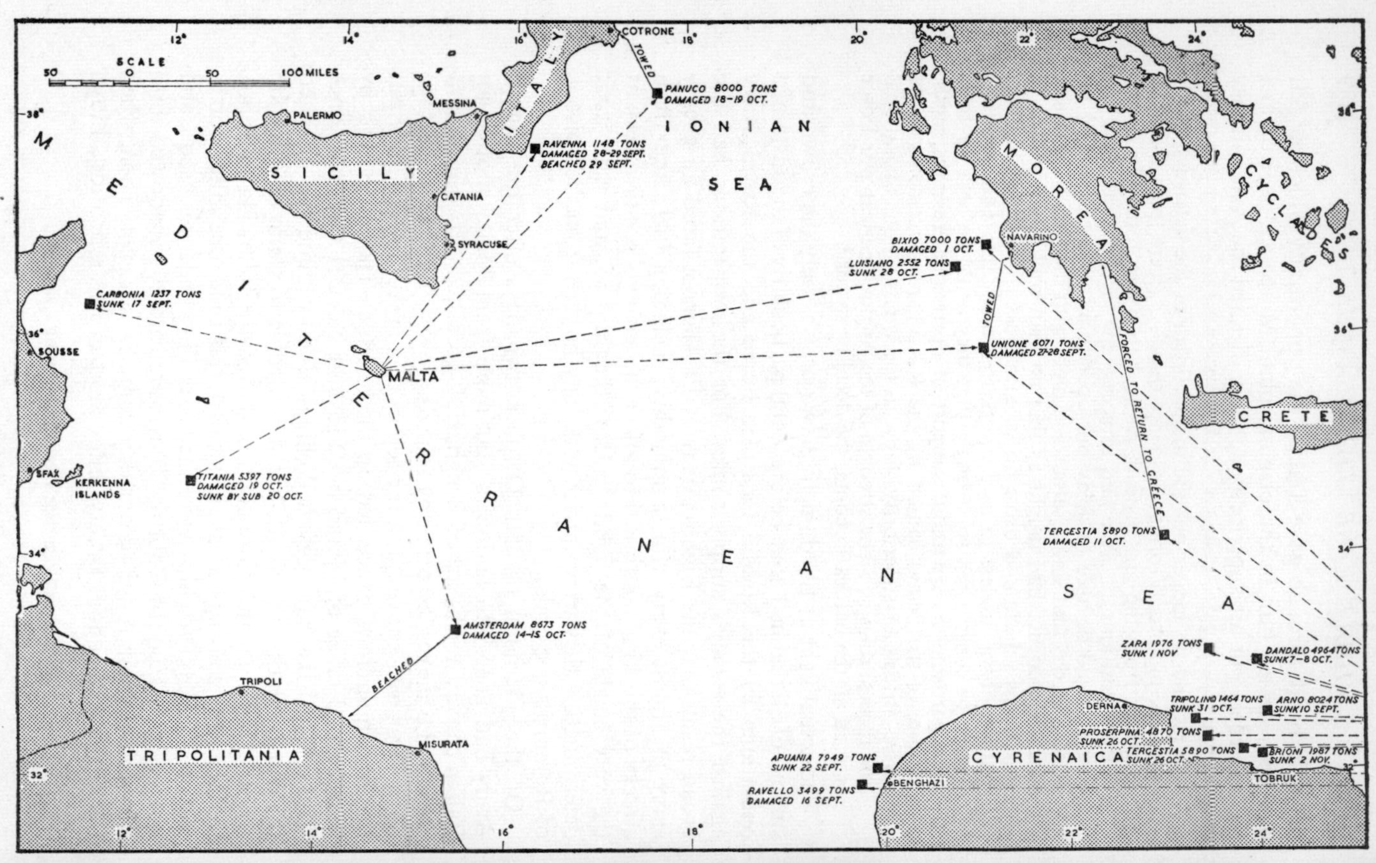

SCALE
50 0 50 100 MILES
MEDITERRANEAN SEA
IONIAN SEA
SICILY
ITALY
MOREA
CYCLADES
CRETE
TRIPOLITANIA
CYRENAICA
PALERMO
MESSINA
CATANIA
SYRACUSE
COTRONE
MALTA
SOUSSE
SFAX
KERKENNA ISLANDS
TRIPOLI
MISURATA
BENGHAZI
DERNA
TOBRUK
NAVARINO
TOWED
BEACHED
FORCED TO RETURN TO GREECE
PANUCO 8000 TONS DAMAGED 18-19 OCT.
RAVENNA 1148 TONS DAMAGED 28-29 SEPT. BEACHED 29 SEPT.
CARBONIA 1237 TONS SUNK 17 SEPT.
TITANIA 5397 TONS DAMAGED 19 OCT. SUNK BY SUB 20 OCT.
AMSTERDAM 8673 TONS DAMAGED 14-15 OCT.
BIXIO 7000 TONS DAMAGED 1 OCT.
LUISIANO 2552 TONS SUNK 28 OCT.
UNIONE 6071 TONS DAMAGED 27-28 SEPT.
TERGESTIA 5890 TONS DAMAGED 11 OCT.
ZARA 1976 TONS SUNK 1 NOV
DANDALO 4964 TONS SUNK 7-8 OCT.
TRIPOLINO 1464 TONS SUNK 31 OCT.
ARNO 8024 TONS SUNK 10 SEPT.
PROSERPINA 4870 TONS SUNK 26 OCT.
TERGESTIA 5890 TONS SUNK 26 OCT.
BRIONI 1987 TONS SUNK 2 NOV.
APUANIA 7949 TONS SUNK 22 SEPT.
RAVELLO 3499 TONS DAMAGED 16 SEPT.

despatched a strike of four Bisleys (a later version of the Blenheim) and five Beauforts, all under Beaufighter escort.

The four Bisleys attacked first. The leading aircraft bombed from twenty feet, scoring hits on the stern of the tanker. The second bomber narrowly missed, fouled the tanker's mast as it pulled away, and crashed into the sea. The third and fourth Bisleys collided and broke up in flames. Then the Beauforts went in. They scored another hit on the tanker and damaged at least one of the merchant vessels. An hour and a half later another Beaufort strike failed to locate the convoy but fought a successful action with enemy aircraft. By then it was dusk, and the task again fell to the Wellingtons. They came up with the convoy just outside Tobruk harbour. For the loss of one aircraft they hit the larger merchant vessel and caused a huge explosion which covered the whole convoy with black smoke and flying debris. The attack was witnessed, according to an enemy prisoner, by a group of high-ranking German officers who had gathered on the cliffs to watch these desperately needed supplies brought into harbour. If this was so, they saw the end, not merely of the convoy, but of Rommel's last hope of victory. Six more Wellingtons went out during the night, but all they could find was the tanker, blazing furiously from stem to stern. 'A black mark for the situation in Libya', noted Ciano, recording the loss, '. . . Rommel is optimistic about the military quality of the troops but he is literally terrified by the supply situation. Just now not only is fuel lacking but also munitions and food'.

* * *

Thirty thousand prisoners and immense quantities of equipment fell to our victorious troops at El Alamein. The subsequent pursuit, however, did not quite satisfy our most ardent desires. It swept across the breadth of Africa; it wore down and greatly reduced the enemy; but it failed to put Rommel and his armoured and mechanized divisions 'in the bag'. For this an unlucky beginning was partly responsible. On 6th November the skies opened in a deluge which lasted for over twenty-four hours. This hampered Coningham's squadrons and proved still more of a hindrance to Montgomery's armour, which was bogged down as it tried to strike across the desert. Meanwhile, the enemy, moving along the coastal road, gained a flying start. By 8th November Rommel was well on his way to escape; and the consequences of this might indeed have been serious. But that morning Anglo-American strategy came into its own as 2,000 miles away, sealing off the enemy's line of retreat, 'Torch' was lit on the beaches of French North Africa.

For weeks which stretched into months the pursuit across Libya rolled on. By 13th November the Eighth Army was in Tobruk and the Western Desert Air Force at Gambut. By 17th November Coningham's fighters were at Gazala and by 19th November at Martuba, just in time to give continuous cover to the convoy that now at last broke the siege of Malta. That same day, while Montgomery's troops were arriving in Benghazi, Rommel reported to the *Führer* that the German motorized formations in the forward area were completely immobile for lack of petrol. A show of fight at El Agheila, however, saved the German commander: the British troops deployed, and it was not until mid-December that they swept into Tripolitania. A month later, on 23rd January, after further deployment and a fight at Buerat, the Eighth Army was entering Tripoli and the Desert Air Force taking over Castel Benito. Throughout all this time the fighter and fighter-bomber squadrons kept pace with the movement of our ground forces; though the bombers, with their bigger requirements and greater dependence on an Army supply system now stretched to its utmost limits, came along more slowly. It was not, perhaps, a classic pursuit: there were no Beda Fomms and the 'left hooks' failed to connect. But it was marked by many notable achievements. On the air side, there was the work of the new transport group (No. 216) under Air Commodore Whitney Straight, magnificently aided by the British Overseas Airways Corporation. There was Coningham's brilliant move, during the pursuit to Benghazi, of two Hurricane squadrons (Nos. 213 and 238) to a position well in advance of our troops, so that convoys of enemy lorries far from the front were suddenly subjected to a rain of bullets which destroyed or damaged some 300 vehicles. There was the promising performance of the newly formed Royal Air Force Regiment; and, ever a source of admiration to the airmen, there was all the skilful and devoted work of the Royal Engineers in making fresh airfields or in restoring and 'de-mining' those lately occupied by the enemy.

It was not annihilation, then, but it was at least sustained pursuit. The fighters hammered away at the enemy all the time, the bombers as their moves permitted. Tedder and Coningham occasionally fretted at what seemed to them unnecessary delays; but their men, like those of General Montgomery, were happy. For they sensed now, that with Stalingrad held, Rommel on the run, and Eisenhower in Tunisia, nothing could cheat them of their final triumph. Their ordeals, they were well aware, were far from over. They had not yet finished with deserts, even if those of Egypt and Libya were at last behind them: there were still the sun and the wind, the dust and the flies and the sores, the interminable bully beef and chlorinated tea. And there was still the certainty of further fighting, suffering, mutilation and death. But nothing of this could stifle the gladness that was now in their hearts. For unquestionably, whatever the difficulties, they were going forward; and this time they would not be coming back.

CHAPTER XII

'Torch' and Tunisia

'No responsible British general, admiral or air marshal is prepared to recommend 'Sledgehammer' as a practicable operation in 1942 . . . I am sure myself that . . . 'Gymnast' is by far the best chance for effecting relief to the Russian front in 1942. This . . . is your commanding idea. Here is the true Second Front of 1942'.

These words of Mr. Churchill's[1], the result of investigations and discussions which had proceeded since the Washington Conference of December, 1941, were despatched to President Roosevelt on 8th July, 1942. 'Sledgehammer' was a project favoured by the Americans for establishing a bridgehead that year in Northern France. 'Gymnast', the operation preferred by the British, was the invasion of French North Africa.

Nine days later the President's 'Three Musketeers'—General Marshall, Admiral King and Mr. Harry Hopkins—paid their second visit of the year to London. Failing to shake the British objections to 'Sledgehammer', they agreed to compromise. All efforts, the Allies decided, would be bent towards invading Europe in the first half of 1943 (Operation 'Round-up'); but if by September 1942 further German successes in Russia had made this impracticable, 'Gymnast'—or, as it now became, 'Torch'—should be mounted before December.

A programme so conditional could hardly appeal for long to leaders as vigorous as the British Prime Minister and the American President. On 30th July Roosevelt cut through the uncertainties by pronouncing definitely for the North African venture that year. As we were already in favour of this course, from 30th July Operation 'Torch' was thus 'on'. From the same date—though this was not yet officially recognized—a cross-Channel invasion in 1943 could be considered 'off'.

There followed what General Eisenhower, who was to command the Allied Expeditionary Force, termed a 'transatlantic essay-contest'. In this the Americans made it clear that they expected opposition to

[1] Quoted in Volume IV of his war memoirs—*The Hinge of Fate* (Cassell)

the venture not only from the French in North Africa but also from Spain. The Germans, too, might move through the Peninsula against Gibraltar. The Americans accordingly emphasized the need to secure Morocco and our communications to the Atlantic coast. The British leaders, less apprehensive on these scores, for their part stressed the importance of landing as far east as possible and forestalling the Axis in Tunisia. From the proposals and counter-proposals there eventually emerged on 20th September an outline plan which took account of both viewpoints. Simultaneous assaults would be aimed at three main objectives—Casablanca on the Atlantic coast, Oran and Algiers on the Mediterranean; but shortage of escorts and landing craft, and the likelihood of heavy losses among our ships from enemy air attack, would rule out any landing farther to the east.

As finally arranged, the burden of the enterprise was to be shared not unequally between the two nations. The Moroccan landings would be all-American affairs, staged directly from America; those in Algeria would be mixed enterprises mounted from the United Kingdom. At Oran the landing force would be American, but the Royal Navy would put it ashore. Air support would be provided initially by the Fleet Air Arm, later by the Americans. At Algiers the first troops ashore would also be American, to lessen the chances of French hostility, but otherwise the operation would be British. 'D Day' was set for 8th November, the earliest date by which all the manifold requirements of the expedition could be satisfied. This allowed a possible three weeks of good weather before the North African winter rains set in.

The Royal Air Force part in the great venture would begin, of course, long before the landings. First would come assistance in the great task, already in progress, of building up powerful American forces in the British Isles. So far as the Royal Air Force was concerned, this involved, among other things, shepherding convoys across the Atlantic and providing bases, facilities and air protection for General Spaatz's Eighth Air Force—from and around which the new formation for 'Torch', the Twelfth Air Force under Major-General James Doolittle, was to be created. Next, considerable developments must be undertaken at the Royal Air Force Station at Gibraltar, the key point for the Mediterranean landings. Thirdly, when the enterprise was actually under way, there would be the work of supporting the invasion convoys, first from the United Kingdom and then from Gibraltar. Finally would come the air operations connected with the campaign itself, including support to the British First Army in its dash for Tunis. In all this it was not visualized that the Royal Air Force in the Middle East would take any part, despite the fact that in Malta the Middle East Command held an obvious control-point for the prevention of enemy reinforcement. The air authorities in the Middle East knew, of course, the rough outline of the plan; but they had no share in drawing it up, and they were not informed of the moment for its execution.

To support the British First Army in its advance on Tunis, and for the associated duties of protecting the land and sea communications east of Cape Tenez, a special Royal Air Force contingent was formed under Air Marshal Sir William Welsh. In distinction from the sphere of operations farther west proposed for the Americans, it was known as the Eastern Air Command. Numerically, but not otherwise, it was to be the junior partner—seven weeks after the landings Welsh was intended to deploy only 450 aircraft as against Doolittle's 1,250. As no provision was made for a separate air commander-in-chief, Welsh and Doolittle were to be alike directly responsible to Eisenhower. The latter, however, would be aided by a special air adviser on his staff—Air Commodore A. P. M. Sanders.

The first 'Torch' convoy sailed from the Clyde on 22nd October. How these and the succeeding vessels reached the Straits of Gibraltar without loss has already been related in Chapter VI. The achievement was due not only to the unfailing efforts of the Navy and Coastal Command, aided by the Germans' preoccupation with the unfortunate convoy from Sierra Leone, but also to the success of our deception measures. These misled the enemy more completely than we could have dared to hope. When the expedition was being assembled the Germans thought we were preparing to invade Norway; when it entered the Mediterranean they assumed—as we intended—that its destination was Malta.

On 2nd November Air Marshal Welsh arrived at Gibraltar to take control of air operations. Three days later he was followed by General Eisenhower, The congestion on the runway was such that the latter's pilot had to circle the Rock for an hour before he could put down. This, however, might almost be considered a tribute to what the energetic direction of Air Vice-Marshal J. M. Robb and others had achieved there during the preceding weeks. For since March the devoted efforts of the Royal Engineers had not only transformed a landing strip 980 yards long by 75 yards wide into a fully tarmacked runway 1,400 yards long—with the last 400 yards protruding into the sea—and 100 yards wide, but had also enlarged and resurfaced the dispersal areas alongside until they could take some 600 aircraft. As the total area available for these purposes had been only 1,000 yards by 800 yards, and had also included the operations block, the administrative buildings, the living quarters and the cemetery, the task had not been easy. High standards of work, however, had not been sacrificed to speed of execution. Over twelve inches of rain fell at Gibraltar in November, 1942—ten inches more than in a normal November—but the deluge made no impression on North Front airfield.

The building of the runway, already decided upon before 'Torch', was the prime requirement at Gibraltar. Without this and the construction of the dispersals, the whole North African enterprise would have been impossible. There were, however, other big undertakings. Among these was the project of sinking bulk fuel tanks into the rocky soil to avoid the risk of relying entirely upon petrol in tins. The chambers were duly excavated, but the ship carrying the tanks was torpedoed, with the result that huge quantities of petrol, in tins, had in fact to be stored on the airfield and among the aircraft. Then, as 'D Day' approached, came the reception and assembly of the shorter range aircraft, which were shipped out in crates from Britain. This involved the use of skilled labour in quantities beyond the resources of the local erection party. A special draft of fitters, flight mechanics and the like was accordingly despatched from home, but by some mistake it finished up in the Middle East. However, soldiers from the Gibraltar garrison promptly took the place of the missing airmen, and to such good effect that 122 Spitfires and Hurricanes were erected in the short space of nine days. To do this the men began work in the early morning, continued throughout the day, toiled on after dusk under searchlights blazing from the Rock, and knocked off only two hours short of midnight. By 6th November the task of assembly was thus complete, but many machines were still unserviceable. An intense effort throughout the ensuing day and night, and by dawn on 8th November the erection crews and their skilful and tireless commander, Flight Lieutenant B. Flannery, could breakfast content. Serviceability, as they intended, was one hundred per cent.

Meanwhile, since 5th November, Gibraltar's Hudsons, Catalinas and Swordfish had been hard at work escorting the assault convoys and hunting down the enemy's submarines. At the same time our photographic reconnaissance aircraft, operating not only from Gibraltar but also from England and Malta, were keeping careful track of the French, Spanish and Italian navies and air forces. From Gibraltar every take-off was painstakingly observed from the roof of La Linea's tallest hotel by an Axis agent with a pair of binoculars, but fortunately there was nothing to tell the 'German Duty Pilot'—as he was known at North Front—whither our aircraft were bound.

By this time the political situation, which was very largely in the hands of our ally, appeared somewhat more favourable. The Americans still expected a strong reaction from Spain or a German march through the Peninsula; but they now hoped that after the initial resistance we should derive a great deal of help from the French. This was the result of contacts at Algiers with General Mast, and of the latter's conviction that if General Giraud could be brought out from Southern France all French North Africa would rally to his banner. The political game naturally involved a number of difficult and delicate moves, and in these the Royal Air Force was twice able to give some assistance. The first occasion was on 24th October, when a Catalina of No. 202 Squadron from Gibraltar picked up Brigadier General Mark Clark, Eisenhower's deputy, from a submarine after his clandestine trip to Algiers to meet Mast and other leaders of the resistance. The second incident was on 7th November, when another Catalina performed the same service for General Giraud after the latter had been smuggled out of France. The second of these episodes was not without what may be described, at this distance, as a touch of comedy. In the course of transfer from submarine to flying-boat the distinguished foreign passenger fell into the sea.

It was not until 7th November, only a few hours before the landings, that the main Mediterranean convoy came under fire. On that day German air attacks developed from Sardinia. The brunt of these, however, fell on Gibraltar's Force H, which was steaming to the north of the assault armada, and it was probably from a U-boat that the first and only casualty of the passage occurred. Despite these attacks the convoy still shaped towards Malta. Then, as darkness fell, it turned on its true course, one part towards Oran, the other towards Algiers.

*   *   *

Punctually at 0100 on 8th November the assault opened—against one of the three selected beaches near Algiers. Various things went amiss at the other two, but with no serious consequences. General Mast quickly proved as good as his word by surrendering a key fortress, and this and the patrols of our naval aircraft greatly eased the task of the invaders. Apart from Algiers itself our first objectives were the local airfields of Maison Blanche and Blida, the former eleven and the latter twenty-five miles distant from the port. Maison Blanche quickly fell to an American combat team. The news, how-

GIBRALTAR

ever, was slow to reach Gibraltar; and it was only by taking the grave risk of having nowhere to land—their fuel endurance was not sufficient to carry them back to the Rock—that eighteen Hurricanes of No. 43 Squadron were able to fly in by 0900 hours. Almost at the same moment a Royal Air Force Servicing Commando Party arrived after marching twelve miles from the beaches in less than three hours. Shortly afterwards Blida surrendered to four Martlets of the Fleet Air Arm. Sporadic resistance, however, still continued from some quarters, and at the airfields the attitude of the local authorities could be described as no better than sullen. But in the course of the afternoon our naval guns and aircraft silenced another of the main forts, and the arrival of Nos. 81 and 242 Squadrons at Maison Blanche further increased our strength in the air. Meanwhile parleys with the French had been complicated by a unexpected factor —the presence in Algiers of Admiral Darlan, who was visiting his sick son. Fortunately, the unwelcome arrival soon saw reason. Pending the discussion of an armistice he called off resistance around Algiers, so ending the local fighting but leaving the position elsewhere still obscure.

The French forces disposed of, there came a challenge from the *Luftwaffe*. On the evening of 9th November a group of some twenty Ju.88's came in to attack the port and Maison Blanche. But Nos. 43, 81 and 242 Squadrons were ready; for Group Captain Edwardes-Jones, the airfield commander, had organized a system of standing patrols and a code of Verey lights to scramble further sections. 'At the time of the scramble', recorded Air Commodore Traill, 'the squadrons were parked on three sides of the airfield. Nearly all pilots, whether at readiness or not—there was nowhere else for them to go—were in or near their aircraft. When the Verey light was fired the first formation of Ju.88's were overhead at 8,000 feet with standing patrol about to engage. The ensuing scramble was an exhilarating spectacle. Singly or in sections from all three sides, the three squadrons poured into the air. Collisions appeared inevitable, especially when at the height of it a B-17 with General Mark Clark aboard came in and landed. Few of our pilots had ever met unescorted bombers before. They all appreciated the experience'.

Oran proved more difficult than Algiers. Vigorous action brought the small harbour of Arzeu and its immediate neighbourhood into Allied hands by 0745 on the 8th; but the attack on the port of Oran failed, and an ambitious attempt by the Americans to land paratroops on the airfields of La Senia and Tafaroui went completely astray. Tafaroui, however, soon succumbed to the ground forces, after effective work by the Fleet Air Arm, and during the evening

Doolittle's aircraft began to fly in from Gibraltar. La Senia, more vigorously defended, fell only on the 10th, when Oran itself surrendered.

The toughest nut, as expected, was Casablanca. Since this was an all-American operation, apart from the help provided by Gibraltar's reconnaissance aircraft, it is unnecessary to follow its fortunes in detail. Three days' stiff fighting enabled the Americans to capture Port Lyautey and converge successfully on their main objective, but it required a broadcast from Darlan to end Noguès' resistance. A broadcast from Giraud, who had flown to Algiers on November 9th, had meantime fallen on completely deaf ears.

By 11th November all the initial objectives had been achieved. But a *modus vivendi* with the French, which could give us valuable military help and secure our highly vulnerable lines of communication, was not at once achieved. For General Giraud, of whom we had hoped so much, began by being a nuisance—at Gibraltar he strove not only to divert the expedition to Southern France but also to displace Eisenhower as its commander—and ended by being a cipher. The Vichy writ, it was all too clear, ran throughout French North Africa; and the obvious representative of Pétain was not Giraud but Darlan. With Darlan, for all the Admiral's fiercely anti-British sentiments, Eisenhower accordingly felt obliged to come to terms. Otherwise, the Allied commander was convinced, there could be no hope of a swift and safe advance into Tunisia. On 13th November Eisenhower accordingly flew to Algiers, and there agreed to conditions, amounting to a temporary and entirely *de facto* recognition of Darlan's position, on which the Admiral would co-operate. The agreement profoundly shocked the British and American publics, who, being farther from the scene of military action than General Eisenhower, could afford to place correspondingly greater emphasis on political principle.

The pact with Darlan assured us of French help. It promised, too, at least a fair chance of rallying to our side the authorities at Dakar and the fleet at Toulon. The first of these hopes was to prove justified, the second vain; but at least when the time came the fleet was scuttled, not surrendered. The agreement came too late, however, to give us an unimpeded approach to the vital ports of Bizerta and Tunis. For though the expedition had caught the Germans completely by surprise, their reaction had been very swift. On the very morrow of the Allied landings German fighters, bombers and transports, the latter loaded with troops, began putting down at El Aouina, the municipal airport of Tunis. There they were officially welcomed by representatives of the French Resident General, Admiral Esteva. Pétain's

France, which fought to keep the Allies out of Morocco and Algeria, let the Germans into Tunisia unopposed.

From Sicily across to Tunis or Bizerta is roughly 100 miles. From Algiers to either of these two places, travelling by road, is over five hundred. Of this situation, and of the passivity of the local French, the Germans quickly took advantage. On 10th November our reconnaissance detected 115 Axis aircraft on the ground at El Aouina; while at Sidi Ahmed, outside Bizerta, air transports were beginning to arrive at the rate of fifty a day. To this was soon to be added a continuous stream of reinforcement by sea—a movement less reported in the newspapers than the corresponding movement by air, but in fact carrying by far the greater part of the traffic. For Hitler, doubtless guided by his infallible intuition, had at last decided to give serious attention to Africa. All that he had denied to Rommel when the latter had stood some chance of success the German *Führer* was now to pour into Tunisia. Far, far too late, his myopic gaze had discerned the red light. If the Axis failed to hold a bridgehead in North Africa, the Anglo-American armies could walk into 'Fortress Europe' by the back door.

The news of the German arrival at Tunis made an instant advance to the east imperative. On 10th November a convoy accordingly left Algiers to seize the port of Bougie, 120 miles along the coast. One ship was detailed to sail on and occupy Djidjelli, thirty miles farther east, so that fighter cover could be supplied from the local airfield over the convoy as it approached Bougie. But a heavy surf on the beaches convinced the Senior Naval Officer that a landing was impossible, and the vessel turned back to join the convoy. Had those on board known, they could have entered Djidjelli harbour unopposed. The attempt to seize this airfield having failed, the convoy was left with only such air support as could be provided by a carrier—which was soon withdrawn—and by fighters operating from Algiers. During the afternoon and evening of 11th November the ships were heavily attacked by German aircraft, and lost two of their number; and they were again attacked in Bougie harbour on the morning of the 12th, suffering further losses and considerable interruption in the work of unloading. This in turn held up the despatch of petrol to Djidjelli airfield, on which a small party had now advanced overland from Bougie. The result was that when No. 154 Squadron flew in to Djidjelli during the early morning of 12th November it found no fuel, put up one patrol of six aircraft only by draining the tanks of the rest of the squadron, and was then completely impotent. The petrol arrived the next day, but by that time the forces at Bougie had lost still more of their equipment.

Despite this series of mishaps, which was fairly typical of the early stages of the campaign, we had gained our first objectives east of Algiers. No opposition had been encountered other than that from Axis aircraft. In these circumstances and in the absence of more than two good roads and one single-line railway, strategy obviously dictated a rapid progress from port to port and airfield to airfield. Accordingly, we now set out to seize the important harbour and airfield of Bone, 175 miles farther along the coast. While No. 6 Commando landed from the sea, on 12th November twenty-six American C.47's of the Twelfth Air Force, escorted by six Hurricanes of No. 43 Squadron, dropped two companies of British paratroops successfully on the airfield. The next day No. 81 Squadron flew in, to be followed on 14th November by No. 111. Unfortunately, the new arrivals were at once attacked by enemy aircraft, which inflicted severe casualties on ground crews and machines alike.

The occupation of these key points enabled General Anderson, the commander of the British First Army, to push the 78th Division forward with all speed. Meantime the French forces in Tunisia had begun to help by engaging the Germans—not, as yet, in combat, but in protracted negotiations. Sustained by the merest trickle of supplies our troops pressed on, and on 15th November occupied the port of Tabarka. They were now sixty-five miles east of Bone, 360 miles east of Algiers, and only eighty miles short of Bizerta. That same day American paratroops dropped at Youks les Bains airfield, near the boundary between Algeria and Central Tunisia. This opened up a threat to the Axis forces from a fresh direction—a threat which increased when the paratroops pushed on to Gafsa and established cordial relations with the French garrison at Tebessa.

While a front or, rather, a series of outposts, was thus coming into being in Central Tunisia, the main movement in the north progressed still further. On 16th November British paratroops dropped from American machines at Souk el Arba, fifty miles south of Tabarka. Next day they moved forward to Béja; and there they encountered the Germans. The enemy, however, was as yet in no great strength, his total forces around Tunis and Bizerta being estimated at some 5,000. Moreover, from the 16th onwards the French had begun to fight, so screening our concentration. Within three or four days the screen was pierced, but against growing opposition the 78th Division pressed on to Mateur and Medjez el Bab. At these points it was some thirty-five miles from both Bizerta and Tunis. By 28th November further fighting had carried our foremost troops to Djedeida, whence the white buildings of Tunis, sixteen miles away, were plainly visible.

This swift advance by a skeleton force was a gamble which very

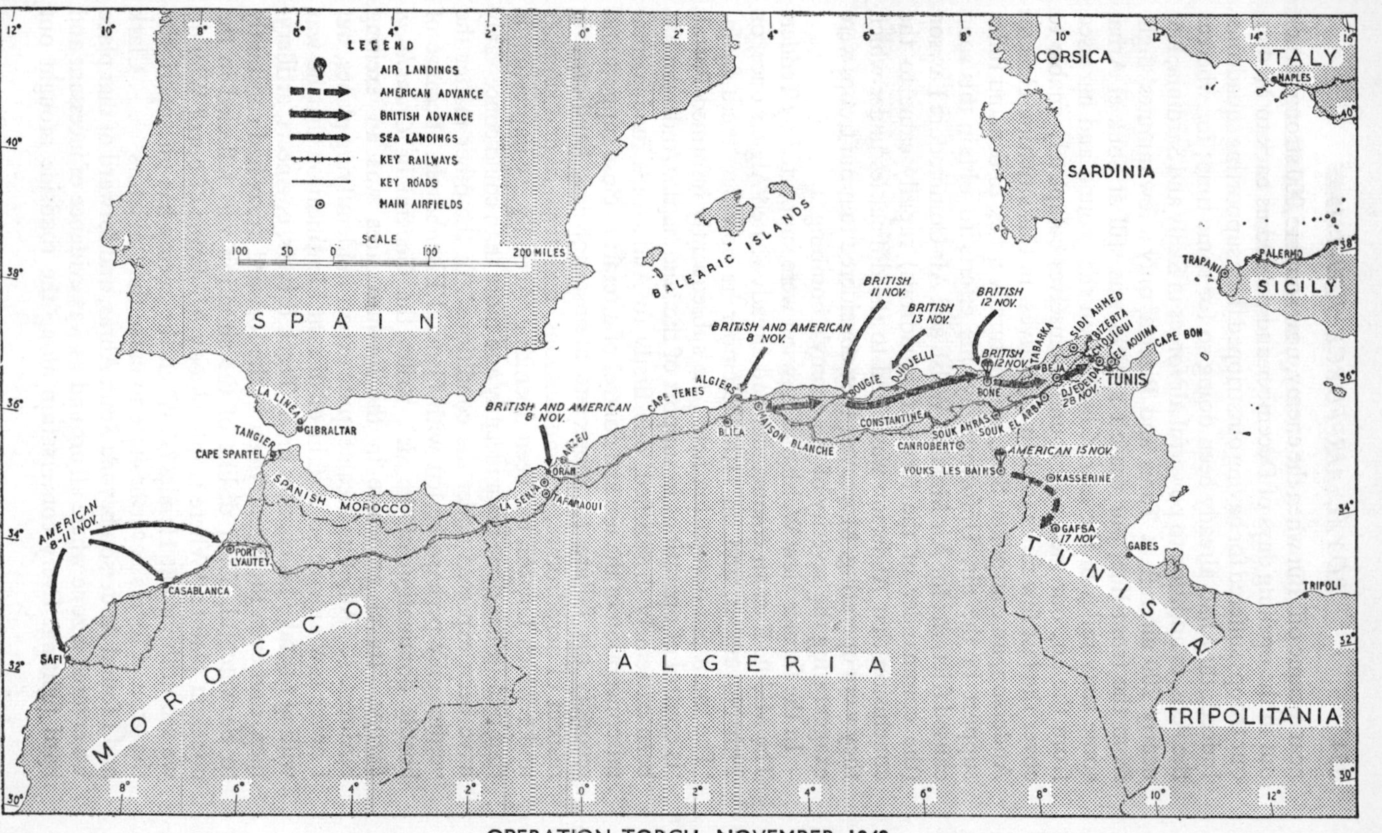

OPERATION TORCH, NOVEMBER 1942

nearly came off. But when the enemy, now some 15,000 strong, struck out in the opening days of December and pushed us back to Medjez, our troops suffered for having outstripped their supporting squadrons. Indeed, they had already been doing so for some time; for whereas the Axis, in addition to powerful air forces in Sicily and Sardinia, had nearly 200 aircraft at Tunis and Bizerta, only a few minutes' flight from the front line, our nearest airfield was still at Souk el Arba, some sixty miles in the rear. Checked on the ground and harassed from the air, our men now found themselves completely unable to cover the last few miles to their objectives. In this situation General Anderson, an outspoken Scot, was naturally quick to demand fuller support in the air. Unfortunately, his efforts to obtain this soon caused friction; for Air Marshal Welsh and Air Commodore Lawson (the commander of the forward squadrons) rapidly came to the conclusion that Anderson was blind to the difficulties under which they were operating. Moreover, they considered that our troops were exaggerating the severity of the enemy's bombing.

In the former view Welsh and Lawson were supported by Tedder. The Middle East air commander had already visited Algiers once, on 29th November, and on 11th December he now flew there again. 'The main pre-occupation here', he subsequently informed Portal, 'is control of operations in support of the land battle. Anderson has been extremely dissatisfied, due firstly to Anderson's fundamental misconception of the use and control of aircraft in close support and secondly his failure to appreciate almost hopeless handicaps in respect of aerodromes, communications, maintenance and supplies under which Lawson has been operating. Actually my impression is that our air has done magnificently and more than could conceivably have been expected under the conditions'. In the other matter the verdict may perhaps be left with General Eisenhower. 'Because of hostile domination of the air', writes the General in *Crusade in Europe*, 'travel anywhere in the forward area was an exciting business. . . . All of us became quite expert in identifying planes, but I never saw anyone so certain of distant identification that he was willing to stake his chances on it. Truck drivers, engineers, artillerymen, and even the infantrymen in the forward areas had constantly to be watchful. Their dislike of the situation was reflected in the constant plaint: "Where is this bloody Air Force of ours? Why do we see nothing but Heinies?" When the enemy has air superiority the ground forces never hesitate to curse the "aviators". . . . Clark and I found Anderson beyond Souk Ahras, and forward of that place we entered a zone where all around us was evidence of incessant and hard fighting. Every conversation along the roadside brought out astounding exaggerations. "Béja has been bombed to rubble". "No one can live on this next stretch of road". "Our troops will surely have to retreat; humans cannot exist in these conditions". Yet on the whole morale was good. The exaggerations were nothing more than the desire of the individual to convey the thought that he had been through the ultimate in terror and destruction—he had no thought of clearing out himself'.

Whatever the truth about the scale of enemy air attack, there was certainly no doubt that Lawson was in a difficult position. Supplies were not coming forward properly over the enormously long, thin lines of communication; airfields were few and far between; wireless messages were received with difficulty because of the mountains, and land lines were utterly inadequate. Operating on a commando basis, the squadrons were still struggling along without their full complement of ground staff and with not a single repair and salvage unit in the forward area. The various Command Headquarters, too, were hopelessly strung out over the 500-mile route. By mid-December Eisenhower was in Algiers, and Welsh a few miles outside; Anderson, having handed over the immediate battle to Corps control, was moving back to Constantine, midway between Algiers and the front; Lawson and the Corps Commander were at Bone; and the forward troops were nearly at Tunis. And even with more airfields Welsh could hardly have concentrated all his forces near the front line; for he had also to protect Algiers, the ports to the eastward, the convoys, and the lines of communication generally, all of which were being subjected to repeated attack.

From the point of view of supporting the forward troops, the lack of conveniently placed airfields was undoubtedly the worst of Welsh's many handicaps. Our advanced lines might be only a score of miles outside Tunis, but our nearest airfield was still at Souk el Arba, sixty miles farther back. On this were soon crowded, apart from American aircraft which followed later, five squadrons of Spitfires—Nos. 72, 81, 93, 111 and 152. Maintenance facilities were such that between them the five squadrons could usually muster no more than forty-five serviceable aircraft. Meanwhile, the bombers—the Bisleys of Nos. 13, 18 (Burma), 114 and 614 Squadrons—were operating, until the early days of December, from as far back as Blida, outside Algiers. Despite the poor performance of their aircraft and the loss of several machines on the long flight from England, the spirit of these squadrons remained high. It needed to be so. Beginning with daylight attacks, notably against the docks and airfields of Tunis and Bizerta, the squadrons had suffered such losses that they were now constrained to operate by night. And in the absence of special training or navigational facilities, night operations conducted at long range over mountainous country might well have daunted the stoutest hearts.

In the opening days of December Welsh tried to remedy matters by sending fighters to operate from Medjez el Bab, almost on top of the front line. But when No. 93 Squadron approached the landing ground the formation was pounced on by Me.109's patrolling overhead. Two of the Spitfires at once succumbed to the enemy's fire; the rest, badly damaged, managed with difficulty to struggle back to Souk el Arba. Greater success attended the movement of the Bisleys forward to Canrobert, 180 miles from Tunis. Even from this point, however, our bombers had a long and difficult flight to their objectives compared with the Germans.

One of the first raids undertaken after the move to Canrobert led to disaster so complete that from then on our crews were firmly committed to a policy of night bombing. On 4th December No. 18 Squadron was detailed to bomb an enemy landing ground at Chouigui. This target had been discovered and attacked by some of the squadron pilots during the morning; they had then returned to Canrobert, re-armed and refuelled, and moved forward to Souk el Arba to be ready for a further attack during the afternoon. At 1515 eleven Bisleys duly prepared to take off. One was held back by a burst tyre and another crash-landed after a few minutes' flight, but the remaining nine got under way successfully. Their task, the crews knew, would be far from enviable; for as our Spitfires were fully occupied trying to protect our troops the mission had to be flown without escort. Nevertheless the Squadron Commander, Wing Commander H. G. Malcolm, had not demurred at the risk. Fully aware that the landing ground would be hotly defended and that he would have no support other than a fighter sweep over the general area of the operation, and entirely conscious from his narrow escapes during the previous few days that his Bisleys were all too vulnerable, he had nevertheless agreed to meet the wishes of our ground forces and lead his squadron against a highly dangerous target. In this he was only acting as he had always acted before: if there was a job to be done, it was not for him to count the cost.

The Bisleys approached the target area at 1,000 feet. As they neared Chouigui their pilots saw a few of our Spitfires engaged high up with a swarm of Me.109's. Then the Germans dived down—some fifty or sixty of them. Within a few seconds our crews were fighting for their lives. At first they strove to force their way through to their objective; then, unable to find the landing ground, they jettisoned their bombs in the neighbourhood and tried to battle their way back to Souk el Arba. One by one they were hacked down. Still maintaining formation, four of the nine regained our lines, only to be shot down within sight of our troops. Almost the last to survive was the aircraft of Wing Commander Malcolm.[1]

Throughout December the First Army built up strength. But so, too, did the Germans confronting it. By 18th December the enemy forces in Tunisia numbered (according to our estimate) some 42,000, of which 25,000 were German. Meanwhile, to add to our difficulties, the weather grew steadily worse. Torrential rain set in, cutting up the soil over which Anderson's men were supposed to advance, turning our airfields into quagmires, and ruining our chances of intercepting German convoys. The enemy air force, however, could operate from hard ground—at El Aouina German planes took off from the road between the airport and Tunis docks—and so remained comparatively unaffected. The result was that our attack on Tunis was successively postponed until 24th December, when the entire project was cancelled. The 'last straw', as far as Eisenhower was concerned, was the spectacle of four men struggling in vain to pull a motor-cycle out of the mud.

Apart from a good meal there was little cheer for our airmen that Christmas. 'A pretty miserable day', recorded No. 111 Squadron at Souk el Arba; 'raining all the time and bogging the aircraft. The pilots spent the day trying to get them out and came back at dusk dead to the world'. 'Rained most of the day', recorded No. 152 (Hyderabad) Squadron at the same place; 'kites bogged, pilots spent most of the day trying to unbog them . . . in fact a shambles for Christmas Day'. On this airfield, as elsewhere, efforts were being made to lay steel matting; but some 2,000 tons of this—or two days' carrying capacity of the entire railway system in the forward area—were required for a single runway. And when laid, it tended simply to disappear into the mud. Like everything else on our side, the provision of hard runways suffered from the long, thin line of communication and the appalling weather.

Such difficulties naturally brought about a decline in our air effort. Moreover, the Bisleys, though now confined to night bombing, were frequently unable to operate. On 6th January Group Captain Sinclair, commanding the Bisley Wing, reported that he had only twelve aircraft serviceable: that half his pilots were unfit to fly on dark nights: and that attacks could be carried out only during moonlight. Welsh,

---

[1] For his determination in trying to fight his squadron through to its objective and back to base, Wing Commander Malcolm was posthumously awarded the Victoria Cross. His name is commemorated in the Royal Air Force Malcolm Clubs, the first of which opened some months later in Algiers.

in fact, would have been virtually without a striking force had not his two Wellington squadrons—Nos. 142 and 150—by now arrived from England. From the closing weeks of 1942 these aircraft delivered repeated and successful attacks by night against Bizerta and the airfields in Sardinia. In gratifying contrast with the unfortunate Bisleys, nearly two months were to elapse before the sturdy 'Wimpies' suffered their first casualty from the guns of the enemy.

* * *

If conditions at the front were at their worst at the end of December, in the rear they showed one significant improvement. German air attacks on Algiers had ceased to be the profitable business they were in November. On the night of 20th November a dozen or so German bombers had destroyed on the ground at Maison Blanche five Beaufighter night-fighters, three Flying Fortresses, and several Spitfires and Lightnings, besides damaging many other aircraft. Losses would have been still heavier but for the courage of several pilots and other aircrew who disregarded the falling bombs and taxied unfamiliar aircraft to safety. The cause of the disaster, and of one or two less serious incidents which followed in the next few nights, was undoubtedly the fact that our night-fighters had no radar; for in the interests of security the Beaufighters had been stripped of their A.I. before flying out to Africa. As the Operations Record Book of No. 255 Squadron ruefully recorded: 'There is nothing more galling than to fly about near the *flak*, with parachute flares dropping from the Hun aircraft, on a bright moonlight night, and yet see absolutely nothing owing to being without radar. The Huns would have been sitting birds on these nights if only our A.I. equipment had been installed in the aircraft'. By the beginning of December, however, No. 255 Squadron had its A.I.—the sets were hastily flown out from England, risk or no risk—and the German successes rapidly came to an end. During December the other Beaufighter squadrons also received their equipment, G.C.I. control was set up, and night patrols were operated with outstanding success not only over Algiers but also over Bone and the forward area.

The growing success of Eastern Air Command in protecting our convoys and the Algerian ports could not, however, disguise the fact that there was still no integrated direction of the British and American air effort. This weakness was the more serious since the Twelfth Air Force, initially handicapped by its deployment so far west, was by now playing a major part in the Tunisian battle. Some of Doolittle's fighters were already based at Souk el Arba, behind the main battle front in the north; while others, operating from Youks les Bains, were supporting the American II Corps as it moved forward in the centre and south. The American long-range bombers, too, had attacked Tunisian ports and airfields from the beginning—despite an early retirement from Maison Blanche to the less congested and more secure Tafaroui. The mud at this airfield might be, in the words of the song, 'deep and gouey', but at least it was spanned by a hard runway. So rare a blessing in French North Africa was ample compensation for the fact that every sortie to Tunis or Bizerta involved a round trip of 1,200 miles.

Eastern Air Command and the Twelfth Air Force, however, were not the only Allied aircraft concerned with Tunisia. By January 1943 the Middle East bombers, including Brereton's Fortresses and Liberators, were playing a vital part in the struggle. The moment the fall of Tripoli was assured these aircraft began to hammer away against the Tunisian ports; while their attacks on Sicily and Southern Italy benefited our forces in Tunisia and Tripolitania alike. Moreover, our reconnaissance and anti-shipping aircraft on Malta were also helping to shape the pattern of events in Tunisia. Long before the Eighth Army reached the Mareth Line all this pointed clearly to the need to integrate the air activity of Middle East, Malta, Eastern Air Command and Twelfth Air Force. Tedder perceived this from the start, and as early as November he was in Algiers urging a single unified air command over the whole of the Mediterranean. The first essential, however, was to produce an efficient organization in French North Africa. Early in December Eisenhower appointed General Spaatz to co-ordinate the operations of Eastern Air Command and the Twelfth Air Force, but this left almost the whole way still to go.

Ultimately the logic of Tedder's proposition proved irresistible. When the Casablanca Conference met in mid-January 1943 it accordingly approved a plan of unification worked out by Tedder in consultation with Eisenhower and Portal. By that time Tedder himself had been designated to the position of Vice Chief of the Air Staff. He was not, however, as yet destined for a desk in Whitehall; for Eisenhower's acceptance of the idea of a single air commander in the Mediterranean was not unconnected with the fact that in Tedder there existed, ready-made, the man with precisely the experience and capacity for the job.

The essence of the scheme accepted at Casablanca was unified air control over the whole of the Mediterranean and North Africa. To achieve this a super-command known as Mediterranean Air Command was to be formed. The Air Commander-in-Chief—Tedder—would be responsible to Eisenhower for operations in connection with Tunisia, but to the British Chiefs of Staff for operations in the Middle East. As Tunisia was the affair of the moment, his headquarters would be alongside Eisenhower's, in Algiers. Thence he could direct, in accordance with a single coherent strategy, his three great operational instruments. Two of these were already in existence—Royal Air Force, Middle East, now under Air Chief Marshal Sir Sholto Douglas, and Royal Air Force, Malta, under Air Vice-Marshal Sir Keith Park. The third was a new formation to be known as the Northwest African Air Forces. Commanded by General Spaatz, it was created by the amalgamation of Eastern Air Command, Twelfth Air Force and the advanced or tactical units from the Middle East.

Though Mediterranean Air Command and Northwest African Air Forces were not brought into being until the third week of February it will be convenient at this point to complete the description of the new arrangements. Spaatz's Command was carefully framed on the functional model which had proved so successful in the Middle East. The Royal Air Force in Egypt and Libya, it will be remembered, had developed along the broad lines of a long-range bomber force (No. 205 Group), a tactical force (A.H.Q. Western Desert) and a maritime force (No. 201 Group). In the Northwest African Air Forces this pattern was repeated. A Northwest African Strategic Air Force was set up under Doolittle, a Northwest African Tactical Air Force under Coningham, and a Northwest African Coastal Air Force under Lloyd. The Coastal Air Force was responsible for air defence in the coastal area, as well as for reconnaissance and anti-shipping strikes at sea. Other functional commands formed at the same level, either at this time or shortly afterwards, were the Northwest African Air Service Command, the Northwest African Training Command, and the Northwest African Troop Carrier Command. The latter controlled air transport generally, besides providing forces for airborne operations. On a smaller scale, but in the same relation to Northwest African Air Forces, was the Northwest African Photographic Reconnaissance Wing under Colonel Elliott Roosevelt.

Perhaps the most remarkable feature of these subordinate commands was that they were genuine Anglo-American entities. Doolittle's Strategic Air Force, for instance, included British Wellingtons as well as American 'heavies'; Coningham's Tactical Air Force comprised not only the Western Desert Air Force (now under Air Vice-Marshal Harry Broadhurst) and No. 242 Group of light bombers and fighters from Eastern Air Command, but also the tactical aircraft of the Twelfth Air Force, known as the Twelfth Air Support Command. Similarly, the British and American maintenance facilities were combined to form the Air Service Command. All this was no mere matter of assigning British units to American control, or vice versa; unification was achieved in the headquarters organization at all levels from Mediterranean Air Command down to the subordinate commands. Tedder, for instance, soon had an American Chief of Staff, Spaatz a British deputy—Air Vice-Marshal Robb, a well-loved figure whose onerous duties included control of N.A.A.F. operations—and Coningham an American second in command. Some of the subordinate Command headquarters were predominantly British, others American, according to the composition of the force they controlled; but a surprising number of offices were manned on the 'one for one' principle—a British head having an American deputy, an American head a British deputy. In theory this was no doubt wasteful. That it was in practice wise, no one who saw it in action can doubt. For though the new headquarters might, and indeed did, contain many who were at first virtually onlookers, it was in these headquarters that large numbers of British and American Air Force officers learnt to know each other. And with knowledge came understanding, respect, liking, and the wholehearted co-operation that distinguishes friends rather than allies.

In the circumstances of early 1943, unified direction of the ground forces was no less important than unified direction of the air forces. The Casablanca Conference also settled this point by nominating General Alexander deputy commander under Eisenhower with special responsibility for land forces. As soon as the Eighth Army approached the Tunisian border Alexander was also to assume the higher direction of the First Army, the American II Corps, and the French XIX Corps. This arrangement, apart from ensuring co-ordinated movement by the three armies, allowed Eisenhower to concentrate on those matters of politics and general strategy which bulked so large in French North Africa. It also enormously simplified the task of the Tactical Air Commander; for Coningham could locate his headquarters alongside Alexander's—just as, at a lower level, he had previously located it alongside Montgomery's. With the full picture before him, he could then rapidly adjust his air effort to meet the varying requirements of the different fronts—to concentrate, in other words, on Southern Tunisia, Central Tunisia or Northern Tunisia as the situation demanded.

The effect of the air reorganization was profound and almost instantaneous. Besides putting at the top men with the requisite ability and experience, it made possible that high degree of flexibility which characterizes correctly organized air power. Under Tedder's direction the air forces in the Mediterranean could now be concentrated to the confusion of the Axis at the decisive points—whether at the fronts, or along the lines of land and sea communication, or far back among the airfields, ports and bases of Italy. The Anglo-American air forces were neither parcelled out to naval and land commanders nor tied down to particular geographical sectors. In all circumstances Tedder could direct, without argument or delay, his total force according to a single coherent plan.

* * *

The reorganization approved at Casablanca was applied at the most critical moment since the landings. During January, Eisenhower had sent the American II Corps forward into Central and Southern Tunisia. His intention was to drive through to the coast at Sfax, so cutting the tenuous link between von Arnim in north-east Tunisia and Rommel in Tripolitania. Unfortunately, II Corps, stretched out between Fondouk in Central Tunisia and Gafsa in the south, was not yet strong enough for the task; indeed, so far from being able to take the offensive, it presented—to an enterprising opponent—a most tempting subject for attack. At the end of January the enterprising opponent arrived. Rommel, still on the long, long trail from Alamein, reached the southern gates of Tunisia.

Taking stock of the situation with his customary speed, the Axis commander at once decided to safeguard his communications—and line of retreat—before giving battle to Montgomery. He had already sent the 21st Panzers ahead to re-equip. On 14th February he launched these formidable warriors against the Americans at Faid.

The blow fell farther south than the Allied intelligence staffs had anticipated; and it fell on inexperienced troops and commanders. It gained added strength from the activity of 371 German aircraft concentrated for the occasion—an occasion known to the enemy staffs, with true German poetic feeling, as Operation '*Frühlingswind*' ('Spring-Breeze'). At the same time another movement still farther south forced the Americans out of Gafsa. Under lowering skies which cut down air activity on both sides, the Germans then pressed on to Kasserine, where on 17th February the two wings of their attack united. At this point the enemy movement, originally designed merely to clear Rommel's flank, developed far more serious implications, for it now threatened to burst through the mountains of Central Tunisia, turn north across the communications of the First Army, and take our whole northern front in the rear.

During these four days and nights of confusion, when the central front was crumbling and the Twelfth Air Force was abandoning its forward airfields, No. 242 Group was able to carry out only one attack in support of the hard-pressed Americans. From 18th/19th February onwards the Bisleys operated every night, but the weather remained so thick that the crews dropped their bombs more in hope than in expectation. But though the Anglo-American air effort was still at the mercy of the elements, from this date onwards it was no longer hampered by factors within Anglo-American control. The reorganized system of command, introduced on 18th February, brought about an instant improvement. Coningham, for instance, at once gave orders that the fighters of No. 242 Group and the Twelfth Air Support Command, which in response to military requests had been doing a great deal of purely defensive flying, should concentrate on offensive patrols in the manner of the Western Desert Air Force. At the same time Spaatz quickly proved the flexibility of the new arrangements by placing most of the strategic bombers at Coningham's disposal for the duration of the crisis. It was not, of course, this reorganization of the Allied air forces that stopped the Germans. That was achieved by the integration of the Allied land forces under Alexander, the latter's skilful diagnosis of the enemy's intentions, and the resolute defence of Tebessa and Thala. But the air reorganization, coupled with better weather, did enable the Anglo-American airmen to play a highly effective part in the later and more favourable stages of the battle.

The Germans began to fall back towards the coast on 23rd February. Taking advantage of the improved weather, our aircraft based in Tunisia harassed this retreat, which was prevented from becoming a rout only by the enemy's skill in planting mines in the path of the pursuers. Meanwhile, the Middle East long-range bombers and the Western Desert Air Force in Tripolitania were already preparing the way for the Eighth Army's next move. For the most part this preparation consisted of two kinds. Raids against the enemy's forward landing grounds near Mareth, Gabes and El Hamma ruthlessly cut down the activity of the German fighter force; raids behind the Mareth positions played havoc with the enemy's transport and supplies.

It was in the midst of these operations that Rommel, having gained more elbow-room at the expense of the Americans, struck out against Montgomery. But the enemy's preparations had been well reported by our air reconnaissance, and the British commander was ready. Launched on 6th March against a massive concentration of guns on high ground near Medenine, the attack met with instant failure; the Axis forces took a beating and retired discomfited to the Mareth positions, leaving behind no less than fifty-two tanks. During this episode low clouds and bad visibility kept the Western Desert Air Force out of the air for many hours, but when conditions permitted Broadhurst's crews took full advantage of their opportunities.

The battle of Medenine was Rommel's last throw. Shortly afterwards, a sick and disillusioned man, he flew back to Germany, and command of the Axis forces passed into the hands of von Arnim in the North, the Italian Messe in the South. By that time the general Allied situation, which a fortnight earlier Tedder had described as 'quite incredibly untidy, both from the operational and organizational point of view', had improved out of all recognition. 'New organization is functioning with remarkably little friction', reported Tedder on 5th March; 'No doubt that establishment of new joint headquarters by Alexander and Coningham has changed the whole atmosphere and outlook of British and American land and air . . . mutual co-operation is good and is improving daily in both operations and administration. One senses a growing feeling of cohesion and concentration, and I think the enemy also senses it. We have a long way to go and many problems to solve before we have welded the two forces into one weapon, but the will exists and we are undoubtedly finding the way'.

* * *

While the various elements in the Allied forces were thus fusing into one, von Arnim had already opened an offensive in Northern Tunisia. This met with some success till the First Army and No. 242 Group (which in the first five days of March flew over 1,000 sorties against ground targets) halted it short of the vital centres of Béja and Medjez el Bab. Frustrated in the north, the enemy then tried again in the south. On 10th March they attacked the gallant band of Frenchmen who had covered the breadth of the Sahara to take their place on the western flank of the Eighth Army; but Leclerc's men, powerfully aided by the Western Desert Air Force, proved more than equal to the occasion. Then Eisenhower and Alexander struck back. On 17th March the American II Corps, with the help of the strategic bombers as well as the American tactical aircraft, began to press the enemy towards the coast. So commenced that brilliantly co-ordinated series of attacks which was to end only when every Axis soldier in Tunisia was killed, wounded, or meekly awaiting the barbed wire.

Gafsa fell to the Americans on 17th March. Within a week their advance came to a halt, but II Corps continued to play its part by holding down the 10th Panzer Division. Meanwhile, the Eighth Army had struck the second blow. After preliminary air operations, less

ITALIAN AIRCRAFT AT CASTEL BENITO, MARCH 1943

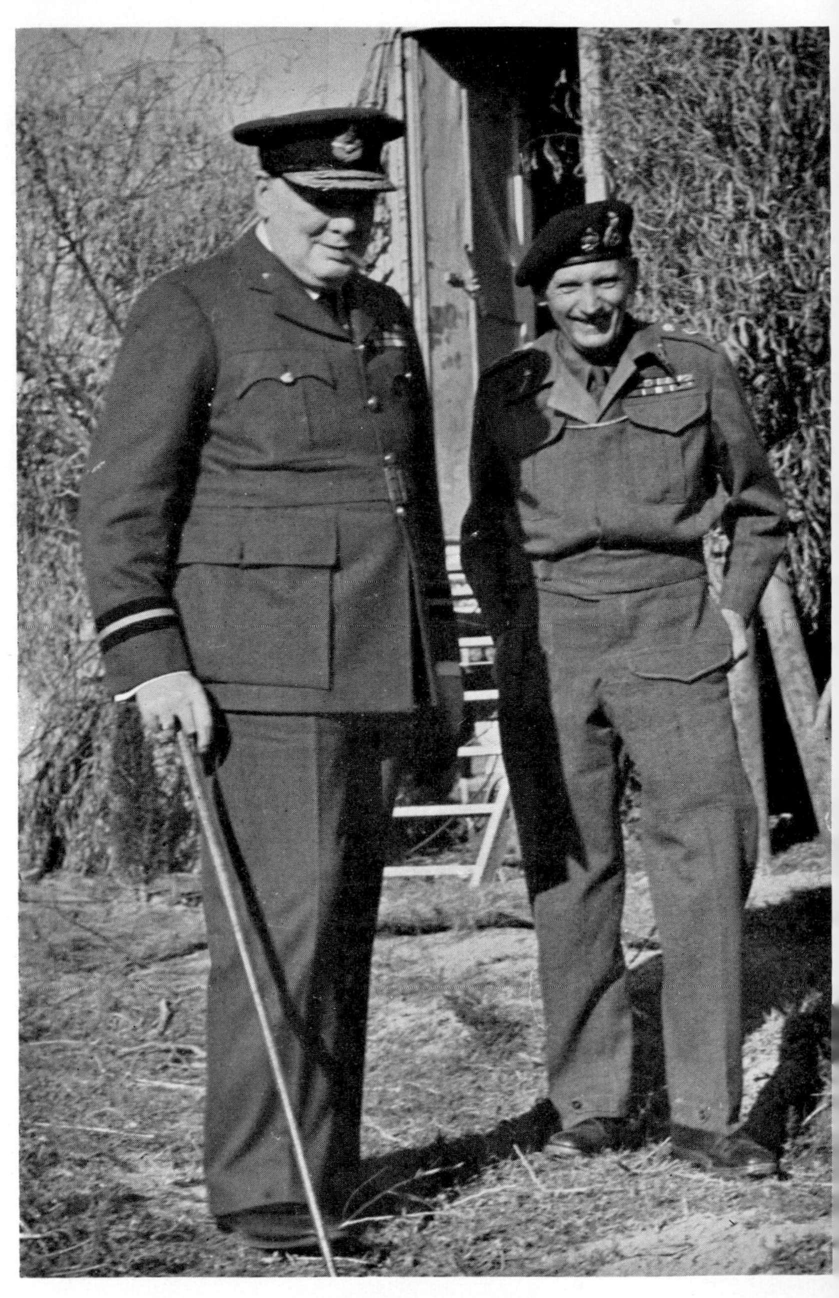

A FAMOUS VISIT

Mr. Churchill and General Montgomery outside the latter's caravan at Castel Benito

intensive than usual on account of the weather, on the night of 20th/21st March Montgomery launched a full-scale attack against the Mareth line.

The task which confronted the Eighth Army and the Western Desert Air Force was the most formidable since El Alamein. The left end of the Mareth line rested on the sea, the right on the Matmata Hills; and beyond the latter the country was so rough that in the considered view of French military science no mechanized force could hope to traverse it. Montgomery accordingly threw the main weight of the assault into a direct blow at the enemy front; but the Eighth Army Commander, having thoughtfully experimented over the territory with the Long-Range Desert Group, was also convinced that an outflanking movement held possibilities unsuspected by the designers of the line, and a subsidiary part of his plan was an extensive circuit west of the Matmata Hills by the New Zealand Corps. This move, which was possible only because of the toughness of our transport and the domination of the skies by our aircraft, began some twenty-four hours before the main attack.

The initial frontal assault carried our forward troops across the Wadi Zigzaou, a steep watercourse at the bottom of which there stood, as it proved, all too much water. Raids on enemy concentrations during 21st March by the Western Desert Air Force helped our men to maintain their foothold on the other side, while attacks on enemy landing grounds by Strategic and Tactical Air Forces alike kept the *Luftwaffe* virtually grounded. At the same time the outflanking move, directed at El Hamma, made good progress. But though the enemy had been thrown off their balance they rapidly recovered. Kittybombers and Hurricane IID's broke up a group of forty tanks which menaced the New Zealanders, but in the main struggle our troops fared less well. In face of the enemy guns few of our tanks could cross the Wadi; and on 22nd March a torrential downpour stopped the Western Desert Air Force operating against the threatened counter-attack. The next day, ten raids against the Mareth positions helped to avert disaster, but could not avail to secure the bridgehead.

With great promptitude Montgomery now withdrew his troops across the Wadi. While appearing to gather strength for a renewed frontal assault he then swung the whole weight of the attack into the outflanking movement. Headquarters X Corps and the 1st Armoured Division went bumping round the Matmata Hills in the tracks of the New Zealanders, while Broadhurst correspondingly transferred his main air effort to the enemy positions south of El Hamma. Here the crucial obstacle before our troops was the funnel between the Jebel

Tebaga and the Jebel Melab, only four miles wide and bristling with enemy guns.

To carry this immensely strong position with the available forces seemed at first sight impossible. Even the indomitable Freyberg believed that there was nothing for it but a further outflanking movement, involving the loss of some ten days. Broadhurst, however, considered that a truly formidable air 'blitz' delivered in conjunction with a frontal assault by the ground forces would suffice. The plan was accepted, and elaborate measures were worked out for denoting targets. There followed two nights of heavy bombing which severed many of the enemy telephone communications and profoundly disturbed the slumbers, such as they were, of the Axis troops. Then, at 1530 on 26th March, the Western Desert Air Force went into action against the enemy soldiery with unprecedented fury. Three squadrons of escorted bombers opened the attack, coming in very low by an evasive route and achieving complete surprise. From then on two and a half squadrons of Kittybombers, briefed first to bomb individual positions and then to shoot up the enemy gun teams, were fed into the area every fifteen minutes. Half an hour after the first bomb fell our infantry went forward, preceded by a creeping barrage which gave our pilots an unmistakable 'bomb-line'. Meanwhile Spitfires, patrolling high above, kept the air clear of the enemy—a task in which other formations of the Northwest African Air Forces again co-operated by raiding landing grounds. More than once our opponents attempted to mass their tanks, but on each sign of this Hurricane IID's swept in and broke up the concentration. Within two and a quarter hours Western Desert Air Force alone, at a cost of eleven pilots, had flown 412 sorties; and the enemy defenders, disorganized and demoralized, had yielded the key-points to our troops. The result was that during the night our armour passed through the bottle-neck virtually unscathed. El Hamma itself still held, but we had turned the Mareth line.

The next night the Axis forces, shielded from our aircraft by a thick haze, pulled out of the whole Mareth position and raced north before our armour could cut across to the coast. Within another twenty-four hours El Hamma and Gabes were in our hands and the enemy was retiring under heavy air attack to his next line of resistance on the Wadi Akarit. 'The outstanding feature of the battle', ran the terse verdict of the Eighth Army Commander, 'was the air action in co-operation with the outflanking forces'.

All this time the medium and heavy bombers, both of the Middle East and the Northwest African Air Forces, continued to attack the ports and airfields of Tunisia, Sardinia, Sicily, and Southern Italy.

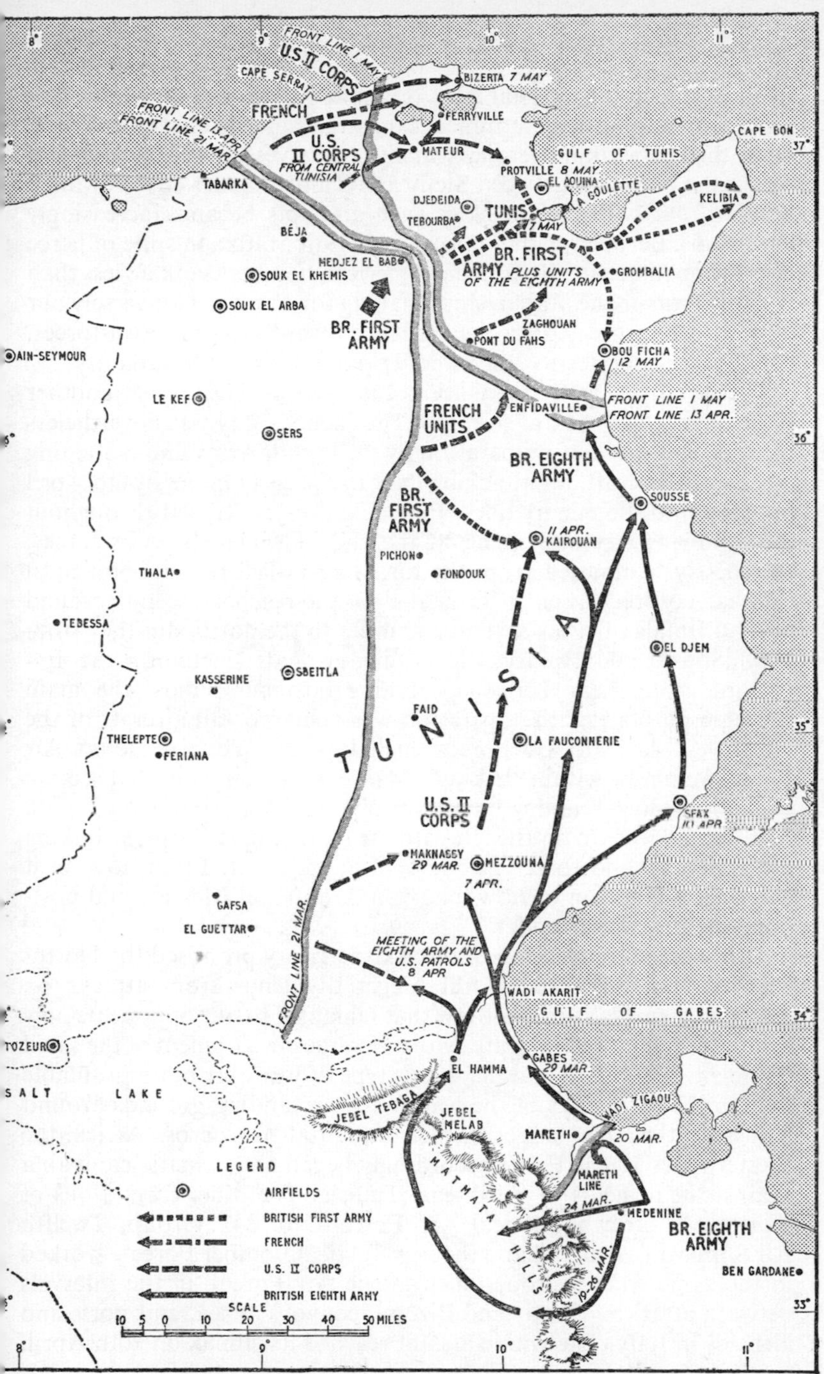

THE TUNISIAN CAMPAIGN, 19 MARCH - 13 MAY 1943

In concert with the Coastal Air Force and our aircraft on Malta they were also waging a determined campaign against enemy convoys. Until the last week in February many enemy vessels were able to slip across the Narrows between Sicily and Tunisia under cover of thick weather, but with clearer skies such attempts became increasingly hazardous. Between 19th February and 19th March, in spite of fierce opposition in the air, British and American bombers sank no less than twenty German and Italian ships making for Tunisia. Conversely our own vessels, protected by the vigilance of our air and naval forces, could carry supplies to Bone and Tripoli almost with impunity.

The Wadi Akarit, dominating the 'Gabes Gap', was another position of great natural strength. The enemy's stay was nevertheless brief. After a week of preparation by the Eighth Army and 'softening up' by our aircraft, an attack by dark in the early hours of 6th April bit deep into the enemy lines. Fierce fighting continued throughout the following day and night, at the end of which the Axis forces, mercilessly hammered from the air, were in full retreat. Not until they had covered the entire coastal plain and reached the high ground beyond Enfidaville, more than 150 miles to the north, did they stop. With Sousse and twenty-two landing-grounds (including the important group near Kairouan) falling into our hands, the main strategic purpose of the operation was achieved; all aircraft of the Northwest African Air Forces, including the Western Desert Air Force, were now within striking distance of any target in that section of Tunisia which remained to the enemy. At the same time the Eighth Army could join up on the left with the American II Corps, so linking the Allied ground forces in one continuous front. From now on it was only a question of how long von Arnim and Messe could postpone the day of surrender.

This violent contraction of the Axis territory promised the Northwest African Air Forces still bigger dividends from attacks on Tunisian airfields; for those few that remained to our opponents now held several hundred aircraft. Moreover, the development of the small fragmentation bomb had made this type of work far more profitable than in the early days of the war. With the landing-grounds around Kairouan their last laager in their immortal trek across Africa, the Western Desert Air Force accordingly began a systematic campaign against the airfields of north-east Tunisia. The other formations of Northwest African Tactical Air Force—No. 242 Group, Twelfth Air Support Command and the new Tactical Bomber Force—worked to the same end; so, too, did Strategic Air Force—in the intervals between attacking Tunis and Bizerta, convoys at sea, and ports and airfields in Italy. The whole assault reached its climax on 20th April, when the Eighth Army moved forward against the Enfidaville line and Northwest African Air Forces flew more than 1,000 sorties. After that, concerted attacks on landing grounds were no longer necessary.

Meanwhile, the bombing of Tunis, Bizerta and the South Italian ports, coupled with our ever-increasing success against convoys at sea, had brought the Axis supply system to the verge of collapse. The German remedy was a still greater use of air transport. During the opening week of April the *Luftwaffe* maintained a daily average of something like 150 sorties on the routes to Tunisia. Already on 5th April a determined effort by Northwest African Air Forces to discourage this traffic, both at source and *en route*, had resulted in the destruction of twenty-seven German aircraft in the air and thirty-nine on the ground, besides damage to another sixty-seven. These figures take no account of Italian losses, which are unknown. Now, with the loss of Sfax and Sousse forcing the enemy to an even greater reliance on air transport, the time was ripe for further blows. On 10th/11th April British and American fighters, sweeping over the Narrows, shot down twenty-four German Ju.52's and fourteen escorts. Many of the quarry were carrying fuel, and blew up in spectacular fashion. Equally impressive was the slaughter on 18th April, when American Warhawks and Royal Air Force Spitfires intercepted about 100 escorted Ju.52's near Cape Bon. Within a few seconds the shore below was strewn with blazing wreckage, fifty-two German machines being destroyed for a loss on the Allied side of seven. The next day our fighters massacred yet another formation, and thereafter the enemy wisely confined the Ju.52's to minor operations by night. One further lesson was needed, however, to complete the Germans' education in the matter. On 22nd April they rashly committed a consignment of petrol to Me.323's—six-engined glider-type aircraft which they had previously employed only in small numbers. Several of these huge machines, each carrying some ten tons, attempted the passage under heavy escort. Intercepted over the Gulf of Tunis by seven and a half squadrons of Spitfires and Kittyhawks, the formation was mown down almost to the last aircraft. The Allies' official 'score', according to our own estimates, was now 432 transports destroyed since 5th April for the loss of thirty-five aircraft, and the Axis had suffered a grievous blow not merely to their hopes in Tunisia but to their whole future prospects of success elsewhere. For the waste of aircraft in Tunisia, coming hard on top of an equally prodigal expenditure at Stalingrad, meant that the Axis transport fleets, so potent an asset at the beginning of the war, were now of little account beside the ever-growing resources of the Allies.

With their bridgehead in Africa fast shrinking, their supply system breaking down, and their landing grounds under remorseless attack, the Germans and Italians were by this time already withdrawing their aircraft to Sicily. The venerable, vulnerable Stukas led the way; other types followed; and only the fighters remained, grouped now for the defence of Tunis and Bizerta. This gave our forces still greater liberty of action, so that among other consequences our aircraft were able to devote even more of their attention to enemy shipping. Western Desert Air Force, now suitably based for the task, took to this type of work with the utmost enthusiasm, and in the month of April destroyed eleven vessels. Many of the fighter pilots were novices so far as attacks on shipping were concerned, but practice soon made perfect.[1]

* * *

The final moves in the campaign opened on the night of 19th/20th April with an attack by the Eighth Army. Enfidaville itself fell rapidly, but the mountains beyond proved a tougher proposition. For once Montgomery found himself up against more than he could manage—doubtless in part because the Western Desert Air Force was preoccupied elsewhere with enemy landing grounds, shipping, and air transport. Lack of success on the southern front, however, did not spoil the general plan, for Alexander had in any case arranged to deliver the *coup de grâce* in the north. Thither, to the extreme coastal sector—clean across the communications of the First Army—he had already transferred the American II Corps. Like the out-

[1] In their desire to become proficient some of the pilots apparently went too far. The following masterly communication from the commanders of three naval vessels at Sousse tells its own story :—

1st May, 1943

To the Mess President of No. 244 *Wing*

Sir,

It has been observed by various individuals of unimpeachable character that Spitfires are making use of valuable dan buoys as targets.

These dans, which mark the way through a minefield, have been laid at enormous expense and with great skill and daring in order to safeguard the shipping bringing you your bully, biscuits, pickles and booze (R) booze. Should the unlikely event occur of one of these buoys being sunk or damaged by your planes, no booze will be forthcoming. Calamity !!!!

For a fee we could lay a very large-sized beacon for you to practise on and perhaps hit.

Should this pernicious habit of buoy-strafing not cease, no further pennies will be contributed to buy you new Spitfires.

Geoffrey R. Price, Lt. R.N.V.R.
Robin Bell, Lt. R.N.V.R.
C. W. Pearce, Lt. R.N.V.R.

flanking of the Mareth line, this was a movement made possible only by the absolute supremacy we had now established in the air

With the Americans on the left advancing along the coast, on 22nd April the First Army struck out for Tunis. Northwest African Air Forces provided support on a lavish scale; each day, to the order of over 1,000 sorties, bombers and fighter-bombers attacked troop positions, while fighters maintained complete mastery over the battlefield. All this helped First Army and II Corps alike to make substantial headway; but a week's fighting made it clear that the end, if certain, would not be swift. On 30th April Alexander accordingly ordered Montgomery, now engaged only in a holding operation, to transfer to the First Army the best formations he could spare. The Eighth Army Commander chose the most seasoned veterans in Africa—7th Armoured Division, 4th Indian Division and the 201st Brigade of Guards. In yet another vast cavalcade, unmolested and apparently even unobserved from the air, this powerful reinforcement now proceeded north.

During the first four days of May bad weather cut down the activity of our aircraft. Fortunately the skies cleared in good time for the attack by the reinforced First Army. On the night of 4th/5th May Wellingtons and Bisleys were out in force against roads and transport in the Tunis sector; the following day, while Fortresses attacked Tunis and La Goulette, and aircraft of the Strategic and Tactical Air Forces alike continued to prey on enemy shipping, Mitchells and Bostons softened up strongholds and troop concentrations in the area where the opening blow was to fall; and after dusk Bisleys, Wellingtons and French Leos continued the good work of the night before. Then at dawn on the 6th the infantry of the First Army moved forward. They were covered not only by artillery fire but by concentrated bombing of a selected area only $4 \times 3\frac{1}{2}$ miles in dimension—a device promptly hailed in the Press as 'Tedder's bomb-carpet'. In conformity with this plan the ground forces scheduled for the attack had been massed on an extremely narrow front, the greater part of the supplies to four divisions being carried over the single bridge at Medjez el Bab—another arrangement possible only by reason of the Allies' complete command in the air.

The infantry did their work well, so that soon the way was clear for our massed armour to go through. At all points of resistance the Tactical Air Force was overhead with bomb and shell, and by the afternoon our tanks had torn the enemy front asunder. Indeed, the First Army advanced so far ahead of schedule, and the situation became so confused, that in the latter part of the day air support was perforce restricted. Meanwhile in the coastal sector the Americans, also with powerful help from the air, were progressing equally fast. All told, the day's total of sorties by Northwest African Air Forces amounted to 2,154, of which 1,663 were flown by Tactical Air Force. Most of the remainder were flown by Strategic Air Force, partly in support of the battle, partly—in case the enemy should attempt evacuation—against the various small craft gathered in the ports of Sicily or bound for Tunis.

After another night's bombing by the Wellingtons the advance was resumed on 7th May. The skies had clouded now, and our aircraft were not out in the same strength as on the previous day. But the work to be done on the ground did not now demand any great help from above. The enemy defenders still in our path were brushed aside, and during the afternoon the foremost elements of the 7th Armoured Division swept into Tunis. Half an hour later the Americans occupied Bizerta. By rapidly switching his forces Alexander then sealed off the Cape Bon peninsula and shattered the enemy's only hope of prolonging resistance.

At this point the Axis fighters departed from Tunisia, leaving the enemy ground forces with no more air support than an occasional raid from Sardinia or Sicily. The remaining days of the campaign, until the capitulation of von Arnim on 12th May and Messe on 13th May, were mainly a matter of rounding up disorganized opponents who knew that only rapid surrender would protect them from unopposed bombing. In these circumstances the air forces were in fact able, during the final week, to devote a large part of their effort to targets in Italy, Sicily and Pantelleria associated with the next stage in Allied strategy.

Against the expected evacuation Admiral Cunningham and Tedder had devised elaborate counter-measures under the code-name 'Retribution'. Their intention was at once to exact revenge for the sufferings of British expeditionary forces in 1940 and 1941, and at the same time to show the Germans how evacuations can be prevented. But Hitler and Mussolini, in face of our air and naval control over the Narrows, knew better than even to attempt a Dunkirk. Had they done so, they would merely have added, to the loss of 250,000 men and vast quantities of equipment, the annihilation of the Italian fleet.

So ended the war in Africa—a war which, though of profound strategic significance, Hitler had never taken seriously until too late. In that war the Royal Air Force, in association first with the Dominion Air Forces and some gallant remnants from France, Greece and Yugoslavia, and subsequently also with increasingly powerful forces from the United States, had played a vital, perhaps a decisive, part. It had won the freedom of the skies against fierce opposition. It had kept the enemy short of supplies, while safeguarding our own. It had preserved the Eighth Army in retreat and speeded it in advance. At every stage, from the first attack on the Italian landing grounds on 10th June, 1940, to the last raid against the 90th Light Division at Bou Ficha on the afternoon of 12th May, 1943, the aircrews of the Royal Air Force had shown the same indomitable spirit. But it was on the theme of co-operation, both within the air forces and between them and the other arms, that Tedder rightly chose to dwell in his final Order of the Day:—

> *To all ranks of the Allied Air Forces.*
>
> By magnificent team work between nationalities, commands, units, officers and men from Teheran to Takoradi, from Morocco to the Indian Ocean, you have, together with your comrades on land and sea, thrown the enemy out of Africa. You have shown the world the unity and strength of air power. A grand job, well finished. We face our next job with the knowledge that we have thrashed the enemy, and the determination to thrash him again.

To that it is perhaps necessary to add only one thing. In Africa first the British, then the Americans, learnt how to fight a war in which action by land, air and sea was closely integrated. In all the fighting of the next two years this knowledge was to prove of inestimable value. For from the African struggle there emerged, not only skilled and seasoned Allied troops, but highly competent Allied staffs and commanders. Eisenhower and Tedder, Montgomery and Coningham—to name only four of the triumphant team—were destined to win, on more fertile soil, a campaign of far greater import. Victory would certainly not have crowned their arms in Europe so swiftly, or at such little cost, but for the lessons learned amid the rocks and sand.

CHAPTER XIII
Casablanca and the Ruhr

THE room in which the Conference sat was in shape semi-circular, one of its walls being curved and composed 'chiefly of large windows fronting the Atlantic'. Through them poured the sunshine which day after day burnished the rolling waters beyond the line of perpetual surf. The Chiefs of Staff had but to rise from the round table in the middle of the room and walk a yard to find themselves gazing at 'villas and farms and the white mass of Casablanca town, the bougainvillaea, the begonias and the green of the orange groves and palm trees', rising from the red soil beneath a sky of unchanging blue. It was in these surroundings that for ten January days in 1943 the political, naval, military and air chiefs of Britain and America deliberated. When they were ended, decisions which made victory certain had been taken. The Casablanca Conference did, indeed, mark a tide in the affairs of the Allies. They took it at the flood, and, though many weary weeks and months had still to pass, from that time onwards the ultimate result was never in doubt. The initiative had passed to them never to be regained by the enemy.

When Churchill, Roosevelt and the Chiefs of Staff met together in that sun-drenched town, the invasion of North Africa had been an accomplished fact for two months, and though nearly four more were to pass before von Arnim surrendered in Tunisia, it was already possible to plan the future conduct of the war. One decision was of cardinal importance and upon it depended the whole course of future operations. Was the prime enemy to be Germany or Japan? The British had no doubts. The 'cleansing of the North African shore', to use a phrase more than once on Churchill's lips in those days, would prepare the 'underbelly' of the Axis to receive the knife of invasion. The Mediterranean would be freed, with all the consequences which would follow—a shortening of the sea routes to the Far East, where the enemy still raged in formidable strength, the release of large armies and air forces for new enterprises, and, very possibly, the disappearance altogether from the struggle of one of the three partners of the Axis.

The American view was not so clear-cut, even though General

Marshall stated at the outset of the talks the premise that seventy per cent of Allied resources should be assigned to the Atlantic theatre and thirty per cent to the Pacific. A year had passsed since the attack on Pearl Harbour and the leaders of the United States were still under its influence. Largely because of that violent and unprovoked assault from the air, followed so soon by the surrender of Singapore, the American fleet in the Pacific was homeless. Covered by its seaborne aircraft and supported by long-range bombers based on small, unheard-of islands, it was operating seven thousand miles from its bases and had not as yet been able to settle the issue. There were great and urgent tasks to be accomplished in the Pacific and in Burma; the condition of China was grave, some thought desperate; the Burma Road was still closed and such supplies as could reach the armies of Chiang Kai-Shek had to be carried by air across the Patkai range of the Naga hills. Since it was not possible to be equally strong on all fronts, might not too grave a risk be run in pressing the war in Europe at the expense of the Far East? Japan had begun the war with some six million tons of shipping, of which she had lost one million in the first twelve months. Reduce this tonnage to four million and she would be hard pressed to maintain her garrisons in the chain of islands running in a great half circle from Burma to New Guinea.

These were powerful considerations, not lightly to be disregarded, and there was another in the background more powerful than any, brooding, as it were, over the subconscious minds of these captains of war. How to use air power to the best advantage was a dominant factor in the deliberations of the Conference. Plans might be made and were, for vast movements of troops and supplies and for the regrouping of navies in each of the seven seas, but all were governed from first to last by the situation in the air. By January 1943 examples of the might of air power were not lacking. They ranged in importance from the capture of Crete, the virtual closing of the Mediterranean, the heavy losses inflicted on the American Pacific Fleet in Pearl Harbour and the sinking of the *Prince of Wales* and the *Repulse* off the East coast of Malaya, to the attacks by the *Luftwaffe* on the small but important port of Bone, which even at that late stage were causing difficulties for the Anglo-American-French army on the march to Tunis. All then, at that round table took it for granted that to ignore the power of the air would be an act of folly.

That being so, the Conference sought to reach agreement in three stages. First, the proportion of effort to be directed against Japan and against Germany had to be settled. Here the Americans, while evidently anxious that Germany should be defeated first, seemed uncertain as to the steps to take to achieve this end without weakening unduly the forces arrayed against Japan. The discussion ranged far and wide, but can be summed up by an observation of one of the senior officers present. 'We are', he said, 'in the position of a testator who wishes to leave the bulk of his fortune to his mistress. He must, however, leave something to his wife, and his problem is to decide how little he can in decency set apart for her'. Eventually, it was agreed that 'the major portion of the forces of the United Nations' should be 'directed against Germany' but that most of the American fleet should remain in the Pacific where a number of operations should be undertaken of which the prime object was to prevent Japan from consolidating her gains.

The next problem was what point on the coast of Europe should be marked down for assault. The claims of the western coast of France as compared with those of Sicily and Italy were examined in detail and it was at one time thought that an invasion of the Pas de Calais or the Cherbourg area might achieve first a bridgehead, then a breach in Germany's West Wall, through which the tide of invasion would pour. Such an attack would achieve three objects. It would, or might, satisfy the demands of the Russians which were being pressed with great vigour, it would give armies which had been training for two and a half years or more their longed-for opportunity to come to grips with the enemy, and it would almost certainly provoke the *Luftwaffe* into intense activity. On the other hand, for the Allies to mount an assault of such a nature with the naval and military forces which were then available, or which might become so during the ensuing twelve months, was soon seen to be hazardous in the extreme. The grave shortage of landing craft alone must limit the size and strength of the operations.

These were some of the reasons why, despite the pressure of the Russian Government, which was calling for an attack in the West large enough to draw off forty German divisions from the Eastern Front, the invasion of France was judged to be impracticable. There remained that stab in the soft underbelly of the Axis which had always been advocated by the British General Staff, and to which the Americans had never been averse. Once Tunisia was cleared of Axis forces, a large number of Allied troops would be immediately available to deliver it. The question was, where? Sicily was poised, a tempting stepping-stone between Africa and Italy. On the other hand, precisely because it was so tempting the enemy might well expect an attack upon it and take measures so to increase its defences as to make an amphibious onslaught costly. The alternative was Sardinia. That island was far more lightly defended; but it was farther away and it would be more difficult to provide an assaulting force with cover from the air. Moreover, its air bases, once captured, were few and far between. The whole matter was summed up by Portal, who pointed out that while to assault northern France might induce the Germans to bring up air forces from the Mediterranean, they would realize that Britain and America were not strong enough to attack simultaneously both in the north and in the south. On the other hand to threaten Italy would cause a dispersal of the *Luftwaffe* and thus achieve that wastage of its strength which was indispensable to the maintenance of a sustained bomber offensive, itself the preliminary to a successful invasion of Europe. Moreover, such a policy, if successful, would provide air bases from which it would be possible to bomb Austria, where no small part of the German aircraft industry, notably the Messerschmitt factories at Wiener Neustadt, was situated, and Rumania, where was to be found the main source of her supplies of natural oil.

These arguments, reinforced as they were by the Chief of the Imperial General Staff and the First Sea Lord, prevailed. To attack Sicily might be a more costly affair than an assault upon Sardinia, but it would yield greater and more immediate results, of which not the least would be the freeing of the Mediterranean for the passage of ships.

Before any invasion could be mounted the enemy must be mastered in two vital elements, the air and the sea. It was here that the views of the Chief of the Air Staff carried special weight. The *Luftwaffe* must be rendered powerless and the best way to achieve this end was to compel the Germans to spread it over as wide an area as could be found. Such a dispersal would not allow it to be strong enough at any given point to offer effective resistance. The position of the German Air Force, said Portal, was critical. The stamina of the crews was not what it was, their training had fallen off, and they were showing less determination than in previous years. Undoubtedly the main cause of this was a shortage of aircraft. There was no depth behind the German front line in the air. Portal's suspicions of the actual strength of the *Luftwaffe* at that time were correct. In fact it possessed no more than 4,207 first-line aircraft of all kinds, of which 2,521 were serviceable. In reserve there were 1,417, of which 735 were ready for action. This was not a large number for a nation marking time in the West while fighting a life and death campaign in the East. General Marshall was strongly of opinion that to compel the Germans to engage in air combat with the air forces of the Allies was the easiest and most effective method of reducing the strength of the *Luftwaffe*. To do so it would be necessary to lure that force by means of operations involving sea and land forces to some place where it would encounter the British and American fighter squadrons and suffer the consequences.

One further requisite for success was needed. The U-boats of Admiral Dönitz must be vanquished and the seas freed from their menace. For Allies separated from each other by thousands of miles of ocean, and compelled by the unalterable logic of geography to fight on exterior lines, the safety of seaborne communications was vital. U-boats must therefore be combated by every means, and wherever they were to be found—in the building yards, at their operating bases, on passage to their hunting grounds and in those grounds themselves. By 1943 attacks of this kind had long lost all elements of novelty. From the very beginning of the war they had been pressed but had never achieved a decision.

For dealing with German submarines two things were necessary—an increase in the activities of Coastal Command, and the intensified bombing of U-boat operational bases and the ports where they were being built or their prefabricated parts assembled. On these two points agreement in the Conference was general and immediate. Pride of place in the directive to the Allied bomber forces, drawn up by the Combined Chiefs of Staff on 21st January, 1943, and immediately approved by the Prime Minister and the President, was therefore given to attacks on 'German submarine construction yards'. This directive, one of the most important of the war, needs careful examination, since within its short compass an attempt was made to outline a programme for what amounted to the annihilation of the enemy and all his works and pomps. It was addressed to the appropriate British and United States Air Force Commanders and by them transmitted almost unaltered to those who were to carry it out. 'Your primary object', ran the instructions sent to Air Marshal Harris, Commander-in-Chief of Bomber Command, 'will be the progressive destruction and dislocation of the German military, industrial and economic system, and the undermining of the morale of the German people to a point where their capacity for armed resistance is fatally weakened'. That, as it were, was the general premise, and having stated it, the Chiefs of Staff then went into details. First in order of attack were the all-important German submarine construction yards. Next came German aircraft industry; the third in the chosen list was German means of transportation; the fourth, oil plants, synthetic or natural; the fifth and last, targets somewhat vaguely defined as situated 'in enemy war industry'. To amplify their instructions the Chiefs of Staff went on to give examples of objectives 'of great importance either from the political or military point of view'. Among these, as might have been expected, were first and foremost 'submarine operating bases on the Biscay coast'. 'If these', they averred, 'can be put out of action, a great step forward will have been taken in the U-boat war. . . . Day and night attacks on these bases have been inaugurated and should be continued, so that an assessment of their effects can be made as soon as possible. If it is found that successful results can be achieved, these attacks should continue whenever conditions are favourable for as long and as often as is necessary'. The second example was of greater political than operational significance. 'Berlin', ran the directive, '. . . should be attacked when conditions are suitable for the attainment of specially valuable results, unfavourable to the morale of the enemy or favourable to that of Russia'. Such were the instructions delivered to Air Marshal Harris and General Eaker. They deserve, and must be accorded, closer examination.

The directive was not a directive in fact at all but something even more important, a general statement of policy set down by the high personages responsible in the last resort for the conduct of the war. In drafting it they were dealing with a situation which was the opposite of stable. By invading North Africa a great effort had been made to increase the scale of the war on land. It was soon to be successful, and its success, though it did not become a fact until May, was, for all intents and purposes, assured in January when the directive was drafted. Moreover, the Germans had of late been hard hit. They had failed to take Stalingrad, the Russians were within fifty miles of Rostov, and most serious of all, the vital oil of the Caucasus was still uncaptured. Against this had to be set an increase in the U-boat campaign and the continued existence of a complex and highly organized industrial machine in Germany itself which, up till then, had been able to work almost unscathed and was capable of much greater efforts.

Faced with this state of affairs, it was not unnatural for those who had the ordering of the fight so to word their commands that not only could advantage be taken of a sudden development, but also that a balance might be struck between those who feared that, unless repeatedly and heavily attacked, the U-boats would gain the upper hand, and those who were convinced that blows, equally heavy or heavier, delivered against the cities and industries of the enemy, would prove decisive. Nevertheless, the mere issue of the directive led to momentous results. Henceforward the ever-increasing bomber strength of Britain and America would be used in combination and each force would play its designed part in the fulfilment of a common purpose. The Americans would carry out precision attacks by day, the British, area attacks by night, but the object of both was the utter destruction of German industrial power. How Bomber Command went forth to battle beneath the 'pitchy mantle' of night must now be told.

At the time the directive was issued, Air Marshal Sir Arthur Harris had been at the head of Bomber Command for not quite a year. He was an airman of very special qualifications and was well fitted to occupy the position, alike by training and temperament. Behind him lay more than a quarter of a century of experience, much of it gained in operating heavy bombers at night in conditions of both peace and war. The long years passed in his country's service had formed his will and matured his judgment. He knew his own mind, and though he did not always chose the best moment to do so, he could express it with force and freedom. An expert in his own profession he was impatient not of criticism but of any lack of a considered policy. His was the responsibility, and, as long as he was in command, he would take it and with it the consequences, whatever they might be. If a firm and consistent line was not, or could not be, taken in Whitehall, that was an annoying but not an insurmountable obstacle. He would persevere but in the last resort he would not forget that he, too, was a man subject to authority. Once it was clear to him that an order had been issued he would obey it without question and he did so. All his life through he had lived under discipline and knew what it could accomplish and what it could not. His very ruthlessness, offspring of Harris's fierce honesty of purpose and singleness of mind, drove him to demand the utmost of his crews, not once but again and yet again, while at the same time with equal vehemence he strove to move mountains on their behalf. When there was an opportunity to strike the enemy hard, he seized it; but every proposal to make use of them for purposes for which he considered them to be untrained, or which were in his view not such as to produce a result worth the risk, he vigorously opposed.

To this formidable man the grim opening words of the Casablanca Directive had the voice of a trumpet. 'At long last', he records, 'we were ready and equipped'[1]. He believed that in his Command he possessed not a mere weapon of war but the vital weapon, the weapon by which alone it could be won, and he intended to use it with all the skill and resolution of his stern nature and fierce heart.

By the end of April, 1943, Bomber Command had at its disposal thirty-six operational and two non-operational heavy squadrons and ten operational and four non-operational Wellington squadrons, a total of 851 heavy aircraft and 237 medium. These included the

---

[1] *Bomber Offensive.* Sir Arthur Harris (Collins).

contribution of the Royal Canadian Air Force, No. 6 Group, formed on 1st January, 1943. Pilots from the Dominions had been serving with the Command from the outset of the war, and by the beginning of that year amounted to more than one-third of the total number. Of these over half had been furnished by Canada. Harris was ready to commit them all to the attack, and he had already chosen the battlefield. It was to be the Ruhr.

Harris was all the more eager to assault this vital region of Germany because he had recently had little opportunity of doing so. A directive, which he had received in the middle of January, a week before that agreed upon at the Casablanca Conference, had chosen a very different type of target. Harris had obeyed. 'It was', he records, 'one of the most infuriating episodes in the whole course of the offensive', and he did not scruple to describe this decision as a misdirection of his force. His opinion was based on the conviction that no damage could be caused to the U-boat pens, for by then they had been completed and were covered with many feet of concrete impenetrable by any bomb then possessed by his force. All that it could achieve would be the devastation of the towns themselves, the destruction of workshops not under cover of the pens and of the hostels and other places of refreshment used by the U-boat crews on their return from a voyage. Bomber Command, Harris protested, should be used for a greater purpose. Such modest achievements as these were unworthy of its energies. But were they?

As far back as 12th October, 1942, the First Sea Lord had pointed out to the Chiefs of Staff that attacks on the bases in the Bay of Biscay were of great importance and had urged that the United States Eighth Army Air Force should be despatched against them. A month later, the First Lord renewed his naval colleagues' request. At this point the Prime Minister intervened. To attack the ports would, he said, undoubtedly cause casualties among their inhabitants, and those inhabitants were French. Public opinion in that unhappy country might well be stirred. This was also the view of the Chief of the Air Staff who maintained that the bombing of the submarine bases would have no effect except the destruction of old French towns. The First Sea Lord, whose main preoccupation was, quite rightly, the prosecution by any and every means of the campaign against the U-boats, remained unconvinced. The question was eventually submitted for decision to the War Cabinet. Three weeks passed and then, two days before Christmas, the War Cabinet made known its decision. Harris was to bomb Lorient, St. Nazaire, Brest and La Pallice in the order named and the directive instructed him to bring about 'the effective devastation of the whole area in which are located the submarines, their maintenance facilities, and the services, power, water, light, communications and other resources on which their operations depend'. The Admiralty had won its point. The U-boat pens might be impenetrable but the damage caused to the plant and installations situated outside their sheltering roofs might well hinder U-boat activities, even though it could not put an end to them. Casualties among French civilian workers would doubtless be caused and this would be very regrettable, but political considerations had to yield to the harsh demands of war.

As has been said, Harris received his orders on the morning of 14th January 1943. That same night, true to his training and philosophy, he put them into execution. Between that day and mid-February some 2,000 aircraft were despatched against Lorient. On the last night of February about 400 attacked St. Nazaire and the attack was repeated twice in the course of the ensuing month. The United States Eighth Army Air Force sustained the attack by day.

Six weeks later Grand Admiral Dönitz informed the Central Planning Office of the *Reich* that 'The towns of St. Nazaire and Lorient have been rubbed out as main submarine bases. No dog nor cat is left . . . nothing but the submarine shelters remain'. These, built by the Todt organization through 'the far sighted vision of the *Führer*' had suffered no damage. Harris's prophecy had proved true. Yet the rate at which U-boats could be repaired had certainly been diminished. A number of slipways had suffered severely; the water mains and electric current were unreliable and by the end of January the German commander on the spot reported that the capacity of the dockyard at Lorient was temporarily reduced by half. Such results, though not decisive, were not wholly negligible. Moreover, fearful for their U-boat bases, the German High Command hastily despatched reinforcements of anti-aircraft guns, and before long Lorient, St. Nazaire, Brest and La Pallice had each received four additional eight-gun batteries of heavy *flak*. The German U-boats continued to use these ports and, although Bomber Command had not entirely failed, the last word lay with Marschall, the German Admiral Commanding in the West, who reported that 'the British have not succeeded in their efforts to eliminate the bases'.

The pens had taken the Todt organization somewhat more than a year to construct. During most of that time they had been very vulnerable, for the heavy concrete roofs were not in position. Yet the pens were not attacked, and the Admiralty does not appear to have made any strong representation that they should be, but to have contented itself with pressing for the bombing, not of the bases where the pens were situated, but of the yards where new U-boats were under construction. The change of policy, when it occurred, came too late. Yet the Admiralty still continued to demand more attacks and seems at that time to have been influenced by an analysis of the German attacks on a number of English towns in 1940. These, so the experts averred, had they been prolonged, would have made it impossible for the factories of the towns to remain in production, for they would have been without gas or electricity. True, such services, though easily damaged, were easily repaired; but a prolonged assault must in the end not only put, but keep, them out of action. The same, *mutatis mutandis*, would be true in the Biscayan ports. Such reasoning made no appeal to Harris when it was applied to sea ports in France for they were not the centres of German industry; and when, on 4th February, he received the Casablanca Directive he felt that he had all the excuse he needed. Bomber Command would now be used not as a defensive weapon, part of the armoury employed to keep open the sea lanes, but in an offensive role against the vitals of the enemy. By the beginning of March, after two preliminary and fairly heavy attacks on Cologne, he felt himself free at last to begin anew the Battle of the Ruhr.

The target chosen was the most important within range from Great Britain. The industrial area of the Ruhr is, or was, the largest centre of heavy industry and coal-mining in Europe. Not only did it provide finished products of all kinds but also the raw material in the form of coal and steel which other industries in Germany needed for the production of war material. Its boundary on the north runs from Wesel to Hamm and is defined on the south by the valley of the Ruhr. On the west the Rhine is the main boundary, but along both its banks stretches a ribbon of industry and transport systems. The great river port of Duisburg-Hamborn at the junction of the Rhine and Herne canals is the western gateway. The heart of this comparatively small and highly compact region is composed of a coalfield lying at the foot of the lower Rhine hills and enclosed between the Lippe and Ruhr rivers.

The history of the Ruhr as an industrial concern began in 1838 and developed rapidly after 1846, when Friedrich Krupp, the founder of the most notorious firm of armament manufacturers the world has ever known, cast his first gun in a small forge in Essen. From that year onwards the Ruhr became Europe's principal producing area of coal, coke, iron and steel. The main area occupied by the metallurgical industries and coke ovens lies in the Bochum and Essen basins, and their presence in that region led to the wide development of other industries. Coal tar and gases from the coke ovens have for fifty years provided raw materials for the chemical industries, and the abundance of coal has led to the smelting and working of metals. But the main industry was, and always has been, the production of iron and steel. The huge works created for this object dominated Duisburg and Oberhausen, Mülheim and Essen, and it was in these towns, too, that the heavy engineering industries were concentrated. Of Germany's needs of coal for coke the Ruhr produced nearly three-quarters and more than sixty per cent of the total production of pig-iron and steel. Two-thirds of all high-grade alloyed steels, indispensable for the forging of a large number of weapons and the building of aircraft engines, came from the Ruhr, and Ruhr coal produced the oil manufactured in ten synthetic oil plants.

This huge concentration of industry in a comparatively small area provided its own means of defence, a screen composed of a natural haze increased by the belching smoke from hundreds of chimneys. It spread a dark pall over all the countryside and, even on a bright moonlight night, its presence made it almost impossible for the crew of a bomber to distinguish landmarks with certainty. To this half natural, half artificial defence, anti-aircraft guns and night fighters were added in abundance.

Such was the formidable target which in March 1943 Harris set out to destroy. Of all parts of it the most important and the most difficult to find was Essen, the business and commercial centre of the coal and iron industries of the Ruhr-Westphalia region. Here was situated the headquarters of the vast Krupps concern, the mining section of the United Steelworks of the Rheinische Coal Syndicate, the Rheinische Steelworks, and the headquarters of many other great firms. The Krupps undertaking produced not only iron, steel, coal and coke, but armaments of every kind, locomotives, tractors and mining machinery.

Here then was the target, its heart was Essen, and at the heart Harris determined to strike. He did so on 5th/6th March and for the first time made use of 'Oboe' on a large scale. The assault was planned with that attention to detail which, always a characteristic of the Command, was to develop as the war went on until it attained a very high degree of complexity and precision. The plan was for the bombs to be dropped from 2100 hours onwards. Eight Mosquitos fitted with 'Oboe' were to lead the attack and they were to be followed closely by twenty-two Pathfinders to act as 'backers-up'. The duty of the Mosquito group was to put down yellow target indicator flares along the line of approach and fifteen miles short of the target. The 'backers-up' were to maintain these pointers to the target by dropping more flares. Having released the yellow target indicators, the Mosquitos were to mark the aiming point—which on this night, as on others, was the centre of the vast Krupps works—with salvoes of red target indicators dropped in accordance with a closely calculated schedule. The first was to fall at Zero hour, the next three minutes later, the next ten minutes later, and so on until the last fell thirty-three minutes after the first. The 'backers-up' were to attack at intervals of from one to two minutes during this period, beginning two minutes after Zero hour and continuing for thirty-six minutes. They were to drop green target indicators and high explosive bombs in salvoes, aiming them at the red target indicators with a delay of one second before releasing the incendiaries.

Following the Mosquitos and 'backers-up' of the Pathfinder Force, the main force, led in its turn by Pathfinders and composed of 417 aircraft, was to attack in three sections. The first, composed of Halifaxes, would complete its attack in eighteen minutes and would finish twenty minutes after Zero hour. Section No. 2, made up of Wellingtons and Stirlings, was to begin the attack a quarter of an hour after Zero and maintain it for ten minutes. Section No. 3, the Lancaster force, was to come in twenty minutes after the first bomb had been dropped, and complete its task, like the Wellingtons and Stirlings, in ten minutes. Each crew of the main force was warned that the method of placing the red target indicators was new and regarded as very accurate. They were, therefore, to use their utmost endeavours to drop their bombs with precision upon them. If the red indicators could not be seen, then they were to bomb the green. Before the attack had been in progress for fifteen minutes no aircraft belonging to the main force was to bomb anything but the target indicators. The bomb loads were to be one-third high explosive and two-thirds incendiaries and of the high explosive bombs one-third again were to be fused for long delay with anti-disturbance mechanism.

Such was the plan. As will be seen it was complicated and depended for success on accurate timing. This was very largely secured, the first Pathfinder dropping its flares at two minutes to nine p.m., the last at thirty-eight minutes past. Of the main force, four aircraft of Section No. 1, the Halifaxes, attacked two minutes early and one a minute late; the remaining seventy attacked within the required period. Of the Wellingtons and Stirlings in Section No. 2 thirty-five attacked early, six late and one hundred on time. Of Section No. 3, the Lancasters, forty-three were ten minutes too soon and eighty-six timed their attack correctly.

As soon as the first red target indicator markers had been dropped, they were bombed by a number of aircraft belonging to the main force, and sticks of incendiaries were seen burning round them. The green target indicators which followed a few minutes later fell very accurately close to the red. The attack had been in progress no more than seven minutes when fires obtained a firm grip of the target, and this indication of success was soon confirmed by 'a tremendous explosion', after which 'fires increased in intensity and by the end the whole target area seemed covered with fire and smoke'. One observer reported that it was surrounded by an almost complete circle of flames, 'miles in diameter'.

The new method had brought about the necessary concentration, and at last the bombs were falling upon what it had been intended they should hit. All the later red target indicators were seen to enter the centre of the fire, except one cluster which, at half past nine, fell to the south-west, an error due to a technical defect in the 'Oboe' mechanism carried by one of the Pathfinder aircraft. Towards the end of the raid two more large explosions were observed and, by the time the last attacker turned on its way home, the Krupps undertaking was filled with fires and craters.

That night an area somewhat larger than 160 acres was laid waste, by far the greater part of it by fire. In the main group of Krupps buildings, fifty-three separate shops were damaged and thirteen destroyed or put virtually out of action. Three coalmines, a sawmill, an iron foundry and a screw works also suffered severely. The plants of the Goldschmidt Company, smelters and makers of sulphuric acid, and of the Machinenbau Union were partly gutted. The power station, gasworks and the municipal tram depot suffered a like fate, as did the goods yard of the Segerth suburban station. Seven hundred houses, blocks of flats, offices and small business premises in or near the centre of the town were utterly destroyed and 2,000 more rendered uninhabitable. A number of hutted camps housing the slave workers of Germany were almost entirely wiped out. The public buildings which suffered very extensive damage, mostly from fire, included the Town Hall, the Exchange, the town baths, four buildings of the Post Office, an enclosed market, nine churches, five schools and a theatre.

Of all this damage, the most satisfactory was that which occurred in the shops devoted to the stamping of sheet metal, to annealing, and to the production of gun parts, pneumatic tools, excavators and gun turrets. Interference with the public services—gas, water and electricity—was less severe, but the main gasometer of the city was never used again and most householders or flat dwellers were without gas for from three to twenty-five days. The principal factories, however, received their full supply of electricity within a very short time.

Such were the main results of a raid carried out by 442 aircraft, of which 367 reached the target. Of those which did not, forty-eight failed to take off owing to some technical defect. The losses from enemy action were light, no more than fourteen. Of these four were shot down by *flak*, five fell to fighters and five disappeared and were entered in the column 'missing, causes unknown'. 'J for Jig' of No. 196 Squadron and 'L for Love' of No. 466 Squadron, Royal Australian Air Force, collided over the North Sea on the way to Essen. Both aircraft were damaged but one held on and reached the target and both returned safely to base. 'Z for Zebra' of No. 429 Squadron, Royal Canadian Air Force, crashed on take-off.

This raid on Essen on the night of 5th/6th March has been described in some detail because it marked a new stage in the development of Bomber Command, an important step forward which brought it nearer to its constant aim—greater precision of bombing. There ensued a pause of a week, then Bomber Command struck a second time at the same spot: 384 bombers attacked Essen for a loss of twenty-three of their number. The assault was repeated on a smaller scale on the night of 3rd/4th April by 348 aircraft, of which twenty-one were lost. When the last fire had been extinguished, 600 acres of the city had been devastated. The destruction in Krupps had been increased, and perhaps as many as half of the 300-odd buildings of the great works had been put, some temporarily, others permanently, out of action. A fourth raid, on the night of 30th April/1st May, inflicted what the Germans reported to be 'total' damage on gas, water and electricity in the Krupps works and very heavy damage on the steel foundry.

The effect on the enemy of these attacks on Essen was very great. 'We arrived in Essen before seven a.m.' runs an entry in Göbbels' diary for the 10th April. '. . . We went to the hotel on foot because driving is quite impossible in many parts of Essen. This walk enabled us to make a first-hand estimate of the damage inflicted by the last three air raids. It is colossal and, indeed, ghastly. . . . The city's building experts estimate that it will take twelve years to repair the damage'. It will be perceived that Göbbels did not spare his words. In a passage too long to quote, taking Field-Marshal Milch as his authority, he inveighs against the negligence of Göring and General Udet, whose sins of omission had been committed 'on a scale deserving to be commemorated by history'. There was little doubt in the mind of Göbbels, even at this comparatively early stage of our bomber offensive, that the situation was serious and that it would remain so for some time. He did not regard Milch, to whose technical opinions he deferred, as a pessimist; but he could not but note that one of the creators of the *Luftwaffe* saw the situation in a sombre light, and he was prepared to admit that, long before it became possible to retaliate effectively 'the English could lay a large part of the *Reich* in ruins, if they go about it the right way'. Such testimony, confided to the secrecy of a private diary, only a few days after the events upon which it comments took place, is of great significance. The Royal Air Force, despite the opposition of the *Luftwaffe*, had delivered a grievous blow upon the most sensitive part of Germany, and the prophecy made two years before that Bomber Command would 'deliver that overwhelming onslaught which will bring the enemy to his knees and then lay him prostrate in the dust of his own ruined cities' was on the way to fulfilment. Sharply criticized at the time, especially by those who still pinned their faith in the omnipotence of sea power, this forecast of the fate of Germany's cities, far from being mere bombast, was a year later seen to be no more than a statement of fact. The tumbling masonry, the roaring fires, the thin screams of the victims in the tortured town of Essen were phenomena soon to be repeated in an even more dreadful form throughout the length and breadth of Germany.

However much this consummation was devoutly wished at the Headquarters of Bomber Command, its achievement was to be a painful process. The first assault on Essen in the opening days of March had been very severe, but it will have been noticed that in number of aircraft despatched and in weight of tons dropped, the attacks had a tendency to grow lighter while our casualties tended to increase. The enemy, struck in a vital spot, was doing his utmost to protect himself. From that time onwards he steadily reinforced his anti-aircraft defence until *Luftgau VI*, though the smallest of the eight *Luftgaue* into which the Third *Reich* was divided, contained no less than forty per cent of the total number of heavy anti-aircraft batteries available. By the summer of 1943 he had increased his night-fighter force from 386 aircraft, at the end of January 1943, to 466. The manner in which they were handled shows the difficulties confronting the defence. It was in the hands of General Josef Kammhuber, who had first concerned himself with the problem at the end of 1940 when he had been given the command of a night-fighter division. He was an insignificant looking little man of about forty and very abstemious, for consumption of alcohol and tobacco in any quantity affected his health. In August 1941 his Division was extended into a *Fliegerkorps* and given the number twelve, and he himself was promoted Lieutenant-General. This Corps was in full operation when the Battle of the Ruhr began. It was comprehensive in character and by then included six night-fighter groups, three

U-BOAT PENS AT BREST

BEFORE AND AFTER—THE MÖHNE DAM

WING COMMANDER GUY GIBSON,
V.C., D.S.O. and bar, D.F.C. and bar

searchlight regiments and an air reporting battalion, whose duties corresponded to those of the Royal Observer Corps. The total number of fighters was therefore in the neighbourhood of 460. They formed the pinnacle of a pyramid—that at least was the opinion of the unhappy General who commanded them—which at the base consisted of ground organizations which, in his view were heavily overstaffed.

Night fighters, for the most part Ju.88's and Me.110's, were controlled from the ground and, when airborne, were sent to circle the radio beacons set up in a long chain stretching from Jutland southwards to Brest. The aircraft worked in pairs, fighter No. 1 being directed by the operators of the *Würzburg* detector, a radar device for picking up attacking aircraft, while fighter No. 2 continued to circle the medium frequency beacon at the reported height of the attacking bombers. When contact had been established by fighter No. 1, he was released from ground control, which switched to fighter No. 2. As soon as the attack, successful or not, had been delivered the night fighter returned to his beacon and continued to circle it. If, however, when so doing, the pilot caught sight of a hostile bomber, his orders were to attack it at once. Wireless silence was maintained except when the aircraft was answering specific questions put by the fighter control officer on the ground. Night fighters who approached the anti-aircraft 'boxes'—areas in which the guns were concentrated so as to cover a fixed section of the sky—were required to fly above 18,000 feet to avoid interfering with their own *flak*. The main 'boxes' were situated in Holland and north-west Germany at Juist, Wangerooge, Cuxhaven and Heligoland. The success of these beacons, round which the night fighters flew, was limited by the range, which for some time was not more than twenty kilometres. This was gradually increased until double that distance could be covered.

The tactics of the German night-fighter pilots were simple and often effective. They carried out their search as directed from the ground, flying at a slightly lower height than the estimated height of the bomber. They were thus searching from below and their gaze was turned upwards in the hope of seeing the dark silhouette of the bomber against the night sky. On seeing their prey they flew ahead of it, climbed and then dropped back to a position above and astern. They then dived to attack, fired and broke away sharply. The range on a dark night was about 100 yards and sometimes as short as thirty-five. On a lighter night it increased to 200. Such tactics were countered by the pilots of Bomber Command by putting their aircraft into a corkscrew flight when the presence of night fighters was known or suspected. This method of evasion would, it was hoped, make it difficult for the night fighter to keep his sights on the target. At the beginning of the corkscrew twist, if the bomber moved toward the night fighter coming in to attack, the mid-upper gunner obtained a good view of the fighter and had therefore an opportunity to open fire. The success of these tactics varied and, as will be seen from the evidence of German pilots quoted in Volume III (Chapter 1), was very far from assured.

Though in 1943 the German night fighter and *flak* defences of the Ruhr were not so highly developed as, with the introduction of a number of radar devices, they later came to be, they were nevertheless far from ineffective. The Battle of the Ruhr was fought with mounting casualties and in the teeth of an opposition steadily growing in strength and skill. Nevertheless it was pressed with the greatest vigour. Between the night 5th/6th March when it opened and 28th/29th June, twenty-six major attacks were delivered on targets in or near the Ruhr. To these must be added three attacks on Berlin, four on Wilhelmshaven, two each on Hamburg, Nuremberg and Stuttgart, and one each on Bremen, Kiel, Stettin, Munich, Frankfurt and Mannheim. All these were made before the end of April. In all, from the beginning of February 1943 until the end of June, Bomber Command was out in force on fifty-two nights—nine in February, thirteen in March, nine in April, eleven in May and ten in June.

In the Ruhr the next town after Essen to suffer assault on a considerable scale was Duisburg, site of a great part of German heavy industry, and a great inland port 'with its complex of industrial satellite towns, rolling mills, etc.' It was attacked five times during the battle and received 5,157 tons of bombs, the two most severe attacks being on the nights of 26th/27th April and 12th/13th May.

Düsseldorf, 'the leading commercial city of Western Germany', was of special importance, for in it was housed the general administrative departments of almost all the important 'iron and steel, heavy engineering and armament concerns of the Ruhr and Rhineland'. The first attack, carried out on the night of 25th/26th May, was not very successful. The second, delivered on 11th/12th June by 693 aircraft, took place in good weather and a strong concentration on the aiming point was achieved. So large were the fires kindled on that occasion that the air raid precautions services in the city were overwhelmed. Photographs showed very great damage, particularly in the engineering works and railways, and some buildings were still smouldering a week later.

Of other attacks during this battle, it is necessary to mention that delivered upon Wuppertal-Barmen on the night of 29th/30th May. The Mosquitos directed by 'Oboe' were not very successful but the thirty-four 'backers-up' and forty-four Lancasters which followed them were able to keep the target marked with ground flares and incendiaries. They performed their task with efficiency, and the main force, in great strength, dropped their bombs in precisely one hour. The results were some of the most remarkable achieved throughout the course of the battle. Nine-tenths of the built-up area attacked was devastated; about 2,450 of the inhabitants lost their lives and a somewhat larger number were seriously injured. At dawn 118,000 found themselves without homes and 34,000 housing units were made uninhabitable.

On this raid 534 bombers were equipped with the navigational aid 'Gee' and most of them were able to use it on their outward and homeward journey, although the distance to the target was 360 miles. Sixty aircraft were damaged by *flak*, six by our own incendiaries when over the target, and thirty-three did not return. When recrossing the North Sea the bombers were subjected to seventy-six attacks, for the German night-fighter defence made great efforts that night and claimed twenty-two victims. They fell to the *Geschwader* operating mainly from the Gilze and Venlo districts of Holland, whose reputation for efficiency was enhanced. Thus, by the end of June, 34,705 tons of bombs had been dropped by Bomber Command on the Ruhr for the loss of 628 aircraft—totals which do not include minor operations.

Two more attacks, one of them outside the Ruhr, made during this period, must be mentioned. On 28th/29th June 540 bombers made a 'blind' attack on Cologne, flying there on 'Gee' and bombing beacons and sky markers dropped by 'Oboe'-directed Pathfinders. The industrial district east of the Rhine and the northern area, including the railways, were badly damaged. It was almost certainly in this raid that the main railway station suffered especially severely, though Cologne Cathedral, only a few hundred yards away, by some extraordinary chance received no major hurt. The other attack, by only nineteen aircraft, was of special importance alike because of the target chosen and of the skill shown by the crews. It had long been determined to add water as well as fire and high explosive to the list of plagues scourging the Ruhr. On the night of 16th/17th May this intention was fulfilled by Wing Commander Gibson, who set out with his Squadron to destroy the Möhne, Eder and Sorpe dams. The Möhne dam controlled the level of the river Ruhr, and the lake which its construction created had a surface of over ten square kilometres and a maximum depth of water of 105 feet. It contained over 130 million tons of water, which were used to supply pumping stations and electric plants in the Ruhr, the quantity available being sufficiently great to enable the supply to be maintained even in periods of drought. To breach the dam meant the release of this water, which, gushing through the valley of the Ruhr would not only cause widespread, possibly disastrous, flooding, but would also affect electricity supplies in the most highly industrialized area possessed by the enemy. The wall of the dam was composed of limestone rubble masonry twenty-five feet thick at the top and 112 feet at the bottom. A series of arched openings pierced the crest to allow the water of the lake to flow out over an apron. At the foot of the dam was a 6,000 kilowatt power station. The Eder dam, of similar construction, had been built to control the River Weser and prevent flooding in the great areas of Westphalia. It was even stronger than the Möhne dam and controlled more water. The Sorpe dam was of different construction but also of great importance. To cause the greatest amount of damage it was necessary to attack the dams when the dry season was at hand and when, therefore, they would be full. The ideal date was found to be the night of 16th/17th May when the water in the Möhne dam would be only four feet from the top.

As soon as the decision had been made, special and urgent preparations to ensure the success of the operation were put in hand. A new squadron, No. 617, marking letters AJ, was formed, attached to No. 5 Group, Bomber Command, and based on Scampton. The command of it was given to Wing Commander Guy Penrose Gibson,[1] later to be killed in action on 19th September, 1944, over München-Gladbach, and he was allowed *carte blanche*, the only stipulation being that all should be ready by 10th May. Gibson, a man of the highest resolution and ability, formed the squadron on 20th March and training began five days later. By the stipulated date the twenty-one picked crews, chosen by himself, were each able to fly long distances at a height of 150 feet or less, and to bomb with a margin of error of not more than twenty-five feet from a height of only sixty feet. To reach this pitch of professional skill they had flown 2,000 hours and dropped some 2,500 practice bombs. The weapon they were to carry with them was of a special type designed by B. N. Wallis, a scientist in the employ of Vickers-Armstrong's, who with Gibson had worked out the very special manner in which it would have to be dropped to make the necessary breach in the dams. Numerous experiments showed that the casing of these mines broke to pieces if they were dropped from a height even as low as 150 feet.

[1] His own account of the raid was published after his death in his book *Enemy Coast Ahead* (Michael Joseph).

Wallis and Gibson were almost in despair when, only a fortnight before the operation, they found that, dropped from 60 feet, the mines remained intact. To fly a four-engined heavy bomber of a total weight of some 63,000 pounds, which included a bulky weapon, at a height so low as this over calm water and in the uncertain light of the moon, required skill of the very highest order. To make certain that that height would be maintained at the moment of the mine's release, two small searchlights were fixed, at the suggestion of Mr. Lockspeiser of the Ministry of Aircraft Production, to the wing tips of each Lancaster. They were set at an angle and, when switched on, their beams intersected at a point exactly sixty feet below the aircraft. To maintain that height it was necessary for the pilot to fly so that the point of intersection rested on the surface of the water. This device was known as the spotlight altimeter calibrator.

By 15th May all was ready. The crews were practised, the route chosen, the models of the dams studied, the mines (still warm from the filling factory, which had placed a special explosive within their skins) were fused and in position, the weather forecast was favourable. As dusk fell, one by one the great aircraft climbed slowly into the air, for they were heavy-laden. 'After they had gone, Lincoln was silent once more; the evening mist began to settle on the aerodrome'.

The attack, carried out by nineteen aircraft, was made in three waves. The leading wave, led by Gibson, attacked first the Möhne dam, then the Eder. The objective of the second wave was the Sorpe dam and the third wave acted as a flying reserve. All aircraft were fitted with very high frequency radio telephone so that each could speak with the other. Flying very low on courses carefully chosen to avoid *flak* positions, especially those in the Western Wall, the first two waves crossed the coast of Holland simultaneously. Eight of the first wave reached the dam, one being shot down on the way. Gibson at the controls of his Lancaster led the attack. 'As we came over the hill', he records, 'we saw the Möhne lake. Then we saw the dam itself. In that light it looked squat and heavy and uncomfortable'. After circling for some time to make sure that he would take the best line of approach Gibson dived down to sixty feet under a brisk fire from two *flak* towers, and approached the dam at 240 miles an hour. The spotlight altimeter calibrator, thrusting down its beams, provided a mark for the very active German gunners, but they were soon vigorously engaged by Gibson's rear gunner, Flight Lieutenant Trevor Roper, who that night fired 12,000 rounds. At precisely the right moment Pilot Officer Spafford released the mine and a few seconds later 'a great thousand feet column of whiteness' rose from the lake. Its surface became instantly disturbed and this delayed the subsequent attacks, for the mines could only be dropped in calm water. The Lancaster flown by Flight Lieutenant Hopgood, who made the second attack, was hit, crashed, and his mine fell on the power house beyond the dam, destroying all the telephone communications. Three other aircraft dropped their mines successfully, while the gunners in Gibson's Lancaster, flying up and down the dam, sprayed the defences with fire and presently mastered them. By now the air was full of spray created by the explosions and a mist had settled upon the wind-screens of the attacking aircraft. Peering through the mist, it seemed to Gibson's straining eyes that the dam still stood unshaken. Then, as he turned to fly yet once more along it, he heard someone shout, 'I think she has gone, I think she has gone'. He looked down, and saw the water of the lake, 'like stirred porridge in the moonlight, rushing through a great breach'. In a few minutes 'the valley was beginning to fill with fog and . . . we saw cars speeding along the roads in front of this great wave of water which was chasing them. . . . I saw their headlights burning and I saw the water overtake them, wave by wave, and then the colour of the headlights underneath the water changing from light blue to green, from green to dark purple until there was no longer anything except the water bouncing down'.

Back in the Operations Room at Grantham the Air Officer Commanding-in-Chief, Bomber Command, the Group Commander, and Wallis, awaited the signal for success. At last it came. The listening operator reported picking up the word 'Nigger',[1] the agreed code word, whereupon Harris and Wallis leapt to their feet in unrestrained relief.

His task accomplished at Möhne, Gibson, at the head of the three aircraft still with their mines on board, went on to the Eder dam. The mines were laid one by one, one of them detonating on the parapet of the dam and destroying the aircraft which had dropped it. Two breaches appeared 'causing a wall of water about thirty feet high to sweep down the valley'. The attack on the Sorpe dam was less successful, but considerable damage was caused. The attacks on the secondary targets, the Lister and Schwelme dams, failed.

On his return Gibson was awarded the Victoria Cross. For the loss of eight aircraft and fifty-four highly trained and gallant men, a heavy blow had been dealt the enemy. On that night the warden of the dam, *Oberförster* Wilkening, finding the main telephone lines out of action, ran wildly to the nearest railway station on the Ruhr-Lippe line and rang up headquarters at Soest. He reported that an immense flood wave twenty-five feet high, moving at a speed of six

[1] Nigger was the name of Gibson's dog, run over and killed just before his master took off on the operation.

yards a second, was pouring through the dam down the Möhne and Ruhr valleys. The *Regierungspräsident* at Arnsberg, in control of Westphalia, was powerless, and spent some time issuing orders which, since they reached no one, could not be obeyed. All lights were extinguished, operators in the candlelit telephone exchange sought to send out flood warnings, but already the water had submerged the lines. The police at Neheim, however, received the message; but since most of the inhabitants were in the air raid shelters, for the sirens had sounded on the approach of Gibson and his men, it proved impossible to tell the people in time. This accounts for the high death roll of 499 Germans, 718 foreign workers and 1,012 head of livestock. The floods spread to the bottom of the Ruhr valley, and overran the district round Schwerte and Hattingen. The Eder valley was in the same case, for both the Möhne and the Eder lakes were emptied. At Bringhausen the storage power station was inundated and Affoldern was under water as was the Wabern and Felsberg district, sixteen miles from the dam. Part of the town of Kassel remained submerged for several days. Many hydro-electric installations, including a large power house on the Möhne itself, were destroyed or heavily damaged. Waterworks and purification plants all along the Ruhr were put out of action for some time, the main line between Hagen and Kassel was washed away and half the station at Fröndenberg completely wrecked. Of the ferro-concrete bridge at Neheim not even the piles remained, and the iron bridge at the same place was washed a hundred yards downstream. Damage to industrial undertakings was extensive, that caused by mud being difficult to repair quickly. Seventy per cent of the harvest and all the root crop was destroyed over a wide area. Seventy-nine houses vanished completely and more than 400 others were damaged more or less severely. It is not surprising that Göbbels had to record in his diary that 'the attacks of British bombers on the dams . . . were very successful. . . . Damage to production was more than normal . . . the *Gauleiters* in all *Gaus* containing dams which have not yet been attacked are very much worried. . . .'

The worst damage of all, and that which Bomber Command had been most anxious to inflict, was caused to the water supply system. The water behind the Möhne dam served the needs of about four and a half million people. Its escape halved the amount available for them, a most serious matter in so highly industrialized an area. Of this the Germans were well aware, and very strenuous efforts were made to repair the dam as quickly as possible. Nineteen thousand cubic metres of concrete washed away or displaced by the bursting of the waters were replaced by the end of September, but the dam was not fully repaired until August 1944. By then its defences had been immensely strengthened to guard against further attacks by similar weapons. 'The next time the dam is attacked', reported *Hauptmann* Freisewinkel, the Officer Commanding its defences, 'I shall be rewarded either with the *Ritterkreuz* or the guillotine'. He had successfully slammed the door of the stable long after the horses, in this case the sea—or rather the lake—horses, had bolted.

Nevertheless, consideration of the evidence available after the war must lead to the conclusion that the damage caused, though great, was not decisive; industry in the Ruhr received a heavy, but by no means a mortal blow. To have dealt this it would have been necessary to breach every dam in the district, especially that at Sorpe. Working literally like beavers, the Germans carried out repairs in a space of time short enough to avoid a disaster.

The damage caused by Gibson and his gallant crews, added to that inflicted upon Essen, Dortmund, Duisburg and the other centres of production in the Ruhr, was by July, 1943, deemed sufficient to warrant a change of target. Moreover, towards the end of the Battle of the Ruhr, the casualties sustained were beginning to rise in a disquieting manner. On 10th June, the Air Ministry noted that the 'increasing scale of destruction being inflicted by our night bomber force and the development of the day bomber offensive had forced the enemy to deploy day and night fighters in increasing numbers on the Western Front'. This was indeed so. Their number had steadily increased and together with the augmented ground defences they were taking such toll that both the United States Eighth Air Force and Bomber Command were in grave jeopardy. Their offensive was, in fact, in the balance. Faced with this situation the Combined Chiefs of Staff decided that in the first instance German fighter forces and the industry upon which they depended should be eliminated. For this purpose they presently issued what was soon known as the Pointblank Plan. Bomber Command prepared to redouble its efforts and now a new weapon came into play. At long last Harris was allowed to make use of 'Window', the code name for strips of metallized paper of various lengths and sizes, which, dropped in showers of silver rain, prevented radar instruments from tracing the course of the attackers. With this device Bomber Command set out upon the next phase of the campaign. This time its objective was the huge seaboard town and port of Hamburg.

Before what befell that city is described, how the air forces fared far away in the south over the barren hills and fertile groves of Sicily must now be set down.

MMAND, 1942—1943

CHAPTER XIV

Now These Things Befell In Sicily

WHILE Bomber Command was seeking to prove that a new form of warfare, first waged by the Zeppelins of Kaiser Wilhelm II a generation before, might, by its direct impact on the general population of the enemy, be able to achieve what had formerly been accomplished by armies and navies, the Allies pressed on with the policy decided upon at Casablanca. The Combined Chiefs of Staff had agreed that Sicily, the stepping-stone to Italy, should be invaded during 'the favourable period of the July moon'.

A Combined Special Planning Staff was established in a High School on the outskirts of Algiers, and here the invasion, to which the code-name 'Husky' was given, was planned. The task was to be entrusted to General Montgomery and the Eighth (British) Army and General Patton and the Seventh American. The naval forces were to be under Admiral Cunningham, and Air Chief Marshal Tedder was to command the combined air forces. The Deputy Commander-in-Chief to Eisenhower was to be Alexander, who, occupied as he was with the critical battles which brought the North African campaign to its conclusion, was not able to review the labours of the planners until the end of April.

The island of Sicily has been compared to a 'jagged arrow-head with the broken point to the West'. Within its area of about 10,000 square miles are many peaks of over 3,000 feet, separated or surrounded by plains of which the largest lies south and west of Catania and is dominated by the volcano of Etna. All round the coast, save for a short stretch to the north, runs a narrow strip of low-lying country traversed by a circular highway ringing the island. The main ports are Messina in the north-east, Palermo in the north and Catania and Syracuse in the east. To capture one or more of them was the first essential step and this in turn depended on the extent and amount of cover which could be provided by the air forces employed. Messina, the largest port, was beyond the range of fighters based on Malta and Tunisia and was, moreover, heavily defended. An assault on Catania could be given cover from the air only at extreme range, but its capture would ensure for the Allies the use of the main group of airfields in Sicily. On the other hand, its unloading facilities were not large enough to maintain more than four, or at the most six, divisions, and the second main port, Palermo, would in the view of the planners also have to be captured.

Next, and indeed of equal importance, were the airfields of Sicily. Of these the Germans and Italians had originally constructed nineteen, a number which had risen to thirty by the time the Allied assault was launched. They were grouped in the east, south-east and west of the island and were all within fifteen miles of the sea. The most important were those forming the eastern group between Catania and Gerbini, and their capture would make it impossible for the enemy's air forces to maintain themselves on the island. They would have to retreat to Naples and Brindisi, some 200 miles away, for the three airfields in the 'toe' of Italy were too small for use except as advanced landing grounds.

In considering his plans, Alexander thought first, as a modern general must, of the probable situation in the air. 'From our bases in Malta and Tunisia', he reports, 'we could give air cover over the southern half of Sicily, south of a line running from Trapani to Catania. . . . These two places, however, were near to the limit of effective air action. The plan, therefore, provided for an early attack on all three groups of airfields, but at the cost of a loss of concentration'. Such an attack would have to be made by seaborne invaders from Africa. Where they should land was the first and most important point. The vital spot was presently seen to be Avola, a small town on the east coast in the centre of the Gulf of Noto. Failure to seize this place would make it impossible to capture the ports of Syracuse, Augusta and Catania, and therefore to overrun the airfields. To provide a force large enough for so great an enterprise was, however, a matter of difficulty, especially when Tedder made it clear that Ponte Olivo 'the airfield centre inland from Gela' had to be taken if our air forces were not 'to labour under an intolerable situation'. Alexander was thus faced with a considerable problem. He must make sure of capturing both the airfield and the ports. How could he do so?

The matter was discussed at a conference on 29th April, at which General Leese, on behalf of the Eighth Army, argued that the destination of the assault should be changed and that it should fall entirely on the east coast of the island so as to ensure the capture of the Pachino Peninsula. To this proposal Tedder raised strong objections. This plan, he said, would leave thirteen landing grounds in enemy hands, far too many to be effectively rendered harmless by attack from the air with the forces at his disposal. Faced with these two opinions, both sound and both irreconcilable, Alexander did not hesitate to change his plan. Abandoning the original design to capture Palermo at an early stage, he decided that both armies, British and American, should assault side by side in the south-east of the island. In taking this decision he ran a grave risk; for, though the airfield at Ponte Olivo would thus be captured, no port large enough to supply both armies would fall into his hands immediately. The Seventh (American) Army would have, therefore, to be supplied entirely across open beaches and the Eighth (British) Army from two small ports of which one, Syracuse, was no more than a naval anchorage. Alexander showed himself to be a bold commander, for, it should be remembered, at that time the enemy was expected, by both Eisenhower and Montgomery, to resist desperately. Could the momentum and vigour of the assault be adequately sustained by supplies brought in in this manner? For two reasons Alexander believed that they could: the weather in July would probably be favourable, and his armies would have at their disposal a newly invented amphibious vehicle, the D.U.K.W., inevitably christened the 'Duck' as soon as it appeared. Thus he showed himself prepared to 'take a calculated administrative risk for operational reasons', the chief of which being the need to capture a group of airfields without delay. Already the conditions in which warfare in the air had to be conducted were imposing themselves upon those prevailing on land and on the sea.

On 13th May, the day on which the German resistance in Tunisia came to an end, the final plan was approved by the Combined Chiefs of Staff. The operation was divided into five phases. The first covered the preparatory measures to be taken by the navy and the air forces 'to neutralise enemy naval efforts and to gain air supremacy'. The second phase, seaborne assaults, would be delivered just before dawn, helped by airborne landings, made 'with the object of seizing airfields and the ports of Syracuse and Licata'. In the third a firm base would be established from which assaults would be made upon Augusta, Catania and 'the Gerbini group of airfields'. The fourth and fifth phases were to come later and would result in the capture of the whole island.

In all five phases the combined air forces of Britain and America under Tedder's command were to play a major part. He was assisted by Air Vice-Marshal Wigglesworth, an officer of great experience, who had served with the Americans in the Northwest African campaign and was well accustomed to their methods of thought and action. Under these two, who were responsible for the general conduct of the fight in the air, were three executive air commanders—

Major-General Carl Spaatz, with Air Vice-Marshal Robb as his deputy, who was in charge of the Northwest African Air Forces taking a direct part in the operation: Air Chief Marshal Sir Sholto Douglas at the head of the Middle East Air Command: and Air Vice-Marshal Sir Keith Park commanding at Malta. The parts to be played by the forces under the command of Douglas and Park in the Sicilian invasion were, after a footing had been gained on the island, less direct than those which fell to the lot of Spaatz and his two chief subordinate commanders Coningham and Doolittle. Air Marshal Sir Arthur Coningham, with his United States deputy, Major-General Cannon, commanded the Northwest African Tactical Air Forces which consisted of the Desert Air Force under Air Vice-Marshal Broadhurst, the United States XII Air Support Command, led by Major-General House, and the Tactical Bomber Force commanded by Air Commodore Sinclair. Thus, Coningham had under his control all those Allied air forces destined to appear over the Sicilian battlefields in immediate or close support of the armies. Major-General Doolittle was in command of the heavy bombers of the Northwest African Strategic Air Force, which consisted of two American bomber wings and the Royal Air Force Wellingtons of No. 205 Group, and operated behind the lines of the enemy. The exploits of Doolittle in leading the first raid on Tokio, and in due course the still more famous raid on the oilfields of Ploesti, provide a pleasing contradiction to his name. To keep watch and ward over Allied sea communications was the task of the Northwest African Coastal Air Force under Air Vice-Marshal Sir Hugh P. Lloyd. Finally, there were the Dakotas of Troop Carrier Command under Brigadier-General Dunn, of the United States, and the Photographic Reconnaissance Wing commanded by Colonel E. Roosevelt.

Considering the number of commanders and the multiplicity of their headquarters dotted over thousands of miles between Malta and Algiers, the degree of unity and therefore of success attained can only be described as remarkable. A certain simplification was presently seen to be inevitable, and as the fight continued through Sicily on into Calabria and then up Italy, the Headquarters of the Northwest African Air Forces merged into those of the Mediterranean Air Command to become Headquarters Mediterranean Allied Air Forces. The speed of the process was unremarkable—more that of the transport Dakota than of the fighting Spitfire—but in the end the required degree of unity was achieved.

The number of squadrons available was 267 of which 146 were American and 121 British. The Americans predominated in heavy and medium bombers and transport aircraft, the R.A.F. was stronger in fighters and fighter-bombers.

A single Tactical Air Force, to which both Allies contributed, had been created and was to render support to two armies fighting side by side. Thus, though administered separately, the two air forces, like the two armies and the two navies, were operationally one. This union on a lower plane was the natural consequence of that achieved on a higher, when in the autumn of 1942 General Eisenhower had been the Allied Commander-in-Chief of the invasion of Northwest Africa. The unity of the two allies aimed at by this appointment and achieved among the stony hills of that inhospitable land, was accepted as a matter of course for the next adventure, and so in the subjugation of Sicily and Italy every plan made, every movement executed, every peril encountered, every triumph won was shared in equal measure by both Allies. For a proper understanding of the war in the air as it was fought over Sicily and Italy it is essential to remember that the two air forces formed a single whole. It is impossible therefore when describing their exploits to separate those of the Royal Air Force from those of the United States Army Air Force. Both entered the battle simultaneously and together under a command common to both; and each contributed to the victory a full share, according to its means.

To them, four main directives were issued. They were first and foremost to maintain 'sustained air operations' in order to paralyse or destroy the air force of the enemy. This essential task, which involved winning the battle in the air before those of the sea and land were begun, was to be performed in the period immediately preceding 'D Day'. Then, as soon as the convoys put to sea, they were to be given close cover from the air. Next, at the actual moment of the landings, which were to take place at eight beaches on the south-east corner of Sicily, their chief duty was to be the protection of ships lying off shore, and the assault by day and by night of the beach defences. Lastly, once the armies were firmly established on land, the air forces were to provide the closest co-operation above and behind the battlefield until Sicily should fall to the Allies.

Even before von Arnim and Messe had surrendered in Tunisia, the first item of this fourfold programme was put into operation by the launching of a series of air attacks against the main enemy airfields in Sicily, Sardinia and southern Italy. They endured for six weeks and throughout this period the Strategic Bomber forces kept the ports and submarine bases in the same areas under bombardment, sought to cut the ferry services in the Strait of Messina and attacked industrial targets in Naples and Bari. To this series of assaults must be added the six attacks made by Bomber Command from bases in the United Kingdom against targets in the north of Italy.

These preliminaries were also marked by two special and necessary operations, the capture of Pantelleria and Lampedusa—two fortified islands lying in the path of those who would invade Sicily from Africa and providing airfields, from which fighters could operate, and valuable radar detection facilities. Pantelleria has been described as the 'Italian Heligoland'. A forbidden zone since 1926, its defences by 1943 were formidable, at least on paper. Rocky and barren, its volcanic soil was sown like the field of Ares with dragon's teeth, in this instance anti-aircraft guns, and, beneath the surface, underground hangars, impervious, it was claimed, to bombs, had been constructed. The garrison were well provisioned and with ample supplies of water. Nevertheless, after sustaining for five days, between the 7th and 11th June, a continuous series of attacks delivered by heavy, medium, light and fighter-bombers, they showed themselves to be in no mood to fight. By the evening of 8th June, the principal batteries to the north of the island had been gravely damaged, and by the morning of the 11th, all the northern defences had been destroyed. A bomb had even been successfully 'skipped' into the entrance of an underground hangar, where it failed to explode—very fortunately, as it turned out, since the hangar was soon one of those in constant use by our air forces after the fall of the island.

The demoralization of the enemy was completed by the dropping of 695 tons of bombs by the heavy bombers of the American Strategic Air Force and by a bombardment carried out by units of the Royal Navy, aided at night by Albacores of the Fleet Air Arm, which dropped flares. On the morning of 11th June, units of 3rd Infantry Brigade Group landed under the cover of heavy air attacks and soon after midday the commander of Pantelleria sent a wireless message to Malta offering to surrender. The offer being accepted, some 11,100 Italians and 78 Germans became prisoners of war. Though the bombing had pulverized the town and harbour, the underground galleries and tunnels had protected the inhabitants and the garrison, whose casualties had, therefore, been few. So bemused, however, were they by the quantity of high explosive which had fallen upon them that no demolitions had been carried out although extensive preparations to do so had been made. Large stocks of stores accordingly fell intact into our hands.

After Pantelleria, it was the turn of Lampedusa, a much smaller island, only fourteen square miles in extent, to be subjected to the new form of combined air and sea attack. On 12th June it received 268 tons of bombs besides numerous shells from bombarding ships of war. Long before the attackers drew off its small garrison was fully prepared to surrender, and the unexpected arrival during the afternoon of 'P for Percy', an Air/Sea Rescue Swordfish, which had been compelled by a defective compass and empty fuel tanks to land upon the airfield, prompted the Italian commander, resplendent in 'leather jacket, shorts and high boots' with a Tyrolean hat set off by a huge plume upon his head, to come to immediate terms. Sgt. Cohen, the pilot of the Swordfish, accepted the surrender, refuelled with enemy petrol, took off, and landed near Sousse. On the evening of the 12th, the captain of a British destroyer completed the formalities and the still smaller islands of Linosa and Lampione surrendered a few hours later. The outposts of Sicily were in our hands a month before the assault was to be delivered.

These operations were mounted from bases in Northern Africa and also from Malta. For that island the wheel had come full circle. Set in the midst of an inland sea under the disputed control of the enemy for two long years, the life of its defenders had been hard. They had borne unflinchingly the insidious assault of hunger and the slings and arrows of bombing. Now, at long last, the Mediterranean was free again; supplies poured in, and by June 1943, Malta's capacity as a base for air forces had been enlarged beyond recognition. A new landing strip, rapidly constructed by American engineers on the neighbouring island of Gozo, added to the airfields available, the latest radar devices were installed and spacious fighter control and filter rooms hewn out of the rock. Malta, it was decided, should be the headquarters of Alexander and those with him who were to direct the invasion. It was accordingly provided with a combined war room, in which the constantly changing situation, on the ground, on the sea and in the air, was recorded hour by hour. That these intense preparations in a war-torn island were so swiftly wrought was due very largely to the energy of Keith Park, the Air Officer Commanding, and to the Works Department of the Air Ministry, whose men laboured with efficiency and despatch, crowding the work of months into weeks, of weeks into days, till all was prepared. As the summer slipped by, more and more aircraft, larger and larger quantities of stores arrived, until upon the eve of battle forty squadrons of fighters awaited the advent of 'D Day' upon Malta, Gozo and Pantelleria.

Arrayed against them was a mixed Italian-German force of about 1,850 aircraft possessing bases in Italy, Sicily, Sardinia and the south of France. Of these about 1,000 were serviceable at the beginning of July. The *Luftwaffe* was at a disadvantage. Not only had its strength in aircraft and spare parts dwindled, but the number of experienced pilots and ground crews captured in Tunisia had much reduced its efficiency. It had proved impossible to replace these 'old campaigners' by men of similar calibre and experience, for the demands of the Russian front were too high. To these tactical difficulties, strategic were added. With the whole of the North African coast, except that of Spanish Morocco, in Allied hands, the position of the Axis forces in Italy and Sicily had greatly deteriorated. For three years the peninsula and the island had linked North Africa with Germany and had provided bases from which the enemy operated by air and sea in the Mediterranean. Now all was changed, and Italy was a vulnerable tongue of land thrusting a still more vulnerable island into a sea daily falling more and more under the dominion of the Allied naval and air forces.

Most serious misfortune of all, perhaps, was the relations of the *Regia Aeronautica* and the *Luftwaffe*. Tactical co-operation between them had never been achieved, not even when their combined presence in the Mediterranean had encountered no serious challenge. No uniform system of air to air or ground to air signalling or of aircraft safety and weather reporting procedure had been introduced, far less enforced, and the ill-assorted partners had throughout shown a marked tendency to keep their own signal codes a closely guarded secret from each other. Only when the campaign was almost over and the situation desperate was any improvement made in this, the most important factor in the operation of a modern air force.

In other scarcely less important respects, co-operation was equally absent. Never cordial, the relations of the German Air Force with its Italian opposite number became more and more strained with every month of war. Long before the invasion of Sicily was under way, the suspicion and distrust of the Italians for their more energetic and ruthless northern Ally had reached a very high pitch. With Latin ingenuity they had created a bureaucratic machine 'of fantastic proportions', whose ponderous revolutions, when they occurred at all, occurred so slowly as to make the movement to an airfield of even a few tons of cement or coal an administrative operation of the first magnitude. All dealings with the *Luftwaffe* passed through the hands of Italian liaison officers, experts in the art of pin-pricking and procrastination. Not even the telephone would perform its office, and slow and fatiguing journeys by car had to take the place of a simple long-distance call.

Nevertheless, the Germans were nothing if not persevering. By the end of June, the quantity of Allied shipping discovered by air reconnaissance in Algiers and Bizerta, combined with the presence of landing craft at Tunis and Malta, pointed with ever-increasing certainty to the imminent invasion on a grand scale of Sicily, and possibly of Sardinia. *Generalfeldmarschall* Freiherr von Richthofen and his subordinate in Sicily, *Generalleutnant* Bülowius, hindered and obstructed though they were by their opposite numbers, General Ambrosio and his successor General Roatta, did their best to prepare for the forthcoming blow. *Luftflotte 2* was reinforced and General Peltz, a young, energetic and capable officer, afterwards to mount the attacks on London in the early months of 1944, known as the 'Little Blitz', was given command of all bomber units in the Italian theatre. Forsaking their bases in Sicily they established themselves on airfields in Apulia between Lecce and Foggia. The fighters remained in Sicily grouped, for the most part, on airfields around Catania and Comiso, hastily enlarged and camouflaged. The torpedo-bomber units, whose duty it was to attack Allied convoys, were transferred to the South of France, to which a number of fighter and reconnaissance units, badly needed in Sicily, had to be sent for their protection. Here the 2nd *Flieger* division was formed as a general reserve which could be sent westwards to the Bay of Biscay or eastwards for operations in the western Mediterranean and the Tyrrhenian Sea. One of its *Geschwader* (K.G. 100) was provided with two *Gruppen* of Dornier 217's, equipped to launch radio-controlled glider bombs. The long-range reconnaissance *Gruppe* was moved from Trapani to Frosinone on the mainland and the transport units were sent as far north as Florence and Pisa. A small force was sent to Sardinia.

To these preparations in the air were added the reinforcement of *flak* units and their deployment in new areas. The *flak* defences of the all-important Strait of Messina were strengthened by units from northern Italy and by the battered remnants of those which had escaped from Tunisia. They were to prove efficient and well served. An attempt to add a balloon barrage to the defence was defeated by the difficulty of obtaining the necessary balloons. More light anti-aircraft batteries were placed round the north Sicilian ports and the airfields and the men serving them attached to the *Flakkampftrupps* recruited from the anti-aircraft regiments and trained for special duties.

Thus did the enemy make ready for battle, the Germans stubbornly, the Italians without hope or heart. One advantage they did possess. The loss of Africa had made it possible to concentrate the forces available, and the German Air Force was now relieved of its heavy and unprofitable task of convoying shipping across the Mediterranean. In all other respects it was less fortunate. A constant watch had to be kept on the whereabouts and movement of Allied shipping, and the photographic reconnaissance at frequent intervals of Algiers, Tunis and Tripoli was of the highest importance. The only aircraft available for these duties were Ju.88's, which were far too slow, and in consequence their losses were heavy. In addition to reconnaissance, attacks had to be made on Allied shipping but not upon warships, for the *Oberkommando der Luftwaffe* (Supreme Command of the *Luftwaffe*) believed that these were a smaller threat to the German army than a merchant vessel laden with stores for troops. Having lost command of the air, the *Luftwaffe* could only attempt to fulfil this part of the programme at night, and this it tried its best to do by flying sorties of fifty to eighty aircraft in loose formation led by 'a master of ceremonies'. A certain success was achieved, and R.A.F. night fighters did not destroy more than five per cent.

By 1st July, the first part of the Allied air attack was over. For the next nine days the bombers of the Northwest African Air Forces turned their attention away from lines of communication to the forthcoming battlefield. Sicilian landing grounds were assaulted by heavy, medium and light bombers, and special attention was paid to the Gerbini airfield and its satellites, upon which, as has been said, the fighters of the *Luftwaffe* were mainly concentrated. By the morning of 'D Day' seven of these were unserviceable and Comiso, Bocca di Falco and Castelvetrano were in the same condition. These attacks, delivered by the Americans by day and by Wellingtons of No. 205 Group by night, provoked the defence, but only spasmodically, the principal engagement being fought on 5th July between United States Fortresses and about 100 German fighters. The scale of attack on communications was, during this period, reduced, not more than seventy-five Wellington sorties being flown against Palermo and twenty-six against Catania.

The effect on the enemy's airfields of the air assault in the period immediately preceding the invasion appears to have been very great. 'In the last few weeks before the landing', said Colonel Christ, Chief of the German Air Operations Staff in that theatre, 'all the aerodromes, operational airfields and landing grounds on Sicily were so destroyed in continuous attacks by massed forces that it was only possible to get this or that airfield in running order again for a short time, mainly by mobilising all available forces, including those of the German and Italian armies'. When 'D Day' came, the *Luftwaffe* appeared to be paralysed and unable to exercise any effect on the course of events.

The second part of the preparatory phase ended on 9th July. On that afternoon the great convoys, made up in all of some 2,000 vessels, began to arrive at their assembly areas east and south of Malta and then to move north. Those from the west were covered by the Northwest African Coastal Air Force, enlarged by the addition of a number of Beaufighter squadrons; those from the east were protected by fighter squadrons under the control of Air Headquarters, Air Defences Eastern Mediterranean. Each half of these covering air forces flew some 1,400 sorties in two days. Opposition was negligible—a few bombs on shipping in Bizerta harbour on the night of 6th/7th July. The Germans were conserving such strength as they possessed with intent to use it against the beaches and the vessels anchored off them.

As the ordered lines of ships moved northwards, the wind began to rise and the sea became choppy. It was a bad beginning to an enterprise which was to culminate in a landing at dawn, but the armada, by then irrevocably committed, sailed on. To none could the worsening weather do more harm than to the airborne forces who, in accordance with the general plan, were to land in advance of the seaborne invasion. They were composed of troops of the British 1st Airborne Division carried from bases in North Africa in gliders towed partly by the Northwest African Troop Carrier Command, flying Dakotas, and partly by the Albemarles and Halifaxes of No. 38 Wing, Royal Air Force. In addition to the glider forces, the U.S. 82nd Airborne Division were to be dropped in the Gela/Licata area by the same American Command. High wind is dangerous, often fatal, to an operation of this kind, and it was therefore in a mood of more than ordinary anxiety that General Alexander went down after dusk to Cape Delimara, the south-eastern point of Malta, to watch the gliders pass. 'As the tandem-wise pairs of tow and glider came flying low', his majestic prose records, 'now in twos and threes, now in larger groups, with the roar of their engines partly carried away by the gale and their veiled navigation lights showing fitfully in the half light of the moon, I took note that the first invasion of European soil was under way. On my right the quiet expanse of Marsa Scirocco waited for the Italian fleet, which two months hence was to anchor there in humble surrender'.

The airborne harbingers of the Eighth Army were carried in two types of gliders, the light Hadrian or Waco of which the maximum load was fourteen men and a handcart, and the larger Horsa which could carry thirty men within its plywood belly. The Horsas had been towed by No. 38 Wing from England to North Africa, a most difficult and hazardous undertaking. The squadron mainly concerned, No. 295, had had to fly within 100 miles of the enemy's air bases in south-western France, and to make the long journey in daylight, for the hazards of flying by night with a glider in tow over so great a distance were regarded as too great. It says much for the skill and determination of the pilots that by 7th July, twenty-seven out of thirty Horsas had reached North Africa. One which failed to do so landed in the sea, the Halifax towing it having been shot down by two Focke-Wulf Condors returning from a raid on an Atlantic convoy. The three glider pilots spent eleven days in a dinghy before being rescued. Major A. J. Cooper, another, had also to take to a dinghy when his Horsa fell into the sea after the tow rope had parted. After ten hours afloat he was picked up and within twenty-four was at the controls of another glider which he brought successfully to its destination.

The Horsas arrived at Kairouan only a week before they were due to take part in the invasion. The pilots of the Wacos had had three weeks' intensive training, during which 1,800 night flights had been carried out without serious casualty. This period of training was not long enough, especially for the American pilots of the tugs, and its shortness was the main cause of the high losses suffered.

The plan was for the 1st Air Landing Brigade of the 1st Airborne Division to land from gliders put down near Syracuse and seize the bridge known as Ponte Grande, south of the town and also its western outskirts. While they were taking these objectives, American parachute troops of the 82nd Division were to drop in the Gela/Licata area farther west. The Air Landing Brigade, comprising some 1,200 men, were conveyed to the battlefield in 137 gliders towed by Dakotas of the U.S. Troop Carrier Command and by twenty-eight Albemarle and seven Halifax aircraft belonging to Nos. 296 and 297 Squadrons of No. 38 Wing. Of the gliders, 127 were the Wacos; the remainder Horsas. This force took the air from six airfields in the neighbourhood of Kairouan. Owing to the difference in speed between the various combinations, the timing had to be carefully calculated. The course flown was to the south-east corner of Malta, then to Cape Passero at the south-east corner of Sicily, and then along the east coast of the island to the landing zone south-west of Syracuse. To avoid anti-aircraft fire the orders were that no combination should approach closer to the shore than 3,000 yards. Covering the aircraft bearing the airborne troops, night-flying Hurricanes of No. 73 Squadron, equipped with cannon, were to put out any searchlight which might be exposed. To distract the defences of the enemy, fifty-five Wellingtons from No. 205 Group were to attack targets in the Syracuse area, nineteen more to bomb Catania, and another nineteen, targets in the area of Caltanissetta and Caltagirone. It was during these attacks that dummy parachutists were dropped to create confusion among the defenders on the ground, an object successfully attained.

From the start the airborne operation showed itself to be one of great difficulty. The pilots of the Dakotas were lacking in experience and were not fully trained in flying at night. They were unused to *flak* and to handling in a high wind an aircraft towing a glider. Though the weather moderated as they approached Sicily, conditions on arrival were far from ideal. They had to judge distance in uncertain moonlight, a difficult task even for very experienced pilots, and they had to do so flying at a low height, which gave almost no opportunity to correct errors. In the circumstances, it is not surprising that these were many, or that of the 137 gliders released, sixty-nine fell into the sea and fifty-six were scattered along the south-eastern coast of Sicily far from their appointed landing places. Only twelve reached the chosen landing zone, and all of them had been towed by the Royal Air Force. One, a Horsa, landed within 300 yards of the bridge, and its passengers made resolutely towards their moonlight objective. It was seized, and by dawn eight officers and sixty-five other ranks were holding the Ponte Grande. Repeated assaults by the enemy delivered throughout the morning and early afternoon failed to dislodge them until half past three, when the survivors, reduced to fifteen in number, were overrun. By then, however, the first elements of the Eighth Army were almost at hand and its advance guard at once retook the bridge which the Germans had not been able to destroy.

The remainder of the force, though it inflicted but little hurt on the enemy—a coast defence battery and two pillboxes were captured—created much alarm and despondency among the tepid ranks of the Italians, whose apprehensions were increased by the arrival over an area of some fifty square miles of the first contingent of the U.S. 82nd Airborne Division which was scattered for miles round Gela and Licata.

While the tugs and their gliders were battling with the high wind the seaborne expedition was moving steadily, if uncomfortably, towards the beaches.

At 4 a.m. on 10th July, 1943, the 5th, 50th and 51st Divisions of the Eighth Army, together with the 231st Brigade, landed at four places in the Gulf of Noto and on the extreme tip of Cape Murro di Porco, while the 1st Canadian Division went ashore upon their immediate left on the Peninsula of Pachino. To the left again the 45th Division, the 2nd Armoured Division, the 1st Division and the 3rd Division of the American Seventh Army assaulted four beaches in the Gulf of Gela. The landings, covered by a naval bombardment, were everywhere successful. Dawn broke upon a scene of amphibious vehicles 'scuttling through the shadows in line astern' followed by infantrymen wading breast deep through the swell, rifles and packs held high above their heads, and behind them, in a series of arcs, a great fleet of vessels ranging from the small landing craft making for the shore and the sand dunes, to their parents, the Infantry Landing Ships farther out, and beyond these the steel-clad men-of-war. The latest of many invasions of Sicily had begun, and the British and American troops, plodding through the shallows and clinging sand, took their place at the head of past invaders. Red-shirted followers of Garibaldi, blue-coated French and red-coated British Marines of Nelson and Napoleon's day, Alphonso's Spaniards, Frederick I's Germans, Guiscard's Normans, Saracens with curved swords, Roman Legionaries with square shields, Athenians with plumed helmets—each in turn had trodden this land, and before them, 2,500 years back from this the new invasion of her soil, Sicily had known the men of Carthage and of Tyre. The fight was to be upon historic ground.

Above the great concourse of ships sped Spitfires and Warhawks, their wings flashing in the first beams of day, the first of the 1,092 sorties flown that day on beach patrol. Most of these were flown by fighters operating from Tunisia, Malta, Gozo and Pantelleria, fighter cover being provided throughout the sixteen hours of daylight over at least two of the beaches in turn, and over all the landing areas for the first two hours of daylight, for two hours in the middle of the day and for two hours at dusk. The adoption of this plan was necessary, for though many more fighter squadrons were available to provide a much greater degree of cover, airfields from which they could fly were not. As matters turned out, the air cover proved more than adequate. In the first twenty-four hours only twelve ships were lost, one of them a hospital ship, although the plan of invasion had allowed for the sinking of 300. The *Luftwaffe* had been powerless to interfere with the landings.

As the day wore on it showed itself equally impotent to prevent the long series of attacks by Allied bombers and fighter-bombers on airfields, defensive positions and lines of communication. The Gerbini group of landing grounds were again assaulted by United States Fortresses, and Mitchells of the same air force attacked the western airfields of Sciacca and Milo. The marshalling yards of Catania were also bombed and the explosions observed showed that ammunition had been hit. To the attacks of the heavy and medium bombers, those of the American A.36's, dive bombers developed from the Mustang, were added.

All these attacks, together with the patrols over the beach-heads, cost the Allies no more than sixteen aircraft, of which eleven were fighters. The pilot of one of them provided an authentic version of the standard R.A.F. tall story which begins, 'There was I upside down at 20,000 feet'. In this instance, the pilot, seeking to fall from his Spitfire, which he had with some difficulty inverted, caught his foot beneath the instrument panel and hung upside down from a shattered aircraft about to plunge to destruction. With a great effort he disentangled himself, his parachute opened just in time, and he was able to make a safe, if prickly, landing in a patch of cactus.

From the outset success everywhere crowned the efforts of the sea-borne invaders. By early afternoon the whole peninsula of Pachino was captured and by sunset Syracuse had fallen. To the left the United States Seventh Army had seized Licata and was moving on Vittoria. When darkness fell, the protection of the beaches was assured by Beaufighters of No. 108 Squadron based on Malta and intruder Mosquitos of No. 23 Squadron. Their operations, which continued throughout the period of the invasion, were made much easier by the putting ashore of a Ground Controlled Interception Unit on the evening of 10th July, and the subsequent speedy extension of warning systems.

The first day had gone well. 'On our journey back to Berlin', says Semmler, a jackal of Doctor Göbbels, 'we heard at Erfurt at three in the morning that the enemy had landed in Sicily. Göbbels looked black and once again cursed our alliance with the "macaroni eaters"' His irritation was justified. They made little or no attempt to resist. In twenty-four hours all the beach-heads had been firmly established. The airfield at Pachino, which had been ploughed up, was being hastily prepared by Royal Engineers assisted by members of No. 3201 R.A.F. Servicing Commando Unit. Coming ashore immediately behind the assault troops they had established themselves on the morning of the 11th on its edge, and had hardly done so when a Spitfire of No. 72 Squadron piloted by Flying Officer D. N. Keith, out of petrol after shooting down two enemy aircraft, landed on the furrowed runway. It was refuelled, rearmed and dragged to a nearby road, from which the pilot contrived to take off, the first aircraft of the Royal Air Force to operate from the soil of Sicily.

Farther along the coast other servicing commandos were ashore at Gela, where presently they became involved in a German counter-attack delivered by the Hermann Göring Division supported by tanks. No. 83 Auxiliary Embarkation Unit was for a short time under heavy fire, but the broadsides of the navy and the resolute handling of the anti-tank guns already ashore, of which one was served in person by

General Patton, the Army Commander, broke up the assault. Apart from this small episode, the all-important ground staffs, though subject to the nuisance of sniping and an occasional bomb, were able to perform their tasks with rapidity and effect.

By 13th July the first Spitfire squadrons of No. 244 Wing arrived from Malta and were in operation. Three days passed and six more R.A.F. Spitfire squadrons had been installed at Comiso and six United States fighter squadrons at Licata and Ponte Olivo. 'Thereafter the transference of Tactical Air Force squadrons to Sicily in accordance with the Air Plan occurred at regular intervals, and full air support to our advancing land forces was continued without a break'.

The conditions in which the pilots lived were not unlike those to which they had been accustomed in the desert, though the countryside, spread with olives and fruit trees, was very different. The ground was too rocky to cut slit trenches and they bivouacked, therefore, in small sangars, breast high. The Mess was often a tarpaulin from a lorry, stretched above a long table set in an olive yard. Aircraft were dispersed in the groves of almonds nearby, and soon the ground crews could be seen in their off duty moments cracking with the blows of a stone the hard shell of the almonds to win enough to send a pound or two home to their families. One luxury everyone enjoyed. The orange crop had long been gathered, but lemons, grapes, melons, tomatoes and wine were all available in the friendly farm-houses, for the population, from the soldier, who had thrown away his rifle, to the ragged urchin whining for chocolate in the dusty streets of baroque Noto, was, with few exceptions, delighted to see them. This first, fine careless rapture did not long endure. As the days advanced, the weather became more and more sultry, and the brownish-white houses, with their faded red roofs, began to waver in the noontide sun. With the heat came dust, flies and fever. At one time a quarter of the officers at the headquarters of the Tactical Air Force were suffering from malaria or dysentery.

While the first fighter squadrons were arriving, a second airborne operation was launched with the object of capturing the important bridge of Primo Sole which carried the main road to Catania across the Simeto. The 1st Parachute Brigade of the 1st Airborne Division, together with a number of glider-borne anti-tank units and some Royal Engineers, were called upon to make the attack, and on the night of 13th/14th July they flew from Kairouan in 107 aircraft and seventeen gliders towed by Halifaxes and Albemarles. On this occasion the ships of the Royal Navy had been warned of their advent, but they were unlucky enough to arrive over the invasion

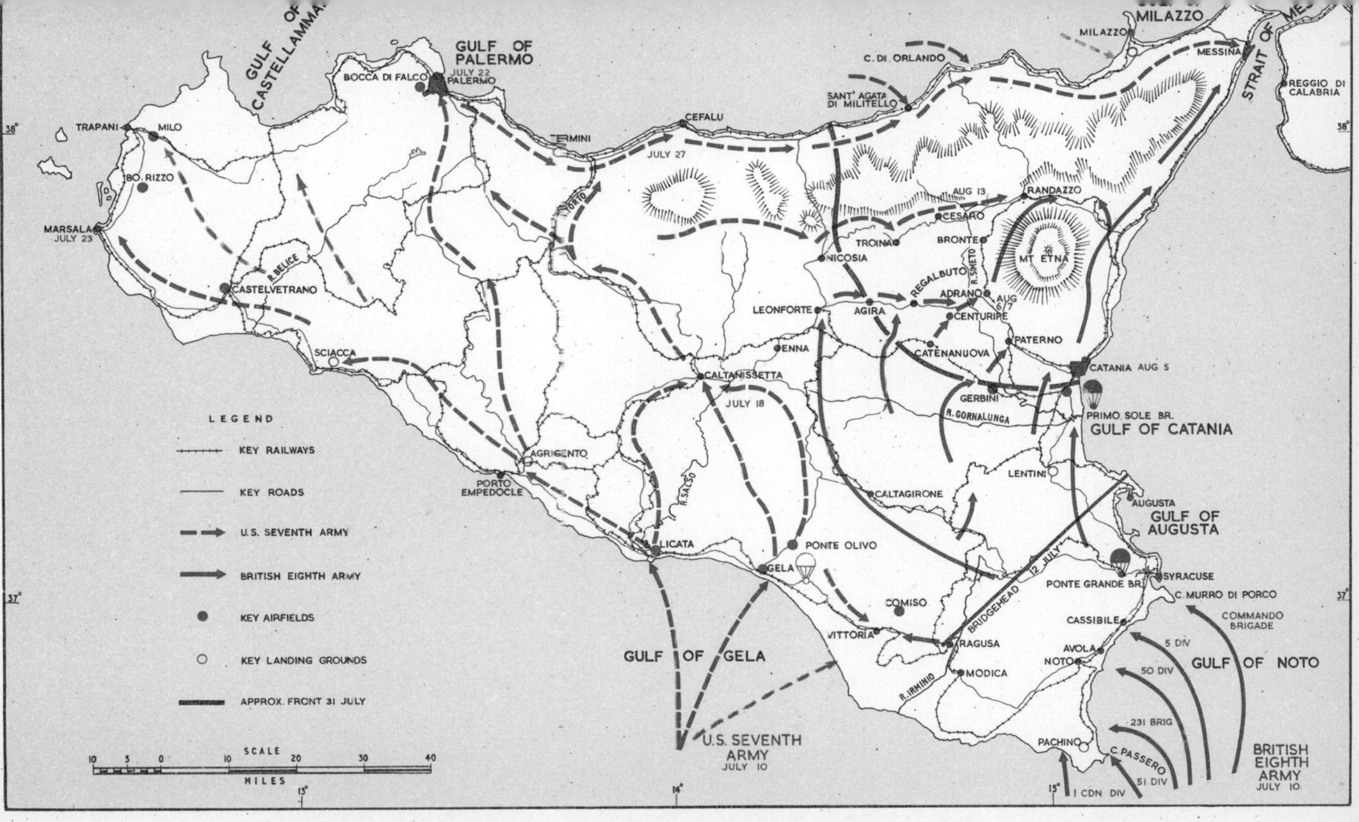

THE INVASION OF SICILY, 10 JULY—17 AUGUST 1943

[facing page 312]

fleet at a moment when it was being attacked by Ju.88's. The anti-aircraft fire in progress caused casualties and a scattering of the force. Twenty-seven aircraft carrying parachute troops lost their way, nineteen returned to base without dropping their passengers, and ten Dakotas, one Halifax and three Albemarles were shot down. This mishap was the cause of much concern to Admiral Cunningham and the Commander-in-Chief and was a partial and melancholy fulfilment of Tedder's forebodings. He had from the start strongly advised the cancellation of the airborne operations for he maintained that they were a 'serious misuse' of airborne troops. Thirteen gliders landed in the correct zone and by dawn on the 14th some 200 parachute troops and five anti-tank guns were installed on the bridge. They removed the charges placed upon it by the Germans and held on until driven off in the evening. The next morning they counter-attacked with the leading unit of the XIII Corps and retook the bridge which, like that at Ponte Grande, was intact. Once more an airborne operation had been successful despite mistakes which, added to the inevitable hazards of war, had caused only one-fifth of the force despatched to arrive at the right place at the right moment. Though these airborne operations were carried out in a confused and uncertain manner by eager but inexperienced men, there is no doubt that they were of considerable assistance to both armies whose commanders reported that the speed of the invasion and of the initial advance had been materially increased by their efforts.

Meanwhile, the resistance of the enemy in the air was daily, hourly, becoming less. The Spitfires and Warhawks based on Malta made attacks by the *Luftwaffe* in daylight hazardous and costly, and at night Beaufighters and Mosquitos in bright moonlight took heavy toll among Peltz's bombers. On the night of 15th/16th July, for example, pilots of No. 256 Squadron shot down five out of six enemy aircraft encountered.

Nevertheless, some German bombers were, on occasion, able to reach their targets and to cause casualties, notably among commando troops making ready to sail from Augusta on a raid. Such incidents, however, were rare and confined for the most part to the hours of darkness. In daylight, by dusk on 13th July, only three days after the assault had begun, the enemy's ability to influence the course of the battle in the air had virtually come to an end. On the 15th, offensive patrols flown over the areas of Catania and Gerbini met with not a single enemy aircraft, and the Allied bombers and fighter-bombers carrying out an almost continuous series of attacks by day and by night were equally unmolested. Their main targets had been Enna in the centre of the island, Messina, and the docks at Milazzo. In addition, enemy transport was attacked wherever seen. Farther afield, the Wellingtons of No. 205 Group were striking at communications in Italy itself. They did so with the object of preventing the enemy's bases in southern Italy from proving effective centres of supply. On the night 14th/15th July, the two Neapolitan airfields of Capodichino and Pomigliano were attacked, together with the docks of Naples, which received two especially heavy assaults on 17th July when the Royal Arsenal was hit. On the next day the marshalling yards of that city were bombed by United States Fortresses, which dropped upon them a load of 212 tons. This attack was in its turn followed on the next night by further attacks carried out by Wellingtons on other marshalling yards in the neighbourhood. To bombs, leaflets were added, 4,348,000 altogether being distributed by air over Rome, Naples and towns in southern Italy. They contained a joint message from Churchill and Roosevelt warning the Italian people of what was about to fall upon them and urging them to abandon a hopeless struggle.

In addition to these onslaughts at long range, the Northwest African Coastal Air Force had been far from idle and had attacked shipping wherever it was to be found. In all they had sunk or damaged ten vessels in a week. These shipping strikes were carried out largely at night by Wellingtons, capable of remaining airborne for ten hours. Skill in flying and the correct use of the radar equipment was necessary for success. The method followed was for groups of three aircraft to patrol the coasts sometimes as much as 300 miles apart in radio touch with each other so that should a convoy be sighted by one the other two would be able, eventually, to attack it. The attacks were made from a very low level with all the consequent dangers.

These squadrons of Coastal Air Force formed part of Mediterranean Air Command. Units of the Royal Air Force and the United States Army Air Force had by then been combined to form a single command with a common Operational Headquarters which co-ordinated the air war in the Mediterranean area. Air Headquarters, Egypt, had become Air Headquarters, Air Defences Eastern Mediterranean, and was responsible for the protection of the coastline and convoys from the Levant to Tripolitania. Northwest African Coastal Air Force assumed, under Air Vice-Marshal Sir Hugh Lloyd, a like responsibility from Tripolitania to French Morocco. It was a mixed force, giving protection to convoys and pursuing the anti-U-boat and anti-shipping campaign. It was also responsible for the fighter defence of an area bounded on the south by some 1,100 miles of African coastline and on the north by an imaginary line running fifty miles behind the battle front. May was an outstanding month for this force because two convoys were able to sail through the Narrows on their way to the Middle East without losing a ship, the first to do so for two long years. The Mediterranean was open again and remained so until the end of the war. On occasion the *Luftwaffe* showed traces of its old spirit. On 26th June a force of over 100 attacked a convoy of forty-two merchant vessels and their twelve escorts passing from Gibraltar to the Middle East and pressed its assaults through the afternoon and into the night. The attack was held at bay by North-west African Coastal Air Force fighters without loss to themselves, but it cost the enemy three Junkers 88's, one Focke-Wulf 190 and two Cant. Z1007's.

By 16th July, not a week after the invasion had begun, the commanders, especially Tedder, could rightly claim that all prospered marvellously. The cover from the air provided in the assault phase had been most effective; in the short space of seventy-two hours the resistance of the *Luftwaffe* had been overcome and was now negligible; four airfields were in our hands and in use, the enemy had been denied the all-important group at Gerbini, and those in the west of the island, five in number, had either been, or were about to be, over-run by the troops of General Patton. The prospect was indeed bright.

Now, however, came a check—not to the forces in the air but to those on the ground. Though the Italians in Sicily were showing little or no resistance, the three German divisions were full of obstinacy and determination. They were now under their own commanders, the chief being the energetic General Hube, and their armoured units, which on 'D Day' had been left for sixteen hours without orders by the Italian officer in command, were now acquitting themselves very well. Moreover, reinforcements consisting of a parachute regiment of the 1st Parachute Division, despatched by air from southern France to Rome and thence to Sicily, had arrived and had gone straight into action. The fighting qualities of these men and of those to whose aid they had come were of the first order. They had food and ammunition, but were grievously lacking in transport. To this handicap Tedder had added another and a greater. The Germans found themselves fighting without the protection and help of an air force. The only service which the *Luftwaffe* was still able to perform was to carry reinforcements to the troops in the field, spare parts to tanks and ammunition to both tanks and infantry. This duty soon became very dangerous, indeed suicidal. By night the Ju.52's had to land and take off on airfields under almost continuous air attack. By day their situation was worse. Allied fighters, only too eager to shoot them down, ranged the pitiless skies. On 25th July, thirty-three Spitfires of No. 322 Wing, operating from Lentini, met a number of Ju.52's circling to land upon an improvised strip on the seashore near Milazzo, on the north coast of Sicily. In a few moments, twelve had been shot down, each and all exploding and bursting into flames as they were hit, for they were loaded with petrol. Within ten minutes, twenty-one had been destroyed together with four Messerschmitt fighters, their outnumbered and outfought escort. 'Flashes, flames, explosions and aircraft dropping into the sea' made up the picture before the eyes of the Spitfire pilots, and the range was so close that fragments of the disintegrating transports struck the attackers and smoke filled their cockpits with acrid fumes.

Yet with every circumstance against them the German troops had no other thought but to fight on. It took them a bare week to recover from the initial shock of the invasion. In the first few days, when the Eighth Army set a confident foot on the south-east coast and the Seventh began to stride forward in the west, something akin to panic seems to have occurred. The immediate breakdown of all Italian resistance and the fact that some of the German units, particularly those which had been on lines of communication, were seeing action for the first time, momentarily upset Teutonic discipline and weakened Teutonic will. Matters were set right by two hard-bitten Generals, Mahncke and Stahel, who, as night fell on 15th July, arrived at Gerbini in Fieseler-Storches. With ruthless efficiency they cleared the roads in the Messina area of retreating Italian transport and succeeded in holding open the routes by which reinforcements and supplies could reach the German divisions south-west of Catania. Towards those who were still their nominal Allies their behaviour was particularly drastic. Italian officers and soldiers, many of them discovered in borrowed civilian clothing, were arrested and shot. By these means order was restored and a respite gained. It endured a month.

The intention of the Germans, having lost Augusta, was to hold Catania, and the troops available for this purpose included the tough Hermann Göring Division, now reinforced by elements of the equally tough First Parachute Division. They had not been able to prevent the Eighth Army from debouching into the plain, for its Commando troops had captured the bridge over the Lentini river and its airborne troops the bridge of Primo Sole, but they had checked a further advance. The next few days saw an increase in German resistance, which grew fiercer and fiercer, for they were determined to carry on their withdrawal from Sicily, which was now seen to be inevitable, in as orderly and as protracted a manner as they could. Their problem was two-fold. It was necessary to remove from the island all troops and as much material as was not absolutely necessary to continue the fight. At the same time those divisions in contact with the Allies had to be kept supplied for as long as possible. The weak link in the chain of communications was the narrow Strait of Messina, and here the Germans established anti-aircraft defences of very great strength. Thirty-five reinforced heavy batteries and numerous light units from the *Luftwaffe* and the Army and Navy were set up to cover that stretch of water. How effective they were very soon became clear, for Allied fighter-bombers, which had been attacking from very low heights the stream of shipping ferrying troops or supplies to and fro, were soon forced to fly higher. The accuracy of their aim was thus spoilt and casualties to enemy shipping fell sharply. The Germans were successful at Messina, but the withdrawal from Palermo and other coastal harbours in the north and west for the most part failed. Here allied air forces were too strong and the enemy suffered accordingly.

By 17th July his plan was clear. He would withdraw into the north-east corner of Sicily and to do so would have to pivot on Catania. This city he had therefore to hold and, as long as he held it, he could continue to deny the Allies 'the greatest prize of the island', the airfields on the plain to the south.

By now the Eighth Army 'were beginning to show definite signs of fatigue owing to the intense July heat and continual marching over the mountainous country'. Montgomery accordingly changed the axis of attack. He abandoned his advance up the east coast against the strongly held Catania position in favour of a move inland, his object being to come behind the enemy between Mount Etna and the northern coast of the island. The first task of the air forces was to attempt the isolation of the Catania area by maintaining a continuous onslaught. This followed what were by then classic principles—constant attacks on targets in the battlefield itself, delivered with the object of helping the infantry to move forward, and attacks made further off on all lines of approach to prevent the arrival of supplies and reinforcements. The ring of roads round the area was kept under constant air bombardment, the junction of Randazzo being singled out for special assault together with Regalbuto, Agira and Troina.

Meanwhile the heavy bombers were being used strategically against communications in southern Italy. The United States Fortresses and Liberators by day and the Wellingtons of the Royal Air Force by night maintained a steady series of raids on Naples, Salerno and Foggia, the object being to create a vast traffic block on roads and railways on both sides of the Apennines. As the days went by and the Germans continued to hold fast to their positions round Etna, these attacks were seen to be not enough. On the morning of 19th July, therefore, after due warning had been conveyed by leaflets, 158 United States Fortresses of the Northwest African Strategic Air Force and 112 Liberators of the United States Ninth Air Force bombed the Lorenzo and Littorio railway yards at Rome, and in the afternoon a slightly larger force attacked Ciampino, its largest airfield. Photographs taken on the following day showed 130 direct hits on railway stock and tracks. Between fifty and sixty wagons were destroyed in Littorio, but the damage at Lorenzo was greater, though the main lines were repaired and in use again within forty-eight hours. The casualties to the Germans were five killed. Though, in general, the aim of the bombers was good, a few bombs fell outside the target and the ancient basilica of St. Lorenzo-without-the-Walls with its twelfth century frescoes was damaged by blast. But these attacks and those in the Naples area created a 200-mile gap in the railway system from the north of Rome to the south of Naples, while Italian aircraft on the airfields at Ciampano sustained severe damage.

The bombing of Rome caused a sensation throughout what was still pleased to call itself the civilized world. Though the squadrons used were all American, they belonged to the Allied Northwest African Air Forces and the British government accepted, as was right, an equal responsibility. Public opinion in England, if the results of a Gallup Poll taken seven weeks later are to be considered accurate, was strongly behind it. To faint protests voiced in the Commons, the Foreign Secretary returned an unequivocal reply. Rome would be bombed 'as heavily as possible if the course of the war should render such action convenient and helpful', and he went on to imply that the attack was a belated retaliation for Mussolini's attempt to bomb London during the Battle of Britain. A day or two later the Secretary of State for Air took a somewhat different view and maintained 'that the policy of an eye for an eye and a tooth for a tooth is entirely foreign to our thought. We are concerned only with bombing important military targets'.

The reaction in America was similar to that in Britain, and the remark of the President that, after the failure of the Allies to persuade the Fascist government of Italy to declare Rome an open city, the bombing of it saved American and British lives in Sicily, was naturally not without great effect. Nevertheless, a number of Roman Catholic bishops protested strongly and their recriminations were echoed as far away as Australia. Though in public the two Allied governments appeared to be in agreement, behind the scenes there was a difference of opinion. The American Government was mildly inclined to refrain from bombing the Eternal City at least while negotiations for declaring it 'open' were in progress. The British refused to agree and continued to urge the bombing of military targets in or near Rome whenever such a course might prove necessary. Their views prevailed and on 13th August the marshalling yards were once again assaulted. The efforts of the Axis powers to make capital out of the first attack had been frustrated by the Pope himself, who in a dignified letter to his Vicar-General in Rome reiterated his oft repeated and studiously neglected advice to all belligerents to concern themselves with 'the safety of peaceful citizens and of religious and cultural monuments'.

Looking back on these two attacks it is hard to say that they were in a military sense indispensable. They were certainly useful for they helped to disrupt Italian communications at the height of a hard-fought campaign; but it is at least possible to argue that had the assaults on the marshalling yards at Naples and Salerno, Battipaglia and Foggia been made with greater frequency and on a larger scale—there would have been no difficulty in increasing both—they would have rendered those on similar targets at Rome superfluous.

Meanwhile, the enemy still stood at Catania and in the little hill towns which were the outposts to Adrano. Only by heavy fighting were they captured, one by one. The most easterly, Leonforte, fell to the Canadians on 23rd July, and Nicosia on the next day. The German 15th Armoured Division then retreated sullenly eastwards suffering heavy casualties from air attack, to make a short stand at Agira, which did not fall until the 29th. With the capture of Catenanuova on the 30th the way was open for an assault on Centuripe, a place 'built on a very high mountain mass and reached by a single road which twists and turns'. If Adrano was the key to the Etna position, Centuripe was the key to Adrano. It was eventually captured by the 78th Division on 3rd August. To these operations the Tactical Air Forces contributed to the best of their abilities, and attacked these and other towns with persistence in an effort to fulfil their original and never abandoned intention to isolate Catania. This town itself was frequently bombed, special attention being paid to the marshalling yards and the railway bridge, while all the time Adrano, Paterno and Cesaro were kept under aerial bombardment to an extent which prompted Montgomery in writing about the campaign afterwards to record that 'our mounting air offensive was achieving outstanding success'[1].

[1] *El Alamein to the River Sangro.* Viscount Montgomery (Hutchinson).

Could that achievement have been greater? At the time, no. The Northwest African Air Forces were still '*in statu pupillari*' so to speak. They had passed their first test with flying colours; the second was more difficult. The country of Sicily with its steep, folded valleys was very different from the wide, stony spaces of North Africa and made co-operation with the army on the ground no easy task. The positions occupied by the German infantry were often hard to discover and harder still to hit; a machine-gun on the roof of the principal church in Regalbuto, which the cannons of a single Spitfire could have destroyed in a few seconds, was able to hold up the advance for half a day. But this was, given the circumstances, probably unavoidable. The means at the disposal of Montgomery's men for signalling targets to their air force comrades were inadequate. Word had to be sent through a chain of command beginning with company headquarters till eventually it reached the air force, which only then took action. Such an arrangement, which had proved far from infallible in mobile desert warfare, was even less readily adaptable to the semi-mobile conditions in Sicily, and the need for a system under which it was possible for forward troops to call for immediate support direct to aircraft was becoming apparent. In due course the 'Cab Rank' and 'Rover David' method of sending fighters and fighter-bombers to immediate targets, to be described in a later chapter, was discovered and perfected. The result in its extreme form was to be seen over the fields of Normandy a year later. In the meantime both air force and army were learning, and if the results achieved in Sicily were by comparison with those of Normandy inadequate, they were at least a beginning, an early link in a chain which, before the war ended, was to bind the enemy fast and paralyse him.

Though the air forces could not quell resistance in the tenaciously held positions round Etna, they greatly discouraged it. This was clear from German reports in which the disappearance from the sky of the *Luftwaffe* was deplored or censured.

There were certain factors which militated against complete success in the air. Local airfields were scarce—not until near the end of the campaign was the Gerbini group opposite Catania in our hands—and the scarcity reduced the number of sorties which could be flown. The targets attacked were not always the most important, nor were they always hit. The town of Randazzo, for example, a road junction to the north of Etna, was not nearly so badly damaged as the reports show; 212 bomber sorties flown in one day against the town of Regalbuto might disorganize but certainly could not overwhelm the enemy, and even in much-bombed Adrano the number of Germans put out of action was very small. On the roads a greater measure of good fortune awaited the air forces. The Germans had soon to abandon vehicles, targets which were vulnerable and easily destroyed from the air, and take instead to mules, stolen from the local peasants. The casualties among these animals were not low, but enough of them remained alive to enable the movement of ammunition and food, through the difficult country over which the battle was fought, to be maintained. The failure on the part of the air forces to achieve perfection does not greatly whittle down the solid core of their achievement. When all is said and done the Germans in Sicily were decisively beaten.

While the Eighth Army was thus heavily engaged in the east of Sicily, the American Seventh Army in the west had met with little resistance. It had therefore been able without much difficulty to reach the northern coast and then, turning eastwards, to make straight for Palermo. The city fell on the evening of 22nd July, and Patton's men presently established themselves facing east before Cesaro. But the German army in the north-east corner of the island still held on, for General Hube was a man of great tenacity. His problems, however, were daily becoming more difficult, for the weight of the assault from the air on his lines of communication was making itself felt. Only through Messina, where the Strait was at its narrowest, could supplies be passed in any quantity. The use of Milazzo as an additional port of entry for his necessities was largely frustrated by a series of attacks carried out from the 24th to 31st July by heavy, medium and light bombers, and there was no other harbour available. Throughout this period the onslaught on the main communications passing through Italy was maintained, the most severe attacks being those made by Fortresses, Wellingtons and Mitchells on Salerno, Battipaglia and Foggia. The passage of supplies was thus made more difficult, but never became impossible. Among the airfields assaulted were Vibo Valentia, Crotone, Grottaglie and Leverano in the toe and heel of Italy, the airfields in the Naples area and those in that of Rome. These operations not only contributed to the conquest of Sicily, they also prepared the way for the next phase, the invasion of Italy.

By 4th August all was ready for the final assault on General Hube and his men, and on the 5th the advance guard of the Eighth Army entered Catania, the troops being met 'by a seething mob of citizens, who expressed delight at the departure of the Germans and begged for food'. 'Relentlessly pounded from the air', Adrano was now almost won and on the night of 6th/7th August its garrison, having fought with the grimmest determination, fell back towards Bronte.

With the capture of Adrano the line of defence across the north-eastern part of Sicily had been broken. The Germans were now in full retreat and suffering heavy losses at the hands of the air forces which anon switched their main attack to Messina. By 8th August that unhappy town was reduced to a condition much the same as that in which it had been left by the earthquake of 1909. The riposte of the enemy in the air was spasmodic, but, in the early hours of 1st August, twenty-five Ju.88's and Dornier 217's made a successful raid on Palermo and put the largest dock temporarily out of commission. Ration and petrol supplies were also destroyed, an ammunition train was blown up and a vessel was sunk. The defence was inadequate and seven only of the enemy were shot down. Such an attack, however, was an isolated effort for by now it was beyond the power of the *Luftwaffe* to stay the onslaught of the triumphant Allied air forces.

After the fall of Adrano, Randazzo was attacked and fell on the 13th. Only one road to Messina was now left to the Germans and they held it as long as they could in order to evacuate such men and supplies as it was still possible to save. The end was now at hand. A tenacious but badly equipped enemy, whose air force had been rendered powerless in the first few days, had been overthrown in the space of little more than a month. By 14th August there remained to him nothing but the port of Messina, and this was to fall on the 16th. Could the Allied victory be completed by preventing the beaten Germans from leaving the island? The answer was No. Hindered he was, but the losses he sustained were not great, and this despite the fact that the beaches and harbours, which he was using on both sides of the Strait, were subjected to continuous attack by fighter-bombers and by the Wellingtons of No. 205 Group, which bombed stretches of shore all along the toe of Italy. As has been said the Strait was heavily defended and, being less than three miles wide, to cross it took but a short time. This physical fact goes far to explain our failure to prevent the enemy's withdrawal. Between the 8th and 17th August some 1,170 sorties were flown against the shipping he used to bring away his defeated but still hard-fighting troops. The peak was reached on the 16th, when pilots of Kittyhawk bombers returned with such reports as 'All bombs fell within thirty yards of Siebel ferry. Vessel stopped'. 'Direct hit scored on two 100-foot barges; both were destroyed'.

Nevertheless, despite these efforts and despite the bombing of railways and roads in southern Italy the Germans could justly claim that they had withdrawn the bulk of the forces which had fought in Sicily. They carried out this hazardous operation with great skill and resolution, bringing back their troops in small parties over a considerable period of time before the end came. Only between the 8th and 17th August did their departure become hurried; even then it was never disorganized.

Yet, when all is said and done, a notable victory had been gained; and the Allied commanders, gazing across the wrecked waterfront of Messina towards the nearby Italian shore, could congratulate themselves on a very successful operation carried out against an enemy who had every advantage but one, air superiority. That had been possessed by the Allies from the beginning, and the shattered remains of 1,100 enemy aircraft strewn over the airfields of Sicily, 189 at Gerbini and 132 at Catania, was proof of its significance. 'The hangars and living quarters smashed into rubble; an ornamental garden with geraniums and oleander still in flower; a plaster statue freakishly wrecked in a garden, close to a solid building ground to dust; the whole area littered with letters and newspapers . . . blowing in the wind'—these and more which met the eyes of the advanced parties of the Royal Air Force when they reached the Gerbini airfields were but a few examples of the meaning of air power.

For a loss of fewer than 400 aircraft, they had destroyed or captured 1,850 aircraft of the enemy. On the ground the Axis had lost about 32,000 men killed and wounded and 162,000 prisoners, mostly Italians. A stepping-stone to Europe had been captured. It was a notable achievement of that combined land/sea/air technique which was to be the keynote of all future operations of the Second World War.

CHAPTER XV

The Fight at Salerno

WHILE these things were happening in Sicily, 'by the yellow Tiber was tumult and afright', especially in high Fascist circles. On 25th July the Grand Council at last found courage to depose Mussolini, and his arrest that same day was ordered by the King. Within a few hours, the latest of Italy's tyrants quitted Rome, to which he had marched twenty years before in the comfort of a first-class sleeping compartment, for the solitude of the Gran Sasso, whither he was conveyed in a closed and guarded ambulance. From this mountain top he was presently rescued by a striking and melodramatic use of air power and established north of the Po, where he sought to pick up the scattered pieces of Fascism with the aid of a yellow-haired mistress, some thousands of fanatical black-shirts and a sullen, but far from conquered, ally. His place at the head of affairs was taken by Badoglio, who, emerging from a retirement which had been almost a prison, sought to alleviate the consequences of his country's folly. The task needed not only cunning, which he felt himself to possess, but courage. An immediate announcement that the war would continue might serve to allay Teutonic suspicions, but for a little while only. At least ten German divisions occupied the north, two of them poised ready to strike an immediate blow at Rome. What remained of four more would shortly arrive in Calabria after their defeat in Sicily, now imminent, and reinforcements of unknown strength were to be expected from beyond the Alps as soon as the news of Mussolini's fall reached the ears of the German General Staff.

Battling in Sicily or waiting poised in Africa, their faces turned northwards, were the British and American armies, and none could doubt that their advent was certain. As soon as the Allies appeared in strength on the mainland, it would be possible to spring to the aid of the victors. For this time there must be no mistake. Having guessed wrong in the summer of 1940, the Italian General Staff were determined not to repeat the blunder in the summer of 1943. Together with their ambiguous chief and his forces of uncertain allegiance they would rally to the true cause; but in the meantime when would its protagonists arrive? For how long would it be safe to run with the hare and hunt with the hounds especially when the hare bore a striking resemblance to a wolf and the hounds appeared to be still so far away? Though the Allies expected overtures of peace, they did not count upon them and continued to press the war-weary and disillusioned Italians with unabated vigour. On 27th July, however, President Roosevelt offered honourable terms in exchange for capitulation, and his words were echoed by General Eisenhower, who, nevertheless broadcast, on the 1st day of August, a sharp reminder that more and heavier air bombardment would follow if the Italians dallied. A week passed, and Bomber Command gave effect to his words.

Milan was subjected to four heavy attacks on the nights of the 7th/8th, 12th/13th, 14th/15th and 15th/16th August, the bombers being led to their targets by Pathfinders using 'H2S'. Smaller forces attacked Turin and Genoa. During the second of these attacks, Flight Sergeant Aaron of No. 218 Squadron, flying a Stirling, was severely wounded in an encounter with a night fighter whose fire hit three out of the four engines, shattered the windscreen, put both turrets out of action and damaged the elevator cables. With his jaw smashed, part of his face torn away, a lung perforated and his right arm broken, the flight sergeant sat beside the bomb-aimer, who had taken over the controls, and showed him by means of directions written with the left hand how to keep the crippled aircraft in the air. By so doing he brought it safely to Bone in North Africa, where, dying of his wounds, he was awarded the Victoria Cross for 'an example of devotion to duty which has seldom been equalled and never surpassed'.

The destruction caused in Milan by these raids was considerable, and after the last of them parts of the city burned for two days. Forty churches, ninety-nine schools, and some hundred factories were damaged or destroyed. About 1,500 houses were razed to the ground and 1,700 badly damaged. The raid of the 12th/13th August was the worst. The Duomo escaped, but the Basilica of San Ambrogio, where Saint Augustine was baptized, was ringed with fire, its northern aisle destroyed and its famous frescoes hideously defaced. Hard-by, the church of Santa Maria delle Grazie was hit, and when day dawned, of its Refectory only one wall remained. Upon it still mouldered, untouched by the blast of bombs and yielding only to the slow assault of time, 'The Last Supper' of Leonardo da Vinci.

Whether the object of these raids, which was to hasten the surrender of Italy, was achieved is hard to say. The Milanese endured them in much the same spirit of indignant fortitude as Londoners had displayed three years before in a worthier cause, and Badoglio remained unmoved. He had already begun negotiations for an armistice by dispatching one Castellano to Madrid. This General arrived on 15th August and at once sought and was granted an interview by Sir Samuel Hoare, our Ambassador. Castellano made it clear that his purpose was not to learn the terms upon which his country might surrender, but the means by which she could transfer her allegiance from Germany to the Allies. By so doing she hoped to assume, when the time came, a modest place in the rear rank of the victorious powers.

There was the rub; for the soldiers of Italy, though in numbers far greater than those of the ally whom she now wished to abandon, were no match for them in the field. The rank and file were dispirited, in this taking their tone from their officers. Yet, given a stiffening, they could still fight. Were the Allies prepared to provide it? The Italian General Staff hoped that they were, but based their calculations on highly misleading information supplied by their Intelligence Services. This together with their own ignorance of 'the difficulties of amphibian warfare', induced them to believe that Eisenhower could put ashore at any point on the coastline of Italy a force so large that, together with the Italian troops available, the Germans would be destroyed or sent reeling back to the Alps. At one moment Castellano even expressed the hope that not less than fifteen divisions would be landed north of Rome, preferably in the country around Leghorn. Among its many deficiencies, such a plan ignored the limitations of air power. These, however, had been constantly in the mind of General Eisenhower and his staff, who, when Castellano arrived, were preparing to initiate the invasion of Italy.

This project, known as Operation 'Avalanche', involved the putting ashore of three divisions at Salerno, the farthest point up the west coast of Italy at which protection from the air could be adequately provided. It was to be preceded by Operation 'Baytown', to be carried out by the Eighth Army which would cross the Strait of Messina and land in the toe of Italy. The advent of Castellano followed by that of another general, Zanussi, did not change these plans. They were kept a close secret from the Italians, who were informed, first at Lisbon whither the negotiations had been transferred and later at Cassibile, in Sicily, that if the Italian Government accepted our terms, the end of the war with Italy would be announced five or six hours before the main force of the Allies landed on her soil. When that moment came, the Allied Commander-in-Chief would broadcast the announcement of an armistice and Badoglio would make a similar announcement at the same time ordering the forces and people in Italy to co-operate with the Allies in fighting the Germans. The Italian fleet was to sail for Allied ports, all units of the *Regia Aeronautica* were to fly to Allied bases, and all Allied prisoners of war were to be released. These terms were set down in two instruments—one long, detailed, and containing political, financial, and economic clauses, the other short and confined solely to military matters. The Combined Chiefs of Staff agreed that Italy's acceptance of the short instrument would entitle her to be granted an armistice.

While Castellano and Zanussi were flitting uneasily and in great secrecy to and fro between Badoglio and Eisenhower, the war in the air against Italy continued. The Northwest African Air Forces fulfilled an extensive programme of bombing, the targets chosen being railways and airfields. The intention was to isolate the German divisions in southern Italy and to drive what remained of the *Luftwaffe* from its landing grounds. During the last fortnight of August, 736 heavy bomber, 1,696 medium, 88 light and 1,009 fighter-bomber sorties were flown with this object. Most effective of these were the attacks on the Foggia marshalling yards carried out on the 19th and 25th August. They undid all the work of repair which had been laboriously completed after the heavy attacks of the 15th and 22nd July, when severe damage had been caused, together with heavy casualties among railway staff, including the station-master and his five immediate subordinates.

The weight of the air attacks increased during the last week of August, and by the 27th a total of 1,542 tons of bombs had been dropped on marshalling yards at Battipaglia, Salerno, Bagnoli, Taranto, Villa Literno, Aversa and Torre Annunziata, and on the airfields at Foggia, Capua and Grazzanise. These assaults were not considered adequate and forty-seven more, in which 2,835 tons of bombs fell, mainly on railway targets as far north as Pisa, were therefore carried out. A glance at the map will show how dependent the northern and southern parts of Italy are for supplies upon the railways which connect them with the industrial north, and this dependence increased as the War went on, for Italian coastal shipping was, by the middle of 1943, almost at a standstill owing to the activities of the coastal air forces. The railway system had to carry not only supplies but also reinforcements, and these had to come from Germany over the Brenner Pass. They followed three main routes—the line running from Bologna to Rome and two lines running along the west and east coasts respectively. On these three lines were three main junctions at Rome, Naples and Foggia. These, it was held, were the crucial points and must therefore be singled out for attack.

While the Northwest African Air Forces were taking the air almost unopposed above Italy, behind the scenes negotiations between Badoglio's emissaries, on the one hand, and General Bedell Smith, Eisenhower's Chief of Staff, and Brigadier Strom, the Head of his Intelligence Service, on the other, had reached a critical stage. The Allies remained firm in their refusal to reveal their plans and made it clear that the Italians would be judged by their deeds alone. From the calm heights of Abraham, beside which the Prime Minister and President were in conference with their Chiefs of Staff, the situation in the smoke-covered streets of Milan and the rumour-ridden capital of Italy may have been viewed in too rosy a light. Fascism had certainly fallen, but its collapse had been due to inherent rottenness. The burning spirit of the *Risorgimento*, which nearly a century before had sent Italian youths shouting to their deaths on the dusty slopes beyond the Janiculum, was conspicuous by its absence. The Germans, however, were present in force, and though the Italians had the weapons, they lacked the will to overcome them. This was made abundantly clear when Bedell Smith and Strom met Castellano and Zanussi for the second time on the Sicilian shore in almond-ringed Cassibile.

For one moment it seemed as though the negotiations might break down, and indeed if the Italians had been aware at that stage that the largest number of Allied troops which could be landed was no more than three divisions, they would undoubtedly have decided 'to postpone capitulation to a more propitious date'. Some action had to be taken to mitigate their far from groundless fears. General Eisenhower offered, therefore, to fly an airborne division to airfields near Rome, provided that the Italians would seize and hold them against German attacks. This they somewhat hesitatingly undertook to do and plans were therefore hastily made to divert the American 82nd Airborne Division, then preparing to drop in the country round Volturno a few hours before the landings at Salerno, to four airfields in the neighbourhood of Rome. Upon these they would alight at 2130 hours British Time on 8th September, the day fixed for the opening of Operation 'Avalanche'. Their strength would then be built up on succeeding nights and supplies of ammunition and heavy weapons despatched to them up the Tiber from a beach-head to be established at Ostia by landing craft. To assist the defence of the airfields and of the Eternal City itself, fighter squadrons of the Royal Air Force, flying Spitfires, and American squadrons of P.40's from their 33rd Fighter Group were to be flown in, together with two Whitley aircraft carrying fighter control equipment. Throughout the early stages the Italians were to provide petrol and maintenance.

So it was planned, and Castellano hurried off to Rome. He returned to Cassibile on 3rd September, and there, at a quarter past five in a tent pitched in an almond grove, he and Zanussi signed the short instrument containing the armistice terms. Some thirteen hours earlier the clamour of 900 guns firing across the Strait of Messina had announced the advent of the Eighth Army.

Its advance guard landed on the Calabrian shore without opposition at Reggio, Gallico and Catona. They were covered by patrols from the Desert Air Force, which on that day and on those which immediately followed, found few targets and almost no enemy aircraft opposed to them. Photographic reconnaissance showed that all airfields in the neighbourhood had been abandoned by the enemy. So negligible was the resistance that, on the 7th, two squadrons of Kittyhawk light bombers brought their bombs back, and the only attack of importance was an assault on the Crotone marshalling yards.

It had been decided to make public the armistice concluded between the Allies and Italy on 8th September, when both sides should broadcast its general terms to the world. While awaiting the announcement, preparations were hastily made throughout the Mediterranean area for the reception of surrendering Italian aircraft. They were to arrive at certain named airfields in Libya, Cyrenaica, Cyprus and Sicily, and since it was essential that when on passage they should not interfere with the Northwest African Air Forces, which would then be fully engaged in supporting the landings at Salerno, a rectangular area covering the battle zone was created, in which all but Allied aircraft were forbidden to fly. The *Regia Aeronautica* had, therefore, to make a detour and at night to burn navigation lights. Their crews were to be treated neither as Allies nor as prisoners of war; but were to be disarmed, segregated, and given certain amenities as an encouragement to hope for better things as soon as the co-operation of their country became more active.

The necessity for extreme secrecy complicated these arrangements, and the orders issued to wings and squadrons and to the anti-aircraft units, created, in consequence, some bewilderment. A hint that a listening watch should be kept on the Rome and Algiers radio was sufficient to man all listening posts by 1830 hours on 8th September. Throughout that day Italian broadcasts had given no hint of what might be in store. Their announcers continued to blare out defiance mingled with assertions of the importance of Italy in Europe. Towards midday a German agency went so far as to say that if Churchill and Roosevelt were awaiting, as was rumoured, the surrender of Italy, they might as well wait for Father Christmas. This taunt was nearer the truth than those who made it knew, for at the last moment the inevitable hitch occurred.

As soon as the terms had been signed on the 3rd, preparations were at once put in hand for the descent of the 82nd Airborne Division on the chosen Roman airfields. First-hand knowledge of the situation in Rome itself was, however, essential before the risk of committing the division to its perilous mission could be taken. Accordingly, Brigadier-General Taylor, an American, later to achieve fame as the defender of Bastogne in December 1944, was sent to Rome, where he arrived late on 7th September, having travelled from Palermo in a British motor torpedo-boat and an Italian naval craft, to which he had trans-shipped at Ustica. He carried with him a code-word, to be broadcast at the appropriate moment. For this purpose he was to use the direct wireless channel which had been established between Allied headquarters and Badoglio.

By the time Taylor had arrived in Rome, the Allied invasion force was already at sea, steering a northerly course before turning east for Salerno; the 1st (British) Airborne Division was ready at Bizerta to sail for Taranto as soon as the armistice was announced; the 82nd (United States) Airborne Division were waiting at Kairouan ready to fly to Rome; in Calabria the Eighth Army was already well established.

All seemed well, when to Eisenhower, Alexander, Tedder and Coningham, assembled in conference at Bizerta, two messages were brought. The first was from Brigadier-General Taylor, and ran simply 'Situation Innocuous'. It was the pre-arranged code and meant that conditions in Rome were not such as to make it possible for the 82nd Airborne Division to carry out its task with any hope of success. The mission was therefore cancelled a bare half hour before the aircraft of Troop Carrier Command were due to take off. This was a serious blow, for by then it was too late to switch the Division to its original target, the country round Volturno.

Its tough and valiant troops would therefore be able to play no part in the impending invasion. The second message was even graver. It came from Badoglio himself. The strength of the German forces in Rome and its neighbourhood, he said, was so great that he could not guarantee the security of the airfields, and that in consequence, since the airborne division could not land upon them, he would not be in a position to announce the armistice until after the invasion by sea had been successful. Was the Marshal seeking to denounce the armistice which his representatives had signed? Was he about to fall into German hands? No one knew, but for Eisenhower the hour for decision had struck. Picking up the telephone he dictated there and then a strongly worded message to General Bedell Smith in Algiers for immediate transmission to Badoglio. 'I intend', said Eisenhower, 'to broadcast the existence of the armistice at the hour originally planned. If you or any of your armed forces fail to co-operate as previously agreed, I will publish to the world the full record of this affair. Today is 'X Day' and I expect you to do your part'. The message went on by a skilful blend of threats and encouragement to draw attention to the serious consequences to Italy which a failure to carry out the terms of the armistice would entail.

Half past six came and went, but Badoglio was silent. Eisenhower made his broadcast, and the world waited for confirmation from Rome. At last it came. At a quarter to eight Badoglio, having overcome a final spasm of vacillation, announced in lugubrious tones that his country had surrendered unconditionally. He then fled hastily with the King and some of the government to Pescara and thence to Brindisi.

The seaborne invasion swept onwards through the night, ready to meet at dawn whatever Fate held in store. In this case it was a hostile, strong and determined enemy. Though taken by surprise the Germans reacted with speed and address to the announcement of the Armistice, heralded as it had been by the news that an invasion fleet had been seen at sea steaming for Salerno. Kesselring had nine hours in which to make his dispositions: it was enough. Germans at once took over all the coastal defences, disarmed their Italian garrisons—'As I expected, they threw their weapons away', wrote a German officer in his diary, 'and showed their joy that the war was now over for them'. The Germans, however, prepared to dispute the imminent landing with the utmost fury.

It took place at dawn on 9th September, 1943, the 36th (United States) Division landing on the right, the 46th and 56th (British) Divisions on the left of the chosen beaches. These were situated on the edge of a level plain running from Salerno in the north to Agropoli in the south. Standing back from its fertile fields and orchards, traversed by three rivers, the Asa, the Tusciano and the Sele, rise the mountains in a semi-circle. At their feet, between the little town of Battipaglia, with its marshalling yards, and the eastern edge of the plain, lay the one airfield, Monte Corvino, of which the capture was an important part of the plan. Though the beaches chosen were very suitable for an amphibious operation, the position to be assaulted was very strong, for the whole plain is dominated by the hills and mountains which surround it on all sides but one. To the north rise the pale yellow and grey buildings of Salerno, broken here and there by a red-tiled roof, and these reach out to the darker grey of the hills where stands the ancient Castello, the crumbled home of Lombard princes long forgotten.

From the town two roads lead to Naples. Of these, one was impassable against even light opposition. Among the more beautiful of the world, it clings to the vine-embroidered skirts of the mountains which rise above the little fishing ports of Vietri and Amalfi, and winding with the convolutions of a snake, reaches at last the dead city of Pompeii, where it joins the main road running through the cleft in the hills by Nocera. It was along this main road that the advance would have to move once the plain of Salerno and the hills beyond were in our hands. Herein lay the difficulty of the operation, for the Germans held the hills which dominated the plain.

Many days before the invasion fleet sighted the beaches, a great and continuous effort had been made by the Northwest African Air Forces to make the position of the enemy as uncomfortable as possible. Railways and highways leading to what was to be the battlefield had been attacked with considerable success—on the north at Aversa, Villa Literno, Grosseto, Cancello and Salerno itself; to the east at Battipaglia and Potenza, and to the south at Cosenza, Lauria and Sapri. The attacks met at first with some opposition from the *Luftwaffe*. As high an average as forty fighters had at one time sought to interfere with daylight raids, but by the first week in September its efforts to defend the situation in the air had almost entirely died away, no more than 300 sorties being flown in the last seven days before the invasion.

The fact was that the *Luftwaffe* was in no position at the time to offer serious resistance. The attacks on its airfields had been too severe. Whereas its aircraft situated at the large bomber bases at Foggia and Viterbo, which were well defended by anti-aircraft guns, had not suffered unduly high losses, the fighter squadrons, especially those in south-eastern Apulia, had been gravely reduced in strength. For fighters to remain in readiness, a higher degree of concentration on the ground is necessary than with bombers. Thus the attacks made on fighter airfields accounted for a larger number of victims, especially when, as happened more than once, the raids of the Northwest African Air Forces were so timed as to surprise the German fighters as they were about to land or when they were taxying to their dispersal points. Night attacks on the airfields—there was a particularly severe series against that at Aquino—also took heavy toll, for the grounded aircraft were not protected by blast- or splinter-proof shelters.

So it was that, at the moment of the invasion, the *Luftwaffe* had been paralysed, thanks to the efforts of the Allied air forces. For three months the assaults upon it had steadily continued, and they had followed principles of air warfare which the Allies had long known in theory to be sound, but which, lacking crews and aircraft, they had not been able to prove by experiment on a large scale. By the high summer of 1943, schemes of expansion, drawn up years earlier, were beginning to achieve results. Aircraft were pouring from the factories of the United States and Great Britain, crews from the training centres in Canada, Texas, Rhodesia and elsewhere; and when the moment came to invade Italy, 461 heavy bombers, 162 medium (night) bombers and 703 medium and light (day) bombers, 1,395 fighters and fighter-bombers and 406 transport aircraft, reaching the imposing total of 3,127 aircraft, were ready for action.

As a climax to a week, which was itself a climax in the air assault, 31 Fortresses attacked the headquarters of the German Army at Frascati, south of Rome. This lovely town, set among the vineyards which produce the golden wine of that name, was gravely damaged, but Kesselring escaped unscathed and casualties among the headquarters of the *Luftwaffe* staff, who numbered more than 1,000, were only some eighty killed. The signals network was disrupted for a certain time, but six hours after the attack headquarters were again in control of their armies.

At a quarter to four on the morning of 9th September, the first wave of the assaulting troops reached the Salerno beaches on time. As dawn broke, above their heads a force of twelve United States Mustangs as low cover, twenty-four Lightnings as medium and eight Seafires of the Fleet Air Arm as high cover were on patrol. The shore-based aircraft came from airfields in Sicily as far distant as Gerbini, and had therefore had to fly a minimum of 175 and a maximum of 220 miles to the scene of action. They were enabled to do so by the use of long-range petrol tanks which could be jettisoned when empty. With this addition to their petrol supply Spitfires arriving at 0830 hours were able to maintain patrols of twenty-five minutes' duration over the beaches, the squadrons succeeding each other throughout the long day. Squadrons of Seafires, based on aircraft carriers, made it possible for high fighter cover to be extended from dawn to dusk over the beaches by maintaining patrols from dawn until 0830 hours, when they were relieved by the shore-based Spitfires, and again in the evening from

1830 hours till dusk. They also provided high and low fighter patrols throughout the day over the northern approaches to the anchorage. At night the work of protection was carried out by Royal Air Force Beaufighters based on Sicily. The assaulting troops had reached the beaches covered by squadrons of the Tactical and Coastal Air Forces. From the beginning of the campaign in July Coastal Air Forces had protected some 140 convoys of which those moving to Salerno were the latest. Pilots and crews, flying many thousands of hours, had sighted thirty-five submarines, made twenty-one attacks and sunk two.

By the hour the first troops set foot upon the beaches, and indeed before it, the Northwest African Air Forces, their Order of Battle very similar to that used for the invasion of Sicily, were in full operation. As before, their composition was international. Broadly speaking, the Twelfth Air Support Command was American, the Tactical and Strategic Bomber Forces of mixed composition, and the Desert Air Force British. But squadrons of other Allies were also present and in action under Tedder's general command.

The attempts of the *Luftwaffe* to attack the assault convoys before they sailed or during passage were very half-hearted. The most considerable was the raid on Convoy FSS.2, at anchor in Bizerta Bay, on the evening of 6th September. A tank landing craft of the Royal Navy, No. 624, sailing in Convoy FSS.1, was sunk on the 8th, fortunately without casualties; but that was the only loss during operations on which some 700 warships and other craft were employed. At the time, the Force Commanders believed this comparative immunity from air attack to be due to shortage of petrol and the damage done to the enemy's airfields, a view substantiated by post-war investigation.

Against their former allies, however, the Germans had better fortune. A number of Dornier 217E's of 2nd *Gruppe* of KG.100, stationed at Istres in southern France, turned their attention to the Italian fleet, then on its way to surrender. Allied reconnaissance aircraft had been keeping its units under close observation, and on 8th September the ships in Taranto, and those, the larger number, in Spezia were seen to be preparing for sea. That evening and on the following morning they put out, those from Taranto proceeding unmolested to Malta, where they surrendered. The three battleships, six cruisers and thirteen destroyers which sailed from Spezia, however, were less fortunate. In the middle of the afternoon of the 9th, Wing Commander H. Law-Wright, the pilot of a Royal Air Force Marauder, flying at a low height round them, was suddenly met with anti-aircraft fire. It was directed not against him, but against a number of Ju.88's, which were attacking the Italian fleet. A hit by a radio-controlled glider-bomb was made on the battleship *Roma* and the Wing Commander saw her 'fold up, break in two and sink'.

In its surrender the *Regia Aeronautica* was luckier than the Italian navy, perhaps because only a small number of its pilots obeyed the order to go over to the Allies. These, to show their enthusiasm and skill, indulged in aerobatics before landing upon the airfields set aside to receive them, but the number of aircraft which thus reached the Allies was little more than 300. They were formed into squadrons and fought for the rest of the war beside the Northwest African Air Forces.

To attack the troops newly arrived on the beaches, the *Luftwaffe* used some thirty or forty Focke-Wulf 190's. Patrolling Spitfires, Lightnings and Mustangs went immediately into action against them and, for the most part, succeeded in keeping them away from the beach-heads. Low-flying German aircraft encountered balloons, which went ashore flying at a height of 200 feet. The crews in charge of them were a happy company and had seen much service from El Alamein onwards up the long length of North Africa to Tunis and Sicily. Now they were among the first to set foot upon European soil, and with them went Blondie, their hen, which 'fed on rice, tea leaves and flies, had laid eggs valiantly since the Battle of the Mareth Line'.

All this time heavy and medium bombers of the Northwest African Air Forces continued to attack roads, railway junctions and bridges in the area of Naples and in the neighbourhood of the Volturno river. The most successful of these operations was that directed against the two bridges at Capua, which were almost completely destroyed.

Though unable to be of great effect over the beaches, the *Luftwaffe* scored a number of successes against ships, the most notable being the severe damage inflicted upon H.M.S. *Warspite* by two radio-controlled glider-bombs. She was forced to withdraw from the fight and remained out of action for six months. These bombs were of two kinds—the PC.1400FX, a modified armour-piercing type of bomb with cruciform stabilizing fins forward and a box tail aft, weighing somewhat more than 3,000 lb., and the Hs.293, a jet propelled missile, in shape and form a miniature monoplane, intended for attacks on merchant vessels. Both were launched from Dornier 217's which carried them beneath their wings. All things considered, it is surprising that the *Luftwaffe* was not able to achieve more in the early days at Salerno, for the Allied fighters, it must be repeated, were operating at extreme range. This state of affairs continued for some days, for though the airfield at Monte Corvino had been captured almost at once it remained dominated by the guns of the enemy situated in the hills above the plain. Recourse was therefore had to the skill and courage of the Allied airfield construction engineers. They were ordered to make four landing strips, one close to each of the three rivers which traversed the plain of Salerno and the fourth to the south hard by the honey-coloured temples of Paestum. Working without pause and under fire, they completed their task by 15th September, but since the strips were small and built on friable soil they could only be used in daylight and in fair weather. The first, at Paestum, some 1,300 yards long and 50 yards in width, was completed by the evening of the 10th and occupied by Lightnings the next day. Twenty-six Seafires landed there on 12th September and they were soon followed by three Spitfire squadrons of No. 324 Wing of the Royal Air Force. These and the other fighters and medium bomber squadrons still based on Sicily were badly needed in the critical days of the 12th to 14th September.

For the first three days of the battle in the beach-head, success seemed to be within the grasp of the Allies. Though progress had not been quite so fast or so far as had been hoped, it had nevertheless been considerable. By the night of 11th September, on the southern flank, VI Corps had penetrated to a line running from Altavilla and Albanella in the foothills of the Apennines down to the coast at Agropoli, an advance at its farthest point of some ten miles. To the north-west Salerno was in our hands and, in the centre, a battalion, fiercely engaged by the enemy, was fighting a desperate battle in the streets of Battipaglia. It was on the 12th that a number of heavy German counter-attacks began, and these were soon to cause 'grave anxiety'. 'The critical period was from the 12th to 14th September'. Issuing from the foothills, the 29th Panzer Grenadier Division and what remained of the 15th and 16th Panzer Divisions advanced with great resolution into the flat plain before them, moving over the cultivated fields, between the olives and the wide-flung coppices of oak trees. Behind the assaulting troops, the gunners firing in their support could survey the whole battlefield from the heights upon which their batteries were sited. No such advantage favoured the invading Allies, whose forward observation officers were forced to look across the plain from a low level. They could not look down upon it and their vision was therefore limited. The troops themselves were inexperienced. Some, like those of the 36th Division, had never been in action before and

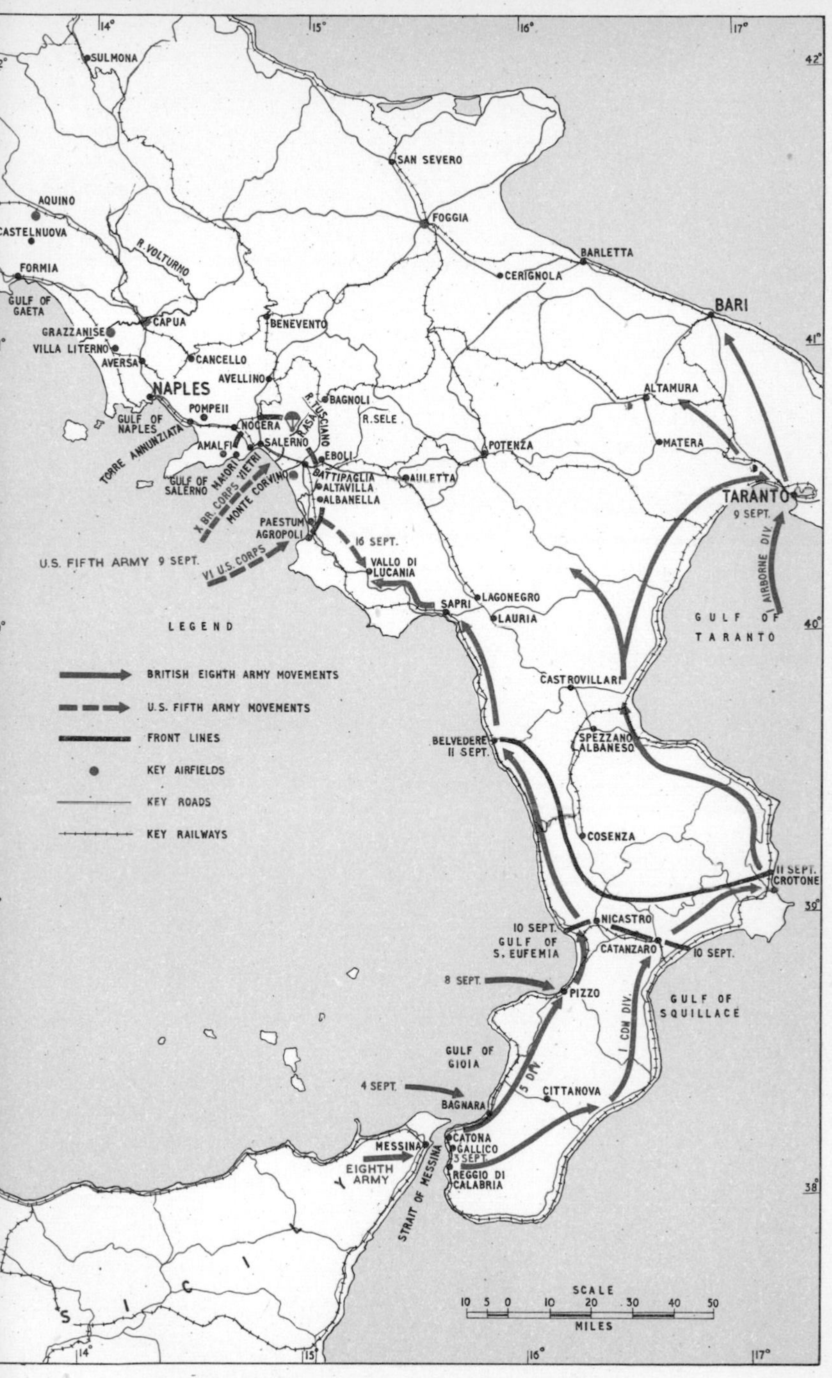

THE INVASION OF ITALY, 3–16 SEPTEMBER 1943

others had not seen much fighting. Yet they were to be victorious, and this for two reasons. The Northwest African Air Forces were in control above the beaches and were able, therefore, to provide observation for the guns beneath, while their bombers attacked targets which those guns could not hit. Moreover, the warships out to sea could bring their broadsides to bear with what proved to be devastating effect. Nevertheless, for three days the issue was in doubt.

By the end of the 13th, Altavilla had been abandoned and the enemy had advanced down both banks of the river Sele and had almost achieved his object, which was to cut the beach-head in half. That night, VI Corps withdrew from Albanella, and Battipaglia was lost. The critical nature of the situation was realized at once at Headquarters at La Marsa, where, at a conference, Tedder, turning to Alexander, promised all the aid the air could muster. The same undertaking was given by Admiral Cunningham speaking for the Navy and he ordered the *Warspite* and *Valiant* at full speed to the scene in spite of the danger of radio-controlled glider-bombs, which as has been recorded, were to put the *Warspite* out of commission for six months.

While the Allied naval forces maintained a fierce bombardment of German positions, the whole weight of the Allied air force available, including all the strategic bombers, was directed against German counter-attacks. On 12th September, fighters sped up and down the battlefield from dawn to dusk. Fighter-bombers were equally active and attacked transport upon roads in the areas of Sapri, Potenza and Auletta. These efforts continued unabated on the 13th and were increased upon the 14th, which witnessed the crisis of the battle. On that day the fighters and fighter-bombers of the Tactical Air Force flew somewhat more than 700 sorties against targets of opportunity wherever they presented themselves. The weight of the fighter-bomber attacks were especially directed against Battipaglia in the battle zone, and Torre Annunziata, the railway junction near Naples. The Desert Air Force took a hand from airfields near Reggio, and attacked German transport near Eboli. The heavy bombers, the United States Fortresses, also joined the battle, bombing Pompeii—'it was not safe even among the ruins' was the comment of an unhappy inhabitant—and Torre Annunziata, and at night Wellingtons of the indefatigable No. 205 Group attacked the same targets, and also road junctions, such as that at Castelnuova, a bridge at Benevento, and stretches of road near Formia.

During these three days the German Air Force made what attempt it could to hold its own, but, as in Sicily, it was overwhelmed and could do little to check the determination of Tedder's combined air forces to help their hard-pressed comrades of the army to the utmost of their ability. Realizing its impotence, the *Luftwaffe*, operating almost entirely at night, concentrated such strength as it still possessed against the beaches and the shipping lying off them, and left the German army units carrying out the counter-attacks without any protection except that which anti-aircraft could provide. These tactics gave our night fighters an opportunity to show their mettle and they took it in no uncertain manner.

One further service the air forces could, and did, render. A bold and imaginative use of airborne troops was made both to reinforce the hard-pressed front line and to harass the enemy in his immediate rear. While on the 14th the Navy was struggling to put more armour ashore on the beaches, the 504th Airborne Regiment of the 82nd U.S. Airborne Division was dropped in friendly territory some five miles behind the thinly held line of the VI Corps on the south-eastern perimeter of the beach-head. They found their dropping zones without difficulty, for they had been marked by navigational aids dropped by three Pathfinder aircraft. All the troops landed within 200 yards of the agreed point and were in the line before dawn. On the next night, the 14th/15th, the 505th United States Airborne Regiment belonging to the same Division was dropped in the same place and with the same happy results. Less than three quarters of an hour after the last aircraft had turned for base, some 2,100 parachute soldiers were on their way to the front near Agropoli. That night, too, a third airborne operation took place, the 509th Airborne Regiment being dropped at Avellino, or rather somewhere in the neighbourhood of that town. Because of the height of the mountains, most of the parachute troops had to leave their aircraft at between three and four thousand feet, and the Regiment was in consequence scattered far and wide. 'I was awakened suddenly by a violent shaking of my arm', says a German officer of the 16th Reconnaissance Unit, 16th Panzer Division, in his diary, 'and found a guard bending over me and pointing towards the sky. . . . I was still half asleep but forced my eyes open and saw the amazing sight for myself . . . fifty to sixty paratroops, still at a height of some 150 metres, swinging towards the ground . . . As it was a bright moonlight night one could recognise every white fleck in the heavens . . . Like cats, the gunners sprang into the turrets and soon . . . some twenty machine-guns were firing on the descending enemy'.

The swift use of airborne troops was one of the factors which kept in good heart the hard fighting Fifth Army during the six days when it was engaged upon that most hazardous operation of war, the carrying out of an opposed landing and the subsequent consolidation of the beach-head thus secured. The two other factors were the bombing of the enemy by the air forces and the gun-fire of the men-of-war. The aid thus given was gratefully acknowledged in a signal sent to Eisenhower by Alexander, who, on the critical 14th, was present in the beach-head and could see the situation for himself. In those three days and nights somewhat more than 2,300 tons of bombs were dropped on the battlefield or on its approaches, while the navy engaged in 129 bombardments of land targets. It was enough. The author of the German war diary kept by General von Vietinghoff, was soon sorrowfully recording that 'the fact that the attacks . . . were unable to reach their objectives owing to the fire from naval guns and low flying aircraft, as well as the slow but steady approach of the Eighth Army, caused the Army Commandant to withdraw from the battle . . . .'

By 15th September, 'Our hold on the mainland of Italy could be considered firm', and those directing the war on behalf of the Allies were able to draw the conclusion, which the raid on Dieppe of a little more than a year before had seemed to contradict, that an amphibious landing, even on coasts held by a resolute and well-prepared enemy, was possible, always provided that air supremacy had been attained. More, it had also been proved that the foothold, once secured, could be maintained by exploiting that supremacy. The Battle of Salerno was won by all three arms. 'The accurate and deadly shooting of the Navy', the stubbornness of the Army, the dash and ubiquity of the Air Forces had each made a vital and co-ordinated contribution, and together, the *tria juncta in uno* had secured victory. The portents were clear, and those already deep in the study of plans for the liberation of France could feel that a way had at last been found to secure the success of the most difficult part of the operation, the initial landing.

Though success was achieved after hard fighting at Salerno, failure attended the efforts of the Allies to mount another, if minor, invasion farther east. While the position in Italy was being secured, preparations were under way in the Middle East to gain a foothold in the Aegean. To seize Rhodes was of special importance, for its capture would prepare the way for the ultimate invasion of Greece. The island would provide the fighter airfields indispensable for such an operation, but its capture required strong air forces. They were not forthcoming, for, though the strength of the Allies in the air was very considerable, it lay rather in bombers and short-range fighters than in long-range fighters. These, however, were indispensable for the success of such an enterprise because of the distance, some 310 miles, separating Rhodes from the nearest Allied air bases in Cyprus and Cyrenaica.

Any hopes that the island would fall into our hands without fighting were still-born; for the Germans, never blind to the importance of Rhodes, had increased their garrisons and, though still far outnumbered, took immediate steps to overcome their erstwhile allies, the Italians. In three days they were in full control. The Allied commanders had, therefore, either to abandon their design altogether or to be content to turn aside, avoid Rhodes, and lay hands instead on Kos, Leros and Samos. This was the course they chose. The position of Kos, with its airfield at Antimachia, made it the pass-key of which the possession would unlock the Aegean. Seize it, and Rhodes would fall, and with Rhodes the other islands of the Archipelago, garrisoned as they were for the most part by Italians, who would certainly surrender at the first approach of invading forces.

Kos was to be taken by a combined assault of all three arms and the part to be played by the air forces followed the usual pattern—first, the bombing of enemy airfields within range in Greece, Rhodes and Crete, and the despatch to them of intruders to prevent the *Luftwaffe* from using them; secondly, attacks on all enemy shipping found in the Aegean; thirdly, the protection of the convoys conveying the assault troops. To these general tasks were added the reconnaissance of Leros, Samos and other islands and the dropping of leaflets by a flight of Wellingtons operating from the Nile Delta. Eight Dakotas from No. 216 Squadron were detailed to carry airborne troops, and departed to Palestine for the purpose of training with them.

The air forces detailed for the conduct of these operations were not large. Apart from the troop-carrying and transport Dakotas, there were two day and two night Beaufighter squadrons, a Wellington (Torpedo Bomber) squadron, three Baltimore and one Hudson (General Reconnaissance) squadrons, three Spitfire and two Hurricane (Fighter) squadrons and a detachment of Photographic Reconnaissance Spitfires. This force was based on the mainland of Africa and in Cyprus. In addition, two heavy bomber squadrons of No. 240 (Royal Air Force) Wing of IX United States Bomber Command took part at a later stage. In all, the number of aircraft amounted to 144 fighters (single and twin-engined), and 116 heavy, medium and torpedo bombers.

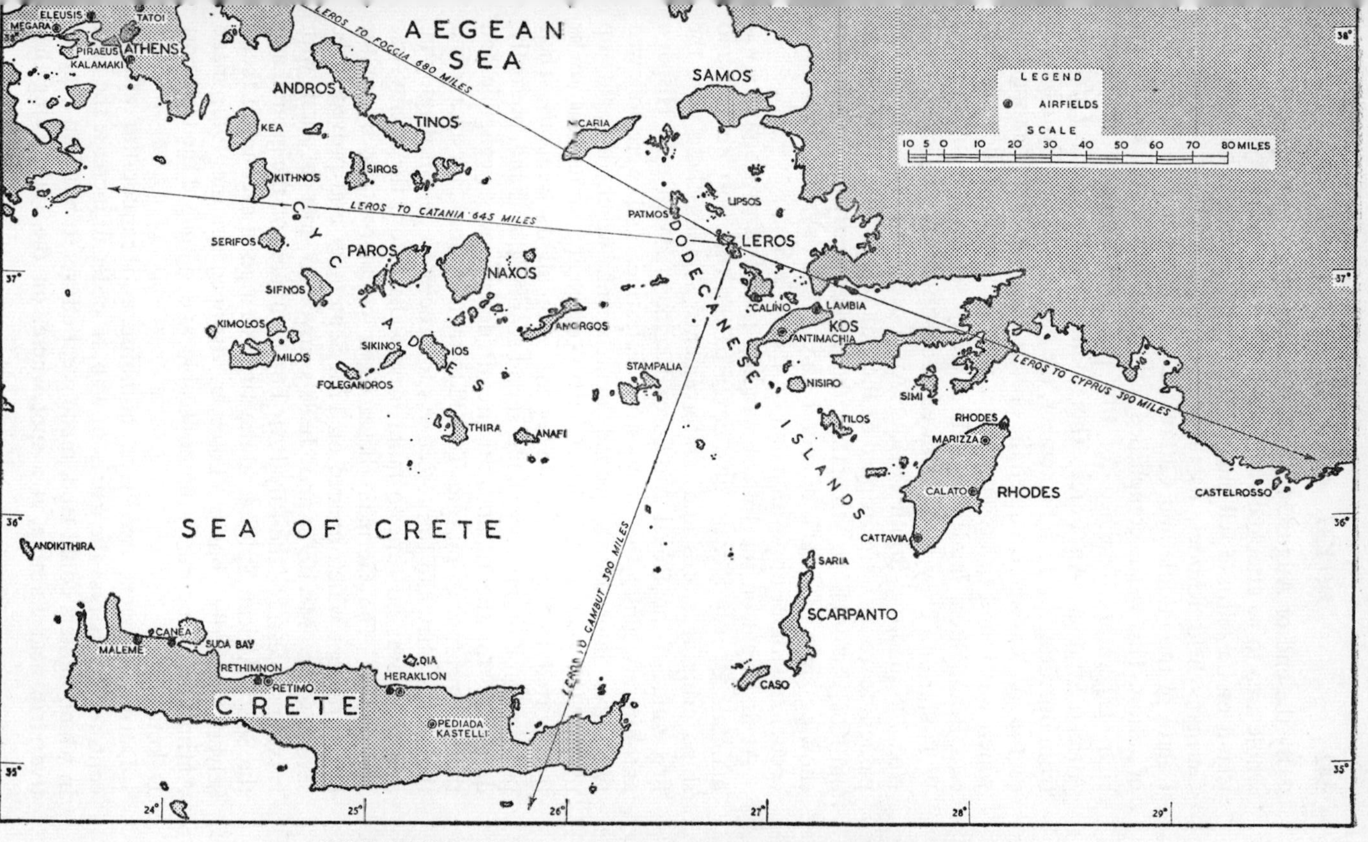

OPERATIONS IN THE AEGEAN, 9 SEPTEMBER - 22 OCTOBER 1943

By the end of August, No. 680 Squadron had photographed the whole area to be attacked and operations began nine days later. The island of Castelrosso fell into our hands immediately, but since the Germans held Rhodes, its three airfields, Marizza in the north, Calato in the middle and Cattavia in the south, had to be put out of action. This was accomplished for a time by the attack of thirty-eight Liberators detached for this purpose from the Northwest African Strategic Air Force. Their bombs prevented the *Luftwaffe* from operating on 13th September, the day on which a British force set foot on Kos and occupied the port and the airfield at Antimachia, which was found to be serviceable. At dawn on the following day, two Beaufighters landed and their crews set up a point-to-point W.T. station. They were followed soon afterwards by Spitfires of No. 7 Squadron, South African Air Force, and that night 120 parachute troops were dropped by the Dakotas of No. 216 Squadron on Kos, in order to strengthen the Italian garrison, which was showing signs of a lack of moral fibre. That day, too, Leros was occupied without opposition and on the 16th, Samos.

At first light on the 15th, a standing patrol of two Spitfires was maintained over Kos to give cover to the transport aircraft and ships bringing stores and reinforcements. Among these were the first units of the Royal Air Force Regiment. With nine Hispano anti-aircraft guns, they flew from Palestine, and were followed two days later by a second detachment, which brought up to strength one of the first of the Regiment's squadrons to be transported to the battlefield by air with all its weapons. Their position on Kos, never enviable, soon became serious and, presently, desperate, for the Italian anti-aircraft defence was negligible and their own resources meagre. To add to their troubles, the area round the airfield they had to protect was too rocky to permit digging in, and there was no time to build blast walls before the enemy was upon them. The Germans began their counter-attack by an air bombardment which opened on 17th September and proved to be severe. The Me.109's and Ju.88's involved met at first with varying success, for the Royal Air Force gunners on the ground and the South African Spitfires in the air gave a good account of themselves. 'Butterfly' bombs, however, dropped on the 19th, made Antimachia temporarily unserviceable and damaged the transport Dakotas.

During the next two days, bombing and cannon-fire attacks continued to harass the garrison, who, in order to increase the area in which fighters could land, made great efforts to build an alternative strip near Lambia, at a spot where, on the 18th, seeing that

Antimachia was under attack, the pilot of a Dakota had landed rather than return to Cyprus with his load. It was completed on the 21st and then ensued a lull which lasted a week. The *Luftwaffe* was building up, and by the end of the month had transferred over 100 aircraft to the Aegean area to bring its strength to over 350, which included ninety Ju.88's and He.111's, fifty Me.109's and sixty-five Ju.87's. These forces had had to be withdrawn from other theatres of operations, and at this time there were only a little over 400 aircraft left in Italy, Corsica and the south of France.

In an attempt to interfere with the enemy's plans, which were daily becoming more obvious, Liberators, Halifaxes, Wellingtons and Hudsons, of No. 240 Wing and No. 201 Group, attacked airfields near Athens on four nights between the 20th and 25th September. Those on Crete and Rhodes also received attention. The attacks do not appear to have had much effect, for on the 26th the enemy was able to resume his air offensive and soon made conditions in Kos very difficult. By the end of that day only four of the Spitfires of No. 7 Squadron were still able to fly, and anti-aircraft gunners of the Royal Air Force Regiment, though reinforced by Bofors manned by the army, were not strong enough to beat off the German bombers. Reinforcements in the form of nine Spitfires of No. 74 Squadron arrived, but were too few to prevent or drive away an enemy smarting under recent reverses and determined to use to the full the local air superiority he had created by moving squadrons so swiftly from bases as far distant as the south of France. A determined raid on 29th September scored forty direct hits on Antimachia, and caused a move to Lambia, where, during the night of 2nd October, urgent supplies were landed by five Dakotas. During their unloading, news came that a small German invasion fleet of ten vessels was at sea. The 880 men of the Army and the 235 of the Royal Air Force Regiment on Kos prepared to defend the island unaided, for by then the Italian garrison had made it clear that in their view the better part of valour was discretion.

At dawn on the 3rd the Germans landed by sea and air, and by midday 1,500 men, well-armed with light artillery and armoured cars, were ashore and in action. Dive-bombing by Ju.87's added to the difficulties of the defence, and in the afternoon Antimachia was overrun. Lambia fell at 0600 hours on the following morning, and what was left of the garrison signalled laconically: 'Kos town untenable. Intend continuing to fight elsewhere. Destroying wireless set'. Kos had been in Allied hands for a bare three weeks.

The next island to be regained by the enemy was Leros, and the same tactics were used. A superior force of the *Luftwaffe* based on airfields in Rhodes, Crete and Greece, all most conveniently close at hand, bombed the island almost at their pleasure. No fighter cover could be given to its small garrison, for the nearest Allied airfields were some 390 miles away. The invasion began on 12th October and by the 16th all was over. As at Kos, it was carried out partly by seaborne troops and partly by airborne, whose standard of training and marksmanship was high. On more than one occasion the magazines of the Bren guns in the hands of the defenders were shot away as soon as they were inserted. The Germans also showed that the link between the *Luftwaffe* above and the troops below was strong and effective, the first instantly responding to all demands made on them by the second.

Mediterranean Air Command had not remained indifferent to the situation in the Middle Eastern theatre. Between 14th October and 16th November, United States Mitchells were sent to attack Greek airfields, and in so doing flew 317 sorties, and the heavier Liberators made a single attack on the airfield at Eleusis. Arrangements were also made for a Mitchell group, armed with 75-mm. cannon, to attack shipping in the area of Kos and Calino, and to do so it flew a total of eighty-six sorties between 16th October and 16th November. These assaults, by sinking a number of the invasion craft, delayed, but could not prevent, the enemy from accomplishing his purpose, and long before the middle of November the situation was lost beyond retrieving. Nevertheless, the bombers, both the Mitchells and the Liberators, continued to operate until 8th December, their targets for the last month being the airfields at Larissa, Eleusis and Kalamaki. The reinforcements of fighters sent were smaller, but No. 603 (Beaufighter) Squadron was transferred to the Aegean on 12th October and was joined by No. 47 Squadron at the end of the month. These reinforcements were adequate to meet the situation, but, though sent as soon as demanded, they arrived too late.

The fact was that the Allies were trying to accomplish too much. Their reach exceeded their grasp and the hoped for heaven turned out to be an operation which was not in fact a feasible operation of war with the means made available.

In this unhappy story the gallantry of the Dakota crews of No. 216 Squadron must not be forgotten. Shortage of shipping placed a great responsibility on transport aircraft for keeping the invading forces supplied and in these operations the Squadron played a notable part. Many of the flights involved had to be undertaken by aircrew inexperienced in supply-dropping. Altogether from the night of 5th/6th October to that of 19th/20th November, when the last sortie was flown to the third of the ill-fated islands—Samos, regained by the enemy on 22nd November—these missions were attempted on twenty-six occasions, involving a total of eighty-seven sorties. The despatchers were volunteer airmen or soldiers who, inspired by the army officer in charge, carried out their task with stout hearts. The outstanding achievement of the Squadron was the dropping on two nights of 200 officers and men of the Greek Sacred Squadron on to the island of Samos, from which they were very soon withdrawn. When the last ship bearing them had sailed away under cover of darkness, the British and Americans in the Aegean were back where they had started.

This rash experiment had cost the lives of some hundreds of troops and airmen, a large quantity of valuable stores and equipment, a number of naval vessels and 115 aircraft. The German losses were as heavy, if not heavier, but they had regained lost ground and by so doing received much-needed encouragement. The operation, ill-judged from the beginning, had been the result of over-confidence, an unconscious flouting of a cardinal principle of modern warfare. Troops and ships in isolated positions without air support cannot long survive if their enemy, moving on interior lines, can bring his air power to bear at the crucial point. Nevertheless, when all is said, the Aegean episode was no more than a setback, humiliating indeed, but with no effect on the final issue.

CHAPTER XVI

The Path to Rome

WHILE the Fifth Army was engaged so sternly on the plains and in the hills about Salerno, the Eighth, encountering but slight resistance, but delayed by demolitions, was moving slowly up from the south and south-east of Italy. On 16th September, patrols from its 1st Airborne Division, which had been landed at Taranto, made contact on their left with the Canadians who, moving steadily to Avigliano, had captured Potenza by the 19th. Here they came into touch with the Fifth Army which had seized the high ground to the north and east of Eboli. For the next few days the enemy continued to withdraw, pivoting on his right flank north of Salerno. It was his plan, now that the whereabouts of the Allied invasion had been discovered and its strength gauged, to hold on a line south of Rome running from Gaeta through Isernia to Vasto; but before retreating to these positions, which were to form the basis of his winter line, he continued to fight a series of delaying actions. During these he lost the large group of airfields around Foggia, of which the capture was one of the strategic objects of the Allies. They fell to the Eighth Army on 27th September. On the next day, Broadhurst's Desert Air Force found themselves entering a bleak plain, and could see upon their right hand the mountainous promontory of Monte Gargano, the spur on the heel of Italy. In the midst of this plain was the dusty town of Foggia, of which the general appearance had not been improved by the frequent air attacks made upon it, and to the south of it, the airfields. They were of great extent and admirably suited for the operations of heavy bombers.

Three days before they suffered this severe loss, the Germans completed their evacuation of Sardinia. This island, which, it will be remembered, had at one time been considered as a possible objective in place of Sicily, had been attacked from the air since the beginning of February, the attacks varying in intensity but becoming severe in April and May. Its main airfields—among them Elmas, Monserrato, Milis, Olbia and Alghero—had been subjected to spasmodic and sometimes violent assault by Wellingtons at night and United States fighter-bombers and Mitchells by day throughout the period immediately before the invasion of Sicily and during it. On the fall of Sicily and with the invasion of Italy imminent, the German High Command decided to cut its losses and the evacuation of both Sardinia and Corsica was decreed and carried out. After rendering the main landing fields unserviceable, and destroying such aircraft as could not be taken away, the *Luftwaffe* moved off almost without loss, save among the seaplanes of the 2nd *Staffel* of No. 196 *Gruppe* which covered the forces retreating by sea, and in so doing lost heavily in combat with Beaufighters. The German Air Force could justly claim that it had successfully withdrawn most of its units, which were then sent to reinforce those in the area of Rome. They were badly needed there, for the *Luftwaffe* in Italy was in a sorry state. Before 1943 was out, their resources, in aircraft and men alike, had fallen far too low to cope with the many demands made upon them, ranging as these did from attacks on Allied shipping carrying reinforcements, to close support over the field of battle.

Having secured the Salerno beach-head, the Allied armies began their advance, and on 1st October the 7th Armoured Division entered Naples. This great town, the largest city captured from the enemy up to that date, had been attacked from the air over fifty times. Some of these onslaughts had been singularly effective especially those directed against the marshalling yards, where much damage had been caused including the destruction of about 600 railway wagons. There is no doubt that the Northwest African Air Forces were very successful in creating at Naples a stumbling-block to the movement of supplies to southern Italy, and their success was enhanced by the destruction at the end of August of an ammunition ship in the harbour. Whether through an act of sabotage or from a cause unknown, she blew up and caused heavy casualties, the shells on board flying 'like meteors through the air' to explode indiscriminately all over the town. Before leaving, the Germans demolished the harbour and the landing gear, including the heavy cranes. They then fell back, abandoning upon the nearby airfields of Capodichino and Pomigliano 145 German and 45 Italian aircraft.

With the capture of Naples, it seemed for the moment that there was a chance of bringing the campaign in Italy to a rapid and triumphant conclusion. The enemy was in retreat and hard pressed. By 6th October, the Fifth Army stood along the line of the Volturno river and the Eighth was opposite Termoli. The second of the four phases, into which Alexander had sought to divide the campaign, had been completed. The third phase, the seizure of Rome and its airfields, now seemed possible, and this would lead to the fourth, the advance to Leghorn, Florence and Arezzo.

The completion of the second phase had one result of outstanding importance to the Allied onslaught upon the *Reich* from the air. The capture of the Foggia group almost completed the circle of airfields lying round Germany. Henceforward and for the rest of the war it was possible to bomb that country from bases as far apart as the levels of Lincolnshire and the plain of Apulia, and not Germany only, but all the Balkan Peninsula, the industrial areas of Silesia, the factories of Czechoslovakia, the oilfields of Rumania. Allied bombers made their first attack from Foggia on the aircraft factories of Wiener Neustadt on 1st October, only three days after the group had fallen into our hands. It was carried out entirely by United States bombers of the Strategic Air Force, whose crews showed a splendid determination to help their comrades of the Eighth American Air Force and of Bomber Command operating from England to fulfil the Casablanca Directive. Between 1st October, 1943 and 8th May, 1945, attacks were launched from Foggia against a great variety of targets. Among those assaulted were Augsburg, Munich, Breslau and Pilsen in Germany and Czechoslovakia, Wiener Neustadt, Innsbruck and Klagenfurt in Austria, Bucharest, the Iron Gate of the Danube, and Ploesti in Rumania, Budapest and Pécs in Hungary, Czechowicka in Poland and Marseilles, Toulon, Lyons and Grenoble in France. From this base, too, the mining operations of No. 205 Group of the Royal Air Force, which did so much damage to hostile shipping in the Danube, and which are described in Volume III (Chapter X), were mounted.

From the point of view of General Alexander, the presence at Foggia of units of the Strategic Air Force was more a liability than an asset. They were engaged in carrying out the strategic bombing programme which had no direct relation to the military operations for which he was responsible. Yet they were based on Italy, then but partially conquered, and, as the months went by, to be the scene of a fierce and long drawn-out campaign. The problem of supplying the heavy bombardment groups stationed at Foggia put a severe strain on the supply services and on shipping, while 'their maintenance requirements were nearly as great as those of the Eighth Army'. On the other hand, one of the main objects of the invasion of Italy had been to secure these bases for the purpose for which they were used.

Though superiority, indeed supremacy, in the air had been virtually achieved in the Central Mediterranean within three days of the Allied landings in Sicily, and though thereafter the *Luftwaffe* gave no cause for anxiety, an occasional success rewarded its spasmodic efforts to play a part altogether beyond its strength. On the night of 2nd/3rd December, preceded by three aircraft flying at 10,000 feet dropping 'Window'—the strips of tinfoil which were proving so baffling to the night-fighter defences of Germany—a force of Ju.88's dropped bombs and parachute mines upon the town and harbour of Bari with devastating effect. A ship carrying ammunition was hit almost at once and her explosion set three others on fire. The conflagration spread until fourteen merchant vessels, with 34,330 tons of cargo on board, were burning or sunk; three more went down, but their cargoes were saved, and six others were damaged; the bulk petrol pipeline was pierced and took three weeks to repair. About 1,000 men, chiefly seamen and soldiers, were killed and injured. By then, it must be admitted, the Allies had grown careless. Bari was defended by a bare minimum of anti-aircraft guns and there were far too few searchlights. On the night of the attack the best sited radar warning set was unserviceable, telephone communication was bad throughout the area, and the defence arrangements suffered from being under too many authorities.

Such a raid, however, could cause no more than a temporary setback. Nor could the German night attacks by Ju.88's on Naples do more than hamper the influx of supplies. Here, too, the Germans used 'Window' with some success, confusing alike the radar warning stations and the fighters sent up to repel the raiders. The anti-aircraft gunners were less affected and it was to their fire that the majority of such as were destroyed fell. Far more serious than the opposition of the *Luftwaffe* was the evil weather, which, persisting, soon became the bane alike of the air forces and of the army. 'The Apennines', said one observer, 'produced Jekyll and Hyde conditions. A blue sky to the west could mask scudding clouds to the east'[1]. Soon squadrons were experiencing every variation of climate at very short notice, and flying conditions, which at the beginning of a sortie were good, often became in the proverbial twinkling of an eye so bad that a closely knit system of diverting and recalling aircraft became urgently necessary. This led to an increase in the labours of those engaged on Flying Control, an organization which, being almost unnecessary in the desert, had up till then hardly existed. The Mobile Operations Room Unit did its best to help pilots who, with long hours of flying in Africa behind them, found the new weather conditions difficult and exasperating. The trials of the Unit were many. 'Daylight found the site an indescribable scene of desolation', records an entry in its diary for 1st January, 1944, when it was at Penna Point. 'In the small hours the abominable

[1] *The Desert Air Force.* Roderic Owen (Hutchinson).

gale returned accompanied by very heavy rain. One and all suffered. The orderly room was flattened and draped half across the road'. The airmen were found shelter in neighbouring houses and the seven officers took refuge in a chapel hard by, whose verger '. . . came in and . . . produced a vast bottle of Vino Rosso and made us all drink to Capo d'Anno. No flying was possible'. Close at hand the 7th South African Air Force Wing on the beach at Trigno was washed out by high waves driven on to the shore by the 'strong northerly gale'.

From October 1943 until well on into the spring of 1944 weather conditions were to prove a potent cause of the delay in the advance of the armies; and with delay came frustration. Long before October was out, Alexander's plan to complete the third phase, the capture of Rome, had gone irretrievably agley. He had hoped that the enemy would retreat north and stand on a line running from Pisa to Rimini, the 'Gothic Line' which the Allied army was eventually to assault many weary months later. Instead, urged by Hitler, who sent imperative orders on 10th October, Kesselring stood to his defence much farther south along what presently became known as the 'Winter Line' and then the 'Gustav Line'—a series of positions defended in depth, based on the Rivers Sangro in the east and Garigliano in the west, and containing among others the strong position of Cassino in the massif of Monte Cairo. An earlier attempt to turn this line by landing Commando troops at Termoli on the east coast had miscarried through failure to exploit their initial success, and with it the last chance of moving speedily up Italy to Rome and beyond.

Throughout this period the bomber forces maintained their attacks whenever possible on targets far and near. The marshalling yards at Civitavecchia, Pisa, Bologna, Mestre and the railway bridge at Bolzano all felt the weight of their assault. Closer at hand, as the weather decreed and opportunity offered, the Tactical Air Force ranged the sky above the battlefield. It was especially to the fore at the crossing of the Volturno and Trigno rivers in the middle of October, and of the Sangro a month later. During these months of bitter fighting on the ground there were no great battles in the air. The tale is rather one of monotonous co-operation, of day-to-day protection afforded to troops in close contact with a resolute foe. Individual combats there were on occasion, such as that which took place one December day between a Spitfire of Desert Air Force flown by a young South African pilot, Lieutenant A. Sachs of No. 92 Squadron, Royal Air Force, who attacked twelve Focke-Wulf 190's seeking to assault our forward troops. He shot down two within a few moments, the second blowing up to the detriment of his own aircraft, which was soon further damaged by the remaining Focke-Wulfs, now roused to fury. Half the tail was shot away, both wings were damaged, and the engine was smashed and set on fire. Then a Focke-Wulf collided head-on with the Spitfire and fell burning to the ground. The Spitfire began to fall too, and Sachs baled out, his parachute opening at the last possible moment. On landing he was surrounded by a number of peasants, who rushed forward and kissed his hands.

Bad weather proved a more redoubtable foe than the *Luftwaffe*. This entered so little into their calculations that the Desert Air Force presently evolved a form of tactical support which was to prove of great, of very great, value in the battles awaiting the Allies in Normandy, Belgium, the Netherlands and Germany. The Eighth Army had stumbled up the comparatively open and unencumbered east coast of Italy and had crossed the Trigno, when the air forces protecting it began to elaborate the system already in use for describing targets on the battlefield the infantry wished to be attacked from the air. Their delineation had for long been the task of the Air Liaison Officers stationed at all Wing and Group headquarters and with the Mobile Operations Room Unit. Targets were accepted or rejected by the Headquarters of the Desert Air Force after consultation with Army Area Headquarters. On acceptance, a single code-word, to which the word 'accept' was added, was sufficient to cause the Mobile Operations Room Unit to allot the target to the appropriate Wing. By the time the acceptance had been received, the Air Liaison Officer was ready to brief the squadrons detailed for the operation.

This practice, with various modifications, had proved successful in the desert. In the closer country, however, in which the army was now operating, something which would achieve much quicker results was necessary. It was discovered by Wing Commander D. Haysom who gave his Christian name to the experiment. Haysom created a Mobile Observation Post situated with the forward troops at Brigade Headquarters, and in direct communication with a squadron or squadrons of aircraft already airborne. The same photographic map with a grid superimposed upon it was used by both pilots and controllers, and by means of it the second gave targets to the first as and when necessary. What happened was this. A squadron of fighters or fighter-bombers patrolled overhead, usually in line astern, and when the army called for an attack to be made upon a specific target, one or more aircraft from the formation, or 'Cab Rank', as it at once came to be known, dived upon it and dropped its bombs or opened fire with its cannon. 'Rover David'—to give this system its code-name—proved an instant success. It was conducted at first from armoured cars fitted with Very High Frequency transmitters, but presently the equipment included a lorry, a jeep and a trailer manned by an army and a R.A.F. officer with a mechanic. What 'Rover' patrols were to be flown was settled on the evening preceding each day of battle at a conference attended by representatives of the army and the air force.

The advantages of the 'Cab Rank' system quickly became obvious. Targets, fixed or moving, could be bombed or subjected to cannon and machine gun fire very swiftly, within a matter of minutes after they had been chosen. Various modifications of the system were tried from time to time as the war went on, but its essential principle remained unchanged.

'Rover David' would have been quite impossible to institute had the *Luftwaffe* been able to dispute the presence of Allied aircraft over the battlefield. That such a system could be adopted and maintained in action from the late autumn of 1943 until the end of the war is one of the many proofs of the supremacy which the Allied air forces established. It had, however, its disadvantages, the principal one being the very large number of aircraft needed to keep it in operation. Only when the air forces of a country have very great resources on which to draw, and the virtual certainty that air opposition will be negligible and will remain so, can they afford the luxury of a 'Cab Rank' system. Fortunately, as the war progressed, the Allies came to be more and more in that happy situation with every day that passed, and there can be no doubt that it proved of great value and saved many lives.

On 10th December, Mediterranean Air Command became Mediterranean Allied Air Forces and into its headquarters was absorbed that of Northwest African Air Forces. The Northwest African Tactical, Strategic and Coastal Air Forces were renamed Mediterranean Allied Tactical, Strategic and Coastal Air Forces respectively. Their activities were unchanged and in fact increased, for better weather in the first half of the month enabled the strategic bombers, particularly those of the Royal Air Force, to attack the Italian railways. Bolzano was again assaulted, together with the marshalling yards at Arezzo; so, too, were the ball-bearing works in Turin. On 2nd December, some precious hours of sunshine enabled the Tactical Air Forces to be directed against targets on the front of the Fifth Army, then preparing to attack south-west of Mignano.

This day marked the end of exactly three calendar months of operations against the enemy in Italy. They had been uniformly

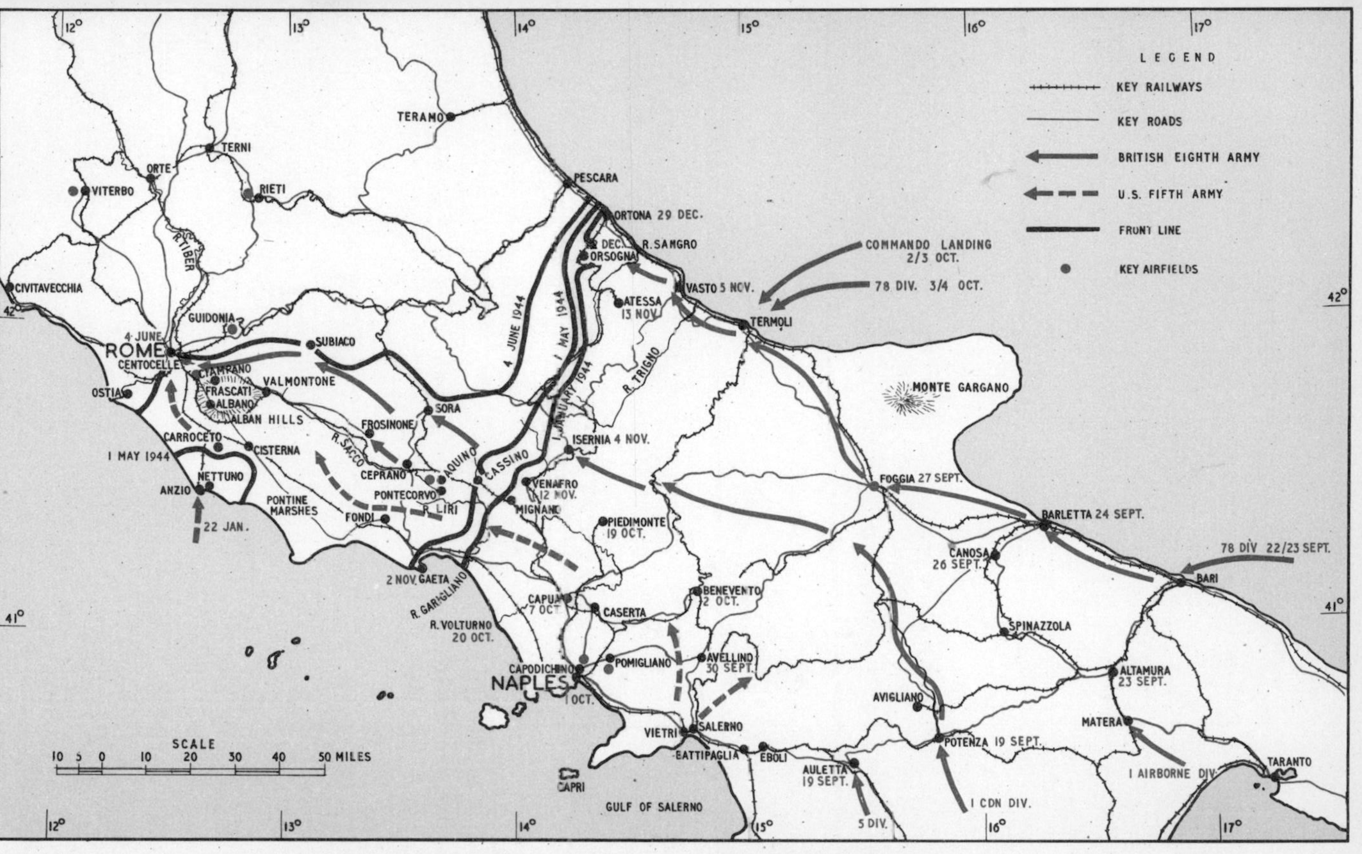

THE ITALIAN FRONT, SEPTEMBER 1943—JUNE 1944

[*facing page 352*]

successful in the air in contrast to those on the ground. The armies had made a good beginning but, losing momentum, had failed to achieve a decision. The fact was that the Germans had throughout shown a great spirit of determination and stubbornness. Their men were resolute, well-trained and quick to profit from the natural advantages afforded by swollen rivers, tumbled mountains and infrequent roads. In strength they were nine divisions, and to oppose them the Allies could muster no more than eleven, 'no great numerical superiority' as Alexander observes in his despatch.

At the beginning of 1944, General Sir H. Maitland Wilson took over supreme command in the Mediterranean from Eisenhower, who was appointed Supreme Commander for the invasion of Normandy. Montgomery was succeeded on 1st January by General Leese, and all the armies concerned were grouped under the general title 'Allied Armies in Italy'. A change of command was also made in the air forces, General I. Eaker, of the United States Army Air Force, taking over from Tedder, who departed to the more important post of Eisenhower's deputy. Eaker had as his second in command Air Marshal Sir John C. Slessor. The new commanders, like the old, were determined to fulfil the general plan to 'contain the maximum number of German divisions in Italy', and duly continued along the thorny path to Rome.

Alexander's first 'knight's move' in October 1943, the outflanking of the German line at Termoli, had not been successful; but now, three months later, a similar operation, carried out on a larger scale on the west coast, within easy distance of Rome, might give him his next and most desired prize, the Eternal City. A successful landing at the two small ports of Anzio and Nettuno, on the western seaboard, followed by the immediate seizure of the Alban Hills, would outflank the defences of Monte Cassino, gateway to the coastal road to Rome, and render a frontal assault, on what had always been considered an impregnable position, unnecessary.

As at Pachino and Salerno, the general task of the air forces at Anzio was, first and foremost, to eliminate all opposition from the air from such of the 555[1] operational aircraft which, it was thought, composed at that time the remaining strength of the *Luftwaffe* in Italy. Next in order of importance came the disruption of the enemy's supply lines, then protection from the air for the assault convoys, and lastly, direct participation in the operation by attacking suitable targets in the battlefield and its neighbourhood. Plans were drawn up with these four ends in view, but their details changed almost as

[1] In fact they numbered no more than 350.

quickly and as often as did the date of the assault, which, for one reason or another, was postponed from week to week until it was finally launched on 22nd January, 1944.

The operation began well by the achievement of complete surprise. This had been secured by the action of the air forces in striking hard at all the central Italian airfields. So effective were these blows, especially those against Ciampino, Centocelle, Guidonia, Rieti and Viterbo, that the *Luftwaffe* was unable to put even one reconnaissance aircraft into the air. In consequence, the convoy of 243 vessels of various kinds and nationalities carrying the assaulting troops was able to reach the Anzio beaches unobserved. Once more, thanks to the power of the air, 50,000 American and British troops had arrived undetected in full battle array, this time many miles behind the enemy's front. Not until twenty minutes past eight on the morning of 22nd January, six hours after the landings had been carried out, did a Messerschmitt 109 succeed in penetrating the air screen and bringing authentic news to Kesselring that the Allies were behind his right flank.

Having at length discovered the new invaders, the *Luftwaffe* did what it could to molest them, but until 2nd February it was never able to fly more than a maximum of 100 sorties a day of which some sixty were by fighters. Fog on the airfields and its own depleted numbers made a stouter effort impossible. Its chief success was the sinking of the British cruiser *Spartan* by glider-bomb on the 29th. The Royal Air Force and the United States fighter squadrons, on patrol above the beach-head, were numerous and alert. Beyond them, in the area between Rome and Anzio, notably at Albano on 2nd February, the bombs dropped by Fortresses and American medium bombers on road junctions and other tactical targets hindered the approach of reinforcements on the ground, and, far away from the immediate battlefield, attacks on Italian railways, notably at Pisa, Empoli and Pontedera, were maintained with good, though not decisive, effect.

For a day or two it seemed that Alexander was at last to reap the reward of his great and sustained efforts. But this was not to be. The troops ashore failed, or were not able, to exploit the surprise they had achieved. General Lucas, their commander, fulfilling the letter rather than the spirit of the plan, chose not a swift dash inland to those delectable mountains, the Alban Hills, but the painstaking consolidation of his bridgehead. In his defence it must be admitted that the beaches were so unsuitable and the little port of Anzio, which a battalion of the 29th Panzer Grenadiers had failed to blow up, of such limited capacity, that the landing of guns, tanks and heavy equipment 'was delayed beyond our expectations'. On the other hand an air force of great, indeed overwhelming, strength was present and active.

Though weak in the air, the enemy was now strong on the ground. A regiment of the 3rd Panzer Grenadier Division, on its way east to oppose the Eighth Army, was brought back to the Alban Hills, where it was joined on the evening of the 23rd by a regimental group of the 15th Panzer Grenadiers. These troops, reinforced by a part of the Hermann Göring Division, were ready to carry out unflinchingly a brusque order from Hitler to 'struggle for every yard'. By 30th January, elements of eight army divisions were assembled south of Rome, hastily organized, it is true, and very mixed in character, but stout-hearted and determined to display the German genius for war. They did so.

By 2nd February General Lucas's advance was halted, and the efforts of the air forces to clear a path for him were unavailing. American bombers attacked Ceprano and Pontecorvo, but not heavily enough to ease the situation. The headquarters of those directing the German forces were also assaulted. On 10th February Allied bombers destroyed the Villa Propaganda at Castel Gandolfo. Some 500 civilians suffered, many being killed; but the German Staff escaped, for they were not in the building. Nor were the Tactical Air Forces, which continued to bomb road junctions immediately beyond the beach-head, more successful. Nevertheless, pressure by the Allied Air Forces was maintained by day and night, and marshalling yards as far distant from the area as Verona were bombed, the object being to cut the line through the Brenner Pass to Bologna along which reinforcements must be carried.

Though unable to produce more fighters, the enemy had brought his strength to 130 by transferring two Junkers 88 *Gruppen* of bombers from Greece and Crete to north Italy, and by reinforcing his striking force in the south of France by twenty-five Dornier 217's equipped with radio-controlled glider-bombs.

The Fifth Army, which at the end of January had attacked across the Garigliano in support of Operation 'Shingle', was given full fighter protection, and the Bostons of the Desert Air Force did all they could at night to prevent the movement of German troops from east to west. They were able to achieve a certain success, for the enemy drivers, faced with difficult Apennines roads, dared not turn off their headlights and therefore provided targets easily visible. Farther away heavy bombers made raids against the Montpellier and Istres le Tubé airfields in the south of France and the Udine group in the north of Italy. The attack on Lavariano, Villaorba, Maniago and Udine of 30th January, 1944, was particularly successful. 215

escorted Fortresses and Liberators dropped some 29,000 twenty-pound fragmentation bombs, which did much execution among German fighters assembled there for the dual purpose of reinforcing Kesselring's hard-pressed air force and of intercepting the long-range Allied bombers operating from Foggia against Austria and southern Germany.

These efforts, which involved the dropping of 12,500 tons of bombs between 22nd January and 15th February, though by no means insignificant, could not prevent Kesselring from launching a strong counter-attack, which came near to complete success. The troops who delivered it were in high fettle and were under the stimulus of a special order from Hitler, who demanded that the abscess, as he called it, should be 'eliminated in three days'. They were further heartened by promises of strong air support and by the use of a new weapon, the Goliath remote-control explosive tank. The counter-attack began at dawn on 16th February, and by the end of the day an advance into our positions of some 2,000 yards had been made. The air strip at Nettuno was under artillery fire and could not be used. On the next day the drive continued until a 'wedge of two and a half miles wide and over a mile deep' had been driven into the positions of the invaders at Anzio. This the enemy had accomplished with very limited help from his air force. On the 16th the *Luftwaffe* was able to fly at most 250 sorties and on the next day about 200. It seemed as though his infantry were capable of achieving victory without air support. Indeed, had this been adequate, the issue would hardly have been in doubt. The 18th was the most critical day. For four hours the battle raged just beyond the 'final beach-head line', which if pierced would entail either the destruction of the force or its hasty withdrawal to the friendly safety of the Tyrrhenian Sea.

By then, as at Salerno, the navy and the air forces had begun to intervene and to play a great, perhaps a decisive part, in preventing the achievement of Kesselring's desire, and this despite the weather, which varied between 'poor' and 'bad'. On 17th February, more than 800 bombers of all kinds, including Wellingtons, dropped 950 tons of bombs in close support of the armies—the heaviest assistance in one day which the Allied Air Forces had yet been able to render. On the 18th, the weather was very bad and no more than forty United States Invaders and eighty-seven Warhawks were able to aid the hard-pressed troops. The weather next day was the same, but on the 20th it improved, and more than 10,000 fragmentation bombs were dropped on enemy concentrations near Carroceto, on the way to Anzio.

The German counter-attack was at last spent, and Alexander felt confident '. . . that the bridgehead could be held'. But the invaders were equally exhausted, and it seemed unwise to their commander to use his 'last fresh troops' to repeat 'our former attacks, unless I could produce some new tactics to give us a better chance of success. In this frame of mind I decided to try the effect of a really heavy air bombardment'. General Cannon, Commanding General of the Tactical Air Force, was anxious to make the experiment too; he hazarded the opinion that, given good weather and all the air resources in Italy, we could 'whip out Cassino like an old tooth'. The General had already witnessed the effects of one such experiment conducted on 15th February when the Monastery on Monte Cassino was destroyed by a concentrated bombing attack. How this came about must now be explained.

In order to support the operations at Anzio an assault against the general Cassino positions had been launched by the 34th American Division of the Fifth Army. By 2nd February it had driven the Germans from Monte Casselone, a nearby bastion, and, advancing along a feature known as Snake's Head Ridge, had reached a point a few hundred yards from Monastery Hill. This advance so encouraged General Clark that he sent a message to Alexander declaring that 'present indications are that the Cassino Heights will be captured very soon'. The General was an optimist, but at that time his optimism seemed well founded. Yet the natural obstacles confronting his troops were among the most formidable in the world. The mountain called Monte Cassino was a position of such strength that it had for years been regarded by the Italian General Staff as the most conspicuous example in Italy of an impregnable site. Such indeed it was. Situated at the mouth of a valley watered by the Garigliano, into which flows the rivers Liri and Rapido, is the town of Cassino. It stands at the foot of a hill some 1,700 feet high, upon whose summit St. Benedict built his first monastery. The saint had a shrewd eye for country, for the hill is a bare and rocky promontory thrust out from the greater mass of Monte Cairo, 'the southernmost peak of a great spur of the Apennines'. The position dominates the road to Rome, the Via Casilina, which runs through the valley until it reaches the Pontine Marshes, which the Germans had attempted, without much success, to flood. Close to the road at the crucial point flows the Rapido, which Alexander in his despatch compared 'to the moat before a castle gate'. Such was the castle which the American 34th Division had come near to taking by storm.

After their gallant efforts a pause ensued while the next step was being considered. It was of the gravest kind. Should the Monastery, one of the most renowned and revered shrines of the Christian world, be bombed or not?

To do so would be to attack one of those historical monuments about which Eisenhower had issued a special directive dated 29th December, 1943, and addressed to all his Army Commanders. It had not been revoked by his successor. 'If', said the American Commander-in-Chief, 'we have to choose between destroying a famous building and killing our men, then our men's lives count infinitely more and the building must go. But the choice is not always so clear-cut as that. In many cases the monuments can be spared without any detriment to operational needs. Nothing can stand against the argument of military necessity. That is an accepted principle. But the phrase "military necessity" is sometimes used where it would be truthful to speak of military convenience or even of personal convenience. I do not want it to cloak slackness or indifference'.

What Generals Wilson and Alexander and their subordinate commanders had therefore to decide was whether the bombing of Monte Cassino was a necessity or a convenience. Alexander seems to have thought that to spare it would be 'to our great disadvantage'. General Wilson was convinced that the Monastery buildings had been occupied by the enemy and he based this view on intelligence reports received for the most part from II Corps. These, which he summarized in a signal sent to the Combined Chiefs of Staff three weeks after the bombing, were of a fragmentary and inconclusive description. With the exception of two, one from an Italian civilian, the other from a German prisoner of war, and of a statement by the Commander of the 133rd United States Infantry Regiment, who reported that a telescope had been seen protruding from a window on the east face of the Abbey, none of these reports stated that the Abbey was garrisoned, but merely that the Germans were dug in close to it. This was true, and subsequent examination of the ground has shown that there were no fixed defences in the immediate neighbourhood of the Abbey. In other words though the hill, Monte Cassino, was part of a complicated and immensely strong defensive position, the Abbey itself was not.

At the time, however, General Wilson was evidently convinced that it was, and General Freyberg, commanding the New Zealanders, had no kind of doubt whatever. 'In the meantime', says the History of the Fifth Army, 'General Freyberg decided that the Abbey of Monte Cassino must be destroyed. Enemy activity round it had been observed for some time. Ammunition dumps were dangerously close to it; observers used it constantly to direct artillery fire; snipers had fired from it and gun emplacements were numerous round it'.

General Tuker, commanding the 4th Indian Division which was to make the attack, was equally definite and desired the Abbey to be bombed whether it was 'occupied by a German garrison or not'. In his view so formidable a position must 'be softened up' before being assaulted by infantry or else 'turned and isolated', a solution which was eventually adopted after all else had failed.

The British Commanders, then, were of one mind; but the American General, Mark Clark, was very doubtful and expressed the view that, once the Abbey was bombed, its ruins would provide excellent cover for the Germans.[1] His subordinate, the General commanding the 34th Division, went further and maintained that there were no Germans in the Monastery. Eaker and Slessor, in command of the air forces, shared General Clark's doubts.

If the testimony of Abbot Gregorio Diamare and Father Oderigio Graziosi living in the Monastery at the time be correct, those doubts were justified. The Germans had resisted the temptation to garrison the Monastery, and this for a very good reason. It was both unnecessary and dangerous to do so. The hill upon which it is built is tall and steep. Though its summit dominates the plain, so also do its upper flanks. In these, observation posts, gun posts and foxholes could be very easily constructed, and they were. In this rocky hillside they proved far less conspicuous than the great mass of stone and marble buildings, which could be seen for miles and was not a suitable defensive position as long as it remained intact, a shining invitation to bombers. The posts established around but some distance below it, might, and indeed did, remain untouched by bombardment. So convinced was the German General Baade, commanding the fanatical parachute troops holding the position, that the Allies would not seek by bombing to transform the Monastery into a useful addition to his defences, that when, on 13th February, leaflets threatening to do so fell, he informed the monks that this was an attempt at bluff, and that he would continue to honour his undertaking not to occupy the Monastery unless it was bombed. His attitude was doubtless influenced by a direct order issued, according to General von Senger, commanding the German XIV Panzer Corps, by Kesselring. No Germans were to enter the Monastery, said the Field-Marshal, and military police were posted at its gates to see that the order was obeyed. They also took care to allow no civilian to leave.

Alexander and his generals, however, were not bluffing and the leaflets meant what they said. At 0830 on the morning of 15th February, 135 United States Fortresses of the Strategic Air Force dropped 287 tons of 500 lb. general purpose bombs and 66 tons of

[1] *Calculated Risk*. General Mark Clark (Harrap).

100 lb. incendiary bombs on the buildings and courtyards of the Monastery, while forty-seven United States Mitchells and forty United States Marauders dropped 140 tons of 1,000 lb. bombs on the same target and the guns of the Fifth Army fired 314 shells of heavy and medium calibre into it. The Monastery was reduced to a heap of smoking ruins; but its outer walls, in places thirty feet thick, remained standing. An unexploded bomb lodged in the pavement before St. Benedict's tomb and was still embedded there in 1948. The saint's cell, hewn partly in the rock where he had established himself in the year 529, survived, but the great church and courtyard were wiped out, together with between 300 and 400 women and children who had taken refuge in the Monastery.

So crumbled to ruin a building erected upon a site venerated by Christendom for more than 1,400 years. It is too early to pass final judgment on this melancholy event; but, while making allowance for the feelings of commanders faced with a task of peculiar difficulty, it may not be out of place to observe that to destroy so famous a shrine on so slender evidence that it was occupied by the enemy even though it stood in the midst of his defences, was to place a very wide interpretation on Eisenhower's directive. Of greater weight, perhaps, is the contention that no troops, not even the New Zealanders and the Gurkhas, Baluchis and Mahrattas of the 4th Indian Division, could have been expected to attack so strong a position as long as the buildings which crowned it stood intact. This may have been true, but what is certain is that the action taken by the commanders on the spot was endorsed by General Wilson and subsequently by the Chiefs of Staff. Future generations alone will be able to decide whether the bombing of the Monastery of Monte Cassino was a necessity.

As soon as the attack was ended, General Baade saw his opportunity, and that same afternoon, while the aged abbot[1] was leading the few survivors down the hill to the dubious safety of the plain, German machine gunners hastened to set up their posts among the ruins and their field kitchens in the cell of St. Benedict. A most useful addition to the defences had, contrary to his expectations, been provided. More than that he was able to counter-attack and by 19th February to drive the assaulting troops east of the Rapido.

Such was the position of the Fifth Army when the German counter-attack in the beach-head at Anzio was brought to a standstill. The

[1] Before he left he wrote and signed a statement dated 15th February in which he says categorically that the only Germans who had ever been within 'the enclosure of the sacred Monastery of Cassino' were three military police who had been withdrawn twenty days before the attack.

The Monastery

The Town

AFTER THE ALLIED ATTACKS AT CASSINO

fighting had been of such severity that, as has been seen, it induced Alexander to try to produce 'new tactics' and with the aid of air power to seek a decision at Cassino. The destruction of the Monastery had failed, that of the town might succeed. On 15th March it was reduced to rubble by eleven groups of the Strategic Air Force heavy bombers and five groups of the Tactical Air Force. The bombing of the town, which was strongly held by determined German parachute troops, lasted with intervals of approximately fifteen minutes from 0830 hours until noon. 1,107 tons of bombs fell and the target was utterly destroyed. Subsidiary attacks were made by about 200 aircraft of XII Air Support Command on the positions of the enemy to the south and south-west, and by fifty-nine Desert Air Force Kittyhawks on gun positions to the north of Aquino. To cover the advance of the infantry, 200 United States Lightnings and seventy-four Royal Air Force Spitfires patrolled the battlefield but found no enemy to engage. Mustang and Spitfire pilots observed for the guns and took photographs.

The bombs which fell upon Cassino proved disruptive, too much so. Huge craters in the streets and masses of brick, rubble and masonry created blocks of formidable size. The German garrison, which at the beginning of the air bombardment had returned to its dug-outs and shelters, came out of them as soon as it was over, manned the ruins and maintained a stubborn and successful resistance. 'A battle on the Stalingrad model developed', says one observer. 'Bombers and snipers laboriously cleared a few yards at a time. . . . Every wall, every cellar window, harboured a paratrooper'. Not until two months later, on 18th May, when the position was finally captured, did this ill-starred battle come to an end.

Long before that date, on 19th March, the most determined of all the efforts of the Mediterranean Allied Air Forces to help the armies in Italy began. Operation 'Strangle' was designed to interrupt, and, if possible, to destroy, the enemy's lines of communication. If successful, the Germans would be without the necessary supplies in their forward areas when the Allied offensive opened in May. The essence of the plan was for the bombers of the Tactical Air Force to assault railway targets, especially bridges, south of the line Pisa/Rimini, and for the fighter-bombers to attack similar targets closer to the front and also repair depots, open stretches of track and places where stores carried by rail were transferred to lorries. As the attack proceeded and these targets were shattered, it was hoped and believed that rolling-stock carrying essential supplies would begin to accumulate in the various marshalling yards of northern Italy where it could be destroyed by the heavy bombers. In order to leave unmolested no means whereby the enemy might supply and reinforce his troops at the front, harbours and coastal shipping were also included in the programme of assault.

The planning of the operation depended upon speed of attack and frequent photographic reconnaissance. The latter was carried out effectively by the Photographic Reconnaissance Wing commanded by Colonel Roosevelt. By the end of March more than 1,000 bombing sorties against the main railway communications had been flown with some not inconsiderable results. The marshalling yards at Campo di Marte and the bridge at Orte had been damaged, and that near Poggibonsi destroyed. The cutting of the viaduct west of Arezzo, the damage to the bridge east of Perugia and the demolition of the Cecina railway bridge must also be noted. Kittyhawks of the Desert Air Force were employed against targets situated on the east coast, including Terni and Ancona, and in fulfilment of the second phase of the plan, the Strategic Air Force and the Wellington bombers attacked junctions along the Milan/Venice railway and the marshalling yards at Verona, Mestre, Turin, Bolzano and Milan. The assault was made in some strength, well over a thousand tons being dropped. As was by then usual, opposition offered by the *Luftwaffe* was very small.

Operation 'Strangle' would have been more effective had not periods of bad weather intervened to prevent the full development of this long series of attacks. Even so, in the month of March 1944 the Mediterranean Strategic, Tactical and Coastal Air Forces were able to drop 19,460 tons of bombs. The attacks continued on an increased scale in April, and by the 6th the interpreters of the photographs reported that the Italian railways had been blocked in ten places.

The effect of this operation, as of those which had preceded it, though far from negligible, was inconclusive. The supply routes of the Germans were constantly cut, but were as constantly repaired, and in spite of the destruction caused to railways, ports, vehicles and dumps, the enemy was still able to keep his troops supplied with their minimum requirements. The fact was that the weight of the air attack throughout the campaign, though heavy, was not nearly sufficient utterly to destroy and disrupt the communications of a country like Italy. Much damage was inflicted from the beginning in September 1943 and at intervals during the autumn, winter and spring which followed; but it was not enough to turn the scale, not even after Operation 'Diadem' had added 51,500 tons to those dropped in Operation 'Strangle'. Nevertheless, though the use of the railways was never entirely prevented, the enemy had largely to increase his use of roads and presently found himself under the necessity of moving convoys by day with disastrous results.

In summing up the first ten months of the war in Italy, it must be said that the air forces were at times hampered in their task by divided counsels. The broad aim as outlined by General Wilson was 'to use the air to deprive the enemy of the ability either to maintain his present positions, or to withdraw his divisions out of Italy'. In theory unassailable, in practice it was unattainable, an unpleasant fact not fully appreciated at the time either at Army or Air Headquarters where two schools of thought, each with much evidence to support it, contended. One was under the influence of Professor S. Zuckerman, technical adviser to those responsible for the bombing policy. Zuckerman, whose advice concerning the bombing of Pantelleria had proved correct and whose opinion therefore carried much weight, urged that the weak link in the Italian railway system was the repair and servicing facilities. Vigorously attacked, they would soon be unable to perform their functions, the quantity of rolling-stock unserviceable would therefore increase more and more and faster and faster until eventually all traffic would be brought to a standstill. Since the repair shops were for the most part situated in or near marshalling yards, these should be immediately attacked. The proverbial two birds could thus be killed by one stone; not only the repair shops, but also many hundreds of wagons in the yards would be destroyed.

The other school, supported by not a few of the Army Commanders, maintained that such a scheme could not achieve a result quickly. It was one of attrition, whereas what was wanted was a policy which would have an immediate effect on the battle. This would be achieved by attacking bridges, viaducts, road junctions, and similar targets so as to isolate the enemy's troops from their supplies. A geographical line of interdiction, through which no train would be able to pass, should be established. This plan was strongly favoured by the American Air Force Commanders who based their views on a study of captured documents and on the interrogation of prisoners. It was Slessor who found the solution. After discussing the problem with Brigadier-General L. Norstad of the U.S. Army Air Force he succeeded in blending the two opposing designs into a single plan. A geographical line of interdiction would be established so as to put an end, if possible, to through traffic on the Italian railways. At the same time the heavy bombers would be used to assault marshalling yards, and therefore repair shops, behind this line. This combination of interdiction and attrition formed the basis of the 'Transportation Plan' afterwards used with such telling effect in

Normandy. It was the origin of new strategy and new tactics which were to make the intervention of the air forces in the battles of Western Europe decisive. This was not so in Italy. That the new policy was sound was soon as obvious as was the fact that it was not achieving overwhelming results. The reason was simple. Large though the Mediterranean Allied Air Forces were, they were not large enough, and the requisite concentration of bombs was beyond the capacity of the heavy bombers. South of Naples and Foggia the only railway target of first-class importance was Brindisi: the others at Potenza, Lecce, Cosenza, and elsewhere being the home of railway shops of secondary importance. Upon these the requisite concentration of bombs to ensure destruction could be dropped and it was. When, however, it became necessary for the bomber offensive to move farther northwards, the number of railway targets which had to be destroyed, especially in the valley of the Po, was too great for this method of concentrated bombing to be followed. The bomber force available, though large, was not large enough to make it possible to paralyse simultaneously, or even for a short period, such railway centres as Turin, Pisa, Piacenza and Florence. Too few bombs were dropped on too many places, too few times. For this the weather must bear a large part of the blame. Bad weather is sometimes a convenient excuse for bad operations—in Italy it was not. It provided the dark curtain of cloud, the blind mist of rain, which must always be the best protection for any target attacked by aircraft not equipped with special devices.

Such conclusions, however, are but wisdom after the event. During the conflict, and at its height, these difficulties, which so greatly prolonged the campaign, were not clearly seen, or if they were, could not be adequately dealt with by the means at the disposal of the commanders. During the winter of 1944-1945 the position so greatly improved that this was no longer so. Then the wisdom of the policy became immediately manifest. With more squadrons, more bombs, it could be applied on the required scale and it was. The results were the same as in Normandy. The enemy's lines of communication were pulverized to an extent which proved decisive in April 1945.

The spring offensive opened on 11th May, 1944, and on 4th June, two days before Montgomery and Bradley went ashore at Normandy, the Allies entered Rome. Much hard fighting had taken place before the polyglot army of Alexander marched beneath a rain of flowers through the roaring streets of the Eternal City. The high hopes entertained after the battle for the Salerno beach-head ten months before had not been fulfilled. The broken country of woods and mountains, with its rain-swollen rivers and its poor communications, the small size of the invading force, the bad weather which bedaubed troops and vehicles accustomed to rock and sand with clogging mud, above all, the stubborn resolution of the enemy, displayed especially on those parts of the battlefield towards the east coast, where the country was more open, were among the main causes of the unsatisfactory nature of the campaign. Though air supremacy had been gained from the outset and was never lost, the bald truth is that it did not avail to achieve swift victory. Without it, no invasion would have been possible; with it, the ultimate result was certain, but the way, nevertheless, long and hard.

APPENDIX I

Members of the Air Council, 1942-43

	Date of Appointment
SECRETARY OF STATE FOR AIR	
The Rt. Hon. Sir Archibald Sinclair, Bart., K.T., C.M.G., M.P.	11th May, 1940
PARLIAMENTARY UNDER-SECRETARY OF STATE FOR AIR	
Captain The Rt. Hon. H. H. Balfour, M.C., M.P.	16th May, 1938
Lord Sherwood (Under-Secretary of State, House of Lords)	22nd July, 1941
CHIEF OF THE AIR STAFF	
Air Chief Marshal Sir Charles F. A. Portal, G.C.B., D.S.O., M.C.	25th October, 1940
AIR MEMBER FOR PERSONNEL	
Air Marshal P. Babington C.B., M.C., A.F.C. ...	1st December, 1940
Air Marshal Sir Bertine E. Sutton, K.B.E., C.B., D.S.O., M.C.	17th August, 1942
AIR MEMBER FOR SUPPLY AND ORGANISATION	
Air Chief Marshal Sir Christopher L. Courtney, K.C.B., C.B.E., D.S.O.	15th January, 1940
AIR MEMBER FOR TRAINING	
Air Marshal A. G. R. Garrod, C.B., O.B.E., M.C., D.F.C.	8th July, 1940
Air Marshal Sir Peter R. M. Drummond, K.C.B., D.S.O., O.B.E., M.C.	27th April, 1943
PERMANENT UNDER-SECRETARY OF STATE FOR AIR	
Sir Arthur W. Street, K.C.B., K.B.E., C.M.G., C.I.E., M.C.	1st June, 1939
ADDITIONAL MEMBERS	
Air Chief Marshal Sir Wilfrid R. Freeman, K.C.B., D.S.O., M.C. (Vice-Chief of the Air Staff)	5th November, 1940- 18th October, 1942
Air Vice-Marshal C. E. H. Medhurst, C.B., O.B.E., M.C. (Acting Vice-Chief of the Air Staff)	19th October, 1942- 20th March, 1943
Air Marshal Sir Douglas C. S. Evill, K.C.B., D.S.C., A.F.C. (Vice-Chief of the Air Staff)	21st March, 1943
Air Marshal F. J. Linnell, C.B., O.B.E. (Controller of Research and Development, Ministry of Aircraft Production)	5th June, 1941- 19th April, 1943
Air Marshal R. S. Sorley, C.B., O.B.E., D.S.C., D.F.C. (Controller of Research and Development, Ministry of Aircraft Production)	20th April, 1943
Sir Harold G. Howitt, D.S.O., M.C., F.C.A.	18th September, 1939
Sir Henry Tizard, K.C.B., A.F.C., F.R.S.	June 1941- August 1943

APPENDIX II

Principal Air Commanders, 1942-43[1]

	Date of Appointment
HOME	
BOMBER COMMAND	
Air Marshal Sir Richard E. C. Peirse, K.C.B., D.S.O., A.F.C.	5th October, 1940
Air Chief Marshal Sir Arthur T. Harris, K.C.B., O.B.E., A.F.C.	22nd February, 1942
FIGHTER COMMAND[2]	
Air Chief Marshal Sir W. Sholto Douglas, K.C.B., M.C., D.F.C.	25th November, 1940
Air Marshal Sir Trafford L. Leigh-Mallory, K.C.B., D.S.O.	28th November, 1942
Air Marshal R. M. Hill, C.B., M.C., A.F.C. ...	15th November, 1943
COASTAL COMMAND	
Air Chief Marshal Sir Philip B. Joubert de la Ferté, K.C.B., C.M.G., D.S.O.	14th June, 1941
Air Marshal Sir John C. Slessor, K.C.B., D.S.O., M.C.	5th February, 1943
ARMY CO-OPERATION COMMAND[3]	
Air Marshal Sir Arthur S. Barratt, K.C.B., C.M.G., M.C.	20th November, 1940
FLYING TRAINING COMMAND	
Air Marshal Sir William L. Welsh, K.C.B., D.S.C., A.F.C.	7th July, 1941
Air Marshal Sir Philip Babington, K.C.B., M.C., A.F.C.	17th August, 1942
MAINTENANCE COMMAND	
Air Marshal Sir John S. T. Bradley, K.C.B., C.B.E.	31st March, 1938
Air Marshal D. G. Donald, C.B., D.F.C., A.F.C. ...	12th October, 1942
TECHNICAL TRAINING COMMAND	
Air Marshal Sir John T. Babington, K.C.B., C.B.E., D.S.O.	7th July, 1941
Air Marshal Sir Arthur S. Barratt, K.C.B., C.M.G., M.C.	1st June, 1943

---

[1] The appointment is that of Air Officer Commanding-in-Chief except where otherwise stated.

[2] Renamed Air Defence of Great Britain, 15th November, 1943.

[3] Disbanded 1st June, 1943.

Date of Appointment

TRANSPORT COMMAND

Air Chief Marshal Sir Frederick W. Bowhill, G.B.E., K.C.B., C.M.G., D.S.O. — 25th March, 1943

ALLIED EXPEDITIONARY AIR FORCE

Air Commander-in-Chief

Air Chief Marshal Sir Trafford L. Leigh-Mallory, K.C.B., D.S.O. — 15th November, 1943

OVERSEAS

MEDITERRANEAN AIR COMMAND[1]

Air Commander-in-Chief

Air Chief Marshal Sir Arthur W. Tedder, G.C.B. — 17th February, 1943

MIDDLE EAST COMMAND

Air Chief Marshal Sir Arthur W. Tedder, G.C.B. — 1st June, 1941

Air Chief Marshal Sir W. Sholto Douglas, K.C.B., M.C., D.F.C. — 11th January, 1943

AIR FORCES IN INDIA

Air Marshal Sir Patrick H. L. Playfair, K.B.E., C.B., C.V.O., M.C. — 26th September, 1940

Air Chief Marshal Sir Richard E. C. Peirse, K.C.B., D.S.O., A.F.C. — 6th March, 1942

EASTERN AIR COMMAND, AFRICA[2]

Air Marshal Sir William L. Welsh, K.C.B., D.S.C., A.F.C. — 2nd November, 1942

AIR COMMAND, SOUTH-EAST ASIA

Air Chief Marshal Sir Richard E. C. Peirse, K.C.B., D.S.O., A.F.C. — 16th November, 1943

R.A.F. FERRY COMMAND[3]

Air Chief Marshal Sir Frederick W. Bowhill, G.B.E., K.C.B., C.M.G., D.S.O. — 18th July, 1941

---

[1] Higher operational control over Middle East Air Forces, including Malta, and over Northwest African Air Forces.

Mediterranean Air Command became Mediterranean Allied Air Forces on 10th December, 1943, into which formation Middle East and Northwest African Air Forces were absorbed.

[2] Absorbed into Northwest African Air Forces (Mediterranean Air Command) 18th February, 1943.

[3] Renamed No. 45 (Ferry) Group, 11th April, 1943 after formation of Transport Command.

APPENDIX III

Royal Air Force Command Organisation, March, 1943

AIR MINISTRY

HOME COMMANDS

- HEADQUARTERS BOMBER COMMAND
  - No. 1 Bomber Group
  - No. 2 Bomber Group
  - No. 3 Bomber Group
  - No. 4 Bomber Group
  - No. 5 Bomber Group
  - No. 6 Bomber Group R.C.A.F.
  - No. 8 P.F.F. Group
  - No. 26 Signals Group
  - No. 91 Bomber O.T.U. Group
  - No. 92 Bomber O.T.U. Group
  - No. 93 Bomber O.T.U. Group
- HEADQUARTERS FIGHTER COMMAND
  - No. 9 Fighter Group
  - No. 10 Fighter Group
  - No. 11 Fighter Group
  - No. 12 Fighter Group
  - No. 13 Fighter Group
  - No. 14 Fighter Group
  - No. 60 Signals Group
  - No. 81 Fighter O.T.U. Group
- HEADQUARTERS COASTAL COMMAND
  - No. 15 G.R. Group
  - No. 16 G.R. Group
  - No. 17 Training Group
  - No. 18 G.R. Group
  - No. 19 G.R. Group
  - H.Q. R.A.F. Gibraltar
  - H.Q. R.A.F. Iceland
- HEADQUARTERS BALLOON COMMAND
  - No. 30, No. 32, No. 33, No. 34 Balloon Barrage Groups
- HEADQUARTERS FLYING TRAINING COMMAND
  - No. 21 Training Group
  - No. 23 Training Group
  - No. 25 Armament Group
  - No. 29 Training Group
  - No. 50 Training Group
  - No. 51 Training Group
  - No. 54 Training Group
- R.A.F. IN NORTHERN IRELAND
- HEADQUARTERS MAINTENANCE COMMAND
  - No. 40 Maintenance Group
  - No. 41 Maintenance Group
  - No. 42 Maintenance Group
  - No. 43 Maintenance Group
- HEADQUARTERS R.A.F. TRANSPORT COMMAND
  - No. 44 Ferry Group
  - Ferry Command
- HEADQUARTERS ARMY CO-OPERATION COMMAND
  - No. 70 Army Co-operation Training Group
  - No. 72 Army Co-operation Group
- HEADQUARTERS TECHNICAL TRAINING COMMAND
  - No. 20 Training Group
  - No. 24 Training Group
  - No. 27 Training Group
  - No. 28 Training Group

OVERSEAS COMMANDS

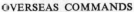

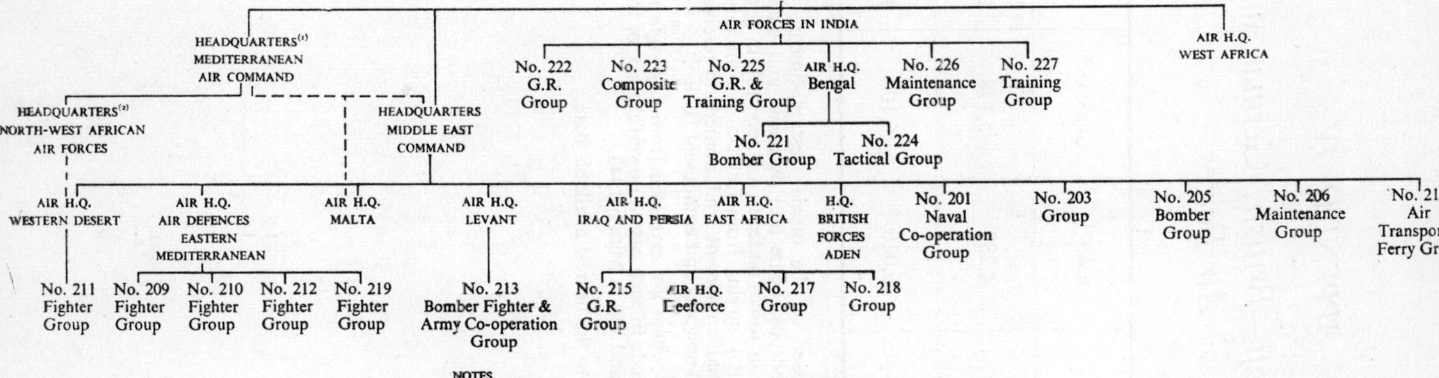

NOTES
(1) - - - Operational Control of Middle East Air Formations
(2) For details of North-West African Air Forces see Appendix XII

Abbreviations

G.R.	General Reconnaissance	P.F.F.	Pathfinder Force
O.T.U.	Operational Training Unit	R.C.A.F.	Royal Canadian Air Force

APPENDIX IV

First-line Aircraft—British, German and Italian Air Forces

DATE	R.A.F.[1]	GERMAN[2]	ITALIAN[3]
1st December 1941 .	4,287	5,178	2,212 (Nov.)
1st March 1943 . .	6,026	6,107	1,947 (May)

[1] These figures are based on the official 'establishment' for the initial equipment (I.E.) of squadrons, home and overseas, and include aircraft of the Dominion and Allied air forces under R.A.F. control. In addition there was an immediate reserve (I.R.) varying from four to five aircraft per squadron. After June 1944 this initial equipment and immediate reserve were grouped together in what became known as unit equipment (U.E.).

[2] The German figures, which are extracted from *Luftwaffe* records, are for actual strength. They include in each case a powerful force of transport aircraft —747 in December 1941 and 753 in March 1943.

[3] Official Italian totals to the nearest available date.

APPENDIX V

Principal Operational Aircraft of the Royal Air Force, 1942-43

BOMBER[1]

AIRCRAFT NAME AND MARK	MAXIMUM SPEED	SERVICE CEILING	RANGE AND ASSOCIATED BOMB LOAD	ARMAMENT
	m.p.h. feet	*feet*	*miles lb.*	
Halifax II	260 at 18,500	21,800	1,900 — 3,000 or 500 — 13,000	8 × ·303″
Halifax II-IA	260 at 19,000	21,000	1,900 — 4,000 or 600 — 13,000	9 × ·303″
Halifax V	260 at 18,500	21,000	1,900 — 4,500 or 650 — 13,000	9 × ·303″
Lancaster I & III [2]	270 at 19,000	22,200	2,350 — 5,500 or 1,000 — 14,000	9 × ·303″
Stirling III	270 at 14,500	17,000	2,010 — 3,500 or 590 — 14,000	8 × ·303″
Wellington III	255 at 12,500	19,500	2,200 — 1,500 or 1,540 — 4,500	8 × ·303″
Wellington X	255 at 14,500	19,600	2,085 — 1,500 or 1,470 — 4,500	6 × ·303″
Mosquito IV	380 at 14,000	33,000	1,620 — 2,000 or 1,450 — 4,000	Nil
Mosquito IX	408 at 26,000	36,000	1,870 — 1,000 or 1,370 — 5,000	Nil
Baltimore III	302 at 11,000	22,000	950 — 2,000	10 × ·30″ 4 × ·303″
Boston III	304 at 13,000	24,250	1,020 — 2,000	8 × ·303″
Mitchell II	292 at 15,000	20,000	1,635 — 4,000 or 950 — 6,000	6 × ·50″

[1] See Notes on page 375.

[2] The essential difference between the Lancaster Marks I and III was in the power units, the former incorporating Merlin XX engines, the latter Merlin 28 (identical with the XX) built in America by Packard.

FIGHTER AND FIGHTER-BOMBER[1]

AIRCRAFT NAME AND MARK	MAXIMUM[2] SPEED	SERVICE[2] CEILING	CLIMB[2]— TIME TO HEIGHT	ARMAMENT[2]
	m.p.h. feet	*feet*	*minutes feet*	
Beaufighter VI-F	333 at 15,600	26,500	7·8 to 15,000	4×20-mm. 6×·303″
Hurricane II-C	339 at 22,000	35,600	9·1 to 20,000	4×20-mm.
Hurricane II-D	316 at 19,000	33,500	·75 to 2,000	2×40-mm. 2×·303″
Kittyhawk I	350 at 15,000	29,000	8·7 to 15,000	4 or 6×·50″
Mosquito II	370 at 14,000	35,000	7 to 15,000	4×20-mm. 4×·303″
Mosquito VI	378 at 14,000	32,000	9·5 to 15,000	4×20-mm. 4×·303″ (4×500 lb. bombs)
Mosquito XII (N/F)	370 at 14,000	35,000	7 to 15,000	4×20-mm.
Mustang I	390 at 8,000	32,000	8·1 to 15,000	4×·50″ 4×·303″
Spitfire V-B	374 at 13,000	36,000	7·5 to 20,000	2×20-mm. 4×·303″ (1×500 lb. bomb)
Spitfire V-B (L/F)	357 at 6,000	35,500	1·6 to 5,000	2×20-mm. 4×·303″ (1×500 lb. bomb)
Spitfire IX	408 at 25,000	43,000	6·7 to 20,000	2×20-mm. 4×·303″ (1×500 lb. and 2×250 lb. bombs)
Typhoon I-B	405 at 18,000	33,000	6·2 to 15,000	4×20-mm. (2×1,000 lb. bombs or 8 ×60 lb. R.P.s)

[1] See Notes on page 375.

[2] Performance data in this table relate to the aircraft operating in a short-range fighter role. When bombs, rockets or drop tanks were added these figures were reduced. The bomb weights are those which could be carried when the aircraft operated as a fighter-bomber.

COASTAL

AIRCRAFT NAME AND MARK	CRUISING SPEED AND ENDURANCE	ASSOCIATED BOMB (OR DEPTH CHARGE) LOAD	ARMAMENT
	knots hours	*lb.*	
Catalina I (F.B.)	100 — 17·6	2,000	6×·303″
	or 25	Nil	
Catalina III	100 — 14·5	2,000	5×·303″
Fortress II	140 — 10·7	1,750	9×·50″
	or 12·9	Nil	
Halifax II	135 — 10·4	2,250	9×·303″
	or 13·3	1,500	
Hampden (T/B)	120 — 7·25	1×18″ torpedo	6×·303″
Hudson VI	140 — 6·9	1,000	7×·303″
Liberator I (V.L.R.)	150 — 16·1	2,000	4×20-mm. 6×·30″
Liberator III	145 — 11·6	3,000	6×·50″
Liberator V	150 — 15·3	1,500	6×·50″
Wellington I-C	120 — 9·3	2,000	6×·303″
Whitley VII	105 — 10·3	2,000	5×·303″
Wellington VIII	120 — 8·8	1,000	6×·303″
Wellington XII	140 — 8·3	2,400	7×·303″
Sunderland II (F.B.)	110 — 11·6	2,000	7×·303″
Sunderland III (F.B.)	110 — 11·9	2,000	7×·303″

NOTES.

(i) MAXIMUM SPEED was only possible for an extremely limited period. Apart from tactical manœuvring, bomber and fighter aircraft, in the main, flew at speeds between 'most economical cruising' and 'maximum continuous cruising'. Varying with the different aircraft, these speeds were respectively between 55-80% and 80-90% of the maximum speed.

(ii) SERVICE CEILING. The height at which the rate of climb has a certain defined low value (in British practice 100 feet per minute). Ceilings quoted are for aircraft with full load.

(iii) RANGE AND ASSOCIATED BOMB LOAD. The main purpose of this table is to give some idea of the relative performances of the various aircraft. The figures quoted relate to aircraft flying at 'most economical cruising' speed at the specified height, i.e. the speed and height at which the greatest range could be obtained. Allowance is made for take-off but not for landing, the range quoted being the maximum distance the aircraft could cover in still air 'flying to dry tanks'. Furthermore in the planning of operations a reduction of range of about 25% had to be made for navigational errors, tactical manœuvring, weather conditions and other factors.

(iv) ENDURANCE. The time an aircraft can continue flying under given conditions without refuelling. This being a vital factor of Coastal Command operations an economical cruising speed, consistent with maximum safe endurance as determined under normal operational conditions, is quoted.

(v) A number of Liberators Marks III and V were modified to achieve a performance similar to that of the V.L.R. Liberator Mark I.

(vi) The Catalina Mark III (amphibian) was known as the Canso.

(vii) ABBREVIATIONS. (N/F) Night-Fighter; (L/F) Low Flying; (R.P.) Rocket Projectile; (F.B.) Flying Boat; (T/B) Torpedo-Bomber; (V.L.R.) Very Long Range.

APPENDIX VI

Principal Operational Aircraft of the German Air Force, 1942-43

BOMBER AND RECONNAISSANCE

AIRCRAFT	MAXIMUM SPEED	SERVICE CEILING	RANGE AND ASSOCIATED BOMB LOAD	ARMAMENT
	m.p.h. feet	*feet*	*miles lb.*	
Junkers (Ju.) 88B3	333 at 20,000	25,000	1,280 — 2,200	2×13-mm. 2×7·9-mm.
Junkers (Ju.) 87D[1]	255 at 13,500 or 232 at 13,500	18,500	720 — 2,200 620 — 4,000	4×7·9-mm.
Junkers (Ju.) 188	325 at 20,000	33,500	1,200 — 4,400	1×20-mm. 2×13-mm. 2×7·9-mm.
Heinkel (He.) 111	240 at 14,000	26,000	1,510 — 2,200	7×7·9-mm. 2×20-mm.
Heinkel (He.) 177	305 at 20,000	21,000	2,650 — 2,200 or 1,150 — 12,320	5×13-mm. 4×13/20-mm.
Focke-Wulf (F.W.) 200[2]	240 at 13,600	20,500	2,150 — 3,600 or 2,700 (Recce only)	3×13-mm. 3×15/20-mm.

[1] The Stuka—dive-bomber. [2] Known as the Condor.

FIGHTER

AIRCRAFT	MAXIMUM SPEED	SERVICE CEILING	CLIMB— TIME TO HEIGHT	ARMAMENT
	m.p.h. feet	*feet*	*minutes feet*	
Junkers (Ju.) 88C5	347 at 20,000	30,200	10·3 to 18,500	6×7·9-mm. 3×20-mm.
Messerschmitt (Me.) 109G	400 at 22,000	38,500	6 to 19,000	2×7·9/13 mm. 3×20-mm.
Messerschmitt (Me.) 110G	368 at 19,000	34,800	7·3 to 18,000	6×7·9-mm. 4×20-mm. 1×37-mm.
Messerschmitt (Me.) 210	370 at 21,000	29,000	11·8 to 19,000	2×20-mm. 2×13-mm. 2×7·9-mm.
Messerschmitt (Me.) 410	395 at 22,000	30,000	11·5 to 19,000	2×20-mm. 2×13-mm. 2×7·9-mm.
Focke-Wulf (F.W.) 190A3	385 at 19,000	36,000	6·5 to 18,000	4×20-mm. 2×7·9-mm.

Notes i - iii on page 375 apply in general to the above tables.

APPENDIX VII

Principal Operational Aircraft of the Japanese Air Forces, 1942-43[1]

BOMBER AND RECONNAISSANCE

MAKER	TYPE	KNOWN AS	MAXIMUM SPEED	SERVICE CEILING	RANGE AND ASSOCIATED BOMB LOAD	ARMAMENT
			m.p.h. feet	*feet*	*miles lb.*	
Nakajima	Navy-96	Nell 23	270 at 19,600	34,250	2,125 — 1,100	4×7·7-mm. 1×20-mm.
Mitsubishi	Army-97	Sally 2	294 at 15,500	30,500	1,635 — 2,200	4×7·7-mm. 1×12·7-mm. 1×20-mm.
Nakajima	Army-100	Helen 2	312 at 16,900	30,900	1,600 — 2,200	3×7·9-mm. 2×12·7-mm. 1×20-mm.
Nakajima	Navy-1	Betty 22	283 at 13,800	30,500	3,075 — 2,200	4×7·7-mm. 4×20-mm.
Nakajima	Navy-2	Liz 11	270 at 16,100	29,100	2,990 — 7,240	no data avail.
Kawasaki[1]	Army-99	Lily 2	228 at 19,900	34,300	1,500 — 880	1×12·7-mm. 3×7·9-mm.
Nakajima	Navy 'Tenzan'	Jill 12	327 at 15,100	35,400	1,740 1 torpedo (1,765 lb.)	2×7·7-mm.
Mitsubishi[2]	Navy-97	Kate 12	225 at 8,000	27,500	645 1 torpedo (1,765 lb.)	4×7·7-mm.
Aichi	Navy-99 (*dive bomber*)	Val 22	281 at 20,300	33,600	965 — 550	3×7·7-mm.

FIGHTER

MAKER	TYPE	KNOWN AS	MAXIMUM SPEED	SERVICE CEILING	CLIMB—TIME TO HEIGHT	ARMAMENT
			m.p.h. feet	*feet*	*minutes feet*	
Nakajima	Army-1	Oscar 3	358 at 21,900	37,400	7·4 to 20,000	2×12·7-mm.
Kawasaki	Army-3	Tony 1	361 at 15,800	35,100	8·5 to 20,000	2×7·7-mm. & 2×12·7-mm. or 4×12·7-mm.
Nakajima[3]	Navy-0[4]	Zeke 52	358 at 22,000	35,100	7·8 to 20,000	2×13·2-mm. 2×7·7/13·2-mm. 2×20-mm.
Kawasaki	Army-2	Nick 1	346 at 21,100	35,000	8 to 20,000	2×12·7-mm. 1×7·9-mm. 1×20-mm.

[1] These data have been taken from official Japanese sources, but the nature of the trials, under which the performances quoted were attained, is unknown.

[2] Also manufactured by Nakajima and Aichi.

[3] Also manufactured by Mitsubishi.

[4] The Zero.

APPENDIX VIII

Order of Battle, Coastal Command, 15th February, 1943

HEADQUARTERS COASTAL COMMAND

No. 15 Group

Squadrons	
Nos. 201, 228, 246, 330, 422 (R.C.A.F.), 423 (R.C.A.F.)	Sunderland
Nos. 206, 220	Fortress
No. 120	Liberator
No. 280 (Det.)	Anson (Air Sea Rescue)
Flights	
No. 1402 (Metcal.)	Spitfire, Hudson, Gladiator

No. 16 Group

Squadrons	
Nos. 143, 236, 254	Beaufighter
Nos. 53, 320, 407 (R.C.A.F.)	Hudson
No. 86	Liberator
No. 415 (R.C.A.F.)	Hampden
No. 521 (Metcal.)	Spitfire, Hudson Mosquito, Gladiator
No. 279	Hudson (Air Sea Rescue)
No. 280	Anson (Air Sea Rescue)
Nos. 833 (F.A.A.), 836 (F.A.A.)	Swordfish
Nos. 540, 541, 542, 543, 544	Mosquito, Spitfire, Wellington, (P.R.)

No. 18 Group

Squadrons	
Nos. 144, 235	Beaufighter
Nos. 455 (R.A.A.F.), 489 (R.N.Z.A.F.)	Hampden
No. 190	Catalina
No. 612	Whitley
No. 540 (Det.)	Mosquito (P.R.)
Flights	
No. 1477	Catalina
No. 1406 (Metcal.)	Spitfire, Hudson

No. 19 Group

Squadrons	
Nos. 172, 179 (Det.), 304, 311, 547	Wellington
No. 224, 1st and 2nd Antisubmarine (U.S.A.A.F.)	Liberator

Nos. 10 (R.A.A.F.), 119, 461 (R.A.A.F.)	Sunderland
Nos. 248, 404 (R.C.A.F.)	Beaufighter
No. 502	Whitley
No. 58	Whitley, Halifax
No. 59	Fortress
No. 210	Catalina
No. 405 (R.C.A.F.) (on loan from Bomber Command)	Halifax
No. 543 (Det.)	Spitfire (P.R.)
Flights, Other Units	
No. 1404 (Metcal.) Flight	Hudson, Ventura, Albemarle
No. 10 O.T.U. (Det.) (on loan from Bomber Command)	Whitley

HEADQUARTERS R.A.F. ICELAND

Squadrons	
No. 269	Hudson
84th (U.S. Navy) Squadron	Catalina
No. 330 (Det.)	Northrop
No. 120 (Det.)	Liberator
Flights	
No. 1407 (Metcal.)	Hudson

HEADQUARTERS R.A.F. GIBRALTAR

Squadrons	
Nos. 48, 233	Hudson
Nos. 202, 210 (Det.)	Catalina
No. 179	Wellington
No. 544 (Det.)	Spitfire (P.R.)

ABBREVIATIONS

Det.	Detachment
F.A.A.	Fleet Air Arm
Metcal.	Meteorological Calibration
O.T.U.	Operational Training Unit
P.R.	Photographic Reconnaissance
R.A.A.F.	Royal Australian Air Force
R.C.A.F.	Royal Canadian Air Force
R.N.Z.A.F.	Royal New Zealand Air Force
U.S.A.A.F.	United States Army Air Force

APPENDIX IX

Order of Battle, Bomber Command, 4th March, 1943

HEADQUARTERS BOMBER COMMAND

No. 1 Group

Squadrons

Nos. 166, 199, 300, 301, 305	Wellington
Nos. 12, 100, 101, 103, 460 (R.A.A.F.). .	Lancaster

No. 2 Group

Squadrons

Nos. 21, 464 (R.A.A.F.), 487 (R.N.Z.A.F.) .	Ventura
Nos. 88, 107, 226	Boston
Nos. 98, 180	Mitchell
Nos. 105, 139	Mosquito

No. 3 Group

Squadrons

Nos. 15, 75, 90, 149, 214, 218	Stirling
No. 115	Lancaster, Wellington
No. 138 (S.D.)	Halifax
No. 161 (S.D.)	Lysander, Halifax, Hudson, Havoc, Albemarle
No. 192 (S.D.)	Halifax, Wellington, Mosquito

No. 4 Group

Squadrons

Nos. 10, 51, 76, 77, 78, 102, 158 . . .	Halifax
Nos. 196, 429 (R.C.A.F.), 431 (R.C.A.F.), 466 (R.A.A.F.)	Wellington

No. 5 Group

Squadrons

Nos. 9, 44, 49, 50, 57, 61, 97, 106, 207, 467 (R.A.A.F.)	Lancaster

No. 6 Group (R.C.A.F.)

Squadrons

Nos. 405 (R.C.A.F.), 408 (R.C.A.F.), 419 (R.C.A.F.)	Halifax
Nos. 420 (R.C.A.F.), 424 (R.C.A.F.), 425 (R.C.A.F.), 426 (R.C.A.F.), 427 (R.C.A.F.) 428 (R.C.A.F.)	Wellington

No. 8 (P.F.F.) Group

Squadrons

No. 7	Stirling
No. 35	Halifax
Nos. 83, 156	Lancaster
No. 109	Mosquito

Abbreviations

P.F.F.	Pathfinder Force
R.A.A.F.	Royal Australian Air Force
R.C.A.F.	Royal Canadian Air Force
R.N.Z.A.F.	Royal New Zealand Air Force
S.D.	Special Duty

APPENDIX X

Order of Battle, Middle East Command, 11th November, 1941

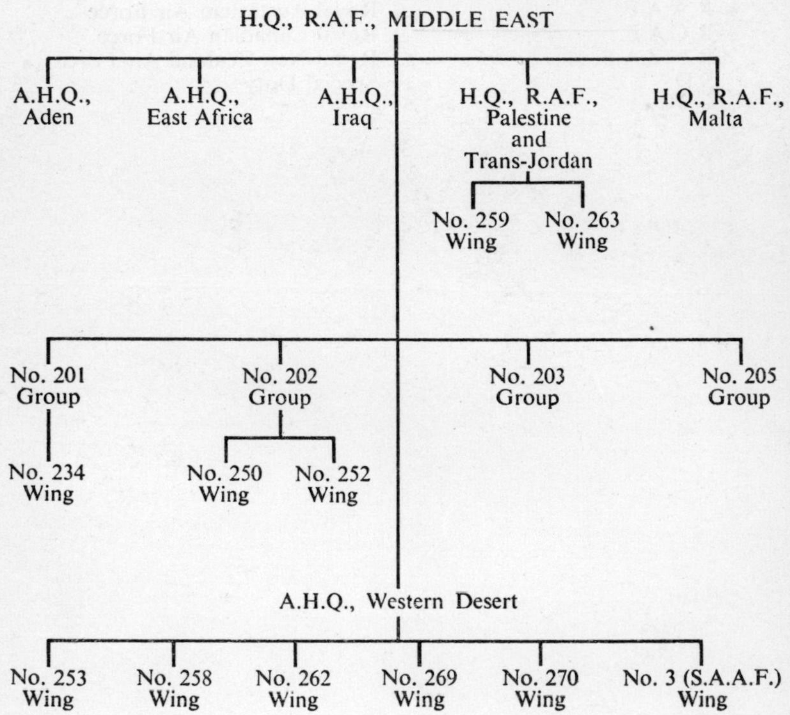

Note. For details of formations see following pages.

HEADQUARTERS, ROYAL AIR FORCE, MIDDLE EAST

No. 267 Squadron	Lodestar, Audax, Proctor
No. 2 Photographic Reconnaissance Unit .	Hurricane, Beaufighter

AIR HEADQUARTERS, ADEN

No. 8 Squadron	Various

AIR HEADQUARTERS, EAST AFRICA

Squadrons	
No. 3 (S.A.A.F.)	Mohawk
No. 15 (S.A.A.F.)	Battle
No. 16 (S.A.A.F.)	Junkers 86, Maryland
No. 41 (S.A.A.F.)	Hartebeeste
Flights	
No. 34 (S.A.A.F.)	Anson
No. 35 (S.A.A.F.)	Junkers 86
No. 51 (S.A.A.F.)	Junkers 52

AIR HEADQUARTERS, IRAQ

Squadrons	
No. 52	Audax
No. 244	Vincent
No. 261	Hurricane

HEADQUARTERS, ROYAL AIR FORCE, PALESTINE AND TRANS-JORDAN

No. 259 Wing	
Squadrons	
No. 213	Hurricane
No. 815 (F.A.A.)	Albacore, Swordfish
No. 263 Wing	
No. 335 Squadron	Hurricane
Free French (Fighter) Squadron . . .	Morane
Free French Flight	Blenheim

HEADQUARTERS, ROYAL AIR FORCE, MALTA

Squadrons	
Nos. 18, 104, 107	Blenheim
No. 40 (Det.)	Wellington
No. 69	Maryland
Nos. 126, 185, 249	Hurricane
Nos. 828 (F.A.A.), 830 (F.A.A.) . . .	Albacore, Swordfish

* * *

No. 201 Group

Squadrons

No. 2 (Yugo-Slav)	Dornier 22, Sim 14
No. 13 (Hellenic)	Anson
Flights	
Sea Rescue Flight	Wellington
R.N. Fulmar Flight	Fulmar
No. 234 Wing	
Squadrons	
No. 39	Boston, Maryland
No. 203	Blenheim, Beaufort
No. 230	Sunderland

No. 202 Group

Squadrons

No. 117	Various
No. 216	Bombay
No. 223 (Acting as Operational Training Unit)	Maryland
No. 250 Wing	
No. 73 Squadron	Hurricane
No. 1 General Reconnaissance Unit	Wellington
No. 252 Wing	
Squadrons	
Nos. 73 (Det.), 213 (Det.)	Hurricane

No. 203 Group

Squadrons

No. 6	Hurricane, Lysander
No. 47	Wellesley

No. 205 Group

Squadrons

Nos. 37, 38, 70, 108, 148	Wellington

* * *

AIR HEADQUARTERS, WESTERN DESERT

Squadrons

Nos. 31 (Det.) 117, (Det.)	D.C.2
No. 33	Hurricane
No. 39 (Det.), 60 (S.A.A.F)	Maryland
No. 113	Blenheim (fighter)
No. 203 (Det.)	Beaufort
No. 216 (Det.)	Bombay
No. 272 (Det.)	Beaufighter
No. 826 (F.A.A.)	Albacore, Swordfish

Flights, Other Units

Strategic Reconnaissance Flight	Maryland
No. 1 R.A.A.F. Ambulance Unit	D.H. 86

No. 253 Wing

Squadrons

Nos. 208, 237, 451 (R.A.A.F.)	Hurricane

No. 258 Wing

Squadrons

Nos. 1 (S.A.A.F.), 94, 238, 274	Hurricane
Nos. 2 (S.A.A.F.), 3 (R.A.A.F.)	Tomahawk

No. 262 Wing

Squadrons

Nos. 4 (S.A.A.F.), 112, 250	Tomahawk
No. 80	Hurricane (bomber)
Nos. 229, 260	Hurricane

No. 269 Wing

Squadrons

No. 30, R.N. (Fighter) Squadron	Hurricane

No. 270 Wing

Squadrons

Nos. 8 (Det.), 14, 45, 55, 84, Lorraine Squadron	Blenheim

No. 3 (S.A.A.F.) Wing

Squadrons

No. 11	Blenheim
Nos. 12 (S.A.A.F.), 21 (S.A.A.F.)	Maryland

ABBREVIATIONS

A.H.Q.	Air Headquarters
Det.	Detachment
R.A.A.F.	Royal Australian Air Force
R.N.	Royal Navy
S.A.A.F.	South African Air Force

APPENDIX XI

Order of Battle, Middle East Command, 27th October, 1942

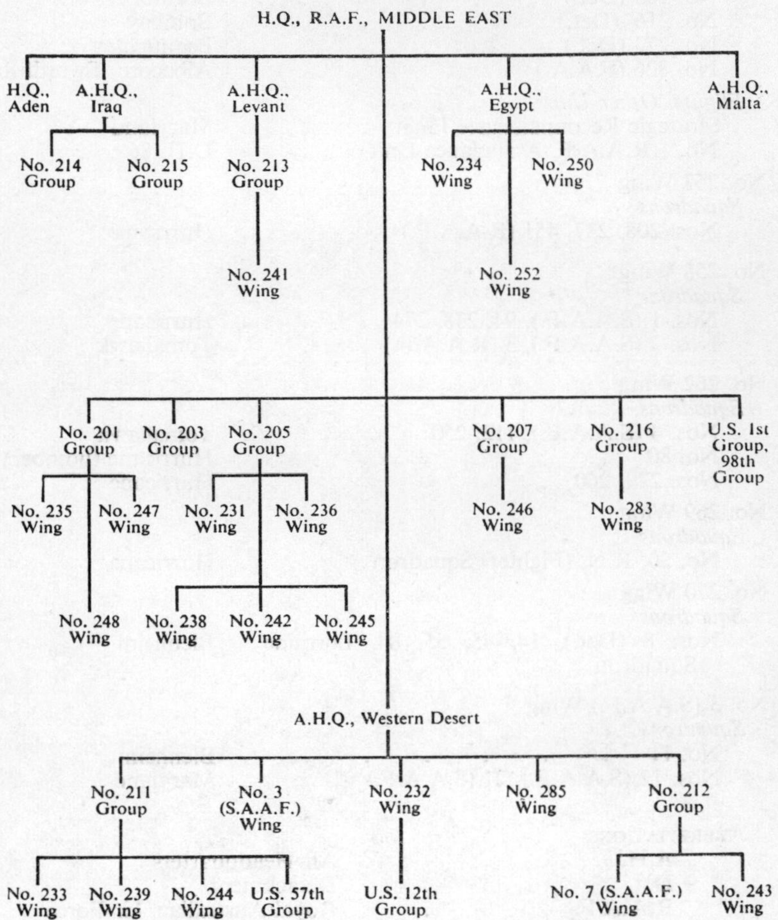

Note. For details of formations see following pages.

HEADQUARTERS, ROYAL AIR FORCE, MIDDLE EAST

Squadrons
No. 60 (S.A.A.F.) (Det.) . . . . . Maryland
No. 162 . . . . Lodestar, Wellington
Flights, Other Units
No. 1411 Met. Flight . . . . . Gladiator
No. 2 Photographic Reconnaissance Unit . Spitfire, Hurricane. Beaufighter

HEADQUARTERS, BRITISH FORCES, ADEN

Squadrons
No. 8 . . . . Blenheim
No. 459 (R.A.A.F.) (Det.) . . . . . Hudson
Flights
Defence Flight . . . . Hurricane

AIR HEADQUARTERS, IRAQ

No. 214 GROUP

No. 237 Squadron . . . . . . Hurricane

No. 215 GROUP

No. 244 Squadron . . . . . . Blenheim, Vincent, Catalina

AIR HEADQUARTERS, LEVANT

No. 1413 Met. Flight . . . . . . Gladiator
No. 1438 Flight . . . . Blenheim
No. 2 Photographic Reconnaissance Unit (Det.) Hurricane

No. 213 GROUP

No. 241 Wing
No. 451 Squadron (R.A.A.F.) . . . . Hurricane

AIR HEADQUARTERS, EGYPT

No. 234 Wing
No. 889 Squadron (F.A.A.) . . . . Fulmar, Hurricane
No. 250 Wing
Squadrons
No. 89 . . . . Beaufighter
No. 94 . . . . Hurricane, Spitfire
No. 252 Wing
Squadrons
No. 46 . . . . Beaufighter
No. 417 (R.C.A.F.) . . . . . . Hurricane, Spitfire

AIR HEADQUARTERS, MALTA

Squadrons

Nos. 89 (Det.), 227	Beaufighter
No. 69	Wellington, Baltimore, Spitfire
Nos. 126, 185, 249	Spitfire
No. 229	Hurricane, Spitfire
No. 828 (F.A.A.) (Det.)	Albacore
No. 830 (F.A.A.) (Det.)	Swordfish

Flights

No. 1435	Spitfire

* * *

No. 201 Group

Squadrons

No. 15 (S.A.A.F.)	Blenheim
No. 47	Beaufort
No. 203	Blenheim, Baltimore, Maryland
No. 230	Sunderland, Dornier 22
Nos. 252, 272	Beaufighter
No. 459 (R.A.A.F.)	Hudson
No. 701 (F.A.A.)	Walrus
Nos. 821 (F.A.A.), 826 (F.A.A.)	Albacore
No. 815 (F.A.A.)	Swordfish

Flights, Other Units

No. 1 General Reconnaissance Unit	Wellington
Sea Rescue Flight	Wellington, Fairchild Ambulance

No. 235 Wing

Squadrons

Nos. 13 (Hellenic), 47 (Det.)	Blenheim
No. 459 (R.A.A.F.) (Det.)	Hudson

No. 247 Wing

Squadrons

No. 203 (Det.)	Maryland, Baltimore, Blenheim
No. 221 (Det.)	Wellington

No. 248 Wing

Squadrons

Nos. 38, 221, 458 (R.A.A.F.)	Wellington
No. 39	Beaufort

No. 203 Group

No. 15 Squadron (S.A.A.F.) (Det.)	Blenheim
No. 1412 Met. Flight	Gladiator

No. 205 Group

Unit	Aircraft
Special Liberator Flight	Liberator
No. 231 Wing	
Squadrons	
Nos. 37, 70	Wellington
No. 236 Wing	
Squadrons	
Nos. 108, 148	Wellington
No. 238 Wing	
Squadrons	
Nos. 40, 104	Wellington
No. 242 Wing	
Squadrons	
Nos. 147, 160	Liberator
No. 245 Wing	
Squadrons	
No. 14	Marauder, Boston
Nos. 227 (Det.), 462 (R.A.A.F.)	Halifax

No. 207 Group

Unit	Aircraft
Squadrons	
No. 16 (S.A.A.F.)	Beaufort, Maryland
Nos. 209, 321	Catalina
Flights	
No. 34 (S.A.A.F.)	Anson
No. 35 (S.A.A.F.)	Blenheim
No. 1414	Gladiator
No. 1433	Lysander
No. 246 Wing	
No. 41 Squadron (S.A.A.F.)	Hartebeeste, Hurricane

No. 216 Group

Unit	Aircraft
Squadrons	
No. 117	Hudson
No. 173	Various
No. 216	Lodestar, Hudson, Bombay
No. 267	Various
No. 283 Wing	
No. 163 Squadron	Hudson
U.S. 1st Bombardment Group (Provisional)	
Squadrons	
9th	Fortress
Halverson Squadron	Liberator
U.S. 98th Bombardment Group	
Squadrons	
343rd, 344th, 345th, 415th	Liberator

* * *

AIR HEADQUARTERS, WESTERN DESERT

No. 1 Air Ambulance Unit	D.H. 86
No. 3 (S.A.A.F.) Wing	
Squadrons	
Nos. 12 (S.A.A.F.), 24 (S.A.A.F.) . .	Boston
No. 21 (S.A.A.F.)	Baltimore
No. 232 Wing	
Squadrons	
Nos. 55, 223	Baltimore
U.S. 12th Bombardment Group	
Squadrons	
81st, 82nd, 83rd, 434th	Mitchell
No. 285 Wing	
Squadrons	
Nos. 40 (S.A.A.F.), 208	Hurricane
No. 60 (S.A.A.F.)	Baltimore
Flights, Other Units	
No. 1437 Strategic Reconnaissance Flight .	Baltimore
No. 2 Photographic Reconnaissance Unit (Det.)	Various
No. 211 Group	
Squadrons	
Nos. 6, 7 (S.A.A.F.)	Hurricane
No. 233 Wing	
Squadrons	
Nos. 2 (S.A.A.F.), 4 (S.A.A.F.) and 260 .	Kittyhawk
No. 5 (S.A.A.F.)	Tomahawk
No. 239 Wing	
Squadrons	
Nos. 3 (R.A.A.F.), 112, 250, 450 (R.A.A.F.) .	Kittyhawk
No. 244 Wing	
Squadrons	
Nos. 92, 145, 601	Spitfire
No. 73	Hurricane
U.S. 57th Fighter Group	
Squadrons	
64th, 65th, 66th	Warhawk
No. 212 Group	
No. 7 (S.A.A.F.) Wing	
Squadrons	
Nos. 80, 127, 274, 335	Hurricane
No. 243 Wing	
Squadrons	
Nos. 1 (S.A.A.F.), 33, 213, 238 . . .	Hurricane

Abbreviations

A.H.Q.	Air Headquarters
Det.	Detachment
F.A.A.	Fleet Air Arm
Met.	Meteorological
R.A.A.F.	Royal Australian Air Force
R.C.A.F.	Royal Canadian Air Force
S.A.A.F.	South African Air Force

APPENDIX XII

Order of Battle, Mediterranean Air Command, 10th July, 1943

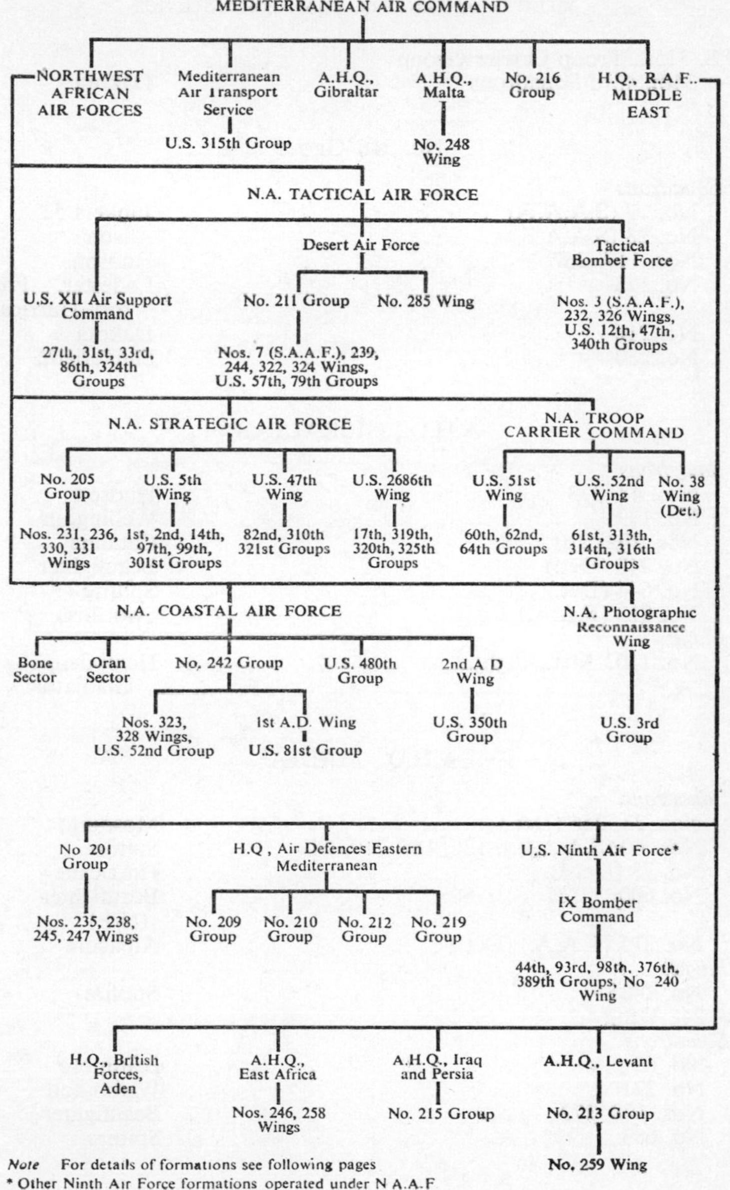

Note For details of formations see following pages

* Other Ninth Air Force formations operated under N A.A.F

MEDITERRANEAN AIR COMMAND

Mediterranean Air Transport Service

Unit	Aircraft
U.S. 315th Troop Carrier Group	
34th, 43rd Squadrons	Dakota

No. 216 Group

Unit	Aircraft
Squadrons	
No. 17 (S.A.A.F.)	Junkers 52
No. 28 (S.A.A.F.)	Anson
Nos. 117, 267	Hudson
No. 173	Lodestar, Proctor, Hurricane
No. 216	Dakota
No. 230	Sunderland

A.H.Q., GIBRALTAR

Unit	Aircraft
Squadrons	
Nos. 48, 233	Hudson
No. 179	Wellington
Nos. 202, 210	Catalina
No. 248 (Det.)	Beaufighter
No. 544 (Det.)	Spitfire
No. 813 (F.A.A.)	Swordfish
Flights	
No. 1403 Met. Flight	Hampden, Gladiator

A.H.Q., MALTA

Unit	Aircraft
Squadrons	
Nos. 23, 256 (Det.)	Mosquito
Nos. 40 (S.A.A.F.), 126, 185, 229, 249	Spitfire
No. 73 (Det.)	Hurricane
No. 600	Beaufighter (N/F)
No. 815 (F.A.A.) (Det.)	Albacore
Flights	
No. 1435	Spitfire
No. 248 Wing	
Squadrons	
No. 69	Baltimore
No. 221	Wellington
Nos. 108, 272	Beaufighter
No. 683	Spitfire

NORTHWEST AFRICAN AIR FORCES

N.A. TACTICAL AIR FORCE

Desert Air Force

Unit	Aircraft
No. 285 Wing	
No. 40 (S.A.A.F.) Squadron (Det.)	Spitfire
No. 60 (S.A.A.F.) Squadron	Mosquito
No. 1437 Flight	Mustang
No. 211 Group	
No. 6 Squadron	Hurricane
No. 7 (S.A.A.F.) Wing	
Squadrons	
Nos. 2 (S.A.A.F.), 4 (S.A.A.F.)	Spitfire
No. 5 (S.A.A.F.)	Kittyhawk
No. 239 Wing	
Squadrons	
Nos. 3 (R.A.A.F.), 112, 250, 260, 450 (R.A.A.F.)	Kittyhawk
No. 244 Wing	
Squadrons	
Nos. 1 (S.A.A.F.), 92, 145, 417 (R.C.A.F.), 601	Spitfire
No. 322 Wing	
Squadrons	
Nos. 81, 152, 154, 232, 242	Spitfire
No. 324 Wing	
Squadrons	
Nos. 43, 72, 93, 111, 243	Spitfire
U.S. 57th, 79th Fighter Groups—six squadrons	Warhawk

U.S. XII Air Support Command

Unit	Aircraft
27th, 86th Fighter-Bomber Groups—six squadrons	Mustang
33rd, 324th Fighter Groups—six squadrons	Warhawk
31st Fighter Group—three squadrons	Spitfire
111th Tactical Reconnaissance Squadron	Mustang

Tactical Bomber Force

Unit	Aircraft
Squadrons	
No. 225	Spitfire
No. 241	Hurricane
No. 3 (S.A.A.F.) Wing	
Squadrons	
Nos. 12 (S.A.A.F.), 24 (S.A.A.F.)	Boston
No. 21 (S.A.A.F.)	Baltimore
No. 232 Wing	
Squadrons	
Nos. 55, 223	Baltimore
No. 326 Wing	
Squadrons	
Nos. 18, 114	Boston
U.S. 12th, 340th Bombardment Groups—eight squadrons	Mitchell
U.S. 47th Bombardment Group—four squadrons	Boston

N.A. STRATEGIC AIR FORCE

No. 205 Group

No. 231 Wing	
Squadrons	
Nos. 37, 70	Wellington
No. 236 Wing	
Squadrons	
Nos. 40, 104	Wellington
No. 330 Wing	
Squadrons	
Nos. 142, 150	Wellington
No. 331 Wing	
Squadrons	
Nos. 420 (R.C.A.F.), 424 (R.C.A.F.), 425 (R.C.A.F.).	Wellington

U.S. 5th Wing

2nd, 97th, 99th, 301st Bombardment Groups—sixteen squadrons	Fortress
1st, 14th Fighter Groups—six squadrons	Lightning

U.S. 47th Wing

310th, 321st Bombardment Groups—eight squadrons	Mitchell
82nd Fighter Group—three squadrons	Lightning

U.S. 2686th Wing

17th, 319th, 320th Bombardment Groups—twelve squadrons	Marauder
325th Fighter Group—three squadrons	Warhawk

N.A. COASTAL AIR FORCE

Squadrons	
Nos. 13, 614	Blenheim
No. 36	Wellington
No. 253	Hurricane
Nos. 500, 608	Hudson
No. 813 (F.A.A.) (Det.)	Swordfish
Nos. 821 (F.A.A.), 828 (F.A.A.)	Albacore
Flights	
No. 1575	Halifax, Ventura
U.S. 480th Antisubmarine Group—two squadrons	Liberator
Bone Sector	
Squadrons	
Nos. 32, 87	Hurricane
No. 219	Beaufighter (N/F)

Oran Sector	
U.S. 92nd Fighter Squadron	Airacobra
2nd Air Defense Wing	
No. 153 Squadron	Beaufighter (N/F)
U.S. 350th Fighter Group—three squadrons	Airacobra

No. 242 Group

No. 323 Wing	
Squadrons	
No. 73	Spitfire
No. 255	Beaufighter (N/F)
Nos. 283, 284	Walrus (A.S.R.)
Nos. II/5, II/7 (French)	Kittyhawk, Spitfire
No. 328 Wing	
Squadrons	
No. 14	Marauder
Nos. 39, 47, 144	Beaufighter
No. 52	Baltimore
Nos. 221 (Det.), 458 (R.A.A.F.)	Wellington
U.S. 52nd Fighter Group—three squadrons	Spitfire
1st Air Defense Wing	
U.S. 81st Fighter Group—two squadrons	Airacobra

N.A. TROOP CARRIER COMMAND

No. 38 Wing (Det.)	
Squadrons	
No. 295 (Det.)	Halifax
No. 296	Albemarle

U.S. 51st Wing

60th, 62nd, 64th Troop Carrier Groups—twelve squadrons.	Dakota

U.S. 52nd Wing

61st, 313th, 314th, 316th Troop Carrier Groups—fifteen squadrons	Dakota

N.A. Photographic Reconnaissance Wing

Squadrons	
Nos. 60 (S.A.A.F.) (Det.), 540 (Det.)	Mosquito
No. 682	Spitfire
U.S. 3rd Photo Reconnaissance Group	
Squadrons	
5th, 12th	Lightning
15th	Fortress

HEADQUARTERS, R.A.F., MIDDLE EAST

Squadrons

No. 148	Liberator, Halifax
No. 162	Wellington, Blenheim
No. 680	Spitfire, Lightning, Hurricane

Flights

Nos. 1411, 1412, 1464 Met. Flights . . .	Hurricane, Gladiator

No. 201 Group

No. 701 Squadron (F.A.A.)	Walrus
No. 235 Wing	
Squadrons	
No. 13 (Hellenic)	Blenheim
No. 227 (Det.)	Beaufighter
No. 454 (R.A.A.F.)	Baltimore
No. 459 (R.A.A.F.)	Hudson
No. 815 (F.A.A.)	Swordfish
No. 238 Wing	
Squadrons	
No. 16 (S.A.A.F.)	Beaufort
Nos. 227 (Det.), 603	Beaufighter
No. 815 (F.A.A.) (Det.)	Swordfish
No. 245 Wing	
Squadrons	
No. 15 (S.A.A.F.)	Blenheim, Baltimore
No. 38 (Det.)	Wellington
Other Units	
No. 1 General Reconnaissance Unit . .	Wellington
No. 247 Wing	
Squadrons	
No. 38	Wellington
No. 203	Baltimore
Nos. 227, 252.	Beaufighter

HEADQUARTERS, AIR DEFENCES, EASTERN MEDITERRANEAN

No. 209 Group

Squadrons

No. 46 (Det.)	Beaufighter
No. 127	Hurricane, Spitfire

No. 210 Group

Squadrons

Nos. 3 (S.A.A.F.), 33, 213, 274	Hurricane
No. 89	Beaufighter (N/F)

No. 212 Group

Squadrons

Nos. 7 (S.A.A.F.), 41 (S.A.A.F.), 94, 123, 134, 237	Hurricane
No. 80	Spitfire
No. 108 (Det.)	Beaufighter (N/F)

Flights

Nos. 1563, 1654 Met. Flights	Gladiator

No. 219 Group

Squadrons

Nos. 74, 238, 335, 336, 451 (R.A.A.F.)	Hurricane
No. 46	Beaufighter (N/F)

UNITED STATES NINTH AIR FORCE

316th Troop Carrier Group (see N.A. Troop Carrier Command)

IX Bomber Command

44th, 93rd, 98th, 376th, 389th Bombardment Groups—twenty squadrons	Liberator
No. 240 Wing	
Squadrons	
Nos. 178, 462 (R.A.A.F.)	Halifax

12th, 340th Bombardment Groups (See N.A. Tactical Air Force)

IX Fighter Command

57th, 79th, 324th Groups (see N.A. Tactical Air Force)

H.Q., BRITISH FORCES, ADEN

No. 8 Squadron	Blenheim
No. 1566 Met. Flight	Gladiator
Catalina Flight	Catalina

A.H.Q., EAST AFRICA

Squadrons	
Nos. 259, 262, 321 (Det.)	Catalina
No. 246 Wing	
Squadrons	
Nos. 209, 265	Catalina
No. 258 Wing	
No. 1414 Met. Flight	Lysander, Anson

A.H.Q., IRAQ AND PERSIA

No. 215 Group

Unit	Aircraft
No. 208 Squadron (Det.)	Hurricane
No. 244 Squadron	Blenheim
No. 1415 Met. Flight	Gladiator

A.H.Q., LEVANT

Unit	Aircraft
No. 208 Squadron	Hurricane
No. 1413 Met. Flight	Gladiator

No. 213 Group

Unit	Aircraft
No. 259 Wing	
No. 1565 Met. Flight	Hurricane

Abbreviations

A.H.Q.	Air Headquarters
A.S.R.	Air/Sea Rescue
Det.	Detachment
F.A.A.	Fleet Air Arm
Met.	Meteorological
N.A.	Northwest African
N/F	Night Fighter
P.R.	Photographic Reconnaissance
R.A.A.F.	Royal Australian Air Force
R.C.A.F.	Royal Canadian Air Force
S.A.A.F.	South African Air Force

APPENDIX XIII

Glossary of Code Names & Abbreviations

'ACROBAT' . . .	Projected British advance from Cyrenaica into Tripolitania—early 1942.
A.I.	Air interception—radar carried by fighters.
A.M.E.S.	Air Ministry Experimental Station (i.e. radar station).
ASDIC	Shipborne apparatus for the detection of underwater objects.
A.S.V.	Air-to-surface vessel—airborne search and homing radar used for anti-U-boat and anti-shipping operations.
'AVALANCHE' . . .	Allied invasion of Italy (Salerno)—September 1943.
'BATTLEAXE' . . .	British operation to relieve Tobruk—June 1941.
'BAYTOWN' . . .	8th Army assault on the toe of Italy—3rd September, 1943.
'CAB-RANK' . . .	Small formations of patrolling fighters and fighter-bombers on immediate call for close tactical support.
'CHANNEL STOP' . .	British air operations to prevent German shipping passing through the Straits of Dover by day.
'C 3' (Italian) . . .	Projected invasion of Malta—1942.
'CRUSADER' . . .	British offensive in Cyrenaica—November 1941.
'DIADEM'	Assault to effect union between main front and Anzio beach-head—May 1944.
'FRÜHLINGSWIND' (German)	Attack against the United States forces in southern Tunisia—February 1943.
'GARDENING' . . .	Sea minelaying by aircraft.
G.C.I.	Ground-controlled interception.
'GEE'	Medium-range radar aid to navigation employing ground transmitters and airborne receiver.
'GYMNAST' . . .	Original plan for Anglo-American operation which eventually became 'Torch'.

'HARPOON'	Covering operations—convoy from U.K. to Malta—June 1942.
'H2S'	Airborne radar navigational and target location aid.
'HERCULES' (German) .	Projected invasion of Malta—1942.
'HUSKY'	Allied invasion of Sicily—10th/17th July, 1943.
'INTRUDER' . . .	Offensive night patrols over enemy territory intended to destroy hostile aircraft and to dislocate the enemy flying organization.
'MATADOR' . . .	Projected operation to seize Singora area of Siam—December 1941.
'MILLENNIUM' . . .	1,000-bomber attack on Cologne—30th/31st May, 1942.
'OBOE'	Ground-controlled radar system of blind bombing in which one station indicates track to be followed and another the bomb release point.
O.T.U.	Operational Training Unit.
'PEDESTAL' . . .	Malta convoy operations—August 1942.
'POINTBLANK' . . .	The attack on German fighter forces and the industry upon which they depended—1943/1944
P.R.U.	Photographic Reconnaissance Unit.
'ROUND-UP' . . .	Projected Anglo-American operation against northern France—1943.
'ROVER DAVID' . . .	Attacks on fleeting tactical targets by 'Cab-rank' fighters and fighter-bombers.
'SHINGLE'	Amphibious operations mounted from Naples to facilitate ultimate capture of Rome—January 1944.
'SLEDGEHAMMER' . .	Projected Anglo-American operation against northern France—1942.
'STRANGLE' . . .	Air operations for the destruction of enemy road, rail and sea communications—Italy, March/May 1944.
'THESEUS' (German) . .	Rommel's offensive in Cyrenaica—May 1942.
TORBEAU	Torpedo-carrying Beaufighter.
'TORCH'	Anglo-American landing operation in French North Africa—November 1942.

TURBINLITE . . .	Searchlight fitted to aircraft for night-fighter operations.
'VIGOROUS' . . .	Covering operations—convoy from Eastern Mediterranean to Malta—June 1942.
V.L.R.	Very Long Range.
'WALTER'	Radar beacon carried in dinghy to facilitate search and homing by aircraft equipped with A.S.V.
'WINDOW' . . .	Metallized paper strips dropped by bomber aircraft in order to disrupt enemy radar system.
WÜRZBURG (German) .	Ground radar system used for controlling searchlights, anti-aircraft guns and night-fighter aircraft.

INDEX

S.O. Code No. 22-209-2*

ROYAL AIR FORCE 1939–1945

VOLUME I

BY DENIS RICHARDS

The Fight at Odds *1939–1941*

Re-armament and pre-war planning. Early war operations. Norway and France. The Battle of Britain and 'The Blitz'. The bombing of Germany. Air operations in the war at sea. The Mediterranean and the Middle East.

VOLUME II

BY DENIS RICHARDS AND HILARY ST. G. SAUNDERS

The Fight Avails *1941–1943*

The Far East. The U-boat war and anti-shipping operations. The Western Desert, Malta and Tunisia. The strategic bombing offensive. Sicily. The invasion of Italy (with subsequent operations up to the fall of Rome, May 1944).

VOLUME III

BY HILARY ST. G. SAUNDERS

With concluding chapter by Hilary St. G. Saunders and Denis Richards

The Fight is Won *1943–1945*

The combined bombing offensive. The Atlantic and the Bay of Biscay. The liberation of North-West Europe—plans and preparations. Normandy and the battle for France. Flying bombs and rockets. Italy and the Balkans. The advance into Germany and the final surrender. Victory in Burma and the Far East. The war in the air—the balance sheet.